PERSONALITY AND PERSONAL GROWTH

THIRD EDITION

James Fadiman, Ph.D.
Robert Frager, Ph.D.

HarperCollins*CollegePublishers*

Acquisitions Editor: Catherine Woods
Project Coordination and Text Design: Proof Positive/
    Farrowlyne Associates, Inc.
Cover Design: Kay Petronio
Photo Researcher: Judy Ladendorf
Production Manager: Kewal Sharma
Compositor: Proof Positive/Farrowlyne Associates, Inc.
Printer and Binder: R. R. Donnelley & Sons Company
Cover Printer: Phoenix Color Corporation

Personality and Personal Growth, Third Edition

Library of Congress Cataloging-in-Publication Data

Fadiman, James, 1939–
     Personality and personal growth / James Fadiman, Robert Frager. —
3rd ed.
          p.   cm.
     Frager's name appears first on the earlier edition.
     Includes bibliographical references and index.
     ISBN 0-06-500772-7
     1. Personality. 2. Psychotherapy. I. Frager, Robert, 1940–
II. Title.
BF698.F22 1994
155.2—dc20   93-21285
                                                                    CIP

93 94 95 96 9 8 7 6 5 4 3 2 1

To our wives: Dorothy and Ayhan
Our children: Renee, Maria, Ariel, Eddie, John, Kenny
and
to our teachers

Contents in Brief

Table of Contents

Chapter Four
Karen Horney and Humanistic Psychoanalysis
(originally prepared for the second edition by Kathleen Speeth)   130

Chapter Five
The Psychology of Women: A Relational Approach
Jean Baker Miller, M.D., Irene Pierce Stiver, Ph.D.,
Judith V. Jordan, Ph.D., Janet L. Surrey, Ph.D.   159

Chapter Six
Erik Erikson and the Life Cycle   180

Chapter Seven
Wilhelm Reich and Somatic Psychology

Chapter Eight
Frederick Perls, Laura Perls, and Gestalt Therapy
(originally prepared for the first edition by Lisby Mayer)

Chapter Twelve
Carl Rogers and the Person-Centered Perspective 417

Chapter Thirteen
Abraham Maslow and Transpersonal Psychology 463

Part Two Introduction to Eastern Theories of Personality

Preface

This edition has numerous improvements. We have updated every chapter, added new sections to many, included hundreds of new references, clarified or deleted sections students found unclear or obscure, dropped ideas no longer of interest, and attempted to keep students abreast of how each theory is being used and how it is regarded by psychology at large. In the process of improving the text, we have added two new chapters. The first, The Psychology of Women: A Relational Approach, was written by a group of women clinicians and scholars from the Stone Center in Wellesley, Massachusetts. We are pleased to be able to give personality development in women the specific attention it deserves. The second new chapter is Cognitive Psychology and the Personal Constructs Theory of George Kelly. It was written by Kaisa Puhakka, who was trained first as a philosopher, then as a clinician and teacher. We have been asked repeatedly to devote space to both the emerging cognitive area and to Kelly's contributions. His brilliant explorations have been widely admired; however, he is not well known outside academia.

We have also rectified an injustice by revising (and retitling) the chapter on Perls and Gestalt therapy to acknowledge the work of Laura Perls, whose contributions are equal in importance to those of her more extroverted husband.

Changes were made in the chapters on Eastern thought for several reasons. We were able to utilize a great deal of original and newly translated material that was previously unavailable. Because more and more instructors have been exposed to Eastern psychologies, we felt it was important that these chapters acknowledge this new awareness.

Finally, we are all gradually learning that teaching psychology as if it were the exclusive province of white males does a disservice to a world that is growing in multicultural awareness. In the spirit of this new awareness, we are happy to report that this text is available in Spanish, Portuguese, and Japanese translations.

With the addition of two new chapters and new material throughout, the total number of chapters and pages is more than can be covered in a quarter-length course. It is a little tight even for a semester. In any case, we know that most instructors tend to choose among many theorists. Therefore, providing a longer book simply allows for more choices as well as greater opportunity for the assignment of extra credit or independent study. Each chapter is discrete, designed to stand alone. Therefore, you may structure the course as you see fit both in terms of length and according to whatever topics you wish.

In our own teaching experience, we have found it best to begin with Chapter 1, Sigmund Freud and Psychoanalysis, because almost every other theorist presented in Part 1 has had to come to terms with Freud's work directly or indirectly. We also strongly recommend that you include Chapter 5, The Psychology of Women: A Relational Approach. Together, these two chapters will tease out most of the pertinent issues that students tend to wrestle with in this class.

Side-by-side comparisons, which paint such good theoretical pictures, are of less interest to students and instructors than they used to be. Our reviewers reminded us that clarity and vitality were more crucial to good learning than the tidiness of chapter outlines. So, those of you who have used earlier editions will notice that certain subdivisions, which we used to compare and contrast each theory, have melted away where they served no purpose.

The end-of-chapter exercises have been changed and now appear *throughout* each chapter as Personal Reflections, to give students a feel for aspects of each theory in context.

Some of our reviewers asked for more research findings, while others thanked us to stay with the theory. We have debated over the issue of research versus theory ourselves as we have worked on each new edition. We conclude that both the quality and quantity of research that all of us want simply does not exist. In the preface to the textbook, *Current Psychotherapies* (Corsini & Wedding, 1989),[1] Wedding writes:

> I had initially wanted to include a section on research for every chapter. However, virtually every chapter author maintained that the research base of his or her system was not sufficiently well developed to justify an exclusive selection devoted to research findings. (1989, p. ix)

Since the most sophisticated experts on each theory have unanimously agreed that the current available research does not merit inclusion in their theoretical reviews, we have felt that it would be wise to include less

---

[1] Corsini, R., & Wedding, D. (Eds.). (1989). *Current psychotherapies* (4th ed.). Itasca, IL: F. E. Peacock Publishers.

research in our presentations as well. So, if any of your students are inclined toward research, *do* inform them that the frontiers are still open.

Every theory in this book has been *use-tested* with thousands of people. Each theory has helped to resolve personal problems, improve child-raising, enhance communication, or support personal growth and spiritual development. Every theory we have included has active adherents, as well as journals and training programs. None have been empirically proved, none have been empirically disproved; all have supporters and critics.

Instead of holding to one viewpoint and defending it, we offer students a full set of choices upon which to make their own decisions. We encourage them to test the validity or utility of each theory against their own experience and their own common sense. Therefore, each chapter focuses more on the stronger aspects of each theory—the reasons for its continuing strength and popularity—than on its weaknesses.

Students have told us that this material is well worth their time. Even if they go no further in psychology, the ideas and issues raised in this book continue to serve them and enrich their lives.

We have developed an instructor's handbook designed to help you teach this course. It includes outlines of each chapter; additional and more current resources; media suggestions; true-false, multiple choice, and essay questions; and additional Personal Reflections for individual or class use. Be sure that you request your copy from HarperCollins.

Thank you for putting this book to use. Please write to us and let us know what you and your students liked as well as how you would have us improve the book to better serve your needs.

Acknowledgments

With gratitude and humility we acknowledge the numerous people who have contributed their wisdom and effort. Their work has been invaluable in improving the second edition.

We are most grateful to Kaisa Puhakka of West Georgia College, whose review of the previous edition was so penetrating and detailed that, in this edition, we invited her to help us implement her own suggestions. Special thanks to Peter Hirose, chief librarian of the Institute for Transpersonal Psychology, who repeatedly solved amazingly difficult bibliographic problems.

We are grateful to the following colleagues for their professional criticism: Peter Carnochan on Freud, Charlotte Lewis on Jung, Bernard Paris on Horney, and Yōzan Dirk Mosig on Zen Buddhism.

We also wish to thank students in the seminar on Personality Theory at the Institute of Transpersonal Psychology for their thoughtful criticisms and recommendations, and the many psychology instructors across the country and abroad who have used this text and given us encouraging and critical feedback.

A deep bow to Merrill Gillaspy of Proof Positive/Farrowlyne Associates, Inc., for vastly improving the clarity of every chapter with her extensive final editing of the entire manuscript. And special thanks to the following professionals, who reviewed the entire manuscript and offered many, many detailed and helpful suggestions, most of which have been incorporated into this edition: Gordon Becker, University of Nebraska at Omaha; John Calhoun, University of Georgia; George Guthrie, Pennsylvania State University; Davis Hayden, Western Washington University; Judy Johnson, Mount Royal College; David Lutz, Southwest Missouri State University; Solomon Schuck, Monmouth College; T. Gale Thompson, Bethany College; and Irving Tucker, Shepherd College.

Any errors of judgment or fact that remain are ours.

James Fadiman
Robert Frager
Palo Alto, California

Introduction

Much to our delight, many students have said that they actually enjoyed reading this book. We hope you will as well.

We first wrote this book because we found that our students were no longer satisfied with the same personality courses that we took as undergraduates. The changing values and interests have supported similar tendencies in our own intellectual development. We have continued to expand and improve this book, because it has proved valuable to a new generation of students. In making these changes, we accepted and incorporated a great deal of student feedback.

In our courses, we have experimented with a wide variety of formats in an attempt to break out of the rigid and passive roles inherent in many of the traditional models of learning. One result is that we have included more and more direct ways to experience new ideas. This structure reflects our ongoing concern that learning should always be an exciting experience for our students.

Our intention is to provide students with a worldwide, cross-cultural body of knowledge that is of practical use in understanding human nature. Most students hope to find in psychology classes a set of structures, concepts, theories, and perspectives that will facilitate their own growth and their capacity to adjust to a rapidly changing, diverse society. We confess that we, as well as our students, found many of the current textbooks too technical, too ponderous, or too concerned with arid academic abstractions to be of personal value. They clearly reflect a very standard and accepted academic perspective.

In recent years, four additional approaches to human nature and functioning have become increasingly important: cognitive psychology, the human potential movement, the psychology of women, and non-Western ideas. The impact of these forces on our own thinking has served to expand the limits and range of our approach to personality theory.

Cognitive psychology has extended into more and more areas of psychology including personality. It is a way of looking at the basic functioning of the mind itself. If we can better understand how we think, observe, attend, and remember, we will be better able to understand how these basic cognitive building blocks lead to fears, illusions, creative works, and all the behaviors and mental events that make us who we are.

The human potential movement, founded in part at the Esalen Institute in California and at the National Training Laboratories in Maine in the 1950s and 1960s, is now a widely accepted cultural force. Growth, or training, centers exist in most major cities, generally offering intensive and powerful weekend or week-long workshops in various kinds of encounter groups, body-oriented work, meditation, and spiritual disciplines. These workshops also offer training in communication, time management, quality control, and stress reduction. Many colleges and universities now offer experientially oriented courses that stress personal involvement and emotional experience, while corporations regularly send their executives to classes and seminars that are rooted in the human potential movement. Group leaders and participants, as well as government and corporate sponsors, generally believe that these changes are beneficial and long lasting.

Unfortunately, over a number of years, along with the emphasis on direct experiential learning and immediate results, there developed an antitheoretical and anticonceptual bias, which sometimes was seen as a deliberate disregard for academic psychology. Conversely, academic psychologists tended to remain ignorant of the movement's very real and important achievements. We realized that the human growth movement has a solid and cogent intellectual framework. To take a single example, the ideas of Fritz and Laura Perls place the experiential aspects of Gestalt therapy on firm theoretical ground, by drawing from phenomenology, holism, psychoanalysis, Reichian theory, and experimental Gestalt psychology.

A third major approach to human nature and functioning, still outside the academic beltway, acknowledges the differences between men and women. It sounds absurd, but most personality theories and most other textbooks still seem to sidestep this issue. When we wrote the first edition in the early 1970s, we included a chapter called, The Psychology of Women. At that time, there was a great deal of interest in the subject, but not much substantial research available. For our second edition, we abandoned the chapter and integrated the question of sexual differences into the body of the text. In this edition, while still maintaining the integration, we were able to work with a group of brilliant scholars and therapists who generously took time away from their own cutting-edge work to write an original exposition of the unique contribution of women's studies to understanding personality.

The fourth perspective on human nature arises from Eastern philosophies. Many of the Eastern systems include a theory of personality structure as well as fundamental rules for behavior and character change. These systems cover many of the same topics as Western personality theories. They tend to deal more explicitly with transpersonal and religious experience and with the role of values and morals in human behavior than some Western theories.

We chose to focus on one facet each of Buddhism, Hinduism, and Islam (the most influential of Eastern disciplines) that is concerned with direct experience and personal growth. These disciplines have been summarized and discussed using the same theoretical structure employed for Western theories. Please look at the introduction to Part 2 for a more complete discussion of why we have included these Eastern ideas.

An Approach to Personality Theory

We approach each theory in the text as positively and as sympathetically as possible. Each chapter has been read and evaluated by theorists and practitioners from each system to help us ensure that our treatment is relatively comprehensive and unbiased. We have avoided, as much as possible, the tendency to criticize or belittle the accomplishments of any theory. Instead, we have tried to highlight the strengths and the effectiveness of each approach. We have sought to be neither partisan nor unthinkingly eclectic. However, we have been purposefully biased in our choice of theorists. We have included those theorists whose importance and utility are evident to us, and left out other well-known theorists who seemed less useful and less congruent with the overall aim of this book.

Each theorist in this book offers something of unique value and relevance, isolating and clarifying very specific aspects of human nature. We feel that each one is essentially "correct" in his or her own area of expertise. Nevertheless, we have attempted to present certain crucial disagreements. The major disagreements among personality theorists often seem to resemble, as in the famous tale, the plight of the blind men and how they "see" an elephant. When each man touches a part of the elephant, he assumes that this one part is the key to the whole animal's appearance.

Each chapter discusses a theory or perspective that adds to our general knowledge of human behavior. We are convinced that, in addition to our innate biological pattern of growth and development, each individual possesses a tendency for psychological development. This has been described by various psychologists as a tendency toward self-actualization: an urge for self-understanding and a need to improve one's awareness and effectiveness—all in order to gain more joy and satisfaction from life.

Structure of Each Chapter

With the exception of Chapter 5, each chapter generally is divided into the following sections (Personal Reflection exercises, like the one on p. xxi, are peppered throughout each chapter):

Personal History

Intellectual Antecedents

Major Concepts

Dynamics

Psychological Growth
Obstacles to Growth

Structure

Body
Social Relationships
Will
Emotions
Intellect
Self
Therapist (or Teacher)/Therapy

Evaluation

The Theory Firsthand

Annotated Bibliography

References

This is not a cookie-cutter text that attempts to fit each theory into a separate mold. Many of the theories *do* overlap and can be compared and contrasted, but each also makes its own discrete and unique contribution to human knowledge.

Personal Reflection ——————————

—————————————————— Life History Questionnaire

Here is the first in a series of exercises in htis text that are intended to bring you closer to the concepts presented.

We are to some extent developed and conditioned by past experience; therefore, we approach any body of material already primed to accept or reject parts of it. Before reading this book, it may be useful for you to begin to review some of the major forces in your own development. Record your answers to the questions that follow. Answer the questions as freely and as fully as you can, as this exercise is designed for your own use.

1. What nicknames do you prefer? Why?

2. What is your ethnic and/or religious identification? If it is different from that of your family, comment on the difference.

3. Describe your siblings and your feelings about them.

4. Describe your parents (stepparents) and your feelings about them.

5. Who in your family do you most resemble? How?

6. What is your current life situation—job, living situation, and so forth?

7. Do you have any recurring dreams/daydreams? What are they?

8. What men or women of the past or present do you appreciate and admire most? Why? Whom might you consider an ideal role model?

9. What books (e. g., poems or works of art) have influenced you most? When and how?

10. What events or inner experiences give or have given you the greatest joy? The greatest sorrow?

11. What occupation would interest you the most if you could become whatever you wanted?

12. Is there anything about yourself that you would like to change?

13. What is there about yourself that you especially like?

Each chapter presents the personal history and the intellectual antecedents of the theorist. We outline the major influences on the theorist's thinking, influences rooted in childhood experiences and from his or her adult life. The bulk of each chapter explores the theory, beginning with a summary of the major concepts. This is followed by sections on psychological development and obstacles to growth. A later section called *structure* covers, depending on the chapter, from some to all of the following seven categories: the body, social relationships, will, emotions, intellect, self, and the therapist (or teacher)/therapy. We have tried to be consistent in order to help you compare and contrast different theories, but not to be so rigid as to be unfair to the theory. The final section of each chapter provides a brief evaluation.

We include an extended passage, whenever possible, from the theorist's own writings, or a description of the system in operation. We feel it is important for you to be exposed to the style and the personality of each theorist. We have also added a number of quotations in the margins. Theorists, their supporters, and even their critics often have unique and fascinating ways of phrasing their ideas and arguments. By using these quotes, we can present other points of view without making the text itself too cumbersome.

Each chapter has sprinkled throughout it a series of Personal Reflections to give you a better feel for some aspects of each theory. Experiential and intellectual learning are complementary rather than contradictory processes. A personal encounter with a concept adds a dimension of immediacy to the theory that cannot be obtained by any other means. The exercises have all been tested, improved, and retested until our students pronounced them helpful.

Finally, each chapter concludes with an annotated bibliography and extensive references. Each chapter is really only an introduction to an involved and complex system of thought. We *hope* you will pursue those theories that you find most interesting and valuable. We have tried to facilitate this next step by suggesting those books that we have found most valuable in understanding each theory.

Introduction to
Personality Psychology

Chapter One

Sigmund Freud and Psychoanalysis

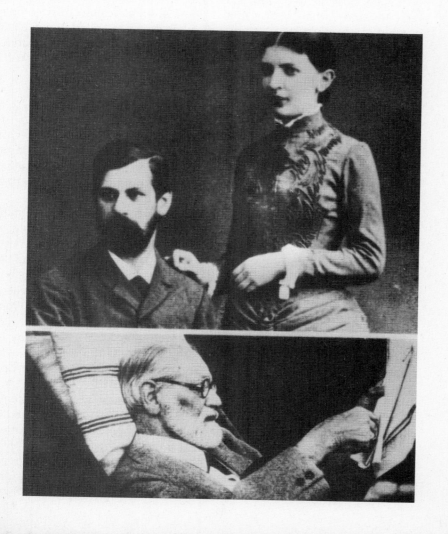

Sigmund Freud's work, originating in the disciplines of biology, neurology, and psychiatry, proposed a new understanding of personality that profoundly affected Western culture. His view of the human condition, striking violently against the prevailing opinions of his era, offered a complex and compelling way to understand normal and abnormal mental functioning.

Freud explored areas of the psyche that had been obscured by Victorian morality and philosophy. He devised new approaches to treat the mentally ill. His work contradicted cultural, religious, social, and scientific taboos. His writings, his personality, and his determination to extend the boundaries of his work kept him at the center of an intense, shifting circle of friends, disciples, and critics. Freud was constantly rethinking and revising his earlier ideas. Interestingly, his harshest critics included those he had personally supervised at various stages in their careers.

It is not possible to discuss all of Freud's contributions in a single chapter. Therefore, what follows is a deliberate simplification of a complex and intricately connected system. It is an overview intended to make later exposure to Freudian ideas more intelligible and to allow a better understanding of other theorists whose works are heavily influenced by Freud.

Personal History

Sigmund Freud was born on May 6, 1856, in Freiberg in Moravia, which is now part of the Czech Republic. When he was 4 years old, his family suffered financial setbacks and moved to Vienna, where Freud remained most of his life. In 1938, he emigrated to England to avoid the German occupation.

During his childhood, Freud excelled as a student. Despite the limited financial position of his family, with all eight members living together in a crowded apartment, Freud, the eldest child, had his own room and even an oil lamp to study by while the rest of the family made do with candles. In "gymnasium" he continued his excellent academic performance. "I was at the top of my class for seven years. I enjoyed special privileges there and was required to pass scarcely any examinations" (Freud, 1925a, p. 9).

Because he was Jewish, he felt that all professional careers, except medicine and law, were closed to him. Such was the prevailing anti-Semitic climate of the time. He chose to enter the Faculty of Medicine at the University of Vienna in 1873.

His experiences at the University of Vienna, where he was treated as both an "inferior and an alien" because of being Jewish, strengthened his capacity to withstand criticism. "At an early age I was made familiar with the fate of being in the opposition and being put under the ban of the 'compact majority.' The foundations were thus laid for a certain degree of independence of judgement" (Freud, 1935, p. 11). He remained a medical student for eight years, three more than was customary.

During these years, he worked in the physiological laboratory of Ernst Brücke, where he did independent research in histology, the study of the minute structure of animal and vegetable tissue, and published articles on anatomy and neurology. At the age of 26, Freud received his medical degree. He continued his work under Brücke for a year, while living at home. He aspired to fill the next open position in the laboratory, but Brücke had two excellent assistants ahead of Freud. He concluded, "The turning point came in 1882, when my teacher, for whom I felt the highest possible esteem, corrected my father's generous improvidence by strongly advising me, in view of my bad financial position, to abandon my theoretical career" (Freud, 1925a, p. 13). In addition, Freud had fallen in love and realized that if he ever were to marry, he would need a better-paying position.

Although he moved reluctantly to a private practice, his primary interests remained in scientific exploration and observation. Working first as a surgeon, then in general medicine, he became a "house physician" at the principal hospital in Vienna. He took a course in psychiatry that furthered his interest in the relationships between mental symptoms and physical disease. By 1885, he had established himself in the prestigious position of lecturer at the University of Vienna. His career began to look promising.

From 1884 to 1887, Freud did some of the first research in cocaine. At first, he was impressed with its properties: "I have tested this effect of coca, which wards off hunger, sleep, and fatigue and steels one to intellectual effort, some dozens of times on myself" (Freud, 1963, p. 11). He wrote about its potential therapeutic uses for both physical and mental disturbances. He later became concerned with its addicting properties and discontinued the research (Byck, 1975).

With Brücke's backing, Freud obtained a travel grant and went to Paris to work under Jean-Martin Charcot, where he studied hypnotic technique and served as Charcot's translator for his lectures (Carroy, 1991). Charcot saw Freud as a capable and understanding student and gave him permission to translate his papers into German upon Freud's return to Vienna.

His work in France increased his interest in hypnosis as a therapeutic tool. With the cooperation of the distinguished older physician Josef Breuer, Freud (1895) explored the dynamics of hysteria. Their findings were summarized by Freud: "The symptoms of hysterical patients depend upon impressive, but forgotten scenes of their lives (traumata). The therapy founded thereon was to cause the patients to recall and reproduce these experiences under hypnosis (catharsis)" (1914, p. 13). He found, however, that hypnosis was not as effective as he had hoped. It did not allow the patient or the therapist to work with the resistance to recalling the traumatic memories. Eventually, Freud abandoned hypnosis altogether. Instead, he encouraged his patients to speak freely by reporting whatever thoughts came to mind, regardless of how these thoughts related to the patients' symptoms.

In 1896, Freud first used the term *psychoanalysis* to describe his methods. His own self-analysis began in 1897. By 1900, he had published *The*

Neither at that time, nor indeed in my later life, did I feel any particular predilection for the career of a physician. I was moved, rather by a sort of curiosity, which was however, directed more towards human concerns than towards natural objects; nor had I grasped the importance of observation as one of the best means of gratifying it. (Freud, 1935, p. 10)

Even a superficial glance at my work will show how much I am indebted to the brilliant discoveries of Freud. (Jung in McGuire, 1974)

Interpretation of Dreams, now considered by many to be his most important work, though at the time it received almost no attention. Freud followed it the next year with another major book titled, *The Psychopathology of Everyday Life.* Eventually, Freud had a following of interested physicians, including Alfred Adler, Sandor Ferenczi, Carl Gustav Jung, Otto Rank, Karl Abraham, and Ernest Jones. The group established a society. Papers were written, a journal was published, and the psychoanalytic movement began to expand.

In 1910, Freud was invited to America to deliver lectures at Clark University. His works were being translated into English. People were becoming interested in the theories of Dr. Sigmund Freud.

Freud spent the rest of his life developing, extending, and clarifying psychoanalysis. He tried to retain control over the psychoanalytic movement by ejecting members who disagreed with his views and by demanding an unusual degree of loyalty to his own position. Jung, Adler, and Rank, among others, left after repeated disagreements with Freud on theoretical issues. Each later founded a separate school of thought.

Freud wrote extensively. His collected works fill 24 volumes and include essays concerning the fine points of clinical practice, a series of lectures outlining the theory in full, and specialized monographs on religious and cultural questions. He attempted to build a structure that would outlive him, one that might eventually reorient all of psychiatry. He was compelling and dogmatic in some areas and open to criticism and revision in others. He feared that analysts who deviated from the procedures he established might dilute the power and the possibilities of psychoanalysis. Above all, he wanted to prevent the distortion and misuse of psychoanalytic theory. When, for example, in 1931 Ferenczi suddenly changed his procedures, making the analytic situation one in which affection might be more freely expressed, Freud wrote him as follows:

> I see that the differences between us have come to a head in a technical detail which is well worth discussing. You have not made a secret of the fact that you kiss your patients and let them kiss you. . . .
>
> Now I am assuredly not one of those who from prudishness or from consideration of bourgeois convention would condemn little erotic gratifications of this kind. And I am also aware that in the time of the Nibelungs a kiss was a harmless greeting granted to every guest. . . . But . . . with us a kiss signifies a certain erotic intimacy. We have hitherto in our techniques held to the conclusion that patients are to be refused erotic gratifications.
>
> Now picture what will be the result of publishing your technique. There is no revolutionary who is not driven out of the field by a still more radical one. A number of independent thinkers in matters of technique will say to themselves: why stop at a kiss? . . . And then bolder ones will come along who go further to peeping and showing . . . resulting in an enormous increase of interest in psychoanalysis among both analysts and patients. . . . The new adherent . . .

As I stepped on to the platform at Worcester to deliver my "Five Lectures" upon psychoanalysis it seemed like some incredible daydream: psychoanalysis was no longer a product of delusion, it had become a valuable part of reality. (Freud, 1925a, p. 104)

the younger of our colleagues will find it hard to stop at the point they originally intended, and God the Father Ferenczi gazing at the lively scene he has created will perhaps say to himself: maybe after all I should have halted in my technique of motherly affection before the kiss. (Jones, 1955, pp. 163–164)

As Freud's work became more widely available, the criticisms increased. In 1933, the Nazis burned a pile of Freud's books in Berlin. Freud commented on the event: "What progress we are making. In the Middle Ages they would have burnt me, nowadays they are content with burning my books" (Jones, 1957).

Perpetually embroiled in battles over the validity or utility of his work, he continued to write. His last book, *An Outline of Psycho-Analysis* (1940), begins with a blunt warning to critics: "The teachings of psycho-analysis are based on an incalculable number of observations and experiences, and only someone who has repeated those observations on himself and others is in a position to arrive at a judgment of his own upon it" (p. 1).

Freud's last years were difficult. From 1923 on, he was in ill health, suffering from cancer of the mouth and jaws. He was in almost continual pain and had a total of 33 operations to halt the spreading cancer. When the Germans took over Austria in 1938, Freud was granted permission to leave for London. He died there a year later.

Unfortunately, Freud's first biographer, Ernest Jones, also a close personal friend, wrote a sanitized account of his life, leaving the writing of a more balanced version to a later generation (Gay, 1988). Others have criticized Freud for a possible affair with his wife's sister (O'Brien, 1991), a lack of professional honesty (Masson, 1984), and a blatant disregard of confidentiality and manipulation within psychoanalysis (Goleman, 1990; Hamilton, 1991). He has also been accused of possibly misrepresenting some of his most famous cases (Decker, 1991) and even of being "the false prophet of the drug world" (Thornton, 1984). Only the continuing importance of Freud's work supports the publication of these attacks.

Freud's ultimate importance can be judged not only by the ongoing interest and debate over aspects of psychoanalytic theory, but, to a greater extent, by appreciating how many of his ideas have become part of the common heritage of the West. We are all in Freud's debt for partially illuminating the world that moves beneath conscious awareness.

> No one who, like me, conjures up the most evil of those half-tamed demons that inhabit the human breast, and seeks to wrestle with them, can expect to come through the struggle unscathed. (Freud, 1905b)

Intellectual Antecedents

Philosophy

While still a student at the university, Freud was influenced by the German romantic poet Clemens Brentano and introduced to the ideas of Friedrich Nietzsche as well (Godde, 1991a). Both Freud and Nietzsche felt, for example, that moral convictions arose from internalized aggression (Roazen,1991).

Freud's ideas are also close to those of Arthur Schopenhauer. They overlap in their view of the will, the importance of sexuality, the domination of reason by the emotions, and the centrality of repression (Godde, 1991b).

Biology

Some of Freud's faith in the biological origins of consciousness may be traced to Brücke's own positions. Brücke once took a formal oath to abide by the following proposition, which was seen as open and optimistic for the time:

> No other forces than the common physical and chemical ones are active within the organism. In those cases which cannot at present be explained by these forces one either has to find the specific way or form of their action by means of the physical-mathematical method or to assume new forces equal in dignity to the chemical-physical forces inherent in matter, reducible to the force of attraction and repulsion. (Rycroft, 1972, p. 14)

I sometimes come out of his lectures [Charcot's] . . . with an entirely new idea about perfection. . . . No other human being has ever affected me in the same way. (Freud in E. Freud, 1961, pp. 184–185)

Charcot demonstrated that it was possible to induce or relieve hysterical symptoms with hypnotic suggestion. Freud observed, as had others, that in hysteria, patients exhibit symptoms that are physiologically impossible. For example, in *glove anesthesia* a person's hand is without feeling, while the sensations in the wrist and arm are normal. Because the nerves run continuously from the shoulder into the hand, there can be no physical cause for this symptom. It became clear to Freud that hysteria was a disorder whose genesis required a psychological explanation.

The Unconscious

Freud did not discover the unconscious. The ancient Greeks, among others, recommended the study of dreams. Just before Freud's time, Johann Wolfgang von Goethe and Friedrich von Schiller "had sought the roots of poetic creation in the unconscious" (Gay, 1988, p. 128), as had many romantic poets and even Freud's contemporary, the novelist Henry James. Freud's contribution lies in his observing this part of the mind, its origins and and contents, with the emerging tools of scientific analysis. His work and the attention it attracted has made the unconscious a part of our public lexicon.

Freud's final attempt to develop a neurologically based psychology (1895) may have arisen from his own earlier and highly sophisticated personal explorations with cocaine (Fuller, 1992). This model, cast aside by Freud, has recently been revived and is seen by some to be a neglected but brilliant precursor to contemporary theories (Pribram, 1962).

Major Concepts

One evening last week when I was hard at work, tormented with just that amount of pain that seems to be the best state to make my brain function, the barriers were suddenly lifted, the veil was drawn aside, and I had a clear vision from the details of the neuroses to the conditions that make consciousness possible. Everything seemed to connect up, the whole worked well together, and one had the impression that the thing was really a machine and would soon go by itself . . . all that was perfectly clear, and still is. Naturally I don't know how to contain myself for pleasure. (Freud, letter to Fliess; in Bonaparte, 1954)

Underlying all of Freud's thinking is the assumption that the body is the sole source of all mental energy. He looked forward to the time when all mental phenomena might be explained with direct reference to brain physiology (Sulloway, 1979).

Many of the most puzzling and seemingly arbitrary turns of psychoanalytic theory . . . are either hidden biological assumptions, or result directly from such assumptions. (Holt, 1965, p. 94)

Psychic Determinism

Freud assumed that there were no discontinuities in mental life and that all thought and all behavior have meaning. He contended that *nothing* occurs randomly, least of all mental processes. There is a cause, even multiple causes, for every thought, feeling, memory, or action. Every mental event is brought about by conscious or unconscious intention and is determined by the events that have preceded it. It appears that many mental events occur spontaneously; however, Freud began to search out and describe the hidden links that join one conscious event to another.

Conscious, Unconscious, Preconscious

Conscious

"The starting point for this investigation is provided by a fact without parallel, which defies all explanation or description—the fact of consciousness. Nevertheless, if anyone speaks of consciousness, we know immediately and from our most personal experience what is meant by it" (Freud, 1940, p. 14). The conscious is only a small portion of the mind; it includes everything that we are aware of in any given moment. Although Freud was interested in the mechanisms of consciousness, he was far more interested in the less exposed and explored areas of consciousness, which he labeled the *preconscious* and the *unconscious* (Herzog, 1991).

There is no need to characterize what we call "conscious." It is the same as the consciousness of philosophers and of everyday opinion. (Freud, 1940, p. 16)

Unconscious

When a conscious thought or feeling seems to have no relation to the thoughts and feelings that preceded it, Freud suggested that the connections are present but unconscious. Once the unconscious links are found, the apparent discontinuity is resolved. "We call a psychical process unconscious whose existence we are obliged to assume—we infer it from its effects—but of which we know nothing" (Freud, 1933, p. 70).

Within the unconscious are instinctual elements, which have never been conscious and which are never accessible to consciousness. In addition, there is material that has been barred—censored and repressed—from consciousness. This material is neither forgotten nor lost, but neither is it remembered. The thought or memory still affects consciousness, but indirectly.

There is a liveliness and an immediacy to unconscious material. Memories that are decades old, when released into consciousness, have lost none of their emotional force. "We have found by experience that unconscious mental processes are in themselves 'timeless.' That is to say to begin with: they are not arranged chronologically, time alters nothing in them, nor can the idea of time be applied to them" (Freud in Fodor & Gaynor, 1958, p. 162).

Preconscious

Strictly speaking, the preconscious is a part of the unconscious, but a part that can easily be made conscious. Those portions of memory that are accessible are part of the preconscious. This might include memories of everything a person did yesterday, a middle name, street addresses, the date of the Norman conquest, favorite foods, the smell of fall leaves burning, an oddly shaped birthday cake eaten during a tenth birthday party, and a host of other past experiences. The preconscious is like a holding area for the memories of a functioning consciousness.

Drives or Impulses

Impulse (*trieb* in German) is incorrectly translated in most older textbooks as "instinct" (Bettelheim, 1982, pp. 87–88). Impulses are pressures to act without conscious thought toward particular ends. Such impulses are "the ultimate cause of all activity" (Freud, 1940, p. 5). Freud labeled the physical aspects of impulses as needs and the mental aspects of impulses as wishes. These needs and wishes propel people to take action.

All impulses have four components: a *source,* an *aim,* an *impetus,* and an *object.* The source, where the need arises, may be a part or all of the body. The aim is to reduce the need until no more action is necessary; that is, to give the organism the satisfaction it now desires. The impetus is the amount of energy, force, or pressure that is used to satisfy or gratify the impulse. This is determined by the urgency of the underlying need. The object of an impulse is whatever thing or action allows satisfaction of the original desire.

Consider the way in which these components appear in a thirsty person. The body gradually dehydrates until it needs more liquids; the source is the growing need for fluids. As the need becomes greater, thirst may be perceived. As this thirst is unsatisfied, it becomes more pronounced. As the intensity rises, so does the impetus or energy available to do some-

Certain inadequacies of our psychic functions and certain performances which are apparently unintentional prove to be well motivated when subjected to psychoanalytic investigation. (Freud, 1901)

There can be no question of restricting one or the other basic impulses to a single region of the mind. They are necessarily present everywhere. (Freud, 1940)

thing to relieve the thirst. The aim is to reduce the tension. The solution is not simply a liquid—milk, water, or beer—but all acts that go toward reducing the tension. These might include getting up, going to the kitchen, choosing among various beverages, preparing one, and drinking it.

The critical point to remember is that the impulse can be fully or partially satisfied in a number of ways, regardless of whether the initial seeking reactions are instinctual. The capacity to satisfy needs in animals is often limited by a pattern of stereotypical behavior. Human impulses only *initiate* the need for action; they do not predetermine the particular action or how it will be completed. The number of solutions open to an individual is a summation of his or her initial biological urge, the mental "wish" (which may or may not be conscious), and a host of prior ideas, habits, and available options.

Freud assumes that the normal, healthy mental and behavioral pattern is aimed at reducing tension to previously acceptable levels. A person with a need will continue seeking activities that can reduce this original tension. The complete cycle of behavior from relaxation to tension and activity and back to relaxation is called a *tension-reduction* model. Tensions are resolved by returning the body to the state of equilibrium that existed before the need arose.

Many seemingly helpful thoughts and behaviors, however, do not seem to reduce tension; in fact, they can create and maintain tension, stress, or anxiety. To Freud, these thoughts and behaviors indicated that the direct expression of an impulse had been redirected or blocked.

Basic Impulses

Freud developed two descriptions of basic impulses. The early model described two opposing forces: the sexual (more generally, the erotic or physically gratifying) and the aggressive, or destructive. Later, he described these forces more globally as either life supporting or death (and destruction) encouraging. Both formulations presupposed a biological, ongoing, and unresolvable pair of conflicts. This basic antagonism is not necessarily visible in mental life, because most of our thoughts and actions are evoked not by one of these instinctual forces in isolation but by both in combination.

Freud was impressed with the diversity and complexity of behavior that arise from the fusion of the basic drives. "The sexual impulses are remarkable for their plasticity, for the facility with which they can change their aims, for their interchangeability—for the ease with which they can substitute one form of gratification for another, and for the way in which they can be held in suspense" (Freud, 1933, p. 97). The impulses are the channels through which the energy can flow. This energy obeys laws of its own.

Libido and Aggressive Energy

Each of these generalized impulses has a separate source of energy. Libido (from the Latin word for *wish,* or *desire*) is the energy available to

A person falls ill of a neurosis if his ego has lost the capacity to allocate his libido in some way. (Freud, 1916)

the life impulses. "Its production, increase or diminution, distribution and displacement should afford us possibilities for explaining the psychosexual phenomena observed" (Freud, 1905a, p. 118).

One characteristic of libido is its "mobility"; that is, the ease with which it can pass from one area of attention to another. Freud pictured the volatile nature of emotional responsiveness as a flow of energy, flowing in and out of areas of immediate concern.

The energy of the aggressive, or the death, impulse has no special name. It has been assumed to have the same general properties as libido, although Freud did not make this clear.

Cathexis

Cathexis is the process by which the available libidinal energy in the psyche is attached to or invested in a person, idea, or thing. Libido that has been cathected is no longer mobile and can no longer move to new objects. It is rooted in whatever part of the psyche has attracted and held it.

The original German word *Besetzung* means both "to occupy" and "to invest." If you imagine your store of libido as a given amount of money, cathexis is the process of investing it. Once a portion has been invested or cathected, it remains there, leaving you with that much less to invest elsewhere.

For example, psychoanalytic studies of mourning interpret the disinterest in normal pursuits and the excessive preoccupation with the recently deceased as a withdrawal of libido from usual relationships and as an extreme cathexis of the lost person.

Psychoanalytic theory is concerned with understanding where libido has been inappropriately cathected. Once released or redirected, this same energy is then available to satisfy other current needs. The need to release bound energies is also found in the ideas of Carl Rogers and Abraham Maslow, as well as in Buddhism and Sufism. Each of these theories comes to different conclusions about the source of psychic energy, but all agree with the Freudian contention that the identification and channeling of psychic energy is a major issue in understanding personality.

> There are certain pathological conditions which seem to leave us no alternative but to postulate that the subject draws on a specific quantity of energy which he distributes in variable proportions in his relationships with objects and with himself. (LaPlanche & Pontalis, 1973, p. 65)

Structure of the Personality

Freud observed in his patients an endless series of psychic conflicts and compromises. He saw impulse pitted against impulse, social prohibitions blocking biological drives, and ways of coping often conflicting with one another. Only late in his career did he order, for himself, this seeming chaos by proposing three basic structural components of the psyche: the *id,* the *ego,* and the *superego.* These are now accepted English terms, but they are artificially abstract and leave a different impression than Freud had intended. His words for each were simple and direct: *Das es* (id) simply means "it," *das Ich* (ego) means "I," and *das uber-Ich* (superego) means "above I." It is too late to correct the damage done by the initial translation of Freud's work into English. His writings were made deliberately obscure so as to sound more scientific, which appealed to the predominant American mind-set of the time (Bettelheim, 1982).

The Id

The id is the original core out of which the rest of the personality emerges. It is biological in nature and contains the reservoir of energy for all parts of the personality. Although the other parts of consciousness develop out of the id, the id itself is primitive and unorganized. "The logical laws of thought do not apply in the id" (Freud, 1933, p. 73). Moreover, the id is not modified as one grows and matures. The id is not changed by experience because it is not in contact with the external world. Its goals are to reduce tension, to increase pleasure, and to minimize discomfort. The id strives to do this through reflex actions (automatic reactions such as sneezing or blinking) and the psychological processes of the other portions of the mind.

The id may be likened to a blind king who has absolute power and authority but whose trusted counselors, primarily the ego, tell him how and where to use these powers.

The contents of the id are almost entirely unconscious. They include primitive thoughts that have never been conscious and thoughts that have been denied and found unacceptable to consciousness. According to Freud, experiences that have been denied or repressed still have the power to affect a person's behavior with undiminished intensity and without any conscious control.

The Ego

The ego is the part of the psyche that is in contact with external reality. It develops out of the id, as the infant becomes aware of its own identity, to serve and placate the id's repeated demands. In order to accomplish this, the ego, like the bark of a tree, protects the id but also draws energy from it. It has the task of ensuring the health, safety, and sanity of the personality. Freud describes the ego's several functions both in relation to the outside world and to the inner world, whose urges it strives to satisfy.

> The principal characteristics of the ego are these. In consequence of the relation which was already established between sensory perception and muscular action, the ego is in control of voluntary movement. It has the task of self-preservation. As regards *external* events, it performs that task by becoming aware of the stimuli from without, by storing up experiences of them (in the memory), by avoiding excessive stimuli (through flight), by dealing with moderate stimuli (through adaptation), and finally by learning to bring about appropriate modifications in the external world to its own advantage (through activity). As regards *internal* events, in relation to the id, it performs that task by gaining control over the demands of the instincts, by deciding whether

In the id there is nothing corresponding to the idea of time, no recognition of the passage of time, and (a thing which is very remarkable and awaits adequate attention in philosophic thought) no alteration of mental processes by the passage of time. . . . Naturally the id knows no values, no good and evil, no morality. (Freud, 1933, p. 74)

they shall be allowed to obtain satisfaction, by postponing that satisfaction to times and circumstances favorable in the external world or by suppressing their excitations completely. Its activities are governed by considerations of the tensions produced by stimuli present within it or introduced into it. The raising of these tensions is in general felt as *unpleasure* and their lowering as *pleasure*. . . . The ego pursues pleasure and seeks to avoid unpleasure. (1940, pp. 2–3)

Thus, the ego is originally created by the id in an attempt to cope with the need to reduce tension and increase pleasure. However, to do this, the ego must in turn control or modulate the id's impulses so that the individual can pursue realistic approaches to life.

The act of dating provides an example of how the ego controls sexual impulses. The id feels tension arising from unfulfilled sexual arousal and, without the ego's influence, would reduce this tension through immediate and direct sexual activity. Within the confines of a date, however, the ego can determine how much sexual expression is possible and how to establish situations in which sexual contact is most fulfilling. The id is responsive to needs, whereas the ego is responsive to opportunities.

The Superego

This last part of the personality's structure develops not from the id but from the ego. The superego serves as a judge or censor over the activities and thoughts of the ego. It is the repository of moral codes, standards of conduct, and those constructs that form the inhibitions for the personality. Freud describes three functions of the superego: conscience, self-observation, and the formation of ideals. As conscience, the superego acts both to restrict, prohibit, or judge conscious activity; but it also acts unconsciously. The unconscious restrictions are indirect, appearing as compulsions or prohibitions. "The sufferer . . . behaves as if he were dominated by a sense of guilt, of which he knows nothing" (Freud, 1907, p. 123).

The superego develops, elaborates, and maintains the moral code of an individual. The child must learn not only the real constraints in a situation, but also the moral views of the parents before being able to act to obtain pleasure or reduce pain. Thus, the superego is not merely based on the behavior of the parents. "A child's superego is in fact constructed on the model, not of its parents but of its parents' superego; the contents which fill it are the same and it becomes the vehicle of tradition and all the time resisting judgments of value which have propagated themselves in this manner from generation to generation" (Freud, 1933, p. 39).

Relationship Between the Three Subsystems

The overarching goal of the psyche is to maintain—and when that is lost, to regain—an acceptable level of dynamic equilibrium that maximizes the pleasure of tension reduction. The energy that is used originates in the id, which has a primitive, instinctual nature. The ego, arising from the id,

[W]e might say that the ego stands for reason and good sense while the id stands for the untamed passions. (Freud, 1933)

[The superego] is like a secret police department, unerringly detecting any trends of forbidden impulses, particularly of an aggressive kind, and punishing the individual inexorably if any are present. (Horney, 1939, p. 211)

exists to deal realistically with the basic drives of the id. It also mediates between the forces that operate on the id, the superego, and the demands of external reality. The superego, arising from the ego, acts as a moral brake or counterforce to the practical concerns of the ego. It sets out a series of guidelines that define and limit the flexibility of the ego.

The id is entirely unconscious, whereas the ego and the superego are only partly so. "Certainly large portions of the ego and superego can remain unconscious, are, in fact, normally unconscious. That means to say that the individual knows nothing of their contents, and that it requires an expenditure of effort to make him conscious of them" (Freud, 1933, p. 69).

Psychoanalysis, in these terms, has a primary goal to strengthen the ego, to make it independent of the overly strict concerns of the superego, and to increase its capacity to deal with material formerly repressed or hidden in the id.

Psychosexual Stages of Development

As an infant becomes a child, a child an adolescent, and an adolescent an adult, there are marked changes in what is desired and how desires are satisfied. The shifting modes of gratification and the physical areas of gratification are the basic elements in Freud's description of the developmental stages. Freud uses the term *fixation* to describe what occurs when a person does not progress normally from stage to stage but remains overly involved with a particular stage. A person fixated in a particular stage will tend to seek gratification of needs in simpler or more childlike ways, rather than as an adult, which would result from normal development.

Psychoanalysis is the first psychology to take seriously the whole human body as a place to live in. . . . Psychoanalysis is profoundly biological. (Le Barre, 1968)

The Oral Stage

Beginning at birth, both needs and gratification are predominantly oral, involving the lips, tongue, and, somewhat later, the teeth. The basic drive of the infant is not social or interpersonal; it is simply to take in nourishment and to relieve the tensions of hunger and thirst. During feeding, the child is also soothed, cuddled, and rocked. The child associates both pleasure and the reduction of tension with the feeding process.

The mouth is the first area of the body that the infant can control; most of the libidinal energy available is directed or focused on this one area. As the child matures, parts of the body develop and become important sites of gratification. However, some energy remains permanently affixed or cathected to the means for oral gratification. In adults, there are many well-developed oral habits and a continued interest in maintaining oral pleasures. Eating, sucking, chewing, smoking, biting, and licking or smacking one's lips are physical expressions of these interests. Constant nibblers, smokers, and those who often overeat may be people who are partially fixated in the oral stage, people whose psychological maturation may be incomplete.

The late oral stage, after teeth have appeared, includes the gratification of the aggressive instincts. Biting the breast, which causes the mother pain and leads to the actual withdrawal of the breast, is an example of this kind of behavior. Adult sarcasm, tearing at one's food, and gossip have been described as being related to this developmental stage.

It is normal to retain some interest in oral pleasures. It can be looked upon as pathological only if it is a dominant mode of gratification; that is, if a person is excessively dependent on oral habits to relieve anxiety or tension.

The Anal Stage

As the child grows, new areas of tension and gratification are brought into awareness. Between the ages of 2 and 4, children generally learn to control the anal sphincter and the bladder. The child pays special attention to urination and defecation. Toilet training prompts a natural interest in self-discovery. The rise in physiological control is coupled with the realization that such control is a new source of pleasure. In addition, children quickly learn that the rising level of control brings them attention and praise from their parents. The reverse is also true: The parents' concern over toilet training allows the child to demand attention both by successful control and by mistakes.

Adult characteristics that are associated with partial fixation at the anal stage are orderliness, parsimoniousness, and obstinacy. Freud observed that these three traits are usually found together. He speaks of the "anal character," whose behavior is closely linked to difficult experiences suffered during this time in childhood.

Part of the confusion that can accompany the anal stage is the apparent contradiction between lavish praise and recognition on the one hand, and the idea that toilet behavior is "dirty" and should be kept a secret on the other. The child does not initially understand that his or her bowel movements and urine are not valued. Small children love to watch the action of the toilet bowl as it flushes, often waving or saying good-bye to their evacuations. It is not unusual for a child to offer part of a bowel movement to a parent as a gift. Having been praised for producing it, the child may be surprised and confused if the parents react with disgust at the gift. Few areas of contemporary life are as saddled with prohibitions and taboos as toilet training and behaviors typical of the anal stage.

The Phallic Stage

Starting as early as age 3, the child moves into the phallic stage, which focuses on the genitals. Freud maintained that this stage is best characterized as phallic, because it is the period when a child either becomes aware of having a penis or becomes aware of lacking one. This is the first stage in which children become conscious of sexual differences.

Freud tried to understand the tensions a child experiences during sexual excitement; that is, pleasure from the stimulation of the genital areas. This excitement is linked in the child's mind with the close physical presence of the parents. The craving for this contact becomes increasingly more difficult for the child to satisfy; the child is struggling for the intimacy that the parents share with each other. This stage is characterized by the child wanting to get into bed with the parents and becoming jealous of the attention the parents give to each other. Freud concluded from his observations that during this period both males and females develop fears about sexual issues.

Freud saw children in the phallic stage reacting to their parents as potential threats to the fulfillment of their needs. Thus, for the boy who wishes to be close to his mother, the father takes on some of the attributes of a rival. At the same time, the boy still wants his father's love and affection, for which his mother is seen as a rival. The child is in the untenable position of wanting and fearing both parents.

In boys, Freud called this conflict the *Oedipal complex,* after the tragic hero in the plays by Greek dramatist Sophocles. In the most familiar version of the myth, Oedipus kills his father and later marries his mother (not knowing either parent). When he is eventually made aware of who he has killed and who he has married, Oedipus disfigures himself by tearing out both of his eyes. Freud believed that every male child reenacts a similar inner drama. He wishes to possess his mother and kill his father to achieve this end. He also fears his father and is afraid that he will be castrated by him, reducing the child to a sexless being. The anxiety around castration, the fear and love for the father as well as the love and sexual desire for the mother, can never be fully resolved. In childhood, the entire complex is repressed. Among the first tasks of the developing superego are to keep this disturbing conflict out of consciousness and to protect the child from acting it out.

For girls the problem is similar, but its expression and solution take a different turn. The girl wishes to possess her father and sees her mother as the major rival. Boys repress their feelings partly out of fear of castration. For girls it is different. The repression of their desires is less severe, less total. This lack of intensity allows the girl to "remain in the Oedipus situation for an indefinite period. She only abandons it late in life, and then incompletely" (Freud, 1933, p. 129).

Whatever form the resolution of the struggle actually takes, most children seem to modify their attachment to their parents sometime after 5 years of age and turn to relationships with peers, school activities, sports, and other skills. This phase, from age 5 to 6 and until the onset of puberty, is called the *latency period.* It is a time when the unresolvable sexual desires of the phallic stage are not attended to by the ego and are successfully repressed by the superego.

So you too are aware that the Oedipus complex is at the root of religious feeling. Bravo! (Freud, letter to Jung; in McGuire, 1974)

Every aspect of the female Oedipus complex has been effectively criticized, using empirical data and methods which did not exist in Freud's lifetime. (Emmanuel, 1992, p. 27)

From then on, until puberty, it goes through the so-called latency period, in which, normally, sexuality makes no progress; on the contrary, the sexual strivings diminish in strength, and much that the child practiced or knew before is given up and forgotten. In this period, after the early blooming of sexual life has withered, are built up such attitudes of the ego as shame, disgust, and morality, designed to stand against the later storms of puberty and to direct the paths of the freshly-awakened sexual desires. (Freud, 1926, p. 216)

The Genital Stage

The final stage of biological and psychological development occurs with the onset of puberty and the consequent return of libidinal energy to the sexual organs. Now boys and girls are made aware of their separate sexual identities and begin to look for ways to fulfill their erotic and interpersonal needs.

Personal Reflection ———————

——————— Psychosexual Stages

The following exercises and questions will give you a chance to experience feelings associated with each developmental stage. (If Freud is correct in his supposition that any remaining fixations from each stage will be linked to anxiety, the following could prove difficult or embarrassing.)

The Oral Stage

Buy a baby bottle with a nipple. Fill it with milk, water, or fruit juice. Either alone or with other members of the class, drink from the bottle. Does drinking, or even the thought of drinking, from a bottle bring up any memories or feelings? If you go ahead and do it, what postures are you most comfortable in? Allow yourself to experience your unfiltered reactions. Share these reactions with the class. Do you find there are responses that are specific to men or women?

The Anal Stage

Notice how much privacy is a consideration in the architecture of public lavatories as well as your bathroom at home. How does privacy play a role in how you behave in the lavatory? Do you avoid meeting anyone's eyes or really even looking at anyone else when you enter a public restroom? Can you imagine urinating in public? In a park? By the side of the highway? In a forest?

Many people have very strongly conditioned toilet behaviors. For example, some people must read while they are sitting on a toilet. What might be the purpose of this behavior?

Share some of your observations with others, and be aware of how it makes you feel to talk about aspects of this exercise. Joking or giggling could be a defense to some discomfort you might have with the topic.

The Phallic Stage

Can you recall what your parents said to you about your genitals when you were little? Can the women in the class recall any thoughts or ideas about boys and their penises? Can the men recall any fear of losing their penises? If you have no memories of these kinds of feelings, is this sufficient reason to assume that there were no such feelings at the time?

The Genital Stage

Write down any misinformation you have had about sexual matters that has been subsequently corrected. (Examples: You were brought by the stork or found at the supermarket. Every time a person has intercourse a pregnancy results.)

Did you think your early sexual experiences have affected your attitudes or beliefs about your own sexuality? Have those experiences reinforced previously held beliefs? How did you feel about your first sexual experience? Do you feel differently now? Can you relate your current attitudes about sexual matters to earlier attitudes or beliefs?

Freud's Views About Women

Freud's ideas about women were based heavily on biological differences between men and women and have come under an ever-increasing volume of attack. Later chapters of this text, especially Chapter 4 (Karen Horney and Humanistic Psychoanalysis) and Chapter 5 (The Psychology of Women: A Relational Approach), discuss current contrasting views. Here, we are presenting only Freud's position so that you understand what other theorists are arguing about.

The desire for a penis and a girl's related realization that she is "lacking" one is a critical juncture in female development. "The discovery that she is castrated is a turning point in a girl's growth. Three possible lines of development diverge from it: one leads to sexual inhibition and to neurosis, the second to a modification of character in the sense of masculinity complex, and the third to normal feminity" (Freud, 1933, p. 126).

This theory has, according to Freud, substantial implications for the development of the female personality. The girl's penis envy persists as a feeling of inferiority and predisposes her to jealousy. Her perpetual desire for a penis, or "superior endowment," is, in the mature woman, converted to the desire for a child, particularly for a son, "who brings the longed-for-penis with him" (Freud, 1933). The woman is never decisively forced to renounce her Oedipal strivings out of castration anxiety. As a consequence, the woman's superego is less developed and internalized than the man's.

Freud asserts that women

> have the hope of someday obtaining a penis in spite of everything. . . . I cannot escape the notion (though I hesitate to give it expression) that for women the level of what is ethically normal is different from what it is in men. . . . We must not allow ourselves to be deflected from such conclusions by the denials of the feminists, who are anxious to force us to regard the two sexes equal in position and worth. (Freud, 1925b, p. 258)

Freud viewed the little girl as a creature in whom phallic strivings were extremely important but inevitably unsatisfied, thus dooming the girl to feelings of perpetual deficiency and inferiority. Yet, despite such assertions (which have, not surprisingly, received much criticism in feminist literature), Freud frequently stated that he never really felt that he understood women or the psychology of women. In fact, he reiterated time and again the tentative nature and value of his own portrayal of female sexuality and its vicissitudes.

Female sexuality is assumed by Freud to constitute disappointed *male* sexuality, rather than the outcome of distinctly female tendencies. Today, this perhaps seems the weakest of suppositions in Freud's theory. Given this central bias, many of Freud's conclusions about the nature of female sexuality and female psychology seem questionable. In fact, some of the phenomena that Freud observed and attempted to describe seem a good deal more plausible when they are stripped of their disappointed-male bias.

The assumption is made in most early psychoanalytic writing that a little girl's lack of a penis leads not only to envy of the boy's penis and *feelings of* inferiority, but also to *actual* inferiority; that is, inferiority in terms of a woman's sense of justice, intellectual curiosity, capacity to implement her ideas independent of a man's approval, and so forth. The notion that penis envy may be a very real and commonly observed clinical phenomenon is dismissed, because it is so intimately connected, in the minds of many people, with the assumption of generalized female inferiority. This is unfortunate because, as Karen Horney (1926) has suggested, penis envy may be a natural experience for females in the same way that envy of pregnancy, childbirth, motherhood, and suckling is a natural experience for males. Even more important, *experiencing envy* does not doom the little girl to perpetual inferiority. Rather, its occurrence, says Horney, may present her with a complex set of feelings, the working through and mastery of which are central to her growth and development as a mature—certainly not inferior—human being.

We may usefully reexamine a traditional psychoanalytic concept—one that has, in fact, received considerable feminist criticism. Instead of eliminating the whole notion of penis envy (and explaining away its frequent clinical manifestations), we may reevaluate the idea that women feel inferior *as a result of penis envy*. The recurring criticism in the feminist litera-

[T]hough anatomy, it is true, can point out the characteristics of maleness and femaleness, psychology cannot. For psychology the contrast between the sexes fades away into activity and passivity, in which we far too readily identify activity with maleness and passivity with femaleness. (Freud, 1930)

ture suggests that Freud's observations about female feelings of inferiority might be reexamined but not dismissed, even if his idea of how they originated does not seem realistic. Learning how to deal (in productive ways) with feelings of envy or of insecurity or of being different from other people is, after all, central to the challenge of growing up.

Ernest Jones, Freud's biographer, was one of the first psychoanalysts who argued that "the little girl's Oedipal attachment develops out of her intrinsic, innate femininity undergoing its own maturation processes" (Fliegel, 1973, p. 387). He also suggested that castration anxiety derives from a basic fear of loss of sexuality and that this fear poses as much threat to the little girl as to the little boy (Jones, 1927).

Dynamics

Psychoanalysis: The Theory

Freud's intention, from his earliest writings, was to better understand those aspects of mental life that were obscure and apparently unreachable. He called both the theory and the therapy *psychoanalysis*.

> Psychoanalysis is the name (1) of a procedure for the investigation of mental processes which are almost inaccessible in any other way, (2) of a method (based upon that investigation) for the treatment of neurotic disorders and (3) of a collection of psychological information obtained along those lines, which is gradually being accumulated into a new scientific discipline. (Freud, 1923, p. 234)

Freud believed that the unconscious material remains unconscious only with considerable and continual expenditure of libido. As this material is made accessible, energy is released that can be used by the ego for healthier pursuits.

The release of blocked materials can minimize self-destructive attitudes. The need to be punished or the need to feel inadequate can be reevaluated by bringing into awareness those early events or fantasies that led to the need. People may then be freed from the suffering they perpetually bring upon themselves. For example, many Americans are concerned about their sexual attractiveness: penises are too short or too thin; breasts are too small, too large, or not well formed; and so forth. Most of these beliefs arise during the teenage years or earlier. The unconscious residues of these attitudes are visible in worries over sexual adequacy, desirability, premature ejaculation, frigidity, and a host of related concerns. If these unexpressed fears are explored, exposed, and relieved, there can be a rise in available sexual energy as well as a lowering of overall tension.

The theory of psychoanalysis suggests that it is possible, but difficult, to come to terms with the recurring demands of the id. "The analysis aims

The more psychoanalysis becomes known, the more will incompetent doctors dabble in it and naturally make a mess of it. This will then be blamed on you and your theory. (Jung, letter to Freud; in McGuire, 1974)

at laying bare the complexes which have been repressed as a result of the painful feelings associated with them, and which produce signs of resistance when there is an attempt to bring them into consciousness" (Freud, 1906, p. 109).

"One of the tasks of psychoanalysis, as you know, is to lift the veil of amnesia which shrouds the earliest years of childhood and to bring the expressions of infantile sexual life which are hidden behind it into conscious memory" (Freud, 1933, p. 28). The goals as described by Freud assume that if one is freed from the inhibitions of the unconscious, the ego establishes new levels of satisfaction in all areas of functioning. Thus, the resolution of anxieties rooted in early childhood frees blocked or displaced energy for more realistic and complete gratification of one's needs.

Dreams and Dreamwork

In listening to the free associations of his patients, as well as in his own self-analysis, Freud began to scrutinize the reports and memories of dreams. In *The Interpretation of Dreams* (1900), he wrote how dreams help the psyche protect and satisfy itself. Obstacles and unmitigated desires fill daily life. Dreams are a partial balance, both physically and psychologically, between instinctual urges and real-life limitations. Dreaming is a way of channeling unfulfilled desires through consciousness without arousing the physical body.

> A structure of thoughts, mostly very complicated, which has been built up during the day and not brought to settlement—a day remnant—clings firmly even during night to the energy which it has assumed . . . and thus threatens to disturb sleep. This day remnant is transformed into a dream by the dream-work and in this way rendered harmless to sleep. (Freud in Fodor & Gaynor, 1958, pp. 52–53)

More important than the biological value of dreams are the psychological effects of *dreamwork*. Dreamwork is "the whole of the operations which transform the raw materials of the dream—bodily stimuli, day's residues, dream-thoughts—so as to produce the manifest dream" (LaPlanche & Pontalis, 1973, p. 125). A dream does not simply appear. It develops to meet specific needs, although these are not clearly described by the dream's manifest content.

Almost every dream can be understood as a *wish fulfillment*. The dream is an alternative pathway to satisfy the desires of the id. While awake the ego strives to allow pleasure and reduce tension. During sleep, unfulfilled needs are sorted, combined, and arranged so that the dream sequences allow additional satisfaction or tension reduction. For the id, it is unimportant whether satisfaction occurs in physical, sensory reality or in internal, imagined dream reality. In both cases, accumulated energies are discharged. The dream plays out, on at least two levels, current issues

We recognize the soundness of the wish-fulfillment theory up to a certain point, but we go beyond it. In our view it does not exhaust the meaning of the dream. (Jung, letter to Freud; in McGuire, 1974)

that are unresolved or that are part of larger, older patterns that have never been resolved.

Repetitive dreams may occur when a daytime event triggers the same kind of anxiety that led to the original dream. For example, an active, happily married woman in her sixties may still dream, from time to time, of going to take a college exam. When she arrives at the classroom, she sees that the examination is over. She has arrived too late. She has this dream when she is anxious over some current difficulty; however, her anxiety is related neither to college nor to examinations, both of which she left behind many years ago.

Many dreams do not appear to be satisfying; some are depressing, some disturbing, some frightening, and many simply obscure. Many dreams seem to be the reliving of past events, whereas some appear to be prophetic. Through the detailed analysis of dozens of dreams, linking them to events in the life of the dreamer, Freud was able to show that dreamwork is a process of selection, distortion, transformation, inversion, displacement, and other modifications of an original wish. These changes render the modified wish acceptable to the ego even if the original wish is totally unacceptable to waking consciousness. Freud suggested reasons for the permissiveness in dreams where we act beyond the moral restrictions of our waking lives. In dreams we kill, maim, or destroy enemies,

> A dream then, is a psychosis, with all the absurdities, delusions and illusions of a psychosis. No doubt it is a psychosis which has only a short duration, which is harmless and even performs a useful function. (Freud, 1940)

> Dreams are not to be likened to the unregulated sounds that rise from a musical instrument struck by the blow of some external force instead of a player's hand; they are not meaningless, they are not absurd; . . . they can be inserted into the chain of intelligible waking mental acts; they are constructed by a highly complicated activity of the mind. (Freud, 1900)

Personal Reflection _____

_____ Investigate Your Own Dreams

Make a dream journal by keeping a pad of paper by your bed. In the morning, before you do anything else, make a few notes about your dreams. Even if you have never remembered dreams before, this procedure will help you to recall them. It has been shown that groups of students given this as an assignment recall dreams regularly within a few days.

Later in the day, write out your dreams in as much detail as you can recall. What are your associations with particular aspects of your dreams? See if these associations point to possible meanings. For example, might your dreams be attempts at wish fulfillment? Try to guess what various segments might mean. Pay attention to those fragments that seem to be part of your "day residue." Do you notice anything that reflects your desires or attitudes toward others?

Keep this journal for several weeks. As you read other parts of this text, you will learn other ways to analyze dreams. From time to time, go over your dream journal, and see if you can make new interpretations. Notice especially any recurrent themes or patterns. (Chapter 2 provides a slightly different approach to recording your dreams.)

relatives, or friends; we act out perversions and take as sexual partners a wide range of people. In dreams, we combine people, places, and occasions that would be an impossible mix in our waking world.

Dreams attempt to fulfill wishes, but they are not always successful. "Under certain conditions, the dream can only achieve its end in a very incomplete way, or has to abandon it entirely; an unconscious fixation to the trauma seems to head the list of these obstacles to the dream functions" (Freud, 1933, p. 29).

Within the context of psychoanalysis, the therapist aids the patient in interpreting dreams to facilitate the recovery of unconscious material. Freud made certain generalizations about special kinds of dreams (e.g., falling dreams, flying dreams, swimming dreams, and dreams about fire), but he makes it clear that the general rules are not always valid. An individual's own dream associations are more important than any preconceived set of rules of interpretation.

Critics of Freud often suggest that he overinterpreted the sexual components of dreams to conform to his overall theory. Freud's rejoinder is clear: "I have never maintained the assertion which has often been ascribed to me that dream-interpretation shows that all dreams have a sexual content or are derived from sexual motive forces" (Freud, 1925a, p. 47). What he stressed was that dreams are neither random nor accidental but are a way to satisfy unfulfilled wishes.

Mental Health and Mental Illness

Anxiety

The major problem for the psyche is how to cope with anxiety. Anxiety is triggered by an expected or foreseen increase in tension or displeasure; it can develop in any situation (real or imagined) when the threat to some part of the body or psyche is too great to be ignored, mastered, or discharged.

Events with a potential to cause anxiety include, but are not limited to, the following:

1. Loss of a desired object—for example, a child deprived of a parent, a close friend, or a pet.

2. Loss of love—for example, rejection, failure to win back the love or approval of someone who matters to you.

3. Loss of identity—for example, castration fears, loss of face, or fear of public ridicule.

4. Loss of love for self—for example, superego disapproval of acts or traits as well as acts which result in guilt or self-hate.

There are two general ways to decrease the anxiety. The first is to deal with the situation directly. We overcome obstacles, either confront or run from threats, and resolve or come to terms with problems to minimize

Dreams are the true interpreters of our inclinations, but art is required to sort and understand them. (Montaigne, 1580, Essays)

Dreams are real while they last—can we say more of life? (Havelock Ellis)

Anxiety makes repression and not, as we used to think, the other way round. (Freud, 1933, p. 69)

their impact. In these ways, we are working to eliminate difficulties, lowering the chances of their recurrence, and also decreasing the prospects of additional anxiety in the future. In Hamlet's words, we "take up arms against a sea of troubles and by opposing end them."

The alternative approach defends against the anxiety by distorting or denying the situation itself. The ego protects the whole personality against the threat by falsifying the nature of the threat. The ways in which the distortions are accomplished are called *defense mechanisms*. These are fully described only by Anna Freud (1936), Freud's daughter, and are widely accepted and have become an integral part of the core concepts of psychoanalysis.

Defense Mechanisms

The defense mechanisms described here are repression, denial, rationalization, reaction formation, projection, isolation, regression, and sublimation. All the defenses except sublimation block direct expression of instinctual needs. Although any of these mechanisms can be found in healthy individuals, their very presence is an indication of possible neurosis.

Repression. "The essence of repression lies simply in turning something away, and keeping it at a distance, from the consciousness" (Freud, 1915, p. 147). Repression forces a potentially anxiety-provoking event, idea, or perception away from consciousness, thus precluding any possible resolution. Unfortunately, the repressed element is still part of the psyche, though unconscious, and still remains active. "Repression is never performed once and for all but requires a constant expenditure of energy to maintain the repression, while the repressed constantly tried to find an outlet" (Fenichel, 1945, p. 150).

Hysterical symptoms are often found to have originated in earlier repression. Some psychosomatic ailments such as asthma, arthritis, and ulcers may be linked to repression. Excessive lassitude, phobias, and impotence or frigidity may also be derivatives of repressed feelings. For example, if you have strongly ambivalent feelings about your father, you might love him and at the same time wish he were dead. The desire for his death, the accompanying fantasies, and your resulting feelings of guilt and shame might all be unconscious because both your ego and your superego would find the idea unacceptable. Should your father actually die, this complex would be still more rigidly repressed. To admit to the feelings would mean you would feel pleasure at his death, a feeling even more unacceptable to your superego than the original resentment or hostility. In this situation, you might appear unaffected or unmoved by his death, the repression withholding your genuine and appropriate grief and loss as well as your inexpressible hostility.

Denial. Denial is the unwillingness to accept an event that disturbs the ego. Adults have a tendency to "daydream" that certain events are not so,

If the ego is obliged to admit its weakness, it breaks out into anxiety—realistic anxiety in regarding the face of the external world, moral anxiety regarding the super-ego, and neurotic anxiety regarding the strength of the passions in the id. (Freud, 1933)

that they didn't really happen. This flight into fantasy can take many forms, some of which seem absurd to the objective observer. The following story is an illustration:

> A woman was brought into court at the request of her neighbor. This neighbor charged that the woman had borrowed and damaged a valuable vase. When it came time for the woman to defend herself, her defense was threefold: "In the first place, I never borrowed the vase. Second, it was chipped when I took it. Finally, your honor, I returned it in perfect condition."

People are in general not candid over sexual matters. They do not show their sexuality freely, but to conceal it they wear a heavy overcoat woven of a tissue of lies, as though the weather were bad in the world of sexuality. (Freud in Malcolm, 1980)

The form of denial found most often in psychotherapy is a remarkable tendency to remember events incorrectly. An example is the patient who vividly recalls one version of an incident, then at a later time may recall the incident differently and become suddenly aware that the first version was a defensive fabrication.

Freud did not claim that his clinical observations were entirely original. In fact, he quotes Charles Darwin's and Friedrich Nietzsche's observations about themselves. Darwin, in his autobiography, noted:

> I had during years followed a golden rule, namely, whenever I came across a published fact, a new observation or idea, which ran counter to my general results, I made a memorandum of it without fail and at once; for I had found by experience that such facts and ideas were far more apt to slip the memory than favorable ones. (Darwin in Freud, 1901, p. 148)

Nietzsche commented on a different aspect of the same process:

> "I have done that," says my memory. "It is impossible that I should have done it," says my pride, and it remains inexorable. Finally my memory yields. (Nietzsche in Freud, 1901, p. 148)

Rationalization. Rationalization is the process of finding acceptable reasons for unacceptable thoughts or actions. It is a process whereby a person presents an explanation that is either logically consistent with or ethically acceptable for an attitude, action, idea, or feeling that arises from other motivating sources. We use it to justify our behavior when in fact the reasons for our actions are not commendable or not even understood by us. The following statements might be rationalizations (the statements in parentheses are possible unexpressed feelings):

"I'm doing this for your own good." (I want to do this to you. I don't want it done to me. I even want you to suffer a little bit.)

"The experiment was a logical continuation of my prior work." (It started as a mistake; I was lucky that it worked out.)

Rationalization is a way of accepting pressure from the superego; it disguises our motives, rendering our actions morally acceptable. As an obstacle to growth, it prevents the person who is rationalizing (or anyone else!) from working with, observing, and understanding the genuine, less commendable motivating forces. Viewed from outside, as in the following story, its foolish aspect is obvious.

Cheese for Choice

"I have chosen," said the mouse, "to like cheese. Such an important decision, needless to say, cannot be arrived at without a sufficient period of careful deliberation. One does not deny the immediate, indefinable aesthetic attraction of the substance. Yet this in itself is possible only to the more refined type of individual—as an example, the brutish fox lacks the sensitive discrimination even to approach cheese.

"Other factors in the choice are not less susceptible to rational analysis: which is, of course, as it should be.

"The attractive colour, suitable texture, adequate weight, interestingly different shapes, relatively numerous places of occurrence, reasonable ease of digestion, comparative abundance of variety in nutritional content, ready availability, considerable ease of transport, total absence of side-effects—these and a hundred other easily defined factors abundantly prove my good sense and deep insights, consciously exercised in the making of this wise and deliberate choice." (Shah, 1972, p. 138)

Reaction Formation.   This mechanism substitutes behaviors or feelings that are diametrically opposed to the actual wish; it is an explicit and usually unconscious inversion of the wish.

Like other defense mechanisms, reaction formations are developed first in childhood. "As the child becomes aware of sexual excitement which cannot be fulfilled, the sexual 'excitations' evoke opposing mental forces which, in order to suppress this unpleasure effectively, build up the mental dams of disgust, shame and morality" (Freud, 1905a, p. 178). Not only is the original idea repressed, but any shame or self-reproach that might arise by admitting such thoughts is also excluded from awareness.

Unfortunately, the side effects of reaction formation may cripple social relationships. The principal identifying characteristics of reaction formation are its excessiveness, its rigidity, and its extravagance. The urge being denied must be repeatedly obscured.

The following letter was written to a researcher from an antivivisectionist. It is a clear example of one feeling—compassion toward all living things—used to disguise another feeling—a desire to harm and torture.

The person who has built up reaction-formations does not develop certain defense mechanisms for use when an instinctual danger threatens; he has changed his personality structure as if this danger were continually present, so that he may be ready whenever the danger occurs. (Fenichel, 1945)

I read [a magazine article] . . . on your work on alcoholism. . . . I am surprised that anyone who is as well educated as you must be to hold the position that you do would stoop to such a depth as to torture helpless little cats in the pursuit of a cure for alcoholics. . . . A drunkard does not want to be cured—a drunkard is just a weak-minded idiot who belongs in the gutter and should be left there. Instead of torturing helpless little cats why not torture the drunks or better still exert your would-be noble effort toward getting a bill passed to *exterminate* the drunks. . . . My greatest wish is that you have brought home to you a torture that will be a thousandfold greater than what you have, and are doing to the little animals. . . . If you are an example of what a noted psychiatrist should be I'm glad I am just an ordinary human being without letters after my name. I'd rather be just myself with a clear conscience, *knowing I have not hurt any living creature,* and can sleep without seeing frightened, terrified dying cats—because I know they must die after you have finished with them. No punishment is too great for you and I hope I live to read about your mangled body and long suffering before you finally die—and I'll laugh long and loud. (Masserman, 1961, p. 38)

Reaction formations may be evident in any excessive behavior. The housewife who is continually cleaning her home may, in reality, be concentrating her awareness on being with and examining dirt. The parent who cannot admit his or her resentment of the children "may interfere so much in their lives, under the pretext of being concerned about their welfare and safety, that [the] overprotection is really a form of punishment" (Hall, 1954, p. 93). Reaction formation masks parts of the personality and restricts a person's capacity to respond to events; the personality may become relatively inflexible.

Projection. The act of attributing to another person, animal, or object the qualities, feelings, or intentions that originate in oneself is called *projection.* It is a defense mechanism whereby the aspects of one's own personality are displaced from within the individual onto the external environment. The threat is treated as if it were an external force. A person can therefore deal with actual feelings, but without admitting or being aware of the fact that the feared idea or behavior is his or her own. The following statements might be projections (the statement in parentheses might be the actual unconscious feeling):

1. "All that men/women want is one thing." (I think about sex a lot.)

2. "You can never trust a wop/spic/nigger/wasp/honkie/college boy/woman/priest." (I want to take unfair advantage of others sometimes.)

3. "You're mad at me." (I'm mad at you.)

Whenever we characterize something "out there" as evil, dangerous, perverted, and so forth, without acknowledging that these characteristics might also be true for us, we are probably projecting. It is equally true that when we see others as being powerful, attractive, capable, and so forth, without appreciating the same qualities in ourselves, we are also projecting. The critical variable in projection is that we do not see in ourselves what seems vivid and obvious in another.

Research into the dynamics of prejudice has shown that people who tend to stereotype others also display little insight into their own feelings. People who deny having a specific personality trait are more critical of that trait when they see it in or project it onto others (Sears, 1936).

Isolation.   Isolation separates the anxiety-arousing parts of a situation from the rest of the psyche. It is the act of partitioning off, so that little or no emotional reaction remains connected to the event.

When a person discusses problems that have been isolated from the rest of the personality, the events are recounted without feeling, as if they had happened to a third party. This stoic approach can become a dominant style of coping. A person may withdraw more and more into ideas, having less and less contact with his or her own feelings.

Children may play at this, dividing their identities into good and bad aspects. They may take a toy animal and have it say and do all kinds of forbidden things. The animal's personality may be tyrannical, rude, sar-

Personal Reflection _____

_____ Regressive Behaviors

Regression is a primitive way of coping. Although it reduces anxiety, it often leaves the source of the anxiety unresolved. Consider the following extensive list of regressive behaviors suggested by Calvin Hall. See if it includes any of your own behaviors.

Even healthy, well-adjusted people make regressions from time to time in order to reduce anxiety, or, as they say, to blow off steam. They smoke, get drunk, eat too much, lose their tempers, bite their nails, pick their noses, break laws, talk baby talk, destroy property, masturbate, read mystery stories, go to the movies, engage in unusual sexual practices, chew gum and tobacco, dress up as children, drive fast and recklessly, believe in good and evil spirits, take naps, fight and kill one another, bet on the horses, daydream, rebel against or submit to authority, gamble, preen before the mirror, act out their impulses, pick on scapegoats, and do a thousand and one other childish things. Some of these regressions are so commonplace that they are taken to be signs of maturity. Actually they are all forms of regression used by adults. (1954, pp. 95–96)

castic, and unreasonable. Thus, a child may be able to display, through the animal, these "splitting" behaviors that parents would not tolerate under normal circumstances.

Freud felt that the normal prototype of isolation is logical thinking, which also tries to detach the content from the emotional situation in which it is found. Isolation becomes a defense mechanism only when it is used to prevent the ego from accepting anxiety-ridden aspects of situations or relationships (1926b).

Regression. Regression is a reversion to an earlier level of development or to a mode of expression that is simpler and more childlike. It is a way of alleviating anxiety by withdrawing from realistic thinking into behaviors that have reduced anxiety in the past. Linus, in the "Peanuts" comic strip, always returns to a safe psychological situation when he is under stress; he feels secure when he is holding his blanket.

Sublimation. Sublimation is the process whereby energy originally directed toward sexual or aggressive goals is redirected toward new aims—often artistic, intellectual, or cultural goals. Sublimation has been called the "successful defense" (Fenichel, 1945). If the original energy can be thought of as a river that periodically floods, destroying homes and property, sublimation is the building of dams and diversionary channels. These in turn may be used to generate electric power, irrigate formerly arid areas, create parks, and open up other recreational opportunities. The original energy of the river has been successfully diverted into socially acceptable or culturally sanctioned channels. Sublimation, unlike the other defenses, actually resolves and eliminates the tension.

Personal Reflection ——————

—————————————— Defense Mechanisms

Recall a time or an event that was psychologically painful; for example, the death of a close friend or relative, or a time when you were deeply humiliated, beaten up, or caught in a crime. Notice first of all your disinterest in recalling the event clearly and, further, your resistance to even thinking about it. Your tendency may be to say: "I don't want to do this. I can skip this exercise. Why should I think about that again?" If you can, overcome your initial defenses with an act of will and try to recall the event. You may be aware of strong feelings all over again. If it is too difficult to stay focused on the memory, notice instead the ways your mind keeps diverting your attention. Can you begin to see the mechanisms people use to avoid psychic tension?

The sublimated energy is responsible for what we call civilization. Freud argues that the enormous energy and complexity of civilization is the result of the desire to find acceptable and sufficient outlets for suppressed energy. Civilization encourages the transcendence of the original drives and, in some cases, creates alternative goals that can be more satisfying to the id than the satisfaction of the original urges. This transformation "places extraordinarily large amounts of force at the disposal of civilized activity, and it does this in virtue of its especially marked characteristic of being able to displace its aim without materially diminishing its intensity" (Freud, 1908, p. 187).

> The forces that can be employed for cultural activities are thus to a great extent obtained through the suppression of what are known as the "perverse" elements of sexual excitation. (Freud, 1908)

Summary of the Defense Mechanisms

The defenses described here are ways the psyche has to protect itself from internal or external tension. The defenses avoid reality (repression), exclude reality (denial), redefine reality (rationalization), or reverse reality (reaction formation). These mechanisms place inner feelings on the outer world (projection), partition reality (isolation), cause a withdrawal from reality (regression), or redirect reality (sublimation). In every case, libidinal energy is necessary to maintain the defense, effectively limiting the flexibility and strength of the ego.

> They tie up psychological energy which could be used for more effective ego activities. When a defense becomes very influential, it dominates the ego and curtails its flexibility and its adaptability. Finally, if the defenses fail to hold, the ego has nothing to fall back upon and is overwhelmed by anxiety. (Hall, 1954, p. 96)

Structure

Energy

At the center of Freud's theories is his concept of energy flow. It is the link between his concepts of the unconscious, psychological development, personality, and neurosis. "His theories on instincts deal with the *source* of energy; his theories on psychosexual development, fixation, and regression deal with the *diversion* of energy; and his theories of the id, ego, and superego deal with *conflicts* of energy" (Cohen, 1982, p. 4).

Body

Freud developed his theories based on physical and biological assumptions. Basic drives arise from somatic sources; libidinal energy is derived from physical energy; responses to tension are both mental and physical. The body is the core of experience. As Sulloway points out, "It was Freud's continued appeal to biological assumptions that justified his personal conviction that he had finally created a universally valid theory of human thought and behavior" (1979, p. 419).

> The ego is first and foremost a body ego. (Freud, 1937)

Moreover, the primary focuses of energy are through the various forms of sexual expression (oral, anal, and genital). Full maturity is partially defined as full genital sexuality in terms of capacity and quality of expression. Many of Freud's critics never looked at his full theory, but instead became obsessed with his reintroduction of physical and sexual concerns into the fields of so-called mental functioning.

In spite of Freud's recognition of the centrality of the body, his own writings on therapy almost totally ignore it. Perhaps the cultural denial of the body that characterized the age in which he lived colored his own apparent lack of interest in gestures, postures, and physical expressions exhibited by his patients. Many of the later Freudians, such as Erik Erikson and Frederick Perls, as well as those theorists who broke from Freud, such as Carl Jung and Wilhelm Reich, paid more attention to the actual physical body but less attention to the biological theories surrounding it.

Social Relationships

> The all-inclusive nature of sex energy has not yet been correctly understood by psychologists. In fact, the very term *reproductive* or *sex energy* is a misnomer. Reproduction is but one of the aspects of the life energy, of which the other theater of activity is the brain. (Gopi Krishna, 1974)

Adult interactions and relationships are greatly influenced by early childhood experiences. The first relationships, those that occur within the nuclear family, are the defining ones. All later relationships relate back to the ways those initial relationships were formed and maintained. The basic patterns of child-mother, child-father, and child-sibling are the prototypes against which later encounters are unconsciously measured. Later relationships are, to some degree, recapitulations of the dynamics, tensions, and gratifications that occurred within the original family.

Our choices in life—lovers, friends, bosses, even our enemies—are derivatives of the parent-child bonds. The natural rivalries are recapitulated in our sex roles and in the way we accommodate the demands of others. Over and over again, we play out the dynamics begun in our homes, frequently picking as partners people who reawaken in us unresolved aspects of our early needs. For some, these are conscious choices. For others, choices are made without conscious knowledge of the underlying dynamics.

> I confess that plunging into sexuality in theory and practice is not to my taste. But what have my taste and feeling about what is seemly and what is unseemly to do with the question of what is true? (Breuer in Sulloway, 1979, p. 80)

People shy away from this aspect of Freudian theory because it suggests that one's future choices are beyond one's control. The issue turns on the question of how much childhood experience determines adult choices. For example, one critical period in developing relationships occurs during the phallic stage, when both sexes first confront their growing erotic feelings toward their parents and the concomitant inability to gratify these urges. According to Freudian theory, even as the resulting Oedipal complications are resolved, these dynamics continue to affect later relationships.

Relationships are built on a foundation of the residual effects of intense early experiences. Teenage, young adult, and adult dating as well as friendship and marriage patterns are a reworking of unresolved childhood issues.

Personal Reflection

Are There Patterns in Your Life?

Here is a way to look at your current relationships as they relate to your relationships with your parents.

Part I 1. Make a list of some of the people you have liked or loved most in your life—excluding your parents. List men and women separately.

2. Describe desirable and undesirable aspects of each person.

3. Notice, reflect on, or record the similarities and differences in your lists. Are there certain traits common to the men and women?

Part II 1. Make a list of the desirable and undesirable characteristics of your parents.

2. List the desirable and undesirable characteristics of your parents as you saw them when you were a child. (The two lists may or may not overlap.)

Part III Compare and contrast the list of attributes of your parents with those of the other important people.

Emotions

What Freud uncovered, in an age that had worshiped reason and denied the value and the power of emotion, was that we are not primarily rational animals, but are driven by powerful emotional forces, the genesis of which is often unconscious. Emotions are the avenues for the release of tension and the appreciation of pleasure. Emotions may also serve the ego by helping it to keep certain memories out of awareness. For example, strong emotional reactions may actually mask a childhood trauma. A phobic reaction effectively prevents a person from approaching an object or class of objects that might trigger a more threatening source of anxiety.

It was through observing both the appropriate and inappropriate expressions of emotion that Freud found the keys to uncovering and understanding the motivating forces within the unconscious.

Intellect

The intellect is one of the tools available to the ego. The person who is most free is the one who is able to use reason when it is expedient and whose emotional life is open to conscious inspection. Such a person is not driven by unfulfilled remnants of past events, but can respond directly to each situation, balancing individual preferences against the restrictions imposed by the culture.

Reason, so Freud felt, is the only tool—or weapon—we have to make sense of life, to dispense with illusions . . . to become independent of fettering authorities, and thus to establish our own authority. (Fromm, 1959)

The most striking and probably the strongest emotional force in Freud was his passion for truth and his uncompromising faith in reason. For him, reason was the only human capacity that could help to solve the problem of existence or at least ameliorate the suffering that is inherent in human life.

For Freud, as for the age in which he lived, the impact of Darwin's work cannot be underestimated. An unquestioned goal of the time was to prove that rational thought placed human beings above the beasts. Much of the resistance to Freud's work arose from the evidence that people were in fact less reasonable, less in control of their emotions, and more like animals than anyone had suspected. Freud's own hope and personal belief was that reason was primary and that the intellect was the most, if not the only, important tool that consciousness possessed to control its darker side.

What Freud realized was that any aspect of unconscious existence, raised into the light of consciousness, might be dealt with rationally. "Where id is, there let ego be" (Freud, 1933, p. 80). Where the irrational, instinctual urges dominate, let them be exposed, moderated, and dominated by the ego. If the original drive is not to be suppressed, it becomes the task of the ego, using the intellect, to devise safe and sufficient methods for satiation. The use of intellect depends entirely on the capacity and strength of the ego.

Self

The self is the total being: the body, the instincts, as well as the conscious and unconscious processes. A self independent of the body or detached from it has no place in Freud's biological beliefs. When such metaphysical questions were raised, Freud asserted that they were not within his province as a scientist. Psychoanalysts have since moved past Freud's position and have written extensively about the self.

Therapist/Therapy

There is still no acceptable evidence to support the view that psychoanalysis is an effective treatment. (Rachman & Wilson, 1980, p. 76)

We have been chiefly concerned with Freud's general theory of personality. Freud himself, however, was involved with the practical applications of his work—the practice of psychoanalysis. The aim of psychoanalysis is to help the patient establish the best possible level of ego functioning, given the inevitable conflicts arising from the external environment, the superego, and the relentless instinctual demands of the id. Kenneth Colby, a former training analyst, describes the goal of the analytic procedure:

> In speaking of the goal of psychotherapy, the term "cure" frequently intrudes. It requires definition. If by "cure" we mean relief of the patient's current neurotic difficulties, then that is certainly our goal. If by "cure" we mean a lifelong freedom from emotional conflict and psychological problems, then that cannot be our goal. Just as a person

may suffer pneumonia, a fracture, and diabetes during his lifetime and require particular medication and separate treatment for each condition, so another person may experience at different times a depression, impotence, and a phobia, each requiring psychotherapy as the condition arises. Our aim is to treat the presenting problems, hoping that the work will strengthen the patient against further neurotic difficulties but realizing that therapy cannot guarantee a psychological prophylaxis. (1951, p. 4)

The Role of the Psychoanalyst

The therapist's task is to help the patient recall, recover, and reintegrate unconscious materials in order that the patient's current life can become more satisfying. Freud says:

> We pledge him to obey the *fundamental rule* of analysis which is henceforward to govern his behavior towards us. He is to tell us not only what he can say intentionally and willingly, what will give him relief like a confession, but everything else as well that comes into his head, even if it is *disagreeable* for him to say it, even if it seems to him *unimportant* or actually *nonsensical*. (1940, p. 31)

The analyst is supportive of these disclosures, and neither critical nor approving of their content. The analyst takes no moral position but serves as a blank screen for the patient's opinions. The therapist presents as little as possible of his or her personality to the patient. This gives the patient the freedom to treat the analyst in a host of ways, transferring to the therapist attitudes, ideas, even physical characteristics that actually belong to persons in the patient's past. This *transference* is critical to the therapeutic process because it brings past events into a new context that fosters understanding. For example, if a female patient starts to treat a male therapist as she treats her father—outwardly submissive and deferential, but covertly hostile and disrespectful—the analyst can clarify these feelings for the patient. He can point out that he, the therapist, is not the cause of the feelings, but that they originate within the patient herself and may reflect aspects of her relationship with her father that she has repressed.

Transference makes the therapy a living process. Rather than just talking about life, the patient forms a critical relationship with the therapist. To aid the patient in making these connections, the analyst interprets some of what the patient is saying, suggesting links that the patient may or may not have previously acknowledged. This process of interpretation is a matter of intuition and clinical experience.

As part of the psychoanalytic process, the patient is encouraged, never pressured, to uncover material. Freud saw analysis as a natural process; the energy that had been repressed slowly emerges into consciousness where it can be used by the developing ego. "Whenever we succeed in analyzing a symptom into its elements, in freeing an impulse from one

To stand firm against this general assault by the patient the analyst requires to have been fully and completely analyzed himself. . . . The analyst himself, on whom the fate of so many people depends, must know and be in control of even the most recondite weaknesses of his own character; and this is impossible without a fully completed analysis. (Ferenczi, 1955)

The concept of Transference . . . contends that the observation, understanding and discussion of the patient's emotional reactions to the psychoanalytical situation constitute the most direct ways of reaching an understanding of his character structure and consequently of his difficulties. It has become the most powerful, and indeed the indispensable, tool of analytical therapy. (Horney, 1939, pp. 33–34)

nexus, it does not remain in isolation, but immediately enters into a new one" (Freud, 1919, p. 161).

The task of the therapist is to expose, explore, and isolate the component impulses that have been denied or distorted by the patient. Reforming or establishing newer and healthier habits occurs without the intrusion of the therapist. "The psychosynthesis is thus achieved during analytic treatment without our intervention, automatically and inevitably" (Freud, 1919, p. 161).

Limitations of Psychoanalysis

Analysis is not for everyone, nor does the proper application of its procedures inevitably lead to improvement. Freud says:

Personal Reflection ——————————
—————————————————————— Early Memories

Freud found that early memories were often indicative of current personal issues. You can try testing this assumption by doing the following exercise.

Find a partner. One of you will recall your earliest memory while the other records it on paper. (You will trade roles so don't worry about who goes first.)

1. The speaker should sit so as not to be looking at the recorder. Recall your earliest memory or any very early memory. Tell it to the person who is the recorder. Talk no more than five minutes. The more clearly and vividly you can recall the memory, the more you may gain from this exercise. Other memories may emerge in addition to the one you are describing. Feel free to mention them as well. Remember, it's the recorder's task to take notes while the speaker talks about past events. Do not interrupt. Pay attention to the importance your partner puts on any aspect of a memory. In your notes, you can use the Freudian terms described in this chapter.

2. After five minutes, stop. Without any discussion, switch roles. The person who was the speaker is now writing down the partner's memories. At the end of another five minutes, stop. Think about what you have said and what you have heard silently for a minute or so.

3. Discuss your notes with each other. Point out any implications and connections you observe. Note differences in feelings expressed by your partner. Remember that defense mechanisms can and do distort or disguise memories. Try to relate aspects of these first memories to current events in your life.

The field of application of analytic therapy lies in the transference neuroses—phobias, hysteria, obsessional neurosis—and further, abnormalities of character which have been developed in place of these diseases. Everything differing from these, narcissistic and psychotic conditions, is unsuitable to a greater or less extent. (1933, p. 155)

Some analysts have said that people who are already functioning well, whose ego structure is healthy and intact, make the best candidates for psychoanalysis. Like any other form of treatment, it has inherent limitations that have been argued from every point of view. It has been compared favorably to Buddhism, because both provide ways to alleviate human suffering (Pruett, 1987). On the other hand, psychoanalysis has been scrutinized to see if it could stand up to a Marxist examination (Volosinov, 1927). Although Freud hoped that psychoanalysis could help explain the whole of human consciousness, he gently chided those who tended to believe that psychoanalytic psychotherapy was the ultimate cure.

> It almost looks as if analysis were the third of those "impossible" professions in which one can be sure beforehand of achieving unsatisfying results. The other two, which have been known much longer, are education and government. (Freud, 1937)

Psychoanalysis is really a method of treatment like others. It has its triumphs and its defeats, its difficulties, its limitations, its indications. . . . I should like to add that I do not think our cures can compete with those of Lourdes. There are so many more people who believe in the miracles of the Blessed Virgin than in the existence of the unconscious. (1933, p. 152)

> Psychoanalysis is an intimate part of the decaying ideology of the bourgeoisie. (Volosinov, 1927, p. 132)

A Contemporary Development: Heinz Kohut

Since Freud, other analysts have extended the limits of psychoanalysis so that it can be used to more fully explore the self and treat an ever widening set of mental illnesses.

An important outgrowth of Freud's work comes from a group of theorists collectively called the object-relations theorists or the self theorists (e.g., Melanie Klein, Ronald Fairbairn, Donald Winnicott, Margaret Mahler, Otto Kernberg, and Heinz Kohut). These thinkers share in common an emphasis on the effects of the young child's relationships with "objects," or significant others (namely, parents or significant caregivers). Maladaptive behavior is the result of abnormalities in object relations. Psychotherapy is an opportunity to provide a client with a special type of parenting that emphasizes support and acceptance. Thus, object-relations therapists play a more active role in therapy than traditional psychoanalysts.

The best known of the self theorists is Heinz Kohut (1913–1981). Raised and educated in Vienna, he was forced to leave in 1939. He finished medical school and did his psychoanalytic training in the United States. His work at the beginning was understood to be a complementary extension of the Freudian model. Eventually, it became a full theory in its own right, spawning its own associations, trainings, and journals.

Lacking any adherence to nineteenth-century biology or physical science, Kohut denied the utility of biological, sociological, and behavioral ways of obtaining data. Instead, he wrote in his first publication that one could learn only from introspection and empathy (Kohut, 1959). As his thinking developed, he weeded out the deterministic, mechanistic, and outmoded aspects of Freudian theory (Tobin, 1990).

Kohut's own theory arose, as had Freud's, from careful observation of his patients and their experiences. Many of Kohut's patients complained of not feeling real, of feeling a sense of inner emptiness, and of lacking a focus, of falling apart. In short, they seemed to suffer from a sense of being incomplete. What disturbed Kohut was that he was unable to explain or treat these patients' concerns within traditional psychoanalytic theory. Their problems arose, not from their anatomy or their biology, but from their lack of self-worth and their low self-esteem. The etiology of their childhood did not demand the existence of the abstract divisions of the psyche (the id, the ego, and the superego). It demanded a simpler observation—that because their childhoods were incomplete, they were not fully formed. Therefore, they were unable to function with zest, happiness, or purpose.

Kohut, in his later writings, defined the self as an organization of experience that is bipolar in structure. A healthy self is balanced between one pole of ambitions and another pole of values, each pulling the individual in a different direction (Kohut, 1977).

> Linking the two poles is a "tension arc" of basic skills and talents with which the individual attempts to perform the life-long balancing act of striving for individual goals while, at the same time, living in conformity with ideals and values which make life meaningful. (Tobin, 1991, p. 15)

Like Freud, Kohut believed that the self is formed during early childhood. Unlike Freud, however, he saw that the process of formation depended on the interpersonal environment, not on the unfolding biological drives that Freud believed to be universal. Kohut observed that the self developed through the interactions of the infant and its parents or caregivers. The amount and kind of accepting, caring, comforting, and approving behaviors determined the strength, resilience, or weakness of the developing self. He felt that the study of these early interactions would explain a lot about adult behavior.

As Kohut saw both childhood and therapy highly defined by relationships, he came to the conclusion that the need for affirming and stabilizing relationships did not end in childhood, but was an ongoing part of normal adult life. "A move from dependence (symbiosis) to independence (autonomy) in the psychological sphere is no more possible, let alone desirable, than a corresponding move from a life dependent on oxygen to a life independent of it in the biological sphere" (1984, p. 47).

Analysis

The primary tool that Kohut emphasized for successful analysis was empathy. Empathy, as he defined it, is "the capacity to think and feel oneself into the inner life of another person. . . . while simultaneously retaining the stance of an observer" (1984, p. 82). Thus, the therapist had to be concerned about his or her effect on the client as a vital part of the therapy. Therapy became a more personal and relational experience for both the therapist and the patient, because only through empathy could the therapist encourage the patient to become more whole.

Kohut's view of the human condition is far less pessimistic than Freud's. He believed that sex and aggression were not basic drives.

> [T]raditional analysis believes that man's essential nature is comprehensively defined when he is seen as "Guilty Man" . . . as an insufficiently and incompletely tamed animal, reluctant to give up his wish to live by the pleasure principle, unable to relinquish his innate destructiveness . . . as [a] man in hopeless conflict between the drives that spring from the biological bedrock . . . and the civilizing influences emanating . . . from the superego. (1982, pp. 401–402)

The healthy person was not dominated by these drives. Only "If the self is seriously damaged, however, or destroyed, then [do] the drives become powerful constellations in their own right" (Kohut, 1977, p. 122).

The purpose of therapy was to establish conditions in which the incomplete self could be restored to wholeness.

> The successful end of the analysis . . . has been reached when the analysand's formerly enfeebled or fragmented nuclear self . . . has been sufficiently strengthened and consolidated to be able to function as a more or less self-propelling, self-directed, and self-sustaining unit which provides a central purpose to his or her personality and gives a sense of meaning to his or her life. (Kohut, 1977, pp. 138–139)

Kohut produced a psychoanalytic theory more consistent with our current understanding of evolution (Kriegman, 1990). Kohut's revisions of Freudian methodology, his more compassionate psychoanalysis coupled with the careful precision of his theoretical contributions, create a bridge between the increasingly formal, and at times gloomy, Freudian position and the more optimistic, but less rigorous, theories encountered later in this text, especially those of Carl Rogers (Rogers, 1986) and Abraham Maslow (Pauchant & Dumas, 1991).

Evaluation

We have presented an overview of the vast and complex theoretical structure that Freud developed. We have not, in this chapter, attempted to add

The mere presence of empathy has also a beneficial, in a broad sense, a therapeutic effect—both in the clinical setting and in human life, in general. (Kohut, 1982, p. 397)

to it the numerous shadings and elaborations of his followers, disciples, detractors, critics, and clients beyond the one example of Kohut's work. We have tried to organize and simplify the outlines of what was, at its inception, a radical and innovative point of view. Freud threw down a gauntlet that few thinkers have been able to leave unchallenged. Most of the theorists in this book acknowledge their debt to Freud, both those who agree with him and those who repeatedly oppose him.

Freud's ideas continue to influence psychology, literature, art, anthropology, sociology, and medicine. Many of his ideas, such as the importance of dreams and the vitality of the unconscious processes, are widely accepted. Other facets of his theory, such as the relationship between the ego, the id, and the superego, or the role of the Oedipal complex in adolescent development, are extensively debated. Still other parts of his work, including his analysis of female sexuality and his theories on the origins of civilization, have been widely criticized.

There continues to be a veritable torrent of books and articles about Freud's ideas as well as an additional stream of journals and monographs about psychoanalytic therapy. There are more publications on Freud each year than on all the other theorists in this book combined. A sampling of the publications from 1991 alone includes writings on almost every aspect of his work. Unpublished manuscripts were discovered and discussed (Bergeret; Nitzschke). Currently, he is being interpreted as far more humanistic, far more flexible, and far more open-minded in his analysis of human experience than had been originally thought. Aspects of his theories are intelligently criticized. For example, Horacek finds his observations on grieving wrong, van Dam attacks his description of the Oedipal complex, while Kerenyi and Hillman say his understanding of the Oedipal myth is flawed. Diller writes that all his other biographers have underplayed how Jewish Freud was. (Psychoanalysis was known for a time as the "Jewish science.") Warner lists reasons why Freud never liked the United States. One was its rule that psychoanalysts must be physicians. And on it goes. There is an international growth industry of Freudian journals, institutes, and presses that have created a world unto themselves. Most of this community is self-involved and self-contained. But, from time to time, a figure like Kohut emerges from this subculture, affecting the whole of psychology.

It is not our intention to predict how Freudian theory will be judged historically. However, we maintain that his ideas are of no less urgent concern today than they were during his lifetime. Those who choose to study the mind or try to understand other human beings must make their own peace with Freud's basic assertions through an examination of their own inner experience.

Our position is to recognize that there are times in a person's life when Freud's picture of the role of the conscious and unconscious seems like a personal revelation. The stunning impact of his thinking can illuminate an aspect of your own or someone else's character and send you scurrying after more of his books. There are other times when he does not seem to be of use, when his ideas seem distant, convoluted, and irrelevant.

At either time, Freud is a figure to be dealt with. His work evokes a personal response. As we looked over his books, accumulated over the years, we reread our own marginal notes, some of praise and some of damnation. He cannot be treated lightly, because he discussed and described issues that arise in everyone's life.

Whatever your response to Freud's ideas, Freud's advice would be to regard your response as an indicator of your own state of mind as well as a reasoned reaction to his work. In the words of the poet W. H. Auden about Freud: "If often he was wrong and at times absurd, to us he is no more a person now, but a whole climate of opinion" (1945).

Implications for Personal Growth

It is possible to examine your own inner world for clues to your own behavior; however, it is an extremely difficult task because you have, with varying degrees of success, hidden these same clues away from yourself.

Freud suggests that all behavior is linked together, that there are no psychological accidents—that your choice of persons, places, foods, and amusements stems from experiences you do not or will not remember. All thoughts and all behaviors have meaning.

If your memory for past events is actually a mixture of accurate remembrances plus slanted, skewed, and distorted ones, how can you ever know what actually happened?

Here is an example of how two people can remember the same event differently:

> I recall with the clarity of personal suffering being forced to eat hot breakfast cereal for a lengthy period in my childhood. I recall it vividly and viscerally. I can evoke the dining room, my place, the table, the feeling of revulsion in my throat, the delaying strategies, waiting until the adults tired of me and left me in solitude with my half-completed bowl of now cold caking cereal; my attempts to kill the taste with all the sugar I could overpower it with are still clear. To this day I cannot look at a bowl of hot oatmeal without this rush of childhood memories. I *know* that I went through months of fighting with my mother over this issue. Several years ago, I discussed it with her. She recalled it clearly, but she *knew* that it was a brief set of events, a few days, perhaps a week or two at best, and she was surprised that I had any memory of it at all. I was left to decide—her memory against mine.

What emerges from reviewing this story is the realization that neither person was consciously lying, yet the stories were conspicuously different. There might be no way of ever knowing the actual events. The historical truth was not available; only the memories remained, and those were colored on both sides by selective repressions and distortions as well as elaborations and projections.

Freud does not suggest any way out of the dilemma. What he does open up is the realization that your memory or your version of your own past holds clues to how you behave and who you are. It is not simply a record of past events laid out neatly for objective examination.

Psychoanalysis uses a set of tools for personal analysis that includes lengthy self-examination, reflection, and dream analysis, while also noting recurrent patterns of thought and behavior. Freud has written of how he used the tools, what he discovered, and what he concluded from his discoveries. Kohut, among others, added to the tools and came to additional conclusions. Although the conclusions are still a question of debate, the tools are at the core of a dozen other systems and may be the most lasting of his contributions to the study of personality.

The Theory Firsthand: Excerpt from *Studies in Hysteria*

The following material comes from one of Freud's early works. Most of it is self-explanatory. It is a glimpse of the way Freud worked with information and the way he pieced together a coherent picture of the cause of a single symptom from a few items of information.

In the summer vacation of the year 189—— I made an excursion into the Hohe Tauern[1] so that for a while I might forget medicine and more particularly the neuroses. I had almost succeeded in this when one day I turned aside from the main road to climb a mountain which lay somewhat apart and which was renowned for its views and for its well-run refuge hut. I reached the top after a strenuous climb and, feeling refreshed and rested, was sitting deep in contemplation of the charm of the distant prospect. I was so lost in thought that at first I did not connect it with myself when these words reached my ears: "Are you a doctor, sir?" But the question was addressed to me, and by the rather sulky-looking girl of perhaps eighteen who had served my meal and had been spoken to by the landlady as "Katharina." To judge by her dress and bearing, she could not be a servant, but must no doubt be a daughter or relative of the landlady's.

Coming to myself I replied: "Yes, I'm a doctor: but how did you know that?"

"You wrote your name in the Visitors' Book, sir. And I thought if you had a few moments to spare . . . The truth is, sir, my nerves are bad. I went to see a doctor in L—— about them and he gave me something for them; but I'm not well yet."

---

[1] [One of the highest ranges in the Eastern Alps.]

So there I was with the neuroses once again—for nothing else could very well be the matter with this strong, well-built girl with her unhappy look. I was interested to find that neuroses could flourish in this way at a height of over 6,000 feet; I questioned her further therefore. I report the conversation that followed between us just as it is impressed on my memory and I have not altered the patient's dialect.[1]

"Well, what is it you suffer from?"

"I get so out of breath. Not always. But sometimes it catches me so that I think I shall suffocate."

This did not, at first sight, sound like a nervous symptom. But soon it occurred to me that probably it was only a description that stood for an anxiety attack: she was choosing shortness of breath out of the complex of sensations arising from anxiety and laying undue stress on that single factor.

"Sit down here. What is it like when you get 'out of breath'?"

"It comes over me all at once. First of all it's like something pressing on my eyes. My head gets so heavy, there's a dreadful buzzing, and I feel so giddy that I almost fall over. Then there's something crushing my chest so that I can't get my breath."

"And you don't notice anything in your throat?"

"My throat's squeezed together as though I were going to choke."

"Does anything else happen in your head?"

"Yes, there's a hammering, enough to burst it."

"And don't you feel at all frightened while this is going on?"

"I always think I'm going to die. I'm brave as a rule and go about everywhere by myself—into the cellar and all over the mountain. But on a day when that happens I don't dare to go anywhere; I think all the time someone's standing behind me and going to catch hold of me all at once."

So it was in fact an anxiety attack, and introduced by the signs of a hysterical "aura"[2] or, more correctly, it was a hysterical attack the content of which was anxiety. Might there not probably be some other content as well?

"When you have an attack do you think of something? and always the same thing? or do you see something in front of you?"

"Yes. I always see an awful face that looks at me in a dreadful way, so that I'm frightened."

Perhaps this might offer a quick means of getting to the heart of the matter.

"Do you recognize the face? I mean, is it a face that you've really seen some time?"

"No."

"Do you know what your attacks come from?"

---

[1] [No attempt has been made in the English translation to imitate this dialect.]

[2] [The premonitory sensations preceding an epileptic or hysterical attack.]

"No."

"When did you first have them?"

"Two years ago, while I was still living on the other mountain with my aunt. (She used to run a refuge hut there, and we moved here eighteen months ago.) But they keep on happening."

Was I to make an attempt at analysis? I could not venture to transplant hypnosis to these altitudes, but perhaps I might succeed with a simple talk. I should have to try a lucky guess. I had found often enough that in girls anxiety was a consequence of the horror by which a virginal mind is overcome when it is faced for the first time with the world of sexuality.[1]

So I said: "If you don't know, I'll tell you how *I* think you got your attacks. At that time, two years ago, you must have seen or heard something that very much embarrassed you, and that you'd much rather not have seen."

"Heavens, yes!" she replied, "that was when I caught my uncle with the girl, with Franziska, my cousin."

"What's this story about a girl? Won't you tell me all about it?"

"You can say *anything* to a doctor, I suppose. Well, at that time, you know, my uncle—the husband of the aunt you've seen here—kept the inn on the ——kogel.[2] Now they're divorced, and it's my fault they were divorced, because it was through me that it came out that he was carrying on with Franziska."

"And how did you discover it?"

"This way. One day two years ago some gentlemen had climbed the mountain and asked for something to eat. My aunt wasn't at home, and Franziska, who always did the cooking, was nowhere to be found. And my uncle was not to be found either. We looked everywhere, and at last Alois, the little boy, my cousin, said: 'Why, Franziska must be in Father's room!' And we both laughed; but we weren't thinking anything bad. Then we went to my uncle's room but found it locked. That seemed strange to me. Then Alois said: 'There's a window in the passage where you can look into the room.' We went into the passage; but Alois wouldn't go to the window and said he was afraid.

[1]I will quote here the case in which I first recognized this causal connection. I was treating a young married woman who was suffering from a complicated neurosis and, once again, was unwilling to admit that her illness arose from her married life. She objected that while she was still a girl she had had attacks of anxiety, ending in fainting fits. I remained firm. When we had come to know each other better she suddenly said to me one day: "I'll tell you now how I came by my attacks of anxiety when I was a girl. At that time I used to sleep in a room next to my parents'; the door was left open and a nightlight used to burn on the table. So more than once I saw my father get into bed with my mother and heard sounds that greatly excited me. It was then that my attacks came on."

[2][The name of the "other" mountain.]

So I said: 'You silly boy! I'll go. I'm not a bit afraid.' And I had nothing bad in my mind. I looked in. The room was rather dark, but I saw my uncle and Franziska; he was lying on her."

"Well?"

"I came away from the window at once, and leant up against the wall and couldn't get my breath—just what happens to me since everything went blank, my eyelids were forced together and there was a hammering and buzzing in my head."

"Did you tell your aunt that very same day?"

"Oh no, I said nothing."

"Then why were you so frightened when you found them together? Did you understand it? Did you know what was going on?"

"Oh no. I didn't understand anything at that time. I was only sixteen. I don't know what I was frightened about."

"Fräulein Katharina, if you could remember now what was happening in you at that time, when you had your first attack, what you thought about it—it would help you."

"Yes, if I could. But I was so frightened that I've forgotten everything."

(Translated into the terminology of our "Preliminary Communication" [p. 12], this means: "The affect itself created a hypnoid state, whose products were then cut off from associative connection with the ego-consciousness.")

"Tell me, Fräulein. Can it be that the head that you always see when you lose your breath is Franziska's head, as you saw it then?"

"Oh no, she didn't look so awful. Besides, it's a man's head."

"Or perhaps your uncle's?"

"I didn't see his face as clearly as that. It was too dark in the room. And why should he have been making such a dreadful face just then?"

"You're quite right."

(The road suddenly seemed blocked. Perhaps something might turn up in the rest of her story.)

"And what happened then?"

"Well, those two must have heard a noise, because they came out soon afterwards. I felt very bad the whole time. I always kept thinking about it. Then two days later it was a Sunday and there was a great deal to do and I worked all day long. And on the Monday morning I felt giddy again and was sick, and I stopped in bed and was sick without stopping for three days."

We (Breuer and I) had often compared the symptomatology of hysteria with a pictographic script which has become intelligible after the discovery of a few bilingual inscriptions. In that alphabet being sick means disgust. So I said: "If you were sick three days later, I believe that means that when you looked into the room you felt disgusted."

"Yes, I'm sure I felt disgusted," she said reflectively, "but disgusted at what?"

"Perhaps you saw something naked? What sort of state were they in?"

"It was too dark to see anything; besides they both of them had their clothes on. Oh, if only I knew what it was I felt disgusted at!"

I had no idea either. But I told her to go and tell me whatever occurred to her, in the confident expectation that she would think of precisely what I needed to explain the case.

Well, she went on to describe how at last she reported her discovery to her aunt, who found that she was changed and suspected her of concealing some secret. There followed some very disagreeable scenes between her uncle and aunt, in the course of which the children came to hear a number of things which opened their eyes in many ways and which it would have been better for them not to have heard. At last her aunt decided to move with her children and niece and take over the present inn, leaving her uncle alone with Franziska, who had meanwhile become pregnant. After this, however, to my astonishment she dropped these threads and began to tell me two sets of older stories, which went back two or three years earlier than the traumatic moment. The first set related to occasions on which the same uncle had made sexual advances to her herself, when she was only fourteen years old. She described how she had once gone with him on an expedition down into the valley in the winter and had spent the night in the inn there. He sat in the bar drinking and playing cards, but she felt sleepy and went up to bed early in the room they were to share on the upper floor. She was not quite asleep when he came up; then she fell asleep again and woke up suddenly "feeling his body" in the bed. She jumped up and remonstrated with him: "What are you up to, Uncle? Why don't you stay in your own bed?" He tried to pacify her: "Go on, you silly girl, keep still. You don't know how nice it is"— "I don't like your 'nice' things; you don't even let one sleep in peace." She remained standing by the door, ready to take refuge outside in the passage, till at last he gave up and went to sleep himself. Then she went back to her own bed and slept till morning. From the way in which she reported having defended herself it seems to follow that she did not clearly recognize the attack as a sexual one. When I asked her if she knew what he was trying to do to her, she replied: "Not at the time." It had become clear to her much later on, she said; she had resisted because it was unpleasant to be disturbed in one's sleep and "because it wasn't nice."

I have been obliged to relate this in detail, because of its great importance for understanding everything that followed.—She went on to tell me of yet other experiences of somewhat later date: how she had once again had to defend herself against him in an inn when he was completely drunk, and similar stories. In answer to a question as to whether on these occasions she had felt anything resembling her later loss of breath, she answered with decision that she had every time felt the pressure on her eyes and chest, but with nothing like the strength that had characterized the scene of discovery.

Immediately she had finished this set of memories she began to tell me a second set, which dealt with occasions on which she had noticed something between her uncle and Franziska. Once the whole family had spent the night in their clothes in a hay loft and she was woken up suddenly by a noise; she thought she noticed that her uncle, who had been lying between her and Franziska, was turning away, and that Franziska was just lying down. Another time they were stopping the night at the inn at the village of N——; she and her uncle were in one room and Franziska in an adjoining one. She woke up suddenly in the night and saw a tall white figure by the door, on the point of turning the handle: "Goodness, is that you, Uncle? What are you doing at the door?"—"Keep quiet. I was only looking for something."—"But the way out's by the *other* door."—"I'd just made a mistake" . . . and so on.

I asked her if she had been suspicious at that time. "No, I didn't think anything about it; I only just noticed it and thought no more about it." When I enquired whether she had been frightened on these occasions too, she replied that she thought so, but she was not so sure of it this time.

At the end of these two sets of memories she came to a stop. She was like someone transformed. The sulky, unhappy face had grown lively, her eyes were bright, she was lightened and exalted. Meanwhile the understanding of her case had become clear to me. The later part of what she had told me, in an apparently aimless fashion, provided an admirable explanation of her behaviour at the scene of the discovery. At that time she had carried about with her two sets of experiences which she remembered but did not understand, and from which she drew no inferences. When she caught sight of the couple in inter- course, she at once established a connection between the new impres- sion and these two sets of recollections, she began to understand them and at the same time to fend them off. There then followed a short period of working-out, of "incubation," after which the symptoms of conversion set in, the vomiting as a substitute for moral and physical disgust. This solved the riddle. She had not been disgusted by the sight of the two people but by the memory which that sight had stirred up in her. And, taking everything into account, this could only be the memory of the attempt on her at night when she had "felt her uncle's body."

So when she had finished her confession I said to her: "I know now what it was you thought when you looked into the room. You thought: 'Now he's doing with her what he wanted to do with me that night and those other times.' That was what you were disgusted at, because you remembered the feeling when you woke up in the night and felt his body."

"It may well be," she replied, "that that was what I was disgusted at and that that was what I thought."

"Tell me just one thing more. You're a grown-up girl now and know all sorts of things . . . "

"Yes, now I am."

"Tell me just one thing. What part of his body was it that you felt that night?"

But she gave me no more definite answer. She smiled in an embarrassed way, as though she had been found out, like someone who is obliged to admit that a fundamental position has been reached where there is not much more to be said. I could imagine what the tactile sensation was which she had later learnt to interpret. Her facial expression seemed to me to be saying that she supposed that I was right in my conjecture. But I could not penetrate further, and in any case I owed her a debt of gratitude for having made it so much easier for me to talk to her than to the prudish ladies of my city practice, who regard whatever is natural as shameful.

Thus the case was cleared up.—But stop a moment! What about the recurrent hallucination of the head, which appeared during her attacks and struck terror into her? Where did it come from? I proceeded to ask her about it, and, as though *her* knowledge, too, had been extended by our conversation, she promptly replied: "Yes, I know now. The head is my uncle's head—I recognize it now—but not from *that* time. Later, when all the disputes had broken out, my uncle gave way to a senseless rage against me. He kept saying that it was all my fault: if I hadn't chattered, it would never have come to a divorce. He kept threatening he would do something to me; and if he caught sight of me at a distance his face would get distorted with rage and he would make for me with his hand raised. I always ran away from him, and always felt terrified that he would catch me some time unawares. The face I always see now is his face when he was in a rage."

This information reminded me that her first hysterical symptom, the vomiting, had passed away; the anxiety attack remained and acquired a fresh content. Accordingly, what we were dealing with was a hysteria which had to a considerable extent been abreacted. And in fact she had reported her discovery to her aunt soon after it happened.

"Did you tell your aunt the other stories—about his making advances to you?"

"Yes. Not at once, but later on, when there was already talk of a divorce. My aunt said: 'We'll keep that in reserve. If he causes trouble in the Court, we'll say that too.'"

I can well understand that it should have been precisely this last period—when there were more and more agitating scenes in the house and when her own state ceased to interest her aunt, who was entirely occupied with the dispute—that it should have been this period of accumulation and retention that left her the legacy of the mnemic symbol (of the hallucinated face).

I hope this girl, whose sexual sensibility had been injured at such an early age, derived some benefit from our conversation. I have not seen her since.[1] (Breuer & Freud, 1895, pp. 125–134)

Annotated Bibliography

Books by Freud

Freud, S. The interpretation of dreams. In J. Strachey (Ed. and Trans.), *The standard edition of the complete psychological works of Sigmund Freud* (Vols. 4, 5 of 24). Hogarth Press, 1953–1966. (Originally published, 1900.) Freud said of it in 1931: "It contains, even according to my present-day judgment, the most valuable of all the discoveries it has been my good fortune to make." We agree. The best of Freud. Read it to appreciate his intuitive genius and his writing style. Most of Freud's writings are available in a variety of inexpensive editions.

————. Introductory lectures on psycho-analysis. *Standard edition* (Vols. 15, 16). (Originally published, 1916–1917.) Two courses of lectures given at the University of Vienna. The first part of the book assumes no knowledge of the subject; the second part assumes familiarity with the first. Lectures to and for students.

————. (1957). *A general selection from the works of Sigmund Freud.* (John Rickman, Ed.). New York: Doubleday. A good set of readings taken from different parts of Freud's work. There are other collections that may be as good. We like this one.

————. (1963). *Three case histories.* New York: Collier Books. Three cases that Freud analyzed. He presents material from the cases, interweaving it with his developing theory. This is as close to seeing Freud in action as can be gleaned from his writings.

Books About Freud and His Ideas

Gay, P. (1988). *Freud, A life for our time.* New York: W. W. Norton. The best biography of Freud available. Gay neither attacks nor defends Freud, which is the fault of most of the other biographies. He understands the era as well as the man.

---

[1](*Footnote added, 1924*) I venture after the lapse of so many years to lift the veil of discretion and reveal the fact that Katharina was not the niece but the daughter of the landlady. The girl fell ill, therefore, as a result of sexual attempts on the part of her own father. Distortions like the one which I introduced in the present instance should be altogether avoided in reporting a case history. From the point of view of understanding the case, a distortion of this kind is not, of course, a matter of such indifference as would be shifting the scene from one mountain to another.

Hall, C. S. (1954). *A primer of Freudian psychology*. New York: New American Library (Mentor Books). A short, readable, and lucid exposition of the major features of Freud's theories. It is compact and accurate. The best easy introduction available.

Hall, C., & Lindzey, G. (1968). The relevance of Freudian psychology and related viewpoints for the social sciences. In G. Lindzey & E. Arronson (Eds.), *The handbook of social psychology* (2nd ed.). Menlo Park, CA: Addison-Wesley. An intermediate-level summary of psychoanalytic thinking with emphasis on its relevance to social psychology; a theoretical rather than clinical focus.

Rapaport, D. (1959). The structure of psychoanalytic theory. In S. Koch (Ed.), *Psychology: The study of a science: Vol. 3. Formulations of the person and the social context*. New York: McGraw-Hill. Among the most sophisticated and complete theoretical statements of psychoanalytic thinking. Not for the fainthearted.

Sulloway, F. J. (1979). *Freud, biologist of the mind: Beyond the psychoanalytic legend*. New York: Basic Books. Suggests that Freud was more aligned with biology than with psychology. A more human, less heroic view of him than usual, solidly based on historical documents. Disagrees with Jones on matters of fact and opinion. Endless references.

Psychoanalytic Books About Women

Jordan, J., Kaplan, A., Miller, J., Striver, I., & Surrey, J. (1991). *Woman's growth in connection*. New York: Guilford. These authors are the best post-Freudian theorists writing about women. Not limited to psychoanalytic concerns.

Mitchell, J. (1974). *Psychoanalysis and feminism*. New York: Pantheon. Mitchell explores at length the usefulness of psychoanalytic theory in contributing to an understanding of women's psychology in Western, male-dominated society. Mitchell is strongly and openly a feminist, and it is as a feminist that she examines psychoanalysis as put forth by Freud and various theorists since Freud. A critique of various feminist criticisms of these same theories—psychoanalysis in particular—is offered.

Ruitenbeck, H. M. (Ed.). (1966). *Psychoanalysis and female sexuality*. New Haven, CT: College and University Press. A collection of psychoanalytic papers on female sexuality. Included are essays by Jones, Thompson, Horney, Freud, Greenacre, Riviere, and, somewhat surprisingly, Maslow.

Contemporary Psychoanalysis

Kohut, H. (1977). *The restoration of the self*. New York: International Universities Press. Hard reading; however, it is the best introduction to his thinking.

Many of the other important current ideas in the Freudian world are contained in the following books:

Bergman, M., & Hartman, F. (Eds.). (1976). *The evolution of psychoanalytic technique*. New York: Basic Books. Collected papers from the first wave of movements and changes, arising out of Freud's original thinking. The work of those who felt that they stayed within the fold. Contributors include Erikson, Fenichel, Ferenczi, Alexander, and Reich, to name a few.

Greenburg, J., & Mitchell S. (1985). *Object relations in psychoanalytic theory*. Cambridge, MA: Harvard University Press. Lays out clearly the different points of view of the major living theorists. Excellent early chapters of Freud's initial descriptions of the nature of the analytic relationship.

Levenson, E. (1972). *The fallacy of understanding: An inquiry into the changing structure of psychoanalysis*. New York: Basic Books. A delightful musing about the way in which we see and interpret Freud's work from a vantage point years later and cultures apart. His sensible rethinking of Freud's basic ideas and how they were first expressed and understood is a fresh look which stresses utility.

Mitchell, S. (1988). *Relational concepts in psychoanalysis: An integration*. Cambridge, MA: Harvard University Press. A valiant and often successful attempt to integrate a number of the successful offshoots from traditional psychoanalysis, including self psychology, existential psychoanalysis, object relations theories, and interpersonal psychoanalysis. Not for the fainthearted.

Pine, F. (1990). *Drive, ego, object, and self: A synthesis for clinical work*. New York: Basic Books. Brings together in a well-written, flowing narrative different perspectives used in clinical practice followed by a series of case examples.

Schafer, R. (1983). *The analytic attitude*. New York: Basic Books. An exploration of the inner workings of the mind of the analyst during therapy itself by a professor of psychiatry at Columbia University Medical Center for Psychoanalytic Training and Research. Widely read, used, and praised by professionals.

References

Auden, W. H. (1945). *The collected poems of W. H. Auden.* New York: Random House.

Bergeret, J. (1991). 1983: The psychoanalytic glasnost. *Revue Franchaise de Psychanalyse, 55*(1), 111–116.

Bettelheim, B. (1982, March 1). Reflections: Freud and the soul. *The New Yorker,* pp. 52–93.

Bonaparte, M. (Ed.). (1954). *The origins of psychoanalysis: Letters to Wilhelm Fliess.* London: Imago.

Breuer, J., & Freud, S. (1953–1966). Studies in hysteria. In J. Strachey (Ed. and Trans.), *The standard edition of the complete psychological works of Sigmund Freud* (Vol. 2). Hogarth Press. (Originally published, 1895.)

Bruner, J. (1956). Freud and the image of man. *Partisan Review, 23,* 340–347.

Byck, R. (Ed.). (1975). *Cocaine papers by Sigmund Freud.* New York: New American Library.

Carroy, J. (1991). "My interpreter with German readers": Freud and the French history of hypnosis. *Psychanalyse a l'Universite, 16*(62), 97–113.

Cohen, M. (1982). *Putting energy back into Freud.* Unpublished doctoral dissertation, California Institute of Transpersonal Psychology.

Colby, K. M. (1951). *A primer for psychotherapists.* New York: Ronald Press.

Decker, H. (1991). *Freud, Dora, and Vienna 1900.* New York: Free Press.

Diller, J. (1991). *Freud's Jewish identity: A case study in the impact of ethnicity.* Rutherford, England: Associated University Presses.

Emmanuel, D. (1992). A developmental model of girls and women. *Progress: Family Systems Research and Therapy, 1*(1), 25–40.

Farber, L. H. (1966). *The ways of the will: Essays toward a psychology and psycho-pathology of will.* New York: Harper & Row.

Fenichel, O. (1945). *The psychoanalytic theory of neurosis.* New York: Norton.

Ferenczi, S. (1955). *Final contributions to the problems and methods of psychoanalysis.* London: Hogarth Press/New York: Basic Books.

Fliegel, Z. O. (1973). Feminine psychosexual development in Freudian theory; a historical reconstruction. *The Psychoanalytic Quarterly, 42*(3), 385–408.

Fodor, N., & Gaynor, F. (1958). *Freud: Dictionary of psychoanalysis.* New York: Fawcett Books.

Freud, A. (1936). *The ego and the mechanisms of defense.* London: Hogarth Press.

Freud, E. (1961). *Letters of Sigmund Freud.* New York: Basic Books.

Freud, S. The neuro-psychoses of defense. In J. Strachey (Ed. and Trans.), *The standard edition of the complete psychological works of Sigmund Freud* (Vol. 3). Hogarth Press, 1953–1966. (Originally published, 1894.)

———. The interpretation of dreams. *Standard edition* (Vols. 4, 5). (Originally published, 1900.)

———. The psychopathology of everyday life. *Standard edition* (Vol. 6). (Originally published, 1901.)

———. Three essays on the theory of sexuality. *Standard edition* (Vol. 7). (Originally published, 1905a.)

———. Fragment of an analysis of a case of hysteria. *Standard edition* (Vol. 8). (Originally published, 1905b.)

———. Psycho-analysis and the establishment of the facts in legal proceedings. *Standard edition* (Vol. 9). (Originally published, 1906.)

———. Obsessive actions and religious practices. *Standard edition* (Vol. 9). (Originally published, 1907.)

———. "Civilized" sexual morality and modern nervous illness. *Standard edition* (Vol. 9). (Originally published, 1908.)

———. Notes upon a case of obsessional neurosis. *Standard edition* (Vol. 10). (Originally published, 1909.)

———. Five lectures on psycho-analysis. *Standard edition* (Vol. 11). (Originally published, 1910.)

———. Formulations on the two principles of mental functioning. *Standard edition* (Vol. 12). (Originally published, 1911.)

———. On the history of the psycho-analytic movement. *Standard edition* (Vol. 14). (Originally published, 1914.)

———. Repression. *Standard edition* (Vol. 14). (Originally published, 1915.)

———. Introductory lectures on psycho-analysis (Part III). *Standard edition* (Vol. 16). (Originally published, 1916.)

———. On the transformations of instinct, as exemplified in anal eroticism. *Standard edition* (Vol. 17). (Originally published, 1917.)

———. Lines of advance in psycho-analytic therapy. *Standard edition* (Vol. 17). (Originally published, 1919.)

———. Beyond the pleasure principle. *Standard edition* (Vol. 18). (Originally published, 1920.)

———. Two encyclopedia articles. *Standard edition* (Vol. 18). (Originally published, 1923.)

———. An autobiographical study. *Standard edition* (Vol. 20). (Originally published, 1925a.) (Also, *Autobiography.* New York: Norton, 1935.)

———. Some psychical consequences of the anatomical distinctions between the sexes. *Standard edition* (Vol. 19). (Originally published, 1925b.)

———. The question of lay analysis. *Standard edition* (Vol. 20). (Originally published, 1926a.)

———. Inhibitions, symptoms, and anxiety. *Standard edition* (Vol. 14). (Originally published, 1926b.)

———. Civilization and its discontents. *Standard edition* (Vol. 21). (Originally published, 1930.)

———. New introductory lectures on psycho-analysis. *Standard edition* (Vol. 22). (Originally published, 1933.) (Also, New York: Norton, 1949.)

——— . Analysis terminable and interminable. *Standard edition* (Vol. 23). (Originally published, 1937.)

——— . An outline of psycho-analysis. *Standard edition* (Vol. 23). (Originally published, 1940.) (Also, New York: Norton, 1949.)

———. (1950). *The origins of psycho-analysis* (including 1895, A project for a scientific psychology). London: Hogarth Press.

———. (1963). *The cocaine papers.* Zurich: Duquin Press. (Papers not reprinted in *The standard edition,* originally published 1884–1887.)

Fromm, E. (1959). *Sigmund Freud's mission: An analysis of his personality and influence.* New York: Harper & Row.

Fuller, R. (1992). Biographical origins of psychological ideas: Freud's cocaine studies. *Journal of Humanistic Psychology, 32*(3), 67–86.

Gay, P. (1988). *Freud, A life for our time.* New York: W. W. Norton.

Godde, G. (1991a). Freud's philosophical discussion circles in his student years. *Jahrbuch der Psychoanalyse, 27,* 73–113.

———. (1991b). Schopenhauer's anticipation of Freudian metapsychology. *Psyche Zeitschrift fur Psychoanalyse und inre Anwendungen, 45*(11), 944–1033.

Goleman, D. (1990, February 7). Freud's reputation shrinks a little. *New York Times,* (c) 1, 4.

Hall, C. S. (1965). *A primer of Freudian psychology.* New York: New American Library (Mentor Books).

Halt, R. R. (1965). A review of some of Freud's biological assumptions and their influence on his theories. In N. S. Greenfield & W. C. Lewis (Eds.), *Psychoanalysis and current biological thought.* Madison: University of Wisconsin Press.

Hamilton, J. (1991). A reconsideration of the Freud-Tausk-Deutch relationship. *Psychoanalytic Review, 78*(2), 267–278.

Herzog, P. (1991). *Conscious and unconscious: Freud's dynamic distinction reconsidered.* Madison, CT: International Universities Press.

Horacek, B. J. (1991). Toward a more viable model of breathing; consequences for older persons. *Journal of Death Studies, 15*(5), 459–472.

Horney, K. (1939). *New ways in psychoanalysis.* New York: Norton.

———. (1967). The flight from womanhood. In H. Kelman (Ed.), *Feminine psychology.* New York: Norton. (Originally published, 1926.)

Jones, E. (1953, 1955, 1957). *The life and work of Sigmund Freud* (3 Vols.). New York: Basic Books.

———. (1966). The early development of female sexuality. In H. Ruitenbeck (Ed.), *Psychoanalysis and female sexuality.* New Haven, CT: College and University Press. (Originally published, 1927.)

Kerenyi, C., & Hillman, J. (1991). *Oedipus variations: Studies in literature and psychoanalysis.* Dallas: Spring.

Kohut, H. (1959). Introspection, empathy and psychoanalysis: An examination of the relationship between modes of observation and theory. *Journal of the American Psychoanalytic Association, 7,* 459–483.

————. (1977). *The restoration of the self*. New York: International Universities Press.

————. (1982). Introspection, empathy, and the semi-circle of mental health. *International Journal of Psychoanalysis, 63,* 395–407.

————. (1984). *How does analysis cure?* Chicago: University of Chicago Press.

Kriegman, D. (1990). Compassion and altruism in psychoanalytic theory: An evolutionary analysis of self psychology. *Journal of the American Academy of Psychoanalysis, 18*(2), 342–367.

Krishna, G. (1974). *Higher consciousness: The evolutionary thrust of kundalini*. New York: Julian Press.

La Planche, J., & Pontalis, J. B. (1973). *The language of psychoanalysis* (D. Nicholson-Smith, Trans.). New York: Norton.

Lauzan, G. (1962). *Sigmund Freud: The man and his theories* (P. Evans, Trans.). New York: Fawcett.

Le Barre, W. (1968). Personality from a psychoanalytic viewpoint. In E. Norbeck, D. Price-Williams, & W. McCord (Eds.), *The study of personality: An interdisciplinary appraisal* (pp. 65–87). New York: Holt, Rinehart and Winston.

McGuire, W. (Ed.). (1974). *The Freud / Jung letters*. Bollingen Series XCIV. Princeton, NJ: Princeton University Press.

Malcolm, J. (1980, November 24 & December 1). The impossible profession. *The New Yorker*.

Masserman, J. H. (1961). *Principles of dynamic psychiatry* (2nd ed.). Philadelphia: Saunders.

Masson, J. (1984). *The assault on truth: Freud's suppression of the seduction theory*. New York: Farrar, Straus & Giroux.

Nitzschke, B. (1991). Freud's lecture at the Israelite social club Vienna of the B'nai B'rith order: "We and Death" (1915): A recovered document. *Psyche Zeitschrift fur Psychoanalyse und ihre Anwendungen, 45*(2), 97–142.

O'Brien, M. (1991). Freud's affair with Minna Bernays: His letter of June 4, 1896. *American Journal of Psychoanalysis, 51*(2), 173–184.

Pauchant, T., & Dumas, C. (1991). Abraham Maslow and Heinz Kohut. *Journal of Humanistic Psychology, 31*(2), 49–71.

Pribram, K. (1962). The Neuropsychology of Sigmund Freud. In A. Bachrach (Ed.), *Experimental foundations of clinical psychology* (pp. 442–468). New York: Basic Books.

Pruett, G. E. (1987). *The meaning and end of suffering for Freud and the Buddhist tradition*. Lantham, MD: University Press.

Rachman, S. J., & Wilson, G. T. (1980). *The effects of psychological therapy* (2nd ed.). New York: Pergamon Press.

Roazen, P. (1991). Nietzsche and Freud: Two voices from the underground. *Psychohistory Review, 19*(3), 327–349.

Rogers, C. (1986). Rogers, Kohut, and Erikson. *Person-Centered Review, 1,* 125–140.

Rycroft, C. (1972). *Wilhelm Reich*. New York: Viking.

Sears, R. T. (1936). Experimental studies of projection: I. Attributions of traits. *Journal of Social Psychology, 7,* 151–163.

Shah, I. (1972). *The magic monastery.* New York: Dutton.

Strachey, J. (Ed. and Trans.). (1953–1966). *The standard edition of the complete psychological works of Sigmund Freud* (Vols. 1–24). London: Hogarth Press.

Sulloway, F. (1979). *Freud, biologist of the mind: Beyond the psychoanalytic legend.* New York: Basic Books.

Thornton, E. M. (1984). *The Freudian fallacy.* Garden City, NY: Dial.

Tobin, S. (1990). Self psychology as a bridge between existential-humanistic psychology and psychoanalysis. *Journal of Humanistic Psychology, 30*(1), 14–63.

———. (1991). A comparison of psychoanalytic self psychology and Carl Rogers' person-centered therapy. *Journal of Humanistic Psychology, 31*(1) 9–33.

van Dam, H. (1991). Ages four to six: The oedipus complex revisited. In S. Greenspan & G. Pollock (Eds.),*The course of life, volume 3, middle and late childhood* (pp. 53–71). Madison, CT: International Universities Press.

Volosinov, V. (1987). *Freudianism, a critical sketch* (I. R. Titunik, Trans.). Bloomington, IN: Indiana University Press. (Originally published in Russian, State Publishing House, Moscow, 1927.)

Warner, S. (1991). Freud's antipathy to America. *Journal of the American Academy of Psychoanalysis, 19*(1), 141–155.

Wollheim, R. (1971). *Sigmund Freud.* New York: Viking Press.

Chapter Two

Carl Gustav Jung and Analytic Psychology

Carl Jung is one of the most important and also one of the most complex and controversial psychological theorists. Jungian psychology focuses on establishing and fostering the relationship between conscious and the unconscious processes. Dialog between the conscious and unconscious aspects of the psyche enriches the person, as the unconscious is heard and understood at the conscious level. Jung believed that without this dialog, unconscious processes can weaken and jeopardize the personality.

In this chapter, we will take a careful look at the basic concepts of Jungian psychology and examine some brief references to the philosophical underpinnings of this psychology. We will explore such concepts as individuation, complex theory, archetypes, the nature of the symbolic, and Jung's structure of the psyche, which includes ego, shadow, anima/animus, and the self.

One of Jung's central concepts is *individuation,* his term for a process of personal development that involves establishing a connection between the ego and the self. The ego is the center of consciousness; the self is the center of the total psyche, including both the conscious and the unconscious. For Jung, there is constant interplay between the two. They are not separate but are two aspects of a single system. Individuation is a process of developing wholeness by integrating all the various parts of the psyche.

Although his greatest efforts were devoted to investigating the farther reaches of human aspiration and achievement, Jung by no means ignored the negative, maladaptive side of human nature. His analysis of human nature includes investigations of Eastern and Western religions, alchemy, parapsychology, and mythology. His initial impact was greater on philosophers, folklorists, and writers than on psychologists or psychiatrists. Today, however, growing concern with human consciousness and human potential has caused a resurgence of interest in Jung's ideas.

Personal History

Any theory is best understood in the context of the theorist's worldview. Jung's theory is no exception. Thus, an appropriate beginning to our study of Jung is a look at the personal, historical, and cultural influences that touched him.

Carl Gustav Jung was born in Switzerland on July 26, 1875. Until the age of nine, when his sister was born, Jung experienced a somewhat isolated childhood, which he filled with solitary play and a rich inner world. "I did not want to be disturbed [at play]. I was deeply absorbed in my games and could not endure being watched" (Jung, 1961, p. 18). His father was a scholar in Oriental languages and an ordained minister. Even as a child Jung was deeply concerned with religious and spiritual questions. In his autobiography *Memories, Dreams, Reflections* (1961), Jung relates two extremely powerful early experiences that strongly influenced his attitude toward religion. Between ages of 3 and 4, he dreamed of a terrifying phallic image standing on a throne in an underground chamber.

I can only hope and wish that no one becomes "Jungian" . . . I proclaim no cut-and-dried doctrine and I abhor "blind adherence." I leave everyone free to deal with the facts in his own way, since I also claim this freedom for myself. (Jung, 1973, p. 405)

The dream haunted Jung for years. It was not until many years later that he realized the image was a ritual phallus; it represented a hidden, "subterranean God" that was more frightful yet much more real and powerful for Jung than Jesus and the church.

The second experience occurred when Jung was 11. He came out of school at noon and saw the sun sparkling on the roof of the Basel church. He reflected on the beauty of the world, the splendor of the church, and the majesty of God sitting high up in the sky on a golden throne. Jung was suddenly gripped with terror refusing to let himself pursue this train of thought, which he felt was highly sacrilegious. He struggled desperately for several days to suppress the forbidden thought. Finally, Jung gave in: He saw the beautiful cathedral and God seated on his throne high above the world, and from under the throne came an enormous piece of excrement, which fell on the cathedral roof, shattering it, and destroying the walls of the cathedral.

Reflecting on this experience, Jung wrote:

> A great many things I had not previously understood became clear to me. In His trial of human courage God refuses to abide by tradition no matter how sacred. . . . One must be utterly abandoned to God; nothing else matters but fulfilling His will. Otherwise all is folly and meaninglessness. (Jung, 1961, pp. 38–40)

In some ways, it may be hard for us today to imagine the terrifying power of Jung's vision. Given the conventional piety and lack of psychological sophistication of society in 1887, such thoughts were not merely unutterable, they were unthinkable. However, following his vision, Jung felt an enormous relief and a sense of grace, instead of the expected guilt. He interpreted what he saw as a sign from God. It was God's will that Jung go against the traditions of the church. From that time on, Jung felt far removed from the conventional piety of his father and his pastoral relatives. He saw how most people cut themselves off from direct religious experience by remaining bound by the letter of church convention, instead of seriously considering the spirit of God as a living reality.

Partly as a result of his inner experiences, Jung felt himself isolated from other people; sometimes he felt almost unendurably lonely. School bored him; however, he developed a passion for reading, an "absolute craving . . . to read every scrap of printed matter that fell into my hands" (Jung, 1961, p. 30).

From childhood on, Jung had been aware that there were two personalities within him. One was the local parson's son, insecure and uncertain. The other was a wise old man, "skeptical, mistrustful, remote from the world of men, but close to nature, the earth, the sun, the moon, the weather, all living creatures, and above all close to the night, to dreams, and to whatever 'God' worked directly in him" (Jung, 1961, pp. 44–45). The parson's son lived an ordinary daily existence as a child growing up in a particular time and place. The wise old man lived in a timeless and

Nobody could rob me of the conviction that it was enjoined upon me to do what God wanted and not what I wanted . . . often I had the feeling that in all decisive matters I was no longer among men but was alone with God. (Jung, 1961, p. 48)

boundless world of wisdom, meaning, and historical continuity. The inter-action of these two personalities, Jung says, occurs in everyone, only most people are unconscious of the second figure. This figure was of major significance in his life. In many ways, Jung's personality theory, in particular his concepts of individuation and the self, stems from his long-time awareness of this inner wisdom.

When it came time to enter the university, Jung chose to study medicine as a compromise between his interests in both science and humanities. He became attracted to psychiatry as the study of "diseases of the personality," though in those days psychiatry was relatively undeveloped and undistinguished. He realized that psychiatry in particular involved both scientific and humanistic perspectives. Jung also developed an interest in psychic phenomena and began an investigation of the messages received by his cousin, a local medium. This investigation became the basis for his thesis: "On the Psychology and Pathology of So-called Occult Phenomena."

In 1900, Jung became an intern at the Burghölzli Medical Hospital in Zurich, one of the most progressive psychiatric centers in Europe. Zurich became his permanent home.

In 1904, Jung set up an experimental laboratory at the Psychiatric Clinic and developed the word association test for psychiatric diagnostic purposes. In this test, the subject is asked to respond to a standard list of stimulus words; any inordinate delay between the stimulus and the response is taken as an indicator of emotional stress related in some way to the stimulus word. Jung also became skillful at interpreting the psychological meanings behind the various associations produced by the subjects. In 1905, at age 30, he became lecturer in psychiatry at the University of Zurich and senior physician at the Psychiatric Clinic. At this time, Jung had already discovered the writings of a man who would become an important teacher and mentor, Sigmund Freud.

Despite the strong criticism leveled at Freud in scientific and academic circles, Jung became convinced of the value of Freud's work. He sent Freud copies of his articles and of his first book, *The Psychology of Dementia Praecox* (1907). Freud responded by inviting him to Vienna. At their first meeting, the two men talked virtually without pause for 13 hours. They corresponded weekly after that, and Freud came to consider Jung his logical successor.

Freud was the first man of real importance I had encountered. (Jung, 1961, p. 149)

Despite their close friendship, the two men had fundamental disagreements. Jung was never able to accept Freud's insistence that the causes of repression are always sexual trauma. Freud, for his part, was always uneasy with Jung's interest in mythological, spiritual, and occult phenomena. The two men had a philosophical and personal break when Jung published *Symbols of Transformation* (1912), which challenged some of Freud's basic ideas. For example, Jung defined libido as generalized psychic energy, whereas Freud stressed sexual energy as the all important element in the psyche. The break with Freud was a painful, traumatic one for Jung, but he was determined to stand behind his own convictions. In his preface to the book, Jung wrote, "The whole thing came upon me like a landslide that cannot be stopped. . . . [I]t was the explosion of all those psychic contents which could find no room, no breathing space, in the constricting atmosphere of Freudian psychology and its narrow outlook" (Jung, 1912, p. xxiii).

For Jung, this break with Freud precipitated a powerful confrontation with the unconscious. In an effort to contain and grow from these intense experiences, Jung began to document them in his personal journals as a kind of self-analysis.

Jung gradually developed his own theories of unconscious processes and dream-symbol analysis. He came to realize that his procedures for analyzing the dream symbols of his patients could also be applied to the analysis of other forms of symbolism—that he held the key to the interpretation of myths, folktales, religious symbols, and art.

His interest in fundamental psychological processes turned Jung to the study of the ancient Western traditions of alchemy and Gnosticism (a Hellenistic religious and philosophical tradition) as well as to the investigation of non-European cultures. Jung made two trips to Africa, and he traveled to New Mexico to visit the Pueblo Indians. Jung also visited India. He was a serious student of Indian, Chinese, and Tibetan thought.

In 1944, when he was 69, Jung nearly died following a severe heart attack. In the hospital, he experienced a powerful vision in which he seemed to be floating high in space, 1,000 miles above the earth, with Ceylon below his feet, India lying ahead of him, and the desert of Arabia off to the left. Jung then entered a great block of stone that was also floating in space. A temple had been hollowed out of the giant block. As he approached the steps leading to the entrance, Jung felt that everything was left behind him. All that remained of his earthly existence was his own experience, his life's history. He saw his life as part of a great historical matrix of which he had never before been aware. Before he could enter the temple, Jung was confronted by his doctor, who told him that he had no right to leave the earth at that time. At that moment, the vision ceased.

For weeks after, as Jung gradually recovered from his illness, he was weak and depressed by day but would awaken each night around midnight with a feeling of deep ecstasy. He felt as if he were floating in a blissful world. His nightly visions would last for about an hour and then he would again fall asleep.

After he recovered, Jung entered a highly productive period in which he wrote many of his most important works. His visions gave him the courage to formulate some of his most original ideas. These experiences also changed Jung's personal outlook to a more deeply affirmative attitude toward his own destiny.

> I might formulate it as an affirmation of things as they are: an unconditional "yes" to that which is, without subjective protests—acceptance of the conditions of existence as I see them and understand them,

Dreams bring to light material which cannot have originated either from the dreamer's adult life or from his forgotten childhood. We are obliged to regard it as part of the *archaic heritage* which a child brings with him into the world, before any experience of his own, influenced by the experiences of his ancestors. We find the counterpart of this philogenetic material in the earliest human legends and in surviving customs. (Freud, 1964, p. 177)

> acceptance of my own nature, as I happen to be. . . . In this way we forge an ego that does not break down when incomprehensible things happen; an ego that endures the truth, and that is capable of coping with the world and with fate. (Jung, 1961, p. 297)

Jung died on June 6, 1961, at the age of 86, after a lifetime of clinical practice, research, and writing.

A few days before his death, Jung had a dream.

> He saw a great round stone in a high place, a barren square, and on it were engraved the words: "And this shall be a sign unto you of Wholeness and Oneness." Then he saw many vessels . . . and a quadrangle of trees whose roots reached around the earth and enveloped him and among the roots golden threads were glittering. (von Frantz, 1975, p. 287)

Intellectual Antecedents

Freud

Although Jung was already a practicing psychiatrist before he met Freud, Freud's theories were clearly among the strongest influences on his thinking. Freud's *The Interpretation of Dreams* (1900) inspired Jung to attempt his own approach to dream and symbol analysis. Freud's theories of unconscious processes also gave Jung his first glimpse into the possibilities of systematically analyzing the dynamics of mental functioning, rather than relying on the superficial classification schemes that typified psychiatry at the time. Jung acknowledged the validity of Freud's achievements in the area of psychopathology; however, he felt that his own theoretical efforts could be devoted more to issues concerning positive growth and individuation.

Jung has written that

> Freud's greatest achievement probably consisted in taking neurotic patients seriously and entering into their peculiar individual psychology. He had the courage to let the case material speak for itself, and in this way was able to penetrate into the real psychology of his patients. . . . By evaluating dreams as the most important source of information concerning the unconscious processes, he gave back to mankind a tool that had seemed irretrievably lost. (1961, pp. 168–169)

The unconscious is on no account an empty sack in which the refuse of consciousness is collected . . . it is the whole other half of the living psyche. (Jung, 1973, p. 143)

Jung's conception of the unconscious is similar to that of psychoanalytic theory. However, Jung formulated both a personal and collective unconscious. The personal unconscious is composed of forgotten memories, repressed experiences, and subliminal perceptions.

The contents of the collective unconscious, also known as the impersonal or transpersonal unconscious are universal and not rooted in our personal experience. This concept is perhaps Jung's greatest departure from Freud as well as his most significant contribution to psychology. (See Major Concepts in this chapter.)

Literature

Disappointed with the one-sided books of his father's theology, Jung almost gave up early on searching to understand God and His Creation. His mother suggested to him that he read Goethe's *Faust*. This work had a major influence on Jung's understanding of the psyche and provided insight into the power of evil and its relation to growth and self-insight. An avid student, Jung became extremely well read in philosophy and literature.

Nietzsche also had a profound effect on Jung. He felt that Nietzsche's work possessed great psychological insight even though his fascination with power tended to overshadow his portrait of the mature and free human being. Jung saw Nietzsche and Freud as representatives of the two greatest themes in Western culture—power and eros. However, he felt that both men had become so deeply involved with these two vital themes that they were almost obsessed by them.

> When people say I am wise, or a sage, I cannot accept it. A man once dipped a hatful of water from a stream. What did that amount to? I am not that stream. I am at the stream, but I do nothing. (Jung, 1961, p. 355)

Alchemy

Jung searched for Western traditions that dealt with the development of consciousness. He was especially interested in the symbols and concepts used to describe this process. Jung discovered the Western alchemical literature, long ignored as magical, prescientific nonsense. He interpreted the alchemical treatises as representations of inner change and purification disguised in chemical and magical metaphors. The transformation of base metals into gold, for example, can be seen as a metaphor for the reformation of the personality and consciousness in the process of individuation. "Only after I had familiarized myself with alchemy did I realize that the unconscious is a process, and that the psyche is transformed or developed by the relationship of the ego to the content of the unconscious" (Jung, 1936b, p. 482).

Eastern Thought

In pursuing his research into myth and symbolism, Jung developed his own theories concerning individuation, or personality integration. Subsequently, Jung became deeply impressed with various Eastern traditions that provided the first outside confirmation of many of his own ideas. In 1928, Richard Wilhelm, a German scholar who had lived in China for many years, sent Jung the manuscript of his translation of an ancient Chinese spiritual text phrased in alchemical terms, in which the Golden Flower is discussed (Wilhelm & Jung, 1962). The Golden Flower is a mandala symbol. Mandala is the Sanskrit word for circle, or a circular

> The Golden Flower is a mandala symbol which I have often met with in the material brought me by my patients. It is drawn either seen from above as a regular geometric ornament, or as a blossom growing from a plant. The plant is frequently a structure in brilliant fiery colours growing out of a bed of darkness, and carrying the blossom of light at the top. (Jung in Wilhelm & Jung, 1962, p. 101)

design or diagram frequently used in meditation and other spiritual practices.

Jung discovered that Eastern descriptions of spiritual growth, inner psychic development, and integration closely corresponded to the process of individuation that he had observed in his Western patients. Jung was particularly interested in the mandala as an image of the self and of the individual process. He found that his analysands spontaneously produced mandala drawings even though they were completely unfamiliar with Eastern art or philosophy. For Jung, because the mandala symbolizes the process of individuation, it tends to appear in the drawings of analysands who have made considerable progress in their own personal growth. The center of the drawing stands for the self, which comes to replace the limited ego as the center of the personality; and the circular diagram as a whole represents the balance and order that develops in the psyche as the individuation process progresses.

Jung was careful to point out important differences between Eastern and Western paths of individuation. The social and cultural framework in which the process of growth takes place differs greatly between the East and the West, as do the prevailing attitudes toward the concept of individuation and those who actively seek this goal. The desirability of inner development and enlightenment is widely accepted in the East, where there are clearly recognized paths and techniques for facilitating the process.

Jung warned against the dangers of over-systematizing Yoga techniques:

> Centuries ago Yoga congealed into a fixed system, but originally the mandala symbolism grew out of the unconscious just as individually and directly as it does with Western man today. . . . Yoga, however, as we know it today, has become a method of spiritual training which is drilled into the initiands from above . . . that is the exact opposite of what I do. (Jung, 1973, pp. 196–197)

Follow that will and that way which experience confirms to be your own, i.e. the true expression of your individuality. (Jung in Serrano, 1966, p. 83)

Jung sought to develop his own theories first, and carefully avoided imitating Eastern thinking. After returning from his trip to India, Jung wrote:

> I studiously avoided all so-called "holy men." I did so because I had to make do with my own truth, not accept from others what I could not attain on my own. I would have felt it as a theft had I attempted to learn from the holy men and to accept their truth for myself. (Jung, 1961, p. 275)

Jung has argued that Eastern paths to individuation, such as Yoga and Buddhism, are generally unsuitable for Westerners. He felt that the cultural contexts and attitudes related to these practices are in many ways alien to those born and raised in the West. Those Westerners who have pursued Eastern disciplines have tended to deny their Western heritage, attempting to imitate as much of Eastern culture as possible and cutting themselves off from important parts of their own psyches.

Jung's observations may have been more true for his day than ours (as thousands of Westerners today are pursuing Eastern spiritual disciplines in a serious, balanced, and grounded manner). The dated nature of Jung's attitude toward Eastern thought is clear in his foreword to D. T. Suzuki's *Introduction to Zen Buddhism* (1964). "Great as is the value of Zen Buddhism for the understanding of the religious transformation process, its use among Western people is very improbable. The spiritual conceptions necessary to Zen are missing in the West." However, Jung's emphasis on our need to retain our connection with the deep psychic roots of our Western heritage merits serious consideration as so many people turn East for spiritual guidance.

Georg Feuerstein (1989), a Western Yoga scholar, has commented that Jung's warnings should be taken seriously. Mere imitation of Eastern cultural trappings does more harm than good. It runs the risk of a kind of inauthentic and shallow role playing. However, Feuerstein questions Jung's contention that Easterners have a radically different psychic constitution from Westerners. He concludes:

> The dialogue between East and West is one of the most significant events of our century. If, as Jung confidently asserted, the West will create its own Yoga in the centuries to come, it will not be on the foundations of Christianity alone, . . . but rather on the new foundations laid as a result of that dialogue between the two halves of planetary humankind. (p. 8)

Major Concepts

The Attitudes: Introversion and Extraversion

Among all of Jung's concepts, *introversion* and *extraversion* have probably gained widest general use. Jung found that each individual can be characterized as being either primarily inwardly or outwardly oriented. The introvert is more comfortable with the inner world of thoughts and feelings. The extravert is more at home with the outer world of objects and other people.

No one is a pure introvert or a pure extravert. Jung compared these two processes to the heartbeat—there is a rhythmic alternation between the cycle of contraction (introversion) and the cycle of expansion (extraversion). However, each individual tends to favor one or the other attitude and operates more often in terms of the favored attitude.

At times, introversion is more appropriate; at other times extraversion is more suitable. The two are mutually exclusive; you cannot hold both an introverted and an extraverted attitude concurrently. Neither one is better

The path to wholeness is made up of fateful detours and wrong turnings. (Jung, 1961, p. 325)

than the other. The ideal is to be flexible and to be able to adopt either attitude when it is most appropriate—to operate in terms of a dynamic balance between the two and not develop a fixed way of responding to the world.

Introverts are interested primarily in their own thoughts and feelings, in their inner world. They tend to be deeply introspective. One danger for such people is that they may become too immersed in their inner world, losing touch with the outer environment. The absent-minded professor is a clear, if stereotypic, example.

Extraverts are concerned with the outer world of people and things; they tend to be more social and more aware of what is going on around them. They need to guard against becoming dominated by externals and alienated from their internal processes.

Introverts see the world in terms of how it affects them, whereas extraverts are more concerned with their impact upon the world.

The Functions: Thinking, Feeling, Sensation, Intuition

Jung identified four fundamental psychological functions: thinking, feeling, sensation, and intuition. Each function may be experienced in an introverted or extraverted fashion. Generally, one of the functions is more conscious, developed, and dominant. This function is the superior one

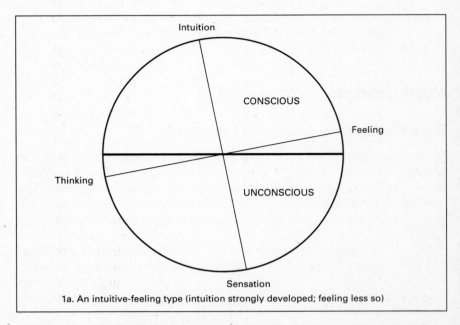

1a. An intuitive-feeling type (intuition strongly developed; feeling less so)

Figure 2.1   **An example of Jung's Functional Typology** Functions above the horizontal line are the better developed, more conscious functions, and those below the line less developed, less conscious.

and operates out of the dominant attitude (either extraversion or introversion). One of the other three remaining functions is generally deep in the unconscious and less developed.

Jung has called the least developed function in each individual the "inferior function." This function is the least conscious and the most primitive, or undifferentiated. It can represent a seemingly demonic influence for some people because they have so little understanding of or control over it. For example, strongly intuitive types may find that sexual impulses seem mysterious or even dangerously out of control because they are so much out of touch with their sensation function. Because it is less consciously developed, the inferior function may also serve as a way into the unconscious. Jung has said that it is through our inferior function, that which is least developed in us, that we see God. It is the struggling with and confronting of inner obstacles that bring us closer to the Divine.

Thinking and feeling are alternative ways of forming judgments and making decisions and discriminations. *Thinking* is concerned with objective truth, with judgment and impersonal analysis. Thinking asks the question, "What does this mean?" Consistency and abstract principles are highly valued. Thinking types (those individuals in whom the thinking function predominates) are the greatest planners; however, they tend to hold on to their plans and theories even when confronted by new and contradictory evidence.

Feeling is focused on value. This may include judgments of good or bad and right or wrong (as opposed to decision making according to criteria of logic or efficiency, as in thinking). Feeling asks the question, "What value does this have?"

Jung classifies sensation and intuition together as ways of gathering information, as opposed to ways of making decisions. *Sensation* refers to a focus on direct sense experience, perception of details, and concrete facts: what one can see, touch, and smell. Tangible, concrete experience is given priority over discussion or analysis of experience. Sensation asks the question, "What exactly am I perceiving?" Sensing types tend to respond to the immediate situation and deal effectively and efficiently with all sorts of crises and emergencies. They generally work better with tools and materials than any of the other types.

Intuition is a way of comprehending sensory information in terms of possibilities, past experience, future goals, and unconscious processes. Intuition asks the question, "What might happen, what is possible?" The implications of experience are more important to intuitives than the actual experience itself. Strongly intuitive people add meaning to their perceptions so rapidly that they often cannot separate their interpretations from the raw sensory data. Intuitives integrate new information quickly, automatically relating past experience and relevant information to immediate experience. Because it often includes unconscious material, intuitive thinking appears to proceed by leaps and bounds.

For the individual, a combination of all four functions results in a well-rounded approach to the world.

> In order to orient ourselves, we must have a function which ascertains that something is there (sensation); a second function which establishes *what* is (thinking); a third function which states whether it suits us or not, whether we wish to accept it or not (feeling); and a fourth function which indicates where it came from and where it is going (intuition). (Jung, 1942, p. 167)

Unfortunately, no one develops all four functions equally well. Everyone has one dominant function and one partially developed auxiliary function. The other two functions are generally unconscious and operate with considerably less effectiveness. The more developed and conscious the dominant and auxiliary functions, the more deeply unconscious are their opposites. (See Figure 2.1.)

One's function type indicates the relative strengths and weaknesses and the style of activity one tends to prefer. Jung's typology is especially useful in helping us understand social relationships; it describes how people perceive in alternate ways and use different criteria in acting and making judgments. For example, intuitive-feeling speakers will not have the same logical, tightly organized, and detailed lecture style as thinking-sensation lecturers. The talks of the former are more likely to ramble, to give the sense of an issue by approaching it from many different angles, rather than developing it systematically.

The Unconscious

Our unconscious mind, like our body, is a storehouse of relics and memories of the past. (Jung, 1968, p. 44)

Jung emphasizes in his writings that the unconscious cannot be known because of its very nature and thus must be described in relationship to consciousness. He writes that consciousness theoretically has no limit.

Further, Jung divides the unconscious into the personal unconscious and the collective unconscious.

Personal Unconscious

The material in the personal unconscious comes from the individual's past. This corresponds to Freud's concept of the unconscious. The personal unconscious is composed of memories that are painful and have been repressed as well as memories that are unimportant and have been simply dropped from conscious awareness. The personal unconscious also holds parts of the personality that have never come to consciousness.

Collective Unconscious

It [the collective unconscious] is more like an atmosphere in which we live than something that is found *in* us. It is simply the unknown quantity in the world. (Jung, 1973, p. 433)

Jung identifies the collective, or transpersonal, unconscious as the center of all psychic material that does not come from personal experience. It extends across time and culture. Some psychologists, such as Skinner, implicitly assume that each individual is born as a blank slate, a tabula rasa; consequently, psychological development can come only from personal experience. Jung postulates that the mind of the infant already possesses a structure that molds and channels all further development and interaction with the environment. This basic structure is essentially the same in all infants. Although we each develop differently and become unique individuals, the collective unconscious is common to all people and is therefore one (Jung, 1951a).

We are born with a psychological heritage as well as a biological heritage, according to Jung. Both are important determinants of behavior and experience. "Just as the human body represents a whole museum of organs, each with a long evolutionary period behind it, so we should expect to find that the mind is organized in a similar way. It can no more be a product without history than is the body in which it exists" (Jung, 1964, p. 67).

> The collective unconscious contains the whole spiritual heritage of mankind's evolution, born anew in the brain structure of every individual. His conscious mind is an ephemeral phenomenon that accomplishes all provisional adaptations and orientations. . . . The unconscious, on the other hand, is the source of the instinctual forces of the psyche. . . . All the most powerful ideas in history go back to archetypes. (Jung in Campbell, 1971, p. 45)

Jung's approach to the collective unconscious can be seen in the following passage from a letter to one of his analysands:

> You trust your unconscious as if it were a loving father. But it is *nature* and cannot be made use of as if it were a reliable human being. It is *inhuman* and it needs the human mind to function usefully for man's purposes. . . . It always seeks its collective purposes and never your individual destiny. Your destiny is the result of the collaboration between the conscious and the unconscious. (Jung, 1973, p. 283)

Archetype

The archetype is probably Jung's most difficult concept. Archetypes are formless, primordial, *a priori* structures of the psyche. They are inherited systems that act as the source point, the ultimate potential energy of the psyche. They are representations of the instinctual energies.

Jung postulated the idea of archetypes from the experiences his patients reported. A number of Jung's patients described dreams and fantasies that included remarkable ideas and images whose content could not be traced to the individual's past experience. Jung discovered a close correspondence between patients' dream contents and the mythical and religious themes found in many widely scattered cultures. "An archetype means a typos (imprint), a definite grouping of characters containing, in form as well as in meaning, mythological motifs" (Jung, 1968, p. 41). Jung suggested that there is a level of imagery in the unconscious common to everyone.

Archetypal imagery can be seen in the mythological themes of the folktales and legends of many different periods and cultures. According to

Primordial means "first" or "original"; therefore a primordial image refers to the earliest development of the psyche. Man inherits these images from his ancestral past, a past that includes all of his human ancestors as well as his prehuman or animal ancestors. (Jung in Hall & Nordby, 1973, p. 39)

Jung, the archetypes are structure-forming elements within the unconscious. These elements give rise to the archetypal images that dominate both individual fantasy life and the mythologies of an entire culture. The archetypes exhibit "a kind of readiness to produce over and over again the same or similar mythical ideas" (Jung, 1917, p. 69). They tend to appear as certain regularities—as recurring situations and figures. Archetypal situations include the hero's quest, the night-sea journey, and the battle for deliverance from the mother. Archetypal figures include the divine child, the double, the old sage, and the primordial mother.

A wide variety of symbols can be associated with a given archetype. For example, the mother archetype embraces not only each individual's real mother but also all mother figures and nurturant figures. This includes women in general, mythical images of women, such as Venus, Virgin Mary, and Mother Nature, and supportive and nurturant symbols, such as the church and paradise. The mother archetype includes not only positive features but also negative ones, such as the threatening, domineering, or smothering mother. In the Middle Ages, for example, this aspect of the archetype was crystallized into the image of the witch.

Each of the major structures of the personality are archetypes. These include the *persona,* the *ego,* the *shadow,* the *anima* (in men), the *animus* (in women), and the *self.*

Generally, archetypal images will have a contemporary form. People today are more likely to dream about fighting with their in-laws than about slaying a dragon.

The archetypes themselves are forms, without content of their own, that serve to organize or channel psychological material. They are somewhat like dry stream beds whose shape determines the characteristics of a river once water begins flowing through them. The archetypes are carriers of energy. When an archetype is activated, it generally unlocks a tremendous amount of energy. All creativity has an archetypal element.

Archetypes form the infrastructure of the psyche. Archetypal patterns are similar to the patterns found in crystal formation. No two snowflakes are exactly alike; however, every single snowflake has the same basic crystalline structure. Similarly, the contents of each individual's psyche as well as each individual's experiences are unique. However, the general patterns into which these experiences fall are determined by universal parameters and generating principles, or archetypes.

In *Hero with a Thousand Faces* (1949), Joseph Campbell, a Jungian scholar, outlines the basic archetypal themes and patterns in the stories and legends of heroes found in cultures throughout history. The story of Oedipus is a good illustration of an archetypal situation that deals with a son's deep love for his mother and conflict with his father. The same basic situation can be found as a theme in many myths and legends and also as a psychological pattern in many individuals. There are numerous other related situations, such as the daughter's relationship to her parents, parents' relationship to children, relationships between men and women, brothers, and sisters, and so forth.

It is essential to insist that archetypes are not mere names, or even philosophical concepts. They are pieces of life itself—images that are integrally connected to the living individual by the bridge of the emotions. (Jung, 1964, p. 96)

Some additional quotes from Jung may help clarify this rich and complex idea:

> The term archetype is often misunderstood as meaning certain definite mythological images or motifs. . . . The archetype is a tendency to form such representations of a motif—representations that can vary a great deal in detail without losing their basic pattern. (Jung, 1964, p. 67)

> These collective patterns I have called archetypes, using an expression of St. Augustine's. An archetype means a typos (imprint), a definite grouping of characters containing, in form as well as in meaning, mythological motifs. (Jung, 1968, p. 41)

Jung lends increasing richness and complexity to the archetypal form as he describes it in the context of mystical experience:

> ". . . Mystics are people who have a particularly vivid experience of the processes of the collective unconscious. Mystical experience is experience of archetypes."
>
> Question: "Is there any difference between archetypal forms and mystical forms?"
>
> Professor Jung: "I make no distinction between them." (Jung, 1968, pp. 110–111)

> The archetypes, which are pre-existant to consciousness and condition it, appear in the part they actually play in reality: as *a priori* structural forms of the stuff of consciousness. They do not in any sense represent things as they are in themselves, but rather forms in which things can be perceived and conceived. (Jung, 1961, p. 347)

Finally, Jung provides a thought-provoking caveat:

> Not for a moment dare we succumb to the illusion that an archetype can be finally explained and disposed of. Even the best attempts at

Personal Reflection ——————————

—————————— Archetypes in Your Own Life

What has been the major archetypal image or theme in your life?

In what ways has it influenced you and those around you? Give some specific examples of how it has actually operated in your life.

Be aware that the first archetype that comes to mind isn't necessarily the most significant one. One way to discover what archetypes are meaningful for you is to think about the themes in literature and film that most appeal to you. Is there a character that you find particularly captivating? Or is there a certain kind of situation that you find particularly alluring, e.g., a doomed great love or a dangerous journey into the unknown?

explanation are only more or less successful translations into another metaphorical language. (Indeed, language itself is only an image.) The most we can do is to *dream the myth onwards* and give it a modern dress. And whatever explanation or interpretation does to it, we do to our own souls as well. (Jung, 1951b, p. 160)

Jung has written that

the contents of an archetype may be integrated into consciousness but they themselves cannot. Archetypes then cannot be done away with through integration any more than by a refusal to admit their contents to enter consciousness. The archetypes remain a source for the channeling of psychic energies throughout the entire lifetime and must be continually dealt with. (Jung, 1951a, p. 20)

The Ego

The ego wants explanations always in order to assert its existence. (Jung, 1973, p. 427)

The ego is the center of consciousness and one of the major archetypes of the personality. The ego provides a sense of consistency and direction in our conscious lives. It tends to oppose whatever might threaten this frag-

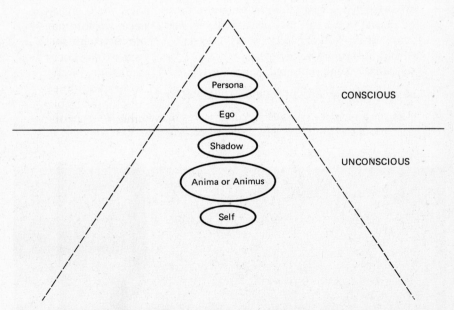

Figure 2.2 The Structure of the Personality This diagram depicts the order in which the major archetypes generally appear in Jungian analysis. However, any two-dimensional representation of Jungian theory is bound to be misleading or even inaccurate. The self, for example, is more deeply unconscious than the other structures of the personality, but, at the same time, it is also the center of the total personality. (Courtesy Thomas Parker)

ile consistency of consciousness and tries to convince us that we must always consciously plan and analyze our experience.

According to Jung, the psyche at first consists only of the unconscious. Similar to Freud's view, Jung's ego arises from the unconscious and brings together various experiences and memories, developing the division between unconscious and conscious. There are no unconscious elements in the ego, only conscious contents derived from personal experience. We are led to believe that the ego is the central element of the psyche, and we come to ignore the other half of the psyche, the unconscious.

The Persona

Our persona is the appearance we present to the world. It is the character we assume; through it, we relate to others. The persona includes our social roles, the kind of clothes we choose to wear, and our individual styles of expressing ourselves. The term *persona* comes from the Latin, meaning "mask," or "false face," as in the *mask* worn by an actor on the Roman stage through which he spoke. (Related to persona is the word *personare,* meaning "to sound through.") We have to play a part in something that defines our roles in order to function socially at all. Even those who try to reject such adaptive devices invariably adopt different ones that represent rejection.

The persona has both positive and negative aspects. A dominant persona can smother the individual, and those who identify with their persona tend to see themselves only in terms of their superficial social roles and facade. Jung also called the persona the "conformity archetype." However, the persona is not all negative. It serves to protect the ego and the psyche from the varied social forces and attitudes that impinge on them. The persona is also a valuable tool for communication. In Greek

Personal Reflection ———————————————————

————————————————————— The Persona

List your favorite articles of clothing, jewelry, or other possessions that you generally carry, a purse or backpack, for example. Choose the one article that you feel most represents *you,* that somehow is an integral part of your self-image. Choose something that you wear or carry most of the time.

1. Go without it for a week and note your reactions to its absence.

2. Lend it to a friend. How does it feel to see it worn or used by someone else?

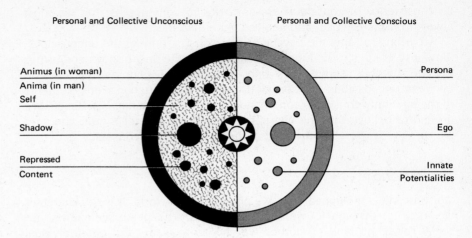

Figure 2.3   General Scheme of the Psyche

Note. From The "I" and the "Not-I" (Diagram 1, Appendix) by M. E. Harding, 1965, New York: Bollingen. Copyright 1965 by Bollingen. Adapted by permission.

drama, the actors' boldly drawn masks informed the entire audience clearly, if somewhat stereotypically, of the character and the attitudes of the role each actor was playing. The persona can often be crucial to our positive development. As we begin to play a certain role, our ego gradually begins to identify with it. This is a central process in personality development.

This process is not always positive, however. As the ego identifies with the persona, people begin to believe that they are what they pretend to be. According to Jung, we eventually have to withdraw this identification and learn who we are in the process of self-realization, or individuation.

Symbols commonly used for the persona include objects we use to cover ourselves (clothing or a veil), symbols of an occupational role (tools or briefcase), and status symbols (car, house, or diploma). All of these symbols can be found in dreams as representations of the persona. For example, someone with a strong persona may appear overdressed, or constricted by too much clothing. A person with a weak persona might appear naked and exposed. One possible expression of an extremely inadequate persona would be to have no skin.

The Shadow

How can I be substantial without casting a shadow? I must have a dark side too if I am to be whole; and by becoming conscious of my shadow I remember once more that I am a human being like any other. (Jung, 1931c, p. 59)

The shadow is an archetypal form that serves as the focus for material that has been repressed from consciousness; its contents include those tendencies, desires, memories, and experiences that are rejected by the individual as incompatible with the persona and contrary to social standards and ideals. The shadow contains all the negative tendencies the

Personal Reflection ⎯⎯⎯⎯⎯⎯⎯⎯⎯⎯

⎯⎯⎯⎯⎯⎯⎯⎯⎯⎯⎯⎯⎯⎯ Seeing Ourselves in Others

List all of the qualities you admire in the person you love or respect most. Then list all of the qualities you dislike in the person you respect the least.

The first list most likely contains your anima or animus projections—those qualities you have inside you that you can develop. The second list contains your shadow projections—those qualities that you must confront within yourself.

individual wishes to deny, including animal instincts as well as undeveloped positive and negative qualities.

The stronger our persona is and the more we identify with it, the more we deny other parts of ourselves. The shadow represents what we consider to be inferior in our personality and also that which we have neglected and never developed in ourselves. In dreams, a shadow figure may appear as an animal, a dwarf, a vagrant, or any other low-status figure.

In his work on repression and neurosis, Freud focused primarily on what Jung calls the shadow. Jung found that the repressed material is organized and structured around the shadow, which becomes, in a sense, a negative self, or the shadow of the ego. The shadow is often experienced in dreams as a dark, primitive, hostile, or repellent figure, because the contents of the shadow have been forcibly pushed out of consciousness and appear antagonistic to the conscious outlook. If the material from the shadow is allowed back into consciousness, it loses much of its dark and frightening quality.

The shadow is most dangerous when unrecognized. Then the individual tends to project his or her unwanted qualities onto others or to become dominated by the shadow without realizing it. Images of evil, the devil, and the concept of original sin are all aspects of the shadow archetype. The more the shadow material is made conscious, the less it can dominate. But the shadow is an integral part of our nature, and it can never be simply eliminated. A person who claims to be without a shadow is not a complete individual but a two-dimensional caricature, denying the mixture of good and evil that is neccessarily present in all of us.

The ancient Chinese sage Chuang-tzu (369–286 B.C.) understood the shadow as well as did the most sophisticated modern psychologist:

There was a man
who was so disturbed
by the sight of his own shadow
and so displeased with his own footsteps
that he determined to get rid of both.

The method he hit upon was to run away from them.
So he got up and ran.

But every time he put his foot down
there was another step,
while his shadow kept up with him
without the slightest difficulty.

He attributed his failure
to the fact that he was not running fast enough.
So he ran faster and faster, without stopping,
until he finally dropped dead.

He failed to realize
that if he merely stepped into the shade,
his shadow would vanish,
and if he sat down and stayed still,
there would be no more footsteps.

(In Merton, 1965, p. 155)

Each repressed portion of the shadow represents a part of ourselves. To the extent that we keep this material unconscious, we limit ourselves.

Personal Reflection

The Shadow

One aspect of the shadow can be personified by a small demon, an imp dedicated to harming you or foiling your best laid plans. It may appear as an implacable inner critic or as you at your worst. The following is intended to help you better understand this aspect of your shadow.

1. Think about how you would describe *in detail* your personal demon and how it operates in your life. When does it appear? Are there any triggers that seem to bring it out?

2. If you were to personify this aspect of the shadow, what would it look like? Does it have a name? How would it dress? What would some of its favorite expressions be?

3. Communicate with this figure. Discuss its good qualities. How has it helped you? Also look at how it has fostered or arrested personal change or growth.

4. What inner figure would be the opposite of the personal demon? With this opposite figure in mind, review steps 1 to 3.

As the shadow is made more conscious, we repossess previously repressed parts of ourselves. Also, the shadow is not simply a negative force in the psyche. It is a storehouse for considerable instinctual energy, spontaneity, and vitality, and it is a major source of our creative energies. Like all archetypes, the shadow is rooted in the collective unconscious, and it can allow the individual access to much of the valuable unconscious material that is rejected by the ego and the persona.

Just when we think we understand it, the shadow will appear in another form. Dealing with the shadow is a lifelong process of looking within and honestly reflecting on what we see there.

The following passage from one of Jung's letters provides a clear illustration of Jung's approach to the shadow and to the unconscious in general.

It is a very difficult and important question, what you call the technique of dealing with the shadow. There is, as a matter of fact, no technique at all, inasmuch as technique means that there is a known and perhaps even prescribable way to deal with a certain difficulty or task. It is rather a dealing comparable to diplomacy or statesmanship. There is, for instance, no particular technique that would help us to reconcile two political parties opposing each other. It can be a question of good will, or diplomatic cunning or civil war or anything. If one can speak of a technique at all, it consists solely in an attitude. First of all, one has to accept and to take seriously into account the existence of the shadow. Secondly, it is necessary to be informed about its qualities and intentions. Thirdly, long and difficult negotiations will be unavoidable. . . .

Nobody can know what the final outcome of such negotiations will be. One only knows that through careful collaboration the problem itself becomes changed. Very often certain apparently impossible intentions of the shadow are mere threats due to an unwillingness on the part of the ego to enter upon a serious consideration of the shadow. Such threats diminish usually when one meets them seriously. Pairs of opposites have a natural tendency to meet on the middle line, but the middle line is never a compromise thought out by the intellect and forced upon the fighting parties. It is rather a result of the conflict one has to suffer. Such conflicts are never solved by a clever trick or by an intelligent invention but by enduring them. As a matter of fact, you have to heat up such conflicts until they rage in full swing so that the opposites slowly melt together. It is a sort of alchemistic procedure rather than a rational choice and decision. The suffering is an indispensable part of it. Every real solution is only reached by intense suffering. The suffering shows the degree in which we are intolerable to ourselves. "Agree with thine enemy" outside and inside! That's the problem! Such agreement should violate yourself as little as your enemy. I admit it is not easy to find the right formula, yet if you find it you have made a whole of yourself and this, I think, is the meaning of human life. (1973, p. 234)

Anima and Animus

Jung postulated an unconscious structure that is the complement of the persona. Jung calls this the *anima* in man and the *animus* in woman. This basic psychic structure serves as a focus for all the psychological material that does not fit with an individual's conscious self-image as a man or woman. Thus, to the extent that a woman consciously defines herself in feminine terms, her animus will include those unrecognized tendencies and experiences that she has defined as masculine.

The animus may be pathologically dominated by identification with archetypal images (e.g., the bewitched prince, the romantic poet, the ghostly lover, or the marauding pirate), and/or by an extreme father fixation. For a woman, the process of psychological development entails entering into a dialog between her ego and her animus. The animus is initially viewed as a wholly separate personality. As the animus and its influence on the individual is recognized, the animus begins to assume the role of liaison between conscious and unconscious until it gradually becomes integrated into the self. Jung views the quality of this union of opposites (in this case, masculine and feminine) as the major determinant of female personality functioning.

A similar process occurs between the anima and masculine ego in the male. As long as our anima or animus is unconscious, not accepted as part of our self, we will tend to project it outward onto people of the opposite sex.

> Every man carries within him the eternal image of woman, not the image of this or that particular woman, but a definitive feminine image. This image is . . . an imprint or "archetype" of all the ancestral experiences of the female, a deposit, as it were, of all the impressions ever made by woman. . . . Since this image is unconscious, it is always unconsciously projected upon the person of the beloved, and is one of the chief reasons for passionate attraction or aversion. (Jung, 1931b, p. 198)

According to Jung, the child's opposite sex parent is a major influence on the development of the anima or animus. All relations with the opposite sex, including parents, are strongly affected by the projection of anima or animus fantasies. This archetype is one of the most influential regulators of behavior. It appears in dreams and fantasies as figures of the opposite sex, and it functions as the primary mediator between unconscious and conscious processes. It is oriented primarily toward inner processes, just as the persona is oriented to the outer processes. It is a source of projections, a source of image making, and a door to creativity in the psyche. (The creative influence of the anima can be seen in artists who have depicted their muses as female goddesses.) Jung also called this archetype the "soul image." Because has the capacity to bring us in touch with our unconscious forces, it is often the key to unlocking our creativity.

The Self

The self is the most important archetype and also the most difficult to understand. Jung has called the self the *central archetype,* the archetype of psychological order and the totality of the personality. The self is the archetype of centeredness. It is the union of the conscious and the unconscious that embodies the harmony and balance of the various opposing elements of the psyche. The self directs the functioning of the whole psyche in an integrated way. According to Jung, "[C]onscious and unconscious are not necessarily in opposition to one another, but complement one another to form a totality, which is the *self*" (Jung, 1928b, p. 175). Jung discovered the self archetype only after his investigations of the other structures of the personality.

The self is often depicted in dreams or images impersonally (as a circle, mandala, crystal, or stone) or personally (as a royal couple, a divine child, or as some other symbol of divinity). Great spiritual teachers, such as Christ, Muhammed, and Buddha, are also symbols for the self. These are all symbols of wholeness, unification, reconciliation of polarities, and dynamic equilibrium—the goals of the individuation process.

The self is a deep, inner, guiding factor, which can seem to be quite different, even alien, from the ego and consciousness. "The self is not only the centre, but also the whole circumference which embraces both conscious and unconscious; it is the centre of this totality, just as the ego is the centre of consciousness" (Jung, 1936b, p. 41). It may first appear in dreams as a tiny, insignificant image, because the self is so unfamiliar and undeveloped in most people. The development of the self does not mean that the ego is dissolved. The ego remains the center of consciousness. However, it becomes linked to the self as the result of the long, hard work of understanding and accepting unconscious processes. The ego becomes less the center of the personality, and more one of the many structures within the psyche.

> The archetype of the individual is the Self. The Self is all-embracing. God is a circle whose center is everywhere and whose circumference is nowhere. (Jung in McGuire & Hull, 1977, p. 86)

> The ego receives the light from the Self. Though we know of this Self, yet it is not known. . . . Although we receive the light of consciousness from the Self and although we know it to be the source of our illumination, we do not know whether it possesses anything we would call consciousness. . . . If the Self could be wholly experienced, it would be a limited experience, whereas in reality its experience is unlimited and endless. . . . If I were one with the Self I would have knowledge of everything, I would speak Sanskrit, read cuneiform script, know the events that took place in pre-history, be acquainted with the life of other planets, etc. (Jung, 1975, pp. 194–195)

Symbols

The symbol has a very complex meaning because it defies reason; it always presupposes a lot of meanings that can't be comprehended in a single logical concept. The symbol has a future. The past does not suffice to interpret it, because germs of the future are included in every actual situation. That's why, in elucidating a case, the symbolism is spontaneously applicable, for it contains the future. (Jung in McGuire & Hull, 1977, p. 143)

According to Jung, the unconscious expresses itself primarily through symbols. Although no specific symbol or image can ever fully represent an archetype (which is a form without specific content), the more closely a symbol conforms to the unconscious material organized around an archetype, the more it evokes a strong, emotionally charged response.

As a plant produces its flower, so the psyche creates its symbols. (Jung, 1964, p. 64)

Jung is concerned with two kinds of symbols: individual and collective. By individual symbols Jung means "natural" symbols that are spontaneous productions of the individual psyche, rather than images or designs created deliberately by an artist. In addition to the personal symbols found in an individual's dreams or fantasies, there are also important collective symbols, which are often religious images, such as the cross, the six-pointed Star of David, and the Buddhist wheel of life.

Symbolic terms and images represent concepts that we cannot clearly define or fully comprehend. For Jung, a sign *stands for* something else, but a symbol, such as a tree, *is* something in itself—a dynamic, living thing. The symbol represents the individual's psychic situation, and it *is* that situation at a given moment.

What we call a symbol is a term, a name, or even a picture that may be familiar in daily life, yet that possesses specific connotations in addition to its conventional and obvious meaning. It implies something vague, unknown, or hidden from us. . . . Thus a word or an image is symbolic when it implies something more than its obvious and immediate meaning. It has a wider "unconscious" aspect that is never precisely defined or fully explained. (Jung, 1964, pp. 20–21)

Active Imagination

Jung valued the use of active imagination as a means of facilitating self-understanding through work with symbols. He encouraged his patients to paint, sculpt, or use some other art form as a way to explore their inner depths. Active imagination is not passive fantasy but an attempt to engage the unconscious in a dialog with the ego, through symbols.

Active imagination refers to any conscious effort to produce material directly related to unconscious processes, to relax our usual ego controls without allowing the unconscious to take over completely. The process of active imagination differs for each individual. Some people use drawing or painting most profitably, whereas others prefer to use conscious imagery, or fantasy, or some other form of expression.

Personal Reflection

Active Imagination

Drawing

Start a sketch diary, a daily collection of sketches and drawings. As you work with the diary, you will gradually see how major changes in your psychological life are related to your drawings. As you draw, you will probably find that you frequently associate certain colors or forms with certain emotions and people, and your drawings will become a clearer medium for self-expression.

Another approach to drawing is to sit down with a pad and crayons and ask your unconscious a question. Then let your imagination find an image; put the image on paper. Do not *think* an answer.

Other Media

Modern technology can serve as an aid in active imagination. Photography and video recording offer many possibilities, including a wide range of special effects. Audio recording is also a readily available vehicle for active imagination. Choose one medium and experiment with it, allowing your unconscious to express itself in the form you have chosen.

Conscious Imaging

Start with a dream image or any image that is particularly powerful or meaningful for you. Contemplate it and observe how it begins to change or unfold. Do not try to make anything happen, just observe what seems to occur spontaneously. Hold to your first image and try to avoid jumping from one subject to another.

You can eventually choose to step into the picture yourself and to address the image and listen to what it has to say.

Jung himself used a variety of outlets to explore his unconscious. He designed his retreat house in Bollingen according to his inner needs, and, as he himself grew, he added new wings to the house. Jung also painted murals on the walls at Bollingen; he inscribed manuscripts in Latin and high German script, illustrated his own manuscripts, and also carved in stone.

Dreams

For Jung, dreams play an important complementary (or compensatory) role in the psyche. The widely varied influences we are exposed to in our conscious life tend to distract us and to mold our thinking in ways that are often unsuitable to our personality and individuality. "The general function of dreams is to try to restore our psychological balance by producing dream material that re-establishes, in a subtle way, the total psychic equilibrium" (Jung, 1964, p. 50).

Jung approached dreams as living realities that must be experienced and observed carefully to be understood. He tried to uncover the significance of dream symbols by paying close attention to the form and content of the dream, and he gradually moved away from the psychoanalytic reliance on free association in dream analysis. "Free association will bring out all my complexes, but hardly ever the meaning of a dream. To understand the dream's meaning I must stick as close as possible to the dream images" (Jung, 1934, p. 149). In analysis, Jung would continually bring his patients back to the dream images and ask them, "What does the *dream* say?" (Jung, 1964, p. 29).

Because the dream deals with symbols that have more than one meaning, there can be no simple, mechanical system for dream interpretation. Any attempt at dream analysis must take into account the attitudes, experiences, and background of the dreamer. It is a joint venture between analyst and analysand. The dreamer interprets the dream with the help and guidance of the analyst. The analyst may be vitally helpful, but in the end only the dreamer can *know* what the dream means.

Jeremy Taylor, a well-known authority on Jungian dream work, postulates certain basic assumptions about dreams (1992, p. 11):

> 1. All dreams come in the service of health and wholeness.
>
> 2. No dream comes simply to tell the dreamer what he or she already knows.
>
> 3. Only the dreamer can say with certainty what meanings a dream may hold.
>
> 4. There is no such thing as a dream with only one meaning.
>
> 5. All dreams speak a universal language, a language of metaphor and symbol.

More important than the cognitive understanding of dreams is the act of experiencing the dream material and taking this material seriously. One Jungian analyst has pointed out the importance of *befriending* our dreams and treating them not as isolated events but as communications from ongoing unconscious processes.

> It is necessary that the unconscious make known its own direction and we must allow it an equal voice with that of the ego, if each side is to be able to adapt to the other. As the ego listens, and the unconscious is encouraged to participate in the dialogue, the unconscious position is transformed from that of an adversary to that of a friend with a somewhat differing but complementary point of view. (Singer, 1972, p. 283)

The image is a condensed expression *of the psychic situation as a whole, not merely, nor even predominantly, of unconscious contents pure and simple. (Jung, 1921, p. 442)*

Personal Reflection ——————————————

————————————————— Dream Journal

Keep a journal of the dreams you have each night. Review the dreams at the end of each week, looking for recurring patterns or symbolism. You can also experiment with different ways of recording your dreams. You can tape them as you wake up, and then write them out; or you can sketch the symbols and images of your dreams.

As you consider your dreams and dream images, ask yourself, "What does this dream have to say to me?"

Dynamics

Psychological Growth

Individuation

According to Jung, every individual possesses a tendency toward individuation, or self-development. Jung believed that the psyche has an innate urge toward wholeness. "Individuation means becoming a single, homogeneous being, and, insofar as 'individuality' embraces our innermost, last, and incomparable uniqueness, it also implies becoming one's own self. We could therefore translate individuation as 'coming to selfhood' or 'self-realization'" (Jung, 1928b, p. 171).

> Individuation is a natural process. It is what makes a tree turn into a tree; if it is interfered with, then it becomes sick and cannot function as a tree, but left to itself it develops into a tree. This is individuation. . . . Consciousness is a part of it, perhaps, yes, but that depends on how much consciousness there is naturally there. Consciousness can also block individuation by not allowing what is in the unconscious to develop. (Jung in McGuire & Hull, 1977, p. 210)

Individuation is a process of developing wholeness and thus moving toward greater freedom. This includes development of a dynamic relationship between the ego and the self, along with the integration of the various parts of the psyche: the ego, persona, shadow, anima or animus, and the other unconscious archetypes. As people become more individuated, these archetypes may be seen as expressing themselves in more subtle and complex ways.

> The more we become conscious of ourselves through self-knowledge, and act accordingly, the more the layer of the personal unconscious that is superimposed on the collective unconscious will be diminished.

In this way there arises a consciousness which is no longer imprisoned in the petty, oversensitive, personal world of objective interests. This widened consciousness is no longer that touchy, egotistical bundle of personal wishes, fears, hopes, and ambitions which always has to be compensated or corrected by unconscious countertendencies; instead, it is a function of relationship to the world of objects, bringing the individual into absolute, binding, and indissoluble communion with the world at large. (Jung, 1928b, p. 176)

Everything that happens to us, properly understood, leads us back to ourselves; it is as though there were some unconscious guidance whose aim it is to deliver us from all this and make us dependent on ourselves. (Jung, 1973, p. 78)

As an analyst, Jung found that those who came to him in the first half of life were relatively uninvolved with the inner process of individuation; they tended to be concerned primarily with emergence as an individual, external achievement, and the attainment of the goals of the ego. Older patients, who had fulfilled such goals reasonably well, tended to develop different aims: to become concerned with integration rather than achievement and to seek harmony with the totality of the psyche.

The individuated human being is just ordinary, therefore almost invisible. . . . His feelings, thoughts, etc., are just anybody's feelings, thoughts, etc.—quite ordinary, as a matter of fact, and not interesting at all. . . . He will have no need to be exaggerated, hypocritical, neurotic, or any other nuisance. He will be "in modest harmony with nature.". . . No matter whether people think they are individuated or not, they are just what they are: in the one case a man plus an unconscious nuisance disturbing to himself—or, without it, unconscious of himself; or in the other case, conscious. The criterion is consciousness. (Jung, 1975, p. 377)

From the point of view of the ego, growth and development consist of integrating new material into one's consciousness; this includes the acquisition of knowledge of the world and of oneself. Growth, for the ego, is essentially the expansion of conscious awareness. However, individuation is the development of the self, and from the point of view of the self, the goal is the union of consciousness with the unconscious.

Unveiling the Persona.   Early in the individuation process, it is necessary to recognize the unveiling of the persona and to view it as a useful tool rather than as a permanent part of oneself. Although the persona has important protective functions, it is also a mask that hides the self and the unconscious.

When we analyze the persona we strip off the mask, and discover that what seemed to be individual is at bottom collective; in other words, that the persona was only a mask for the collective psyche. Fundamentally the persona is nothing real: it is a compromise between individual and society as to what a man should appear to be. He takes a name, earns a title, represents an office, he is this or that. In a certain sense all this is real, yet in relation to the essential individuality of the person concerned it is only secondary reality, a product of compromise, in making which others often have a greater share than he. (Jung, 1928b, p. 156)

Confronting the Shadow.   When we look beyond mere appearances, we are forced to confront the shadow. We can become free of the shadow's influence to the extent that we accept the reality of the dark side and simultaneously realize that we are more than the shadow.

Confronting the Anima or Animus.   A further step is to confront the anima or animus. This archetype must be dealt with as a real person or persons that one can communicate with and learn from. Jung would ask the anima figures that appeared to him about the interpretation of dream symbols, like an analysand consulting an analyst. The individual also becomes aware that the anima or animus figures have considerable autonomy and that they are likely to influence or even dominate those who ignore them or who blindly accept their images and projections as their own personal productions.

The unconscious mind of man sees correctly even when conscious reason is blind and impotent. (Jung, 1952b, p. 386)

Developing the Self.   The goal and culmination of the individuation process is the development of the self. "The self is our life's goal, for it is the completest expression of that fateful combination we call individuality" (Jung, 1928b, p. 238). The self replaces the ego as the midpoint of the psyche. Awareness of the self brings unity to the psyche and helps to integrate conscious and unconscious material. "The aim of individuation is nothing less than to divest the self of the false wrappings of the persona on the one hand, and of the suggestive power of primordial images on the other" (Jung, 1945, p. 174). The ego is still the center of consciousness, but it is no longer seen as the nucleus of the entire personality.

Jung writes that

> one must be what one is; one must discover one's own individuality, that centre of personality, which is equidistant between the conscious and the unconscious; we must aim for that ideal point towards which nature appears to be directing us. Only from that point can one satisfy one's needs. (In Serrano, 1966, p. 91)

It is necessary to keep in mind that although it is possible to describe individuation in terms of stages, the individuation process is considerably more complex than the simple progression outlined here. All of the steps listed overlap, and one continually returns to old problems and issues (hopefully from a different perspective). Individuation might be represented as a spiral in which one keeps confronting the same basic questions, each time in a finer form. (This concept is closely related to the Zen Buddhist conception of enlightenment, in which an individual never solves a personal *koan*, or spiritual problem, and the searching is seen as a goal in itself.)

Obstacles to Growth

Individuation, consciously undertaken, is a difficult task, and the individual must be relatively psychologically healthy to handle the process. The ego must be strong enough to undergo tremendous changes, to be turned inside out in the process of individuation.

> One could say that the whole world with its turmoil and misery is in an individuation process. But people don't know it, that's the only difference. . . . Individuation is by no means a rare thing or a luxury of the few, but those who know that they are in such a process are considered to be lucky. They get something out of it, provided they are conscious enough. (Jung, 1973, p. 442)

This process is especially difficult because it is an individual enterprise, often carried out in the face of the rejection or, at best, indifference of others. Jung writes that

> nature cares nothing whatsoever about a higher level of consciousness; quite the contrary. And then society does not value these feats of the psyche very highly; its prizes are always given for achievement and not for personality, the latter being rewarded for the most part posthumously. (1931a, p. 394)

Each stage in the individuation process is accompanied by difficulties. First is the danger of identification with the persona. Those who identify with the persona may try to become too "perfect," unable to accept their mistakes or weaknesses as well as any deviations from their idealized self-concepts. Those *fully* identified with the persona will tend to repress all of those tendencies that do not fit and project them onto others; the job of acting out aspects of the repressed, negative identity will be assigned to other people.

Filling the conscious mind with ideal conceptions is a characteristic feature of Western theosophy. . . . One does not become enlightened by imagining figures of light, but by making the darkness conscious. (Jung, 1954a, pp. 265–266)

The shadow can also become a major obstacle to individuation. People who are unaware of their shadows can easily act out harmful impulses without ever recognizing them as wrong or without any awareness of their own negative feelings. In such people, the initial impulses to harm or do wrong are instantly rationalized as they fail to acknowledge the presence of such impulses in themselves. Ignorance of the shadow may also result in an attitude of moral superiority and projection of the shadow onto others. For example, those most in favor of censorship of pornography tend to be fascinated by the materials they want to ban; they may even convince themselves of the need to study carefully all the available pornography in order to be effective censors.

Confronting the anima or animus brings with it the problem of relating to the collective unconscious. The anima may bring on sudden emotional changes or moodiness in a man. The animus often manifests itself as irrational, rigidly held opinions in the woman. (We should remember that

Jung's discussion of anima and animus is not a description of masculinity and femininity in general. The content of the anima or animus is the complement of our conscious conception of ourselves as masculine or feminine, which, in most people, is strongly determined by cultural values and socially defined sex roles.)

Once the individual is exposed to collective material, there is a danger of becoming engulfed by the unconscious. According to Jung, this can take one of two forms. First, there is the possibility of ego inflation, in which the individual claims all the virtues of the collective psyche. The other reaction is that of ego impotence; the person feels that he or she has no control over the collective psyche and becomes acutely aware of unacceptable aspects of the unconscious—irrationality, negative impulses, and so forth.

As in many myths and fairy tales, the greatest obstacles are those found closest to the goal. When the individual deals with the anima and animus, tremendous energy is unleashed. This energy can be used to build up the ego instead of developing the self. Jung has referred to this as identification with the archetype of the mana-personality. (*Mana* is a Melanesian word for the energy or power that emanates from people, objects, or supernatural beings; energy that has an occult or bewitching quality.) The ego identifies with the archetype of the wise man or wise woman, the sage who knows everything. (This syndrome is not uncommon among older university professors, for example.) The mana-personality is dangerous because it is an exaggeration of power. Individuals stuck at this stage try to be both more and less than they really are: more, because they tend to believe they have become perfect, holy, or even godlike; but actually less, because they have lost touch with their essential humanity and the fact that no one is perfectly wise, infallible, and flawless.

Jung sees temporary identification with the archetype of the self or the mana-personality as being almost inevitable in the individuation process. The best defense against the development of ego inflation is to remember one's essential humanity, to stay grounded in the reality of what one can and must do, not what one *should* do or be.

> Not perfection, but completeness is what is expected of you. (Jung, 1973, p. 97)

Structure

Body

In his voluminous writings, Jung did not deal explicitly with the role of the body, but chose to direct his efforts to analyzing the psyche. He has argued that physical processes are relevant to us only to the extent that they are represented in the psyche. The physical body and the external world can be known only as psychological experiences. "I'm chiefly concerned with the psyche itself, therefore I'm leaving out body and spirit. . . . Body and spirit are to me mere aspects of the reality of the psyche.

> Psyche and body are not separate entities, but one and the same life. (Jung, 1917, p. 113)

Psychic experience is the only immediate experience. Body is as metaphysical as spirit" (Jung, 1973, p. 200).

Social Relationships

Social interaction is important in the formation and development of the major personality structures: persona, shadow, and anima or animus. The contents of social experiences help determine the specific images and symbols associated with each structure; at the same time, these basic archetypal structures mold and guide our social relationships.

Jung stresses that individuation is essentially a personal endeavor; however, it is also a process that develops through relationships with other people.

> As nobody can become aware of his individuality unless he is closely and responsibly related to his fellow beings, he is not withdrawing to an egoistic desert when he tries to find himself. He only can discover himself when he is deeply and unconditionally related to some, and generally related to a great many, individuals with whom he has a chance to compare, and from whom he is able to discriminate himself. (Jung in Serrano, 1966, pp. 83–84)

Individuation does not isolate, it connects. I never saw relationships thriving on unconsciousness. (Jung, 1973, p. 504)

Will

Jung defines the will as the energy that is at the disposal of consciousness or the ego. The development of the will is associated with learning cultural values, moral standards, and the like. Will has power only over conscious thought and action and cannot directly affect instinctual or other unconscious processes, although it has substantial, indirect power over them through conscious processes.

Jung felt that individual will is a relatively recent human development. In primitive cultures, rituals (such as hunting dances) work tribal members into a state of action, a state that substitutes for our modern willpower.

> The will was practically nonexistent and it needed all the ceremonial which you observe in primitive tribes to bring up something that is an equivalent to our word "decision." Slowly through the ages we have acquired a certain amount of willpower. We could detach so much energy from the energy of nature, from the original unconsciousness, from the original flow of events, an amount of energy we could control. (Jung in McGuire & Hull, 1977, p. 103)

In my medical experience as well as in my own life I have again and again been faced with the mystery of love, and have never been able to explain what it is. (Jung, 1961, p. 353)

Emotions

Jung stresses the central role that the study of the emotions must play in psychology.

Psychology is the only science that has to take the factor of value (i.e., feeling) into account, because it is the link between psychical events and life. Psychology is often accused of not being scientific on this account; but its critics fail to understand the scientific and practical necessity of giving due consideration to feeling. (Jung, 1964, p. 99)

Psychic material that is directly related to the archetypes tends to arouse strong emotions and often has an awe-inspiring quality. When Jung discusses symbols, he is not writing about lifeless words or empty forms, but about powerful, living realities by which men and women live their lives and for which many have died. According to Jung, emotion accompanies all psychic changes. It is the force behind the process of individuation. "Emotion is the chief source of consciousness." (Jung, 1954b, p. 96)

Intellect

For Jung, the intellect refers to directed, conscious thought processes. Jung distinguishes intellect from intuition, which draws strongly on unconscious material. The intellect has an important, but limited, role in psychological functioning. Jung stresses that a purely intellectual understanding cannot be complete. "A psychology that satisfies the intellect alone can never be practical, for the totality of the psyche can never be grasped by intellect alone" (Jung, 1917, p. 117).

> Psychic development cannot be accomplished by intention and will alone; it needs the attraction of a symbol. (Jung, 1928a, p. 25)

Therapist

Jung emphasized that therapy is a joint effort between analyst and analysand working together as equals. Because the two form a dynamic unit, the analyst must also be open to change as a result of the interaction. Jung felt that therapy involves primarily the interaction of the analyst's unconscious with that of the analysand, who can advance in therapy only as far as the analyst has.

> A therapist who has a neurosis does not deserve the name, for it is not possible to bring the patient to a more advanced stage than one has reached oneself. (Jung, 1973, p. 95)

It is a remarkable thing about psychotherapy: you cannot learn any recipes by heart and then apply them more or less suitably, but can cure only from one central point; and that consists in understanding the patient as a psychological whole and approaching him as a human being, leaving aside all theory and listening attentively to whatever he has to say. (Jung, 1973, p. 456)

Jung tried to avoid reliance on theory and on specific techniques in the process of therapy. He believed that this tends to make the analyst mechanical and out of touch with the analysand. The therapist does not merely treat parts of the psyche like a mechanic patching up an old car that needs a new carburetor or muffler. The aim of therapy is to approach the analysand as a whole individual through a genuine relationship.

Jung generally saw people only once or twice a week. He tried to foster a sense of autonomy in analysands and would often give them homework. He might ask them to analyze their own dreams, for example. He would also insist that his clients take occasional vacations from analysis in order to avoid becoming dependent on him and on the analytic routine.

Jung has outlined two major stages of the therapeutic process, each of which has two parts. First comes the *analytic stage*. It consists initially of *confession*, in which the individual begins to recover unconscious material. Ties of dependency on the therapist tend to develop at this stage. Next comes *elucidation* of the confessional material, where greater familiarity and understanding of psychic processes develops. The person remains dependent on the therapist.

The second stage of therapy is the *synthetic*. First comes *education*, in which Jung stressed the need to move from psychological insight to actual new experiences that result in individual growth and the formation of new habits. The final part is the *transformation*. The analysand-analyst relationship is integrated, and dependency is reduced as the relationship becomes transformed. The individual experiences a highly concentrated individuation process, though archetypal material is not necessarily confronted. This is the stage of self-education in which the individual takes more and more responsibility for his or her own development.

Evaluation

An Open System of Psychology

Jung has often been criticized for his lack of a coherent, clearly structured system of thought. His writing often seems to go off on tangents, rather than presenting ideas in a formal, logical, or even systematic fashion. Also, Jung often uses varying definitions for the same terms at different times. He was aware of this difficulty in his writing but did not see it as necessarily a drawback. Jung believed that life rarely follows the logically coherent pattern that has become the standard for scientific and academic writing, and his own style may be closer to the rich complexity of psychological reality.

Jung deliberately developed an open system, one that could admit new information without distorting it to fit an inclusive, theoretical structure. He never believed that he knew all the answers or that new information would merely confirm his theories. Consequently, his theorizing lacks a tight, logical structure that categorizes all information in terms of a small number of theoretical constructs.

Religion and Mysticism

Because he dealt with religion, alchemy, spirituality, and the like, some critics have labeled Jung a mystic rather than a scientist. But it is clear that Jung's attitude was always that of an investigator rather than that of a

Any of my pupils could give you so much insight and understanding that you could treat yourself if you don't succumb to the prejudice that you receive healing through others. In the last resort every individual alone has to win his battle, nobody else can do it for him. (Jung, 1973, p. 126)

The serious problems in life, however, are never fully solved. If ever they should appear to be so it is a sure sign that something has been lost. The meaning and purpose of a problem seem to lie not in its solutions but in our working at it incessantly. (Jung, 1931a, p. 394)

I am a researcher and not a prophet. What matters to me is what can be verified by experience. But I am not interested at all in what can be speculated about experience without any proof. (Jung, 1973, p. 203)

believer or disciple. He viewed mystical belief systems as important expressions of human ideals and aspirations. Spiritual experiences were treated as data that should not be ignored by anyone concerned with the full range of human thought and behavior.

> No matter what the world thinks about religious experience, the one who has it possesses a great treasure, a thing that has become for him a source of life, meaning, and beauty, and that has given a new splendour to the world and to mankind. . . . Where is the criterion by which you could say that such a life is not legitimate, that such an experience is not valid . . . ? Is there, as a matter of fact, any better truth about the ultimate things than the one that helps you to live? . . . No one can know what the ultimate things are. We must therefore take them as we experience them. And if such experience helps to make life healthier, more beautiful, more complete and more satisfactory to yourself and to those you love, you may safely say: "This was the Grace of God." (Jung, 1938, p. 105)

Jung saw clearly that religious issues and concerns were closely related to psychological health:

> Among all my patients in the second half of life—that is to say, over thirty-five—there has not been one whose problem in the last resort was not that of finding a religious outlook on life. It is safe to say that every one of them fell ill because he had lost what the living religions of every age have given to their followers, and none of them has been really healed who did not regain his religious outlook. (Jung, 1932, p. 334)

Jung's stress on the practical importance of spirituality is evident in a letter that he wrote to Bill Wilson, the cofounder of Alcoholics Anonymous. In the letter, Jung wrote about his alcoholic patient Roland H., saying that his addiction to alcohol was hopeless unless "he could become the subject of a spiritual or religious experience—in short a genuine conversion." Jung greatly influenced Wilson in his own conversion and cure as well as in his cofounding AA in 1934. The following is an excerpt from the letter Jung wrote to Wilson:

The main interest of my work is not concerned with the treatment of neuroses but rather with the approach to the numinous [a sense of the holy]. But the fact is that the approach to the numinous is the real therapy and inasmuch as you attain to the numinous experiences you are released from the curse of pathology. (Jung, 1973, p. 377)

> I had no news from Roland H. and often wondered what has been his fate. . . . His craving for alcohol was the equivalent, on a low level, of the spiritual thirst of our being for wholeness, expressed in medieval language: the union with God.
>
> How could one formulate such an insight in a language that is not misunderstood in our days?
>
> The only right and legitimate way to such an experience is that it happens to you in reality, and it can only happen to you when you walk on a path which leads you to higher understanding. You might

be led to that goal by an act of grace or through a personal and honest contact with friends, or through a higher educational education of the mind beyond the confines of mere rationalism. . . .

You see, "alcohol" in Latin is *spiritus,* and you use the same word for the highest religious experience as well as for the most depraving poison. The helpful formula therefore is: *spiritus contra spiritum.* (Jung, 1984, pp. 197–198)

The Analysis of Symbols

Jung's recognition of the psychological importance of symbols and his detailed analysis of symbols and their interpretations are his most important contributions to psychology. Jung was centrally concerned with the complexity of symbolism and with the need to analyze symbols without oversimplifying. He was drawn to mythology, folklore, and alchemy because they provided various contexts that shed light upon the complex symbolic productions he came upon in analysis.

Although Jung's writing is difficult to comprehend, it is perhaps more valuable because it conveys the richness of his thinking. His flexibility and open-mindedness, his concern for the deeper truths of human existence, give Jung's work a breadth and complexity virtually unmatched in psychology.

Recent Developments: Jung's Influence

Jung's ideas have been growing steadily in popularity and influence. The Jung Institute in Zurich continues to train analysts from all around the world. There are also Jungian institutes in several countries and in many major American cities. They offer Jungian books and libraries, lecture series, weekend workshops, and long-term training in Jungian analysis.

Based on Jung's theory of types, the Meyers-Briggs Type Indicator has become one of the most popular psychology tests in the world. It is widely used today in business and in education. Millions of people have taken it. Each individual is scored on introversion versus extraversion, thinking versus feeling, intuition versus sensation, and also perception versus judgment. This final category was later added to Jung's basic scheme. Perception refers to an openness to new evidence and new experience. Judgment refers to the shutting out of new perceptions and coming to a decision.

Jung's ideas have been applied and furthered by a great many writers and scholars. Joseph Campbell was a prominent Jungian scholar and applied Jung's ideas to topics including myth (1985, 1988) and the hero archetype (1949). James Hillman (1975, 1989) strongly influenced by Jung, developed an approach he calls *archetypal psychology.* Jean Shinoda Bolen (1984, 1989) has written two best-selling books on the archetypes of the goddesses in women and the gods in men. Robert Bly (1990), who is one of the founders of the men's movement, has been strongly influenced by Jung's ideas.

There is a whole literature relating Jungian psychology and spirituality, primarily from a Christian perspective. This literature includes writings by Kelsey (1974, 1982) and Sanford (1968, 1981). Caprio and Hedberg's (1986) *Coming Home: A Handbook for Exploring the Sanctuary Within* is a practical guide for spiritual work in the Christian tradition. It includes striking personal stories, excellent illustrations, and useful exercises.

For an excellent look at the relationship between Jungian psychology and Buddhism, see Spiegelman and Miyuki (1985). Spiegelman (1982) has also written on the relationship between Jungian psychology and Jewish mysticism, as well as on the relationship between Jungian psychology and Hinduism (Spiegelman & Vasavada, 1987).

Jung's rich, complex, and sophisticated ideas are gradually gaining the widespread acceptance they so well deserve.

Everything men assert about God is twaddle, for no man can know God. (Jung, 1975, p. 377)

The Theory Firsthand: Excerpts from *Analytic Psychology*

Word Association

Jung's first introduction to *depth* psychology came with his experiments in word association. He developed great expertise at interpreting associations. His intuitive abilities were often astonishing.

> Many years ago, when I was quite a young doctor, an old professor of criminology asked me about the experiment [in word association] and said he did not believe it. I said: "No, Professor? You can try it whenever you like." He invited me to his house and I began. After ten words he got tired and said: "What can you make of it? Nothing has come of it." I told him he could not expect a result with ten or twelve words; he ought to have a hundred and then we would see something. He said: "Can you do something with these words?" I said: "Little enough, but I can tell you something. Quite recently you have had worries about money, you have too little of it. You are afraid of dying of heart disease. You must have studied in France, where you had a love affair, and it has come back to your mind, as often, when one has thoughts of dying, old sweet memories come back from the womb of time." He said: "How do you know?" Any child could have seen it! He was a man of 72 and he had associated *heart* with *pain*—fear that he would die of heart failure. He associated *death* with *to die*—a natural reaction—and with *money* he associated *too little,* a very usual reaction. Then things became rather startling to me. To *pay,* after a long reaction time, he said *La Semeuse,* though our conversation was in German. That is the famous figure on the French coin. Now why on

earth should this old man say *La Semeuse?* When he came to the word *kiss* there was a long reaction time and there was a light in his eyes and he said: *Beautiful.* Then of course I had the story. He would never have used French if it had not been associated with a particular feeling, and so we must think why he used it. Had he had losses with the French franc? There was no talk of inflation and devaluation in those days. That could not be the clue. I was in doubt whether it was money or love, but when he came to *kiss/beautiful* I knew it was love. He was not the kind of man to go to France in later life, but he had been a student in Paris, a lawyer, probably at the Sorbonne. It was relatively simple to stitch together the whole story. (Jung, 1968, p. 57)

Dream Analysis

The following excerpt illustrates Jung's approach to dream analysis:

My colleague was an alienist at a clinic, and the patient was a distinguished young Frenchman, twenty-two years of age, highly intelligent, and very aesthetic. He had travelled in Spain and had come back with a depression which was diagnosed as manic-depressive insanity, depressive form. The depression was not very bad, but bad enough for him to be sent to the clinic. After six months he was released from confinement, and a few months later he committed suicide. He was no longer under the depression, which was practically cured; he committed suicide apparently in a state of calm reasoning. We shall understand from [a] dream why he committed suicide. This is the dream, and it occurred at the beginning of the depression:

Underneath the great cathedral of Toledo there is a cistern filled with water which has a subterranean connection with the river Tagus, which skirts the city. This cistern is a small dark room. In the water there is a huge serpent whose eyes sparkle like jewels. Near it there is a golden bowl containing a golden dagger. This dagger is the key to Toledo, and its owner commands full power over the city. The dreamer knows the serpent to be the friend and protector of B—— C——, a young friend of his who is present. B—— C—— puts his naked foot into the serpent's jaws. The serpent licks it in a friendly way and B—— C—— enjoys playing with the serpent; he has no fear of it because he is a child without guilt. In the dream B—— C—— appears to be about the age of seven; he had indeed been a friend of the dreamer's early youth. Since this time, the dream says, the serpent has been forgotten and nobody dared to descend into its haunts.

This part is a sort of introduction, and now the real action begins.

The dreamer is alone with the serpent. He talks to it respectfully, but without fear. The serpent tells the dreamer that Spain belongs to *him as he is B——— C———'s friend, and asks him to give back the boy. The dreamer refuses to do this and promises instead that he himself will descend into the darkness of the cave to be the friend of the serpent. But then he changes his mind, and instead of fulfilling his promise he decides to send another friend, a Mr S———, to the serpent. This friend is descended from the Spanish Moors, and to risk the descent into the cistern he has to recover the original courage of his race. The dreamer advises him to get the sword with the red hilt which is to be found in the weapons factory on the other bank of the Tagus. It is said to be a very ancient sword, dating back to the old Phocaeans.* S——— gets the sword and descends into the cistern, and the dreamer tells him to pierce his left palm with the sword. S——— does so, but he is not able to keep his countenance in the powerful presence of the serpent. Overcome by pain and fear, he cries out and staggers upstairs again without having taken the dagger. Thus S——— cannot hold Toledo, and the dreamer could do nothing about it and had to let him stay there as a mere wall decoration.*

. . . We make no mistake when we assume that the dreamer has picked out Toledo for a particular reason—both as the object of his trip and of his dream; and the dream brings up material which practically everybody would have who had seen Toledo with the same mental disposition, the same education and refinement of aesthetic perception and knowledge. Toledo is an extremely impressive city. It contains one of the most marvelous Gothic cathedrals of the world. It is a place with an immensely old tradition. . . . The cathedral of Toledo, being such an impressive and beautiful building, naturally suggests all that it represents: the greatness, the power, the splendour, and the mystery of medieval Christianity, which found its essential expression in the Church. Therefore the cathedral is the embodiment, the incarnation, of the spiritual kingdom, for in the Middle Ages the world was ruled by the Emperor *and* by God. . . .

The dream says that underneath the cathedral there is a mysterious place, which in reality is not in tune with a Christian church. What is beneath a cathedral of that age? There is always the so-called under-church or crypt. You have probably seen the great crypt at Chartres; it gives a very good idea of the mysterious character of a crypt. The crypt at Chartres was previously an old sanctuary with a well, where the worship of a virgin was celebrated—not of the Virgin Mary, as is done now—but of a Celtic goddess. Under every Christian church of the Middle Ages there is a secret place where in old times the mysteries were celebrated. . . .

The crypt is probably taken over from the cult of Mithras. In Mithraism the main religious ceremony took place in a vault half sunk into the earth, and the community remained separated in the main church above. There were peepholes so that they could see and hear

But we must not forget that only a very few people are artists in life; that the art of life is the most distinguished and rarest of all the arts. (Jung in Campbell, 1971, p. 19)

the priests and the elect ones chanting and celebrating their rites below, but they were not admitted to them. That was a privilege for the initiates. In the Christian church the separation of the baptistry from the main body of the building derives from the same idea, for baptism as well as the communion were mysteria of which one could not speak directly. One had to use a sort of allegorical allusion so as not to betray the secrets. . . .

The idea of the crypt or mystery-place leads us to something below the Christian *Weltanschauung,* something older than Christianity, like the pagan well below the cathedral at Chartres, or like an antique cave inhabited by a serpent. The well with the serpent is of course not an actual fact which the dreamer saw when he travelled in Spain. This dream-image is not an individual experience and can therefore only be paralleled by archaeological and mythological knowledge. I have to give you a certain amount of that parallelism so that you can see in what context or tissue such a symbolical arrangement appears when looked at in the light of comparative research work. You know that every church still has its baptismal font. This was originally the piscina, the pond, in which the initiates were bathed or symbolically drowned. After a figurative death in the baptismal bath they came out transformed . . . as reborn ones. So we can assume that the crypt or baptismal font has the meaning of a place of terror and death and also of rebirth, a place where dark initiations take place.

The serpent in the cave is an image which often occurs in antiquity. It is important to realize that in classical antiquity, as in other civilizations, the serpent not only was an animal that aroused fear and represented danger, but also signified healing. Therefore Asklepios, the god of physicians, is connected with the serpent; you all know his emblem which is still in use. In the temples of Asklepios . . . which were the ancient clinics, there was a hole in the ground, covered by a stone, and in that hole lived the sacred serpent. . . .

The serpent is not only the god of healing; it also has the quality of wisdom and prophecy. The fountain of Castalia at Delphi was originally inhabited by a python. Apollo fought and overcame the python, and from that time Delphi was the seat of the famous oracle and Apollo its god, until he left half his powers to Dionysus, who later came in from the East. In the underworld, where the spirits of the dead live, snakes and water are always together, as we can read in Aristophanes' *The Frogs.* The serpent in legend is often replaced by the dragon; the Latin *draco* simply means snake. . . .

Very often these caves, like the cave of Castalia, contain springs. These springs played a very important role in the cult of Mithras, from which many elements of the early Church originated. Porphyry relates that Zoroaster, the founder of the Persian religion, dedicated to

Mithras a cave containing many springs. . . . We know of other religious ideas in antiquity, for instance of the Orphic cult, which always associate the underworld with water.

This material will give you an idea that the serpent in the cave full of water is an image that was generally known and played a great role in antiquity. As you have noticed, I have chosen all my examples exclusively from antiquity; I could have chosen other parallels from other civilizations, and you would find it was the same. The water in the depths represents the unconscious. In the depths as a rule is a treasure guarded by a serpent or a dragon; in our dream the treasure is the golden bowl with the dagger in it. In order to recover the treasure the dragon has to be overcome. The treasure is of a very mysterious nature. It is connected with the serpent in a strange way; the peculiar nature of the serpent denotes the character of the treasure as though the two things were one. Often there is a golden snake with the treasure. Gold is something that everyone is seeking, so we could say that it looks as if the serpent himself were the great treasure, the source of immense power. . . .

That prepares us a little for understanding the golden bowl and the dagger in our dream. If you have seen Wagner's *Parsifal* you know that the bowl corresponds to the Grail and the dagger to the spear and that the two belong together; they are the male and the female principle which form the union of opposites. The cave or underworld represents a layer of the unconscious where there is no discrimination at all, not even a distinction between the male and the female, which is the first differentiation primitives make. . . .

When the unconscious brings together the male and the female, things become utterly indistinguishable and we cannot say any more whether they are male or female. . . . So we see that the bottom of the cistern in our dream is characterized by a complete union of opposites. This is the primordial condition of things, and at the same time a most ideal achievement, because it is the union of elements eternally opposed. Conflict has come to rest, and everything is still or once again in the original state of indistinguishable harmony. . . .

When the dreamer comes to these symbols he reaches the layer of complete unconsciousness, which is represented as the greatest treasure. It is the central motif in Wagner's *Parsifal* that the spear should be restored to the Grail because they belong eternally together. This union is a symbol of complete fulfillment—eternity before and after the creation of the world, a dormant condition. That is probably the thing which the desire of man is seeking. That is why he ventures into the cave of the dragon, to find that condition where consciousness and the unconscious are so completely united that he is neither conscious nor unconscious. Whenever the two are too much separated, con-

To understand is my one great passion. But I also possess the physician's instinct. I would like to help people. (Jung, 1961, p. 322)

sciousness seeks to unite them again by going down into the depths where they once were one. . . .

The bowl is a vessel that receives or contains, and is therefore female. It is a symbol of the body which contains the anima, the breath and liquid of life, while the dagger has piercing, penetrating qualities and is therefore male. It cuts, it discriminates and divides, and so is a symbol of the masculine Logos principle.

In our dream the dagger is said to be the key to Toledo. The idea of the key is often associated with the mysteries in the cave. . . .

. . . so we have to consider the symbolic meaning of Toledo and of the city. As the old capital of Spain, Toledo was a very strong fortification and the very ideal of a feudal city, a refuge and stronghold which could not easily be touched from outside. The city represents a totality, closed in upon itself, a power which cannot be destroyed, which has existed for centuries and will exist for many centuries more. Therefore the city symbolizes the totality of man, an attitude of wholeness which cannot be dissolved.

The city as a synonym for the self, for psychic totality, is an old and well-known image. . . .

So these depths, that layer of utter unconsciousness in our dream, contain at the same time the key to individual completeness and wholeness, in other words to healing. The meaning of "whole" or "wholeness" is to make holy or to heal. The descent into the depths will bring healing. It is the way to the total being, to the treasure which suffering mankind is forever seeking, which is hidden in the place guarded by terrible danger. This is the place of primordial unconsciousness and at the same time the place of healing and redemption, because it contains the jewel of wholeness. It is the cave where the dragon of chaos lives and it is also the indestructible city, the magic circle or *temenos,* the sacred precinct where all the split-off parts of the personality are united. . . .

The serpent in the cave in our dream is the friend of B—— C——, the hero of the dreamer's early days, into whom he projected everything he wanted to become and all the virtues to which he was aspiring. That young friend is at peace with the serpent. He is a child without guile, he is innocent and knows as yet of no conflict. Therefore he has the key to Spain and the power over the four gates. (Jung, 1968, pp. 124–138)

We are . . . fully justified in speaking of an unconscious psyche. It is not directly accessible to observation—otherwise it would not be conscious. (Jung in Campbell, 1971, p. 28)

* [The people of ancient Phocaea, on the western coast of Asia Minor, founded Massilia (Marseilles) and colonies on the east coast of Spain.]

Annotated Bibliography

Jung, C. G. (1961). *Memories, dreams, reflections.* New York: Random House (Vintage Books). An autobiography that helps place Jung's multi-faceted thinking in perspective and provides an excellent introduction to Jung's thought. Includes a glossary with discussions of Jung's major concepts.

———. (Ed.). (1964). *Man and his symbols.* London: Aldus Books. Contains an extremely clear essay by Jung called, "Approaching the Unconscious." The book is amply illustrated, one of the best integrations of text and pictures in psychology. There is an inexpensive Dell paperback edition, but the Doubleday hardcover edition has more photos, many in color.

———. (1967). *Collected works of C. G. Jung* (H. Read, M. Fordham, & G. Adler, Eds.). Princeton, NJ: Princeton University Press. (Published under the sponsorship of the Bollingen Foundation; English edition, London: Routledge & Kegan Paul; American edition volumes issued 1953–1967, Pantheon Books.) For those seriously interested in exploring Jung in depth, this includes virtually all of Jung's writings.

———. (1968). *Analytic psychology: Its theory and practice.* New York: Pantheon Books. A clear account of Jung's theories, containing transcripts of a series of lectures he gave in London.

Many of Jung's essays are now available in paperback editions. Of special interest are: *Two Essays on Analytical Psychology,* an overview of the entire theoretical system, and *Psychological Types,* especially Chapter 10, "General Descriptions of Types," and Chapter 11, "Definitions," both of which describe the major Jungian concepts.

Good Secondary Sources

Dry, A. (1961). *The psychology of Jung.* New York: Wiley.

Fordham, F. (1953). *An introduction to Jung's psychology.* London: Penguin Books.

Hall, C., & Nordby, V. (1973). *A primer of Jungian psychology.* New York: New American Library (Mentor Books). Clear and well-written overview of Jungian psychology.

Jacoby, J. (1959). *Complex, archetype, symbol in the psychology of C. G. Jung.* New York: Pantheon Books.

Serrano, M. (1966). *C. G. Jung and Hermann Hesse: A record of two friendships*. London: Routledge & Kegan Paul. Includes some fascinating conversations between Jung and Serrano, a Chilean poet and novelist who lived in India for several years.

Singer, J. (1972). *Boundaries of the soul: The practice of Jung's psychology*. New York: Doubleday. A clear account of the dynamics of Jungian theory and therapy, by a modern Jungian analyst.

References

Adler, G. (1918). *Studies in analytical psychology*. New York: Norton.

Bolen, J. (1984). *The goddesses in everywoman*. San Francisco: Harper & Row.

———. (1989). *The gods in everyman*. San Francisco: Harper & Row.

Bly, R. (1990). *Iron John*. Menlo Park, CA: Addison-Wesley.

Brookes, C. (1991). Jung's concept of individuation. *Journal of the American Academy of Psychoanalysis, 19,* 307–315.

Campbell, J. (1949). *Hero with a thousand faces*. New York: Harcourt Brace Jovanovich.

———. (1985). *The inner reaches of outer space: Metaphor as myth and as religion*. New York: A. van der Marck.

———. (1988). *The power of myth*. New York: Doubleday.

———.(Ed.). (1971). *The portable Jung*. New York: Viking Press.

Caprio, B., & Hedberg, T. (1986). *Coming home: A manual for spiritual direction*. New York: Paulist Press.

Dry, A. (1961). *The psychology of Jung*. New York: Wiley.

Evans, R. (1964). *Conversations with Carl Jung*. New York: Van Nostrand.

Feuerstein, G. (1989). *Yoga: The technology of ecstasy*. Los Angeles: Jeremy P. Tarcher.

Fordham, F. (1953). *An introduction to Jung's psychology*. London: Penguin Books.

Freud, S. The interpretation of dreams. In J. Strachey (Ed. and Trans.), *The standard edition of the complete psychological works of Sigmund Freud* (Vols. 4, 5). London: Hogarth Press, 1953–1966. (Originally published, 1900.)

———. (1964). *An outline of psychoanalysis*. Standard edition (Vol. 23). London: Hogarth Press and Institute of Psychoanalysis.

Glover, E. (1950). *Freud or Jung?* New York: Norton.

Hall, C., & Nordby, V. (1973). *A primer of Jungian psychology*. New York: New American Library (Mentor Books).

Harding, M. E. (1965). *The "I" and the "Not-I."* New York: Bollingen.

———. (1970). *The way of all women*. New York: C. G. Jung Foundation for Analytical Psychology.

Hillman, J. (1975). *Re-Visioning psychology*. New York: Harper & Row.

———. (1989). *A blue fire: Selected writings by James Hillman*. New York: Harper & Row.

Jacobs, H. (1961). *Western psychotherapy and Hindu-sadhana*. London: Allen & Unwin.

Jacoby, J. (1959). *Complex, archetype, symbol in the psychology of C. G. Jung*. New York: Pantheon Books.

Jung, C. G. The psychology of dementia praecox. In H. Read, M. Fordham, & G. Adler (Eds.), *Collected works of C. G. Jung* (Vol. 3). (Published under the sponsorship of the Bollingen Foundation; English edition, London: Routledge & Kegan Paul; American edition volumes issued 1953–1967, Pantheon Books.) (Originally published, 1907.) Princeton, NJ: Princeton University Press, 1967.

———. Symbols of transformation. In *Collected works* (Vol. 5). (Originally published, 1912.)

———. The transcendent function. In *Collected works* (Vol. 8). (Originally published, 1913.)

———. The psychology of the unconscious. In *Collected works* (Vol. 7). (Originally published, 1917.)

———. Psychological types. In *Collected works* (Vol. 6). (Originally published, 1921.)

———. On psychic energy. In *Collected works* (Vol. 8). (Originally published, 1928a.)

———. The relations between the ego and the unconscious. In *Collected works* (Vol. 7). (Originally published, 1928b.)

———. The stages of life. In *Collected works* (Vol. 8). (Originally published, 1931a.)

———. Marriage as a psychological relationship. In *Collected works* (Vol. 17). (Originally published, 1931b.)

———. Problems of modern psychotherapy. In *Collected works* (Vol. 16). (Originally published, 1931c.)

———. Psychotherapists or the clergy. In *Collected works* (Vol. 11). (Originally published, 1932.)

———. (1933). *Modern man in search of a soul*. New York: Harcourt Brace Jovanovich.

———. The practical use of dream analysis. In *Collected works* (Vol. 16). (Originally published, 1934.)

———. The concept of the collective unconscious. In *Collected works* (Vol. 9, Part 1). (Originally published, 1936a.)

———. Individual dream symbolism in relation to alchemy. In *Collected works* (Vol. 12). (Originally published, 1936b.)

———. The archetypes and the collective unconscious. In *Collected works* (Vol. 9, Part 1). (Originally published, 1936c.)

———. Psychology and religion. In *Collected works* (Vol. 2). (Originally published, 1938.)

———. Conscious, unconscious, and individuation. In *Collected works* (Vol. 9, Part 1). (Originally published, 1939.)

———. A psychological approach to the dogma of the Trinity. In *Collected works* (Vol. 11). (Originally published, 1942.)

———. The relations between the ego and the unconscious. In *Collected works* (Vol. 7). (Originally published, 1945.)

———. Instinct and the unconscious. In *Collected works* (Vol. 8). (Originally published, 1948.)

———. A study in the process of individuation. In *Collected works* (Vol. 9, part 1). (Originally published, 1950.)

———. Aion. In *Collected works* (Vol. 9, Part 2). (Originally published, 1951a.)

———. The psychology of the child archetype. In *Collected works* (Vol. 9, Part 1). (Originally published, 1951b.)

———. Symbols of transformation. In *Collected works* (Vol. 5). (Originally published, 1952a.)

———. Answer to Job. In *Collected works* (Vol. 12). (Originally published, 1952b.)

———. The philosophical tree. In *Collected works* (Vol. 13). (Originally published, 1954a.)

———. Psychological aspects of the mother archetype. In *Collected works* (Vol. 9, Part 1). (Originally published, 1954b.)

———. The undiscovered self (present and future). In *Collected works* (Vol. 10). (Originally published, 1957.)

———. (1961). *Memories, dreams, reflections*. New York: Random House.

———. (1968). *Analytical psychology: Its theory and practice*. New York: Random House.

———. (1973). *Letters* (G. Adler, Ed.). Princeton, NJ: Princeton University Press.

———. (Ed.). (1964). *Man and his symbols*. New York: Doubleday.

———. (1975). *Letters, Vol. II: 1951–61*. (G. Adler, Ed.). Princeton, NJ: Princeton University Press.

———. (1984). *Selected letters of C. G. Jung, 1909–1961*. (G. Adler, Ed.). Princeton, NJ: Princeton University Press.

Kelsey, M. (1974). *God, dreams, and revelation: A Christian interpretation of dreams*. Minneapolis: Augsburg Publishing House.

———. (1982). *Christo-psychology*. New York: Crossroad.

McGuire, W. (Ed.). (1974). *The Freud-Jung letters: The correspondence between Sigmund Freud and C. G. Jung*. Princeton, NJ: Princeton University Press.

McGuire, W., & Hull, R. F. C. (Eds.). (1977). *C. G. Jung speaking*. Princeton, NJ: Princeton University Press.

Merton, C. (Trans.). (1965). *The way of Chuang Tzu*. New York: New Directions, p. 155.

Neumann, E. (1954). *The origins and history of consciousness*. Princeton, NJ: Princeton University Press.

Pearson, C. (1989). *The hero within: Six archetypes we live by*. New York: Harper & Row.

Progoff, I. (1953). *Jung's psychology and its social meaning.* New York: Julian Press.

Riesman, D. (1950). *The lonely crowd.* New Haven, CT: Yale University Press.

Sanford, J. A. (1968). *Dreams: God's forgotten language.* Philadelphia: Lippincott.

———. (1981). *The man who wrestled with God: Light from the Old Testament on the psychology of individuation.* Ramsey, NY: Paulist Press.

Serrano, M. (1966). *C. G. Jung and Hermann Hesse: A record of two friendships.* London: Routledge & Kegan Paul.

Singer, J. (1972). *Boundaries of the soul: The practice of Jung's psychology.* New York: Doubleday.

Spiegelman, J. (1982). *Jungian psychology and the tree of life.* Phoenix, AZ: Falcon Press.

Spiegelman, J., & Miyuki, M. (1985). *Buddhism and Jungian psychology.* Phoenix, AZ: Falcon Press.

Spiegelman, J., & Vasavada, A. (1987). *Hinduism and Jungian psychology.* Phoenix, AZ: Falcon Press.

Suzuki, D. T. (1964). *An introduction to Zen Buddhism.* New York: Grove Press.

Taylor, J. (1992). *Where people fly and water runs uphill: Using dreams to tap the wisdom of the unconscious.* New York: Warner Books.

von Frantz, M. (1975). *C. G. Jung: His myth in our time.* New York: Putnam.

———. (1991). *Dreams.* Boston, MA: Shambhala Publications.

Whitmont, E. (1969). *The symbolic quest.* New York: Putnam.

Wilhelm, R., & Jung, C. G. (1962). *The secret of the golden flower.* London: Routledge & Kegan Paul.

C h a p t e r   T h r e e

Alfred Adler and Individual Psychology

Alfred Adler is the founder of the holistic system of individual psychology, which emphasizes an approach to understanding each person as an integrated totality within a social system. He called his approach individual psychology, because it stresses the uniqueness of each individual, rather than the universalities of behavior espoused by Freud.

Adler's followers established centers throughout Europe, England, and the United States, and many of his original ideas have become widely accepted in psychology and psychotherapy today. Probably more people have heard of Adler's concept of the *inferiority complex* than of any other single idea in psychology.

His major principles are holism, the unity of the individual's style of life, social interest or community feeling, and the importance of goal-directed behavior. Adler argued that goals and expectations have a greater influence on behavior than past experiences. This was one the major causes of his break with Freud. Adler also believed that everyone is motivated primarily by the goal of superiority or conquest of the environment. He stressed the effect of social influences on each individual and emphasized the importance of social interest: a sense of community, cooperation, and concern for others. Adler felt that life is essentially a movement toward better adaptation to the environment and greater cooperation and altruism.

Adler's individual psychology is similar to behaviorism in its stress on overt behaviors and their consequences as well as in its postulation that concepts must be concrete and related to actual behavior. In contrast to most of the other psychological theories covered in this text, individual psychology is not a *depth* psychology; that is, it does not postulate intangible forces and constructs deep within the psyche. Adler developed a *context* psychology in which behavior is understood in terms of its larger context, a context that the individual generally is not aware of. Adler was the first to practice family therapy, which he first introduced in 1920. Adlerians have made important contributions to group therapy, *brief* therapy, and to applications of psychology in education.

Personal History

Alfred Adler was born in a suburb of Vienna on February 7, 1870, the son of a middle-class Jewish merchant. The Adler family was extremely musical. Alfred's sister was an excellent pianist, one brother became a violin teacher, and Alfred himself had such a beautiful voice he was often encouraged to seek a career in the opera. As a child, he suffered from a number of serious illnesses, including rickets. He also suffered from an extremely jealous rivalry with his older brother. He once commented, "My elder brother . . . was always ahead of me—he is *still* ahead of me" (Adler in Bottome, 1957, p. 27)!

Adler struggled hard to overcome his physical weakness. Whenever possible, young Alfred ran and played away from home with other children, with whom he was popular. He seemed to gain a sense of equality and self-esteem from his friends that he did not find at home. These experiences can be seen later in Adler's stress on the community sharing of feelings and values, which he called *social interest,* and through which Adler believed a person could find his or her potential as a productive member of society.

During his sickly youth, Adler read voraciously. In his adult years, his knowledge of and familiarity with literature, the Bible, psychology, and German philosophy made him popular in Viennese society and later as a lecturer throughout the world.

> The hardest things for human beings to do is to know themselves and change themselves. (Adler, 1928, p.11)

As a child, Adler was closely confronted with death on several occasions. His younger brother died in the bed they shared when Adler was 3 years old. In addition, Adler twice narrowly escaped being killed in street accidents; and, at the age of 5, he contracted a severe case of pneumonia. The family physician believed the case to be hopeless, but another doctor managed to save him. As a result of this experience, Adler decided that he wanted to be a doctor.

At the age of 18, Adler entered the University of Vienna to study medicine. He was deeply interested in socialism and attended a number of political meetings. It was at one of these meetings that he met his wife Raissa, a Russian student, who was attending the University of Vienna.

Adler received his medical degree in 1895. He established a practice first in ophthalmology and then in general medicine. Because of his growing interest in nervous system functioning and adaptation, Adler's professional interests later shifted to neurology and psychiatry. In 1901, Adler, a rising young physician, strongly defended in print Freud's new book, *The Interpretation of Dreams.* Although Freud had never met Adler, he was deeply touched by Adler's courageous defense of his work, and he wrote to thank and invite Adler to join a newly formed discussion group on psychoanalysis.

This group developed into the Vienna Psychoanalytic Society. Adler entered the group as a young professional who was already developing his own theoretical orientation. He was not a follower of Freud. He was never Freud's "pupil" and never underwent a training analysis. Nevertheless, in 1910, Adler became president of the Vienna Psychoanalytic Society and coeditor of one of its journals.

By 1911, just one year later, Adler's increasingly divergent theoretical orientation had become unacceptable to Freud and to many other members of the society. Adler resigned as president and left the society along with nine like-minded colleagues. The rest, only 14 others, remained with Freud. Adler founded his own organization, the Association for Individual Psychology, which gradually spread throughout Europe.

Adler and his followers became active in the field of education, especially in teacher training, because Adler believed it was extremely important to work with those who shaped the minds and characters of the young. Endorsed by the Minister of Education, Adler and his associates established child guidance centers in the public schools, where children and their families could receive counseling. By the 1930s, there were 30 such clinics in Vienna alone. From 1921 until 1927, when he went to teach in America, Adler lectured and took demonstration cases twice a month to colleagues, parents, and teachers alike.

An eminent medical colleague stated, "The whole approach of the Viennese School of Medicine to their patients was altered . . . by Adler's teaching. I do not believe a single doctor of any standing in Vienna failed to attend, at one time or another, Adler's lectures and to profit by them" (Bottome, 1957, p. 209).

Adler's wisdom and compassion were evident to virtually everyone who came in contact with him. The desk clerk at a hotel in which Adler often stayed mentioned to one of Adler's colleagues, "You can hardly keep the bell-boys or the porter out of his room. They'll take *any* excuse to talk to him, and as far as that goes, I'm not much better myself" (Bottome, 1957, p. 54)!

Adler published numerous papers and monographs and also began to devote a great deal of time to lecture tours throughout Europe and the United States. Between World Wars I and II, there were Adlerian groups in 20 European countries and also in the United States. In 1927, Adler was appointed lecturer at Columbia University. In 1928, he lectured at the New School for Social Research in New York, and a year later returned to give a series of lectures and clinical demonstrations. Adler left Vienna permanently in 1932 because of the rise of Nazism. He settled in the United States and accepted a visiting professorship in medical psychology at the Long Island Medical College. Adler died in Scotland in 1937, at the age of 67, while on a European lecture tour.

Intellectual Antecedents

Evolution

Adler was strongly influenced by Darwin's theory of evolution, as were most of his contemporaries. His theory of individual psychology is based on the premise that adaptation to the environment is the most fundamental aspect of life.

Most psychology theorists are primarily concerned with intrapsychic dynamics. Adler was not. He was an *ecological psychologist,* focusing on the relations between individual and environment. Adler's early book on organ inferiorities and compensation was largely an application of the Darwinian view of medicine. It was considered a psychological complement to psychoanalytic theory and was well received by Freud. Adler's later work can be viewed as a refutation of Social Darwinism, which emphasized the survival of the fittest and the elimination of the unfit. Adler believed that organic inferiority can stimulate us to superior attainments, instead of necessarily causing defeat in the struggle of life. Also, Adler argued that cooperation and community feeling are more important than competitive struggle in the process of human evolution.

Individual Psychology stands firmly on the ground of evolution and in the light of evolution regards all human striving as a struggle for perfection. (Adler, 1964a, pp. 36–37)

Psychoanalysis

Adler had begun his own theoretical work and had already published papers in the areas of social medicine and education before he met Freud. Although he never really accepted the concepts of libido or the Oedipal complex, Adler was profoundly influenced by psychoanalytic theory, especially the importance of early childhood experiences and the mother-child relationship, the purposefulness of neurotic symptoms, and the meaningfulness of dreams.

Freud considered Adler to have been his pupil, which Adler consistently denied. Rather than building upon psychoanalytic theory, Adler developed his own independent theoretical position, often in response to Freud's views. They had fundamentally different approaches to understanding human nature. Freud was interested in the analysis of parts and stressed divisions. Adler always insisted that each person's "wholeness" was the key to understanding. Symptoms had significance only as a part of the individual personality. Adler used to say, "You must not only ask yourself what effect a bacillus has on a body—it is also important to know what is the effect of the body on the bacillus" (Adler in Bottome, 1957, p. 72)!

Adler disagreed with Freud on several major points. He could never accept Freud's theory that the repressed, unconscious, sexual material of childhood was the core of all neuroses. Adler saw sexuality as an expression of one's personality and not its fundamental motivator, opposing Freud's assertion of the primacy of the libido. Adler suggested a different fundamental drive, the drive for power. He saw this as the child striving to become strong and take power to dominate others. The major biological fact for Adler was not the child's instinctive sexual behavior, but the child's smallness and helplessness in relation to the surrounding adult world. According to Adler, children's early attempts to adapt to their environment may easily result in choosing the exercise of power over others as a means to gain self-esteem and to achieve success.

Adler was strongly critical of Freudian analysis, which he felt was without moral orientation and resulted in antisocial, selfish individuals. "It is a spoilt child psychology, but what can be expected from a man who asks, 'Why should I love my neighbor'" (Adler in Bottome, 1957, p. 256)?

Friedrich Nietzsche

Adler was also affected by Friedrich Nietzsche's powerful writings, as were virtually all intellectuals of his generation. However, he was not a superficial imitator of Nietzsche as some critics have maintained. Although his earliest conceptualization of the aggressive instincts did have much in common with Nietzsche's will to power, Adler's later formulation of the striving for superiority is a much broader concept than striving for power; it emphasizes the role of creative growth and development. In addition, Adler's concept of social interest stands in diametric opposition to Nietzsche's individualistic perspective.

All neurotic symptoms are safeguards of persons who do not feel adequately equipped or prepared for the problems of life. (Adler, 1964b, p. 95)

Adler would always say to new patients, "The Doctor sits in your chair." (Adler in Bottome, 1957, p. 217)

The Philosophy of "As If"

Adler was significantly influenced by the writings of Hans Vaihinger, a philosopher who proposed that there are social "fictions" that have no basis in reality but become critical determinants of human behavior. Vaihinger believed that people, confronted by a welter of facts and experiences, create systems to organize and systematize their experiences. They then assume that these mere systems are the truth. These fictions become some of the most important influences on our behavior. Vaihinger argued that people are more affected by their *expectations* than their actual experiences. He called this approach *fictionalism, or the philosophy of "as if."* In *The Neurotic Constitution* (1912), Adler suggests that all human behavior, thought, and feeling proceed along *as if* lines. Beginning in childhood, we all attempt to adapt our environment and overcome any felt weakness. We create for ourselves an idealized goal of perfect adaptation, then struggle toward it as if the goal equals success, happiness, and security.

Holism

Fifteen years after his exposure to Vaihinger, Adler's thinking was affected by the holistic philosophy of Jan Smuts. Smuts was a South African military leader, statesman, and philosopher, whose work on holism influenced many contemporary thinkers. The two men corresponded, and Adler was instrumental in having Smuts's work published in Europe. Smuts believed that whole systems often have properties that are distinct from the properties of their parts; that there is an impulse toward increasing organization, toward wholeness in every individual. Adler found in holistic philosophy a confirmation of many of his own ideas and an important philosophical basis for individual psychology.

> There is a logic from the head; there is also a logic from the heart; and there is an even deeper logic from the whole. (Adler in Bottome, 1957, p. 80)

Major Concepts

Inferiority and Compensation

Adler's monograph on organ inferiority, which first appeared in 1907, attempted to explain why illness affects different people in different ways. At the time, Adler wrote as a physician who was concerned primarily with physiological processes. He suggested that in each individual certain weaker organs are particularly susceptible to illnesses and diseases. Adler also noted that organic weaknesses can be overcome through diligent training and exercise. In fact, a weakness can be developed to such a degree that it becomes a person's greatest strength. Adler wrote, "In almost all outstanding people we find some organ imperfection; and we gather the impression that they were sorely confronted at the beginning of life but struggled and overcame their difficulties" (Adler, 1931, p. 248).

> The important thing is not what one is born with, but what use one makes of that equipment. (Adler, 1964b, p. 86)

Adler extended his investigation of organ inferiority to the study of the psychological sense of inferiority. He coined the term *inferiority complex*. He claimed that all children are deeply affected by a sense of inferiority, which is an inevitable consequence of the child's size and lack of power. Adler's own childhood experiences led him to stress the central importance of this concept.

> One of my earliest recollections is of sitting on a bench, bandaged up on account of rickets, with my healthy elder brother sitting opposite me. He could run, jump and move about quite effortlessly, while for me movement of any sort was a strain and an effort. (Adler in Bottome, 1957, p. 30)

Adler believed that the life experiences of all children involve feelings of weakness, inadequacy, and frustration.

Children are relatively small and helpless in the world of adults. For children, controlling their own activities and breaking free from domination is of primary concern. Their own wants are secondary. From this perspective, power is seen as the first good and weakness as the first evil. The struggle to attain power is the child's first compensation for a sense of inferiority.

Moderate feelings of inferiority can motivate the individual to constructive achievements. However, a strong sense of inferiority will impede positive growth and development.

Inferiority feelings are not in themselves abnormal. They are the cause of all improvements in the position of mankind. (Adler, 1956, p. 117)

> He [the child] realizes at an early age that there are other human beings who are able to satisfy their urges more completely, and are better prepared to live. . . . [H]e learns to over-value the size and stature which enable one to open a door, or the ability to move heavy objects, or the right of others to give commands and claim obedience to them. A desire to grow, to become as strong or even stronger than all others, arises in his soul. (Adler, 1928, p. 34)

It is important to remember that virtually all progress is the result of attempts to compensate for inferiority feelings. These feelings motivate us in our most significant achievements.

Aggression and Striving for Superiority

In his early writings, Adler emphasized the importance of aggression and striving for power. He did not equate aggression with hostility, however. Adler equated aggression with a sense of strong initiative in overcoming obstacles as in an aggressive salesman, for example. Adler asserted that human aggressive tendencies have been crucial in individual and species survival. Aggression may manifest itself in the individual as *the will to power*, a phrase of Nietzsche's that Adler used. Adler pointed out that sexuality is often used to satisfy the urge for power.

In his later theorizing, Adler viewed aggression and the will to power as manifestations of a more general motive, the goal of superiority or perfection; that is, motivation to improve ourselves, to develop our own capacities and potential. Adler believed that all healthy individuals are motivated to strive for perfection, to seek continuous growth and improvement. "The striving for perfection is innate in the sense that it is a part of life, a striving, an urge, a something without which life would be unthinkable" (Adler, 1956, p. 104).

The goal of superiority can take either a positive or a negative direction. When the goal includes social concerns and interest in the welfare of others, it develops in a constructive and healthy direction. It takes the form of a striving to grow, to develop one's skills and abilities, and to work for a superior way of living. However, some people strive for *personal* superiority; they try to achieve a sense of superiority by dominating others rather than by becoming more useful to others. For Adler, striving for personal superiority is a neurotic perversion, the result of a strong sense of inferiority and a lack of social interest. Personal superiority generally fails to bring the recognition and personal satisfaction that the individual is seeking.

> The feeling of personal worth can only be derived from achievement, from the ability to overcome. (Adler, 1964b, p. 91)

The goal of superiority has its roots in the evolutionary process of continuous adaptation to the environment. All species must evolve toward more effective adaptation or else suffer extinction, and thus each individual is driven to strive toward a more perfect relationship with the environment. "If this striving were not innate to the organism, no form of life could preserve itself. The goal of mastering the environment in a superior way, which one can call the striving for perfection, consequently also characterizes the development of man" (Adler, 1964b, p. 39).

> To live means to develop. (Adler, 1964b, p. 31)

Adler once said to a patient:

> What do you first do when you are learning to swim? You make mistakes, do you not? And then what happens? You make other mistakes, and when you have made *all* the mistakes you possibly can with-

Personal Reflection ─────────────────────────────

─────────────────────────────────────── Power

Adler wrote a great deal about having a sense of power in one's environment. Imagine that you had the power to accomplish almost anything. What would you do? How would having real power affect your life? Would you have more or fewer friends? Would you be happier or sadder—in what ways?

Where and when have you felt powerless in your life? What was it like? Are there some areas in which you still feel powerless? How might you change that?

out drowning—and some of them many times over—what do you find? That you can swim? Well—life is just the same as learning to swim! Do not be afraid of making mistakes, for there is no other way of learning how to live! (Adler in Bottome, 1957, p. 37)

Everyone wants to be a worthy human being. According to Adler, the "supreme law" of life is that "the sense of worth of the self shall not be allowed to be diminished" (Adler, 1956, p. 358).

Life Goals

> The goal of superiority with each individual is personal and unique. It depends upon the meaning he gives to life. This meaning is not a matter of words. It is built up in his style of life and runs through it. (Adler, 1956, p. 181)

Adler viewed the goal of mastering the environment as being too broad a concept to explain logically how people choose a direction in life. Therefore, Adler turned to the idea that each individual develops a specific life goal that serves as a focus for achievement. Each individual's life goal is influenced by personal experiences, values, attitudes, and personality. The life goal is not a clear and consciously chosen aim. As adults, we may have definite, logical reasons for our career choices. However, the life goals that guide and motivate us were first formed early in childhood and remain somewhat obscured from consciousness. For example, Adler mentions that many physicians chose their careers in childhood, as he did, as a means of coping with their insecurity concerning death.

> Man is but a drop of water . . . but a very conceited drop. (Adler in Way, 1950, p. 167)

The formation of life goals begins in childhood as compensation for feelings of inferiority, insecurity, and helplessness in an adult world. Life goals generally serve as a defense against feelings of impotence, as a bridge from the unsatisfying present to a bright, powerful, and fulfilling future. These goals are always somewhat unrealistic and may become neurotically overinflated if inferiority feelings are very strong. For the neurotic, there is generally a large gap between conscious aims and unconscious, self-defeating life goals. Fantasies of personal superiority and self-esteem are given more attention than goals involving real achievement. Adler's favorite question to his patients was, "What would you do if you had not got this trouble?" In their answers, he usually discovered what his patients' symptoms helped them to avoid.

Life goals provide direction and purpose for our activities; they enable an outside observer to interpret various aspects of thought and behavior in terms of these goals. For example, someone who strives for superiority by seeking personal power will develop various character traits necessary to attain this goal—traits such as ambition, envy, and distrust. Adler points out that these character traits are neither innate nor unalterable, but were adopted as integral facets of the individual's goal orientation. "They are not primary but secondary factors, forced by the secret goal of the individual, and must be understood teleologically" (Adler, 1956, p. 219).

Style of Life

Adler emphasized the need to analyze each individual as a unified totality. Life-style is the unique way that an individual chooses to pursue his or her

Personal Reflection —————————————

——————————————— Understanding Goals

Adler emphasized more the pull of the future than the pressure of the past. For Adler, where we hope to *go* is more important than where we have *been*. In order to discover the relationship between your life goals and daily activities, try the following exercises.

Part 1 Set aside 15 minutes for this exercise. Sit down with four sheets of paper and a pen or pencil. Write at the top of the first sheet, "What are my lifetime goals?" Take two minutes to answer this question. Put down whatever comes into your mind, no matter how general, abstract, or trivial it may seem. You may want to include personal, family, career, social, community, or spiritual goals. Then give yourself an additional two minutes to go over your list and make any additions or alterations. Set aside this first sheet.

Take your second sheet and write at the top, "How would I like to spend the next three years?" Take two minutes to answer this question. Then take two more minutes to go over your list. This should help you pinpoint your goals more specifically than you did with the first question. Again, set aside this list.

For a different perspective on your goals, write on your third sheet, "If I knew my life would end six months from today, how would I live until then?" The purpose of this question is to find out if there are things that are important to you that you are not doing or even considering now. Again, write for two minutes; go back over your answers for another two minutes, and set this sheet aside.

On your fourth sheet of paper, write down the three goals you consider most important out of all the goals you have listed.

Compare all four lists. Are there any themes running through the various goals you have given? Are most of your goals in one category, such as social or personal? Are there some goals that appear on all of the first three lists? Do the goals you have chosen as most important differ in some way from the other goals on your lists?

Although this method of analyzing life goals does not fully uncover the unconscious life goals that Adler discussed, it can be a powerful way of discovering the relationship between your goals and your daily activities. It is also a useful exercise to repeat every six months or so in order to see what changes may have occurred. (Adapted from Lakein, 1974)

Part 2 You have found an old, sealed bottle that has washed up on shore. When you open it, a genie appears and grants you three wishes. As you contemplate your wishes, remember that they should be within the realm of the humanly attainable. They should be exciting, yet believable.

1. Write out your three wishes.

2. Choose the one that is the most important to you.

3. Write out your wish clearly and in detail, as a central life goal.

4. What are you doing or planning to do in order to attain this goal?

5. What are the obstacles to your attaining your goal?

6. What feelings come up when you do this—when you write out your goals and take them seriously?

life goal. It is an integrated style of adapting to and interacting with life in general.

According to Adler, the key to understanding a person's behavior is found in hidden purposes to which all energies are directed. These purposes reveal all, not just external facts or situations. For example, if I believe that my father mistreated me as a child and blame a life of failure on this, then I have orchestrated my own failure. The fact of how I was actually treated is immaterial. If I believe that I was abused, then this is true psychologically. Further, I have made this mistreatment a reality to fit my chosen style of life, a life of failure.

> It is, as we have already seen, in the first four or five years of life that the individual is establishing the unity of his mind and constructing the relationship between mind and body. He is taking his hereditary material and the impressions he receives from the environment and is adapting them to his pursuit of superiority. By the end of the fifth year his personality has crystallized. The meaning he gives to life, the goal he pursues, his style of approach, and his emotional disposition are all fixed. They can be changed later; but they can be changed only if he becomes free from the mistake involved in his childhood crystallization. Just as all his previous expressions were coherent with his interpretation of life, so now, if he is able to correct the mistake, his new expressions will be coherent with his new interpretation. (Adler, 1931, p. 34)

Seemingly isolated habits and behavior traits gain their meaning within the larger context of the individual's life and goals, and thus psychological and emotional problems must be treated within this context. The whole style of life must be addressed in treatment, because a given symptom or trait is but an expression of the unified life-style of the individual.

> The science of Individual Psychology developed out of the effort to understand that mysterious creative power of life which expresses itself in the desire to develop, to strive, to achieve. . . . This power is *teleological,* it expresses itself in the striving after a goal, and, in this striving, every bodily and psychological movement is made to cooperate. It

The foremost task of Individual Psychology is to prove this unity in each individual—in his thinking, feeling, acting; in his so-called conscious and unconscious—in every expression of his personality. (Adler, 1964b, p. 69)

is thus absurd to study bodily movements and mental conditions abstractly without relation to an individual whole. (Adler, 1956, p. 92)

Mosak (1989) has listed the following dimensions of life-style:

1. The *self-concept*—conceptions about oneself, who one is.

2. The *self-ideal*—notions of what one *should* be. (Adler developed this concept in 1912.)

3. The *image of the world*—convictions about such things as the world, people, and nature as well as about what the world demands.

4. *Ethical convictions*—a personal ethical code.

The Schema of Apperception

As part of the life-style, each individual develops a conception of self and of the world. Adler called this the schema of apperception. Apperception is a psychological term that refers to perception involving a subjective interpretation of what is perceived.

Adler emphasized that it is one's conception of the world that determines behavior. If someone believes that a coil of rope in a dark corner is a snake, his or her fear can be as intense as if a snake were actually present. Adler reminds us that "our senses do not receive actual facts, but merely a subjective image of them, a reflection of the external world" (Adler, 1956, p. 182). The schema of apperception is generally self-reinforcing. For example, when we are afraid, we are more likely to perceive threats in the environment, which reinforces our original belief that the environment is a threatening one. Adler's work on the schema of apperception is an important precursor to cognitive psychology and cognitive therapy. (See Chapter 11.)

Adler knew how to use this principle in therapy with great effectiveness. One patient came to him with a long history of failure. He was a man of considerable ability who had no self-confidence. Adler pointed out that his "ability" at failure could be used to his advantage. "A success is very important for you, I admit; then why not try to fail, since according to your own evidence, you would be almost certain to succeed in bringing it off " (Adler in Bottome, 1957, p. 100)? This was a real turning point for the individual, who could not help laughing at himself.

> You find what you planned to find. (Adler, 1964b, p. 100)

The Creative Power of the Individual

Adler pointed out that we respond actively and creatively to the various influences affecting our lives. We are not inert objects, passively accepting all outside forces; we actively seek out certain experiences and reject others. We selectively codify and interpret experience, developing an individualized schema of apperception and forming a distinct pattern of relating to the world.

It is futile to attempt to establish psychology on the basis of drives alone, without taking into consideration the creative power of the child which directs the drive, molds it into form, and supplies it with a meaningful goal. (Adler, 1956, p. 177)

Adler believed that each individual has a center where he or she is free. Since we are free, we are also responsible for our actions and for our lives.

Adler always stressed the individual's positive, creative, healthy capacities. When a patient came to see him, Adler did not ask himself "How ill is she?" but always "How much in her is healthy?" He believed that the basis of any cure lay not in the strength of the illness but in the individual's power of resistance (Bottome, 1957).

At the core of Adler's model of human nature is creativity—the capacity to formulate (consciously or unconsciously) goals and the means of achieving them. This culminates in the development of a life plan, which organizes one's life into a self-consistent life-style.

Each individual arrives at a concrete goal of overcoming through his creative power, which is identical with the self. (Adler, 1956, p. 180)

For Adler, this process of the formation of a life goal, life-style, and schema of apperception is essentially a creative act. It is the creative power of the personality, or of the self, that guides and directs the individual's response to the environment. Adler attributes to the individual uniqueness, awareness, and control over his or her own destiny—qualities he felt that Freud did not sufficiently stress in his conception of human nature. Adler emphasized that we are not powerless pawns of external forces. We mold our own personalities. "Every individual represents both a unity of personality and the individual fashioning of that unity. The individual is thus both the picture and the artist. He is the artist of his own personality" (Adler, 1956, p. 177).

Social Interest

Adler's theories regarding aggression and the striving for power have been oversimplified and overemphasized by many critics. Adler's later concept of social interest is central to his later writing. (A better translation of his original German term, *Gemeinschaftsgefühl,* might be "community feeling.") By social interest, Adler means "the sense of human solidarity, the connectedness of man to man . . . the wider connotation of a 'sense of fellowship in the human community'" (Wolfe in Adler, 1928, p. 32n). Community feeling refers to the interest we take in others not simply to serve our own purposes, but "an interest in the interests" of others.

All failures . . . are products of inadequate preparation in social interest. They are all non-cooperative, solitary beings who run more or less counter to the rest of the world; beings who are more or less asocial if not antisocial. (Adler, 1964b, p. 90)

From his holistic perspective, Adler saw the individual not only as a unified whole, but as a part of larger wholes—family, community, society, and humanity. Our lives and all of our activities are carried out within a social context.

> Any man's value is determined by his attitude toward his fellow man, and by the degree in which he partakes of the division of labor which communal life demands. His affirmation of this communal life makes him important to other human beings, makes him a link in a great chain which binds society, the chain which we cannot in any way disturb without also disturbing human society. (Adler, 1928, p. 121)

In one sense, all human behavior is social because, as Adler argued, we develop in a social environment and our personalities are socially formed. Social interest is more than concern for one's immediate community or society. It includes feelings of kinship with all humanity and relatedness to the whole of life. Social interest in its broadest sense refers to concern for "the ideal community of all mankind, the ultimate fulfillment of evolution" (Adler, 1964b, p. 35).

Cooperation

One important aspect of social interest is the development of cooperative behavior. From an evolutionary point of view, the ability to cooperate in food gathering, hunting, and defense against predators has been one of the most important factors in the survival of the human race and the most effective form of adaptation to the environment.

Adler believed that only through cooperation with others and operating as valuable, contributing members of society can we overcome our actual inferiorities or our sense of inferiority. He wrote that those who have made the most valuable contributions to humanity have been the most cooperative individuals, and the works of the great geniuses have always been oriented in a social direction (Adler, 1931). On the other hand, a lack of cooperation and a resulting sense of inadequacy and failure are at the root of all neurotic or maladaptive styles of life. Adler believed that "if a person cooperates, he will never become a neurotic" (Adler, 1964b, p. 193).

The only individuals who can really meet and master the problems of life, however, are those who show in their striving a tendency to enrich all others, who go ahead in such a way that others benefit also. (Adler, 1956, p. 255)

Personal Reflection ———————

——————————— Practicing Cooperation

In order to understand more clearly what Adler meant by cooperation and social interest, devote as much time in one week as you can to helping others. Keep a record of your behavior and how you felt. Resolve that you will not refuse any reasonable requests from others, even if they take up some of your valuable time, energy, or even some money. (If you want to make the exercise more demanding, let all of your friends know that you are carrying out this exercise and that you will be available to serve them for a week!) Don't simply wait for someone to ask you, but actively look for opportunities to offer your help to others.

At the end of the week, review your experiences. How did other people react to you? What were your reactions to helping others? What did you learn from the exercise?

Adler on Women

Alfred Adler made the somewhat radical suggestion that psychological differences between the sexes are entirely the result of cultural attitudes. He also pointed out that a culture's attitude toward gender differences affects an individual's development from birth more profoundly than most other cultural attitudes. He condemned society's conception of women in which they are viewed as inferior in order to perpetuate societal systems of male domination and male privilege. He suggested that a

> girl comes into the world with a prejudice sounding in her ears which is designed only to rob her of her belief in her own value, to shatter her self-confidence, and destroy her hope of ever doing anything worthwhile. . . . The obvious advantages of being a man (in our society) have caused severe disturbances in the psychic development of women. (Adler, 1973, pp. 41–42)

Basic Principles of Adlerian Theory

Mosak (1989) has outlined the basic assumptions of Adlerian psychology. They are summarized as follows:

1. All behavior occurs in a social context. People cannot be studied in isolation.

2. The focus is on interpersonal psychology. Most important for the individual is the development of a feeling of being an integral part of a larger social whole.

3. Individual Psychology stresses holism rather than reductionism. All functions are subordinate to the person's goals and style of life.

4. Adlerian psychology treats the unconscious as an adjective rather than as a noun. Unconscious processes are purposeful and serve the individual's goals, as do conscious processes.

5. To understand the individual, you must understand his or her style of life, or cognitive organization. This is the lens through which everyone views themselves and their lives.

The life of the human soul is not a "being" but a "becoming." (Adler, 1929, p. ix)

6. Although behavior may change, the style of life and long range goals of the individual remain relatively constant, unless the individual's fundamental convictions are transformed. This is one of the main tasks of therapy.

7. Behavior is not determined by the past, but by either heredity or environment. Individuals are motivated by self-selected goals, which they feel will bring them success and happiness.

8. The central motivation for each individual is to strive for perfection or superiority. (This is comparable to Horney's concept of self-realization and Maslow's self-actualization.)

9. The individual is confronted with many different life choices. He or she may choose healthy, socially useful goals or neurotic, socially useless ones.

10. Adlerian psychology focuses primarily on process. There is relatively little attention paid to labeling individuals.

11. Whatever meaning life has is what we attribute to it ourselves. A healthy conception of life always includes a sense of the importance of helping others and contributing to society.

Dynamics

Psychological Growth

Psychological growth is primarily a matter of moving from a self-centered goal of personal superiority to an attitude of constructive mastery of the environment and socially useful development. Constructive striving for superiority plus strong social interest and cooperation are the basic traits of the healthy individual.

Life Tasks

Adler discussed three major life tasks that confront each individual: work, friendship, and love. They are determined by the basic conditions of human existence.

> These three main ties are set by the facts that we are living in one particular place in the universe and must develop with the limits and possibilities which our circumstances set us; that we are living among others of our own kind to whom we must learn to adapt ourselves; and that we are living in two sexes with the future of our race dependent on the relations of these two sexes. (Adler, 1931, p. 264)

Work includes all those activities that are useful to the community, not simply those occupations for which we receive an income. For Adler, work provides a sense of satisfaction and self-worth only to the extent that it benefits others. The importance of our work is ultimately based upon our dependence on the physical environment.

> We are living on the surface of this planet, with only the resources of this planet, with the fertility of its soil, with its mineral wealth, and with its climate and atmosphere. It has always been the task of mankind to find the right answer to the problem these conditions set us. . . . [I]t

has always been necessary to strive for improvement and further accomplishments. (Adler, 1956, p. 131)

Friendship is an expression of our membership in the human race and our constant need to adapt to and interact with others of our species. Our specific friendships provide essential links to our communities because no individual ever relates to society in the abstract. Friendly, cooperative endeavor is also an important element in constructive work.

Love is discussed by Adler in terms of heterosexual love. It involves a close union of mind and body and the utmost cooperation between two people of the opposite sex. Love comes from intimacy, which is essential to the continuance of our species. Adler writes that the close bond of marriage represents the greatest challenge to our ability to cooperate with another human being, and a successful marriage creates the best environment for promoting cooperation and social interest in children.

Adler stressed that these three tasks (work, friendship, and love) are interrelated.

> A solution of one helps toward the solution of the others, and indeed we can say that they are all aspects of the same situation and the same problem—the necessity for a human being to preserve life and to further life in the environment in which he finds himself. (Adler, 1956, p. 133)

Obstacles to Growth

Organ Inferiority, Pampering, and Neglect

Adler specified three childhood situations that tend to result in a lack of social interest, isolation, and the development of a noncooperative style of life based on an unrealistic goal of personal superiority. These are organ inferiority, pampering, and neglect.

Children who suffer from illnesses or disease tend to become strongly self-centered. They withdraw from interaction with others out of a sense of inferiority and inability to compete successfully with other children. However, those children who overcome their difficulties tend to overcompensate for their original weakness and develop their abilities to an unusual degree.

Pampered or spoiled children also have difficulties in developing a sense of social interest and cooperation. They lack confidence in their own abilities because others have always done things for them. Rather than cooperate with others, they tend to make one-sided demands on friends and family. Social interest is usually minimal, and Adler found that pampered children generally have little genuine feeling for the parents they manipulate so well.

Neglect is the third situation that tends to strongly impede a child's development. A neglected or unwanted child has never known love and cooperation in the home, and therefore finds it extremely difficult to develop these capacities. Such children have no confidence in their ability to be useful and to gain affection and esteem from others. They tend to become cold and hard as adults.

> The traits of unloved children in their most developed form can be observed by studying the biographies of all the great enemies of humanity. Here the one thing that stands out is that as children they were badly treated. Thus they developed hardness of character, envy and hatred; they could not bear to see others happy. (Adler, 1956, p. 371)

The Basic Dynamics of Neurosis

In 1913, Adler and his group published an Adlerian approach to neurosis (Bottome, 1957). The following points provide an illustration of how Adler's main ideas can be applied to understanding and working with human problems:

1. Every neurosis can be understood as an attempt to overcome a feeling of inferiority and to gain a feeling of competence.

2. Neurosis tends to isolate the individual because it leads away from social functioning and the solving of real-life problems.

3. The neurotic individual's relations with others are severely limited by a combination of hypersensitiveness and intolerance.

4. Estranged from reality, the neurotic tends to live a life of imagination and fantasy, avoiding responsibilities and service to society.

5. Illness and suffering become a substitute for the original, healthy goal of superiority.

6. The neurosis represents an attempt to be free of all the constraints of society by establishing a *counter-compulsion*. This may take the form of anxiety attacks, sleeplessness, compulsions, hallucinations, hypochondria, and so forth.

7. Even logical thinking becomes dominated by the counter-compulsion.

8. Logic, love, compassion, and the will to live, all arise from social life. Neurotic isolation and striving for power is directed against this.

9. The neurotic is constantly seeking personal power and prestige, looking for excuses to leave real-life problems unsolved, and consequently never develops social interest.

10. To cure a neurosis, it is necessary to change completely the individual's orientation, which results from his or her whole upbringing, and turn the person back into society.

No act of cruelty has ever been done which has not been based upon a secret weakness. The person who is really strong has no inclination to cruelty. (Adler, 1956, p. 390)

Striving for Personal Superiority

When inferiority feelings predominate or when social interest is underdeveloped, individuals tend to seek personal superiority, because they lack confidence in their ability to function effectively and to work constructively with others. The trappings of success, prestige, and esteem become more important than concrete achievements. Such individuals contribute nothing of real value to society and become fixed in self-centered behavior patterns that inevitably lead to a sense of failure. "They have turned away from the real problems of life and are engaged in shadow-fighting to reassure themselves of their strength" (Adler, 1956, p. 255).

Structure

Body

The body is a major source of inferiority feelings in the child, who is surrounded by those who are bigger and stronger and who function more effectively physically. Adler has also pointed out that what is most important is our attitude toward our bodies (Adler, 1964b). Many attractive men and women have never resolved childhood feelings of ugliness and unacceptability, and they still behave as if they were unattractive. On the other hand, those who have physical deficiencies may through compensation strive hard and develop their bodies to a greater than average extent.

Social Relationships

Social relationships are of central importance in Adler's theories. They are a direct expression of social interest and are essential in developing a fulfilling, constructive life-style.

Will

For Adler, will is another name for striving for superiority and actualizing life goals. As such, it is a central element in his theory.

Emotions

Adler writes of two kinds of emotions: socially disjunctive emotions, which are related to individual goal attainment, and socially conjunctive emotions, which tend to promote social interaction. Disjunctive emotions, such as anger, fear, or disgust, are intended to bring about a positive change in the life situation of the individual, although sometimes at the expense of others. They result from a sense of failure or inadequacy and serve to mobilize the individual's strength to make fresh efforts (Adler, 1956). Conjunctive emotions tend to be socially oriented, as in the desire to share our joy and laughter with others. The emotion of sympathy is "the purest expression of social interest" and reveals the extent to which we can relate to others (Adler, 1956, p. 228).

Intellect

Adler distinguishes between reason and intelligence. Neurotics, criminals, and others who have failed to function successfully in society are often quite intelligent. Frequently, they give perfectly logical arguments and justifications for their behavior. However, Adler has called this kind of intelligence *personal intelligence,* or thinking that is bound by the individual's goal of personal superiority rather than by socially useful considerations. Reason is "the kind of intelligence which contains social interest and which is thus limited to the generally useful" (Adler, 1956, p. 150). Reason is in accord with common sense, which comes out of basic cultural attitudes and values.

Self

The "self" *is* the individual's style of life. It is the personality viewed as an integrated whole.

> In real life we always find a confirmation of the melody of the total self, of the personality, with its thousandfold ramifications. If we believe that the foundation, the ultimate basis of everything has been found in character traits, drives, or reflexes, the self is likely to be overlooked. Authors who emphasize a part of the whole are likely to attribute to this part all the aptitudes and observations pertaining to the self, the individual. They show "something" which is endowed with prudence, determination, volition, and creative power without knowing that they are actually describing the self, rather than drives, character traits, or reflexes. (Adler, 1956, p. 175)

For Adler, the self is a dynamic, unitary *principle* rather than a structure to be found within the psyche. "[In Adlerian psychology] the self is not considered as an entity. . . . There is literally no self to actualize but through transactions with its world" (Ansbacher, 1971, p. 60). Adler's position concerning the self strongly resembles the concept of "selflessness" in Buddhist psychology.

Therapist

The aim of Adlerian psychotherapy is to help the individual reconstruct assumptions and goals in accord with greater social usefulness. Adler defines three major aspects of therapy: understanding the specific lifestyle of the patient, helping patients understand themselves, and strengthening social interest.

There must be uncovered, step by step, the unattainable goal of superiority over all; the purposive concealment of this goal; the all-dominating, direction-giving power of the goal; the patient's lack of freedom and his hostility toward mankind, which are determined by the goal. (Adler, 1956, p. 333)

Understanding the Life-style

Therapy requires cooperation. One of the first tasks is to address the goals and expectations of each patient. Patients often expect from the therapist the kind of response they have gotten from everyone else. The patient may feel misunderstood, unloved, or unfairly treated. The therapist must carefully avoid meeting these unconscious expectations.

Because the life-style forms a basically consistent whole, the therapist looks for themes that run through the individual's behavior. In order to determine their life-styles, Adler always asked patients for their earliest memories, the most salient events from early childhood. "There are no 'chance memories'; out of the incalculable number of impressions which meet an individual, he chooses to remember only those which he feels, however darkly, to have a bearing on his situation" (Adler, 1931, p. 73).

Adler assumed that the patient's life plan had developed under negative conditions, so the therapist should be sensitized to look for organ inferiority, pampering, or neglect in childhood.

Adler also emphasized the importance of expressive behavior, including posture and intonation. "I have found it of considerable value to conduct myself as during pantomime, that is, for a while not to pay any attention to the words of the patient, but instead to read his deeper intention from his bearing and his movements within a situation" (Adler, 1956, p. 330).

Promoting Self-understanding

Adler viewed the major problem of most patients as being their erroneous schema of apperception determined by an unattainable and unrealistic goal of superiority over all others. One of the major tasks of the therapist is to help patients understand their own life-styles, including their basic approaches to life. Only after self-understanding is reached can people correct their nonadaptive style of life. "A patient has to be brought into such a state of feeling that he likes to listen, and wants to understand. Only then can he be influenced to live what he has understood" (Adler, 1956, p. 335). This approach will succeed only when the therapist's explanation is clear and detailed and speaks directly to the experience of the patient.

Self-understanding means learning to see the mistakes we are making in coping with daily situations. It involves gaining a better understanding of how the world is run and of our place in it. Adler stressed the importance of learning to understand the consequences of our behavior rather than learning more about our inner experience. For Adler, insight is not merely intellectual understanding. It is understanding translated into constructive action.

Adler emphasized that success in therapy is always up to the patient.

Even when a patient lies it is of value to me . . . it is his lie and nobody else's! What he cannot disguise is his own originality. (Adler in Bottome, 1957, p. 162)

> The actual change in the nature of the patient can only be his own doing. . . . One should always look at the treatment and the cure not as the success of the consultant but as the success of the patient. The

adviser can only point out the mistakes, it is the patient who must make the truth living. (Adler, 1956, p. 336)

Strengthening Social Interest

Therapy is a cooperative enterprise between therapist and patient, a supportive relationship that helps the patient develop a sense of cooperation and social interest. "The task of the physician or psychologist is to give the patient the experience of contact with a fellow man, and then to enable him to transfer this awakened social interest to others" (Adler, 1956, p. 341).

Adler pointed out that the therapist often has to provide the care, support, and sense of cooperation that the patient never received from his or her own parents. Adler was convinced that concern for self rather than for others is at the core of most psychological problems. He felt that the major task of the therapist is to gradually guide the patient away from exclusive interest in self toward working constructively for others as a valuable member of the community. In caring for the patient, the therapist serves as a role model for social interest.

The Role of the Therapist

Adler stressed the importance of establishing a sense of equality between patient and therapist. He preferred facing the person to sitting behind a reclining patient as Freud did. Adler also emphasized engaging in a free discussion, not free association. His beliefs and attitudes concerning the therapeutic relationship seem to foreshadow the work of Carl Rogers.

Adler strongly believed in empowering others. He felt that patients had to work to change themselves. The therapist could provide only insight and support. "A patient is like a person in a dark room. He complains to me, 'I cannot get out.' I switch on the light and point out the door-handle. If he still says that he cannot get out—I know that he does not wish to get out" (Adler in Bottome, p. 101)!

> We can succeed only if we are genuinely interested in the other. We must be able to see with his eyes and listen with his ears. He must contribute his part to our common understanding. . . . Even if we felt we'd understood him we should have no witness that we were right unless he also understood. (Adler, 1929, p. 340)

Adlerian psychology distinguishes between psychotherapy and counseling. Therapy seeks to bring about a fundamental change in an individual's unhealthy life-style. Counseling is aimed at changing behavior within an existing life-style.

Evaluation

Adler's theories have had a great impact on humanistic psychology, psychotherapy, and personality theory. Many of his concepts have been inte-

Psychotherapy is an exercise in cooperation and a test of cooperation. We can succeed only if we are genuinely interested in the other. (Adler, 1956, p. 340)

I tell [patients] "You can be cured in fourteen days if you follow this prescription. Try to think every day how you can please someone." (Adler, 1956, p. 347)

grated into other schools of thought. Adler's stress on social interest has made psychotherapy much more social in orientation. Also, his concern with conscious, rational processes has created the first ego psychology. In fact, it has been suggested that *neo-Adlerian* is a more accurate term than neo-Freudian for theorists such as Erich Fromm, Karen Horney, and Harry Stack Sullivan (Wittels, 1939). One writer has pointed out that "most observations and ideas of Alfred Adler have subtly and quietly permeated modern psychological thinking to such a degree that the proper question is not whether one is Adlerian but how much of an Adlerian one is" (Wilder, 1959, p. xv). Adler's thoughts have had a major influence on many other eminent psychologists, yet astonishingly he is relatively unknown outside the field.

Viktor Frankl and Rollo May, noted existential analysts, have regarded Adler's psychology as an influential precursor to existential psychiatry (Frankl, 1970; May, 1970), and Adler's interest in holism, goal-directedness, and the role of values in human behavior anticipated many of the developments of humanistic psychology. Abraham Maslow wrote:

> For me Alfred Adler becomes more and more correct year by year. As the facts come in, they give stronger and stronger support to his image of man . . . in one respect especially the times have not yet caught up with him. I refer to his holistic emphasis. (1970, p. 13)

However, Adler has failed to receive the credit he really deserves. Concepts original to Adler are often seen as derivatives of psychoanalytic theory or as self-evident or trivial. In his survey of major psychiatric schools of thought, Ellenberger writes:

> It would not be easy to find another author from which so much has been borrowed from all sides without acknowledgment than Alfred Adler. His teaching has become . . . a place where anyone and all may come and draw anything without compunction. An author will meticulously quote the source of any sentence he takes from elsewhere, but it does not occur to him to do the same whenever the source is individual psychology; it is as if nothing original could ever come from Adler. (1970, p. 645)

One reason for Adler's relative lack of popularity lies in his writing style. He was an excellent speaker and much preferred lecturing to writing. His writing is not always precise, and his theorizing tends to be phrased in a simple, commonsensical manner that often seems superficial or shallow. Adler was more interested in practice than in theory. He was at his best in dealing with actual case materials; thus his work has tended to be most popular among teachers, social workers, clinical practitioners, and others who require practical psychological skills in their professional work. Adler's seminal contributions to the development of modern psychology include the inferiority complex, the role of power and aggression in human behavior, the concept of unity of the personality, and the significance of nonsexual factors in development.

Recent Developments: Adler's Influence

Many of Adler's pioneering ideas have become so well accepted that they are taken for granted today. Adler is virtually the father of psychosomatic medicine in his pioneering work on the interaction of psychological and physical elements in organ inferiority. Adler is also the father of the increasingly popular field of parenting. Virtually every modern book on parenting makes use of Adler's principles of child discipline, generally without giving him much credit. Adler's student Rudolf Dreikurs has had a powerful influence on this field. His book, *Children: The Challenge* (1964), has become a classic.

Adlerian psychology is flourishing. Adler's influence on leading psychologists, such as Abraham Maslow, Carl Rogers, and Rollo May has been well documented (Ansbacher, 1990). Adlerian training institutes, family education centers, study groups, and professional societies are growing in size and influence (Mosak, 1989). The first Adlerian psychology textbook written in English, *Individual Psychology* (Manaster & Corsini, 1982), has generated widespread interest. *A Bibliography of Adlerian Psychology* in two volumes covers over 10,000 references to the literature of Adlerian psychology (Mosak & Mosak, 1975a, 1975b).

The Theory Firsthand: Excerpt from *What Life Should Mean to You*

The following passage provides an example of Adler's analytic methods. Adler discusses the theoretical importance of first memories and then demonstrates his technique of analyzing them.

Early recollections have especial significance. To begin with, they show the style of life in its origins and in its simplest expressions. We can judge from them whether the child was pampered or neglected; how far he was training for cooperation with others; with whom he preferred to cooperate; what problems confronted him, and how he struggled against them. In the early recollections of a child who suffered from difficulties in seeing and who trained himself to look more closely, we shall find impressions of a visual nature. His recollections will begin, "I looked around me . . . ," or he will describe colors and shapes. A child who had difficulties of movement, who wanted to walk or run or jump, will show these interests in his recollections. Events remembered from childhood must be very near to the main interest of the individual; and if we know his main interest we know his goal and his style of life. It is this fact which makes early recollections of such value in vocational guidance. We can find, moreover, the child's relations towards his mother, his father and the other members of the family. It is comparatively indifferent whether the memories are accurate or inaccurate; what is of most value about them is that they represent the individual's judgment, "Even in childhood, I was such and such a person," or, "Even in childhood, I found the world like this."

Most illuminating of all is the way he begins his story, the earliest incident he can recall. The first memory will show the individual's fundamental view of life; his first satisfactory crystallization of his attitude. It offers us an opportunity to see at one glance what he has taken as the starting point for his development. I would never investigate a personality without asking for the first memory. Sometimes people do not answer, or profess that they do not know which event came first; but this itself is revealing. We can gather that they do not wish to discuss their fundamental meaning, and that they are not prepared for cooperation. In the main people are perfectly willing to discuss their first memories. They take them as mere facts, and do not realize the meaning hidden in them. Scarcely anyone understands a first memory; and most people are therefore able to confess their purpose in life, their relationship to others and their view of the environment in a perfectly neutral and unembarrassed manner through their first memories. Another point of interest in first memories is that their compression and simplicity allows us to use them for mass investigations. We can ask a school class to write their earliest recollections; and, if we know how to interpret them, we have an extremely valuable picture of each child.

Let me, for the sake of illustration, give a few first memories and attempt to interpret them. [Adler had members of the audience write down their first memories on slips of paper and hand them to him.] I know nothing else of the individuals than the memories they tell—not even whether they are children or adults. The meaning we find in their first memories would have to be checked by other expressions of their personality; but we can use them as they stand for our training, and for sharpening our ability to guess. We shall know what might be true, and we shall be able to compare one memory with another. In especial we shall be able to see whether the individual is training towards cooperation or against it, whether he is courageous or discouraged, whether he wishes to be supported and watched, or to be self-reliant and independent; whether he is prepared to give or anxious only to receive.

It is important to notice which people in the environment occur in first memories. When a sister occurs, we can be pretty sure that the individual has felt greatly under her influence. The sister has thrown a shadow over the other child's development. Generally we find a rivalry between the two, as if they were competing in a race; and we can understand that such a rivalry offers additional difficulties in development. A child cannot extend his interest to others as well when he is occupied with rivalry as when he can cooperate on terms of friendship. We shall not jump to conclusions, however: perhaps the two children were good friends.

"Since my sister and I were the youngest in the family, I was not permitted to attend [school] until she (the younger) was old enough to go." Now the rivalry becomes evident. My sister has hindered me! She was younger, but I was forced to wait for her. She narrowed my possibilities! If this is really the meaning of the memory, we should expect this girl or boy to feel, "It is the greatest danger in my life when some one restricts me and prevents my free development." Probably the writer is a girl. It seems less likely that a boy would be held back till a younger sister is ready to go to school.

"Accordingly we began on the same day." We should not call this the best kind of education for a girl in her position. It might well give her the impression that, because she is the older, she must stay behind. In any case, we see that this particular girl has interpreted it in this sense. She feels that she is slighted in favor of her sister. She will accuse some one of this neglect; and probably it will be her mother. We should not be surprised if she leaned more towards her father, and tried to make herself his favorite.

"I recall distinctly that mother told every one how lonely she was on our first day at school. She said, 'I ran out to the gate many times that afternoon and looked for the girls. I just thought they would never come.'" Here is a description of the mother; and a description which does not show her behaving very intelligently. It is the girl's portrait of her mother. "Thought we should never come"—the mother was obviously affectionate, and the girls knew of her affection; but at the same time she was anxious and tense. If we could speak to this girl, she could tell us more of the mother's preference for the younger sister. Such a preference would not astonish us, for the youngest child is almost always pampered. From the whole of this first memory, I should conclude that the older of the two sisters felt hindered through the rivalry of the younger. In later life we should expect to find marks of jealousy and fear of competition. It would not surprise us to find her disliking women younger than herself. Some people feel too old all through their lives, and many jealous women feel inferior towards members of their own sex who are younger than they. (Adler, 1931, pp. 74–78)

Annotated Bibliography

Adler, A. (1929). *The practice and theory of individual psychology*. London: Routledge & Kegan Paul. A collection of essays and discussions on neurosis and psychological problems, including considerable case material.

———. (1931). *What life should mean to you*. Boston: Little, Brown. A clearly written exposition of Adler's basic concepts, for the layperson.

———. (1956). *The individual psychology of Alfred Adler: A systematic presentation in selections from his writings.* (H. L. Ansbacher & R. R. Ansbacher, Eds.). New York: Harper & Row. The best introduction to Adler's work; it includes materials that are not available elsewhere in English. Two major sections: personality theory and abnormal psychology.

———. (1964). *Superiority and social interest: A collection of later writings.* (H. L. Ansbacher & R. R. Ansbacher, Eds.). New York: Viking Press. Includes sections on theory, case studies, religion, and various applications of individual psychology. Also includes an essay on the increasing recognition of Adler, a biography, and a definitive bibliography of Adler's writings.

Dreikurs, R. (1957). *Psychology in the classroom: A manual for teachers.* New York: Harper & Row. An application of Adler's theories to education, including extensive case material.

Manaster, G. J., & Corsini, R. J. (1982). *Individual psychology.* Itasca, IL: F. E. Peacock. The first textbook of Adlerian psychology written in English. It includes a complete Adlerian psychotherapy case summary and also a section on research in Adlerian psychology.

References

Ackerknecht, L. (n.d.). *Recent influences of Adlerian psychology on general psychology.* Unpublished manuscript.

Adler, A. (1912). *The neurotic constitution.* New York: Moffat, Yard.

———. (1928). *Understanding human nature.* London: Allen & Unwin.

———. (1929). *The practice and theory of individual psychology.* London: Routledge & Kegan Paul.

———. (1930). *The science of living.* London: Allen & Unwin.

———. (1931). *What life should mean to you.* Boston: Little, Brown.

———. (1956). *The individual psychology of Alfred Adler: A systematic presentation in selections from his writings.* (H. L. Ansbacher & R. R. Ansbacher, Eds.). New York: Harper & Row.

———. (1964a). *Social interest: A challenge to mankind.* New York: Capricorn Books.

———. (1964b). *Superiority and social interest: A collection of later writings.* (H. L. Ansbacher & R. R. Ansbacher, Eds.). New York: Viking Press.

———. (1973). Sex. In J. Miller (Ed.), *Psychoanalysis and women.* Baltimore: Penguin.

Adler, K. & Deutsch, D. (Eds.). (1959). *Essays in individual psychology.* New York: Grove Press.

Ansbacher, H. L. (1971). Alfred Adler and humanistic psychology. *Journal of Humanistic Psychology, 2,* 53–63.

———. (1974). The Adlerian and Jungian schools. [Part] A: Individual psychology. In S. Arieti (Ed.), *American handbook of psychiatry.* New York: Basic Books.

———. (1990). Alfred Adler's influence on the three leading cofounders of humanistic psychology. *Journal of Humanistic Psychology, 30,* 45–53.

Bottome, P. (1957). *Alfred Adler: A portrait from life.* New York: Vanguard Press.

Dreikurs, R. (1950). *Fundamentals of Adlerian psychology.* New York: Greenberg.

———. (1957). *Psychology in the classroom: A manual for teachers.* New York: Harper & Row.

———. (1964). *Children: The challenge.* New York: Dutton.

Ellenberger, H. (1970). *The discovery of the unconscious: The history and evolution of dynamic psychiatry.* New York: Basic Books.

Frankl, V. (1970). Tributes to Alfred Adler on his hundredth birthday. *Journal of Individual Psychology, 26,* 12.

Hall, C., & Lindzey, G. (1957). *Theories of personality.* New York: Wiley.

Lakein, A. (1974). *How to get control of your time and your life.* New York: New American Library.

Manaster, G. J., & Corsini, R. J. (1982). *Individual psychology.* Itasca, IL: F. E. Peacock.

Maslow, A. (1970). Tributes to Alfred Adler on his hundredth birthday. *Journal of Individual Psychology, 26,* 13.

May, R. (1970). Tributes to Alfred Adler on his hundredth birthday. *Journal of Individual Psychology, 26,* 13.

Mosak, H. (1989). Adlerian psychotherapy. In R. Corsini & D. Wedding (Eds.), *Current psychotherapies* (4th ed.). Itasca, IL: F. E. Peacock.

Mosak, H., & Mosak B. (1975a). *A bibliography of Adlerian psychology* (Vol. 1). Washington, DC: Hemisphere Publishing.

Mosak, H., & Mosak B. (1975b). *A bibliography of Adlerian psychology* (Vol. 2). Washington, DC: Hemisphere Publishing.

Orgler, H. (1939). *Alfred Adler: The man and his work.* London: Daniel.

Way, L. (1950). *Adler's place in psychology.* London: Allen & Unwin.

Wilder, J. (1959). Introduction. In K. Adler & D. Deutsch (Eds.), *Essays in individual psychology.* New York: Grove Press.

Wittels, F. (1939). The neo-Adlerians. *American Journal of Sociology, 45,* 433–445.

Chapter Four

Karen Horney and Humanistic Psychoanalysis

Karen Horney was a pioneer in the exploration of the social and cultural aspects of personality. Although, as a practicing psychoanalyst, she revered Freud's revolutionary clinical observations and insights, she was one of the first of Freud's followers to openly and cogently disagree with many of his fundamental assumptions.

Horney rejected Freud's impulse-oriented theoretical stance and questioned the universality of key Freudian concepts. These included the Oedipus complex, the opposition of the life and death impulses, and the overriding importance of sexual factors in neurosis. Her work on the psychology of women foreshadowed the current recognition of a feminine psychology. Against the sober pessimism of psychoanalytic theory, she developed and promulgated an open, optimistic, and self-actualizing view of the human condition.

Horney (1937) asserted that neurosis was the product of cultural influences—economic, social, and educational forces. Neurosis was not, as Freud assumed, only the product of dammed-up impulses in a restrictive environment. In her later works, where she continued to develop the thesis that everyone has the capacity for personal growth, she popularized psychoanalytic insights and attempted to demystify the therapeutic process. With her clients, she addressed current conflicts, needs, and possible solutions to restore a true sense of self and assure continued psychological growth.

Personal History

The first daughter and second child of Berndt and Clothilde Danielsen, Karen Horney was born in Hamburg, Germany, on September 16, 1885. Her family was Protestant and comfortably well-off. They were basically settled except that the father was the captain of a commercial ship and sometimes took his young daughter with him on long voyages. These unusual early experiences may have contributed to her cross-cultural sensitivity. However, the trips were merely brief punctuations to a more usual life at home with her mother and older brother Berndt, her father's namesake and mother's favorite.

As a student, Karen Danielsen's performance was outstanding. Even though it was rare for a girl to study medicine in her day, she decided at the age of 12, against her father's strong opposition, to prepare for medical school. Her interest in psychological self-study was also precocious. At the age of 13, she began a diary that she kept until she completed psychoanalysis ten years later (Horney, 1980).

At the age of 21, after studying in Freiberg and Göttingen, Germany, Karen Danielsen went to medical school in Berlin. She married Oscar Horney two years later. In 1910, she went into analysis with a staunch Freudian, Karl Abraham. After receiving her medical degree in 1915, she joined the Berlin Psychoanalytic Society. Soon thereafter, she became a practicing psychoanalyst herself, then a training analyst at the Berlin Psychoanalytic Institute, founded in 1920 (Kelman, 1971).

[Horney writes at the age of 17:] I should not read anything—I mean no books, but only myself. For half of my being lives, the other observes, criticizes, is given only to irony. (Horney, 1980, p. 57)

Horney studied and practiced in Berlin in the ferment of the very beginnings of psychoanalysis. Freud was still generating startling insights in Vienna and evolving his theories of anxiety, defense mechanisms, the unconscious, and the id-ego-superego map of the mind. Horney participated by writing over 20 articles, several of which were important theoretically, including those on the psychology of women. From the beginning of her career, she felt the female was inadequately understood by her male colleagues. She also participated in a famous discussion of lay analysis with Freud himself.

At this time, there was also political unrest in Germany. A polarity was emerging in which the Second Reich, under the domination of the kaiser, was evolving into what would ultimately become Fascism, countered by a movement toward Marxism. With her colleagues Erich Fromm and Wilhelm Reich, Horney chose a position close to the Marxist left.

In 1932, on the invitation of Franz Alexander, Horney emigrated to the United States to become Associate Director of the Chicago Psychoanalytic Institute. She had separated from her husband before moving to America. The association with Alexander did not work out, and, two years later, Horney moved again, this time to New York. She settled down to clinical work and active participation in the New York Psychoanalytic Society and Institute.

After two decades of classical psychoanalytic practice, Horney began to write books that criticized and revised the Freudian view of human growth, neurosis, and psychotherapy. Her first book, *The Neurotic Personality of Our Time,* appeared in the United States in 1937. Horney wrote this book for the layperson. *New Ways in Psychoanalysis,* a point-by-point revision of Freud's theory, was published in 1939, the year of Freud's death. The publication of this book, as well as her outspoken criticisms of the way analysis was being taught, shocked the more orthodox of her colleagues into direct action. In 1941, during a tempestuous meeting of the New York Psychoanalytic Society, she was officially demoted. After the vote, she rose and,with a number of her supporters, walked out of the meeting. Three days later, the group sent this letter of resignation to the Society:

For the last few years it has become gradually more apparent that the scientific integrity of the New York Psychoanalytic Society has steadily deteriorated. Reverence for dogma has replaced free inquiry; academic freedom has been abrogated; students have been intimidated; scientific sessions have degenerated into political machinations.

When an instructor and training analyst is disqualified solely because of scientific convictions, any hopes we may have harbored for improvement in the politics of the Society have been dispelled.

We are interested only in the scientific advancement of psychoanalysis in keeping with the courageous spirit of its founder, Sigmund

Freud. This obviously cannot be achieved within the framework of the New York Psychoanalytic Society as it is now constituted.

Under the circumstances we have no alternative but to resign, however much we may regret the necessity for this action. (Rubins, 1978, p. 240)

In September of that year, Horney and 20 other analysts formed the Association for the Advancement of Psychoanalysis.

From that crucial year in 1941 until the end of her life 11 years later, Horney was involved in personal and political struggles within the psychoanalytic world and with debates involving articles and rebuttals in the respective journals of the two competing organizations. After raising her children, she maintained a full career, which was unusual for the time. In addition, she took up painting, and enjoyed a wide circle of friends that included dramatists, theologians, philosophers, and anthropologists.

Apart from clinical psychoanalytic articles, Horney wrote a remarkable series of books designed for the public that were not at all to the taste of her more orthodox colleagues. Some were never reviewed in professional journals and others were roundly attacked when they were given any official recognition. Horney continued to express her own ideas and theories as they evolved from her clinical experience. The social and economic upheavals in Germany as well as the enormous personal changes in her own life (her marriage, separation, and move to America), sensitized Horney to the importance and impact of social factors on personality. Never comfortable with the Freudian idea of biological determinism, which ignored cultural issues and indirectly denigrated her for being a woman, she brought a new awareness to the psychoanalytic movement of the need to include family and society in any discussion of the genesis and maintenance of neurosis.

With her writings, Horney opened up a new set of possibilities for all people, men as well as women, who were concerned with self-understanding. She became the first major psychoanalytic writer who dared suggest that, although psychoanalysis was valuable, it was possible to gain insights outside of therapy—through self-analysis (1942).

As she became friends with the Zen teacher D. T. Suzuki, she became interested in Eastern thought, once asking one of her Zen teachers if her concept of *basic anxiety* was close to the Buddhist idea of *dukkha*, or "suffering" (Quinn, 1987). She even traveled to Japan and stayed in Zen monasteries. Drawn to the study of Zen practice, she explored the uses of meditation as utilized by a *roshi*, or "teacher" (DeMartino, 1991).

Karen Horney died at age 67 in New York City on December 4, 1952. Four years later, her students and admirers were among the diverse organizers of the the American Academy of Psychoanalysis, which has been active since that time. Her books have never been out of print. They continue to educate each new generation in the optimistic possibilities inher-

[Japan] is overwhelming. The art of the gardens, the simplicity of the homes, the feeling of deep inner meaning in the monasteries. (Horney in Quinn, 1987, p. 376)

ent in her view of human functioning. There also is an active International Karen Horney Society devoted to the continued exploration of her ideas.

Intellectual Antecedents

Sigmund Freud and Psychoanalysis

Horney readily acknowledged her indebtedness to Freud. She embraced his theory of psychic determinism, on which psychoanalysis is founded, as well as Freud's emphasis on the importance of unconscious motivation and the primacy of emotional over rational forces in the mind. She agreed with the basic Freudian insight that adult neurosis is due to the persistence of childhood influences. She also accepted the doctrine of repression and resistance as well as the basic idea of neurotic conflict. In her psychotherapeutic work, she used the basic Freudian techniques of free association, dream interpretation, and analysis of transference.

[T]he system of theories which Freud has gradually developed is so consistent that when one is once entrenched in them it is difficult to make observations unbiased by his way of thinking. (Horney, 1939, pp. 7–8)

Her own work, although derived from traditional psychoanalytic thinking, was original. Rejecting Freud's biological, genetic, and mechanistic orientation, she pursued a social and interpersonal one. Her exploration of the feminine was a reaction to the Freudian dictum, "Anatomy is destiny." Eventually, she came to view orthodox psychoanalytic explanations as simplistic, culture-bound, and theoretically inadequate. Her own method of doing therapy arose, in part, as a reaction to the standard practice of nondirectness. Also, she reacted to the avoidance of value judgments with respect to the client's life. In addition, her method arose out of the evaluation of her successes and failures during the first fifteen years of her more orthodox practice (Rendon, 1984). In Horney's work, we see the rejection of Freudian dualism, the endless and static opposition of forces (sexual versus aggressive or life versus death), and her espousal of an integration of psychological material in a recurring cycle of growth.

Hegel and Dialectical Materialism

Horney grew up in Germany at a time when the ideas of Georg Hegel (1770–1831) were widely discussed. He proposed that the natural sequence of ideas—the thought process itself—moves in a three-beat rhythm called the *dialectic*. One has an idea, or a *thesis*. Then one proceeds to develop its opposite or the *antithesis*. Finally, the mind recognizes the relationship between the thesis and antithesis and weaves them into a *synthesis*. This synthesis becomes the thesis of the next cycle. Karl Marx worked with the idealism of Hegel as part of his own formulation of the doctrine of dialectical materialism. This doctrine proposes that the social development of a culture moves, much like Hegel's dialectic, from thesis to antithesis (in this case, revolution) to synthesis. Horney took a number of Hegel's terms, including the real self, the actual self, alienation, and *shoulds* as core ideas in her own formulation of human behavior (Rendon, 1991).

Other Intellectual Influences

Horney's idea neurosis does not originate from the frustration of instinctual drives, but from feeling alienated from the real self comes, at least in part, from existentialism. Horney's understanding of the despair that one feels when cut off from the real self reflects the thinking of philosopher Søren Kierkegaard. She was also influenced by Adler, whose theory of the striving for power and superiority may be the root of Horney's more extensive concept of "the search for glory." She learned about human nature from such diverse sources as the innovative theater of Max Reinhardt, the philosophy of Georg Simmel, and the discoveries of contemporary anthropologists. She saw in anthropological reports the evidence to support her own perspective: the idea that culture is the critical factor in personality development and that different cultures could and did produce radically different kinds of persons.

Major Concepts

Basic Anxiety

Normal growth toward *actualization of the real self* (the full realization of one's potential) can be distorted and blocked by factors in one's childhood environment. If in the early years, a child's real needs are ignored or given too little respect, or if the parents are untrustworthy, the child may develop *basic anxiety*, a diffuse, uncertain sense of isolation and helplessness in a potentially hostile world (Horney, 1945). Neurotic processes arise out of the need to fend off awareness of this basic anxiety. The following description of basic anxiety, as Horney observed it over and over again, underscores the extraordinary lengths to which people go to avoid experiencing this anxiety.

> [Basic anxiety develops when] the environment is dreaded as a whole because it is felt to be unreliable, mendacious, unappreciative, unfair, unjust, begrudging and merciless. According to this concept the child not only fears punishment or desertion because of forbidden drives, but he feels the environment as a menace to his entire development and to his most legitimate wishes and strivings. He feels in danger of his individuality being obliterated, his freedom taken away, his happiness prevented. In contrast to the fear of castration this fear is not fantasy, but is well founded on reality. In an environment in which the basic anxiety develops, the child's free use of energies is thwarted, his self-esteem and self-reliance are undermined, fear is instilled by intimidation and isolation, his expansiveness is warped through brutality, standards or overprotective "love."
>
> The other essential element in the basic anxiety is that a child is rendered helpless to defend himself adequately against infringements. Not

"If it were not for reality, I would be perfectly all right." (Horney, quoting a patient, 1950, p. 37)

> only is he biologically helpless and dependent on the family, but every kind of self-assertion is discouraged. He is usually too intimidated to express his resentment or his accusations, and when he does express them he is made to feel guilty. The hostility which has to be repressed precipitates anxiety, because hostility is a danger when directed against someone on whom one feels dependent. (1939, pp. 75–76)

Horney observed that most people use some combination of three protective mechanisms to minimize this basic anxiety. These are compliance (itself a blend of affection and submission), aggression, and withdrawal. As we will see later, each of these leads to the formation of distinctive personality types (Zabriskie, 1976). Although all of these types manage to minimize basic anxiety in their own way, none of them do so in a completely healthy manner (Horney 1950).

Safety

Contrary to Freud, who saw humans as being driven by sexual urges, Horney perceived the sexual urge to be a manifestation of a more fundamental need, the need to be loved. Being loved can be nonsexual and can satisfy the wish to be accepted. It is this wish to be accepted that Horney suggests is the most visible sign of the need for "safety."

> [People] are not ruled by the pleasure principle alone but by two guiding principles: safety and satisfaction. . . . People can renounce food, money, attention, and affection as long as they are only renouncing satisfaction, but they cannot renounce these things if without them they would feel in danger of destitution or starvation or of being helplessly exposed to hostility, in other words, if they would lose their feelings of safety. (1950, p. 73)

It is the drive to be safe that precedes the satisfaction of pleasure. One cannot enjoy the pleasures of food, rest, or even sex if one is afraid. Thus, the drive to eliminate situations that might lead to fear or anxiety is the goal of both healthy *and* neurotic behavior.

The Idealized Self

The child whose need for safety within the family is unsatisfied may fantasize that he or she is *never* anxious or afraid. Gradually, this fantasy evolves into an *idealized self*. The child then attempts to *become* this fantasy and begins a process of alienation from or denial of the real self. In so doing, an inner bargain, a Faustian agreement of sorts, is made in which the part of the self that is genuine is disowned in favor of a façade. Protective in nature rather than creative, and compulsive rather than spontaneous, this contrived self is manipulative, guarded, and lacking in its capacity to express genuine feelings.

In a letter to Horney, one of her patients described the process:

> How is it possible to lose a self? The treachery, unknown and unthinkable, begins with our secret, psychic death in childhood—if and when we are not loved and are cut off from our spontaneous wishes. . . . It is a perfect double crime in which . . . the tiny self gradually and unwittingly takes part. He has not been accepted for himself, *as he is.* Oh, they love him, but they want him or force him or expect him to be different! Therefore *he must be unacceptable.* He himself learns to believe it and at last even takes it for granted. He has truly given himself up. No matter now whether he obeys them, whether he clings, rebels or withdraws—his behavior and his performance is all that matters. His center of gravity is in them, not in himself—yet if he so much as noticed it he would think it natural enough. And the whole thing is entirely plausible; all invisible, automatic and anonymous. . . . He has been rejected, not only by them but by himself. (1949, p. 3)

The Real Self

There is, says Horney (1950), "a central inner force, common to all human beings and yet unique in each, which is the deep source of growth" (p. 17). This is the *real self,* the inborn potential, the core of the personality. This real self is sharply different from the Freudian ego that must borrow its energy from a primitive id to maintain a precarious balance among impulses, environmental conditions, and moral prohibitions.

> [Given the proper conditions] the human individual . . . will develop then the clarity and depth of his own feelings, thoughts, wishes, interests; the ability to tap his own resources, the strength of his will power . . . the faculty to express himself and to relate himself to others with his spontaneous feelings. . . . In short, he will grow substantially undiverted toward self-realization. (Horney, 1950, p. 17)

These proper conditions include family warmth, to give an individual inner security and inner freedom; the goodwill of others, to encourage mature and fulfilling behavior; and "healthy friction with the wills and wishes of others" (Horney, 1950, p. 18), to develop inner strength.

The search for unity is one of the strongest motivating forces for human beings and it is even more important for the neurotic. (Horney, 1950, p. 240)

Basic Conflict

A child with basic anxiety is in conflict between his or her actual dependence on the parents and the need to rebel against insensitive parenting, thereby preserving the real self. Anger and aggression must be repressed because of the situation of dependence. Thus, the child is rendered unaware of real dangers to the self and produces an indiscriminate compliance. Therefore, the child's helplessness actually increases. Compliance is necessary, yet it produces a defenselessness that in turn fosters a

Personal Reflection

The Real Self

Horney says that basic anxiety results when a child moves further and further from his or her real self. Test the applicability of this idea in your own life with the following exercise.

1. Close your eyes, relax, and remember a typical day when you were 13 or 14 years old. From the time you woke up in the morning, recall your experience as you worked and played at school and the quality of your contact with family and friends in the afternoon and evening. Write down a description of that day, including specific thoughts and feelings as well as your general mood.

2. Now do the same for a day when you were 4 or 5 years old. Take a few minutes to relax to help you remember.

3. Compare the two days. Is there any difference in the degree of your spontaneity? Did your interests become less or more your own as you grew up? Did your life become constricted by conflicting *shoulds*, or were you able to keep a genuine sense of what was right for you? Did your love for yourself and others change?

4. Form groups of up to six people. Each person can describe and compare his or her own two days and listen to the accounts of others.

process by which the child loses touch with self-love, identifying instead with the idealized self constructed in response to family requirements. The basic internal conflict rages between necessary compliance and the aggression generated by that very compliance (Horney, 1945).

Horney (1937) describes four ways to minimize the conflict and to escape from basic anxiety: to rationalize it, deny it, narcotize it, or to avoid situations, thoughts, and feelings that might bring it into awareness.

Rationalization. Some people try to turn basic anxiety into "rational" fear. They worry unrealistically about situations over which they have little control. This worry may be seen in excessively worried parents or in the fear of earthquakes, car accidents, or loss of income. The anxiety may be a response to something very real, but the quality of the anxiety is excessive, compulsive, and desperate.

Denial. Denial takes two forms. In the first form, a person will try to exclude the anxiety from consciousness; to be unaware of it. What appears are the physical symptoms, such as nervous twitching, sweating, accelerated heartbeat, and so on; and/or the mental symptoms, such as feeling restless, being rushed or agitated, or being immobile and unable to function.

In the second form of denial, a person will try consciously to override the anxiety simply by an act of will. It is an attempt at bravery; recognizing the fear and acting anyway. It has practical value in that it does allow a person to function in spite of personal fears, but the underlying personality dynamics remain unchanged. The control over the fear cannot be relaxed.

Narcotization.   This is an attempt to lower general awareness of anxiety and other feelings by external means. Devices might include the use of drugs or alcohol as well as overindulging in certain social activities (to avoid facing loneliness), excessive work and insufficient leisure time, excessive sleep without feeling rested, or promiscuity (to feel wanted).

Inhibition.   With inhibition, a person avoids parts of experiences that trigger awareness of basic anxiety. Inhibition consists of an inability or unwillingness to feel, think, or do certain things. Its function is to avoid the anxiety that could arise if the person did feel, think, or do these things.

Dynamics

Neurotic Trends

Many people do not feel safe either as children or as adults. This feeling develops in various ways,

> but when summarized, they all boil down to the fact that the people in the environment are too wrapped up in their own neuroses to be able to love the child, or even to conceive of him as the particular individual he is; their attitudes toward him are determined by their own neurotic needs and responses. In simple words, they may be dominating, overprotective, intimidating, irritable, overexacting, overindulgent, erratic, partial to other siblings, hypocritical, indifferent, etc. It is never a matter of just a single factor, but always the whole constellation that exerts the untoward influence on a child's growth. (Horney, 1950, p. 18)

This thwarted development is called *neurosis*. For Horney, there are three paths that an individual may take to regain the feeling of safety and satisfaction: moving toward others, moving away from others, or moving against others in an attempt to escape a feeling of inner anxiety and loss of acceptance. To the extent that these tendencies distort either inner reality (lying to oneself) or outer reality, they will be unsuccessful. However, they can also become compulsive, dominant trends as a person unconsciously attempts to resolve inner conflicts by creating artificial harmony.

Moving Toward People: Compulsive Compliance

Someone in whom this trend predominates is self-effacing and has a constant need for love and approval. This type of person "needs such acceptance in whatever form it is available: attention, approval, gratitude, affection, love, sex. . . . [T]he self-effacing type measures his value in the currency of love. . . . He is worth as much as he is liked, needed, wanted, or accepted" (Horney, 1950, p. 227).

To be loved and to have a partner whom one can love is a vital part of the solution to the problem of safety. This type needs someone to help, to take care of, or to perform for. In order to be loved, one's own needs must be submerged; assertiveness, criticism of others, and getting one's own way must be repressed in favor of idealized lovableness.

Sacrifice is another theme. The self-effacing person does not like to win—at games or in any situation where winning might offend or displease someone else. Success frightens this individual, and he or she will often devalue or deny his or her own achievements. What is important to this person is to be useful to others and to support others' goals.

> While curtailed in any pursuit on his own behalf, he is not only free to do things for others but, according to his inner dictates, should be the ultimate of helpfulness, generosity, considerateness, understanding, sympathy, love and sacrifice. In fact, love and sacrifice in his mind are closely intertwined: he should sacrifice everything for love—love is sacrifice. (Horney, 1950, p. 220)

Moving Against Others: Compulsive Aggression

We all experience basic anxiety, but coping strategies differ from person to person. The aggressive individual will make every effort to mask any evidence of weakness or fear. The compulsive needs of this type are to dominate and control others, to exploit and outsmart them, and to prevail over them. This domination results in a philosophy of the jungle that is often rationalized as realism. Consciously, such a person feels tough minded, hard driving, efficient, and comparatively uninhibited. Actually, however, what appears as expansiveness and lust for life is an insatiable need to appear big and tough, acquired at the price of a ruthless disregard for the feelings and rights of others, which isolates the individual from humanity and from the tender feelings within. Horney describes this individual as follows:

> He glorifies and cultivates in himself everything that means mastery. Mastery with regard to others entails the need to excel and to be supe-

rior in some way. He tends to manipulate or dominate others and to make them dependent upon him. . . . Whether he is out for adoration, respect, or recognition, he is concerned with their subordinating themselves to him and looking up to him. He abhors the idea of his being compliant, appeasing, or dependent. . . .

Mastery with regard to himself means that he is his idealized proud self. Through will power and reason he is the captain of his soul. . . . It disturbs him inordinately to recognize a conflict within himself, or any problem that he cannot solve (master) right away. Suffering is felt as a disgrace to be concealed. . . . Nothing should push him around. . . . He abhors being helpless toward anything in himself as much as or more than being helpless toward any external factor. (1950, pp. 214–215)

Moving Away from People: Compulsive Detachment

Compulsive detachment predominates in the world's outsiders, those who construct a kind of invisible shield around themselves that no one may actually penetrate. Estranged from themselves as well as from others, these people restrict personal needs to maintain self-sufficiency, even eating and drinking less than others. The need for privacy and independence makes for a kind of hypersensitivity to any demands, requests, or even influences from outside, which are felt as intrusive, coercive, and domineering. Horney provides further insight into the compulsively detached:

Another characteristic of a resigned person is his hyper-sensitivity to influence, pressure, coercion or ties of any kind. This is a relevant factor too in his detachment. Even before he enters into a personal relationship or a group activity the fear of a lasting tie may be aroused. And the question as to how he can extricate himself may be present from the very beginning. When this type of person is contemplating marriage, for example, this fear may grow into panic.

What he resents and sees as coercion varies. It may be any contract, such as signing a lease or any long-term engagement. It may be any physical pressure, even collars, girdles, shoes. It may be an obstructed view. He may resent anything that others expect, or might possibly expect, from him—like Christmas presents, letters, or paying his bills at certain times. This resistance may extend to institutions, traffic regulations, conventions, government interference. He does not fight all of this because he is no fighter; but he rebels inwardly and may consciously or unconsciously frustrate others in his own passive way by not responding or by forgetting. (1950, p. 266)

Within this splendid isolation, the individual feels unique, special, and secretly important. His or her efforts are negatively oriented: *not* to need anybody, *not* to be involved, *not* to be influenced by others are the goals. All feelings, whether positive or negative, are suppressed in favor of detached observation, because *any* attachment might endanger the compulsion to avoid relationships. This person is an onlooker who lives "as if he were sitting in the orchestra and observing a drama acted on the stage" (Horney, 1950, p. 261).

Research

Psychoanalysis is often criticized for proposing theories that are impossible to prove through research. Horney may have suffered less from this kind of criticism. Leland Van den Daele (1987) recognized that the three compulsions described by Horney "appear specific, readily operationiz-

---

Personal Reflection ————————
———————————————— A Matter of Philosophy

In the beginning of *Neurosis and Human Growth* (1950, pp. 14–15), Horney distinguishes three concepts of morality that rest on three views of human nature:

1. If the human being is by nature sinful or ridden by primitive impulses, the goal of morality must be to curb them, tame them, overcome them.

2. If there is something inherently "good" in human nature and something inherently "bad," the goal of morality must be to ensure the eventual victory of the good by suppressing the bad and directing or reinforcing the good elements, using will, reason, and strength.

3. If human nature is seen as inevitably evolving toward self-realization by an intrinsic tendency, not by will, then the goal of morality becomes one of removing obstacles in the way of that evolution in order to provide maximum opportunity for the spontaneous forces of growth to manifest.

Having read Horney's three concepts, you can try the following exercise.

1. In a group of at least three students, discuss the three positions and tentatively choose one to support.

2. Horney embraced the third concept of morality. Discuss what implications this philosophy had on her attitude toward psychotherapy.

3. Whichever position you have chosen, ask yourself if you actually live by this position? How do you behave that shows this to be true? Share your answers with the group.

able and conceptually congruent with the requirements of psychological measurement." Indeed, a number of psychoanalytic studies with different populations have been undertaken. Results from work with nurses (Liddle, Heywood, Hankey, & Morman, 1971; Rendon, 1987), athletes (Speciale, Ponticelli, & Rinaldi, 1987), diabetics (Bergman, Aiken, & Fetig, 1990), and heart patients (Roomer, 1987) all yielded the results successfully predicted from Horney's theory.

Neurotic Claims

Having forgotten the real self and having identified with the idealized self, the three compulsive types described by Horney must maintain the illusion of who they are by diminishing their faults and exaggerating their importance. We have all had the experience of observing other people blatantly denying something they did. It is not lying, because lying suggests that the person is aware of the lie; rather, it is a compulsive reframing of reality to protect the idealized image from being exposed as fraudulent.

Imagination plays a crucial role in this neurotic process. The person puffs up his or her desirable qualities and downplays or ignores the fact that his or her weaknesses affect others. However, it is the imagined self, not the *actual* self, that must be honored and given its reward. Therefore, the individual feels entitled to whatever is desired. Each of the three compulsive types has different neurotic claims; nevertheless, these varying claims achieve the same end, the maintenance of illusion. The self-effacing type (the mover toward people), who needs above everything else to be lovable, will claim the right to be loved regardless of callous, hurtful, or objectionable behavior. For the person driven to mastery (the mover against people), the idealized self must always be right. This individual claims immunity from criticism, regardless of the cruelty or oppression of his or her acts. The person who has been driven into self-sufficiency (the mover away from people) will insist that others make no demands and that they go away when told to do so.

The Pride System

To monitor their success, neurotics must inevitably compare themselves to others. There is always the possibility of shame and humiliation rather than the sought-after, vindictive triumph that will signal that the idealized self is for the moment safe. The pride system is made up not only of the idealized image of the self and whatever defenses are necessary to maintain it, but of a fundamental conflict between this idealization and hate, which is directed toward the real self. Other conflicts occur between incompatible drives: "The central inner conflict, however, is between healthy and neurotic, constructive and destructive forces" (Horney, 1950, p. 113). The behavior that results from this inner conflict takes the form of reality distortions and unrealistic expectations (Lauer, 1985).

One simply cannot be unrealistic about oneself and remain entirely realistic in other respects. (Horney, 1950, p. 31)

Personal Reflection
Do I Make Neurotic Claims?

Horney suggested that studying your own reactions can lead you to observe your own neurotic patterns. She said, "It is in our real interest to examine our own reactions when we become preoccupied with a wrong done to us, or when we ponder the hateful qualities of somebody or when we feel the impulse to get back at others" (1950, p. 57).

The following questions may help you to explore your own patterns:

1. Can you recall a time when you asked for something that was unrealistic and you became upset when you did not get what you wanted?

2. Can you recall a time when you agreed to do something that you really did not want to do?

3. Can you recall a time when you were very critical of someone else because they did not meet your *own* standards of right and wrong?

4. Can you recall a time when your pride was hurt?

Constant demands for exceedingly high standards of performance make for a "tyranny of shoulds" (Horney, 1950), torrents of self-recriminations, and feelings of hopelessness. Freud saw these *shoulds* as part of normal development. Horney (1950) disagreed. She saw them as the neurotic counterfeits of normal moral strivings. The pursuit of the ideal self leads inevitably away from truth, dignity, and vitality into a morass of neurotic ambitions and conflicts that are accompanied by feelings of futility, vulnerability, and failure. According to Kerr (1984), another way to understand this inner movement is in the idea that "shoulds generate self-hate with no capacity for forgiveness."

The Search for Glory

In the neurotic, the energy of self-realization is turned toward self-idealization—that is, the maintenance of the ideal self. Self-glorification promises feelings of superiority to compensate for the actual feelings of fear and unacceptance. Horney calls the search to justify and substantiate the idealized self the *search for glory*. One idealizes the neurotic trend that one has developed to cope with anxiety. "Compliance becomes goodness, love, saintliness; aggressiveness becomes strength, leadership, heroism, omnipotence; aloofness becomes wisdom, self-sufficiency, independence.

What—according to his particular solution—appears as shortcomings or flaws are always dimmed out or retouched" (Horney, 1950, p. 22).

In the search for glory, doing a task is colored by the neurotic need for perfection; ambition becomes an insatiable drive for greater and greater success, whereas working with others is oriented toward vindictive triumph. According to Horney, the neurotic process is a set of compulsive and conflicting drives to actualize and maintain the fictional idealized self. This hoped-for, glorious version of oneself is substituted for the lost or hidden real self. Lacking an authentic sense of identity, the neurotic person strains to be somebody. Eventually, psychic energy is used primarily for this struggle. The compulsion to become special, superior, and untouchable overshadows any interest in self-development. Much of the search for glory takes place in the imagination, where the hoped-for, ideal being can be seen, praised, and respected. However, the neurotic's inner life is filled with visions of unattainable success as well as fantasies of devastating failures. Ongoing activities and interactions display an actual disregard for the real self and are clearly perceived as self-destructive to outside observers.

This strange conflict (idealization versus self-effacement) occurs because neurotics strive to glorify their false self-portraits, while at the same time truly hating themselves. To the degree that they have invested in an idealized, dazzling self-image, they correspondingly despise their actual being and attainments. The neurotic enhancement of the false self and the devaluation of the real self is summarized by Horney in the concept of the pride system.

The Neurotic Core

For Horney, the four elements of the neurotic core (claims, shoulds, pride, and self-hate) are interwoven. Claims are unrealistic expectations of how the world should treat us, shoulds are unrealistic expectations of how we should be, pride is the unrealistic expectation that our shoulds will be fulfilled, and self-hate is how we feel when we or the world fails to fulfill them.

The Psychology of Women

Horney's exploration of the psychological meaning of the important events in a woman's life is intrinsically worthwhile and historically significant in the reorientation of social values toward the equality of women.

Throughout her life, Karen Horney attempted to counteract those flaws in psychoanalytic theory that were based on Freud's failure to understand female development. In his paper on infantile genital organization, Freud (1923) asserted that for both sexes only the male's genitalia is important. In this paper, he asserted "the primacy of the phallus" for both men and women. At about the same time, Horney presented the first of her own papers on the feminine. In it she stated "that one half of the human race is discontented with the sex assigned to it and can overcome this discontent only in favorable circumstances . . . is decidedly unsatisfying" (1967, p. 38).

It is easy to attack Freud for his conventional notions. But it is also easy to understand the anger felt by female psychoanalysts like Horney, upon reading such statements as,

> Behind this envy for the penis, there comes to light the woman's hostile bitterness against the man, which never completely disappears in the relations between the sexes, and which is clearly indicated in the strivings and in the literary productions of the "emancipated" woman. (Freud, 1918, p. 205)

At this point, I, as a woman, ask in amazement, and what about motherhood? And the blissful consciousness of bearing a new life within oneself? And the ineffable happiness of the increasing expectation of the appearance of this new being? And the joy when it finally makes its appearance and one holds it for the first time in one's arms? And the deep pleasurable feeling of satisfaction in suckling it and the happiness of the whole period when the infant needs her care? (Horney, 1967, p. 60)

Horney (1926a) wrote a paper that gently but directly opposed the one-sidedness of the Freudian position. She points out, "Psychoanalysis is the creation of a male genius and almost all those who have developed his ideas have been men" (1967, p. 54). Freud had made efforts to account for the patterns of psychological growth in little girls, but always in terms of a felt lack of male genitals. Horney refused to see girls merely as castrated boys—pseudomales who lack a penis and are bound to suffer for it, psychologically, their whole lives.

The concept of penis envy was based on clinical observations that were undoubtedly accurate: women *did* remember the childhood wish to have a penis. But to Horney that was only half of the story. The other half had been neglected because of the male-oriented preconceptions of the observers. Horney's female clients did recall wanting to have a penis. In fact, these women were much less interested in possessing the male organ than they were in having the rights and privileges they saw accorded their fathers and brothers. They felt cheated and with good reason: The culture favored males and was controlled by men. Freud saw anatomy as destiny and therefore assumed that a girl's focus was on having a penis, whereas Horney saw that a girl wished for much more. She wanted the cultural advantages that were given to men. Horney found a parallel in the male for Freud's notion of penis envy. Her male patients routinely reported their envy of the female's experience of pregnancy and childbirth. As well, they envied the female breast and the female cultural advantage of not having to compete. Thus, each sex yearned for the advantages of the other. In the case of penis envy, it was simply that the yearning of women was more obvious in a culture in which they were truly socially inferior. Horney did not believe penis envy to be the problem; rather, she saw *envy,* in men *or* women, as the underlying pathology (Kerr, 1987–1988).

In addition to clarifying the concept of penis envy in girls, Horney contributed to the understanding of masochism in women. Masochistic attitudes appear in fantasies of pleasure involving suffering, or the importation of suffering into situations in which others would not find it. People with masochistic character structures feel weak, helpless, and emotionally dependent. They see themselves as inferior, hide their aggressions, and tend to feel abused. Covertly, they use their weaknesses as a way of manipulating others.

Like Freud, Horney found that this particular type of personality structure occurs far more frequently in women than in men. Rejecting biological reasons for this difference between the sexes, she pointed instead to significant cultural influences (Westkott, 1986a).

In the first decades of this century, women were frustrated by the lack of opportunities for career advancement imposed by the number of children they had. There were social conventions restricting women to jobs such as school teaching and charity work that emphasized sentiment and emotion rather than intellectual creativity. Therefore, child rearing was a woman's primary means of building self-esteem. Horney agreed with philosopher Georg Simmel's view of the subtle and pervasive attitudes of both men and women. Simmel noted that social attitudes assumed male superiority and stereotyped women as "just a little" inferior (in Horney, 1967, p. 58). The very fabric of Western culture was based on such dubious preconceptions. Data on Native-American society and Trobriand Islanders (Mead, 1949) indicated that this denigration of the female was a cultural, not a biological, event. Little girls in these cultures did not seem to be particularly masochistic. Thus, on the basis of anthropological evidence unavailable to Freud in his early period of theory building, Horney (1935) suggested that far from being woman's biological destiny, masochism was a culturally learned pattern of behavior. In any culture in which women are both devalued and expected to care for others, it is not surprising that a neurotic solution might be surface compliance and sub-surface rage (Westkott, 1986b). The very act of caring for men, made into a cultural duty, has been seen as a way to ensure that men's needs take precedence over women's (Westkott, 1989).

Horney (1934) also collected observations of adolescent girls who showed neurotic tendencies at the onset of menstruation. She grouped these difficulties into four major types.

1. A girl who worked and played well as a preadolescent might become boy-crazy and have no concentration left for her schoolwork.

2. A girl might suddenly lose interest in everything, while developing some mental or religious fixation.

3. A girl might suddenly develop a preference for homosexuality. [Note: Homosexuality was considered a pathology in Horney's day.]

4. A girl might show a slackening of interest in everything, as if caring about nothing and renouncing all intense concerns was expected of her.

Horney noticed that although each of the four behavior patterns seemed different, they had the same common denominator: deeply repressed self-rage as well rage directed at the mother and generalized to other females. These four tendencies served as safety mechanisms to prevent what the neurotic adolescent perceived as the threat of competition and aggressive confrontation from other females.

Menstruation was another topic that had been neglected by earlier psychoanalytic thinkers. Based upon observations of many women in therapy, Horney (1931a) suggested that premenstrual tension was related to conflicting unconscious tendencies involving the wish for a child. She was the first to note that functional female disorders, such as menstrual cramps and vaginal infections, were a regular occurrence in disturbed women, regardless of the nature of their neurotic symptoms. She also observed that frigidity was not a natural feminine attitude, as was commonly believed, but a sign of psychological problems (1926b). The sexual feelings of women are much more closely related to their emotional lives than is true of men so that neurotic conflicts are more likely to appear as sexual dysfunction.

Horney made other significant contributions to the psychology of women. She studied the origins and traditions of the fear of women in ancient and modern cultures (1932a) and examined the patterns of distrust between the sexes (1931b). Analyzing the problems of contemporary marriage (1932b), she described how the unconscious expectation that the spouse can be a substitute for the beloved parent can lead only to disappointment. She argued that the Freudian view that men were more polygamous was without clinical substantiation and was even (perhaps) a masculine rationalization. Being a psychoanalyst, a wife, and a mother, she explored maternal conflicts, including the meaning of pregnancy and childbirth.

Her contributions to the psychology of women are best described by Horney herself. In an early paper, she foreshadowed her later work:

> In the foregoing discussion I have put a construction upon certain problems of feminine psychology, which in many points differs from current views. It is possible and even probable that the picture I have drawn is one-sided from the opposite point of view. But my primary intention in this paper was to indicate a possible source of error arising out of the sex of the observer, and by so doing, to make a step forward toward the goal that we are all striving to reach: to get beyond the subjectivity of the masculine or the feminine standpoint and to obtain a picture of the mental development of woman that will be more true to the facts of her nature—with its specific qualities and its differences from that of man—than any we have hitherto achieved. (1967, p. 70)

Interestingly enough, Horney's later works do not dwell much on gender differences. Once she had determined that attitude was culturally determined, not sex-linked as Freud had insisted, she renewed her inter-

---

Always, everywhere, the man strives to rid himself of his dread of women by objectifying it. "It is not," he says, "that I dread her; it is that she herself is malignant, capable of any crime, a beast of prey, a vampire, a witch, insatiable in her desires. She is the very personification of what is sinister." May not this be one of the principal roots of the whole masculine impulse to creative work—the never ending conflict between his longing for the woman and his dread of her? (Horney, 1967, p. 135)

est in basic psychodynamics, which could illuminate the behavior and character of men and women alike (Eckardt, 1991). She argued that character structure as it affects a person's world view can transcend anatomy (Rubin,1991).

Psychological Growth

Normal human development in a healthy, interpersonal setting, with sensitivity to the child's real needs, results in the natural fulfillment of his or her potential. This tendency to evolve toward what we are destined to become is intrinsic in all humanity as well as in all living things.

In the person who is evolving toward inner harmony, the forces that are distorted in the neurotic (toward people, against people, away from people) become harmonized. "Most of us want and appreciate affection, self-control, modesty, consideration of others. . . . Self-sufficiency, independence and guidance through reason are generally regarded as valuable goals" (Horney, 1942, p. 56). It is the development of the real self, the forgotten self, that is the mark of psychological growth. This requires no effort of will, only the absence of hindrances.

> The difference, then, between healthy strivings and neurotic drives for glory is one between spontaneity and compulsion; between recognizing and denying limitations; between a focus on a vision of a glorious end product and a feeling of evolution; between seeming and being, fantasy and truth. (Horney, 1950, p. 38)

The Process of Psychotherapy

Although Horney put much effort into her popular books, for her, the real work was in psychoanalytic psychotherapy. Her theory of personality development, recognition of safety needs, the role of anxiety, the idealized self, and the neurotic trends all arose from sensitive interaction with her clients. She describes some of this interaction in the following excerpt:

> A crescendo of observation opened my eyes to the significance of such conflicts. What first struck me most forcibly was the blindness of patients towards obvious contradictions within themselves. When I pointed these out they became elusive and seemed to lose interest. After repeated experiences of this kind, I realized that the elusiveness expressed a profound aversion to tackling these contradictions. Finally, panic reactions in response to a sudden recognition of a conflict showed me I was working with dynamite. Patients had good reason to shy away from these conflicts: they dreaded their power to tear them to pieces. (Horney, 1945, p. 15)

In her book *New Ways in Psychoanalysis,* Horney describes her primary objective in therapy:

> According to my slant on neurosis, the main neurotic disturbances are the consequences of the neurotic trends. Hence my main objective in therapy is, after having recognized the neurotic trends, to discover in detail the functions they serve and the consequences they have on the patient's personality and his life. (Horney, 1939, p. 281)

In an even larger perspective, the aim of psychotherapy in Horney's view is the restoration of the constructive forces inherent in the individual so that his or her life can become an expression of the real self.

> In order to arrive at a rough estimate of the difficulties of the therapeutic process we must consider what it involves for the patient. Briefly, he must overcome all those needs, drives, or attitudes which obstruct his growth: only when he begins to relinquish his illusions about himself and his illusory goals has he a chance to find his real potentialities and to develop them. Only to the extent to which he gives up his false pride can he become less hostile to himself and evolve a solid self-confidence. Only as his shoulds lose their coercive power can he discover his real feelings, wishes, beliefs, and ideals. Only when he faces his existing conflicts has he the chance for a real integration—and so forth. (Horney, 1950, p. 334)

This objective is accomplished through the therapist's emphasis on present-day problems, conflicts, anxieties, and defenses. Although such an exploration into personal motivations inevitably mobilizes important memories, relating these memories to present problems is not considered as valuable as relating the character trends to one another and thus delineating opposing tendencies and unconscious conflicts. The subjective value of each trend in the character and its life toll must be acknowledged in specific detail.

In the process of self-discovery there are always moments of painful awareness upon accepting the truth about oneself, instead of the ideal image. Also, there are times of anxiety when unconscious conflicts come into conscious awareness. The personal bravery required to sustain this oftentimes painful process is easier to accomplish in the context of a trusting relationship in which the therapist supports, guides, and helps the patient. Thus, Horney recommended that the analyst and the patient sit face to face so that the therapist could be seen, could be supportive, and could be fully participatory during the therapeutic process.

In her work training analysts, she stressed first the humanness of the analyst and then the uniqueness of the patient. "One of the great handicaps in our analytical work is our remaining personal neurotic difficulties. . . . Technique can only be taught to a limited extent because ultimately technique depends on inner freedom, ingenuity, and finger-tip feelings" (Horney, 1987, p. 17).

Every piece of analytic work well done changes these conditions in that it makes a person less helpless, less fearful, less hostile, and less alienated. (Horney, 1945, p. 19)

Horney's psychotherapeutic tools are basically Freudian. They include free association, interpretation, the analysis of dreams, and the sensitive appreciation of patterns of interaction between patient and therapist. For Horney, the analyst must not be merely passive, but must question, probe, and directly influence the patient to make real-life changes after insight into problems has been attained. Horney taught that the analyst should deliberately guide the psychotherapeutic process and not leave its direction up to the patient's free associations. The analyst's direction must necessarily involve value judgments.

As analysis proceeds, motivation to live fully and happily should increase, in Horney's view, because her method of exposing neurotic conflicts allows patients to get detailed and compelling insights into their actual suffering. For Horney, the goal of therapy went beyond simple insight. As neurotic conflicts are banished through insight, an individual becomes increasingly able to solve life's problems without outside support, reducing by stages the dependence upon the analyst. At the completion of therapy he or she will have regained the courage and the capacity to recognize and to actualize the real self (Horney, 1991).

> Observation and critical intelligence are no substitute for that inner certainty with reference to others which is possessed by a person who is realistically aware of himself as himself and others as themselves, and who is not swayed in his estimate of them by all kinds of compulsive needs. (Horney, 1950, p. 295)

Self-analysis

Karen Horney was outstanding among psychoanalytic theorists in that she attempted to expand the scope of therapy to include exercises that could be undertaken by interested people without professional help. In *Self-Analysis* (1942) she asks,

> If the analyst relies on the patient's unconscious mental activity, if the patient has the faculty to work alone toward the solution to some

---

Personal Reflection _____

_____ Self-analysis

Try this exercise in self-analysis. In a quiet, private place, with this textbook and a notebook, take a half hour to do the following:

1. Identify one personal issue for you. After you have made your choice, write it down as succinctly as possible.

2. With as much of the objectivity of an outside observer as you can muster, write a paragraph or two describing what your behavior is around this issue.

3. Reread the section in Neurotic Trends on moving toward, moving against, and moving away from others. Note if these trends and their compulsive shoulds enter into your problem.

4. Is the issue a relatively minor difficulty that arises only under special conditions? Or is it ever-present, ongoing, and entangled with other conflicts?

5. Make a list of the benefits or costs involved, both psychologically and in terms of other real-life losses and gains.

6. Imagine yourself in the middle of this problem. Have you ever felt this way before? If memories arise, make a note of them.

7. If possible, read your notes to another person. Notice what happens when you communicate your self-analysis: How do you feel during different parts of the reading? What do you censor? What do you feel a need to explain further?

problem, could this faculty be utilized in some more deliberate fashion? Could the patient scrutinize his self-observations or his associations with his own critical intelligence? . . . Granted it would be a hard job, fraught with hazards and limitations . . . [but] these difficulties should not prevent us from raising the question is it impossible to analyse oneself? (pp. 16–17)

In considering this possibility Horney, in her characteristic way, was following Freud's personal example (he analyzed himself). It was also another radical departure from what psychoanalysts recommended. For theoretical and technical reasons, classical analysts consider it foolhardy, if not downright impossible, to undertake such a venture alone.

Conclusion

Karen Horney belongs among the social and cultural left wing of Freud's followers, along with Erich Fromm, Harry Stack Sullivan, and Wilhelm Reich. In emphasizing the constructive, evolutionary nature of human development and the great modifiability of human nature, Horney rejected the orthodox, genetic position that "anatomy is destiny" in favor of a more optimistic stance.

For Horney, the four essential constituents at the core of emotional conflict are neurotic claims, shoulds, pride, and self-hate. All of these constituents represent unrealistic expectations and are linked as follows: Neurotic claims dictate how the world should treat a person. Shoulds tell how a person should be. Pride is the way in which a person tries to fulfill the shoulds. Finally, self-hate is what a person feels when he or she fails to fulfill the shoulds.

Horney contributed much to the understanding of women's problems and prospects. Not only did she work to dispel male-oriented myths about female psychodynamics, but she also gave needed attention to such previously neglected, but centrally important, topics as frigidity, menstruation, pregnancy, childbirth, and motherhood.

Evaluation

Horney's work, important as a one of the counterweights to Freud's formulations, is now recognized and becoming more widely studied as an original and still vital formulation of the feminine point of view. She was one of the first theorists to demand not only an appreciation of women, but an understanding of the cultural determinants of personality. Chodorow (1989) asserts that Horney's theories "form the basis, acknowledged or unacknowledged, for most of the recent revisions of psychoanalytic understandings of gender" (p. 3). She has been called a liberator of psychoanalysis (Ingram, 1985) as well as the proponent of a moral philosophy (Mullan, 1988). She is a forerunner of humanistic psychology with her emphasis on the centrality of a healthy core striving for self-realization (O'Connell, 1990).

She possessed an optimism about a person's inner capacities that she felt made self-analysis possible. In her books, she examined the structure of personality and offered solutions to basic neurotic conflicts. Her books, written directly to the public and unfiltered by the psychoanalytic establishment, continue to influence the psychological climate. A constant theme in her writings is a hopeful trust in humanity and the human capacity for change:

> Albert Schweitzer uses the terms "optimistic" and "pessimistic" in the sense of "world and life affirmation" and "world and life negation." Freud's philosophy, in this deep sense, is a pessimistic one. Ours, with all its cognizance of the tragic element in neurosis, is an optimistic one. (Horney, 1950, p. 378)

The Theory Firsthand: Excerpt from *Neurosis and Human Growth*

The following excerpt outlines and illustrates Horney's (1950) concept of "the tyranny of the should," the process by which compulsive, neurotic trends construct, support, and maintain a fictional, idealized image.

> We have discussed so far chiefly how the neurotic tries to actualize his idealized self with regard to the *outside world*. . . .
> We shall now discuss that aspect of self-actualization, briefly mentioned in the first chapter, in which the focus is *within himself.* Unlike Pygmalion, who tried to make another person into a creature fulfilling his concept of beauty, the neurotic sets to work to mold himself into a supreme being of his own making. He holds before his soul his image of perfection and unconsciously tells himself: "Forget about the dis-

graceful creature you actually *are;* this is how you *should be;* and to be this idealized self is all that matters. You should be able to endure everything, to understand everything, to like everybody, to be always productive"—to mention only a few of these inner dictates. Since they are inexorable, I call them "the tyranny of the should."

The inner dictates comprise all that the neurotic should be able to do, to be, to feel, to know—and taboos on how and what he should not be. I shall begin by enumerating some of them out of context, for the sake of a brief survey. (More detailed examples will follow as we discuss the characteristics of the shoulds.)

He should be the utmost of honesty, generosity, considerateness, justice, dignity, courage, unselfishness. He should be the perfect lover, husband, teacher. He should be able to endure everything, should like everybody, should love his parents, his wife, his country; or, he should not be attached to anything or anybody, nothing should matter to him, he should never feel hurt, and he should always be serene and unruffled. He should always enjoy life; or, he should be above pleasure and enjoyment. He should be spontaneous; he should always control his feelings. He should know, understand, and foresee everything. He should be able to solve every problem of his own, or of others, in no time. He should be able to overcome every difficulty of his as soon as he sees it. He should never be tired or fall ill. He should always be able to find a job. He should be able to do things in one hour which can only be done in two to three hours.

This survey, roughly indicating the scope of inner dictates, leaves us with the impression of demands on self which, though understandable, are altogether too difficult and too rigid. If we tell a patient that he expects too much of himself, he will often recognize it without hesitation; he may even have been aware of it already. He will usually add, explicitly or implicitly, that it is better to expect too much of himself than too little. But to speak of too high demands on self does not reveal the peculiar *characteristics of inner dictates.* These come into clear relief under closer examination. They are overlapping, because they all result from the necessity a person feels to turn into his idealized self, and from his conviction that he can do so.

What strikes us first is the same *disregard for feasibility* which pervades the entire drive for actualization. Many of these demands are of a kind which no human being could fulfill. They are plainly fantastic, although the person himself is not aware of it. He cannot help recognizing it, however, as soon as his expectations are exposed to the clear light of critical thinking. Such an intellectual realization, however, usually does not change much, if anything. Let us say that a physician may have clearly realized that he cannot do intensive scientific work in addition to a nine-hour practice and an extensive social life; yet, after abortive attempts to cut down one or another activity, he keeps going at the same pace. His demands that limitations in time and energies should not exist for him are stronger than reason. Or take a more subtle illustration. At an analytic session a patient was dejected. She had talked with a friend about the latter's marital problems, which were complicated. My patient knew the husband only from social situations. Yet, although she had been in analysis for several years and had enough understanding of the psychological intricacies involved in any relationship between two people to know better, she felt that she should have been able to tell her friend whether or not the marriage was tenable.

I told her that she expected something of herself which was impossible for anybody, and pointed out the multitude of questions to be clarified before one could even begin to have a more than dim impression of the factors operating in the situation. It turned out then that she had been aware of most of the difficulties I had pointed out. But she had still felt that she *should* have a kind of sixth sense penetrating all of them. . . . .

The inner dictates, exactly like political tyranny in a police state, operate with a supreme *disregard for the person's own psychic condition*—for what he can feel or do as he is at present. One of the frequent shoulds, for instance, is that one should never feel hurt. As an absolute (which is implied in the "never") anyone would find this extremely hard to achieve. How many people have been, or are, so secure in themselves, so serene, as never to feel hurt? This could at best be an ideal toward which we might strive. To take such a project seriously must mean intense and patient work at our unconscious claims for defense, at our false pride—or, in short, at every factor in our personality that makes us vulnerable. But the person who feels that he should never feel hurt does not have so concrete a program in mind. He simply issues an absolute order to himself, denying or overriding the fact of his existing vulnerability. . . . .

Most neurotic disturbances resist even the most strenuous efforts at control. Conscious efforts simply do not avail against a depression, against a deeply ingrained inhibition to work, or against consuming daydreams.

Many reactions of despondence, irritability, or fear occurring during analysis are less a response to the patient's having discovered a disturbing problem in himself (as the analyst tends to assume) than to his feeling impotent to remove it right away. (pp. 64–67, 71–72)

Annotated Bibliography

(Note: Most of Horney's books—unlike her articles—were written for the layperson.)

Horney, K. (1937). *The neurotic personality of our time.* New York: Norton. General review of neurosis as influenced by culture, human relationships, and tendencies toward helplessness, isolation, and hostility.

————. (1939). *New ways in psychoanalysis*. New York: Norton. Evaluation and expansion of Freudian theory, with particular emphasis on character structure, environmental factors in neurosis, and self-realization with respect to therapeutic goals.

————. (1942). *Self-analysis*. New York: Norton. A description of the possibilities, techniques, and difficulties of self-analysis. Through case description and theoretical discussion, Horney describes the techniques of self-analysis.

————. (1945). *Our inner conflicts*. New York: Norton. Described in detail are the three ways of responding to life situations—moving toward, away from, and against other people. Also described are the ways in which these trends can become neurotic. In addition, neurosis as inner conflict between the *real self* and *the idealized image* is explained.

————. (1950). *Neurosis and human growth*. New York: Norton. Probably the most substantial of all her books and the one to read first. It includes a synthesis of some of the material from earlier works. The concept of moral evolution as humans' spontaneous nature is explored in detail.

Kelman, H. (Ed.). (1967). *Feminine psychology*. New York: Norton. The collected papers and articles of Karen Horney dealing mostly with specific Freudian concepts that are related to various aspects of sexuality; explores in detail the problems of the psychology of women in Freudian theory.

Weiss, F. (1991). Karen Horney, A bibliography. *American Journal of Psychoanalysis, 51*(3), 343–347. If you ever need to track anything by or about Horney, this is the place to start.

References

Bergman, M., Aiken, S., & Fetig, P. (1990). Understanding the diabetic patient from a psychological dimension: Implications for the patient and the provider. *American Journal of Psychoanalysis, 50*(1), 25–33.

Chodorow, N. (1989). *Feminism and psychoanalytic thought*. New Haven, CT: Yale University Press.

DeMartino, R. (1991). Karen Horney, Daisetz T. Suzuki, and Zen Buddhism. *American Journal of Psychoanalysis, 51*(3), 267–283.

Eckardt, M. (1991). Feminine psychology revisited: A historical perspective. *American Journal of Psychoanalysis, 51*(3) 235–243.

Freud, S. The taboo of virginity. In J. Strachey (Ed. and Trans.), *The standard edition of the complete psychological works of Sigmund Freud* (Vol. 11 of 24, pp. 203–211). London: Hogarth Press, 1953–1966. (Originally published, 1918.)

————. The infantile genital organization: An interpolation into the theory of sexuality. In J. Strachey (Ed. and Trans.), *The standard edition of the complete psychological works of Sigmund Freud* (Vol. 19 of 24, pp. 41–49). London: Hogarth Press, 1953–1966. (Originally published, 1923.)

Horney, K. (1967). The flight from womanhood: The masculinity complex in women as viewed by men and by women. In H. Kelman (Ed.), *Feminine psychology*. New York: Norton. (Originally published, 1926a.)

————. Inhibited feminity: Psychoanalytical contributions to the problem of frigidity. In *Feminine psychology*. (Originally published, 1926b.)

————. Premenstrual tension. In *Feminine psychology*. (Originally published, 1931a.)

————. The distrust between the sexes. In *Feminine psychology*. (Originally published, 1931b.)

————. The dread of woman: Observations on a specific difference in the dread felt by men and women respectively for the opposite sex. In *Feminine psychology*. (Originally published, 1932a.)

————. Problems of marriage. In *Feminine psychology*. (Originally published, 1932b.)

————. Psychogenic factors in functional female disorders. In *Feminine psychology*. (Originally published, 1933.)

————. Personality changes in female adolescents. In *Feminine psychology*. (Originally published, 1934.)

————. The problem of female masochism. In *Feminine psychology*. (Originally published, 1935.)

————. (1937). *The neurotic personality of our time*. New York: Norton.

————. (1939). *New ways in psychoanalysis*. New York: Norton.

————. (1942). *Self-analysis*. New York: Norton.

————. (1945). *Our inner conflicts*. New York: Norton.

————. (1949). Finding the real self: A letter with a foreword by Karen Horney. *American Journal of Psychoanalysis, 9*(3).

————. (1950). *Neurosis and human growth*. New York: Norton.

————. (1980). *The adolescent diaries of Karen Horney*. New York: Basic Books.

————. (1987). *Final lectures*. New York: Norton.

————. (1991). The goals of analytic therapy. *American Journal of Psychoanalysis, 5*(3), 219–226.

Ingram, D. (1985). Karen Horney at 100: Beyond the frontier. *American Journal of Psychoanalysis, 45*(4), 305–309.

Kelman, H. (Ed.). (1967). *Feminine psychology*. New York: Norton.

————. (1971). *Helping people: Karen Horney's psychoanalytic approach*. New York: Science House.

Kerr, N. (1984). The tyranny of the shoulds. *Perspectives in Psychiatric Care, 22*(2), 16–19.

————. (1987–1988). "Wounded womanhood": An analysis of Karen

Horney's theory of feminine psychology. *Perspectives in Psychiatric Care, 24*(3–4), 132–141.

Lauer, K. (1985). His husband/her wife: The dynamics of the pride system in marriage. *Journal of Evolutionary Psychology, 6*(3–4), 329–340.

Liddle, R., Heywood, H., Hankey, R., & Morman, R. (1971). Predicting baccalaureate degree attainment for nursing students: A theoretical study using the TAV selection system. *Nursing Research, 20*(3), 258–261.

Mead, M. (1949). *Male and female.* New York: Morrow.

Mullan, H. (1988). Horney's contribution to a rational approach to morals. *American Journal of Psychoanalysis, 48*(2), 127–137.

O'Connell, A. (1980). Karen Horney: Theorist in psychoanalysis and feminine psychology. *Psychology of Women Quarterly, 5*(1), 81–93.

Quinn, S. (1987). *A mind of her own: The life of Karen Horney.* New York: Summit Books.

Rendon, D. (1987). Understanding social roles from a Horneyan perspective. *American Journal of Psychoanalysis, 47*(2), 131–142.

Rendon, M. (1984). Clinical work in the Horney tradition. *American Journal of Psychoanalysis, 44*(30), 319–333.

———. (1991). Hegel and Horney. *American Journal of Psychoanalysis, 51*(3), 285–299.

Roomer, W. (1987). An application of the interpersonal models developed by Karen Horney and Timothy Leary to Type A-B behavior patterns. *American Journal of Psychoanalysis, 47*(2), 116–130.

Rubin, T. (1991). Horney, here and now: 1991. *American Journal of Psychoanalysis, 51*(3), 313–318.

Rubins, J. (1978). *Karen Horney: Gentle rebel of psychoanalysis.* New York: Dial Press.

Speciale, G., Ponticelli, R., & Rinaldi, T. (1987). Team players: Athletes practicing two antagonist sports, and individual athletes: A classification proposal according to individual personality traits. *Movimento, 3*(1), 50–52.

Symonds, A. (1991). Gender issues and Horney theory. *American Journal of Psychoanalysis, 51*(3), 301–312.

Van den Daele, L. (1987). Research in Horney's psychoanalytic theory. *American Journal of Psychoanalysis, 47*(2), 99–104.

Westkott, M. (1986a). *The feminist legacy of Karen Horney.* New Haven, CT: Yale University Press.

———. (1986b). Historical and developmental roots of female dependency. *Psychotherapy, 23*(2), 213–220.

———. (1989). Female relationality and the idealized self. *American Journal of Psychoanalysis, 49*(3), 239–250.

Zabriskie, C. (1976). A psychological analysis of biblical interpretations pertaining to women. *Journal of Psychology and Theology, 4*(4), 304–312.

Chapter Five

The Psychology of Women: A Relational Approach

Jean Baker Miller, M.D., Irene Pierce Stiver, Ph.D.,
Judith V. Jordan, Ph.D., Janet L. Surrey, Ph.D.

Women have a profound stake, beyond the personal, of describing our reality as candidly and as fully as we can to each other. (Adrienne Rich)

In the 1970s, a number of theorists began to examine the importance of gender differences in understanding women's psychological development. These theorists fell into two groups. One group focused on modifying existing theories, working with Freudian or Jungian concepts, for example. The second group proposed that the close study of women's experience leads to new values, categories, and terms (Belenky, Clinchy, Goldberger, & Tarule, 1986; Gilligan, 1982; Jordan, Kaplan, Miller, Stiver, & Surrey, 1991; Miller, 1976).

This second group offers up a psychology of women with assumptions that differ from those that underlie prior theories. This chapter will provide an illustration of this second group's approach. (For a succinct review of the first group's approach, see Johnson and Ferguson, *Trusting Ourselves* [1990].)

Jean Baker Miller's *Toward a New Psychology of Women* (1976) offered a new perspective on the psychology of women, which challenged the basic assumptions of traditional theories. At the same time, Carol Gilligan, a developmental psychologist, was gathering empirical data that reflected fundamental gender differences in the psychological and moral development of women and men. She noted that prior research in women's development was based on sample populations consisting entirely of men. Her book, *In a Different Voice* (1982), presented the new understanding that emerges when women are included in such studies.

The writings of Miller and Gilligan quickly attracted many women in the psychological professions who were becoming more and more dissatisfied with prevailing theories. Although their work has continued to capture the attention and imagination of growing numbers of women, it has taken over a decade for "mainstream" psychiatry and psychology to begin to acknowledge, respect, and assimilate these newer approaches.

Major Concepts

A Relational Approach

In a reframed psychology of women, Miller presented three central themes in the context of a relational approach.

The Cultural Context.   The first theme recognizes the powerful impact of the cultural context on women's lives. In a patriarchal culture, where women have less power than men, women are always attempting to adapt to relationships that are unequal and essentially nonmutual. As a result, women often do not feel sufficiently empowered to have an impact on the important relationships in their lives or, by extension, on society. In such settings, the ways in which the less powerful group adapts and differs from the dominant group are apt to be unnoticed and misunderstood. This dynamic perpetuates the disempowered status of the subordinate group.

Relationships. The second theme stresses the importance of relationships as the central, organizing feature in women's development. Instead of struggling toward independence and autonomy, which is how most developmental models of growth and maturity are characterized, women are more often searching to participate in connection with others. Traditionally, these relationships have been directed toward fostering the development of others, children certainly, but also other adults. Women's relational style is increasingly apparent in other arenas. For example, in the workplace, the collaborative approach of women managers is drawing considerable attention (Godfrey, 1992; Helgesen, 1990; Rosener, 1990).

Pathways to Growth. Miller's third theme acknowledges women's relational qualities and activities as potential strengths that provide pathways to healthy growth and development. This theme stood in stark contrast to the prevailing view that interpreted many of women's most valuable qualities as defects or deficiencies. In traditional theory, women's ability to more freely express emotions and their attention to relationships often led to pathologizing them with labels like *hysterical,* or *too dependent* (Chesler, 1972; Houck, 1972). A review of the descriptions of criteria for diagnosis of "mental illness" in psychiatry's official *Diagnostic and Statistical Manual of Mental Disorders* demonstrates how biased against women these categories really are. Taking issue with this bias, Kaplan humorously suggests adding two new characterizations more applicable to male psychopathology, "The Independent Personality Disorder" and "The Restricted Personality Disorder" (Kaplan, 1983).

> Humanity has been held to a limited and distorted view of itself—from its interpretation of the most intimate of personal emotions to its grandest vision of human possibilities—precisely by virtue of its subordination of women. (Miller, 1976)

Personal Reflection
The Centrality of Relationships

To better understand the importance of relationships in your life, try this exercise.

1. Think of about five to seven important relationships or relational contexts in your life (for example: parents, grandparents, siblings, friends, teachers, groups, classes, clubs, or teams).

2. Describe how each relationship has affected your development. How have you changed through these relationships, either positively or negatively? How have you contributed to these relationships?

3. How do you think these relationships will contribute to shaping your future? Specifically, how do you predict they will shape your sense of self, self-esteem, career development, relational capacities, and your personal values?

More recently, we have begun to explore the ways in which traditional theories of development also misinterpret men's experience. Bergman (1991) notes that society pressures boys to move away from a more connected and empathic relational context into one of competition, power, and disconnection.

Gilligan noted that women's sense of self and morality revolves around issues of responsibility for, and care of, other people. It is embedded in a compelling appreciation of context. While women's orientation is toward relationships, men's tends toward separation. Gilligan also portrayed the woman's dilemma of trying to find a way to include her perspectives and desires in her relationships.

Gilligan's work has expanded over the years to explore the importance of relationships for women at many ages (Brown & Gilligan, 1992; Gilligan, Lyons, & Hammer, 1990). In particular, her research highlights the crisis girls face at adolescence. She demonstrates how hard it is for girls to maintain a strong sense of self and inner "voice," when to do so means risking disconnection in a world that does not honor their relational desires and needs.

A Paradigm Shift

Over the past 15 years, a number of theorists have been developing a relational model of women's psychology, which has grown out of the contributions of Miller, Gilligan, and others. This is a "theory in progress." Many people have been building new parts of it each year. The basic model affirms the power of connection and the terrors of disconnection for women at all ages. As a result, this approach requires a paradigm shift that has led to the reframing of key concepts in psychological development, theory, and practice.

Reframing the central ideas in the psychology of women has broader implications for understanding women and women's place in our societal institutions—especially in the workplace and the family. Women's experiences in work settings often reflect the tensions between their relational style and the focus on independence and hierarchy that dominates most work environments (Stiver, 1991a). In the family, women's relationships with their mothers is another example of a misunderstood area. Although conflict often arises in the mother-daughter relationship, mothers and daughters nevertheless exhibit strong yearnings for connection. This is an area that has not been adequately explored. Originally, this struggle was formulated in terms of Freud's female Oedipus complex. Today, the psychology of women offers a completely novel way of looking at this and other family relationships (Lewis & Herman, 1986; Stiver, 1991c).

Another misunderstood area in the psychology of women is the struggle for power. Miller (1982) observed how much women feel that they are not supposed to have power. Yet, she notes, women exert enormous power in their role of fostering the growth of others. For women, empowering others is seen as enhancing the growth of others in addition to the

Personal Reflection ————————————

—————————— Exploring Parental Relationships

Try these exercises as a means of exploring parental relationships.

Describe a recent interaction with your mother (or father) to another person. Now, describe the same interaction again, but this time imagine that your parent is in the room listening to you. Does your description change? How? What accounts for the differences?

With a partner or in small group, role play one of your parents. Tell the story of your parent's life from his or her perspective, noting in particular the major events and transitions. Reflect on your presentation. How did this affect your feelings and your understanding of your mother or father?

self. This is a counterpoint to the notion that power means "power over," controlling and directing others (Jordan, 1991a). In other words, in empowering another we seek to assist the other person in developing a sense of confidence and self-worth, which will allow him or her to move into the world with vitality and a personal sense of creativity.

When we exercise "power over" others, we seek to ensure our position of dominance and control. We are interested in attaining only our own self-defined goals, with little consideration or respect for the values and goals of others. Often this position is predicated on the use of force— social (silencing and shaming minority opinions), psychological (creating self-doubt or fear), or physical (threatening or actually using physical force or starting war).

In this relational approach to the psychology of women, every prior description of women requires reexamination. For example, the diagnosis of Dependent Personality Disorder and the more general use of the word *dependent* as pejorative and often pathological, is recast (Stiver, 1991b). Women's search for connection and the relative ease with which they express their vulnerabilities and needs, are often mislabeled as dependent—and thus, *neurotic, regressed,* and *infantile.* In recognizing the empowering value of relationships for women, dependency is seen as positive movement along the path of healthy growth and development. This reframing moves us out of a value-laden and blaming mode into an empowering mode. The blaming mode originates in over-valuing independence and self-sufficiency and devaluing relationships, which are more collaborative and mutually empowering.

When you cease to make a contribution, you begin to die. (Eleanor Roosevelt)

Model of Self

This reexamination, an essential task in its own right, serves to reconceptualize notions of the self, not just in women but in all people. Traditional theories of development have emphasized the growth of an autonomous self with firm boundaries, separated out from context and moving toward greater use of abstract logic and self-sufficiency. Miller (1976), Gilligan (1982), and Jordan et al. (1991) have posited a more contextual, relational paradigm for the study of what has traditionally been called *self-experience*. Rather than stress a perspective based largely on the "bounded" and contained self, these approaches emphasize the importance of the connected and relationally emergent nature of human experience. The movement of relating, of mutual initiative and responsiveness, is the ongoing, centrally organizing dynamic in women's lives. This shift in paradigm also means that we no longer look at the self as the primary focus of interest and study. Instead, we increasingly focus on relational development: people engaged in relationships (Jordan, 1989).

Mutual empathy and mutual empowerment are at the core of growth-enhancing relationships. Empathy involves a motivational component (the desire to know the other), a perceptual component (the ability to perceive verbal and nonverbal signals), an affective component (the capacity to resonate with another person's feelings), and a cognitive component (the ability to make sense of this joining resonance).

Empathy always involves a movement toward understanding; it is never a perfect matching, or "mirroring," of another person's experience. Mutuality is another characteristic of "good" connection; it involves openness to change and growth in both people. Each person is respectful of the other's experience (Jordan, 1986). It is the movement of relationship, not just the development of self, that provides the focus for our interest.

Other theorists have built upon these insights. For example, they have found a relational approach helpful in understanding broader cultural contexts. The reframing of the concept of dependency has suggested an explanation of certain characteristics of the Japanese culture (Kobayashi, 1989). Turner (1987) explored the ways in which the relational approach reflects and validates African-American women's experience. It also illuminates some of the specifics of lesbian development. For example, the relational model offers a new perspective on the concept of *fusion* when applied to lesbian women as well as other issues in lesbians' lives. The significant characteristics of fusion are seen as intense intimacy, a lack of separation, and overidentification (Mencher, 1990).

Connections

The experience of connection and disconnection are the central issues in personality development. It is necessary to describe further what these terms really mean.

Extending the concept of empathy is basic to this new understanding that the human connection is fundamental to psychological development. In the late 1970s, Jordan, Kaplan, and Surrey (1982) began to elaborate on the concept of empathy, describing it as a complex cognitive-affective ability rather than the mysterious, intuitive, and even regressive experience that others have suggested. Jordan later developed its implications for psychological development along with an elaboration of the concept of mutuality (1986). Mutual empathy experientially alters the sense of a separate self in profound ways. In true empathic interaction, each person is mutually engaged in affecting and being affected, knowing and being known, assisting each other in coming more fully into clarity and relatedness. Working along similar lines, Surrey (1991b) suggested that the underlying processes of psychological development are mutual engagement, mutual empathy, and mutual empowerment. The goal of psychological development is the participation in mutually empathic and mutually empowering relationships rather than the separation from others.

This vignette of two women interacting serves to illustrate the powerful process and consequences of mutual empathy and mutual empowerment.

> Ann has just heard from her friend Emily that Emily may have a serious illness. Ann is telling another friend, Beth, about this. Tears are in Ann's eyes and her voice sounds sad and fearful. Beth says, "Oh, how sad." Ann then adds, "Yes, sad, but I have this other awful feeling—like fear. Like I'm scared—as if it could happen to me." Beth replies, "Me, too. It is frightening to hear this. Maybe we all feel as if it's happening to us when we hear things like this."

As they continue, both Ann and Beth feel more in touch with what they suspect Emily may be feeling. They come to a deep appreciation for Emily's feelings and also will do whatever is possible for and with Emily.

This example may sound ordinary, as if many people do it all the time. Many people *do* do it all the time, especially women, but it is not ordinary in terms of its value. Furthermore, the valuable actions Ann and Beth demonstrate are often unrecognized. We believe these kinds of interactions contain the key features that make for psychological growth and development in children and adults.

Dynamics

Key Features in Psychological Growth and Development

First, the *process* of psychological growth requires that the participants respond empathically to each other. This is mutual empathy. Because each feels this empathic response, each is able to "take off" from this empathic base and add further thoughts and feelings as they arise. These additions create the interplay, the flow. This mutually empathic interplay is created by both people and builds new psychological experience, that is, growth, for both.

The result of this process is that both people develop psychologically in at least five important ways (Miller, 1986):

1. Both feel a connection with each other that gives them a sense of increased *zest*, or energy. This is familiar to those who know

the feeling of a sense of connection to another person. Its opposite is also familiar, the *down* sort of feeling that follows when one has been unable to connect with another person.

2. Both are active in the immediate relationship, and they feel more empowered to act beyond the relationship.

3. Each person has a bit more self-knowledge as well as knowledge of the other person; more is learned about feelings and thoughts and how they are for each person.

4. Because these processes have occurred, both people feel a greater sense of self-worth.

5. Both desire more connection beyond this one as a result.

It is important to note that in mutual interactions it is not a question of giving or getting, of helping or being helped, or of being dependent or depended upon. It is a question of whether both people *participate,* both people grow, and whether both therefore want more of the same.

Mutual empathy in the process of psychological growth can be seen in relational contexts, particularly with women. They become energized, empowered, feel greater self-worth, and greater clarity of their feeling-thoughts. This process also provides a baseline against which one can identify those circumstances and nonrelational contexts that lead to disconnections and thus to pathological development.

Disconnections

Because women rely so heavily on relationships in the process of psychological growth, disconnections can lead to especially serious consequences in their lives. Disconnections occur whenever a child or adult is prevented from participating in a mutually responsive and mutually enhancing relationship. Clearly, these disconnections exist when a child or an adult suffers major mistreatment, such as sexual and/or physical abuse or when the surrounding relational context is grossly unresponsive. However, many disconnections occur all through childhood and adult life. Most do not lead to serious trouble, especially if there are sufficient empowering connections. The key ingredients that allow for growth when there is a threat of disconnection are (1) the possibility that the child or adult can take action within the relationship to represent her experience, and (2) that the others in the relationship can respond in a way that leads back toward a reconnection (Miller, 1988).

To take a familiar example, suppose a 9-month-old infant is playing and suddenly, for no apparent reason, starts to scream and cry. The parents don't deal with this well initially and respond with angry rebukes. The infant may now feel startled and afraid, in addition to the original distress. However, if the infant can turn again to the parents and, in this second effort, find that they are more responsive to this expression of distress, the infant will feel more effective in communicating with them.

Indeed, the infant has played a part in turning the interaction around and so have the parents. Several infant researchers have documented this ability, in infants as young as 3 months (Gianino & Tronick, 1985; Stern, 1985).

A more serious disconnection can be seen in a variation on the previous vignette involving Emily, Ann, and Beth. Substitute Tom, Ann's husband, for her friend Beth. Tom's response to Ann's tearful sadness and fearful voice is, "Well, it's a terrible thing. In the end, she'll have to do the best she can. She should get a second opinion. Have you called her back yet? Did you call my sister Helen about the birthday party she's arranging for my mother for next week?"

One episode like this does not, however, lead to psychopathology, but this kind of disconnection can lead to serious immediate and long-term consequences if it continues over time without a change in direction. Using this example, assume for a moment that this topic did arouse sadness and fear in Tom. The difference, then, between Tom's and Ann's reactions, is that Tom has not learned how to experience these feelings in connection with others. In fact, he becomes angry if anyone threatens to evoke these feelings in him. Ann may sense some of Tom's feelings but, in contrast to her interaction with Beth, the feelings and thoughts cannot be *between them* or *with both of them*. Instead, it begins to feel as if the emotions are all hers.

In addition, Ann now feels angry. First, she picks up Tom's anger but then she also becomes angry at his response. The anger becomes tied to and confused with her other feelings. Ann is now in greater distress. Precisely because she feels in more distress, her basic reaction is to want even more to connect with the other person. Suppose, again for the sake of example, she tries to express some of this to Tom. In response, he becomes only more angry and attacking and/or withdrawn. Now, Ann's confused feelings and their intensity increase greatly.

Here, Ann has been unable to have an impact, to alter the course of the interaction, and the person in her relational context has been unresponsive to her attempts to represent her experience. She believes her feelings-thoughts helped to create a better connection that would, in turn, lead to more action and empowerment. Instead, she begins to believe that something is deeply wrong with her important feelings because they lead to such trouble. Ann feels the problem is in her.

In contrast to the good things that flow from mutually empowering connections, Ann, in this instance, will feel less energetic (more depleted), less self-worth, less clear about her feelings-thoughts, less able to take action, and less motivated to seek other connections. Most important, she feels that her actions, feelings, and thoughts lead to less connection with the important other person in her life; she not only feels less connection, but a confusing sense of disconnection and isolation.

Clinical experience suggests that perhaps one of the most terrifying human experiences is psychological isolation. This is not isolation just in the sense of loneliness. It is the feeling of being locked out of the possibili-

I understand the rising up of women in this century to be the human race's response to the threat of its own self-annihilation and the destruction of the planet. (Sally Miller Gearheardt)

ty of human connection. This feeling of desperate isolation is usually accompanied by the feeling that people, themselves, are the reason for the exclusion. It is because of who they are. They feel helpless, powerless, unable to act to better the situation. People will go through amazing psychological maneuvers to escape this combination of condemned isolation and powerlessness.

Personal Reflection —————————————
————————————— Experience of Connection and Disconnection

Think about an experience, a moment, or a time in your life when you felt a sense of connection in an important relationship. Also, think about a time when you felt a sense of disconnection in a relationship. In each kind of relationship:

1. What led up to this?

2. What were your feelings?

3. What was the outcome?

4. How did this change you or the relationship?

Psychological Consequences of Repeated Disconnections

In the face of the terror of condemned isolation and powerlessness, people in Ann's position try even harder to make connections with the other individuals in their lives. This attempt leads to the next set of consequences, consequences that often proceed over many years.

If a woman cannot find ways to have an impact on available relationships, she will take the only possible step. She will attempt to change the only person possible to change, herself. Specifically, she tries to alter her internal image of herself and others as well as her view of the connections between herself and others. She must attempt this alteration alone, since the available relationships preclude doing it in interaction with others.

In essence, the child or adult tries to construct some kind of image of herself and others that will allow her to enter into relationships with the people available. In order to twist herself into a person acceptable in "unaccepting" relationships, she will have to move away from and redefine a large part of her experience—those parts of her experience that she believes are not allowed.

We can think of this process occurring in a child within a family. It occurs with varying degrees of complexity depending on the child's age. In settings that are consistently nonresponsive and that violate the child's experience, the child learns that the only way to connect to the significant figures in her life is to become what she thinks others want her to be. For example, she may learn that only a bad person has feelings such as sadness, fear, and the like. Therefore, she tries to become a person who never has such feelings. When events occur that would likely cause any of the now unacceptable emotions, she feels greatly upset; she cannot be certain what she is experiencing, except that she should not be feeling whatever it is she is feeling.

While there is confusion about many feelings, certain feelings become especially prominent over time. One is anxiety. A child growing up in anxiety-provoking settings becomes increasingly anxious about other people. Any person is likely to evoke some of the "forbidden" thoughts and feelings that threaten narrowly constructed images of herself and others. One prominent feeling that threatens these constructed images is anger. No person can withstand violations of her own experience and long-term threats to connection without eventually feeling intense anger.

Most important, this process leads to a major paradox. In order to try to connect in the only relationships available, the child will be keeping more and more of her authentic self out of her relationships. She will be trying to maintain relationships at the price of failing to represent her own experience in them. In this process, she is moving further and further away from connection with her own experience—and she is losing the main source of psychological growth: interactions within relationships. The parts of herself that she has excluded are unable to change from experience. That is, her continuous construction of a sense of herself and of others cannot benefit from the interchange provided by relationships—precisely the source of knowledge and clarity needed for the development of an increasingly accurate image of self and others. She is constructing inner images of relational possibilities—and impossibilities—with less and less actual learning from action within relationships. It is striking to note that in studying girls moving into adolescence Gilligan (Brown & Gilligan, 1992) described a very similar paradox.

This process of repeated disconnections sometimes (though not always) leads to anxious depressive immobilization and complete disconnection (Hamilton & Jensvold, 1992). This immobilizing path probably exists for almost all women in patriarchal societies to some degree. It underlies many of women's psychological troubles including phobias, addictions, eating disorders, depression, dissociative states, and paranoid ideas as well as many of the problems labeled as personality disorders (Brown, 1992). In each of these situations, the woman elaborates specific images of herself and others and specific forms of action that come to seem the only possible forms of action within the framework of the relational images she has constructed.

Implications for Personality Development

We have found that framing psychological development and problems in terms of this central paradox helps us to understand both sexes better, and also helps us understand how psychological troubles arise. Most important, it helps us to find ways to work that are clarifying and empowering. That is, *psychological problems represent the mechanisms people construct that keep them out of connection while they simultaneously are seeking connection.*

Stiver (1990a) has shown how this paradox develops in families labeled *dysfunctional* (for example, alcoholic, incestuous, and Holocaust-survivor families). Several theorists have elucidated other problems with this paradox in mind. Surrey (1984), Steiner-Adair (1991), and Mirkin (1990) have reported on adolescents' development of eating disorders and have illustrated how this connection-disconnection construct unfolds in individual and family therapy. In the same way, Jack (1991), Kaplan (1984), and Stiver and Miller (1988) have described a relational understanding in the treatment of depression. Saunders and Arnold (1990) have recast the major characteristics and treatment of women who are diagnosed with borderline personality disorders. They have illustrated ways of working that differ from the former pejorative and destructive treatment methods.

Kilbourne and Surrey (1991) and Gleason (1992) have discussed the origins, prevention, and recovery from addictions using this more relational approach. They also offered an understanding of the currently popular *codependency* formulation in terms of a lack of mutuality in women's available relationships rather than viewing women as pathological who struggle to make connections when mutuality is not possible. Kaplan and Klein (1990) have examined women's suicide and suicide attempts as they differ from men's and have suggested explanations for these findings in the differing relational experiences of women and men.

Beyond specific clinical formulations, a relational model alters numerous overarching concepts, such as conflict, anger, and shame. Conflict and anger are seen as necessary features occurring in the movement of all relationships (Jordan, 1990; Miller & Surrey, 1989). Jordan (1989) describes shame as the feeling of being excluded from connection and the sense of *loss of empathic possibility*. All of these authors illustrate how a relational approach leads to a reframing of central concepts in women's therapy (Miller & Stiver, 1991).

Relational Therapy

To understand how this paradox of connection-disconnection operates, we can examine the conditions in families that impede rather than foster growth-enhancing connections.

There are many kinds of family systems that have been characterized as *dysfunctional,* including alcoholic, incestuous, and Holocaust-survivor families. In these families, secrecy, inaccessibility to parents, and parentification of children contribute to chronic and sustained disconnections among family members. Children in these families develop a range of strategies, including emotional disengagement, role-playing, and replication, to find ways to make connections, while keeping important parts of

Personal Reflection ————————————

————————————— A Relational Inventory

Take a relational inventory by making a special appointment with a friend or lover to discuss the qualities of your relationship.

Thinking of particular examples in your relationship, discuss the following relational concepts described in this chapter: empathy, authenticity, mutual empathy, mutual empowerment, connection, disconnection, reconnection, anger, conflict, isolation.

themselves out of connection. A sensitivity to these family contexts can help therapists attend empathically to the ways in which children learn to stay disconnected in the face of their longing for connection (Stiver, 1990b).

For example, a woman who grew up in an alcoholic home recalls how, as a child, she was aware that her father drank too much and that he would upset her mother and frighten her and her siblings. When she tried to tell her father that he shouldn't drink so much, he would become enraged with her. He would insist that his drinking was not a problem and that she was a troublemaker. Her mother was also angry at her for upsetting her father. She learned very early on to keep silent about what she saw, which lead her to begin doubting her own experience. While growing up, she became very diplomatic in her dealings with others. She was careful to avoid offending anyone or causing trouble. This early memory of confronting her father about his alcoholism and the family's response were pivotal to an understanding in therapy of her deep sense of isolation despite her apparently well-developed social skills.

This paradox of connection-disconnection becomes the central framework for guiding the therapist. The therapist cues her listening, her understanding of the material that emerges, and her emotional attunement in the context of how connected or disconnected both the therapist and patient are.

We are all familiar with some of the ways our patients move out of connection—for example, the person who talks most of the session leaving no room for any form of exchange, or the person who appears very compliant and yet nothing moves in the process. But we had not previously thought of everything that happens in therapy as reflections of movement toward or away from connection.

We are making the bold statement, then, that we see *all* of the problems that emerge in therapy to be, on one level or another, reflections of this central paradox. This focus on connection-disconnection as the central guide in therapy can develop only in a setting of safety and mutuality. Such a setting becomes defined by the therapist's empathic participation in the relationship. It is the therapist's authenticity and presence, rather

Without a rigorous and consistent evaluation of what kind of a future we wish to create, and a scrupulous examination of the expressions of power we choose to incorporate into all our relationships, including our most private ones, we are not progressing, but merely recasting our own characters in the same old weary drama. (Audre Lourde)

Feminism must be on the cutting edge of real social change if it is to survive as a movement in any particular country. (Audre Lourde)

than the *neutral,* nonengaged stance advocated by Freudians and other psychoanalysts, that makes an enlarged sense of connection possible. Through this relationship, therapist and patient are empowered to grow and change.

This emphasis on building empowering connections has led to new ways to conceptualize group therapy (Fedele & Harrington, 1990). It has also become the basis for the creation of mental health services. An example is women's inpatient psychiatric and alcoholism programs (Fedele & Miller, 1988).

Evaluation

We believe that the emphasis on connection and disconnection in a relational approach speaks to the core of the human condition, a core that has remained out of focus in traditional psychodynamic approaches. Traditional theories *have* spoken about relationships. However, the core of these theories remains obscure because they emerge from an underlying preoccupation with individual gratification and power disguised by terms like *separation* and *individuation.* Such a preoccupation could arise only from the thinking of a dominant group and inevitably distorts the *total* human condition. Once we examine more accurately the lives of all people, we find ourselves moving away from this preoccupation and toward a recognition of the need for human connection and the sources and consequences of disconnection.

The Theory Firsthand: Excerpt from *Women's Growth in Connection*

The following excerpt taken from *Women's Growth in Connection*[1] by Jordan, Kaplan, Miller, Stiver, and Surrey illustrates how the maintenance of distance between patient and therapist is a masculine model that does not work well.

> At first blush the connection between caring and psychotherapy seems obvious, and yet for many of us trained in the traditional model of therapy, caring about one's patients often is seen as something that may get in the way of effective treatment. The maintenance of distance between therapist and patient as well as general prohibitions against the expression of caring can be attributed to two major assumptions underlying this traditional model. The first assumption is tied to a broader model of treatment in which the treatment of the

[1]From "The Meaning of Care: Reframing Treatment Models" (pp. 250, 251, 255–257, 266, 267) by I. P. Stiver in *Women's Growth in Connection* by J. V. Jordan, A. G. Kaplan, J. B. Miller, I. P. Stiver, and J. L. Surrey. New York: Guilford Press. Copyright 1991 by Guilford Press. Reprinted by permission.

patient requires that the treater be objective, nonemotional, and relatively impersonal in order to be most helpful to the patient. . . .

The second assumption is that growth and change can occur only if the therapist does not gratify the patient. The experience of frustration and learning how to tolerate and respond to deprivations in therapy are seen as valuable and therapeutic. . . .

. . . I believe that this model is essentially a masculine model, since it reflects a style much more congenial and familiar to men than to women, that is, objective, nonemotional, impersonal attitudes, and so forth. For precisely this reason, this model does not seem to work very well with women, and perhaps not with some men either. The need to erect barriers to create distance from patients may also then reflect countertransference reactions among male therapists toward their female patients, who are different from them in important ways. . . .

. . . Such terms as *manipulative, seductive, controlling, needy, devouring, frigid, castrating, masochistic* and *hysterical* have been used pervasively, primarily to describe female patients, with the clear implications that such patients are hard to tolerate, and almost impossible to treat and that if one does not manage them carefully one will be taken over, fused with, devoured, and so forth. Even when the perception of the patient is more benign, the labels of "dependent," "seductive," and so forth are at best patronizing. The end result of such labeling is that the patient is not understood and not cared about.

Let me share with you a brief clinical example. I was asked to consult about a young woman who had become anxious and depressed enough to require rehospitalization after a period of fairly good adjustment. She is a young, attractive 19-year-old honor student at an Ivy League college, and is highly intelligent, very sensitive, and articulate. She talked readily to me on several occasions about the anguish she often experienced in a world that felt unreal to her. When I approached one of the administrative psychiatrists to discuss the case, he told me immediately that she was "very manipulative" and was going to be "a handful." I was a bit surprised, since she was always well mannered and quite cultivated with me and I asked him what he meant. "Oh, when we do rounds, if you look around at the group talking to her, everyone looks tense and uncomfortable." As I mused about this curious definition of "manipulative," I thought about what her major concerns were—she was always afraid that her ability to put up a good facade, to be so well socialized and so successful at academic pursuits, and so forth, would hide what she called her "true self," the self that was so terrified, so uncertain, and so confused. Her concern was that she would be misunderstood. I was often very moved in her presence by her unusual capacity to communicate the power of her frustration and pain. I could imagine her "performing" at rounds, while at the same time being vigilant about how others would respond to her, and feeling helpless and even desperate if they did not see what was underneath the facade. I also know that once she felt the other person did not understand her, she gave up trying, with a deep sense of disappointment and underlying rage. That her anxiety and anger at being misunderstood were communicated to those conducting rounds must have contributed to feelings of discomfort among them; I also believe they needed to ward off the intensity of her underlying feelings. The labeling of her as manipulative also created a climate that kept her at a distance and cut off the possibility of understanding her or of engaging with her in a meaningful way.

Male patients certainly may be misunderstood, but I am focusing here on the specific kinds of language that affect women. I would like to suggest that when the language is pejorative and serves to maintain distance between the therapist and the patient, women are more likely to be victimized in the process than are men. We know that the greater number of patients in therapy are women and, among therapists, men represent a significantly higher proportion than women. But it is not even that simple. Women who enter this profession have largely been taught by men (and treated by men) and in order to survive in their careers have often needed to adapt to the standards and values that have been associated with their professions; thus most therapists, male or female, may be very much influenced by those standards classifying mental health and illness that reflect the masculine model of therapy described above. . . .

It is most important to note that styles of caring in therapy do not seem linked in a simple one-to-one fashion with sex of the therapist. That is, some women therapists have in a sense overconformed with the distancing, "masculine model" of therapy as a result of trying to survive, to be successful and adept in this field. On the other hand, I have known "caring" male therapists who are able to be flexible and responsive to both their male and female patients in a genuine, empathic, and nonauthoritarian fashion. We are all aware that selective factors operate that make it more likely that such men, rather than, if you will, hypermasculine, unemotional men, will enter this field. However, what I have also noticed is that often these men are apt to apologize for or hide this style lest they be criticized and devalued by their male colleagues.

Let me close with an example that nicely illustrates this curious dilemma. A woman psychiatrist told me about her termination with a female patient in her last year of training. She was leaving the clinic setting and moving to another city. Because she felt connected to this patient and sad about terminating, when the patient asked where she was going and if she could contact her, she told her, and added that she would be glad to hear from her. When she reported this to her supervisor, a male psychoanalyst, he told her she had been very seductive, had behaved inappropriately and was too involved with her patient. She felt bad and accepted his criticism. She was also terminating her own therapy with a senior male analyst. When asked if she could see him again when she visited Boston he said, "Certainly, I would love to hear from you." She felt vindicated and said, "What goes on behind closed doors! There are all these analysts secretly acting like human beings but nobody is supposed to know it!" I do believe that good caring treatment does go on behind closed doors, but it is time to take it out of the closet. Let us give legitimacy and value to a model of therapy that takes into account the unique aspects of female experience and development and that also allows a more egalitarian "caring about" our patients to become a matter of prime importance.

Annotated Bibliography

Belenky, M., Clinchy, B., Goldberger, N., & Tarule, J. (1986). *Women's ways of knowing.* New York: Basic Books. This book explores the basic patterns of knowing and interacting with the world that characterize women's experience. Based on interviews with one hundred women, the book also delineates the ways in which women are silenced by male standards of knowing and learning.

Brown, L. M., & Gilligan, C. (1992). *Meeting at the crossroads: Women, psychology and girls' development.* Cambridge, MA: Harvard University Press. Delineated are the dilemmas faced by adolescent girls when they begin to feel that they must keep their true selves out of relationships in order to participate in relationships. Also described is the idea that the authenticity and vitality available to young girls in relationships is often lost as girls attempt to meet standards of femininity that silence their real knowledge of the world of relationships.

Gilligan, C. (1982). *In a different voice.* Cambridge, MA: Harvard University Press. Already a classic in the rethinking of the psychology of women, this book begins by reexamining the differing paths of moral development in girls and boys. It explores the differences between a morality of justice and a morality of care. It is a must for anyone interested in new understandings of women's development.

Jordan, J. V., Kaplan, A. G., Miller, J. B., Stiver, I. P., & Surrey, J. L. (1991). *Women's growth in connection.* New York: Guilford Press. A collection of the early papers out of the Stone Center at Wellesley College. This book introduces the reader to some of the core concepts of a relational model of development: mutuality, empathy, mutual empowerment, the sense of self in women, and dependency.

Miller, J. B. (1976). *Toward a new psychology of women.* Boston, MA: Beacon Press. A ground-breaking work that has often been described as revolutionary, this book forms the core of the Stone Center's approach to understanding women. It addresses the societal forces that have shaped women's development and notes in particular the considerable, although often devalued, strengths that women bring to relationships and the culture. Essential reading for anyone who wishes to understand women and the cultural dynamics shaping women's lives.

Stone Center Working Paper Series (1982–1992). *Stone Center works in progress* (Nos. 1–59). (Available from Stone Center, Wellesley College, Wellesley, MA 02181-8268). A wide-ranging series of papers including issues about power, courage, lesbian perspectives, black women's development, and more. Considered by many to be at the cutting edge of new approaches to the psychology of women.

References

Belenky, M., Clinchy, B., Goldberger, N., & Tarule, J. (1986). *Women's ways of knowing.* New York: Basic Books.

Bergman, S. (1991). Men's psychological development: A relational perspective. *Work in progress* (No. 48). Wellesley, MA: Stone Center Working Paper Series.

Brown, L. M., & Gilligan, C. (1992). *Meeting at the crossroads: Women, psychology and girls' development.* Cambridge, MA: Harvard University Press.

Brown, L. S. (1992). A feminist critique of the personality disorders. In L. S. Brown & M. Ballou (Eds.), *Personality and psychopathology: Feminist reappraisals.* New York: Guilford Press.

Chesler, P. (1972). *Women and madness.* New York: Doubleday.

Fedele, N., & Harrington, B. (1990). Women's groups: How connections heal. *Work in progress* (No. 47). Wellesley, MA: Stone Center Working Paper Series.

Fedele, N., & Miller, J. B. (1988). Putting theory into practice: Creating mental health programs for women. *Work in progress* (No. 32). Wellesley, MA: Stone Center Working Paper Series.

Gianino, A., & Tronick, E. (1985). The mutual regulation model: The infant's self and interactive regulation and coping defensive capacities. In P. Field, P. McCabe, & N. Schneiderman (Eds.), *Stress and coping.* Hillsdale, NJ: Lawrence Erlbaum.

Gilligan, C. (1982). *In a different voice.* Cambridge, MA: Harvard University Press.

Gilligan, C., Lyons, N., & Hammer, T. J. (Eds.). (1990). *Making connections.* Cambridge, MA: Harvard University Press.

Gleason, N. (1992). *Towards a model for preventing alcohol abuse by college women: A relational perspective.* Washington, DC: U.S. Dept. of Education (Fund for the Improvement of Post Secondary Education).

Godfrey, J. (1992). *In our wildest dreams.* New York: HarperCollins.

Hamilton, J. A., & Jensvold, M. (1992). Personality, psychopathology and depression in women. In L. S. Brown & M. Ballou (Eds.), *Personality and psychopathology: Feminist reappraisals* (pp. 116–143). New York: Guilford Press.

Helgesen, S. (1990). *The female advantage: Women's way of leadership.* New York: Doubleday.

Houck, J. H. (1972). The intractable female patient. *American Journal of Psychiatry, 129,* 27–31.

Jack, D. J. (1991). *Silencing the self: Women and depression.* Cambridge, MA: Harvard University Press.

Johnson, K., & Ferguson, T. (1990). *Trusting ourselves: The sourcebook on psychology of women.* New York: The Atlantic Monthly Press.

Jordan, J. V. (1984). Empathy and self boundaries. In J. V. Jordan, A. G. Kaplan, J. B. Miller, I. P. Stiver, & J. L. Surrey, *Women's growth in connection* (pp. 67–80). New York: Guilford Press (1991).

———. (1986). The meaning of mutuality. In J. V. Jordan, A. G. Kaplan, J. B. Miller, I. P. Stiver, & J. L. Surrey, *Women's growth in connection* (pp. 81–86). New York: Guilford Press (1991).

———. (1989). Relational development: Therapeutic implications of empathy and shame. *Work in progress* (No. 39). Wellesley, MA: Stone Center Working Paper Series.

———. (1990). Courage in connection: Conflict, compassion, creativity. *Work in progress* (No. 45). Wellesley, MA: Stone Center Working Paper Series.

———. (1991a). The movement of mutuality and power. *Work in progress* (No. 53). Wellesley, MA: Stone Center Working Paper Series.

———. (1991b). The relational self: A new perspective for understanding women's development. In J. Strauss & G. Goethals (Eds.), *The self: Interdisciplinary approaches.* New York: Springer Verlag.

Jordan, J. V., Kaplan, A. G., Miller, J. B., Stiver, I. P., & Surrey, J. L. (1991). *Women's growth in connection.* New York: Guilford Press.

Jordan, J. V., Kaplan, A. G., & Surrey, J. L. (1982). Women and empathy. *Work in progress* (No. 2). Wellesley, MA: Stone Center Working Paper Series.

Kaplan, A. G. (1984). The "self-in-relation": Implications for depression in women. *Work in progress* (No. 14). Wellesley College, MA: Stone Center Working Paper Series.

Kaplan, A., & Klein, R. (1990). Women and suicide: The cry for connection. *Work in progress* (No. 46). Wellesley, MA: Stone Center Working Paper Series.

Kaplan, M. (1983). A woman's view of DSM III. *American Psychologist, 38,* 786–792.

Kilbourne, J., & Surrey, J. (1991). Women, addiction, and codependency. *Colloquium Presentation*. Stone Center, Wellesley College.

Kobayashi, J. S. (1989). Depathologizing dependency: Two perspectives. *Psychiatric Annals, 19,* 653–658.

Lewis, H. B., & Herman, J. L. (1986). Anger in the mother-daughter relationship. In T. Bernay & D. W. Cantor (Eds.), *The psychology of today's woman: New psychoanalytic visions* (pp. 139–163). Hillside, NJ: Lawrence Erlbaum.

Mencher, J. (1990). Intimacy in lesbian relationships: A critical re-examination of fusion. *Work in progress* (No. 42). Wellesley, MA: Stone Center Working Paper Series.

Miller, J. B. (1976). *Toward a new psychology of women*. Boston, MA: Beacon Press.

———. (1982). Women and power. In J. V. Jordan, A. G. Kaplan, J. B. Miller, I. P. Stiver, & J. L. Surrey, *Women's growth in connection* (pp. 197–205). New York: Guilford Press (1991).

———. (1986). What do we mean by relationships? *Work in progress* (No. 22). Wellesley, MA: Stone Center Working Paper Series.

———. (1988). Connections, disconnections and violations. *Work in progress* (No. 33). Wellesley, MA: Stone Center Working Paper Series.

Miller, J. B., & Stiver, I. P. (1991). A relational reframing of therapy. *Work in progress* (No. 52). Wellesley, MA: Stone Center Working Paper Series.

Miller, J. B., & Surrey, J. L. (1989). Revisioning women's anger: The personal and the global. *Work in progress* (No. 43). Wellesley, MA: Stone Center Working Paper Series.

Mirkin, M. (1990). Eating disorders: A feminist structural family therapy perspective. In M. Mirkin (Ed.), *The social and political contexts in family therapy*. Boston, MA: Allyn & Bacon.

Rosener, J. (1990). Ways women lead. *Harvard Business Review, 90,* 119–125.

Saunders, E. A., & Arnold, F. (1990). Borderline personality disorder and childhood abuse: Revisions in clinical thinking and treatment approach. *Work in progress* (No. 51). Wellesley, MA: Stone Center Working Paper Series.

Steiner-Adair, C. (1991). New maps of development, new models of therapy: The psychology of women and treatment of eating disorders. In C. Johnson (Ed.), *Psychodynamic treatment of anorexia nervosa and bulimia*. New York: Guilford Press.

Stern, D. (1985). *The interpersonal world of the infant*. New York: Basic Books.

Stiver, I. P. (1990a). Dysfunctional families and wounded relationships, Part I. *Work in progress* (No. 41). Wellesley, MA: Stone Center Working Paper Series.

———. (1990b). Dysfunctional families and wounded relationships, Part II. *Work in progress* (No. 44). Wellesley, MA: Stone Center Working Paper Series.

————. (1991a). Work inhibitions in women: Clinical considerations. In J. V. Jordan, A. G. Kaplan, J. B. Miller, I. P. Stiver, & J. L. Surrey, *Women's growth in connection* (pp. 223–236). New York: Guilford Press.

————. (1991b). The meanings of "dependency" in female-male relationships. In J. V. Jordan, A. G. Kaplan, J. B. Miller, I. P. Stiver, & J. L. Surrey, *Women's growth in connection* (pp. 143–161). New York: Guilford Press.

————. (1991c). Beyond the oedipus complex: Mothers and daughters. In J. V. Jordan, A. G. Kaplan, J. B. Miller, I. P. Stiver, & J. L. Surrey, *Women's growth in connection* (pp. 97–121). New York: Guilford Press.

Stiver, I. P., & Miller, J. B. (1988). From depression to sadness in the psychotherapy of women. *Work in progress* (No. 36). Wellesley, MA: Stone Center Working Paper Series.

Surrey, J. L. (1991a). Eating patterns as a reflection of women's development. In J. V. Jordan, A. G. Kaplan, J. B. Miller, I. P. Stiver, & J. L. Surrey, *Women's growth in connection* (pp. 237–249). New York: Guilford Press.

————. (1991b). The "self-in-relation": A theory of women's development. In J. V. Jordan, A. G. Kaplan, J. B. Miller, I. P. Stiver, & J. L. Surrey, *Women's growth in connection* (pp. 51–66). New York: Guilford Press.

Turner, C. (1987). Clinical applications of the Stone Center theoretical approach to minority women. *Work in progress* (No. 28). Wellesley, MA: Stone Center Working Paper Series.

Chapter Six

Erik Erikson and the Life Cycle

Erik Erikson is the most widely read and influential post-Freudian theorist, both in psychology and in the popular press. His books have sold hundreds of thousands of copies, and, in 1970, Erikson was featured on the covers of both *Newsweek* and *The New York Times Magazine*. His book on Mohandas Gandhi (1969) was awarded the Pulitzer Prize and the National Book Award.

Erik Erikson has extended the insights of psychoanalysis through cross-cultural studies of child rearing, psychological biographies of great men and women, and interfacing psychological and social dynamics. Erikson's life-span theory of ego development has had enormous influence within psychology and related fields. He is also the founder of modern psychohistory.

Erikson's work is solidly based on psychoanalytic theory; no one else since Freud has done as much to elaborate on and apply the principles of psychoanalysis to new fields and to the problems of today's world. In the process, Erikson developed an original theory rooted in psychoanalytic understanding, yet significantly different in scope, concept, and emphasis. He has been called a "nondogmatic, emancipated Freudian." Erikson's concepts of identity and identity crisis have had major professional influence throughout the social sciences. They have also become household words.

Erikson is a brilliant, insightful theorist and an elegant writer. At the core of his work is his theory of the human life cycle, a model that integrates human growth and development from birth to old age. He made three major contributions to the study of personality: (1) that along with Freud's psychosexual developmental stages a person simultaneously goes through psychosocial and ego-development stages, (2) that personality development continues throughout life, and (3) that each stage of development can have both positive and negative outcomes.

Personal History

Erikson has unusual, even obscure, roots. He was born on June 15, 1902. His mother left Denmark for Germany while pregnant, and remarried a Jewish physician, named Dr. Homburger. Erikson considered himself German in spite of his Danish parentage, yet his German classmates rejected him because he was Jewish. At the same time, his Jewish friends called him the *goy* (the non-Jew) because of his blonde, Aryan appearance.

Erikson grew up as Erik Homburger and first published under that name. Later, he wrote under the name Erik Homburger Erikson, and eventually settled on Erik Erikson (literally, Erik, son of Erik). A Dane by parentage and a German by upbringing, he later became an American by choice.

Erikson's formal academic education lasted until he was 18, when he graduated from a classical *gymnasium*. There, he had studied Latin, Greek, German literature, and ancient history. He was not a particularly devoted student. After graduation, Erik began traveling through Europe. Along with many of his generation, Erik was trying to "find himself." After a year of travel, he returned home and enrolled in art school. He studied art in Munich, then went to live in Florence. The artist's life was good for a young man as yet unwilling to settle down; it gave him great latitude and time for self-exploration.

Erikson returned home at the age of 25, intending to settle down and teach art. He was invited to Vienna to teach at a new school for the children of families that had come to Vienna for psychoanalysis. He taught art, history, and various other subjects. Erikson was given a free hand to create an ideal educational program.

The psychoanalytic community was much less formal in the 1920s. Analysts, patients, and their families and friends attended picnics and other social events together. At these affairs, Erikson became acquainted with Anna Freud and other prominent psychoanalysts. Erikson was screened informally and judged to be a suitable candidate for analytic training. In 1927, Erikson began daily analysis with Anna Freud in the house she shared with her father.

To be surprised belongs to the discipline of a clinician. (Erikson, 1963, p. 100)

When he expressed doubts about the possibility of an artist becoming a psychoanalyst, Anna Freud replied that psychoanalysis would need people who help others *see*. Much of Erikson's long and rich career can be viewed as an attempt to do just that: drawing exquisite word pictures of new concepts and perspectives.

Erikson also studied the Montessori system and was one of only two men who graduated from the Montessori Teachers' Association at that time. His interest in play therapy and child analysis came from his ongoing teaching, influenced by his Montessori education.

In 1929, at a Mardi Gras masked ball in a Viennese castle, Erikson met a young woman, Joan Serson, and fell in love almost immediately. They were married several months later. Joan's interests were similar to Erikson's. A teacher of modern dance, she had received a B.A. in education and a master's degree in sociology, and had been in psychoanalysis with one of Freud's early followers.

In 1933, Erikson finished his analytic training and was accepted as a full member of the Vienna Psychoanalytic Society. Due to the growth of fascism in Europe, Erikson, as well as many other psychoanalysts, decided to leave for the United States. The move was made easier by his wife's Canadian-American ancestry. The Eriksons settled in Boston, where he became the city's first child psychoanalyst. He was offered positions at Harvard Medical School and at the prestigious Massachusetts General Hospital. In addition, he began private practice and became associated with Harvard's Psychological Clinic, run by Henry Murray. During these years, he had contact with a variety of brilliant and influential thinkers, including Henry Murray, anthropologists Ruth Benedict and Margaret Mead, and social psychologist Kurt Lewin.

In 1936, Erikson accepted a position at Yale Medical School. While at Yale, he took his first anthropological field trip to observe Sioux Indian children in South Dakota. His paper on the Sioux combines the cultural richness of an anthropological field report with the psychologically rich perspective of a highly trained clinician. Among the Sioux, Erikson observed a new phenomenon. He noticed psychological symptoms, including the lack of clear self-image or identity, that were related to a sense of loss of cultural tradition. Erikson later observed a similar confusion of identity among emotionally disturbed World War II veterans.

In 1939, the Eriksons moved to California, where they spent 10 years in the San Francisco area. Erikson continued his analytic work with children and worked on research projects at the University of California at Berkeley.

In 1950, Erikson's best-known book, *Childhood and Society,* was first published. This book contains the fundamental formulations of virtually all of Erikson's major contributions: identity, the life cycle, cross-cultural studies, and psychobiography. *Childhood and Society* has been translated into a dozen languages and used as a textbook in psychiatric training centers, psychology courses, and many other disciplines at the graduate and undergraduate levels.

That same year, Erikson left Berkeley because he refused to sign a state loyalty oath. The Eriksons returned to Massachusetts to the Austin Riggs Center, a leading center for psychoanalytic training and research. While at Austin Riggs, Erikson did a psychological study of Martin Luther, entitled *Young Man Luther.* An exciting and innovative combination of psychoanalysis, biography, and history, the book stirred great interest among psychoanalysts, psychologists, historians, and other social scientists.

In 1960, Erikson was appointed a professor at Harvard. It was in 1969, while at Harvard, that he published his study of Gandhi. In 1975, after retiring from Harvard, Erikson moved back to the San Francisco area to write and teach.

Intellectual Antecedents

Psychoanalysis

Throughout his career, Erikson has viewed himself as a psychoanalyst. In his application of psychoanalysis to new areas and his incorporation of recent developments in anthropology, psychology, and other social sciences, Erikson inevitably developed ideas that were significantly different from Freud's basic theories. However, Erikson's writings reveal his indebtedness to Freud. Rather than label himself *neo-Freudian,* Erikson prefers the more neutral term *post-Freudian.*

Erikson's work on in-depth psychological biographies and on child and adult development are essentially psychoanalytic in nature. In dealing with new material, however, Erikson's psychoanalytic understandings have been reshaped and expanded. "I spoke of 'insight,' rather than

Psychoanalysis is unique. It is *the* treatment situation in which intellectual insight is forced to become emotional insight under very carefully planned circumstances defined by technical rules. But outside of that situation, interpretations cannot do what they can do within a disciplined setting. (Erikson in Evans, 1969) knowledge or fact, because it is so difficult to say in the study of human situations what you can really call knowledge" (Evans, 1969).

> When I started to write about twenty-five years ago, I really thought I was merely providing new illustrations for what I had learned from Sigmund and Anna Freud. I realized only gradually that any original observation already implies a change in theory. An observer of a different generation, in a different scientific climate, cannot avoid developing in a field if it is a vital one. Even a great breakthrough like Freud's is characterized by a passionate concern to bring order into data which "haunted him," to use Darwin's phrase, for very complex reasons of his own and of his time. One can follow such a man only by doing likewise, and if one does so, one differs. I say this because some workers want to improve on Freud, as if his theories were opinions, and because they prefer nicer or nobler ones. (Erikson in Evans, 1969, p. 13)

Anthropology

In 1937, Erikson traveled to South Dakota to investigate the cause of apathy among Sioux schoolchildren. He discovered that they were caught between conflicting value systems: the traditional tribal values they learned in early childhood and the white middle-class values taught in school.

Several years later, Erikson visited the Yurok Indians living by the Klamath River in northern California. He was particularly interested in comparing the childhood training and personality styles of these relatively sedentary fishermen with those of the plains hunters he had studied earlier. Erikson found that acquisition of possessions was a continuing preoccupation among the Yuroks. Acquisitiveness was learned early in childhood as Yurok children were taught to be frugal, to value long-term gain over immediate impulses, and to engage in fantasies of catching salmon and accumulating money.

Erikson's work with the Sioux and Yurok Indians had an important influence on his thinking. His field work also reveals his remarkable ability to enter the world views and modes of thinking of cultures far different from his own. On both field trips, Erikson was accompanied by anthropologists who had developed long-standing friendships with the older people of the tribes. Their assistance gave him access to informants and information never before available to a psychoanalyst. Before going into the field, he read anthropological reports on both tribes. Erikson found virtually no details on childhood training in these reports. A good part of his field research consisted of asking the grandmothers, "Before the white men came, how were your children brought up?" He found they loved to talk about it; they had wondered why no one ever asked.

Erikson's later theoretical developments evolved partly from his cross-cultural observations. He found that Freud's pregenital stages of development were intrinsically related to the technology and worldview of Western culture. Erikson's own theoretical focus on healthy personality development was very strongly influenced by firsthand knowledge of other cultures.

Major Concepts

An Epigenetic Model of Human Development

Erikson's model of the stages of human development is the first theory to detail human development from infancy to adulthood and old age. Erikson suggests that the psychological growth of the individual proceeds in a manner similar to that of an embryo. *Epi* means upon and *genesis* means emergence. Epigenesis suggests that each element develops *on top of* other parts. Erikson's model is structurally similar to that of embryonic growth in that the development of each successive stage is predicated on the development of the previous one.

Each organ system of the body has its own special time for growth and development. It follows a predetermined sequence. Erikson explains the epigenetic principle as "anything that grows has a *ground plan,* and that out of this ground plan the *parts* arise, each part having its *time* of special ascendancy, until all parts have arisen to form a *functioning whole*" (Erikson, 1980a, p. 53).

Erikson's scheme of human development has two basic underlying assumptions:

> (1) That the human personality in principle develops according to steps predetermined in the growing person's readiness to be driven forward, to be aware of, and to interact with a widening social radius; and (2) that society, in principle, tends to be so constituted as to meet and invite the succession of potentialities for interaction and attempts to safeguard and to encourage the proper rate and the proper sequence of their unfolding. (1963, p. 270)

Each stage is characterized by a specific developmental task or *psychological crisis* that must be resolved in order to proceed to the next stage. The strengths and capacities developed through successful resolution at each stage are related to the entire personality. They can be affected by either later or earlier events. However, these psychological capacities are generally affected most strongly during the stage in which they are developed. Erikson stresses that each stage is systematically related to all the others and must develop in given sequence.

Table 6.1 is taken from Erikson's first discussion of the eight stages in *Childhood and Society*. It illustrates the progression from one stage to another over time. Also, each attribute exists in various forms before and after its critical stage. *Trust,* for example, takes one form in adolescence

With each passage from one stage of human growth to the next we must shed a protective structure. We are left exposed and vulnerable—but also yeasty and embryonic again, capable of stretching in ways we hadn't known before. (Sheehy, 1977, p. 29)

and yet another in old age; both are based on a sense of trust developed in infancy.

Crises in Development

In Chinese, the word for *crisis* is composed of two characters, "danger" and "opportunity."

Each stage has a period of crisis in which the strengths and skills that form essential elements of that stage are developed and tested. By crisis, Erikson means a turning point, a critical moment, such as the crisis in a fever. When it is resolved successfully, the fever breaks and the individual begins to recover. Crises are special times in each individual's life, "moments of decision between progress and regression, integration and retardation" (Erikson, 1963, pp. 270–271). Each stage is a crisis in learning—allowing for the development of new skills and attitudes. The crisis may not seem dramatic or critical; the individual can see only later that a major turning point was reached and passed.

Erikson has pointed out that successful resolution of the crisis of each stage of human development promotes a certain psychosocial strength or virtue. Erikson uses *virtue* in its old sense, as in the virtue of a medicine. It refers more to potency than morality. The individual emerges from each crisis with an greater sense of inner unity, clearer judgment, and greater capacity to function effectively.

Eight Stages of Human Development

Erikson's first three stages are essentially an amplification of Freud's work. Freud discussed four major stages: oral, anal, phallic, and genital, which are tied to specific organs or specific cultures. Erikson expands these to universal issues of human development.

Babies control and bring up their parents as much as they're controlled by them. (Erikson, 1963, p. 69)

1. Basic Trust Versus Basic Mistrust. This stage occurs at a time when we are the most helpless and totally dependent on others for physical and emotional nourishment. When we begin life, we each develop a relative sense of trust and mistrust of the world around us. Crucial to this development is our experience with our mother. If a mother, or primary caregiver, is sensitive and responsive to her child, the infant's sense of security increases and the frustrations of hunger and discomfort are tolerable. Development of a strong sense of basic trust "implies not only that one has learned to rely on the sameness and continuity of the outer providers, but also that one may trust oneself and the capacities of one's own organs to cope with urges" (Erikson, 1963, p. 248).

The relationship between mother and child is focused around the mouth and the experience of nursing. This relationship is tested during the biting stage, which is the beginning of the infant's ability to cause pain. The capacity to express anger and rage as well as the desire to harm is also connected to the pain of teething, a pain the infant must learn to endure because it cannot be alleviated as simply as can hunger. According to Erikson, this inner pain and the growing ability to inflict pain are the child's first experiences of a sense of evil and malevolence.

A sense of trust develops not so much from the complete satisfying of hunger or demonstrations of love as from the quality of maternal care. Mothers who trust their ability to care for their babies and trust in the healthy development of their children communicate this, creating the infant's sense of trust in self and in the world.

The virtue or strength that results from achieving a balance between basic trust and mistrust is *hope*. *"Hope is the enduring belief in the attainability of fervent wishes, in spite of the dark urges and rages which mark the beginning of existence"* (Erikson, 1964, p. 118). Hope lays the foundation for the development of faith.

Hope is established as a basic strength, relatively independent of specific hopes, goals, and desires. As the individual continues to develop, this strength is verified at each stage; rewarding experiences inspire new hopefulness. At the same time, the individual develops a capacity for renunciation and an ability to cope with disappointment. Also, the individual develops imaginable dreams and focuses expectations realistically.

The strength of hope emerges from three essential sources. First is the mother's relation to her own childhood—her desire and need to pass on the hope transmitted from her mother and from her culture. Second is the mother-child relationship itself, the mutuality and sensitivity that can develop when it is healthy. Finally, the infant's hope is maintained through social institutions that confirm and restore it through religious ritual, inspired advice, or otherwise. The mature form of an infant's hope is faith. The rituals and practices of religion are designed to support, deepen, and restore faith.

Personal Reflection _____
_____ Trust

Share a "trust walk" with a classmate or friend. Blindfold yourself and have your partner guide you for at least 15 to 20 minutes. Your partner should try and give you a variety of experiences—different surfaces to walk on, things to touch, smell, and even taste. Then, switch roles.

After you have both finished, take a little time to discuss your experiences. Was it difficult to trust your partner at times? How did it feel to be so dependent on another person?

2. Autonomy Versus Shame and Doubt.　　The next stage develops at the time of muscular maturation and the accompanying ability to hold on or let go. At this stage, children rapidly develop a variety of new mental and physical abilities. They begin to walk, climb, hold on, and communicate more effectively. The child interacts with the world in new ways—in grasping and dropping objects and in toilet training. The child begins to exert control over self and also over parts of the outside world.

The basic modalities of this stage are to hold on and to let go. Freud focused on one aspect of this in his writings on the anal stage. Holding on and letting go have both positive and negative aspects. Holding on can become cruel restraint or it can be a pattern of caring. Letting go can be a release of destructive forces, or it can be a relaxed allowing, a letting be.

A sense of autonomy develops with the sense of free choice. It is promoted by a feeling of being able to choose what to keep and what to reject. The infant's basic faith in existence, a lasting result of the first stage, is tested in sudden and stubborn wishes to choose—to grab demandingly or to eliminate inappropriately. Parenting experts have

Table 6.1 Erikson's Eight Stages and Related Virtues

		1	2	3
Old Age	VIII			
Adulthood	VII			
Young Adulthood	VI			
Adolescence	V			
School Age	IV			
Play Age	III			Initiative v Guilt PURPOSE
Early Childhood	II		Autonomy vs. Shame, Doubt WILL	
Infancy	I	Basic Trust vs. Basic Mistrust HOPE		

(From Erikson, 1982, pp. 56–57)

called this age *the terrible twos*. The two-year-old's favorite word is *no*, a clear bid for increased autonomy.

Some children turn this urge to control against themselves by developing a rigid, demanding conscience. Rather than mastering the outer environment, they judge and manipulate themselves, which often results in a strong sense of shame or self-doubt.

Shame stems from a sense of self-exposure, a feeling that one's deficiencies are exposed to others and that one is "caught with one's pants down." Shame is also associated with the child's first experience of standing upright, in which the child feels small, wobbly, and powerless in an adult world.

Doubt is more closely related to the consciousness of having a front and a back. Our front is the acceptable face that we turn toward the

				Integrity vs. Despair WISDOM
			Generativity vs. Stagnation CARE	
		Intimacy vs. Isolation LOVE		
	Identity vs. Identity Confusion FIDELITY			
Industry vs. Inferiority COMPETENCE				
4	5	6	7	8

world. The back part of the body cannot be seen by the child. It is unknown and unexplored territory and yet, at the stage of toilet training, the child's backside can be dominated by the will of others. Unless the split between front and back is reduced, the child's feelings of autonomy will become tinged with doubt.

The strength acquired at this stage is *will*. To have will does not mean being willful, but controlling one's drives with judgment and discrimina-

Table 6.2 Eight Stages of Human Development

Stages	Psychosexual Stages and Modes	Psychosocial Crises	Radius of Significant Relations
I Infancy	Oral-Repiratory, Sensory-Kinesthetic (Incorporative Modes)	Basic Trust vs. Basic Mistrust	Maternal Person
II Early Childhood	Anal-Urethral, Muscular (Retentive-Eliminative Modes)	Autonomy vs. Shame, Doubt	Parental Persons
III Play Age	Infantile-Genital, Locomotor (Intrusive, Inclusive Modes)	Initiative vs. Guilt	Basic Family
IV School Age	"Latency"	Industry vs. Inferiority	"Neighborhood," School
V Adolescence	Puberty	Identity vs. Identity Confusion	Peer Groups and Outgroups; Models of Leadership
VI Young Adulthood	Genitality	Intimacy vs. Isolation	Partners in Friendship, Sex, Competition, Cooperation
VII Adulthood	(Procreativity)	Generativity vs. Stagnation	Divided Labor and Shared Household
VIII Old Age	(Generalization of Sensual Modes)	Integrity vs. Despair	"Mankind" "My Kind"

(From Erikson, 1982, pp. 32–33)

tion. The individual learns to make decisions and act decisively in spite of inevitable frustration. "Will, therefore, is the unbroken determination to exercise free choice as well as self-restraint, in spite of the unavoidable experience of shame and doubt" (Erikson, 1964, p. 119).

Infant will develops into the adult ability to control drives and impulses. Ideally, the individual's will joins with others in a way that permits all to retain a sense of power, even when restrained by rules and reason.

Basic Strengths	Core Pathology: Basic Antipathies	Related Principles of Social Order	Binding Ritualizations	Ritualism
Hope	Withdrawal	Cosmic Order	Numinous	Idolism
Will	Compulsion	"Law and Order"	Judicious	Legalism
Purpose	Inhibition	Ideal Prototypes	Dramatic	Moralism
Competence	Inertia	Technological Order	Formal (Technical)	Formalism
Fidelity	Repudiation	Ideological Worldview	Ideological	Totalism
Love	Exclusivity	Patterns of Cooperation and Competition	Affiliative	Elitism
Care	Rejectivity	Currents of Education and Tradition	Generational	Authoritism
Wisdom	Disdain	Wisdom	Philosophical	Dogmatism

Will forms the basis of our acceptance of law and external necessity. It is rooted in an appreciation that parental training is guided and tempered by a spirit of justice. The law is a social institution that gives concrete form to our ego's control of our drives. We surrender our willfulness to the majesty of the law with ambivalence and inevitable small transgressions.

Personal Reflection ———————————
——————————————————— Autonomy

Make an agreement with a partner that, for at least half a day, you will follow his or her directions in whatever you are told to do. In a sense, your partner gets to play "parent" and you agree to be an obedient "child." (Make some clear limits. For example, you will not be made to do anything that is illegal, unethical, or embarrassing to yourself or someone else.)

How does it feel to have someone tell you what to do—what to eat, when to sit down or stand up, how to act, and so on? In many ways, you are duplicating the experience of the average 2-year-old, who has very little say in his or her life.

Discuss your experience with your partner after you are done. It may be better *not* to switch roles afterward. Knowing that you are going to switch may inhibit your partner from being really creative in ordering you around. (And, after all, very few parents anticipate switching roles with their children.)

3. Initiative Versus Guilt.   At this stage, the child experiences greater mobility and inquisitiveness, significant growth in language and imagination, and an expanding sense of mastery and responsibility. Play is the most basic activity of this stage. The child is "into everything," finding joy in attack and conquest over the environment. This stage is analogous to Freud's phallic stage. The child is eager to learn and to perform well. Language and imagination develop. The favorite word at this stage is *why*. There is tremendous curiosity and openness to new learning. The child begins to learn to plan ahead and starts to develop a sense of direction and purpose.

This new sense of mastery is tempered by feelings of guilt. The child's new freedom and assertion of power almost inevitably create anxiety. The child develops a conscience, a parental attitude that supports self-observation, self-guidance, and also self-punishment. At this stage, the child can do more than ever before and must learn to set limits.

Purpose, the virtue of this stage, is rooted in play and fantasy. Play is to the child what thinking and planning are to the adult. It provides the rudiments of purpose: focus and direction given to concerted activity.

Personal Reflection _____

_____ Initiative

This exercise is very much like the previous autonomy experience. Again, with a partner, agree to follow his or her directions. Only this time, you can say *no*. Your partner gets to make all the suggestions about possible activities. You can respond with a *yes* or *no*, but you cannot suggest any ideas on your own.

For instance, if the two of you are in a restaurant, your partner can suggest various foods that you might like. You can accept or refuse, but you do not get to make any suggestions on your own. Or, if the two of you are going out to a movie, your partner can suggest films to go to. You can agree or disagree, but you cannot suggest any specific films on your own.

After you have finished, discuss what it felt like to be deprived of a sense of initiative.

"Purpose, then, is the courage to envisage and pursue valued goals uninhibited by the defeat of infantile fantasies, by guilt and by the foiling fear of punishment" (Erikson, 1964, p. 122).

Purpose provides aim and direction, fed by fantasy yet rooted in reality, limited but not inhibited by guilt. The development of fantasy forms the roots of dance, drama, and ritual in adult life.

4. Industry Versus Inferiority.

This stage marks the beginning of entrance into life outside the family. It corresponds to Freud's latency stage. In our culture, school life (between ages 6 and 11) begins. In other social systems, during this stage, the child may become an apprentice or a working assistant to the father or mother.

This is a stage of systematic instruction, a movement from play to a sense of work. Earlier, the child could *play at* activities. No attention was given to the quality of results. Now, the child needs to perform and develop a sense of satisfaction in a job well done. At this stage, children are expected to master new tasks and skills that are valued in society. The attitudes and opinions of others are particularly important. Now, children need to achieve and to earn the respect of their parents, teachers, and peers. Otherwise, they may develop a sense of inferiority or inadequacy.

The virtue of this stage is *competence,* which is based on a sense of workmanship, the development of practical skills, and general capacities. "Competence, then, is the free exercise of dexterity and intelligence in the completion of tasks, unimpaired by infantile inferiority" (Erikson, 1964, p. 124).

Competence is the psychological basis for technology. At this stage, we have just begun to become productive members of our culture; we have just begun to master our culture's technology.

The adult once was child and a youth. He will never be either again; but neither will he ever be without the heritage of those former states. (Erikson, 1987, p. 332)

5. Identity Versus Identity Confusion.

As childhood ends, adolescents begin to integrate their past experiences into a new whole. They question role models and identifications of the past and try out new roles. The great question of this stage is "Who am I?" A new sense of ego identity develops.

This sense of identity includes the individual's ability to integrate past identifications with present impulses, aptitudes, and skills, as well as with opportunities offered by society. "The sense of ego identity, then, is the accrued confidence that the inner sameness and continuity prepared in the past are matched by the sameness and continuity of one's meaning for others, as evidenced in the tangible promise of a 'career'" (Erikson, 1963, pp. 261–262).

For Erikson, because adolescence is the transition between childhood and adulthood it is a particularly crucial stage. It is generally a period during which a psychological moratorium is called. The adolescent takes "time out" to devote to role experimentation. This period can be strongly affected by social limitations and pressures. The adolescent is likely to suffer from some role confusion. It may be difficult for the adolescent to envision any future occupational role or imagine finding a meaningful place in society. Doubts about sexual attractiveness and sexual identity are also common. An inability to "take hold" and develop a sense of identification with an individual or cultural role model who provides inspiration and direction can lead to a period of floundering and insecurity. Another common reaction at this stage is overidentification (to the point of apparent loss of identity) with youth-culture heroes or clique leaders. The individual often feels isolated, empty, anxious, or indecisive. Under pressure to make important life decisions, the adolescent feels unable, even resistant, to do so.

The basic strength of this stage is *fidelity*. At the threshold of adulthood, each individual faces a need for commitment to a career and a lasting set of values. "Fidelity is the ability to sustain loyalties freely pledged in spite of the inevitable contradictions of value systems" (Erikson, 1964, p. 125). Fidelity is the cornerstone of identity; it requires the validation of acceptable social ideologies and the support of peers who have made similar choices.

It is this stage that we incorporate our culture's ethical values and belief systems. At the same time, the culture itself is renewed by the affirmation of each generation; it is revitalized as adolescents selectively offer their loyalties and energies, supporting some traditions and changing others. Those who cannot pledge their loyalties either remain deviant or commit themselves to revolutionary goals and values.

For most of those in the twenties, a fantastic mystery story waits to be written over the next two decades. It races with excitement and jeopardy . . . and leads us down secret passageways in search of our missing personality parts. (Sheehy, 1977, p. 166)

6. Intimacy Versus Isolation.

This stage generally occurs in young adulthood. It may begin any time from the late teens to mid-twenties or later. It usually encompasses the period from the end of adolescence to the beginning of adulthood. It is a time for developing a sense of independence from parents and school, establishing intimate friendships and relationships with others, and developing a sense of adult responsibility.

Only after a relatively firm sense of identity is established are we capable of developing a close and meaningful relationship with another. Only then can we think of committing ourselves to partnership, affiliation, and intimacy with another person. The critical commitment that generally occurs at this stage is based on true mutuality with a love partner. This level of intimacy is significantly different from the earlier sexual exploration and intense search for sexual identity.

Without a sense of intimacy and commitment, we may become isolated, unable to sustain nourishing personal relationships. If our sense of identity is weak and threatened by intimacy, we may turn away from or even attack whatever encroaches.

The virtue developed in this stage is *love*. Erikson (1964) argues that this is the greatest virtue. He points out that it takes many forms: Early in life, it is the infant's love for its mother, the child's love for parents, and adolescent infatuation. When real intimacy develops between adults, love includes a shared identity and the validation of each partner in the other. This virtue can manifest itself in a romantic, sexual relationship, but also in deep ties developed in joint service of ideals, home, or country. The virtue of love manifests itself in true mutuality and intimacy. "Love, then, is mutuality of devotion forever subduing the antagonism inherent in divided functions" (Erikson, 1964, p. 129).

7. Generativity Versus Stagnation.
This stage generally spans most of our adult years, from the twenties to the fifties or even later. Intimate commitment to others widens to a more general concern for guiding and supporting the next generation. Generativity includes concern for our own children and for the ideas and other products that we have created. It includes productivity and creativity in work and in our personal lives.

The mere fact of having and wanting children does not achieve generativity. (Erikson, 1963, p. 267)

We are teaching as well as learning beings. Creation is important, as is ensuring the ongoing health and maintenance of our creations, ideals, and principles. Unless the sphere of our care and productivity widens, we fall prey to a sense of boredom and stagnation.

Erikson (1982) writes that social institutions tend to reinforce the function of generativity. They provide a continuity of knowledge and structure from one generation to another. Those with a healthy sense of generativity actively participate in these institutions, seeking to maintain and enhance future generations.

The strength developed at this stage is *care*. The care and nurturing of children is at the core of this virtue. This includes not only the care of offspring, but also of the children of our minds and hearts—our ideas, ideals, and creations. Unique to our species is the fact that care for and education of the young extends over a very long period.

As adults, we need to be needed, or else we suffer from narcissism and self-absorption. In terms of human psychosocial evolution, we are essentially a teaching species. We must teach to fulfill our identity and to keep alive our skills and knowledge. "Care is the widening concern for what has been generated by love, necessity, or accident; it overcomes the ambivalence adhering to irreversible obligation" (Erikson, 1964, p. 131).

Personal Reflection

Erikson's Stages: A Personal Assessment

One of Erikson's core concepts focuses on major life stages that inevitably lead to crises in human growth and development. Which of Erikson's stages is the most significant (or powerful, or difficult) for you?

What combination of factors makes this stage so important for you? What are the personality elements, family events, environmental influences, societal forces, and so on that are the most significant in your experience?

How is your own experience of this stage related to your earlier and later development? How is it related to the stage and the growth crisis you find yourself in now?

8. Integrity Versus Despair.   This final stage of life comes with old age, and occurs from the fifties or sixties until death. It is a time of dealing with what Erikson has called *ultimate concerns*. The sense of ego integrity includes the individual's acceptance of a unique life cycle with its own history of triumphs and failures. It brings a sense of order and meaning, personally and in the world around us, as well as a new and different love of parents. A sense of ego integrity includes an awareness of the value of many other life-styles, including those that differ widely from one's own. Integrity brings with it a perspective of wholeness, an ability to see one's life as a whole, and also an ability to view human problems in a comprehensive way.

If we have not gained a measure of self-acceptance, we are likely to plunge into despair over the feeling that time is short—too short to start over. Those who end up in despair may become bitter over what might have been, constantly lamenting "if only. . . ." Despair may manifest itself in fear of death or result in contempt and rejection of other values, institutions, and life-styles.

Erikson (1982) has indicated that the role of old age has been changing. When *Childhood and Society* was first published in 1950, the cultural view of old age was very different from what it is today. Then, the most predominant model was that of the *elders,* those relative few who lived to a decrepit age, but embodied the values of dignity, wisdom, and integrity.

Today, as life expectancy continues to increase, we have an ever increasing population of relatively healthy and active elderly. Our model of the stage of old age will continue to develop as the parameters of aging continue to change.

The strength of wisdom develops out of encounters with both integrity and despair as the individual is confronted with ultimate concerns. Wisdom maintains the integrity of one's accumulated knowledge and experience. Those who have developed wisdom are models of wholeness and completeness. They are inspirational examples to younger generations who have adopted similar values and life-styles. This sense of wholeness and meaning can also alleviate the feelings of helplessness and dependence that mark old age. "Wisdom, then, is detached concern with life itself, in the face of death itself" (Erikson, 1964, p. 133).

Personal Reflection

The Later Stages of the Life Cycle

Rent a videotape of the Ingmar Bergman classic motion picture *Wild Strawberries* (Wilmette, IL: Janus Films, 1957). Give your own analysis of Dr. Borg's dream, and look at the events in the film from the perspective of the stages of the life cycle, especially the last three life stages—Intimacy/Isolation, Generativity/Stagnation, and Integrity/Despair.

Compare your own analysis with Erikson's, which is published as a chapter in *Vital Involvement in Old Age* (Erikson, Erikson, & Kivnick, 1986). This is a unique chance to compare your own analysis of a case study with that of a gifted clinician. You share the same data, as presented in the film. (For many years, Erikson used this exercise with his own students in his Harvard course, The Human Life Cycle.)

Ratio and Balance

At each stage there is a dynamic ratio between two poles. Erikson's terms for these opposite poles tend to be misleading because, inevitably, one seems extremely desirable and the other extremely undesirable. However, both poles at each stage are *undesirable* from the very fact that they are extreme. This may be seen as follows:

(unhealthy)	(healthy)	(unhealthy)
Extreme trust	Basic trust Basic mistrust	Extreme mistrust

Erikson has been frequently misunderstood as advocating only the positive pole for each stage. He has pointed out that ". . . people often take away mistrust and doubt and shame and all of these not so nice, 'negative' things and try to make an Eriksonian achievement scale out of it all, according to which in the first stage trust is 'achieved'" (Erikson in Evans, 1969, p. 15). However, an individual who develops an unbalanced sense of trust can become a Pollyanna, as out of touch with reality as the individual paralyzed with extreme mistrust. We must be able to discriminate between situations in which we can trust and those in which some mistrust, or anticipation of danger or discomfort, is appropriate. Healthy ratios vary widely from relative trust to relative suspicion, but in every case elements of both trust and mistrust are present.

Similarly, unbalanced autonomy can become unreasonable stubbornness. Unbalanced initiative is a self-centered preoccupation with one's own goals and concerns. A sense of industry without a sense of limitation leads to an inflated appreciation of one's abilities. An overdeveloped sense of identity is rigid and inflexible and is likely to clash with external reality, and so on.

Personal Reflection

Examples of Erikson's Stages

Think of three people who you feel are in different Eriksonian stages. You may wish to include a parent, yourself, and someone much younger. Does each person seem to fit his or her designated stage? What is the central issue that you see in the life of each? What are the major strengths? Major weaknesses? Can you see how the current life of each person is related to the past? How has each evolved from past strengths and past issues?

Does framing the concerns, strengths, and critical issues for the three people help you understand them, their differences, possible difficulties in communication, and so on?

Modes of Relating to the Environment

Whereas Freud based his description of the stages of human development on specific organ-related experiences, Erikson's stages are based on more general styles of relating to and coping with the environment. Although styles are often initially developed through a particular organ, they refer to broad patterns of behavior. For instance, the mode learned in the first stage, basic trust versus basic mistrust, is *to get*—that is, the ability to receive and to accept what is given. (This stage corresponds to Freud's oral stage.) At this time, the mouth is the primary organ of interchange

The infant may equally absorb the milk of wisdom where he once desired more tangible fluids from more sensuous containers. (Erikson, 1963, p. 62)

between the infant and the environment. However, an adult who is fixated on *getting* may exhibit forms of *dependency* unrelated to orality.

In the second stage, autonomy versus shame and doubt, the modes are *to let go* and *to hold on*. As with Freud's anal stage, the modes are fundamentally related to retention and elimination of feces; however, the child at this stage also alternates between possessing and rejecting parents, favorite toys, and so on.

The mode of the third stage, initiative versus guilt, Erikson calls *to make*. In one sense, the child is "on the make," focused on the conquest of the environment. This includes a phallic-intrusive attitude and also a seductive-manipulative quality. Play is important, from making mud pies to imitating the complex sports and games of older children.

The fourth stage, industry versus inferiority, includes the modes *to do well* and *to work*. There is no single organ system associated with this stage; rather, productive work and accomplishment are central.

Erikson does not discuss in detail the modes involved with the remaining stages. These later stages, less related to Freud's developmental stages, seem less rooted in a particular activity or organ mode.

Identity

Erikson has developed the concept of identity in greater detail than the concepts discussed in the eight stages. He first coined the phrase *identity crisis* to describe the mental state of many of the soldiers he treated at Mt. Zion Veterans Rehabilitation Clinic in San Francisco. These men were easily upset by any sudden or intense stimulus. Their egos seemed to have lost any shock-absorbing capacity. Their sensory systems were in a constant "startled" state, thrown off by external stimuli as well as a variety of bodily sensations, including hot flashes, heart palpitations, intense headaches, and insomnia. "Above all, the men felt that they 'did not know who they were': There was a distinct loss of ego identity. The sameness and continuity and the belief in one's social role were gone" (Erikson, 1968, p. 67).

The term *identity* brings together the theories of depth psychology with cognitive and ego psychologies. Early Freudian theory tended to ignore the important role of the ego as, in Erikson's terms, "a selective, integrating, coherent and persistent agency central to personality function" (Erikson, 1964, p. 137). The concept of identity also provides a meeting place for psychology, sociology, and history. Because of its complexity, Erikson has wisely avoided giving identity a single definition:

> I can attempt to make the subject matter of identity more explicit only by approaching it from a variety of angles. . . . At one time, then, it will appear to refer to a conscious *sense of individual identity;* at another, to an unconscious striving for *a continuity of personal character;* at a third, as a criterion for the silent doings of *ego synthesis;* and, finally, as a maintenance of an *inner solidarity* with a group's ideals and identity. (1980a, p. 109)

Erikson spells out these aspects of identity as follows (adapted from Evans, 1969, pp. 218–219):

1. *Individuality*—a conscious sense of one's uniqueness and existence as a separate, distinct entity.

2. *Sameness and continuity*—a sense of inner sameness, a continuity between what one has been in the past and what one promises to be in the future, a feeling that one's life has consistency and meaningful direction.

3. *Wholeness and synthesis*—a sense of inner harmony and wholeness, a synthesis of the self-images and identifications of childhood into a meaningful whole that produces a sense of harmony.

4. *Social solidarity*—a sense of inner solidarity with the ideals and values of society or a subgroup within it, a feeling that one's identity is meaningful to significant others and corresponds to their expectations and perceptions.

Further, in the following excerpt, Erikson describes identity in the transition from childhood to adulthood.

Like a trapeze artist, the young person in the middle of vigorous motion must let go of his safe hold on childhood and reach out for a firm grasp on adulthood, depending for a breathless interval on a relatedness between the past and the future, and on the reliability of those he must let go of, and those who will "receive" him. Whatever combination of drives and defenses, of sublimations and capacities has emerged from the young individual's childhood must now make sense in view of his concrete opportunities in work and love . . . [and] he must detect some meaningful resemblance between what he has come to see in himself and what his sharpened awareness tells him others judge and expect him to be. (Erikson, 1964, p. 90)

The concept of identity has become particularly popular because it is generally recognized as the major life crisis in the United States today—and perhaps in all of modern society. Our cultural emphasis on extended education as well as the complexity of most modern vocations make the development of a sense of identity particularly difficult in our society. The struggle to gain a healthy, clear sense of identity frequently continues beyond adolescence, erupting later in mid-life crises.

Years ago, most children took on their parents' adult roles. Girls learned to run households and boys followed their fathers' vocations. Children began to learn adult skills, attitudes, and potential adult roles early in life; their parents' vocations were generally integrated with family life. Given our changing values and social roles, not only are children unlikely to take on their parents' roles, but there may not be any clear adult role models available to them. The Western adolescent's earlier childhood

Personal Reflection ——————————————

—————————————————————————— Identity

To get an idea of how your identity develops, try this exercise.

1. Relax and think of a time when you felt you had a strong sense of identity. Describe that time. What were the components of that identity (for example, captain of the high school football team, oldest daughter in a large family, good student)?

2. List ten words that describe you then—your sense of self, crucial life issues, and so on.

3. How would you describe your *present* identity? Make a second list.

4. Have there been significant changes? What continuity do you notice in your sense of self over this period of time? What changes?

5. Was the transition from one sense of identity to another smooth and gradual or abrupt?

6. Do you feel your present identity will remain relatively stable or do you foresee major changes? If you foresee major changes, why might these occur?

identifications and experiences are clearly inadequate in the task of anticipating a career and making a major vocational role commitment.

Erikson has pointed out that there is a sense of negative identity that is mixed with the positive identity. This negative identity may include what the individual has been punished or made to feel guilty for. There may also be a role model for a negative identity. An example of such a model might be an uncle or a friend who is labeled an alcoholic or a failure in some way. (For more on negative identity, see Obstacles to Growth in this chapter.)

Erikson found that the development of a sense of identity is frequently preceded by a "psychosocial moratorium," a period of time off in which the individual may be occupied with study, travel, or a clearly temporary occupation. This provides time to reflect, to develop a new sense of direction, new values, new purpose. The moratorium may last for months or even years.

Erikson (1980a, pp. 120–130) has stressed that the development of a sense of identity has both psychological and social aspects:

1. The individual's development of a sense of personal sameness and continuity is based, in part, on a belief in the sameness and continuity of a shared worldview.

2. Although many aspects of the search for a sense of identity are conscious, unconscious motivation may also play a major role. At this stage, feelings of acute vulnerability may alternate with great expectations of success.

3. A sense of identity cannot develop without certain physical, mental, and social preconditions (outlined in Erikson's developmental stages). Also, it must not be unduly delayed because future stages of development depend on it. Psychological factors may prolong the crisis as the individual seeks to match unique gifts to existing social possibilities. Social factors and historical change may also postpone adult commitment.

4. The growth of a sense of identity is dependent on the past, present, and future. This growth requires the resources of clear identifications made in childhood. It relies on whatever current role and career models are available. It also relies on a sense that one's chosen roles will be viable in the future in spite of inevitable inner and outer changes.

Erikson has pointed out that problems of identity are not new, though they may be more widespread today than ever before. Many creative

Table 6.3   Identity and the Eight Stages of Development

Old Age	VIII				
Adulthood	VII				
Young Adulthood	VI				
Adolescence	V	Temporal Perspective vs. Time Confusion	Self-Certainty vs. Self-Consciousness	Role Experimentation vs. Role Fixation	Apprenticeship vs. Work Paralysis
School Age	IV				INDUSTRY vs. INFERIORITY
Play Age	III			INITIATIVE vs. GUILT	
Early Childhood	II		AUTONOMY vs. SHAME, DOUBT		
Infancy	I	BASIC TRUST vs. BASIC MISTRUST			

Note. From *Identity, Youth and Crisis* (p. 94) by E. Erikson, 1968, New York: Norton. Copyright 1968 by Norton. Reprinted by permission.

individuals have wrestled with the problems of identity in carving out new careers and social roles for themselves. Some especially creative people contributed major social innovations, thus offering new role models for others. Freud, for example, began his career as a conventional doctor and neurologist. Only in mid-career did he create a new role for himself (and many others) by becoming the first psychoanalyst.

Psychohistory

Erikson expanded psychoanalysis by studying major historical personalities. By analyzing their psychological growth and development, he came to understand the psychological impact they had on their generation. In addition to his books on Martin Luther and Mohandas Gandhi, Erikson's

			INTEGRITY vs. DESPAIR, DISGUST
		GENERATIVITY vs. STAGNATION	
	INTIMACY vs. ISOLATION		
IDENTITY vs. IDENTITY CONFUSION	Sexual Polarization vs. Bisexual Confusion	Leadership and Fellowship vs. Authority Confusion	Ideological Commitment vs. Confusion of Values
Task Identification vs. Sense of Futility			
Anticipation of Roles vs. Role Inhibition			
Will to Be Oneself vs. Self-Doubt			
Mutual Recognition vs. Autistic Isolation			

psychobiographies have included Maxim Gorky, Adolf Hitler, George Bernard Shaw, Sigmund Freud, Thomas Jefferson, and Woodrow Wilson.

Erikson's major psychobiographical subjects were Luther and Gandhi. He combined clinical insight with historical and social analysis. Erikson illuminated the forces that helped shape these two great men and also the impact they in turn had on their societies.

This interest in combining psychoanalysis and history began when Erikson left Europe for the United States as Hitler came to power. On the ship to America he wrote of the central reasons that German youths turned toward Hitler. Because of his own background, Erikson was deeply affected by developments in Germany. Although born a Dane, he grew up in Germany and considered it his home. But German friends had turned Nazi and were killing other friends and classmates who shared Erikson's Jewish roots. He analyzed what was happening in Germany without writing off the Nazis as "others," as depraved criminals essentially different from the rest of humanity. These notes led to Erikson's first psychohistorical study, which appeared as a chapter on Hitler in *Childhood and Society*.

> Psychohistory, essentially, is the study of individual and collective life with the combined methods of psychoanalysis and history. . . . Bridge-heads must be built on each side in order to make a true span possible. But the completed bridge should permit unimpeded two-way traffic; and once this is done, history will be simply history again, but now a history aware of the fact that it has always indulged in a covert and circuitous traffic with psychology which can now be direct, overt, and aware. By the same token, psychoanalysis will have become conscious of its own historical determinants, and *case history* and *life history* will no longer be manners of speaking. (Erikson, 1974, p. 13)

Erikson made a major contribution to the study of historical figures by applying the same methods used in psychoanalytic case histories for reconstructing the life of a historical figure. Erikson realized that in making the transition from case history to life history the psychoanalyst must broaden his or her concerns and take into account the subject's activities in the context of the opportunities and limitations of the outside world. This appreciation of the interaction of psychological and social currents in turn affected Erikson's theoretical work.

There is one major difference between psychological biographies and case histories. In a case history, a therapist tries to understand why the patient has fallen apart. In a life history, an investigator tries to understand how the person manages to stay whole and function creatively and effectively in spite of conflicts, complexes, and crises.

The Study of "Great Individuals"

In his psychobiographical work, Erikson brought the insights of a trained psychoanalyst to the careful study of critical periods in the lives of influential individuals. He was particularly interested in men and women whose identity conflicts mirrored the conflicts of their era and whose greatness lay in their finding a personal solution to their own identity crisis, a solution that became a model for others. Often, they were individuals who had deep personal conflicts. The crisis of the age seemed to be intensified in each of them; yet each brought a special urgency and focus to the solution of the crisis.

In his first major psychobiography, Erikson laid out his fundamental approach to the study of great men and women. He argued that Luther was great because of his struggle "to lift his individual patienthood to the level of a universal one and to try to solve for all what he could not solve for himself alone" (Erikson, 1958, p. 67).

Although they all were creative, energetic, and powerful people, they were not without fear, anxiety, and unhappiness. Their lives were often dominated by a sense, stemming from childhood, that they needed to *settle* or *live down* something. They were generally tied to their fathers in a way that precluded overt rebellion; they also learned a great deal from and felt needed and specially chosen by their fathers. These individuals frequently had early, sensitive senses of conscience and paid early attention to ultimate values, sometimes convinced they carried special responsibility for part of humankind. These productive men and women might have simply become misfits and cranks except for their ability, energy, concentration, and spiritual devotion.

> And then, there are the great adults who are adult and are called great precisely because their sense of identity vastly surpasses the roles foisted upon them, their vision opens up new realities, and the gift of communication revitalizes actuality. (Erikson, 1987, p. 335)

Dynamics

Positive Growth

This focus on positive characteristics developed at each stage distinguishes Erikson's schema from Freud's and from many other personality theorists. Erikson views basic strengths, or virtues, as more than psychological defenses against mental illness or negativity and more than simply attitudes of nobility or morality. These virtues are *inherent* strengths and are characterized by a sense of potency and positive development. As mentioned earlier in the chapter, *hope* is the virtue of the first stage of trust versus mistrust. *Will* is the strength that arises from the crisis of autonomy versus shame and doubt. Purpose is rooted in the initiative versus guilt stage. *Competence* is the strength resulting from the stage of industry versus inferiority. *Fidelity* comes from identity versus identity confusion. *Love* is the virtue that develops from intimacy. *Care* originates in generativity. *Wisdom* is derived from the crisis of integrity versus despair.

Obstacles to Growth

Negative Identity

Our sense of identity always comprises positive and negative elements. These elements include things we want to become and others we do not want to be or know we should not be. Under extremely negative social conditions, it may be impossible for the majority of healthy young men and women to become committed to anything positive and large scale. The Nazi era in Germany is an example.

Lack of a healthy sense of identity may be expressed in hostility toward available social goals and values. This hostility can include any role aspect: one's sexuality, nationality, class, or family background. Children of immigrant families may display contempt for their parents' backgrounds, and descendants of established families may reject everything American and overestimate everything foreign.

Many conflicted adolescents would rather be someone bad than a nobody. Thus, the choice of a negative identity is based on those roles that have been presented as undesirable or dangerous. If the adolescent feels unable to make a commitment to more positive roles, the negative ones become the most real. These may include the drug dealer, prostitute, or any model that represents failure in the eyes of society.

Structure

Body

Experience is anchored in the ground-plan of the body. (Erikson, 1963, p. 108)

The role of the bodily organs is especially important in Erikson's early stages. Later in life, development of physical as well as intellectual skills strongly affects the growth of a sense of competence and an ability to choose demanding roles in our complex society.

As a psychosocial theorist, Erikson is aware of the constant interaction of body, psychological processes, and social forces.

Social Relationships

Social relationships are central in virtually every stage. Interaction with one's parents, family, and peers is crucial in the first five stages of development. The development of a sense of identity is strongly affected by the presence of affirming peers. The stage of intimacy brings opportunities for new and deeper social relationships. Another qualitative change occurs during the stage of generativity, when each individual learns caring for and nurturing of those who are younger, weaker, and less knowledgeable.

A stage has a new configuration of past and future, a new combination of drive and defense, a new set of capacities fit for a new setting of tasks and opportunities, a new and wider radius of significant encounters. (Erikson, 1964, p. 166)

Erikson's basic epigenetic principle states, "Personality . . . can be said to develop according to steps predetermined in the human organism's readiness to be driven toward, to be aware of, and to interact with a widening radius of significant individuals and institutions" (1968, pp. 92–93).

Will

Erikson details the development of will in his discussion of autonomy versus shame and doubt. The development of a healthy and balanced will (and goodwill) continues throughout life. Crucial to the development of a healthy sense of identity is the sense that "I am what I can *will* freely."

Traditional psychoanalysis deals primarily with the analysis of an individual's conception of reality, focusing on thoughts, emotions, and essentially private behavior. Erikson emphasizes, in addition, the importance of will and action in the world. He feels that one of the goals of psychoanalysis is to restore "a productive interplay between psychological reality and historical actuality" (1964, p. 201); that is, to integrate inner, subjective experiences with the details of external actions and events. Erikson suggests that reality refers to "the world of phenomenal experience, perceived with a minimum of distortion" (1964, p. 165). Although dealing with distortion and misunderstanding is essential, Erikson stresses the need for an understanding of actuality, "the world of participation, shared with other participants" (1964, p. 165).

Reanalyzing Freud's classic case study of Dora, Erikson points out that although Freud did a brilliant job of analyzing Dora's personality dynamics and distortions, he failed to consider her real powerlessness as a young girl in a middle-class Viennese family. Dora initially saw Freud for three months, when she was 19 years old. She had been propositioned at the age of 16 by Mr. K, a friend of the family. Her father had brought her to Freud to "bring her to reason." It turned out that Dora's father was having an affair with Mr. K's wife, and he seemed willing to allow Mr. K's advances to his daughter. To further complicate matters, everyone seemed to make Dora their confidante—her father and mother, Mr. K and Mrs. K.

Dora tried to confront her parents with the situation. Freud saw this as acting out, but Erikson disagrees. He sees Dora as someone who was actively searching for honesty and fidelity, qualities that the adult role models in her life were sorely lacking.

Successful action requires both social and historical possibilities and will. To see accurately does not guarantee that one can act effectively.

Emotions

As a psychoanalyst, Erikson stresses the importance of the emotional component of psychological processes. His treatment of the role of the emotions is implicit throughout his theories. As a theorist, his focus has been on adding new cognitive, historical, and social elements to a psychoanalytic framework. However, Erikson does not discuss explicitly the emotions as a distinct aspect of psychological processes.

Intellect

Similar to emotion, the intellect is seen as an essential element in psychological processes. Erikson does not pay specific attention to the role of intellectual capacities. He does point out, however, that the development of intellectual skills is critical in the formation of a sense of competence.

Cognitive skills are essential if one is to master the technological skills of society, form a sense of identity, and choose acceptable social roles and a career.

Self

For Erikson, sense of identity can be seen as the development and flowering of a sense of self:

> The ego, if understood as a central and partially unconscious organizing agency, must at any given stage of life deal with a changing Self which demands to be synthesized with abandoned and anticipated selves. . . . What could consequently be called the *self-identity* emerges from experiences in which temporarily confused selves are successfully reintegrated in an ensemble of roles which also secure social recognition. Identity formation, thus, can be said to have a self-aspect and an ego aspect. (Erikson, 1968, pp. 210–211)

Therapist

Psychoanalysis is the first systematic and active "consciousness-expansion," and such expansion may be necessary as man concentrates on the conquest of matter and is apt to overidentify with it. (Erikson in Evans, 1969, p. 98)

Erikson has pointed out that a competent therapist has a strong sense of the patient's potential growth and development. The therapist's job is to foster that growth rather than impose his or her own future or past on the patient. This focus is implicit in the requirement that each psychoanalyst undergo training analysis and in the stress on the role of *transference* and *countertransference* in psychoanalysis. Transference refers to the positive or negative feelings that patients develop for their therapists. These feelings are often strong and irrational and rooted in childhood feelings for parents. Conscious understanding of the dynamics of transference can be an extremely valuable part of psychotherapy. Countertransference refers to the positive or negative feelings that therapists frequently develop for their patients. Jung had said that every patient who came to him took his life in his own hands. In response, Erikson commented, "This is true, but one must add that he came to *me,* and not to somebody else, and after that he will never be the same—and neither will I" (Erikson in Evans, 1969, p. 103).

Every therapist must be prepared to understand and identify with a variety of alternative life-styles. Issues of values and morality are central to therapy. The notion of the impersonality of the classical analyst is, according to Erikson, a misunderstanding of the role of impartial acceptance of the patient's free associations and past history. The therapist is always there as an individual, with the freedom to express whatever he or she wishes, ideally without distortion from irrational countertransference.

Erikson has reformulated the Golden Rule in light of modern psychological understanding. He writes that truly worthwhile, moral acts strengthen the doer even as they strengthen the other, and enhance the relationship between the two individuals. In therapy, this version of the Golden Rule encourages the therapist to develop as a practitioner and as a person, even as the patient is cured as a patient and as a person. For a real cure transcends the transitory state of patienthood. It is an experience which enables the cured patient to develop and to transmit to home and neighborhood an attitude toward health, which is one of the most essential ingredients of an ethical outlook (Erikson, 1964, pp. 236–237).

Evaluation

Erikson has been criticized for his vagueness. He is an artist with words rather than a logician. His beautiful and brilliant formulations can appear to dissolve into conceptual sketches rather than develop into linear, logical analysis. For example, Erikson's discussion of identity consists of a diverse collection of ideas that are often more confusing than clarifying.

As one reviewer has commented,

> Reading Erikson is like walking in a dense and beautiful forest with a thousand paths leading through it. The very richness of the forest can be confusing. There is so much there. . . . Erikson has never watered down or simplified his writing. Thank God! They [his books] are written with a kind of magnificent obscurity. . . . His work needs to be read and reread; his books need to be outlined and meditated on. They have a lasting quality. (Gross, 1987, p. 3)

Critics (for example, Appadurai, 1978; Roazen, 1976) have raised questions about the universality of Erikson's theories. Can his epigenetic model be applied as successfully to non-Western cultures both past and present? For example, viewing adolescence as a distinct developmental stage is a relatively new phenomenon. Also, issues like autonomy, initiative, and identity may not be central in other cultures such as in India or in tribal societies.

Other questions have been raised about the applicability of Erikson's developmental model even in the West. For example, Erikson proposes that generativity begins with parenthood. That this is not necessarily true is proven by teenage pregnancy. Young mothers and fathers, as yet uneducated as to the terms of generativity, are often dragged kicking and screaming into parenthood. Also, Erikson's work has been criticized as being focused primarily on male development, and relatively unclear about the particular issues of female development (Gilligan, 1982).

Erikson has been limited by psychoanalysis. His tools are those of a clinician, developed for treatment of unwell patients. Application of these tools to the development of the healthy personality is not always satisfactory. This is evident in Erikson's studies of great individuals. In his analysis of Gandhi, for example, Erikson applies brilliantly the tools and insights of the psychoanalyst. He does not, however, address seriously the role of Gandhi's spiritual ideals and spiritual discipline. The dynamics of Gandhi's life and thought are seen largely in terms of dysfunction rather than in terms of psychological and spiritual transformation. Gandhi's inner state may have been qualitatively different from that of the average patient in therapy. Also, Erikson has been criticized for underestimating the role of Indian culture and the social context of many of the key events in Gandhi's life (Appadurai, 1978).

Erikson's psychoanalytic tools are not always adequate for the tasks he takes on. By using these tools he has expanded psychoanalysis while at the same time revealing its limitations. In a sense, Erikson has smuggled the concept of the human spirit into psychoanalytic theory. This is one of the secrets of his great appeal.

Erikson provides a stimulating, relevant reformulation of psychoanalysis. He has successfully brought Freud's brilliant system of thought into a new era. Erikson's concern for social and cultural determinants of behavior and his integration of psychology, sociology, and anthropology with the insights of psychoanalysis predict the future of the psychology of personality.

The Theory Firsthand: Excerpts from *Identity, Youth and Crisis* and *Childhood and Society*

The Roots of the Concept of Identity

In the following excerpt, Erikson shows the early formulations of the concept of identity with a discussion of James's and Freud's constructs.

Before we try to understand the meaning of the present-day echo of our terms, let me take a long look back to our professional and conceptual ancestors. Today when the term identity refers, more often than not, to something noisily demonstrative, to a more or less desperate "quest," or to an almost deliberately confused "search" let me present two formulations which assert strongly what identity feels like when you become aware of the fact that you do undoubtedly *have* one.

My two witnesses are bearded and patriarchal founding fathers of the psychologies on which our thinking on identity is based. As a *subjective sense of an invigorating sameness* and *continuity,* what I would call a sense of identity seems to me best described by William James in a letter to his wife:

A man's character is discernible in the mental or moral attitude in which, when it came upon him, he felt himself most deeply and intensely active and alive. At such moments there is a voice inside which speaks and says: "This is the real me!"

Such experience always includes

. . . an element of active tension, of holding my own, as it were, and trusting outward things to perform their part so as to make it a full harmony, but without any guaranty that they will. Make it a guaranty . . . and the attitude immediately becomes to my consciousness stag-

nant and stingless. Take away the guaranty, and I feel (provided I am ueberhaupt in vigorous condition) a sort of deep enthusiastic bliss, of bitter willingness to do and suffer anything . . . and which, although it is a mere mood or emotion to which I can give no form in words, authenticates itself to me as the deepest principle of all active and theoretic determination which I possess. . . .

James uses the word "character," but I am taking the liberty of claiming that he describes a sense of identity, and that he does so in a way which can in principle be experienced by any man. To him it is both mental and moral in the sense of those "moral philosophy" days, and he experiences it as something that "comes upon you" as a recognition, almost as a surprise rather than as something strenuously "quested" after. It is an active tension (rather than a paralyzing question)—a tension which, furthermore, must create a challenge "without guaranty" rather than one dissipated in a clamor for certainty. But let us remember in passing that James was in his thirties when he wrote this, that in his youth he had faced and articulated an "identity crisis" of honest and desperate depth, and that he became *the* Psychologist-Philosopher of American Pragmatism only after having experimented with a variety of cultural, philosophic, and national identity elements: the use in the middle of his declaration of the untranslatable German word *"ueberhaupt"* is probably an echo of his conflictful student days in Europe.

One can study in James's life history a protracted identity crisis as well as the emergence of a "self-made" identity in the new and expansive American civilization. . . . [F]or the sake of further definition, let us now turn to a statement which asserts a unity of *personal and cultural* identity rooted in an ancient people's fate. In an address to the Society of B'nai B'rith in Vienna in 1926, Sigmund Freud said:

What bound me to Jewry was (I am ashamed to admit) neither faith nor national pride, for I have always been an unbeliever and was brought up without any religion though not without a respect for what are called the "ethical" standards of human civilization. Whenever I felt an inclination to national enthusiasm I strove to suppress it as being harmful and wrong, alarmed by the warning examples of the peoples among whom we Jews live. But plenty of other things remained over to make the attraction of Jewry and Jews irresistible—many obscure emotional forces, which were the more powerful the less they could be expressed in words, as well as a clear consciousness of inner identity, the safe privacy of a common mental construction. And beyond this there was a perception that it was to my Jewish nature alone that I owed two characteristics that had become indispensable to me in the difficult course of my life. Because I was a Jew I found myself free from many prejudices which restricted others in the use of their intellect; and as a Jew I was prepared to join the Opposition, and to do without agreement with the "compact majority."

No translation ever does justice to the distinctive choice of words in Freud's German original. "Obscure emotional forces" are *"dunkle Gefühlsmächte"*; the "safe privacy of a common mental construction" is *"die Heimlichkeit der inneren Konstruktion"*—not just "mental," then, and certainly not "private," but a deep communality known only to those who shared in it, and only expressible in words more mythical than conceptual.

These fundamental statements were taken not from theoretical works, but from special communications: a letter to his wife from a man who married late, an address to his "brothers" by an original observer long isolated in his profession. But in all their poetic spontaneity they are the products of trained minds and therefore exemplify the main dimensions of a positive sense of identity almost systematically. Trained minds of genius, of course, have a special identity and special identity problems often leading to a protracted crisis at the onset of their careers. Yet we must rely on them for formulating initially what we can then proceed to observe as universally human.

This is the only time Freud used the term identity in a more than casual way and, in fact, in a most central ethnic sense. And as we would expect of him, he inescapably points to some of those aspects of the matter which I called sinister and yet vital—the more vital, in fact, "the less they could be expressed in words." For Freud's "consciousness of inner identity" includes a sense of bitter pride preserved by his dispersed and often despised people throughout a long history of persecution. It is anchored in a particular (here intellectual) gift which had victoriously emerged from the hostile limitation of opportunities. At the same time, Freud contrasts the *positive identity* of a fearless freedom of thinking with a *negative* trait in "the peoples among whom we Jews live," namely, "prejudices which restrict others in the use of their intellect." It dawns on us, then, that one person's or group's identity may be relative to another's, and that the pride of gaining a strong identity may signify an inner emancipation from a more dominant group identity, such as that of the "compact majority." An exquisite triumph is suggested in the claim that the same historical development which restricted the prejudiced majority in the free use of their intellect made the isolated minority sturdier in intellectual matters. To all this, we must come back when discussing race relations.

And Freud goes farther. He admits in passing that he had to suppress in himself an inclination toward "national enthusiasm" such as was common for "the peoples among whom we Jews live." Again, as in James's case, only a study of Freud's youthful enthusiasms could show how he came to leave behind other aspirations in favor of the ideology of applying the methods of natural science to the study of psychological "forces of dignity." It is in Freud's dreams, incidentally, that we have a superb record of his suppressed (or what James called "abandoned," or even "murdered") selves—for our "negative identity" haunts us at night. (Erikson, 1968, pp. 19–22)

Son of a Bombardier

In this passage, Erikson, revealing his keen psychoanalytic skills, provides a real-life example of a young boy in a crisis of role identification.

During the last war a neighbor of mine, a boy of five, underwent a change of personality from a "mother's boy" to a violent, stubborn, and disobedient child. The most disquieting symptom was an urge to set fires.

The boy's parents had separated just before the outbreak of war. The mother and the boy had moved in with some women cousins, and when war began the father had joined the air force. The women cousins frequently expressed their disrespect for the father, and cultivated babyish traits in the boy. Thus, to be a mother's boy threatened to be a stronger identity element than to be a father's son.

The father, however, did well in war; in fact, he became a hero. On the occasion of his first furlough the little boy had the experience of seeing the man he had been warned not to emulate become the much-admired center of the neighborhood's attention. The mother announced that she would drop her divorce plans. The father went back to war and was soon lost over Germany.

After the father's departure and death the affectionate and dependent boy developed more and more disquieting symptoms of destructiveness and defiance, culminating in fire setting. He gave the key to the change himself when, protesting against his mother's whipping, he pointed to a pile of wood he had set afire and exclaimed (in more childish words), "If this were a German city, you would have liked me for it." He thus indicated that in setting fires he fantasied being a bombardier like the father, who had told of his exploits.

We can only guess at the nature of the boy's turmoil. But I believe that we see here the identification of a son with his father, resulting from a suddenly increased conflict at the very close of the Oedipus age. The father, at first successfully replaced by the "good" little boy, suddenly becomes both a newly vitalized ideal and a concrete threat, a competitor for the mother's love. He thus devaluates radically the boy's feminine identifications. In order to save himself from both sexual and social disorientation, the boy must, in the shortest possible time, regroup his identifications; but then the great competitor is killed by the enemy—a fact which increases the guilt for the competitive feeling itself and compromises the boy's new masculine initiative which becomes maladaptive.

A child has quite a number of opportunities to identify himself, more or less experimentally, with habits, traits, occupations, and ideas of real or fictitious people of either sex. Certain crises force him to make radical selections. However, the historical era in which he lives offers only a limited number of socially meaningful models for workable combinations of identification fragments. Their usefulness

depends on the way in which they simultaneously meet the requirements of the organism's maturational stage and the ego's habits of
synthesis.

To my little neighbor the role of the bombardier may have suggested a possible synthesis of the various elements that comprise a budding identity: his temperament (vigorous); his maturational stage (phal-
lic-urethral-locomotor); his social stage (Oedipal) and his social
situation; his capacities (muscular, mechanical); his father's temperament (a great soldier rather than a successful civilian); and a current
historical prototype (aggressive hero). Where such synthesis succeeds, a
most surprising coagulation of constitutional, temperamental, and
learned reactions may produce exuberance of growth and unexpected
accomplishment. Where it fails, it must lead to severe conflict, often
expressed in unexpected naughtiness or delinquency. For should a
child feel that the environment tries to deprive him too radically of all
the forms of expression which permit him to develop and to integrate
the next step in his identity, he will defend it with the astonishing
strength encountered in animals who are suddenly forced to defend
their lives. And indeed, in the social jungle of human existence, there is
no feeling of being alive without a sense of ego identity. Deprivation of
identity can lead to murder.

I would not have dared to speculate on the little bombardier's conflicts had I not seen evidence for a solution in line with our interpretation. When the worst of this boy's dangerous initiative had subsided,
he was observed swooping down a hill on a bicycle, endangering, scar-
ing, and yet deftly avoiding other children. They shrieked, laughed, and
in a way admired him for it. In watching him, and hearing the strange
noises he made, I could not help thinking that he again imagined himself to be an airplane on a bombing mission. But at the same time he
gained in playful mastery over his locomotion; he exercised circumspec-
tion in his attack, and he became an admired virtuoso on a bicycle. . . .

Our little son of a bombardier illustrates a general point.
Psychosocial identity develops out of a gradual integration of all identifications. But here, if anywhere, the whole has a different quality from
the sum of its parts. Under favorable circumstances children have the
nucleus of a separate identity early in life; often they must defend it
even against the necessity of overidentifying with one or both of their
parents. These processes are difficult to study in patients, because the
neurotic self has, by definition, fallen prey to overidentifications which
isolate the small individual both from his budding identity and from his
milieu. (Erikson, 1963, pp. 238–241)

Annotated Bibliography

Erikson, E. (1963). *Childhood and society* (2nd ed.). New York: Norton. Erikson's first and most seminal book. It includes his most detailed description of the eight stages of human development, papers on his work with the Sioux and Yurok, and psychobiographies of Hitler and Gorky, which provide a look at the psychological implications of German and Russian culture.

————. (1964). *Insight and responsibility*. New York: Norton. A brilliant set of essays, including a psychobiographical look at Freud, an analysis of psychosocial strengths, psychological reality, and historical actuality, and a discussion of the Golden Rule today.

————. (1969). *Gandhi's truth*. New York: Norton. An epic psychobiography of Gandhi, which provides a model for looking at a great figure in history through psychological eyes. Also a useful example of the limits of psychoanalysis in its neglect of the spiritual and transpersonal aspect of Gandhi's life.

References

Appadurai, A. (1978). Understanding Gandhi. In P. Homans (Ed.), *Childhood and selfhood*. Cranbury, NJ: Associated University Presses.

Coles, R. (1970). *Erik Erikson: The growth of his work*. Boston: Little, Brown.

Cote, J., & Levine, C. (1987). A formulation of Erikson's theory of ego identity formation. *Developmental Review, 7*, 273–325.

Erikson, E. (1958). *Young man Luther*. New York: Norton.

————. (1963). *Childhood and society* (2nd ed.). New York: Norton.

————. (1964). *Insight and responsibility*. New York: Norton.

————. (1965). *The challenge of youth*. New York: Doubleday Anchor Books.

————. (1968). *Identity, youth and crisis*. New York: Norton.

————. (1969). *Gandhi's truth*. New York: Norton.

————. (1974). *Dimensions of a new identity*. New York: Norton.

————. (1975). *Life history and the historical moment*. New York: Norton.

————. (1977). *Toys and reasons*. New York: Norton.

————. (1978). *Adulthood*. New York: Norton.

————. (1980a). *Identity and the life cycle*. New York: Norton.

————. (1980b). *On the generational cycle: An address*. New York: Norton.

————. (1981). *The Galilean sayings and the sense of "I."* New York: Norton.

————. (1982). *The life cycle completed*. New York: Norton.

————. (1983). Reflections: On the relationship of adolescence and par-enthood. *Adolescent Psychiatry, 2,* 9–13.

————. (1985). Reflections on the last stage—and the first. *The Psycho-analytic Study of the Child, 39.*

————. (1987). *A way of looking at things: Selected papers from 1930 to 1980.* New York: Norton.

Erikson, E., Erikson, J., & Kivnick, H. (1986). *Vital involvement in old age.* New York: Norton.

Evans, R. (1969). *Dialogue with Erik Erikson.* New York: Dutton.

Gilligan, C. (1982). *In a different voice.* Cambridge, MA: Harvard University Press.

Gross, F. (1987). *Introducing Erik Erikson: An invitation to his thinking.* Lanham, MD: University Press.

Homans, P. (Ed.). (1978). *Childhood and selfhood: Essays on tradition, religion, and modernity in the psychology of Erik Erikson.* Cranbury, NJ: Associated University Presses.

Levene, M. (1990). Female adolescent development: Reflections upon relational growth. *Melanie-Klein-and-Object-Relations, 8,* 31–42.

Roazen, P. (1976). *Erik Erikson: The power and limits of a vision.* New York: Free Press.

Sheehy, G. (1977). *Passages.* New York: Basic Books.

Chapter Seven

Wilhelm Reich and Somatic Psychology

> The body's life is the life of sensations and emotions. The body feels real hunger, real joy in the sun or the snow, . . . real anger, real sorrow, real tenderness, real warmth, real passion, real hate, real grief. All the emotions belong to the body and are only recognized by the mind. (D. H. Lawrence, 1955)

Reich, perhaps more consistently than anyone else, worked out the critical and revolutionary implications of psychoanalytic theory. (Robinson, 1969, p. 10)

In this chapter, we will first discuss the work of Wilhelm Reich, the founder of what might be called somatic psychology and body-oriented psychotherapy. He is the godfather of all current therapies that work with the emotional life of the body. Wilhelm Reich was a member of the psychoanalytic inner circle in Vienna and led the technical training seminar for young analysts. In his therapeutic work, Reich gradually came to emphasize the importance of dealing with the physical manifestations of an individual's character, especially the patterns of chronic muscle tension that he called *body armor*. He was also concerned with the role of society in creating instinctual—especially sexual—inhibitions in the individual.

Reich's unique contributions to psychology include (1) his insistence on the unity of mind and body; (2) his inclusion of the body in psychotherapy; and (3) his concept of character armor. Reich approached each patient as an *organism,* whose emotional difficulties could be explained only upon consideration of the total being. Reich was also a pioneer in sex education and hygiene, the psychology of politics, social responsibility, and the interfacing of psychology, biology, and physics. Reich was a courageous and stubborn innovator whose ideas were far ahead of the time.

Reich's theories of body-mind interaction are integral to many other body-oriented theories. The second part of this chapter consists of brief summaries of several major body-oriented approaches to therapy and personal growth. These fall into three main areas: (1) body-oriented therapy: bioenergetic analysis; (2) systems of improving body structure and function: structural integration, the Alexander technique, the Feldenkrais method, and sensory awareness; and (3) Eastern body-oriented disciplines: hatha-yoga, t'ai chi ch'uan, and aikido.

Personal History

Wilhelm Reich was born on March 24, 1897, in Galicia, a German-Ukrainian area in Austria. He was the son of a middle-class Jewish farmer, a jealous, authoritarian man who dominated his wife and children. The father provided no religious upbringing for his children and insisted that only German be spoken at home. Consequently, Wilhelm was isolated from both the local Ukrainian peasant children and from the Yiddish-speaking Jewish children. He had one brother, three years his junior, who was both companion and competitor.

Reich idolized his mother. She committed suicide when he was 14 years old, apparently after Reich revealed to his father that she was having an affair with the boys' tutor. Reich's father was devastated by his wife's death. He contracted pneumonia that developed into tuberculosis and died three years later. Reich's brother also died of tuberculosis, at the age of 26. Reich was severely affected by this series of family tragedies.

After his father's death, Reich managed the family farm but continued his studies. In 1916, when war spread throughout his homeland, the family property was destroyed. Reich joined the Austrian army. He fought as an officer in Italy. In 1918, Reich entered medical school at the University of Vienna. Within a year, he became a practicing member of the Vienna Psychoanalytical Society. He received his medical degree in 1922, at the age of 25.

Reich was involved in politics as a student, and subsequently sought to reconcile the theories of Freud and Marx. At the university, Reich met his first wife Annie Pink, who was also a medical student and who later became a psychoanalyst.

In 1922, when Freud established a psychoanalytic clinic in Vienna, Reich was his first clinical assistant, and he later became vice director. In 1924, Reich became the director of the Seminar for Psychoanalytic Therapy, the first training institute for psychoanalysts. Many young analysts came to him for personal analysis as well as for training.

Reich underwent personal analysis at different times with several different psychoanalysts, but for various reasons he broke off from each one. In 1927, Reich sought analysis with Freud, who refused to make an exception to his policy of not treating members of the psychoanalytic inner circle. At this time, Reich developed a serious conflict with Freud. It stemmed partly from Freud's refusal to analyze Reich but also partly from their theoretical differences. Freud was at odds with Reich's uncompromising insistence that neurosis was rooted in sexual dissatisfaction. Reich developed tuberculosis at this time and spent several months recovering in a sanatorium in Switzerland.

When he returned to Vienna after his illness, Reich assumed his previous duties. He also became extremely active politically and, in 1928, joined the Communist party. In 1929, Reich helped found the first sex hygiene clinics for workers, which provided free information on birth control, child rearing, and sex education.

In 1930, Reich moved to Berlin mainly because he sought personal analysis with Rado (a leading psychoanalyst). However, he searched for an analyst outside Vienna, because Viennese psychoanalysts had become uncomfortable with his political activities. In Berlin, Reich became more deeply involved with the communist-oriented hygiene movement. He traveled throughout Germany, lecturing and helping to establish hygiene centers.

Before long, Reich was unpopular with both the psychoanalysts and the communists as a function of his politics on the one hand and his radi-

> [W]here and how is the patient to express his natural sexuality when it has been liberated from repression? Freud neither alluded to nor, as it later turned out, even tolerated this question. And, eventually, because he refused to deal with this central question, Freud himself created enormous difficulties by postulating a biological striving for suffering and death. (Reich, 1973, p. 152)

cal sex education programs on the other. In 1933, Reich was expelled from the German Communist party. Then, in 1934, he was expelled from the International Psychoanalytical Association.

Later in his career, Reich rejected communism and socialism, because he felt that both were committed to an ideology at the expense of human considerations. He came to think of himself more as an individualist and was deeply suspicious of politics and politicians.

Because of Hitler's rise to power, Reich emigrated to Denmark in 1933. He separated from his wife when they left Berlin due to personal, political, and professional differences. A year earlier, Reich had met Elsa Lindenberg, a ballet dancer and a member of his Communist party cell. She joined Reich in Denmark and became his second wife. Because of his controversial theories, Reich was expelled from Denmark and Sweden. He and Elsa moved to Oslo, Norway, in 1934, where he lectured and conducted research in psychology and biology for over five years.

Within a period of six months, Reich had been expelled from his two major affiliations—the Communist party and the psychoanalytic movement—and from three different countries. It is not surprising that his subsequent writing is somewhat defensive and polemical. In Reich's case, a certain amount of paranoia was not irrational or unjustified but represented a fairly realistic assessment of his situation.

After three years of relative quiet in Norway, Reich became the target of a vicious newspaper campaign that attacked his emphasis on the sexual basis of neurosis and his laboratory experiments with bioenergy. He became increasingly isolated and consequently his relations worsened with Elsa, who finally separated from him.

In 1939, Reich was offered the position of associate professor of medical psychology at the New School for Social Research in New York. He packed up his laboratory and moved to the United States. In New York, he met Ilse Ollendorf, a German refugee who became his laboratory assistant and later his third wife.

[T]he life process is identical with the sexual process—an experimentally proven fact. . . . In everything living, sexual vegetative energy is at work. (Reich, 1961, p. 55)

Reich founded the Orgone Institute to support research on *orgone* energy, or life energy. He concluded from his laboratory experimentation that there is a basic life energy present in all living organisms and that this energy is the biological force that underlies Freud's concept of libido. Reich began experimentation with orgone energy accumulators: boxes and other devices that, he claimed, store and concentrate orgone energy. Reich found that various diseases resulting from disturbances of the "automatic apparatus" could be treated with degrees of success by restoring the individual's normal orgone energy flow. This could be accomplished through exposure to high concentrations of orgone energy in the accumulators. The targeted illnesses included cancer, angina pectoris, asthma, hypertension, and epilepsy.

In 1954, the Food and Drug Administration obtained an injunction against the distribution and further use of the accumulators. The FDA alleged that Reich's claim that the orgone energy accumulators successfully treated disease was unfounded. The FDA also enjoined the sale of most of Reich's books and journals. Reich violated the injunction by continuing his research, and he insisted that the courts were not competent to judge matters of scientific fact. He eventually was convicted of contempt of court and sentenced to two years' imprisonment. The FDA burned his books and other publications related to the sale or manufacture of orgone accumulators. Reich died in 1957 of heart disease in federal prison.

Intellectual Antecedents

Psychoanalysis

Much of Reich's work is firmly rooted in psychoanalytic theory. His early contributions are primarily based on his concepts of character and character armor, which developed out of the psychoanalytic conception of the ego's need to defend itself against instinctual forces. According to Reich, an individual's character shows consistent, habitual patterns of defenses. Reich came to associate these defenses with specific patterns of muscular armorings. In other words, each pattern of character defenses had a corresponding pattern of physical gestures and postures. Reich emphasized the importance of loosening and dissolving muscular armoring in addition to dealing analytically with psychological material. By so doing, the process of psychoanalysis was powerfully assisted, because the client released emotions locked into muscular armoring that was forged in early childhood.

Reich's later work with life energy, or orgone energy, is derived in great part from Freud's conception of libido. Later psychoanalytic theorists have tended to deemphasize Freud's libido concept; for Freud, however, especially in his early writings, libido was a real and potentially measurable psychic energy.

[T]he patient must, through analysis, arrive at a regulated and gratifying genital life—if he is to be cured and permanently so. (Reich, 1976, p. 17)

> [Libido] possesses all the characteristics of quantity (though we have no means of measuring it), which is capable of increase, diminution, displacement, and discharge, and which is spread over the memory traces of ideas somewhat as an electric charge is spread over the surface of a body. (Freud in Rycroft, 1971, pp. 14–15)

Reich extended Freud's libido theory to include all basic biological and psychological processes. Reich viewed pleasure as a movement of energy from the core of the organism toward the periphery and the external world; anxiety is represented as a retraction of energy, or movement away from the external world. Reich eventually came to view therapy as a process of allowing free flow of energy throughout the body by systematically dissolving blocks of muscular armoring. He found that these blocks distort and destroy natural feeling and inhibit, in particular, sexual feelings and prevent complete and fulfilling orgasm.

Neuroses are the result of a stasis (damming-up) of sexual energy. . . . Everyday clinical experience leaves no doubt: the elimination of sexual stasis through orgastic discharge eliminates every neurotic manifestation. (Reich, 1961, p. 189)

Marxism

Reich was seriously concerned with the theories of Freud and Marx; he attempted to reconcile these two systems and wrote several books on this subject (Robinson, 1969). Reich argued that (1) psychoanalysis is a "materialistic science" in that it deals with real human needs and experiences; (2) psychoanalysis is based on a dialectical theme of psychic conflict and resolution; and (3) psychoanalysis is a revolutionary science in that it supplements Marx's critique of bourgeois economics with a critique of bourgeois morality based on sexual repression.

In *The Mass Psychology of Fascism* (1970b) Reich provides an important analysis of the roots of ideology in the individual character, a topic he felt was insufficiently covered by Marx. Twenty years before the publication of social science research on the authoritarian personality, Reich discussed the relationship between the German predilection for authoritarianism and the character formation of children in the German lower-middle-class family.

Reich's political interests sparked even greater controversy in psychoanalytical circles than did his theoretical innovations. In the tense political climate of Austria and Germany during the 1930s, Reich's membership in the Communist party and his public political activities created tension among his fellow analysts. Reich was asked to discontinue his political activities. When he refused, he was dropped from the German Psychoanalytic Association.

> Every social order produces in the masses of its members that structure which it needs to achieve its aims. (Reich, 1970b, p. 23)

Major Concepts

Bioenergy

In his work on muscular armoring, Reich discovered that the loosening of chronically rigid muscles often resulted in peculiar physical sensations—feelings of hot and cold, prickling, itching, and emotional arousal. He concluded that these sensations were due to movements of freed biological energy, or bioenergy, which he was later to call *orgone* energy.

Reich also found that the mobilization and discharge of bioenergy are essential stages in the process of sexual arousal and orgasm. He called this the *orgasm formula,* a four-part process that he felt was characteristic of all living organisms (1973):

1. Sexual organs fill with fluid—mechanical tension.

2. Intense excitation results—bioenergetic charge.

3. Sexual excitation discharged in muscular contractions—bioenergetic discharge.

4. Physical relaxation follows—mechanical relaxation.

After physical contact, energy is built up in both bodies and finally discharged in the orgasm, which is essentially a phenomenon of bioenergy discharge.

Orgone Energy

Reich gradually extended his concern with patients' physical functioning to laboratory research in physiology and biology and eventually to research in physics. He came to believe that the bioenergy in the organism is one aspect of a universal energy present in all things. He coined the term *orgone* energy from "organism" and "orgasm." He explained it in this way: "Cosmic orgone energy functions in the living organism as specific biological energy. As such, it governs the entire organism; it is expressed in the emotions as well as in the purely biophysical movement of the organs" (Reich, 1976, p. 393).

Orgone energy has the following major properties (Kelley in Mann, 1973):

1. Orgone energy is mass-free; it has no inertia or weight.

2. It is present everywhere, although in differing concentrations, even in a vacuum.

3. It is the medium for electromagnetic and gravitational activity, the substratum of most basic natural phenomena.

4. Orgone energy is in constant motion.

5. High concentrations of orgone energy attract orgone energy from less-concentrated surroundings (which contradicts the law of entropy).

6. Orgone energy forms units that become centers of creative activity. These units include cells, plants and animals, and also clouds, planets, stars, and galaxies.

Reich's extensive research on orgone energy and related topics has been ignored or dismissed by most critics and scientists. His findings contradict a number of established theories in physics and biology, and Reich's work is certainly not without its experimental weaknesses. However, his research has not been disproved or even carefully reviewed and responsibly criticized by reputable scientific critics. One psychologist who worked with Reich has pointed out:

> In the twenty-plus years since Reich announced the discovery of orgone energy, no good-faith repetition of *any* critical orgone energy experiment has ever been published refuting Reich's results. . . . The fact is, despite (and partly because of) the ridicule, defamation, and attempts by the orthodox to "bury" Reich and orgonomy, *there is no counter evidence to his experiments in any scientific publication,* much

In an ultimate sense, in self-awareness and in the striving for the perfection of knowledge and full integration of one's bio-functions, *the cosmic orgone energy becomes aware of itself.* (Reich, 1961, p. 52)

Orgastic longing, which plays such a gigantic role in the life of animals, appears now [in humans] as an expression of this *striving beyond oneself,* as *longing* to reach out beyond the narrow sack of one's own organism. (Reich, 1960, p. 355)

less a systematic refutation of the volumes of scientific work which support his position. (Kelley, 1962, pp. 72–73)

Human Sexuality

Reich's concern with sexuality formed a major theme that he pursued throughout his career. As a young medical student, Reich first visited Freud to seek his help in establishing a seminar on sexology in the medical school Reich attended (Higgens & Raphael, 1967). And Reich's major political activity consisted of helping to establish communist-sponsored sex hygiene clinics for the working class in Austria and Germany.

Reich's ideas and his clinics far ahead of their time. In the 1930s (around the time Margaret Sanger was imprisoned for advocating planned parenthood for married couples), Reich's program for his clinics included features that were astonishingly radical then and still controversial today (Boadella, 1973):

1. Free distribution of contraceptives to everyone who wants them; intensive birth control education.

2. Complete legalization of abortion.

3. Abolition of the legal distinction between the married and unmarried; freedom of divorce.

4. Elimination of venereal disease and avoidance of sexual problems through education.

5. Training of doctors, teachers, and others in all relevant matters of sexual hygiene.

6. Treatment of rather than punishment for sexual offenses.

Reich came to stress the free expression of sexual and emotional feelings within a mature, loving relationship. He emphasized the essentially sexual nature of the energies with which he dealt, and he found that the pelvic area of his patients was the most blocked. Reich came to believe that the goal of therapy must be to free all the blocks in the body and to attain full capacity for sexual orgasm, which he felt was blocked in most people.

Reich's radical views concerning sexuality resulted in misunderstanding, distortion, and vicious (and unfounded) attacks on all areas of his work, as well as on him personally.

Character

The concept of character was first discussed by Freud in 1908. Reich elaborated this concept: He was the first analyst to treat patients by interpreting the nature and function of their character, not their symptoms.

According to Reich, the character is composed of a person's habitual attitudes and pattern of responses to various situations. It includes psy-

Every person who has succeeded in preserving a certain amount of naturalness knows this: those who are psychically ill need but one thing—complete and repeated genital gratification. (Reich, 1973, p. 96)

The "how" . . . the form of the behavior and of the communications, was far more important than what the patient told the analyst. Words can lie. The expression never lies. (Reich, 1973, p. 171)

chological attitudes and values, style of behavior (shyness, aggressiveness, and so forth), and physical attitudes (posture, habits of holding and moving the body).

Character Armor

Reich felt that the character structure forms as a defense against the child's anxiety over intense sexual feelings and the accompanying fear of punishment. The first defense is repression, which temporarily restrains the sexual impulses. As ego defenses become chronically active and automatic, they develop into stable character traits that combine to form the individual's system of character armoring. Character armor includes all repressing defensive forces, which form a coherent pattern within the ego.

Character traits are not neurotic symptoms. The difference, according to Reich, lies in the fact that neurotic symptoms (such as irrational fears or phobias) are experienced as alien to the individual, as foreign elements in the psyche, whereas neurotic character traits (extreme orderliness or anxious shyness, for example) are experienced as integral parts of the personality. One may complain about being shy, but this shyness does not seem to be meaningless or pathological, as are neurotic symptoms. The character defenses are difficult to eradicate because they are well rationalized by the individual and experienced as part of the individual's self-concept.

Reich continually attempted to make his patients more aware of their character traits. He frequently imitated their characteristic gestures (a nervous smile, for example) and postures, or had patients repeat and exaggerate them themselves. As patients ceased taking their character make-ups for granted, their motivation to change was enhanced.

Genital Character

Freud used the term *genital character* to refer to the final level of psychosexual development. Reich applied it to persons with orgastic potency: "Orgastic potency is the capacity to surrender to the flow of biological energy, free of any inhibitions; the capacity to discharge completely the dammed-up sexual excitation through involuntary, pleasurable convulsions of the body" (1973, p. 102). Reich found that as his patients relinquished their armoring and developed orgastic potency, many areas of neurotic functioning changed spontaneously. In the place of rigid neurotic controls, individuals developed a capacity for *self-regulation*. Reich described self-regulated individuals as naturally rather than compulsively moral. They act in terms of their own inner inclinations and feelings rather than following external codes or demands prescribed by others.

After Reichian therapy, many patients who were formerly neurotically promiscuous developed greater tenderness and spontaneously sought more lasting and fulfilling relationships. Also, those in loveless marriages found that they could no longer make love with their spouses merely as a duty.

The patient's behavior (manner, look, language, countenance, dress, handshake, etc.) not only is vastly underestimated in terms of its analytic importance but is usually completely overlooked. (Reich, 1976, p. 34)

A conflict which is fought out at a certain age always leaves behind a trace in the person's character . . . revealed as a hardening of the character. (Reich, 1973, p. 145)

I say on the basis of ample clinical experience that only in a few cases in our civilization is the sexual act based on love. The intervening rage, hatred, sadistic emotions and contempt are part and parcel of the love life of modern man. (Reich in Rycroft, 1971, p. 81)

Individuals who Reich viewed as genital characters were not imprisoned in their armor and psychological defenses. They were able to shield themselves, only when necessary, against a hostile environment. However, they did this fairly consciously and they could dispense with the armor when it was no longer needed.

Reich wrote that genital characters have worked through their Oedipal complex, so that the Oedipal material is no longer strongly charged or repressed. The superego has become "sex-affirmative," and thus id and superego are generally in harmony (Reich, 1976). The genital character is able to experience sexual orgasm freely, discharging all excess libido. The climax of sexual activity is characterized by surrender to sexual experience and uninhibited, involuntary movement, as opposed to the forced or even violent movements of the armored individual.

Dynamics

Psychological Growth

It is solely our *sensation* of the natural process inside and outside ourselves, which holds the keys to the deep riddles of nature. . . . Sensation is the sieve through which all inner and outer stimuli are perceived; sensation is the connecting link between ego and outer world. (Reich, 1961, p. 275)

Reich defined growth as a process of dissolving one's psychological and physical armoring, gradually becoming a more free and open human being, capable of enjoying full and satisfying orgasm.

Reich found that muscular armoring is organized into seven major segments, composed of muscles and organs with related expressive functions. These segments form a series of seven roughly horizontal rings, at right angles to the spine and torso. They are centered in the eyes, mouth, neck, chest, diaphragm, abdomen, and pelvis. Reich's seven armor segments are closely related to the seven chakras of kundalini-yoga discussed in Chapter 14, although the fit is not a perfect one. It is interesting to note that Reich moves from the top down; the patient is finished once the pelvis, the most important armor segment, is opened and energized. In kundalini-yoga, the movement is from the base of the spine upward, and the yogi is "finished" once the thousand-petaled lotus of the brain, the most important chakra, is opened and energized. Boadella (1987) offers a more complete discussion of this relationship.

According to Reich, orgone energy naturally flows up and down the body, parallel to the spine. The rings of armor are formed at right angles to this flow and interrupt it. Reich points out that it is no accident that in Western culture we have learned to say *yes* by moving our heads up and down, in the direction of energy flow in the body, whereas we say *no* by moving our heads from side to side, the direction of the armoring.

It is possible to get out of a trap. However, in order to break out of a prison, one first must confess to *being in a prison. The trap is man's emotional structure, his character structure. There is little use in devising systems of thought about the nature of the trap if the only thing to do in order to get out of the trap is to know the trap and to find the exit. (Reich, 1961, p. 470)*

Armoring restricts the flow of energy and stops free expression of emotion. What begins as a defense against overpowering anxiety becomes a physical and emotional straitjacket.

In armored human organisms, the orgone energy is bound in the chronic contraction of the muscles. The body orgone does not begin to flow freely as soon as the armor ring has been loosened. . . . As soon as the first armor blocks have been dissolved, the movement expressive of "surrender" appears more and more, along with the orgonotic currents and sensations. However, its full unfolding is hindered by those armor blocks that have not yet been dissolved. (Reich, 1976, pp. 411–412)

The primary goal of Reichian therapy is to dissolve the armor in each of the seven segments, beginning with the eyes and ending with the pelvis. Each segment is more or less an independent unit and must be dealt with separately.

Loosening the Muscular Armor

Reich found that each character attitude had a corresponding physical attitude expressed in the body as muscular rigidity or muscular armoring. He began to work directly on the muscular armoring in conjunction with his analytic work. He found that loosening the muscular armor freed libidinal energy and aided the process of psychoanalysis. Reich's psychiatric work increasingly dealt with freeing the emotions (pleasure, rage, anxiety) through work with the body. He found that this led to intense experiencing of the psychological material uncovered in analysis.

Reich first applied the techniques of character analysis to physical attitudes. He analyzed in detail his patients' posture and physical habits to make them aware of how they suppressed vital feelings in different parts of the body. Reich would have patients intensify particular tensions to become more aware of them and to elicit the emotion that had been bound up in that part of the body. He found that only after the bottled-up emotion was expressed could the chronic tension be fully abandoned. Reich began to work directly on tense muscles with his hands to release the emotions bound up in them.

> In the final analysis, I could not rid myself of the impression that somatic rigidity represents the most essential part in the process of repression. All our patients report that they went through periods in childhood in which, by means of certain practices . . . (holding the breath, tensing the abdominal muscular pressure, etc.), they learned to suppress their impulses of hate, anxiety, and love. . . . It never ceases to be surprising how the loosening of a muscular spasm not only releases the vegetative energy, but, over and above this, reproduces a memory of that situation in infancy in which the repression of the instinct occurred. (Reich, 1973, p. 300)

Reich found that chronic muscular tension serves to block one of the three basic biological excitations: anxiety, anger, or sexual excitation. He concluded that the physical and psychological armor were essentially the same:

> Character armorings were now seen to be functionally identical with muscular [hypertension]. The concept, "functional identity," which I

The spasm of the musculature is the somatic side of the process of repression, and the basis of its continued preservation. (Reich, 1973, p. 302)

[The] armor could lie on the "surface" or in the "depth," could be "as soft as a sponge" or "as hard as a rock." Its function in every case was to protect the person against unpleasurable experiences. However, it also entailed a reduction in the organism's capacity for pleasure. (Reich, 1973, p. 145)

had to introduce means nothing more than that muscular attitudes and character attitudes have the same function in the psychic mechanism: they can replace one another and can be influenced by one another. Basically, they cannot be separated. They are identical in their function. (Reich, 1973, pp. 270–271)

Three major tools are used in dissolving the armor: (1) building up energy in the body through deep breathing; (2) directly attacking the chronically tense muscles (through pressure, pinching, and so on) to loosen them; and (3) maintaining the cooperation of the patient by dealing openly with whatever resistances or emotional restrictions arise. Reich used these tools in each of the seven armor segments as follows:

1. *The eyes.* Armoring of the eyes is expressed by an immobility of the forehead and an "empty" expression of the eyes, which look out from behind a rigid mask. The armor is dissolved by having patients open their eyes wide, as if in fright, in order to mobilize the eyelids and forehead by forcing an emotional expression and by encouraging free movement of the eyes—rolling the eyes and looking from side to side.

2. *The mouth.* The oral segment includes the muscles of the chin, throat, and back of the head. The jaw may be very tight or unnaturally loose. The emotional expressions of crying, angry biting, yelling, sucking, and grimacing are all inhibited by this segment. The armor may be loosened by encouraging the patient to imitate crying, making sounds that mobilize the lips, biting, gagging, and by direct work on the muscles involved.

3. *The neck.* This segment includes the deep neck muscles and also the tongue. The armor functions mainly to hold back anger or crying. Direct pressure on the deep neck muscles is not possible, so screaming, yelling, and gagging are all important means for loosening this segment.

4. *The chest.* The chest segment includes the large chest muscles, the shoulder muscles, the muscles of the shoulder blades, the entire chest cage, and the hands and arms. This segment serves to inhibit laughter, rage, sadness, and longing. Inhibition of breathing, which is an important means of suppressing any emotion, occurs to a great extent in the chest. The armoring may be loosened through work with breathing, especially developing complete expiration. The arms and hands are used to hit, tear, choke, pound, and reach out with longing.

5. *The diaphragm.* This segment includes the diaphragm, stomach, solar plexus, various internal organs, and muscles along the lower thoracic vertebrate. Armoring is expressed by a forward curvature of the spine so that, when the patient is seated in a

chair, there is considerable space between the patient's lower back and the back of the chair. It is much harder to breathe out than to breathe in. The armoring mainly inhibits extreme rage. The first four segments must be relatively free before the diaphragm can be loosened through repeated work with breathing and with the gag reflex. (People with strong blocks in this segment find it virtually impossible to vomit.)

6. *The abdomen*. The abdominal segment includes the large abdominal muscles and the muscles of the back. Tension in the lumbar muscles is related to fear of attack. Armoring in a person's flanks produces ticklishness and is related to inhibition of spite. Dissolution of the armoring in this segment is relatively simple once the higher segments are open.

7. *The pelvis*. This last segment is comprised of all the muscles of the pelvis and lower limbs. The stronger the armoring, the more the pelvis is pulled back and sticks out in the rear. The gluteal muscles are tight and painful; the pelvis is rigid, "dead," and asexual. Pelvic armoring serves to inhibit anxiety and rage as well as pleasure. The anxiety and rage result from inhibitions of sexual pleasure sensations, and it is impossible to experience pleasure freely in this area until the anger has been released from the pelvic muscles. The armoring can be loosened by first mobilizing the pelvis and having the patient repeatedly kick with the feet and also strike, for example, a couch with his or her pelvis.

The capacity of the vegetative organism to participate in the tension-charge function in a unified and total way is undoubtedly the basic characteristic of psychic and vegetative health. . . . Disturbances of self-perception do not really disappear until the orgasm reflex has been fully developed into a unified whole. (Reich, 1973, p. 355)

Personal Reflection ——————————

—————————————— Armor in Your Life

Read over the description of armoring in the text. Which is your most *important* armoring segment? How has this part of your body functioned in your life? How has your strong armoring here affected your experience? (Be as specific as possible.) Has this armoring segment made you particularly vulnerable, or instead, particularly rigid and unfeeling?

Reich found that as his patients began to develop the capacity for "full genital surrender," their whole being and life-style changed.

The unification of the orgasm reflex also restores the sensations of depth and seriousness. The patients remember the time in their early childhood when the unity of their body sensation was not disturbed. Seized with emotion, they tell of the time as children when they felt at one with nature, with everything that surrounded them, of the time they felt "alive," and how finally all this had been shattered and crushed by their education. (Reich, 1973, pp. 357–358)

These individuals began to feel that the rigid norms of society, which previously they had taken for granted, were alien and unnatural. Attitudes toward work also changed noticeably. Many who had done their work as a mechanical necessity quit their jobs to seek new and vital work that fulfilled their inner needs. Often those who were interested in their vocation blossomed with fresh energy and ability.

Obstacles to Growth

Armoring

The armoring is the major obstacle to growth according to Reich.

> The armored organism is incapable of breaking down its own armor. But it is equally incapable of expressing its elemental biological emotions. It is familiar with the sensation of tickling but has never experienced orgonotic pleasure. The armored individual cannot express a sigh of pleasure or consciously imitate it. When he tries to do so, the result is a groan, a suppressed, pent-up roar, or even an impulse to vomit. He is incapable of venting anger or of banging his fist in an imitation of anger. (Reich, 1976, p. 402)

Boadella (1987) has pointed out that almost everyone suffering from emotional maladjustment lives as though in a permanent state of emergency. Only by changing this state of chronic tension can individuals approach their environment rationally and healthfully.

Reich (1961) felt that the process of armoring has created two distorted intellectual traditions that form the basis of civilization: mystical religion and mechanistic science. Mechanists are so well armored that they have no real sense of their own life processes or inner nature. They have a basic fear of deep emotion, aliveness, and spontaneity. They tend to develop a rigid, mechanical conception of nature and are interested primarily in external objects and in the natural sciences.

> A machine has to be *perfect.* Hence the thinking and acts of the physicist must be "perfect." *Perfectionism* is an essential characteristic of mechanistic thinking. It tolerates no mistakes; uncertainties, shifting situations are unwelcome. . . . But this principle, when applied to processes in nature, inevitably leads into confusion. *Nature is inexact. Nature operates not mechanically, but functionally.* (Reich, 1961, p. 278).

In contrast to the mechanists, the religious mystics have not developed their armoring so completely, according to Reich; they remain partly in touch with their own life energy and are capable of great insight because of this partial contact with their innermost nature. Reich believed this insight was distorted, however. Ascetic and antisexual religions lead us to reject our own physical natures and to lose contact with our bodies. They deny the origin of the life force in the body and locate it in a hypothetical soul that has only a tenuous connection with the body.

> In the disruption of the unity of body feeling by sexual suppression, and in the continual longing to re-establish contact with oneself and with the world, lies the root of all sex-negating religions. "God" is the mysticized idea of the vegetative harmony between self and nature. (Reich, 1973, p. 358)

> It was only the mystics who—far removed from scientific insight—always kept in contact with the function of the living. Since, thus, the living became the domain of mysticism, serious natural science shrank from occupying itself with it. (Reich, 1961, pp. 197–198)

Sexual Repression

Another obstacle to growth is the social and cultural repression of the natural impulses and sexuality of the individual. Reich felt this repression to be the major source of neurosis and that it occurs during three principal phases of life: early infancy, puberty, and adulthood (Reich, 1973).

Infants and young children are confronted with an authoritarian, sex-suppressing family atmosphere. For this period of life, Reich reaffirms Freud's observations concerning the negative effects of parental demands for early toilet training, self-restraint, and "good" behavior.

During puberty, young people are kept from attaining a real sexual life; masturbation is prohibited. Even more important, our society generally makes it impossible for adolescents to attain a meaningful working life. And this unnatural life-style makes it especially difficult for adolescents to outgrow infantile attachments to their parents.

Finally, as adults (and this was more true in Reich's time), many people become trapped in unsatisfying marriages for which they are sexually unprepared because of demands for premarital continence. Reich also points out that there are built-in conflicts within marriage in our culture.

> The destructiveness which is bound up in the character is nothing but anger about frustration in general and denial of sexual gratification in particular. (Reich, 1973, p. 219)

> Marriages fall to pieces as a result of the ever deepening discrepancy between sexual needs and economic conditions. The sexual needs can be gratified with one and the same partner for a limited time only. On the other hand, the economic tie, moralistic demand, and human habit foster the permanency of the relationship. This results in the wretchedness of marriage. (Reich, 1973, p. 202)

The family situation recreates the same neurotic environment for the next generation of children.

Reich felt that individuals who are brought up in an atmosphere that negates life and sex develop a fear of pleasure, represented in their muscular armoring. "This characterological armoring is the basis of isolation, indigence, craving for authority, fear of responsibility, mystic longing,

> The life process is inherently "rational." It becomes distorted and grotesque when it is not allowed to develop freely. (Reich, 1973, p. 19)

sexual misery, and neurotically impotent rebelliousness, as well as pathological intolerance" (Reich, 1973, p. 7).

Reich was not optimistic concerning the possible effects of his discoveries. He believed that most people, because of their strong armoring, would be unable to understand his theories and would distort his ideas.

> A teaching of living Life, taken over and distorted by armored man, will spell final disaster to the whole of mankind and its institutions. . . . By far the most likely result of the principle of "orgastic potency" will be a pernicious philosophy of 4-lettering all over the place everywhere. Like an arrow released from the restraining, tightly tensed spring, the search for quick, easy and deleterious genital pleasure will devastate the human community. (Reich, 1961, pp. 508–509)

The armoring serves to cut us off from our inner natures and from social misery outside.

> Nature and culture, instinct and morality, sexuality and achievement become incompatible as a result of the split in the human structure. The unity and congruity of culture and nature, work and love, morality and sexuality, longed for from time immemorial, will remain a dream as long as man continues to condemn the biological demand for natural (orgastic) sexual gratification. Genuine democracy and freedom founded on consciousness and responsibility are also doomed to remain an illusion until this demand is fulfilled. (Reich, 1973, p. 8)

Structure

Body

Reich viewed mind and body as a unit. As described earlier, he gradually moved from analytic work, relying solely on language, to analysis of both the physical and psychological aspects of character and character armor. Then, he emphasized the dissolving of muscular armor and the developing of a free flow of orgone energy.

Social Relationships

Reich believed social relationships are determined by the individual's character. The average individual sees the world through the filter of his or her armoring. Genital characters, having loosened their rigid armoring, are the only ones who are truly able to react openly and honestly to others.

Reich strongly believed in the ideals, enunciated by Marx, of "free organization, in which the free development of each becomes the basis of the free development of all" (Boadella, 1973, p. 212). Reich formulated the concept of work-democracy, a natural form of social organization in which people cooperate harmoniously to further their mutual needs and interests, and he attempted to actualize these principles in the Orgone Institute.

Will

Reich did not concern himself directly with the will, although he did stress the importance of meaningful and constructive work.

> You don't have to do anything special or new. All you have to do is to continue what you are doing: plough your fields, wield your hammer, examine your patients, take your children to the school or to the playground, report on the events of the day, penetrate ever more deeply into the secrets of nature. All these things you do already. But you think all this is unimportant. . . . All you have to do is to continue what you have always done and always want to do: your work, to let your children grow up happily, to love your wife. (Reich, in Boadella, 1973, p. 236)

You do not strive to make your heart beat or your legs move, and you do not, by the same token, "strive" for or seek truth. Truth is in you and works in you just as your heart or your eyes work, well or badly, according to the condition of your organism. (Reich, 1961, p. 496)

Emotions

Reich found that chronic tensions block the energy flow that underlies powerful emotions. The armoring prevents the individual from experiencing strong emotions; it limits and distorts the expression of feeling. Emotions that are blocked in this way are never eliminated, because they can never be fully expressed. According to Reich, only by fully experiencing a blocked emotion can an individual become free of it.

Reich also noted that the frustration of pleasure often leads to anger and rage. These negative emotions must be dealt with in Reichian therapy before the positive feelings (which underlie the negative emotions) can be completely experienced.

Intellect

Reich (1976) opposed any separation of intellect, emotions, and body. He pointed out that the intellect is actually a biological function and that the intellect may have an energetic charge as strong as any of the emotions. He argued that full development of the intellect requires the development of true genitality: "The hegemony of the intellect not only puts an end to irrational sexuality but has as its precondition a regulated libido economy. Genital and intellectual primacy belong together" (1976, p. 203).

Reich believed that the intellect also operates as a defense mechanism. "The spoken word conceals the expressive language of the biological core. In many cases, the function of speech has deteriorated to such a degree that the words express nothing whatever and merely represent a continuous, hollow activity on the part of the musculature of the neck and the organs of speech" (1976, p. 398).

Intellectual activity can be structured and directed in such a way that it looks like a most cunningly operating apparatus whose purpose is precisely to avoid cognition, i.e., it looks like an activity directing one away from reality. In short, the intellect can operate in the two fundamental directions of the psychic apparatus: toward the world and away from the world. (Reich, 1976, p. 338)

Self

For Reich the self is the healthy, biological core of each individual. Most individuals are not in touch with the self; they are too armored and defended.

> What was it that prevented a person from perceiving his own personality? After all, it is what he is. Gradually, I came to understand that it is the entire being that constitutes the compact, tenacious mass which obstructs all analytic efforts. The patient's whole personality, his character, his individuality resisted analysis. (Reich, 1973, p. 148)

In penetrating to the deepest depth and the fullest extent of emotional integration of the Self, we not only experience and feel, we also learn to *understand,* if only dimly, the meaning and working of the cosmic orgone ocean of which we are a tiny part. (Reich, 1961, pp. 519–520)

According to Reich, the repressed impulses and repressing defensive forces together create a layer of contactlessness. Contactlessness is an expression of the concentrated interplay of the two (Reich, 1973). Contact requires free movement of energy. It only becomes possible as the individual dissolves his or her armor and becomes fully aware of the body and its sensations and needs, coming in contact with the core, the primary drives. Where blocks are present, energy flow and awareness are restricted, and self-perception is greatly diminished or distorted (Baker, 1967).

Therapist

In addition to training in therapeutic technique, the therapist must progress in his or her own personal growth. In working both psychologically and physically with an individual, the therapist must have overcome any fears of overtly sexual sounds and of "orgastic streamings"—the free movement of energy in the body.

Elsworth Baker, one of the leading Reichian therapists in the United States, cautions that "no therapist should attempt to treat patients who have problems he has not been able to handle in himself nor should he expect a patient to do things he cannot do and has not been able to do" (1967, p. 223). Another eminent Reichian has written that

> The indispensable prerequisite for whatever methods the therapist uses to release the emotions held in the musculature is that he is in touch with his own sensations and able to empathise fully with the patient and to feel in his own body the effect of particular constrictions on the patient's energies. (Boadella, 1973, p. 120)

Reich himself was considered a brilliant and tough-minded therapist. Even as an orthodox analyst, he was extremely honest, even brutally direct, with his patients. Nic Waal, one of the foremost psychiatrists in Norway, wrote about her experiences in therapy with Reich:

> I could stand being crushed by Reich because I liked truth. And, strangely enough, I was not crushed by it. All through this therapeutic

attitude to me he had a loving voice, he sat beside me and made me look at him. He accepted me and crushed only my vanity and falseness. But I understood at that moment that true honesty and love both in a therapist and in parents is sometimes the courage to be seemingly cruel when it is necessary. It demands, however, a great deal of the therapist, his training and his diagnosis of the patient. (Boadella, 1973, p. 365)

Evaluation

Reich is the leading pioneer in somatic psychology and body-oriented therapy. Only a small minority of psychologists have seriously concerned themselves with somatic psychology. However, appreciation of physical habits and tensions as diagnostic cues is steadily growing. Many therapists have been influenced by the work of Fritz Perls, who was in analysis with Reich and owes much to Reich's theories.

Reich's focus on muscular armoring and emotional release through body work has attracted less interest than it deserves. The encouragement of the expression of suppressed emotions, such as rage, fear, and aggression, is still a controversial issue in psychology.

Leonard Berkowitz (1973), who has studied violence and aggression experimentally for many years, has attacked what he calls the *ventilationist* approach to therapy, in which the main emphasis is placed on expressing bottled-up emotions. Berkowitz cites a number of experimental studies that show that encouraging the expression of aggression results in increased aggression or hostility. According to behaviorist theory, encouraging the expression of a given emotion serves to reward that behavior, making it more likely that the emotion will be expressed in the future.

This criticism represents a shallow understanding of Reich's work, in which emotional release is never simply encouraged for its own sake. It may be true that the discharge of strong emotions leads to increased occurrence of these emotions. However, Reich's emphasis was always on dissolving the armoring, the blocks to feeling that distort an individual's psychological and physical functioning.

A more cogent criticism of Reich's theories concerns his concept of the genital character as an achievable ideal state. Kelley (1971) has pointed out that Reich developed a system that seems to promise a cure-all. A successful treatment is supposed to leave the individual free of all armor, a "finished product" with no need for further growth or improvement.

The underlying model is a medical disease model in which the patient comes to the doctor in order to be "cured." This model pervades much of therapy, but it is especially strong where there is the assumption that the therapist is fully healthy (unarmored) and that the patient is ill. Patients stay "one down" to the therapist; they are generally placed in a passive role, relying on the omnipotent, "perfected" therapist for some sort of dramatic or magical cure. This model also places a tremendous strain on the therapist, who must always appear superior to patients and is permitted no mistakes or fallibility.

Learning to free oneself from inappropriate blocks to feeling is only one aspect of an individual's total growth. Self-control and goal-directed behavior are also essential, and they require a certain amount of control over one's immediate feelings.

> The blocks to feeling that Reich calls "the armor" . . . are a product of the capacity of man to control his feelings and behavior, and so to direct his life along a path he has chosen. One aspect of this is protection of the self from incapacitating emotions, a second the channeling of behavior towards goals. (Kelley, 1971, p. 9)

Thus, the individual never can nor should become totally "unarmored." Reich did not consider how to balance self-control and free expression as part of a continual process of growth.

With his emphasis on dissolving blocks to emotion, Reich tended to overestimate the role of armoring and resistance in the individual. He defined character almost solely in terms of armoring. "Character operates to produce almost constant resistance in psychoanalysis. For him [Reich] character is an armor formed through chronic 'hardening' of the ego. The meaning and purpose of this armor is protection from inner and outer dangers" (Sterba, 1976, p. 278). Yet, character certainly consists of more than rigidity and defenses.

Reich's theories concerning therapy and psychological growth are generally clear and straightforward, as are his therapeutic techniques. He has provided considerable clinical as well as experimental evidence for his work, although to date his ideas have been too controversial to gain widespread acceptance. Interest in Reich and his ideas concerning the body is increasing, and the growth of body-oriented work is one of the more exciting possibilities in the future development of psychology.

The Theory Firsthand: Excerpt from *Me and the Orgone*

The following passages are taken from Orson Bean's book *Me and the Orgone* (1971, pp. 17–20, 29–31, 34–36), an account of the actor's experiences in Reichian therapy with Dr. Elsworth Baker, a prominent Reichian therapist.

> Dr. Baker sat down behind his desk and indicated the chair in front of it for me. . . . "Well," he said, "take off your clothes and let's have a look at you." My eyes went glassy as I stood up and started to undress—"You can leave on your shorts and socks," said Baker, to my relief. I laid my clothes on the chair against the wall in a neat pile, hoping to get a gold star. "Lie down on the bed," said the doctor. . . .

He began pinching the muscles in the soft part of my shoulders. I wanted to smash him in his sadistic face, put on my clothes and get the hell out of there. Instead I said, "Ow." Then I said, "That hurts."

"It doesn't sound as if it hurts," he said.

"Well, it does," I said, and managed an "Ooo, Ooo."

"Now breathe in and out deeply," he said and he placed the palm of one hand on my chest and pushed down hard on it with the other. The pain was substantial. "What if the bed breaks?" I thought. "What if my spine snaps or I suffocate?"

I breathed in and out for a while and then Baker found my ribs, and began probing and pressing. . . . He began to jab at my stomach, prodding here and there to find a tight little knotted muscle. . . . He moved downward, mercifully passing my jockey shorts, and began to pinch and prod the muscles of my inner thighs. At that point I realized that the shoulders and the ribs and the stomach hadn't hurt at all. The pain was amazing, especially since it was an area I hadn't thought would ever hurt. . . .

"Turn over," said Baker. I did and he started at my neck and worked downwards with an unerring instinct for every tight, sore muscle. . . . "Turn back over again," said Dr. Baker and I did. "All right," he said. "I want you to breathe in and out as deeply as you can and at the same time roll your eyes around without moving your head. Try to look at all four walls, one at a time, and move your eyeballs as far from side to side as possible." I began to roll my eyes, feeling rather foolish but grateful that he was no longer tormenting my body. On and on my eyes rolled. "Keep breathing," said Baker. I began to feel a strange pleasurable feeling in my eyes like the sweet fuzziness that happens when you smoke a good stick of pot. The fuzziness began to spread through my face and head and then down into my body. "All right," said Baker. "Now I want you to continue breathing and do a bicycle kick on the bed with your legs." I began to raise my legs and bring them down rhythmically, striking the bed with my calves. My thighs began to ache and I wondered when he would say that I had done it long enough, but he didn't. On and on I went, until my legs were ready to drop off. Then, gradually, it didn't hurt anymore and that same sweet fuzzy sensation of pleasure began to spread through my whole body, only much stronger. I now felt as if a rhythm had taken over my kicking which had nothing to do with any effort on my part. I felt transported and in the grip of something larger than me. I was breathing more deeply than I ever had before and I felt the sensation of each breath all the way down past my lungs and into my pelvis. Gradually, I felt myself lifted right out of Baker's milk chocolate room and up into the spheres. I was beating to an astral rhythm. Finally, I knew it was time to stop. . . .

The Wednesday morning after my first visit to Baker I woke up, after about five hours sleep, feeling exhilarated. My coffee tasted better than it ever had and even the garbage floating down the East River seemed to me to have a lightness and symmetry to it. The feeling lasted for the rest of the day. It was a sense of well-being and at-peace-with-the-world-ness. My body felt light and little ripples of pleasure rolled up and down my arms, legs, and torso. When I breathed, the sensation of movement continued down into the base of my torso and it felt good. I felt vaguely horny in a tender way and the thought of women in general filled me with love. . . .

I was starting to unwind. The pleasurable ripples were lessening and a sense of anxiety was starting to take over. Brownish marks that would be black and blue by the next day began to appear on my body where Baker had pinched and gouged at me. . . .

I got into bed, realized that I was cold and reached down to the foot of the bed for the extra blanket. Then it occurred to me that I was cold with fear. I tried to examine my feelings as I had learned to do in psychoanalysis. It was a different kind of dread than I had ever experienced before. I thought of a marionette show I had seen as a kid with skeleton puppets who danced to the music of the *Danse macabre* and then began to fly apart, with legs and arms and head coming off and ribs and pelvis coming apart. I felt like I too was starting to come apart. The anxiety was terrific and I was aware that I was involuntarily tightening up on my muscles to hold myself together. The wonderful joyous liberated feeling was going away and in its place was a sense of holding on for dear life. My armoring, if that's what it was, seemed like an old friend now. People say, "I'd rather die in the electric chair than spend my life in prison," but prisoners never say that. A life in chains is better than no life at all, except in theory.

I realized it was going to take all the courage I could muster to de-armor myself. I knew I would fight Dr. Baker every step of the way but I also remembered how I had felt for that thirty-six hours or so after my first treatment and I wanted it more than anything else in the world. . . .

"What kind of week did you have?" asked Baker and I told him.

"Your reaction of clamping down after a period of pleasurable sensations was completely natural and to be expected," he said. "You won't always have those nice feelings but it's important to remember what they were like so you can work towards them again. It will help you tolerate the fear you'll feel as your armor breaks down." . . .

For several weeks on Tuesdays at two, I breathed and kicked. (I have since found out that my chest and breathing were being worked on first to mobilize energy in my body, which would help in the de-armoring process. Energy is built up with the intake of air.) Baker now had me pounding with my fists on the bed as I kicked. I would pound and kick and breathe and the rhythm would take me over and I would be transported. . . .

To start freeing my eye armoring, Dr. Baker held a pencil in front of me and told me to keep looking at it. He then moved it around quickly in random patterns which forced me to look about spontaneously. This would be kept up for what seemed like fifteen or twenty minutes and the results were amazing to me. My eyes felt free in my head and I could sense a direct connection between them and my brain. Then, he would have me roll my eyes about without moving my head, forcing them to focus on each wall in the room as their glance lit upon it. All the time I was doing this I would have to keep breathing deeply and rhythmically.

He would tell me to grimace and make faces (I felt like a fool). He would have me try to make my eyes look suspicious or attempt to get them to express longing. All of these things gradually made my eyes feel like they were being used again for the first time in many many years and it felt wonderful. . . .

On the following Tuesday, instead of a pencil, Dr. Baker pulled out a fountain-pen flashlight. He turned out the lights and shone it in my eyes and moved it around. It was a psychedelic effect. I followed it with my eyes as it made patterns in the dark and the effect was startling. I could actually feel the unlikely sensation of my brains moving in my head. Baker waved the flashlight around in front of me for about fifteen minutes and then he turned on the lights and looked deep into my eyes and said, "They're coming along nicely." Everything about the way he worked with me and the way he passed judgment on how I was responding was not mechanical but was the result of one human being's ability to put himself in touch with the feelings and energy charges of another. . . .

"Make a face at me," said Baker and I turned on him with a stupid leer. "Now accentuate it," he said. I twisted my face into a hideous gargoyle's expression. "What does it make you feel?" he asked.

"I dunno," I lied.

"It must make you feel something."

"Well, I guess . . . contemptuous."

"You guess?" . . .

"All right, dammit, it's a lot of crap . . . lying here rolling my eyes around."

"Stick your finger down your throat," said Baker.

"What?" I said.

"Gag yourself."

"But I'll throw up all over your bed."

"If you want to you can," he said. "Just keep breathing while you do it."

I lay there breathing deeply and stuck my finger down my throat and gagged. Then I did it again.

"Keep breathing," said Baker. My lower lip began to tremble like a little kid's, tears began to run down my face and I began to bawl. I sobbed for five minutes as if my heart would break. Finally, the crying subsided.

"Did anything occur to you?" asked Baker.

"I thought about my mother and how much I loved her and how I felt like I could never reach her and I just felt hopeless and heartbroken," I said. "I felt like I was able to feel these things deeply for the first time since I was little, and it's such a relief to be able to cry and it isn't a lot of crap, I was just scared."

"Yes," he said. "It is frightening. You have a lot of anger to get out, a lot of hate and rage and then a lot of longing and a lot of love. Okay," he said, "I'll see you next time."

And I got up and got dressed and left.

Body-oriented Systems of Growth

The body-oriented systems covered in this section are by no means all that are available. Dozens of excellent systems work primarily with the body, concerned with improving psychological and physical functioning. The disciplines and techniques mentioned in this chapter are perhaps better known and more available than some others. They are also systems that have theoretical significance for somatic psychology.

Bioenergetic Analysis

Bioenergetics might be called neo-Reichian therapy. It was founded by two of Reich's students, Alexander Lowen and John Pierrakos, and focuses on the role of the body in character analysis and in therapy. Lowen has used more easily acceptable terms than Reich—bioenergy for orgone energy, for example—and his work has generally met with less resistance than Reich's. There are many more bioenergetic practitioners than Reichians in this country.

Everybody is seeking aliveness, everybody wants to be more alive. What we don't consider is that you have to learn to bear being more alive, to assimilate it, to permit an energetic charge to go through your body. (Keleman, 1971, p. 39)

Lowen (1989) has summarized the major changes introduced by bioenergetic analysis:

1. Pleasure is emphasized more than sexuality, without denying the great importance of sexuality.

2. The concept of grounding is added to Reich's original concepts. Patients lie on a bed in traditional Reichian work. In bioenergetic analysis, other positions are used, including an emphasis on standing and how the legs can support the individual.

3. Physical exercises are taught and patients can practice many of them at home.

Bioenergetics includes Reichian breathing techniques and many of Reich's emotional release techniques, such as allowing patients to cry, scream, and hit. Lowen also utilizes various exercises and stress postures in order to energize parts of the body that have been blocked. In these postures, stress is increased in chronically tense body parts until the tension becomes so great that the individual is eventually forced to relax his or her armoring. These postures include bending down to touch the floor, arching back with the fists at the base of the spine, and bending backward over a padded stool.

Lowen found that Reich's approach to reducing armoring through muscular relaxation could be supplemented with the opposite process: encouraging patients to mobilize the feelings expressed by tense muscles. For example, encouraging a patient's aggression will facilitate the ability to surrender to tender feelings. But if one's only focus is on letting go and "giving in," therapy often results in feelings of sadness and anger exclu-

It delights me to say that I am my body, with full understanding of what that really means. It allows me to identify with my total aliveness, without any need to split myself. (Keleman, 1971, p. 28)

sively. In order to avoid this, Lowen found that the two approaches are best used alternately.

Bioenergetics stresses the need for grounding, or being anchored in one's own physical, emotional, and intellectual processes. Bioenergetic work often concentrates on the legs and pelvis to establish a better, more firmly rooted connection with the ground. This is essentially the opposite of Reich's top-to-down approach. "We begin with the legs and the feet because they are the foundation and support of the ego structure. But they have other functions. It is through our legs and our feet that we keep contact with the one invariable reality in our lives, the earth or the ground" (Lowen, 1971, p. 99). Lowen found that his patients lacked a sense of having their feet planted firmly on the ground, which corresponded to their being out of touch with reality.

> Bioenergetics is a therapeutic technique to help a person get back together with his body and to help him enjoy to the fullest degree possible the life of the body. The emphasis on the body includes sexuality, which is one of its basic functions. But it also includes the even more basic functions of breathing, moving, feeling and self-expression. A person who doesn't breathe deeply reduces the life of his body. If he doesn't move freely, he restricts the life of his body. If he doesn't feel fully, he narrows the life of his body. And if his self-expression is constricted, he limits the life of his body. (Lowen, 1975, p. 43)

Lowen and his colleagues have continued to write influential and thoughtful books (Keleman, 1976, 1979; Lowen, 1975, 1980, 1984; Pierrakos, 1976) and also to train many others in the techniques of bioenergetic analysis.

In the hands of a well-trained practitioner, bioenergetics is an excellent system that provides many of the benefits of orthodox Reichian analysis—opening up blocks to feeling, energizing parts of the body that have been ignored, and so on.

Bioenergetic work can have a powerful spiritual or transpersonal dimension. John Pierrakos, the cofounder of bioenergetics, has made the transpersonal a central feature of his new system of core energetics:

> After many years of bioenergetics work, I came to feel that something was lacking. Though bioenergetics provided a beautiful clinical approach to resolving blocks, difficulties, and neurotic symptoms, it lacked a fundamental philosophy because it did not incorporate the spiritual nature of human beings. (1987, p. 276)

The Alexander Technique

The Alexander technique is designed to improve awareness of one's habits of movement. Alexander students learn how they use their bodies

Personal Reflection ――――――――――――

――――――――――――――― Stress Postures

Try these excercises. According to bioenergetic theory, they are designed to bring energy to parts of the body that are chronically tense.

Stand with legs about shoulder width apart and knees slightly bent; without straining, bend over to touch the floor. Let your body stay loose and your head hang down freely. Hold this posture for several minutes. You may find that your legs begin to shake or quiver, or you may notice other changes in your body. Keep breathing freely and naturally, and don't try to *make* anything happen.

Slowly come up from this position, feeling your spine gradually come to a vertical position, vertebra by vertebra.

Next, try a position that will curve the spine the other way. Stand with feet apart and your knees pointing slightly out. Put your fists in the small of your back and bend backward (be *very careful* not to strain your back). Again, keep your neck relaxed and your head hanging back freely, and breathe freely.

Any muscle quivering that might accompany these two postures is an indication of the relaxing and energizing of armored parts of the body.

improperly and inefficiently and how they can prevent this when active or at rest. By *use*, Alexander refers to our habits of holding and moving our bodies, habits that directly affect the way we function physically, mentally, and emotionally.

F. Mathias Alexander was an Australian Shakespearean actor who originated this system in the late nineteenth century. He suffered from recurring loss of voice, for which there seemed to be no organic cause. Alexander spent nine years of painstaking self-observation and self-study in a three-way mirror; he discovered that his loss of voice was related to a backward and downward pressing movement of his head. By learning to inhibit this tendency, Alexander found that he no longer developed laryngitis, and, in addition, the inhibition of pressure on the back of his neck had positive effects throughout his body. Out of this self-study, Alexander developed a technique for teaching integrated movement based on a balanced relationship between the head and the spine.

One teacher describes the Alexander work as follows:

> In the lessons, first of all, the student is asked to do nothing. Even if I want the student to sit down on a chair, I don't want him to *do* it. He has to leave himself alone entirely, and let me move him. We are not super-imposing something on top of the habits that he already has; we are stopping him from using the habits he has. He is to be free, open

[Alexander] established not only the beginnings of a far-reaching science of the apparently involuntary movements we call reflexes, but a technique of correction and self-control which forms a substantial addition to our very slender resources in personal education. (Shaw in Jones, 1976, p. 52)

Personal Reflection

Body Awareness

Although this exercise does not come from the Alexander technique, it is designed to give you a sense of the dynamics of body use that Alexander stresses (adapted from Barlow, 1973).

You are probably either sitting or lying down as you read this. Are you aware of how you are holding the book, of the way your fingers and your arms are taking the weight of the book? How are you sitting or lying? Is the weight of your body more on one buttock than the other? How are you holding your arms? Is there excess tension in your chest, shoulders, and forearms, or throughout your body?

Do you feel that you want to shift to a more comfortable position? If so, your habits of using your body may not be as efficient or effective as they could be. Because of these habits, we tend to sit and move in ways that are less than optimally comfortable or useful; it is not until we get back in touch with our own bodies that we can recognize this.

and neutral in order to experience something else. What he is going to experience is the way he used to function once upon a time, before the poor habits took over. (Stransky, 1969, p. 7)

Alexander believed that a prerequisite for free and efficient movement is the lengthening of the spine. He did not mean a forced stretching, but a gentle *upward lengthening*. Alexander students work primarily with the following formula: Let the neck be free to let the head go forward and up, to let the back lengthen and widen. The aim is not to try to engage in muscular activity; it is to allow the body to adjust automatically while the individual concentrates on repeating the formula and responding to the guiding touch of the teacher. The movements covered in the lesson are taken from common activities, and the student learns gradually to apply the Alexander principles. This balance between head and spine allows for release of physical tensions, improved alignment, and better muscular coordination. On the other hand, interference with this relationship results in tension, misalignment of the body, and poor coordination.

The Alexander teacher is trained to detect ways we block free movement or anticipate moving with preliminary tension. By moving and readjusting the student's body in subtle ways, the teacher gradually gives the student the experience of resting and acting in an integrated, aligned manner. Alexander lessons typically concentrate on sitting, standing, and walking in addition to *table work*, in which the student lies down and experiences, through the teacher's hands, a greater sense of energy flow

Mr. Alexander has demonstrated a new scientific principle with respect to the control of human behavior, as important as any principle which has ever been discovered in the domain of external nature. (John Dewey, 1976, p. 104)

and length and width in the body. The table work is designed to give the student a sense of freedom and space in all the joints. This experience gradually reeducates the individual by providing an alternative to chronic tightening and cramping of the joints brought on by habitual tension. The Alexander work has been especially popular with actors, dancers, and other performing artists. It has also been used with great effectiveness with the physically handicapped and those suffering from chronic physical illnesses.

The Feldenkrais Method

The Feldenkrais method is designed to help people recover the natural grace and freedom they enjoyed as children. Feldenkrais works with patterns of muscular movement that help the individual find the most efficient way of moving, eliminating the unnecessary muscular tensions and inefficient patterns we have learned over the years.

Feldenkrais often quoted the Chinese proverb, "I hear and I forget, I see and I remember, I do and I understand." His work focuses on understanding through doing, which is why he calls his exercises "awareness through movement."

Moshe Feldenkrais received a doctorate in physics in France and worked as a physicist until 1944, when he was 40 years of age. He became deeply interested in judo and founded the first judo school in Europe, eventually developing his own judo system. Feldenkrais also worked with F. Mathias Alexander and studied Yoga, Freud, Gurdjieff, and neurology. After World War II, he devoted himself to work with the body. Feldenkrais uses a tremendous variety of exercises, which differs from lesson to lesson. They generally begin with very small movements, which are combined in larger patterns. The aim is to develop ease and freedom of movement in every part of the body.

Feldenkrais points out that we need to take responsibility for ourselves to understand how our bodies operate and to learn to live in accordance with our natural constitution and gifts. He contends that the nervous system is primarily concerned with movement. Every action involves muscular activity, including seeing, talking, even hearing (muscles regulate the tension of the eardrum to adjust for sound level). Feldenkrais stresses the need to relax and find one's own rhythm, one's natural pattern of activity, to overcome poor habits. We need to relax, play, and experiment to learn something new. Whenever we are under pressure or tension, or in a hurry, we learn nothing new; we repeat old patterns. Feldenkrais exercises generally serve to break down a single activity into sets of related movements in order to unlock old patterns and develop new possibilities of movement.

For Feldenkrais, growth is the gradual acquisition of more effective action patterns. Rather than abandon old habits, the goal is to increase our repertoire; for example, when we begin to type, most of us use just two fingers. Then, we learn touch-typing with ten fingers, but this skill

I read a lot of physiology and psychology and to my great astonishment I found that in regard to using the whole human being for action, there was ignorance, superstition, and absolute idiocy. There wasn't a single book that dealt with *how* we function. (Feldenkrais, 1966, p. 115)

takes time to develop. Touch-typing is easier and faster than the old two-finger method, and we come to prefer the new way.

If new habits are no longer useful or reliable (because of injury or other damage), old habits are available. Feldenkrais recommends gradual and natural change that does not threaten to destroy useful patterns.

We each have one experience at a time. Because we experience with our whole selves, we cannot *do* and *not do* at the same time or say *yes* and *no* simultaneously. According to Feldenkrais, we learn in every trial. However, old learnings and attitudes impinge on the new; therefore, we have to repeat new learning in different ways and in different contexts to gain real mastery.

To be aware is to be in the present: to be fully focused on what is happening now, without being bored or concerned with results or anticipating what comes next. In the Feldenkrais movement exercises, students pay attention to the whole body, not just to parts that *seem* most involved with movement. Attention broadens naturally and the entire body, the entire self, participates. The ideal is to move without trying, as if the thought of moving is all that is necessary.

What is attention? If you spot a tiger, your whole being is naturally attentive. This is the ideal level of attention in "awareness through movement," but most of us do not achieve it easily. At the start, almost no one performs the movements effectively, but, later, Feldenkrais students attend to more of themselves, their whole systems becoming more effective. Eventually, the movements come easily and naturally for virtually everyone.

Feldenkrais was often heard saying, "If you know what you are doing, you can do what you want." The aim of his exercises is to get you to do what you want, to understand the easiest patterns of movement for you in each new situation.

Feldenkrais works to reestablish connections between the motor cortex and the musculature, connections that have been distorted by habits, tension, or trauma. According to Feldenkrais, increased awareness and flexibility can be achieved through balancing and quieting the motor cortex. The more active the cortex, the less we are aware of subtle changes. One of the fundamental principles of his work is Weber's Law, which states that our sensitivity to change is proportional to our current level of stimulation. If you are carrying a piano, for example, you cannot feel a matchbook added to the load. But if you are carrying one match, the weight of a matchbook is immediately evident.

This explains why most people with bad posture are not aware that they do in fact have bad posture. By the same token, such people are unlikely to notice any worsening in their posture, because they use so much effort just to stand and walk. On the other hand, those with good posture are likely to improve. They are aware of subtle physical changes in themselves and can use this awareness for self-improvement. By balancing the motor cortex and by reducing the level of excitation, Feldenkrais found that we expand awareness and try new movement

To learn we need time, attention, and discrimination; to discriminate we must sense. This means that in order to learn we must sharpen our powers of sensing, and if we try to do most things by sheer force we shall achieve precisely the opposite of what we need. (Feldenkrais, 1972, p. 58)

combinations that were not possible when the motor cortex and musculature were locked into old patterns.

Our actions are formed by the interaction of four elements: skeleton, muscles, nervous system, and environment. "There four elements interact from birth until death and there are feedback and feedforward operations all along the loop" (Feldenkrais, 1981, p. 22).

Personal Reflection ————————————————————
———————————————————— Turning the Head

To get a general idea of how the Feldenkrais method operates, try this exercise.

Sit on the floor or in a chair and slowly turn your head to the right, without straining. Note how far your head will turn, and how far to the rear you can see. Turn your head back to the front.

Turn your head to the right again. Leave your head in place, and move your eyes to the right. See if your head can move further to the right. Repeat this three to four times.

Turn your head to the right. Now move your shoulders to the right and see if you can turn your head further to the rear. Repeat this three to four times.

Turn your head to the right. Now move your hips to the right and see if you can turn your head further to the rear. Repeat this three to four times.

Finally, turn your head to the right, and leaving your head in its right-turned position, move your eyes, shoulders, and hips to the right. How far can you see now?

Now, turn your head to the *left.* How far can you see? Continuing with the left side, repeat each step of the exercise you did with the right side, but *mentally only.* Visualize the movement of your head and visualize your eyes to the left. Visualize each step three to four times. Then, turn your head to the left and move your eyes, shoulders, and hips to the left. How far can you turn now? What do you think happened?

Your range of movement increased because you broke up old movement patterns. You improved by loosening up your brain rather than loosening up your muscles.

Structural Integration (Rolfing)

Structural integration is a system of reshaping and realigning body posture through deep and often painful stretching of the muscle fascia by direct manipulation. Structural integration is often called *rolfing* after its founder, Ida Rolf. Rolf received a doctorate in biochemistry and physiology in 1920 and worked as an assistant in biochemistry at the Rockefeller Institute for 12 years. For over 40 years, she devoted herself to teaching

Personal Reflection —————————————————
—————————————————— Posture Observation

Although it is not possible for anyone to experience the process of structural integration without a trained practitioner, anyone can learn more about the postural principles central to rolfing. Do this exercise with a partner. Have your partner stand naturally, and observe his or her posture carefully. (Form-fitting clothing or a bathing suit will work best.)

Is one shoulder higher than the other? Is the head balanced on top of the neck, or is it held forward or backward? Is the chest caved in or stuck out? Is one hip higher than the other? Is the pelvis stuck out to the rear? Are the knees held directly over the feet? Are the feet straight, or the toes pointed either in or out?

Look at your partner from the front, sides, and back. Then have your partner walk slowly while you observe from all angles. Finally, you might want to have your partner stand against a straight, vertical line drawn on the wall (the line formed by a door will serve) to observe alignment more carefully.

Then, discuss what you have observed. Also, imitate your partner's posture and walk in order to illustrate your points. When you have finished, switch roles.

This exercise is not intended as a critique of you or your partner. No one has perfect posture. Make your observations of each other in an objective and positive way, and receive them with the same attitude.

In any attempt to create an integrated individual an obvious starting place is his physical body, if for no other reason than to examine the old premise that a man can project only that which is within. . . . In some way, as yet poorly defined, the physical body is actually the personality, rather than its expression. (Rolf, 1962, p. 6)

and perfecting her system until her death in 1979.

The aim of structural integration is to bring the body into better muscular balance, better alignment with gravity, and closer to an optimal posture so that, theoretically, a straight line can be drawn through the ear, shoulder, hip bone, knee, and ankle. This leads to balanced distribution of the weight of the major parts of the body—head, chest, pelvis, and legs—and also more graceful and efficient movement. When the body is aligned, the individual is able to function more effectively and with less muscular effort, because the body structure is aligned in its gravitational field.

According to Rolf, the basic order inherent in the body is inevitably disturbed in the course of growing up. Physical and emotional traumas, chronic tension, and similar disorders have permanent effects on posture and alignment. These influences create "random bodies." Structural integration treatments are designed to restore the body's ordered and effective patterns.

Rolfing works primarily with the fascial system, connective tissue that supports and connects the muscle and skeletal systems. Rolf (1977) discovered that psychological trauma or even minor physical injury may result in subtle but relatively permanent changes in the body. Bone or muscle tissue becomes displaced; thickening of connective tissue locks these changes into place. Misalignment will occur not only in the immediate area of an injury but also at distant points in the body out of compensation. For example, favoring a sore shoulder over a time may affect the neck, the other shoulder, and the hips.

Rolfing works directly on the tissue to reestablish balance and flexibility. Most structural integration work involves lengthening and stretching tissues that have grown together or have become unnaturally thickened.

> In order to accomplish a permanent change, it is usually necessary that the actual position or distribution of muscular fibres be very slightly altered. This happens spontaneously as individual fibres stretch or as fascial sheaths again slide over each other instead of being glued on some adjacent sheath. Unless such a change is made the body reverts to its original posture and the restrictions to fluid flow and to interpersonal communication are rebuilt. (Rolf, 1962, p. 13)

Structural integration is generally carried out in a series of 10 one-hour sessions, which include the following areas of work (Rolf, 1962):

Session 1. Includes much of the body, with special focus on muscles of the chest and abdomen that govern breathing, and the hip joint, which controls pelvic mobility.

Session 2. Concentrates on the feet, reforming the foot and ankle hinges and aligning the legs with the torso.

Session 3. Lengthens the sides, especially the large muscles between the pelvis and rib cage.

Sessions 4 to 6. Free the pelvis. Most people hold their pelvis rotated toward the rear. Because of the tremendous importance of the pelvis in posture and in movement, a the major emphasis of rolfing is to make the pelvis more flexible and better aligned with the rest of the body.

Session 7. Concentrates on the neck and head and also on the muscles of the face.

Sessions 8 to 10. Organize and integrate the entire body.

Work on some areas of the body may trigger memories or a deep emotional discharge. However, rolfing is aimed primarily at *physical* integration, and the psychological aspects of the process are not dealt with directly. Many individuals who have combined rolfing with some form of psychological therapy or other growth work have reported that rolfing helped to free their psychological and emotional blocks.

Rolfing, though almost anyone can benefit from it, is especially useful for those persons whose bodies have become seriously misaligned as a result of physical or psychological trauma. Many of the changes from rolfing seem to be relatively permanent, but maximum benefit comes only if the individual remains aware of the changes in body structure and functioning facilitated by the rolfing process. A system called *structural pat-*

Man is an energy field, as the earth and its outward envelope of forces is an energy field. How well a man can exist and function depends on whether the field which is himself, his psychological and physical personality, is reinforced or disorganized by the field of gravity. (Rolf, 1962, p. 12)

terning was developed for this purpose. It consists of a set of exercises involving minor and subtle shifts in body position and balance.

Sensory Awareness

Sensory awareness work emphasizes relaxation and focusing one's attention on immediate experience. It focuses on direct perception, on distinguishing sensations from learned interpretations that overlay our experience. The simple act of sensing can provide astonishing and rich experience, from which we frequently cut ourselves off by living "in our heads." It requires a sense of awareness and of inner quiet, an ability to just let things happen, without force.

The system of sensory awareness is taught in the United States by Charlotte Selver, Charles Brooks, and their students. Their method is based on the work of Elsa Gindler and Heinrich Jacoby, two of Selver's European teachers.

> The study of this work is our whole organismic functioning in the world we perceive, of which we are a part—our personal ecology: how we go about our activities, how we relate to people, to situations, to objects. We aim to discover what is natural in this functioning and what is conditioned: what is our nature, which evolution has designed to keep us in touch with the rest of the world, and what has become our "second nature," as Charlotte likes to call it, which tends to keep us apart. (Brooks, 1974, p. 17)

Typically, children are in touch with their bodies and senses. As they grow up, however, they gradually lose this ability. Sensory awareness is a process that helps people get back in touch with their bodies and senses. This gradual loss of awareness begins at an early age. Parents tend to react to children in terms of their own preferences instead of what actually enhances the child's functioning. Children are taught what things and activities are "good" for them—how long to sleep and what to eat—instead of how to judge for themselves out of their own experience. "Good" children learn to come whenever mother calls, cutting off their natural rhythms and stopping activities immediately for the convenience of parents and teachers. After many such interruptions, the child's innate sense of rhythm becomes confused and so does any inner sense of the value of his or her experience.

The lily is not to be simply watered but must be gilded. (Selver & Brooks, 1966, p. 491)

Another problem is that of *making efforts*. So many parents urge their children to sit, stand, walk, and talk as early as possible, thereby forcing development. These children begin to feel that the future is pressing in on them; they learn striving instead of relaxed play. They learn to *overdo*. This begins with the parents' unnatural use of baby talk, artificial gestures, and noises in relating with their infants. By their example, parents teach that even communication cannot be peaceful and simple, that so much more is needed. This attitude is carried out in many other areas as well.

Many exercises in sensory awareness involve the basic activities of lying, sitting, standing, and walking. These activities offer the best opportunity for discovering our attitudes in relation to the environment and for developing our conscious awareness. Sitting on a stool without padding or a back allows one to sense the support of the stool, the pull of gravity, and the inner-life process that occur in relation to these and other forces. Standing also offers rich possibilities for sensing. Few people learn to stand comfortably as an end in itself; most of us approach standing as the starting point for other activity. Standing allows one to explore *balancing* and moving from familiar postures to new coordination and being.

Another aspect of sensory awareness work involves interaction with others. Many people need to learn how to touch one another and how to receive touch. Various ways of touching can be explored: tapping, slapping, and so forth. The quality of touch can reveal timidity, aggressiveness, impatience, tenderness, and the like.

Most sensory awareness exercises have an inward, meditative orientation. Selver and Brooks have pointed out that as inner quiet develops, unnecessary tension and activity diminish, and receptivity to inner and outer events is heightened; other changes occur simultaneously throughout the whole person. This is essentially the same process that Feldenkrais describes.

> The closer we come to such a state of greater balance in the head, the quieter we become, the more our head "clears," the lighter and more potent we feel. Energy formerly *bound* is now more and more at our disposal. Pressure and hurry change into freedom for speed. We find ourselves being more one with the world where we formerly had to

Personal Reflection ———————————

——————————— Body Awareness, Lying Down

Try this exercise in body awareness.

Lie on the floor and relax. You may be aware of the floor pressing on part of your body, and you may feel free in some parts and constricted in others. One person may feel light, another heavy. One may become refreshed, another tired. Receive and accept any messages from inside or outside without evaluation or labeling. Do not try to rush your awareness; experiencing will come in its own time. It is not wrong to feel constricted or right to feel free. These categories are inappropriate as this is an exercise in *experiencing*.

As tendencies to *anticipate* diminish, sensations generally become more rich and full. You may become aware of changes that happen by themselves. Tenseness may change to relaxation and the floor may feel more comfortable. You may become conscious of changes in breathing.

cross barriers. Thoughts and ideas "come" in lucidity instead of being produced. . . . Experiences can be allowed to be more fully received and to mature in us. (Selver & Brooks, 1966, p. 503)

Hatha-yoga

Hatha-yoga is the name given to a wide number of practices and disciplines designed to control the body and the *pranas*, or vital energies, of the body. It is often thought of as a preliminary discipline to purify the body and overcome physical obstacles with meditation and other spiritual practices of Yoga.

Swami Radha is a European-born Yoga teacher, who received her training in India and returned to the West in 1956 to spread Yogic teachings. She is the founder and spiritual director of a Yoga center in British Columbia, and is a well-known authority on kundalini, mantras, and other Yoga practices. Swami Radha stresses that each Yoga posture has physical, emotional, symbolic, and spiritual significance. In her book on hatha-yoga, she writes,

> The human being functions in polarity and this is expressed in the meaning of the word *Hatha*. *Ha* means "the sun, heat, light, energy, creativity, activity, passion, positive," and *tha* means "the moon, cool, reflective, receptive, negative." . . . The ultimate goal of yogic practices is to be in the center. (Radha, 1987, pp. 3–4)

In the West, hatha-yoga is the practice of Yoga postures. Its main aim is to develop a healthy body. In India, this is known as *physical* Yoga rather than hatha-yoga. These two approaches have practices in common; it is the attitudes and goals of practice that are different, as traditional hatha-yoga is essentially a religious discipline.

The most detailed and also the best-known aspect of hatha-yoga is the practice of Yoga postures—the headstand, lotus posture, and so forth. One aim of posture practice is to enable the individual to sit for long periods of time without physical discomfort, which would interfere with meditation. Certain postures are designed to keep the body limber, exercise the spine, stimulate various nerves and organs, and increase breathing capacity.

The first principle behind the practice of Yoga postures is to accustom the body to a given pose and then gradually lengthen the time in that posture. In various postures, pressure is taken off some parts of the body and intensified in others, blood flow is increased to certain body parts, and organs are stretched or compressed. Combinations of postures can provide balanced stimulation for the entire body. Many people in India practice routines of 15 to 20 postures daily. A given posture may have several variations, each designed to exercise different muscles or different organs. It is best to study hatha-yoga under a qualified teacher, who can correct major mistakes and also provide individualized instruction suited to a person's specific build and other physical characteristics.

Hatha-yoga is a system of health and hygiene involving both body and mind. It aims at the whole man for his full development and self-realization. It takes into account not only the proper growth, strength and tone of the different muscles of the body but also the efficiency and function of the basic factors of constitutional health, namely, the inner organs and the glands. (Majumdar, 1964, p. 99)

One of the aims of hatha-yoga is to purify and strengthen the body as a vehicle for vital energies. There are five major forms of vital energy discussed in the Upanishads, the ancient Indian scriptures; they are respiration, digestion, elimination, circulation, and crystallization. These and other vital energies flow through subtle channels in the body, known as *nadis*. Many hatha-yoga practices are designed to open and purify the *nadis*, which become clogged as a result of faulty diet and unhealthy living patterns. Hatha-yoga includes teachings concerning diet and fasting as well as breathing techniques designed to promote energy flow in the body. *Prana* means breath and vital energy in Sanskrit. The two are seen as closely connected in India (and in many other cultures as well).

There are other methods of purifying the body in hatha-yoga. These include techniques of washing and cleansing the nasal passages and the digestive system and exercises for the muscles of the stomach and internal organs.

According to Swami Radha, "Hatha Yoga is a human science that takes into consideration bodily pains, poor posture, faulty breathing, and incorrect walking, teaching greater awareness of the body as a whole, without separating it from the mind and the influences of all the senses" (Radha, 1987, p. 5).

> There are, in each of us, profound depths of stillness, serenity and wisdom, hidden under restless passions and desires, under our fears, anxieties and illusions—depths we can reach through meditation and by letting go. (Majumdar, 1964, p. 173)

Personal Reflection

The Corpse Pose

This pose is designed for deep relaxation. It is practiced at the end of a series of postures or when the individual desires to relax. It is best to practice on a thick carpet or pad.

Lie on your back with your arms resting on the floor, palms up. Close your eyes and consciously relax every part of your body, starting with the feet. Feel your body sinking into the floor as you relax. Imagine that you have abandoned your body completely so that it lies perfectly limp, detached from your mind. Observe your body as if you were outside of it. Observe your breath as it flows in and out, without any attempt to control it. After some time, gradually lengthen your breathing and make it rhythmical. Practice from 10 to 20 minutes.

T'ai Chi Ch'uan

It has been said that t'ai chi ch'uan practice leads to the flexibility of a child, the health of a lumberjack, and the peace of mind of a sage. *T'ai chi ch'uan* literally means "supreme ultimate boxing." As an exercise for health, sport, and self-defense, t'ai chi has long enjoyed great popularity among the Chinese, and is rapidly becoming better known in the West.

Chinese of all ages and backgrounds practice this rhythmical, balletlike exercise at dawn and at dusk.

There are a number of theories concerning the origin of t'ai chi ch'uan. The most popular holds that Chang San-feng, a Taoist priest who lived in the thirteenth century, learned the method of t'ai chi in a dream. Another theory dates it back to the T'ang dynasty (618–907). Other historians attribute the development of t'ai chi to the Ch'en family, whose generations spanned the fourteenth to eighteenth centuries.

T'ai chi ch'uan is known as an intrinsic energy system. One aim of practice is to develop *ch'i,* or vital energy, in the body. The t'ai chi student must learn to relax completely while training, seeking to eliminate all tension in the body so that *ch'i* can flow unobstructed. In time, the energy of the body becomes integrated and centered in the area of the navel. Eventually, every movement of t'ai chi ch'uan becomes coordinated with the flow of *ch'i.* As well as learning to move in a fully relaxed manner, the student must keep the spine straight and hold the head as if the entire body were suspended by the top of the head from the ceiling. This allows free flow of energy in the spine and neck and enables the body to move as a single unit.

The mind must be calm and concentrated on the movements. Alertness is extremely important; t'ai chi ch'uan has been called *moving meditation.*

Another important quality in t'ai chi practice is slow, fluid movement. Movements are done slowly. The postures flow evenly from one to the next, without pauses to break the fluid movement and block the flow of *ch'i.* The student learns to move as if swimming in the air, coming to feel the air as heavy and resistant, just like water, and developing a sense of lightness and buoyancy in the body.

The following excerpt from the t'ai chi classics gives a sense of the philosophical and theoretical bases of the art:

> In any action the entire body should be light and agile and all of its parts connected like pearls on a thread.
>
> The *ch'i* should be cultivated; the spirit of vitality should be retained internally and not exposed externally.
>
> The entire body is so light that a feather will be felt and so pliable that a fly cannot alight on it without setting it in motion.
>
> Stand like a balance and move actively like a cart wheel.
>
> The mind directs the *ch'i,* which sinks deeply and permeates the bones. The *ch'i* circulates freely, mobilizing the body so that it heeds the direction of the mind.
>
> In resting, be as still as a mountain; in moving, go like the current of a great river.
>
> When you act, everything moves, and when you stand still, everything is tranquil.
>
> Walk like a cat and mobilize your energy as if pulling silken threads from a cocoon. (Chen & Smith, 1967, pp. 106–111)

There are a number of different schools of t'ai chi ch'uan. Some styles tend to stress the practical fighting aspects; others, the exercise aspect. The traditional t'ai chi form consists of 128 postures, including many repetitions. A full round takes over 15 minutes when done at the proper speed. However, a number of teachers have developed their own short form of approximately 40 to 50 postures, which eliminates many of the repetitions of the longer form. This shorter version can generally be completed in 10 minutes.

Although there are a number of books available on t'ai chi, it is essential to study directly with a teacher. The movements are too subtle and complex to learn correctly without direct supervision.

Personal Reflection

A Basic T'ai Chi Pose

In order to develop *ch'i,* or intrinsic energy, t'ai chi students hold one posture for long periods of time. While holding a single pose, the student tries to remain as relaxed as possible, sensing that the body is supported by the flow of energy more than by muscle tension.

One basic pose is to stand with feet shoulder-width apart and parallel. Keep knees slightly bent and hands held in front as if holding a large bell. The elbows are slightly bent, the palms facing inward, and the fingertips of each hand facing each other several inches apart. The arms form a large ring of energy.

The position is held for 5 minutes at first. Serious t'ai chi students may work up to 30 minutes or longer. Try this pose.

Aikido

Aikido is a martial art founded in the 1920s by Master Morihei Ueshiba, who studied many of the traditional Japanese martial arts, including judo, jujitsu, sword, spear, and staff arts. He was also deeply involved in the practice of the spiritual disciplines of Buddhism and Shintoism. In time, Master Ueshiba changed aikido from a way of becoming strong in order to defeat others to a method of self-development and personal and spiritual growth.

> Aiki is not a technique to fight with or defeat the enemy. It is the way to reconcile the world and make human beings one family.
>
> The secret of Aikido is to harmonize ourselves with the movement of the universe and bring ourselves into accord with the universe itself. He who has gained the secret of Aikido has the universe in himself and can say, "I am the universe."

> Aikido is non-resistance. As it is non-resistant, it is always victorious.
> Winning means winning over the mind of discord in yourself.
> A mind to serve for the peace of all human beings in the world is
> needed in Aikido, and not the mind of one who wishes to be strong or
> who practices only to fell an opponent.
> True *budo* [martial arts] is a work of love. It is a work of giving life
> to all beings, and not killing or struggling with each other. Love is the
> guardian deity of everything. Nothing can exist without it. Aikido is the
> realization of love. (Ueshiba, 1963, pp. 177–179)

There is no competition in aikido. The aim of practice is to learn to harmonize with the movements of a partner rather than to see who is stronger. The term *aikido* might be translated as "a way of spiritual harmony"; *ai* means to unite, bring together, or harmonize; *ki* is life energy, will, vital force, or spirit; and *do* means path or way.

One principle of aikido practice is that the mind leads the body. If you can lead your partner's mind, his or her body will follow easily. One aspect of this principle is to learn not to fight force with force, but first to go with the partner's energy and then seek to redirect it. Another important aspect of using mind and body together is using relaxed, fluid, and circular movements, seeking to blend with a partner rather than forcing the partner to move in a certain way. The more tense we are, the more our partners become tense. The more relaxed we become, the more our partners naturally relax.

In order to practice effectively, the aikido student must learn to remain *centered*. In aikido, centering refers to an awareness of the lower abdomen, or *hara* in Japanese. In Japan, this is thought of as one's physical and emotional center. The more one can concentrate one's mind on the lower abdomen and move from that center, the more relaxed, fluid, and effective the movement will be. In Japanese psychology, to develop one's *hara* is to become more calm, more mature, and more empathic. Because of its immediate relevance to psychology, aikido has been seriously studied and its principles applied practically by a number of psychologists (Frager, 1977, 1980; Heckler, 1985; Tart, 1989).

Aikido is different from most martial arts in its lack of competition and in its emphasis on working *with* a partner rather than fighting *against* an opponent. Aikido and t'ai chi ch'uan are very similar in that both emphasize personal development. Also, both emphasize centering and the use of vital energy.

Aikido must be practiced with a partner, and blending with a partner's movements is an essential aspect of the art. By contrast, some t'ai chi forms are practiced slowly without a partner in order to accustom the body to the proper soft, flowing movements. Other t'ai chi exercises are done with a partner, however. Another subtle difference between aikido and t'ai chi lies in the fact that aikido arts are oriented to throwing, whereas t'ai chi ch'uan is based primarily on kicking and striking movements.

Personal Reflection _____

_____ Blending in Aikido

In order to get an understanding of the emphasis in aikido, try the following exercise.

Have a partner stand 10 to 15 feet away and slowly approach you, pointing his or her finger with the intention of poking you (lightly) in the chest. Try the following three responses:

1. Stand in place observing your partner approach. (How does your body feel as he or she comes close?)

2. Back up and try to avoid the finger, as if your partner were actually attacking you.

3. Look upon your partner's motion as merely a flow of energy. Instead of trying to step back out of the way, as your partner approaches, turn to face the direction the partner's finger is pointing. The turn should move you slightly out of the way, so that your partner's hand passes by your body. Think of letting the hand and the energy go by you, instead of trying to stop it or get out of its way.

These three ways of responding generally feel quite different, both to the person approaching and to the person being approached. The first is an example of a clash of energy, the second is a negative drawing back, and the third is an exercise in blending with someone else without being drawn off center.

Evaluation

The various body-oriented systems, which have developed independently in widely different parts of the globe, have much in common. They all advocate *nondoing,* learning to let the body operate naturally and smoothly. All favor relaxed instead of tense activity and try to teach the individual to reduce habitual tensions in the body. All of these systems treat mind and body as a single whole, an ongoing psychophysiological process in which change at any level will affect all other parts.

There are also some interesting differences among these systems. Each seems to specialize in a slightly different area of physical functioning. Reichian and bioenergetic therapies deal with emotionally charged blocks in the body, whereas rolfing works to restructure body misalignments that may have been brought about by physical injury or various other causes. The Alexander technique focuses on body use rather than structure. The Feldenkrais method also deals with use; however, Feldenkrais exercises include considerably more complex behavior patterns in order to restore physical effectiveness and efficiency. Sensory awareness focuses on the senses, on touching and being touched, and on becoming more aware of the body and the surrounding world. Hatha-yoga is a discipline for strengthening and purifying the body. T'ai chǐ ch'uan and aikido are derived from the martial arts of the Far East; their movements originally evolved as effective fighting techniques, but now they are practiced primarily as centering, balance, and awareness exercises.

All of these systems attempt to teach students to be more relaxed and more "natural," both at rest and during activity. They are all concerned with eliminating the unnecessary tensions that we carry around with us and with bringing us back to *nondoing* action. By this action, we learn to allow the body to operate naturally and effectively rather than to strain, push, or overdo. These systems share a conviction that we need not learn something brand new or develop new muscles. The most important thing is to unlearn the poor habits we have picked up as children and adults, and to return once again to the natural wisdom, coordination, and balance of the body

Annotated Bibliography

Wilhelm Reich

Reich, W. (1961). *Selected writings*. New York: Farrar, Straus & Giroux (Noonday Press). An excellent introduction to the full range of Reich's thought. Includes chapters on therapy, orgone theory, and orgone research.

———. (1973). *The function of the orgasm.* New York: Touchstone. Reich's best book, it includes excellent material on character analysis, bioenergy, genital character, and Reichian therapy.

(1976). *Character analysis.* New York: Pocket Books. A classic work, this book represents Reich's contributions to psychoanalysis; rewritten from the first edition to fit his later theoretical perspectives.

Baker, E. (1967). *Man in the trap.* New York: Avon Books. Detailed discussion of Reichian therapy and theory by an eminent Reichian therapist.

Boadella, D. (1973). *Wilhelm Reich: The evolution of his work.* London: Vision. The best secondary source on Reich; details the historical development of his theories.

Bioenergetics

Keleman, S. (1971). *Sexuality, self and survival.* San Francisco: Lodestar Press. A lively treatment of bioenergetics, including transcripts of work sessions; by a major practitioner.

Lowen, A. (1975). *Bioenergetics.* New York: Penguin Books. The best introduction to Lowen's writings on bioenergetics.

Lowen, A., & Lowen, L. (1977). *The way to vibrant health: A manual of bioenergetic exercises.* New York: Harper & Row. Superb do-it-yourself manual of bioenergetic exercises by Alexander and Leslie Lowen. Fully illustrated, with pictures of the couple.

Alexander Technique

Alexander, F. (1969). *The resurrection of the body.* New York: Dell (Delta Books). A collection of Alexander's writings. Rich but difficult material.

Barlow, W. (1973). *The Alexander technique.* New York: Knopf. A clear discussion of the theory behind the technique, with various case studies. Written by an eminent practitioner.

Feldenkrais Method

Feldenkrais, M. (1972). *Awareness through movement.* New York: Harper & Row. Theoretical discussion plus a number of fascinating exercises.

———. (1977). *The case of Nora: Body awareness as healing therapy.* New York: Harper & Row. A brilliant case study that provides insight into Feldenkrais's work as a therapist.

———. (1985). *The potent self.* San Francisco: Harper & Row. A posthumous collection of Feldenkrais's writings on motivation, resistance, habit formation, wellness, and the development of full human potential.

Structural Integration (Rolfing)

Rolf, I. (1977). *Rolfing: The integration of human structures.* Santa Monica, CA: Dennis-Landman. The major work on structural integration, written by the founder.

Schutz, W., & Turner, E. (1977). *Body fantasy*. New York: Harper & Row. A detailed case study involving the creative integration of Rolfing and psychotherapy.

Sensory Awareness

Brooks, C. (1974). *Sensory awareness*. New York: Viking Press. The only extensive study of this work. Excellent, clearly written with many fine illustrative photos.

Gunther, B. (1968). *Sense relaxation*. New York: Collier Books. Marvelous photos and exercises. An extremely influential book, it was a best-seller for several years.

Schutz, W. (1967). *Joy*. New York: Grove Press. Excellent exercises and discussion by participants of their experiences with each exercise.

Hatha-yoga

Danielou, A. (1955). *Yoga: The method of re-integration*. New York: University Books. Includes summaries and selections from classical Indian texts on hatha-yoga.

Iyengar, B. (1972). *Light on Yoga*. New York: Schocken Books. For advanced students. Detailed, technical explanations.

Vishnudevananda. (1972). *The complete illustrated book of yoga*. New York: Pocket Books. One of the best, most available paperbacks on hatha-yoga.

T'ai Chi Ch'uan

Chen, M., & Smith, R. (1967). *T'ai-chi*. Rutland, VT: Tuttle. An excellent book of t'ai-chi theory and practice.

Huang, A. (1973). *Embrace tiger, return to mountain—The essence of t'ai chi*. Moab, UT: Real People Press. T'ai-chi practice and principles applied to calligraphy, movement, and centering exercises.

Aikido

Heckler, R. (Ed.). (1985). *Aikido and the new warrior*. Berkeley, CA: North Atlantic Books. A collection of articles on the effects and applications of aikido to psychology, conflict resolution, and personal growth.

Ueshiba, K. (1963). *Aikido.* New York: Japan Publications. Excellent material on the history and the founder of aikido; fine photos.

Westbrook, A., & Ratti, O. (1970). *Aikido and the dynamic sphere.* Rutland, VT: Tuttle. Marvelous and ample illustrations that illuminate aikido principles and the Japanese martial arts in general.

References

Alexander, F. (1969). *The resurrection of the body.* New York: Dell (Delta Books).

Baker, E. (1967). *Man in the trap.* New York: Macmillan.

Barlow, W. (1973). *The Alexander technique.* New York: Knopf.

Bean, O. (1971). *Me and the orgone.* New York: St. Martin's Press.

Berkowitz, L. (1973). The case for bottling up rage. *Psychology Today, 7*(2), 24–31.

Boadella, D. (1973). *Wilhelm Reich: The evolution of his work.* London: Vision.

———. (1987). *Lifestreams: An introduction to biosynthesis.* New York: Routledge & Kegan Paul.

Brooks, C. (1974). *Sensory awareness.* New York: Viking Press.

Chen, M., & Smith, R. (1967). *T'ai-chi.* Rutland, VT: Tuttle.

Danielon, A. (1955). *Yoga: The method of re-integration.* New York: University Books.

Feldenkrais, M. (1950). *Body and mature behavior.* New York: International Universities Press.

———. (1966). Image, movement, and actor: Restoration of potentiality. *Tulane Drama Review, 3,* 112–126.

———. (1972). *Awareness through movement.* New York: Harper & Row.

———. (1977). *The case of Nora: Body awareness as healing therapy.* New York: Harper & Row.

———. (1981). *The elusive obvious.* Cupertino, CA: Meta Publications.

———. (1985). *The potent self.* San Francisco: Harper & Row.

Frager, R. (1977). Aikido—A Japanese approach to self-development and mind-body harmony. In C. Garfield (Ed.), *Rediscovery of the body.* New York: Dell.

———. (1980). Aikido. In R. Herink (Ed.), *The psychotherapy handbook.* New York: Meridan.

Frey, A. (1965). Behavioral biophysics. *Psychological Bulletin, 63,* 322–337.

Gunther, B. (1968). *Sense relaxation.* New York: Collier Books.

———. (1971). *What to do till the Messiah comes.* New York: Macmillan.

Heckler, R. (Ed.). (1985). *Aikido and the new warrior.* Berkeley, CA: North Atlantic Books.

Higgens, M., & Raphael, C. (1967). *Reich speaks of Freud.* New York: Farrar, Straus & Giroux.

Huang, A. (1973). *Embrace tiger, return to mountain—The essence of t'ai chi.* Moab, UT: Real People Press,.

Iyengar, B. (1972). *Light on Yoga.* New York: Schocken Books.

Jones, F. (1967). *Body awareness in action.* New York: Schocken Books.

Keen, S. (1970a). Sing the body electric. *Psychology Today, 5,* 56–58, 88.

———. (1970b). My new carnality. *Psychology Today, 5,* 59–61.

Keleman, S. (1971). *Sexuality, self and survival.* San Francisco: Lodestar Press.

———. (1973a). *Todtmoos.* San Francisco: Lodestar Press.

———. (1973b). *The human ground.* San Francisco: Lodestar Press.

———. (1976). *Your body speaks its mind.* New York: Pocket Books.

———. (1979). *Somatic reality.* Berkeley, CA: Center Press.

Kelley, C. (1962). *What is orgone energy?* Santa Monica: Interscience Workshop.

———. (1970). *Education in feeling and purpose.* Santa Monica, CA: Interscience Workshop.

———. (1971). *Primal scream and genital character: A critique of Janov and Reich.* Santa Monica, CA: Interscience Workshop.

———. (1972). *The new education.* Santa Monica, CA: Interscience Research Institute.

Lawrence, D. H. (1955). *Sex, literature and censorship.* London: Heinemann.

Leibowitz, J. (1967–1968). For the victims of our culture: The Alexander technique. *Dance Scope, 4,* 32–37.

Linklater, K. (1972). The body training of Moshe Feldenkrais. *The Drama Review, 16,* 23–27.

Lowen, A. (1969). *The betrayal of the body.* New York: Macmillan.

———. (1971). *The language of the body.* New York: Macmillan.

———. (1975). *Bioenergetics.* New York: Penguin Books.

———. (1980). *Fear of life.* New York: Macmillan.

———. (1984). *Narcissism: Denial of the true self.* New York: Macmillan.

———. (1989). Bioenergetic analysis. In R. J. Corsini & D. Wedding (Eds.), *Current psychotherapies* (4th ed.). Itasca, IL: F. E. Peacock.

———. (1990). *The spirituality of the body.* New York: Macmillan.

Lowen, A., & Lowen, L. (1977). *The way to vibrant health: A manual of bioenergetic exercises.* New York: Harper & Row.

Macdonald, P. (1970). Psycho-physical integrity. *Bulletin of Structural Integration, 2,* 23–26.

Majumdar, S. (1969). *Introduction to Yoga principles and practices.* New Hyde Park, NY: University Books.

Mann, W. (1973). *Orgone, Reich and eros.* New York: Simon & Schuster.

Pierrakos, J. (1976). *Human energy systems theory.* Institute of New Age of Man.

———. (1987). *Core energetics*. Mendocino, CA: Life Rhythm.

Radha, Swami S. (1987). *Hatha yoga: The hidden language*. Porthill, ID: Timeless Books.

Reich, I. (1969). *William Reich: A personal biography*. New York: St. Martin's Press.

Reich, W. (1961). *Selected writings*. New York: Farrar, Straus & Giroux (Noonday Press).

———. (1970a). *The sexual revolution*. New York: Farrar, Straus & Giroux.

———. (1970b). *The mass psychology of Fascism*. New York: Farrar, Straus & Giroux.

———. (1973). *The function of the orgasm*. New York: Touchstone.

———. (1976). *Character analysis*. New York: Pocket Books.

Robinson, P. (1969). *The Freudian left*. New York: Harper & Row.

Rolf, I. (1962). *Structural integration: Gravity, an unexplored factor in a more human use of human beings*. Boulder, CO: Guild for Structural Integration.

———. (n. d.). Exercise. *The Bulletin of Structural Integration Anthology, 1*, 31–34.

———. (1977). *Rolfing: The integration of human structures*. Santa Monica, CA: Dennis-Landman.

Rycroft, C. (1971). *Wilhelm Reich*. New York: Viking Press.

Schutz, W. (1967). *Joy*. New York: Grove Press.

———. (1971). *Here comes everybody: Body-mind and encounter culture*. New York: Harper & Row.

Schutz, W., & Turner, E. (1977). *Body fantasy*. New York: Harper & Row.

Selver, C., & Brooks, C. (1966). Report on work in sensory awareness and total functioning. In H. Otto (Ed.), *Explorations in human potentialities*. Springfield, IL: Thomas.

Sterba, R. (1976). Clinical and therapeutic aspects of character resistance. In M. Bergmann & F. Hartman (Eds.), *The evolution of psychoanalytic technique*. New York: Basic Books.

Stransky, J. (1969). An interview with Judith Stransky. *Bulletin of Structural Integration, 2*, 5–11.

Tart, C. (1989). *Open mind, discriminating mind*. San Francisco: Harper & Row.

Tohei, K. (1966). *Aikido in daily life*. New York: Japan Publications.

Ueshiba, K. (1963). *Aikido*. New York: Japan Publications.

———. (1969). *Aikido*. Tokyo: Hozansha.

———. (1984). *The spirit of Aikido*. Tokyo: Kodansha International.

Vishnudevananda (1972). *The complete illustrated book of yoga*. New York: Pocket Books.

Westbrook, A., & Ratti, O. (1970). *Aikido and the dynamic sphere*. Rutland, VT: Tuttle.

Chapter Eight

Frederick Perls, Laura Perls, and Gestalt Therapy

Frederick (Fritz) and Laura Perls, the originators of Gestalt therapy, occupy a unique position in the framework of this text. Unlike Freud, Jung, Adler, James, and others, their contributions to a psychology of personality are primarily in the practice of psychotherapy rather than in personality theory. However, the fact that the Gestalt approach is used in a widening variety of contexts other than the therapeutic suggests that this view of human beings is worth examining. In fact, the lack of a strictly theoretical emphasis in much of the Perlses' later work reflects the direction in which they were trying to take psychology. Fritz, in particular, was convinced that a genuinely holistic and productive view of people and psychotherapy would require substantial deintellectualization, Western intellect having become, in his words, "the whore of intelligence . . . the poor, pallid substitute for the vivid immediacy of sensing and experiencing" (F. Perls, 1967, p. 15).

Toward the end of his life, however, Fritz realized some theoretical statement of the Gestalt approach was needed in order to prevent these ideas from being reduced to a set of gimmicks and attempts at instant psychotherapeutic cures. Fritz never completed his last manuscript (*The Gestalt Approach,* 1973), but even in its unfinished form it provides, along with his other less specifically theoretical works, a basis for understanding the Gestalt view of the psychology of personality. During Fritz's life, Laura Perls's contributions were overshadowed by those of her husband, who not only wrote more but reveled in his celebrity. However, from the beginning and after Fritz's death, Laura continued to train therapists and to expand the ideas of Gestalt therapy (Serlin, 1992). It is fitting that Gestalt, with its emphasis on relationships between the parts, should have developed within a partnership.

Personal History

Frederick S. Perls was born in Berlin in 1893, the son of lower-middle-class Jewish parents. In his autobiography, *In and Out of the Garbage Pail* (1969b), Fritz describes himself as a black-sheep son, often angry and scornful of his parents, who was expelled from school after twice failing seventh grade and who was in trouble with authorities throughout his adolescence.

He managed nonetheless to finish his schooling and receive a medical degree, specializing in psychiatry. While finishing his medical training, he joined the German army and served as a medic during World War I. After the war, Fritz worked in Frankfurt where he met Laura. The two of them, along with many of their friends, were in psychoanalysis with an early disciple of Freud. It was there that they began to formulate some of the philosophical ideas that were to provide a basis for the development of Gestalt therapy.

Laura Perls was born in 1905. Early in life she was attracted by psychoanalysis, reading Freud's *The Interpretation of Dreams* when she was sixteen. She studied with Paul Tillich, Martin Buber, and the early Gestaltists.

In and out the garbage pail
Put I my creation
Be it lively, be it stale
Sadness or elation.
Joy and Sorrow as I had
Will be re-inspected;
Feeling sane and being mad,
Taken or rejected.
Junk and chaos come to halt
'Stead of wild confusion,
Form a meaningful gestalt
At my life's conclusion.
(Perls, 1969b)

In 1926, Fritz worked with Kurt Goldstein at the Institute for Brain-injured Soldiers. Through his work with Goldstein, he developed some sense of the importance of viewing the human organism as a whole rather than as a conglomeration of disparately functioning parts.

In 1927, the Perlses moved to Vienna where Fritz began psychoanalytic training. He was in analysis with Wilhelm Reich and was supervised by several other major figures of the early psychoanalytic movement, among them: Karen Horney, Otto Fenichel, and Helene Deutsch. Fritz and Laura were married in 1930.

In 1933, with the approach of Hitler, the Perlses fled to Holland and then to South Africa where they established the South African Institute for Psychoanalysis. While they practiced what Laura called "straight analysis," she had already begun to sit facing her clients and to pay attention to bodily postures and gestures, drawing from her background in body work and modern dance (Serlin, 1992). Fritz returned to Germany in 1936 to deliver a paper at the Psychoanalytic Congress and to meet Sigmund Freud, which Fritz had anticipated for years. The meeting was an immense disappointment to him. He recalls that it lasted for perhaps four minutes and offered no opportunity for exploring Freud's ideas.

In 1946, they emigrated to the United States, still considering themselves psychoanalysts. They proceeded to develop what became Gestalt therapy. In 1952, at first in their apartment, they established the New York Institute for Gestalt Therapy. Later, Fritz moved to Los Angeles and then, in the early 1960s, to the Esalen Institute in Big Sur, California. There, he offered workshops, taught, and was soon to become well known as the exponent of a viable new philosophy and method of psychotherapy. Shortly before his death, his interest turned to the establishment of a Gestalt kibbutz. He died in 1970 on Vancouver Island, the site of the first Gestalt therapeutic community (Gaines, 1979; Shepard, 1975). While Fritz lived, there was a confusion between his personal style, which was often abrasive, and Gestalt therapy, which was confrontational and yet offered support. Fritz left behind a trail of people who admired the theorist but disliked the man.

Laura remained in New York, running the New York institute and training therapists. In the last 20 years of her life, she felt she had to counteract the prevailing beliefs attributed to Gestalt, especially the idea that it devalued the intellect (L. Perls, 1992). It was one of the areas in which Fritz and Laura stood in quiet disagreement. Laura valued the intellect, calling it "your foremost human attribute" (L. Perls in Serlin, p. 63). Her opinion contrasted sharply to the devaluing of the intellect that Fritz espoused and that was later echoed by many of his students. Laura died on a visit to her home town in Germany in 1990.

My break with the Freudians came a few years later (after my meeting with Freud), but the ghost was never completely laid. . . . I had tried to make psychoanalysis my spiritual home, my religion. . . . Then the enlightenment came. . . . I had to take all responsibility for my existence myself. (F. Perls, 1969b, pp. 59–60, parentheses added)

Intellectual Antecedents

The major intellectual trends that influenced the Perlses were psychoanalysis, Gestalt psychology, as well as existentialism and phenomenology. Fritz also incorporated some techniques from his interest in theater (Serlin, 1992) and ideas from general semantics (Barlow, 1986). Laura describes the philosophy and practice of Zen as an important influence on both of them, but this was explicitly visible only in Fritz's later work (Gordon, 1987; Wheeler, 1991).

Psychoanalysis

Freud

The first book that the Perlses wrote, *Ego, Hunger and Aggression* (1942), was intended to provide a revision of psychoanalytic theory, rather than a new theory of personality. A good part of their early efforts was devoted to developing what they saw to be extensions of Freud's work. Even after their formal break with Freud, the Perlses continued to view their own ideas as revisions of psychoanalysis—a few ideas among many from the psychoanalytic second generation. Their disagreements with Freud had primarily to do with Freud's psychotherapeutic treatment methods rather than with Freud's more theoretical expositions of the importance of unconscious motivations, the dynamics of personality, patterns of human relationships, and so on. "Not Freud's discoveries but his philosophy and technique have become obsolete" (F. Perls, 1969b, p. 14).

The Perlses felt that Freud's work was essentially limited in its failure to stress a holistic approach to organismic functioning, in which the individual and the environment are viewed as constantly interacting parts of a single field. This holistic approach, in which every element of an organism's expression is intimately connected to the whole, led them to place particular emphasis, in contrast to Freud, on *obvious* rather than deeply repressed material in the understanding and working through of intrapsychic conflict. Also in contrast to Freud, the Perlses stressed the importance of examining one's situation in the present rather than investigating the past. They believed that the awareness of *how* one behaves, moment to moment, is more relevant to self-understanding and capacity for change than an understanding of *why* one behaves as one does.

Their initial departure from Freud's approach concerned Freud's theory of impulses and libido. For them impulses are not basic drives that dictate human behavior, but are the espression of biological and emotional needs. The Perlses suggested that the psychoanalytic methods of interpretation and free association constitute avoidance of direct experience and are therefore inefficient and often ineffective methods of self-exploration.

Freud's emphasis on the importance of what causes resistance shifts in the Perlses' view to an emphasis on how resistance is carried out. That is, they stress the importance of decreasing avoidance behavior rather than getting bogged down in examining exactly what is being avoided.

They disagreed with Freud's supposition that the important therapeutic task is the freeing of repressions, following which the working through or assimilation of the material can occur naturally. The Perlses thought that every individual, simply by existing, has plenty of material with which to

None of us, probably with the exception of Freud himself, realized the prematurity of applying psychoanalysis to treatment. . . We did not see it for what it actually was: a *research project.* (F. Perls, 1969b, p. 142)

work in therapy. The difficult and important task is the assimilation process itself, the integrating of previously introjected traits, habits, attitudes, and patterns of behavior.

For the Perlses, the Gestalt approach represents an alternative *Weltanschauung* (worldview) to that from which psychoanalytic theory emerges. Yet, given an understanding of this difference in worldview (which leads to utterly different styles and characteristics between psychoanalytic and Gestalt work), a great deal of psychoanalytic theory finds its counterpart in Gestalt work.

Some of the shared characteristics may be found in the following general pairs of concepts: Freudian cathexis and the Gestalt foreground; Freudian libido and Gestalt basic excitement; Freudian free association and the Gestalt continuum of awareness; Freudian consciousness and Gestalt awareness; the Freudian focus on resistance and the Gestalt focus on avoidance of awareness; Freudian repetition compulsion and the Gestalt unfinished situations; Freudian regression and Gestalt withdrawal (from the environment); the Freudian therapist who permits/encourages transference and the Gestalt therapist who is a "skillful frustrator"; the Freudian neurotic defense-impulse configuration and the Gestalt rigid configuration; and the Freudian projection transference and the Gestalt projection.

Reich

The other major psychoanalytic influence on the Perlses was one of Fritz's analysts, Wilhelm Reich (Smith, 1975). Reich developed the notion of "muscular armor"; he also stressed the importance of understanding character (or habitual ways of reacting) in determining how a person functions. He suggested that character develops early in the individual's life and serves as a kind of armoring against internal or external stimuli that the individual finds threatening. This character armor is physiologically rooted (in muscle, specifically), and functions to prevent insight or psychological change. Reich's early work heavily influenced the Perlses, particularly their view of the body in relation to the psyche (F. Perls, 1979).

Gestalt Psychology

The practical focus on body awareness, however, became part of Gestalt therapy not only through Reich, but through my lifelong experience with modern dance . . . and my awareness of Alexander and Feldenkrais and other body therapies. (L. Perls, 1992, pp. 52–53)

A gestalt is an irreducible phenomenon. It is an essence that is there and that disappears if the whole is broken up into its components. (F. Perls, 1969b, p. 63)

Gestalt theory was introduced in the late 1800s in Germany and Austria. It developed as a protest against atomistic analysis—analysis in which elements of an experience are reduced to their simplest components and then each component is analyzed apart from the others, so that the experience is understood simply as the sum of these components. The very notion of a *gestalt* contradicts the validity of this kind of atomistic analysis. Although there is no precise English equivalent for the German word *gestalt,* the general meaning is a pattern or configuration—a particular organization of parts that makes up a particular whole. The chief principle of the Gestalt approach suggests that an analysis of parts can never provide an understanding of the whole, because the whole is defined by the interactions and interdependencies of the parts. Parts of a gestalt cannot maintain their identity when they are independent of their function to and place in the whole.

In 1912, Max Wertheimer published a paper that is generally considered to be the founding work of the Gestalt school. His paper described an experiment he performed with two colleagues—also central figures in the Gestalt movement—Wolfgang Köhler and Kurt Koffka. Their experiment was designed to explore certain aspects of the perception of motion. They flashed in rapid succession two closely spaced points of light in a dark room, varying the time intervals between the flashes. They found that when the interval between the flashes was less than three hundredths of a second, the flashes appeared simultaneous. When the interval was about six hundredths of a second, the observer reported seeing the flash move from the first point to the second. When the interval was twenty hundredths of a second or more, the points of light were observed as they actually were: two separate flashes of light. The crucial finding of the experiment involved the perception of motion when the flashes were approximately six hundredths of a second apart; the apparent movement was not a function of the isolated stimuli but was dependent upon the relational characteristics of the stimuli and the neural and perceptual organization of the stimuli in a single field.

The results of this experiment led to some major reformulations in the study of perception. From the 1920s to the 1940s, Gestalt theory was applied to the study of learning, problem solving, motivation, social psychology, and, to a certain degree, personality theory.

A major contribution of the Gestaltists involved, as already briefly mentioned, the exploration of how parts constitute and are related to a whole. One aspect of this is seen in how an organism, in a given field, makes his or her perceptions meaningful, how he or she distinguishes between *figure* and *ground*. Figure 8.1 is an example of how a given stimulus may be interpreted as representing different things depending upon what is perceived as figure and what as ground.

> A gestalt is an irreducible phenomenon. It is an essence that is there and that disappears if the whole is broken up into its components. (F. Perls, 1969b, p. 63)

> Every organ, the senses, movements, thoughts, subordinate themselves to this emerging need and are quick to change loyalty and function as soon as that need is satisfied and then retreat into the background. . . . All the parts of the organism *identify* themselves temporarily with the emergent *gestalt*. (F. Perls, 1969b, p. 115)

Figure 8.1   An Example of the Figure-Ground Phenomenon

If the white is viewed as figure and the black as ground, a white chalice appears; if, on the other hand, the black is viewed as figure and white as ground, we see two heads in silhouetted profile. The Gestalt school expanded the phenomenon represented by this picture to describe how an organism selects what is of interest to that organism at any particular moment. To a thirsty person, a glass of water placed in the midst of favorite foods emerges as figure against the background of the food; how one perceives such a picture is a function of personal needs. Once the thirst is satisfied, perception of what is figure and what is ground will probably change in accordance with a shift in dominant need and interest.

Although, by 1940, Gestalt theory had been applied in many areas of psychology, it had been for the most part ignored as a tool for examining the dynamics of personality structure and personal growth. Therefore, there was as yet no formulation of Gestalt principles for use in psychotherapy. In spite of the fact that Laura and Fritz both stressed the importance of the psychophysical in Gestalt work, some scholars still feel that there is no evidence to support a mind-body connection (Henle, 1978; Sherrill, 1986).

Existentialism and Phenomenology

The Perlses described Gestalt as an existential therapy, based in existential philosophy and utilizing principles generally considered to be both existential and phenomenological.

Most generally, the Gestaltists objected strenuously to the notion that the study of human beings could encompass an entirely rational, mechanistic, natural-scientific approach. Following from this, the Perlses aligned themselves with most existentialists. They insisted that the experiential world of an individual can be understood only through that individual's direct description of his or her own unique situation.

The idea that mind and body constitute two different and wholly separable aspects of existence was a notion that the Perlses, in company with most existentialists, found insupportable (F. Perls, 1978). They believed that people create and constitute their own worlds; for a given individual, the world exists only in so far as his or her discovery of it. The world that the individual encounters cannot be seprated from personal experience.

Two major themes in most existentialist thinking are the experience of nothingness and concern with death and dread. As we shall see in examining the Perlses' view of the structure of neurosis, these also constitute important elements in their theory of psychological functioning.

The phenomenological method of understanding through description is basic to the Perlses' thought; all actions imply choice, all criteria in making choices are themselves chosen, and causal explanations are not sufficient to explain one's actions or choices. And the phenomenological reliance on intuition in the knowing of essences resembles the Gestalt reliance on what came to be called the intelligence or wisdom of the organism.

I feel rather desperate about this manuscript. I've got a view looking at a tapestry, nearly completely woven, yet unable to bring across the total picture, the total gestalt. Explanations don't help much towards understanding. . . . I would not be a phenomenologist if I could not see the obvious, namely the experience of being bogged down. I would not be a Gestaltist if I could not enter the experience of being bogged down with confidence that some figure will emerge from the chaotic background. (F. Perls, 1969b)

Other Influences

Laura made it clear that, while the theory came in part from Gestalt psychology, the transformation of theory into therapy required the seminal ideas of later thinkers. "Anybody who wants fully to understand Gestalt therapy would do well to study Wertheimer on productive thinking, Lewin on the incomplete gestalt and the crucial importance of interest for gestalt formation, and Kurt Goldstein on the organism as an indivisible totality" (L. Perls, 1992).

Major Concepts

The Organism as a Whole

The Perlses insisted that human beings are unified organisms, that mental and physical activity work in tandem. They defined mental activity simply as activity of the whole person that is carried on at a lower energy level than physical activity.

Fritz suggested that any aspect of an individual's behavior may be viewed as a manifestation of the whole—the person's being (F. Perls, 1978). Thus, in therapy, what the patient does—how he or she moves, speaks, and so on—provides as much information about the patient as what he or she thinks and says.

Gestalt stresses the importance of viewing the individual as being perpetually a part of a wider field, which includes both the organism and the organism's environment. Just as the Perlses protested against the notion of a mind-body split, they also protested against an inner-outer split and viewed the question of whether people are ruled by internal or external forces as essentially meaningless. There is however a *contact boundary* between the individual and his or her environment; it is this boundary that defines the relationship between them. In a healthy individual, this boundary is fluid, perpetually permitting contact with, then withdrawal from, the environment. Contacting constitutes the forming of a gestalt; withdrawing represents its closure. In neurotic individuals, the contact and withdrawal functions are disturbed, and these people find themselves faced with a conglomerate of gestalten that are in some sense unfinished—neither fully formed nor fully closed.

The Perlses suggested that the cues for this rhythm of contact and withdrawal are dictated by a *hierarchy of needs*. Dominant needs emerge as either figure or ground against the backdrop of the total personality; effective action is directed toward the satisfaction of a dominant need. Neurotics are often unable either to sense which of their needs are dominant or to define their relationship to the environment in such a way that their dominant needs are satisfied.

The organism acts with and reacts to its environment with greater or lesser intensity; as the intensity diminishes, physical behavior turns to mental behavior. As the intensity increases, mental behavior turns into physical behavior. (F. Perls, 1973, p. 13)

Here and Now Emphasis

The holistic view places particular emphasis on the importance of an individual's immediate self-perception in relation to his or her environment. Neurotics are unable to live in the present. They chronically carry with them unfinished "business" from the past. Because their attention is focused on what is unfinished, they have neither the awareness nor the energy necessary to deal fully with the present. The destructive quality of this unfinished "business" is all too evident in their current lives; therefore, they experience themselves as unable to live successfully in the present. The Gestalt approach does not examine the past for memories of trauma or unfinished situations, but has the patient simply focus on becoming aware of his or her *present* experience, assuming that the bits and pieces of unresloved conflicts from the past will inevitably emerge as part of that present experience. As these unfinished situations appear, the patient is asked to reenact them, to reexperience them in order to finish and assimilate them in the present.

Although this focus on the present is an approach particular to Gestalt work, it actually derives from the psychoanalytic notion that one's past is neurotically *transferred* into the present. Thus, in both psychoanalytic and Gestalt work, one attempts to *finish* in the present unfinished situations from the past (L. Perls, 1986).

Anxiety is the gap, the tension between the *now* and the *then*. The inability of people to tolerate this tension causes them to fill the gap with planning, rehearsing, and attempts at making the future secure. This not only absorbs energy and attention away from the present (thereby perpetually creating unfinished situations), it also prevents the kind of openness to the future that growth and spontaneity imply.

In addition to the strictly therapeutic nature of this focus on present awareness, an underlying current to Gestalt work is that attending to the present, rather than the past or future, is in itself something good, because it is the path to psychological growth.

As Claudio Naranjo has pointed out in his article "Present-Centeredness: Technique, Prescription and Ideal" (Fagan & Shepherd, 1970), the attitude that present-centeredness leads to psychological growth is central to many Eastern psychologies. In a passage of the *Pali Canon*, Buddha suggests:

> Do not hark back to things that passed,
> And for the future cherish no fond hopes;
> The past was left behind by thee,
> The future state has not yet come.
> But who with vision clear can see
> The present which is here and now
> Such wise one should aspire to win
> What never can be lost or shaken.
>
> (In Fagan & Shepherd, *Gestalt Therapy Now*, 1970, p. 67)

And from the Sufi tradition, Omar Khayyám suggests:

Never anticipate tomorrow's sorrow
live always in this paradisal Now— . . .
Rise up, why mourn this transient world of men?
Pass your whole life in gratitude and joy.

(From the Rubáiyát of Omar Khayyám, 1968, p. 54)

Importance of *How* Over *Why*

A natural outcome of this orientation is the stress on the importance of understanding experience in a descriptive fashion. Structure and function are identical; if an individual understands how he or she does something, that person is in a position to understand the action itself. The causal determination—the why—of the action is irrelevant to the full understanding of it. Every action may be the result of many different causes. To focus on one or another of the causes can lead a person farther and farther away from observing the action itself.

Awareness

The three major concepts examined thus far—the organism as a whole, the here and now emphasis, and the importance of *how* over *why*—constitute a foundation for examining awareness, the focal point of the Perlses' therapeutic approach. The process of growth is, in Gestalt terms, a process of expanding areas of self-awareness; the major factor inhibiting psychological growth is avoidance of awareness.

The Perlses believed strongly in "the wisdom of the organism." They saw the healthy, mature individual as a self-supporting, self-regulating individual. The cultivation of self-awareness was to be directed toward recognizing this self-regulating nature of the human organism. Following Gestalt theory, the Perlses suggested that the hierarchy-of-needs principle is always operating in the individual. In other words, the most urgent need, the most important, unfinished situation will always emerge if one is simply *aware* of one's experience of oneself, moment to moment.

> I believe that this is a great thing to understand: that awareness per se— by and of itself—can be curative. (F. Perls, 1969a, p. 16)

To be aware is to pay attention to the perpetually emerging foreground of one's own perception. To avoid awareness is to rigidify the naturally free-flowing delineation of foreground and background.

The Perlses suggested that for every individual there are three zones of awareness: awareness of self, awareness of the world, and awareness of what lies between—a kind of intermediate fantasy zone. They saw the exploration of this last zone as Freud's great contribution. However, they felt that Freud focused on this intermediate zone to the exclusion of the other two zones, which are important in developing an awareness of the self and the world. By contrast, much of the Perlses' approach involves a very deliberate attempt to gain awareness of and direct contact with oneself and the world.

> I propose a useful hypothesis that runs counter to this tending to treat ourselves as things. We are awareness rather than have awareness. (F. Perls, 1977, p. 70)

Personal Reflection ———————

————————————— Continuum of Awareness

This excercise in awareness requires much practiced discipline, yet, paradoxically, it serves to develop one's spontaneity.

Part I Begin by noticing your breathing. Is it regular or not? Deep or shallow? Notice the room around you, the temperature, the light, the furniture, and the other people. Just be aware, from second to second, of what you are experiencing, how you experience your existence—Now. And now. And now.

Observe the progress of your awareness. Do you interrupt yourself with planning, rehearsing, fantasizing, remembering? Do you evaluate rather than permit pure awareness? What does awareness feel like?

Pay particular attention to the ways in which you sabotage your own attempts at sustained awareness. Are these ways in which you often prevent yourself from fully contacting your own experience?

Part II This is more difficult. Try to prolong and stay in contact with the moment at which you want to avoid continued awareness. Can you get a sense of what you are avoiding? Does a situation emerge that you feel is unfinished?

Dynamics

Psychological Growth

> Any disturbance of the organismic balance constitutes an incomplete gestalt, an unfinished situation forcing the organism to become creative, to find means and ways to restore that balance. . . . And the figure/background foundation which is the strongest will temporarily take over the control of the total organism. Such is the basic law of organismic self-regulation.
> (F. Perls, 1969b, pp. 79, 92)

Psychological health and maturity is defined as the capacity to exchange environmental support and regulation for self-support and self-regulation. The crucial element in both self-support and self-regulation is balance. One of the basic propositions of Gestalt theory is that every organism possesses the capacity to achieve an optimum balance within itself and in relation to its environment. The conditions for achieving this balance involve an unimpeded awareness of the hierarchy of needs.

A full appreciation of this hierarchy of needs can be achieved only through an awareness that involves the whole organism. This is because the organism experiences needs throughout its system, so that hierarchy of these needs is established only by accounting for the organisms as a whole.

Gestalt views the rhythm of contact with and withdrawal from the environment as the major component of organismic balance. Immaturity and neurosis imply either an inappropriate perception of what this rhythm constitutes or an incapacity to regulate its balance.

Self-regulating, self-supporting individuals are characterized by freely flowing and clearly delineated figure-ground formations (definitions of meaning) in the expression of their needs for contact and withdrawal.

They recognize their own capacity to choose the means of fulfilling needs as such needs emerge. They are aware of the boundaries between themselves and others and are particularly aware of the distinction between their fantasies of others and what they actually experience through direct contact.

In stressing the *self*-supporting, *self*-regulating nature of psychological well-being, the Perls do not suggest that an individual can exist in any sense separate from his or her environment. In fact, organismic balance presumes a constant interaction with the environment. The crucial point is that we can choose *how* we relate to the environment; we are self-supporting and self-regulating in that we recognize our own capacity to determine how we support and regulate ourselves within a field that includes much more than just ourselves.

Fritz Perls (1969a) describes several ways in which psychological growth is achieved. The first involves the finishing of unfinished situations. He also suggests that neurosis may be loosely viewed as a kind of five-layered structure, and that growth (and eventually freedom from the neurosis) occurs in the passage through these five layers.

He calls the first layer the *cliché layer*, or the *layer of token existence*. It includes such tokens of contact as *good morning, hello,* and *nice weather, isn't it?* The second layer is the *role layer*, or *game-playing layer*. This is the *as-if* layer, where we pretend to be the person we would most like to be; for example, the always competent businessman, the perpetually nice little girl, or the very important person.

Having reorganized these two layers, Fritz suggests that we reach the *impasse layer,* also called the *anti-existence layer* or *phobic avoidance layer*. Here, we experience emptiness, nothingness; this is the point at which, by avoiding the nothingness, we generally cut off our awareness and retreat back to the role-playing layer. If, however, we are able to maintain awareness of ourselves in this emptiness, we reach the *death* or *implosive* layer. This layer appears as death or as fear of death, because it consists of a paralysis of opposing forces; in experiencing this layer we contract and compress ourselves—we implode.

But if we can stay in contact with this deadness, we reach the last layer, the *explosive layer*. He suggests that becoming aware of this level constitutes the development of the authentic person, the true self, the person capable of experiencing and expressing emotion. Fritz Perls warns his readers:

> Now, don't be frightened by the word *explosion* [italics added]. Many of you drive a motor car. There are hundreds of explosions per minute in the cylinder. This is different from the violent explosion of the catatonic—that would be like an explosion in a gas tank. Also, a single explosion doesn't mean a thing. The so-called breakthroughs of the Reichian therapy, and all that, are as little useful as the insight in psychoanalysis. *Things still have to work through* [italics added]. (F. Perls, 1969a, p. 56)

There are four basic kinds of explosions that an individual may experience when emerging from the death layer. There is the explosion of *grief* that involves the working through of a loss or death that was previously unassimilated. There is the explosion into *orgasm* in people who are sexually blocked. There is the explosion into *anger* when the expression of anger has been repressed. And, finally, there is the explosion into what Fritz calls *joie de vivre*—joy and laughter, the joy of life.

The structure of our role playing is cohesive, because it is designed to absorb and control the energy of these explosions. The basic misconception that this energy needs to be controlled derives from our fear of emptiness and nothingness (the third layer). Fritz suggests that Eastern philosophies, particularly Zen, have a good deal to teach us about the life-affirming, positive aspect of nothingness and about the importance of permitting the experience of nothingness without interrupting it.

Throughout these descriptions of how an individual develops, the Perlses maintain the notion that change cannot be forced and that psychological growth is a natural, spontaneous process.

Obstacles to Growth

Gestalt views avoidance of awareness and the resultant rigidities in perception and behavior as the major obstacles to psychological growth. Neurotics (those who interrupt their own growth) cannot see their own needs clearly, nor can they make appropriate distinctions between themselves and the rest of the world. Consequently, they are unable to find and maintain the proper balance between themselves and the rest of the world. Neurosis consists of defensive maneuvers designed to protect oneself against and balance oneself in the impinging world.

Gestalt suggests that there are four basic boundary disturbances, which are neurotic mechanisms that impede growth. These are *introjection, projection, confluence,* and *retroflection.*

Introjection

Introjection, or "swallowing whole," is the mechanism by which individuals incorporate standards, attitudes, and ways of acting and thinking that are not their own and that they do not assimilate or digest sufficiently to make their own. Introjecting individuals find it very difficult to distinguish between what they really feel and what others want them to feel—or simply what others feel. Introjection can also constitute a disintegrating force in the personality. Because the concepts or attitudes that are swallowed are incompatible with one another, the introjecting individuals will find themselves conflicted.

Projection

Another neurotic mechanism is *projection;* it is, in a sense, the opposite of introjection. Projection is the tendency to make others responsible for what originates in the self. It involves a disowning of one's impulses, desires, and behaviors, placing what belongs to the self outside.

There are a couple of points absolutely crucial to Gestalt. One is that you already know everything you need to know to lead a fully satisfying, happy, effective life. (Enright, 1980, p. 17)

[These concepts] are the chief actors in the endless self-nagging and inner argument between ideal and real self in which so many people fritter away their lives. (Enright, 1975, p. 20)

Personal Reflection _____

_____ Projection

Try doing this exercise on projection in a small group, and listen and reflect on one another's descriptions. Look around the room, pick out a object that stands out vividly for you. Try identifing with the object; describe yourself in terms of the object. Describe the object, but instead of "it" say "I." After several minutes, discuss with the group what your descriptions might be saying about you.

For example, a woman who identified with a beam in the ceiling described it partly as follows: "I'm very old-fashioned and uselessly ornate. . . . I have a heavy load to bear."(Adapted from Enright, 1977)

The introjector does as others would like him to do, the projector does unto others what he accuses them of doing to him, the man in pathological confluence doesn't know who is doing what to whom, and the retroflector does to himself what he would like to do to others. . . . As introjection displays itself in the use of the pronoun " I" when the real meaning is "they"; as projection displays itself in the use of the pronouns "it" and "they," when the real meaning is "I"; as confluence displays itself in the use of the pronoun "we" when the real meaning is in question; so retroflection displays itself in the use of the reflective [sic] "myself." (F. Perls, 1973, pp. 40–41)

Confluence

The third neurotic mechanism is *confluence*. (Fritz Perls differentiated between confluence in a normal sense and the *neurotic* confluence discussed here.) In confluence, individuals experience no boundary between themselves and the environment. Confluence makes a healthy rhythm of contact and withdrawal impossible because both contact and withdrawal presuppose an *other*.

Retroflection

The fourth neurotic mechanism is *retroflection*. Retroflection means, literally, "turning back sharply against"; retroflecting individuals turn against themselves, and instead of directing their energies toward changing and manipulating their environment, they direct these energies toward themselves. They split themselves and become both subject and object of all of their actions; they are the target of all of their behavior.

Fritz points out that these four mechanisms rarely operate in isolation from one another, though people balance their neurotic tendencies among the mechanisms in varying proportion. The crucial function that all of these mechanisms serve is to hamper boundary discrimination. Given this confusion of boundaries, an individual's well-being—defined as the capacity to be self-supporting and self-regulating—is severely circumscribed.

Fritz's view of these four mechanisms is basic to his psychotherapeutic approach. For example, he saw introjection as being central to what he called the "top dog–underdog struggle." The top dog consists of a bundle of introjected standards and attitudes. Fritz suggests that as long as the top dog (what Freud might call the superego) remains introjected and unassimilated, the demands expressed by the top dog will always seem unreasonable and imposed from outside. Projection is crucial in the formation and understanding of dreams. In Fritz's view, all of the parts of a

I especially prefer to work with dreams. I believe that in a dream we have a clear existential message of what's missing in our lives, what we avoid doing and living, and we have plenty of material to reassimilate and re-own the alienated parts of ourselves. (F. Perls, 1969a, p. 76)

dream are projected, disowned fragments of ourselves. Every dream contains at least one unfinished situation that involves these projected parts. To work on the dream is to reown these projected parts, thereby bringing closure to the unfinished gestalt.

Structure

Body

The Perlses' view the mind-body split of most psychologies as both arbitrary and misleading. Mental activity is simply activity that proceeds at a level that is less intense than physical activity. Thus, our bodies are direct manifestations of who we are. By simply observing our most apparent physical behaviors—posture, breathing, movements—we can learn an immense amount about ourselves.

Social Relationships

The individual exists in a field from which he or she is differentiated but also inseparable. Contact and withdrawal functions are crucial in determining an individual's existence; one way in which contact and withdrawal from the environment is played out is through the individual's relationships with other people. In fact, the sense of relatedness to a group is the individual's primary psychological survival impulse. Neurosis results from rigidities in defining the contact boundary with regard to other people and an inability to find and maintain a proper balance between the boundary and others.

Will

Gestalt stresses the importance of being aware of one's preferences and being able to act on them. Knowing one's own preferences entails knowing one's needs; emergence of the dominant need is experienced as preference for what will satisfy the need. Fritz's discussion of preference is very close to what is generally called *will*. In choosing to use the term *preference*, emphasis is placed on the organismic, natural quality of healthy willing. Willing is simply one of various mental activities; it entails the limiting of awareness to certain areas in order to carry through a set of actions directed toward satisfying specific needs.

Emotions

Gestalt views emotion as the force that energizes all action. Emotions are the expression of our basic excitement, the ways and means of expressing our choices as well as satisfying our needs. Emotion is differentiated according to varying situations—for example, by the adrenal glands into

Emotions are the very life of us . . . emotions are the very language of the organism; they modify the basic excitement according to the situation which has to be met. (F. Perls, 1973, p. 23)

anger and fear or by the sex glands into libido. The emotional excitement mobilizes the muscular system. If muscular expression of emotion is prevented, we build up anxiety, which is the bottling up of excitement. Once we are anxious, we try to desensitize our sensory systems in order to reduce the built-up excitement; it is at this point that symptoms, such as frigidity or a phobic reaction—what Fritz calls the "holes in our personalities''—develop. This emotional desensitizing is at the root of the avoidance of awareness that is basic to neurosis.

Intellect

Both Fritz and Laura believed that the intellect in our society has been overvalued and overused, particularly in attempts to understand human nature. They believed strongly in what Fritz (1969a) called *the wisdom of the organism,* but they saw this wisdom to be a kind of intuition based more in emotion than in intellect and more in nature than in conceptual systems.

The intellect, Fritz frequently asserted, has been reduced to a computerlike mechanism used for playing a series of fitting games. Preoccupation with asking *why* things happen prevents people from experiencing *how* they happen; thus, genuine emotional awareness is blocked in the interest of providing explanations. *Explaining* is the property of the intellect and constitutes something much less than understanding.

Fritz felt more strongly than Laura that certain forms of verbal communication, expressions of the intellect, are particularly overvalued in our culture. He suggests that there are three levels of such communication: chickenshit (social chitchat), bullshit (excuses, rationalization), and elephantshit (theorizing, particularly of a philosophical/psychological sort) (1969a).

With full awareness you become aware of this organismic self-regulation, you can let the organism take over without interfering, without interrupting; we can rely on the wisdom of the organism. And the contrast to this is the whole pathology of self-manipulation, environmental control, and so on, that interferes with this subtle organismic self-control. (F. Perls, 1969a)

Self

The Perlses had no interest in glorifying the concept of self to include anything beyond the everyday, obvious manifestations of who we are. We are who we are; maturity and psychological health are responsible for any claims to this statement. It is counterproductive to get caught up in feeling that we are who we should be or we are who we would like to be. Our self-boundaries are constantly shifting as we interact with our environments. We can, given some level of awareness, rely on our organismic wisdom to define these boundaries and to direct the rhythm of contact with and withdrawal from the environment.

For Gestalt, the notion of *self* or *I* is not a static, objectifiable notion. The *I* is identified with whatever the emerging figure-ground experience happens to be; all aspects of the healthy organism (sensory, motor, psychological, and so on) identify themselves temporarily with the emergent gestalt, and the experience of *I* is this totality of identifications.

In Gestalt Therapy we write the "self" with lower case "s" not capital S. Capital S is a relic from the time when we had a soul, or an ego, or something extra special; "self" means just yourself—for better, for worse, in sickness, in health and nothing else. (F. Perls, 1969a, p. 76)

Therapy

Therapist

The Perlses suggest that the therapist is basically a screen on which the patient sees his or her own missing potential; the task of therapy is the patient's reowning of this potential. The therapist is, above all, a skillful frustrator. The patient has the therapist's attention and acceptance. At the same time, it is the therapist's task to frustrate the patient by refusing to provide the support that the patient lacks within. The therapist acts as a catalyst in helping the patient break through avoidance and impasse points; the therapist's primary catalytic tool is helping the patient to see *how* he or she consistently interrupts himself or herself, avoids awareness, plays roles, and so forth.

The therapist is human, and the therapist's encounter with a patient involves the meeting of two people, which includes but is not limited to the role-defined, therapist-patient encounter. Laura Perls (1985) stressed, however, that the committed therapist must recognize and be able to control his or her own ambition, competitiveness, and anxiety in relation to the patient.

Fritz believed that individual therapy was obsolete, both inefficient and often ineffective. He suggested that work in groups had a good deal more to offer, whether the work actually involved the entire group or became an interaction between the therapist and one individual within the group. He suggested that the group can be enormously valuable as a microcosm of family and society in which people can explore their attitudes and behavior toward one another. Group support in the *safe emergency* of the therapeutic situation can be extremely useful to an individual, as can the identification with and working through of other members' conflicts.

> When I work, I am not Fritz Perls. I become nothing—no thing, a catalyst, and I enjoy my work. I forget myself and surrender to your plight. And once we have closure I come back to the audience, a prima donna demanding appreciation. I can work with everybody. I cannot work successfully with everybody. (F. Perls, 1969b, pp. 228–229)

Work with Dreams

Fritz suggests that dreams are messages that can help us to understand our unfinished situations, including what we are missing in our lives, what we are avoiding doing, and how we are avoiding and disowning parts of ourselves. This leads to an approach that is very different from the way Freud worked with dreams (Dublin, 1976). Fritz describes the opportunities for growth through work with dreams as follows:

> In Gestalt Therapy we don't interpret dreams. We do something more interesting with them. Instead of analyzing and further cutting up the dream, we want to bring it back to life. And the way to bring it back to life is to re-live the dream as if it were happening now. Instead of telling the dream as if it were a story in the past, act it out in the present, so that it becomes a part of yourself, so that you are really involved.

If you understand what you can do with dreams, you can do a tremendous lot for yourself on your own. Just take any old dream or dream fragment, it doesn't matter. As long as a dream is remembered, it is still alive and available, and it still contains an unfinished, unassimilated situation. When we are working on dreams, we usually take only a small bit from the dream, because you can get so much from even a little bit.

So if you want to work on your own, I suggest you write the dream down and make a list of *all* the details in the dream. Get every person, every thing, every mood, and then work on these to become each one of them. Ham it up, and really transform yourself into each of the different items. Really *become* that thing—whatever it is in a dream—*become* it. Use your magic. Turn into that ugly frog or whatever is there—the dead thing, the live thing, the demon—and stop thinking. Lose your mind and come to your senses. Every little bit is a piece of the jigsaw puzzle, which together will make up a much larger whole—a much stronger, happier, more completely *real* personality.

Next, take each one of these different items, characters, and parts, and let them have encounters between them. Write a script. By "write a script," I mean have a dialogue between the two opposing parts and you will find—especially if you get the correct opposites—that they always start out fighting each other. All the different parts—any part in the dream is yourself, is a projection of yourself, and if there are inconsistent sides, and you use them to fight each other, you have the eternal conflict game, the self-torture game. As the process of encounter goes on, there is a mutual learning until we come to a oneness and integration of the two opposing forces. Then the civil war is finished, and your energies are ready for your struggles with the world. . . .

We find all we need in the dream, or in the perimeter of the dream, the environment of the dream. The existential difficulty, the missing part of the personality, they are all there. It's a kind of central attack right into the midst of your non-existence.

The dream is an excellent opportunity to find the holes in the personality. So if you work on dreams it is better if you do it with someone else who can point out where you avoid. Understanding the dream means realizing when you are avoiding the obvious. The only danger is that this other person might come too quickly to the rescue and tell you what is going on in you, instead of giving yourself the chance of discovering yourself.

And if you understand the meaning of each time you identify with some bit of a dream, each time you translate an *it* into an *I*, you increase in vitality and in your potential. (F. Perls, 1969a, pp. 68–70)

Dreamwork Sample

The following excerpt is an excellent example of how Fritz Perls helped patients bring dreams "back to life":

LINDA: *I dreamed that I watch . . . a lake . . . drying up, and there is a small island in the middle of the lake, and a circle of . . . porpoises—they're like porpoises except that they can stand up, so they're like porpoises that are like people, and they're in a circle, sort of like a religious ceremony, and it's very sad—I feel very sad because they can breathe, they are sort of dancing around the circle, but the water, their element, is drying up. So it's like a dying—like watching a race of people, or a race of creatures, dying. And they are mostly females, but a few of them have a small male organ, so there are a few males there, but they won't live long enough to reproduce, and their element is drying up. And there is one that is sitting over here near me and I'm talking to this porpoise and he has prickles on his tummy, sort of like a porcupine, and they don't seem to be a part of him. And I think that there's one good point about the water drying up, I think—well, at least at the bottom, when all the water dries up, there will probably be some sort of treasure there, because at the bottom of the lake there should be things that have fallen in, like coins or something, but I look carefully and all that I can find is an old license plate . . . That's the dream.*

FRITZ: *Will you please play the license plate.*

LINDA: *I am an old license plate, thrown in the bottom of a lake. I have no use because I'm no value—although I'm not rusted—I'm outdated, so I can't be used as a license plate . . . and I'm just thrown on the rubbish heap. That's what I did with a license plate, I threw it on a rubbish heap.*

FRITZ: *Well, how do you feel about this?*

LINDA: (quietly) *I don't like it. I don't like being a license plate—useless.*

FRITZ: *Could you talk about this. That was such a long dream until you come to find the license plate, I'm sure this must be of great importance.*

LINDA: (sighs) *Useless. Outdated . . . The use of a license plate is to allow—give a car permission to go . . . and I can't give any more permission to do anything because I'm outdated . . . In California, they just paste a little—you buy a sticker—and stick it on the car, on the old license plate.* (faint attempt at humor) *So maybe someone could put me on their car and stick this sticker on me, I don't know . . .*

FRITZ: *OK, now play the lake.*

LINDA: *I'm a lake . . . I'm drying up, and disappearing, soaking into the earth . . .* (with a touch of surprise) *dying. . . . But when I soak into the earth, I become part of the earth—so maybe I water the surrounding area, so . . . even in the lake, even in my bed, flowers can grow* (sighs) *. . . New life can grow . . . from me* (cries) *. . .*

FRITZ: *You get the existential message?*

LINDA: *Yes.* (sadly, but with conviction) *I can paint—I can create—I can create beauty. I can no longer reproduce, I'm like the porpoise. . . . but I . . . I'm . . . I . . . keep wanting to say I'm food . . . I . . . as water becomes . . . I water the earth, and give life—growing things, the water—they need both the earth and water, and the . . . and the air and the sun, but as the water from the lake, I can play a part in something, and producing— feeding.*

FRITZ: *You see the contrast: On the surface, you find something, some artifact—the license plate, the artificial you—but then when you go deeper, you find the apparent death of the lake is actually fertility. . . .*

LINDA: *And I don't need a license plate, or a permission, a license in order to . . .*

FRITZ: (gently) *Nature doesn't need a license plate to grow. You don't have to be useless, if you are organismically creative, which means if you are involved.*

LINDA: *And I don't need permission to be creative. . . . Thank you.*

(F. Perls, 1969a, pp. 81–82)

Evaluation

Gestalt therapy is, above all, a synthesis of approaches to understanding human psychology and behavior. The fact that it represents a synthesis does not take away from either its uniqueness or its usefulness; in true Gestalt fashion, uniqueness and usefulness are characteristic of the whole rather than the derivation of parts.

As such a synthesis, Gestalt therapy has usefully incorporated a great deal from psychoanalytic and existential psychology, as well as bits and pieces from behaviorism (the emphasis on behavior and the obvious), psychodrama (the enacting of conflicts), group psychotherapy (work in groups), and Zen Buddhism (the emphasis of wisdom over intellectualization and the focus on present awareness). The spirit of Gestalt therapy is a humanistic, growth-oriented one, which, in addition to the Perlses' associations with the Esalen Institute, has made Gestalt therapy a major force in the human-potential movement. The commonsense, conversational nature of the literature of Gestalt therapy, as well as the attitudes of many Gestalt therapists, has contributed to a demystification of psychotherapy that many people welcome.

The work of Fritz and Laura Perls was more explicitly focused on the practice of psychotherapy than on a theory of personality. Not surprisingly, this makes it difficult to extrapolate a cohesive theory out of their work. However, this fact in itself is consistent with their view of the usefulness of theory as theory. If the attitude and the experience that comprise the Gestalt approach fit in some basic way with our own attitudes

Learning is discovery. . . . And I hope I can assist you in learning, in discovering something about yourself. (F. Perls, 1969a, p. 25)

If you see the events of your life clearly, then your living goes well, without confusion and unnecessary misery. . . . with awareness, you can minimize the pain and maximize the joys and satisfactions. (Stevens & Stevens, 1977)

and experience, the Gestalt approach can do much to help expand our own awareness.

Because Gestalt took a strong stand against many prevailing ideas and partly due to Fritz's personality, (F. Perls, 1989), it never lacked for critics. Gestalt's emphasis on feelings over thoughts and process over content was criticized (Jurjevich, 1978; Becker, 1982). Some singled out the Gestalt prayer as irrational (Morris & Ellis, 1975), while others questioned Gestalt's most fundamental assumptions. "[Some of Gestalt's] theses are not only false, but dangerous. A human being functions best when left alone. Human nature is itself good. . . . All thinking is neurotic and imma-ture . . ." (Cadwallader, 1984, p. 193).

Gestalt therapy developed in reaction to what the Perlses and many others saw as the increasing tendency toward rigidity and dogmatism in psychology, particularly psychoanalytic psychology. The Perlses and their followers made a significant contribution to a holistic psychology of the human organism and to the psychology of human awareness. More than a therapeutic method, Gestalt became, to many, a philosophy that inte-grated the physical, mental, emotional, and social aspects of living (Ginger, 1984). Gestalt's unique stress on individual responsibility echoes traditional American values (Binderman, 1974). The values of Gestalt dif-fer from those held by many other schools of therapy and personality (Tillett, 1984). By the early 1990s, there were 62 Gestalt training centers worldwide, teaching therapists and refining the ideas that originated from the life experience of Fritz and Laura Perls.

The Theory Firsthand: Excerpt from *Gestalt Therapy Verbatim*

This is the introduction to *Gestalt Therapy Verbatim*. It is a compressed yet cogent example of Fritz Perls's point of view.

I want to talk about the present development of humanistic psycholo-gy. It took us a long time to debunk the whole Freudian crap, and now we are entering a new and more dangerous phase. We are entering the phase of the turner-onners: turn on to instant cure, instant joy, instant sensory-awareness. We are entering the phase of the quacks and the con-men, who think if you get some breakthrough, you are cured—disregarding any growth requirements, disregarding any of the real potential, the inborn genius in all of you. If this is becoming a fad-dism, it is as dangerous to psychology as the year-decade-century-long lying on the couch. At least the damage we suffered under psycho-analysis does little to the patient except for making him deader and deader. This is not as obnoxious as this quick-quick-quick thing. The psychoanalysts at least bring good will with them. I must say I am *very* concerned with what's going on right now . . .

. . . We are here to promote the growth process and develop the human potential . . . In therapy, we have not only to get through the role-playing. We also have to fill in the holes in the personality to make the person whole and complete again. And again, as before, this can't be done by the turner-onners. In Gestalt Therapy we have a better way, but it is no magic shortcut. You don't have to be on a couch or in a Zendo for twenty or thirty years, but you have to invest yourself, and it takes time to grow.

The conditioners also start out with a false assumption. Their basic premise that behavior is "law" is a lot of crap. That is: we learn to breathe, to eat, we learn to walk. "Life is nothing but whatever conditions into which it has been born." *If,* in the behaviorist reorganization of our behavior, we get a modification towards better self-support, and throw away all the artificial social roles we have learned, then I am on the side of the behaviorists. The stopping block seems to be anxiety. Always anxiety. Of course you are anxious if you have to learn a new way of behavior, and the psychiatrists usually are afraid of anxiety. They don't know what anxiety *is.* Anxiety is the excitement, the *élan vital* which we carry with us, and which becomes stagnated if we are unsure about the role we have to play. If we don't know if we will get applause or tomatoes, we hesitate, so the heart begins to race and all the excitement can't flow into activity, and we have stage fright. So the formula of anxiety is very simple: anxiety is the gap between the *now* and the *then.* If you are in the now, you can't be anxious, because the excitement flows immediately into ongoing spontaneous activity. If you are in the now, you are creative, you are inventive. If you have your senses ready, if you have your eyes and ears open, like every small child, you find a solution.

A release to spontaneity, to the support of our total personality— yes, yes, yes. . . .

. . . I am what I am, and at this moment I cannot possibly be different from what I am. That is what this book is about. I give you the Gestalt prayer, maybe as a direction. The prayer in Gestalt Therapy is:

> *I do my thing, and you do your thing.*
> *I am not in this world to live up to your expectations*
> *And you are not in this world to live up to mine.*
> *You are you and I am I,*
> *And if by chance we find each other, it's beautiful.*
> *If not, it can't be helped.*

(Perls, 1969a, pp. 1–4)

Annotated Bibliography

Perls, F. S. (1969). *Ego, hunger, and aggression.* New York: Random House. (Originally published, 1947.) Perls's most intellectually oriented work, it explains in detail the theory of Gestalt therapy in its development from psychoanalysis and Gestalt psychology. It includes several chapters by Laura Perls as well.

————. (1969). *Gestalt therapy verbatim*. Lafayette, CA: The Real People Press. An excellent discussion of the basics of Gestalt therapy, including transcripts of therapy sessions.

————. (1969). *In and out of the garbage pail*. Lafayette, CA: The Real People Press. Perls's autobiography, full of anecdotes and written in a casual, humorous style; an experience in Gestalt writing that describes the origins and development of Gestalt therapy.

————. (1973). *The Gestalt approach; Eyewitness to therapy*. Ben Lomond, CA: Science and Behavior Books; New York: Bantam, 1976. Perls's last manuscripts, published together and posthumously. *The Gestalt Approach* offers an excellent, readable, and theoretical exposition of Gestalt therapy, while *Eyewitness to Therapy* includes the transcripts from a series of films of therapy sessions, which Perls planned to use as teaching material.

Fagan, J., & Shepherd, I. (Eds.). (1970). *Gestalt therapy now*. Palo Alto, CA: Science and Behavior Books. Includes papers by a number of Gestalt therapists in addition to several of Fritz Perls's lectures. It offers an interesting selection of viewpoints concerning the theory, techniques, and applications of Gestalt therapy.

Yontef, G., & Simpkin, J. (1989). Gestalt therapy. In R. Corsini & D. Wedding (Eds.), *Current Psychotherapies* (4th ed.) (pp. 323–361). Itasca, IL: Peacock. A good, short, overall introduction to Gestalt therapy. Both authors are Gestalt practitioners and write from long experience.

References

Barlow, A. (1986). The role of semantics in Gestalt therapy. *Gestalt Journal, 9*(2), 67–76.

Becker, E. (1982). Growing up rugged: Fritz Perls and Gestalt therapy. *ReVISION, 5*(2), 6–14.

Binderman, M. (1974). The issue of responsibility in Gestalt therapy. *Psychotherapy Theory, Research, and Practice, 11*(3), 287–288.

Cadwallader, E. (1984). Values in Fritz Perls's Gestalt therapy: On the dangers of half-truths. *Counseling and Values, 28*(4), 192–201.

Dublin, J. (1976). The demise of the traditional dream symbol in psychotherapy: goodbye and good riddance. *International Journal of Symbology, 7*(1), 11–21.

Enright, J. (1975). An introduction to Gestalt therapy. In F. D. Stephenson (Ed.), *Gestalt therapy primer*. Springfield, IL: Charles C. Thomas.

———. (1977). Thou art that: Projection and play. In J. Stevens (Ed.), *Gestalt is*. New York: Bantam, 152–159.

———. (1980). *Enlightening Gestalt: Waking up from the nightmare*. Mill Valley, CA: Pro Telos.

Fagan, J., & Shepherd, I. (Eds.). (1970). *Gestalt therapy now*. Palo Alto, CA: Science and Behavior Books.

Gaines, J. (1979). *Fritz Perls: Here and now*. Millbrae, CA: Celestial Arts.

Ginger, S. (1984). Fantasy in Gestalt therapy. *Etudes Psychotherapiques, 15*(2), 99–106.

Gordon, D. (1987). Gestalt therapy: The historical influences of Frederick S. Perls. *Gestalt Journal, 9*(10), 28–39.

Henle, M. (1987). Gestalt psychology and Gestalt therapy. *Journal of the History of the Behavioral Sciences, 14*(1), 23–32.

Humphrey, K. (1986). Laura Perls: a biographical sketch. *Gestalt Journal, 9*(1), 5–11.

Jurjevich, R. (1978). Emotionality and irrationality in psychotherapeutic fads. *Psychotherapy Theory, Research, and Practice, 15*(2), 168–179.

Khayyám, O. (1968). *The Rubáiyát of Omar Khayyám* (R. Graves and O. Ali-Shah, Trans.). New York: Doubleday.

Morris, K., & Ellis, A. (1975). The Perls perversion. *Personnel and Guidance Journal, 54*(2), 90–93.

Naranjo, C. A. (1973). *The techniques of Gestalt therapy*. Berkeley, CA: SAT Press.

Perls, F. S. (1969). *Ego, hunger and aggression*. New York: Random House. (Originally published, 1947.)

———. (1967). Workshop vs. individual therapy. *Journal of Long Island Consultation Center, 15*(2), 13–17.

———. (1969a). *Gestalt therapy verbatim*. Lafayette, CA: The Real People Press.

———. (1969b). *In and out of the garbage pail*. Lafayette, CA: The Real People Press.

———. (1976). *The Gestalt approach: Eyewitness to therapy*. Ben Lomond, CA: Science and Behavior Books, 1973; New York: Bantam.

———. (1977). Resolution. In J. Stevens (Ed.), *Gestalt is*. New York: Bantam, 70–75.

———. (1978). Psychiatry in a new key. *Gestalt Journal, 1*(1), 32–53.

———. (1979). Planned psychotherapy. *Gestalt Journal, 2*(2), 5–23.

———. (1989). Theory and technique of personality integration. *TACD Journal, 17*(1), 35–52.

Perls, F. S., Hefferline, R. F., & Goodman, P. (1951). *Gestalt therapy*. New York: Dell.

Perls, L. (1992). Concepts and misconceptions of Gestalt therapy. *Journal of Humanistic Psychology, 32*(3), 50–56. (Originally published in *Voices, 14*[3]).

————. (1986). Opening address: 8th annual conference on the theory and practice of Gestalt therapy—May 17, 1985. *Gestalt Journal, 9*(1), 12–15.

Rosenfeld, E. (1978). An oral history of Gestalt therapy. Part I: A conversation with Laura Perls. *Gestalt Journal, 1*(1), 8–31.

Serlin, I. (1992). Tribute to Laura Perls. *Journal of Humanistic Psychology, 32*(3), 57–66.

Shepard, M. (1975). *Fritz: An intimate portrait of Fritz Perls and Gestalt therapy.* New York: (Saturday Review Press) Dutton.

Sherrill, R. (1986). Gestalt therapy and Gestalt psychology. *Gestalt Journal, 9*(2), 53–66.

Smith, E. (1975). The role of early Reichian theory in the development of Gestalt therapy. *Psychotherapy Theory, Research, and Practice, 12*(3), 268–272.

Stevens, J., & Stevens B. (1977). Introduction. In J. Stevens (Ed.), *Gestalt Is.* New York: Bantam, vii–xi.

Stewart, D. (1974). The philosophical background of Gestalt therapy. *Counseling Psychologist, 4*(4), 13–14.

Tillett, R. (1984). Gestalt therapy in theory and in practice. *British Journal of Psychiatry, 145,* 231–235.

Wheeler, G. (1991). *Gestalt reconsidered: A new approach to contact and resistance.* New York: Gardner Press.

Chapter Nine

William James and the Psychology of Consciousness

William James's contributions to psychology are emerging from a period of relative obscurity. His interest in inner experiences passed out of fashion as psychology became more involved in psychoanalysis, psychotherapy, and the hard science orientation of behaviorism. Moreover, the increasing fixation on objective data left little room for James's brilliant and incisive speculations.

Since the 1960s, however, there has been a sustained wave of research into the nature of consciousness. Researchers concerned with the implications of altered states of consciousness, paranormal phenomenon, and intuitive states are returning to and expanding James's original expositions. His ideas are once again being debated and tried in education. His theory of emotions has been returned to center stage in psychophysical circles, while his philosophical contribution, pragmatism, has been so gradually and completely absorbed into mainstream thinking that its originator is largely forgotten.

James's works are free of the kind of petty arguments that currently divides psychological theorists. He was more concerned with clarifying the issues than with developing a unified approach, and he understood that different models were necessary to understand different kinds of data. His explorations and findings defined the field of psychology. He anticipated, among other things, Skinner's behaviorism, existential psychology, much of cognitive psychology, Gestalt theory, and the Rogerian self-concept.

James was a self-confessed "moral" psychologist, a term that has almost vanished from our modern vocabulary. Fully aware that no researcher can be truly objective, he reminded other teachers that their actions always had ethical and moral implications: If your students believe what you are teaching them and act on these beliefs, only then does your teaching have real consequences. James himself took full responsibility for his actions and worked passionately for the side he advocated.

> I can't bring myself, as so many men seem able to, to blink the evil out of sight, and gloss it over. It's as real as the good, and if it is denied, good must be denied too. It must be accepted and hated, and resisted while there's breath in our bodies. (H. James, 1926, Vol.1, p. 158)

His major works, *The Principles of Psychology* (1890), *The Varieties of Religious Experience* (1902), and *Pragmatism* (1907), continue to be studied. The questions that he posed remain largely unanswered but are more and more at the center of the current controversies within psychology and philosophy.

Personal History

William James was born into a well-to-do New England family on January 11, 1842. In his early years, he traveled with his parents to Newport, New

William James is a towering figure in the history of American thought—without doubt the foremost psychologist this country has produced. His depiction of mental life is faithful, vital, subtle. In verve he has no equal. (Allport, 1961, p. xiii)

York, Paris, London, Geneva, Boulogne, and Bonn. He studied painting for a year, then he became interested in science. He entered Harvard, unsure of what area to pursue. Initially, he studied chemistry, then comparative anatomy. In 1863, he transferred to Harvard's medical school. Then, in 1865, he took a leave of absence to accompany the naturalist Louis Agassiz on an expedition to the Amazon Basin. The hazards and discomforts of the trip convinced James that he was better suited to thinking and writing about science than engaging in active scientific exploration:

> My coming was a mistake. . . . I am convinced now, for good, that I am cut out for a speculative rather than an active life. . . . I had misgivings to this effect before starting: but I was so filled with enthusiasm, and the romance of the thing seemed so great, that I stifled them. Here on the ground the romance vanishes and the misgivings float up. (James, 1926, Vol. 1, pp. 61–63)

He returned to Harvard for another year but left again to study in Germany. When he returned again to Harvard it was only after a series of illnesses that he was finally able to earn his medical degree in 1869 (Feinstein, 1984). Upon graduating, he entered into a long, pronounced depression. He experienced himself as worthless; several times he considered suicide. One incident occurred during this period that had a lasting and profound effect on his life:

> Whilst in this state of philosophic pessimism and general depression of spirits about my prospects, I went one evening into a dressing-room in the twilight to procure some article that was there; when suddenly there fell upon me without any warning, just as if it came out of the darkness, a horrible fear of my own existence. Simultaneously there arose in my mind the image of an epileptic patient whom I had seen in the asylum, a black-haired youth with greenish skin, entirely idiotic, who used to sit all day on one of the benches, or rather shelves against the wall, with his knees drawn up against his chin, and the coarse gray undershirt, which was his only garment, drawn over them inclosing his entire figure. He sat there like a sort of sculptured Egyptian cat or Peruvian mummy, moving nothing but his black eyes and looking absolutely non-human. This image and my fear entered into a species of combination with each other. *That shape am I,* I felt, potentially. Nothing that I possess can defend me against that fate, if the hour for it should strike for me as it struck for him. There was such a horror of him . . . it was as if something hitherto solid within my breast gave way entirely, and I became a mass of quivering fear. After this the universe was changed for me altogether. I awoke morning after morning with a horrible dread at the pit of my stomach, and with a sense of the insecurity of life that I never knew before, and that I have never felt since. . . . It gradually faded, but for months I was unable to go out into the dark alone.

In general I dreaded to be left alone. I remember wondering how other people could live, how I myself had ever lived, so unconscious of that pit of insecurity beneath the surface of life. My mother in particular, a very cheerful person, seemed to me a perfect paradox in her unconsciousness of danger, which you may well believe I was very careful not to disturb by revelations of my own state of mind. (James, 1902/1958, pp. 135–136)

James's diary and letters recorded the steps in his recovery:

February 1, 1870: Today I about touched bottom, and perceive plainly that I must face the choice with open eyes: shall I *frankly* throw the moral business overboard, as one unsuited to my innate aptitudes, or shall I follow it, and it alone, making everything else merely stuff for it? I will give the latter alternative a fair trial. (In Perry, 1935, Vol. 1, p. 322)

The depression continued, however, until April 30, 1870, when James put a conscious and a purposeful end to it. He chose to believe in free will. "My first act of free will shall be to believe in free will. For the remainder of the year, I will voluntarily cultivate the feeling of moral freedom" (H. James, 1926, Vol. 1, p. 147). James understood that freedom, in its essential nature, was not an arbitrary or a capricious act. It could neither be derived from nor restricted by any other condition. Therefore, to act with freedom was to act for himself, something that, given his upbringing, was never easy to do.

After his recovery, James took a teaching position at Harvard. He taught first in the department of anatomy and physiology; several years later, he taught the first courses in psychology.

In 1878, he married and began to work on his textbook *The Principles of Psychology*, published in 1890. His colorful style of communicating as well as his concern with moral and practical issues made him a popular lecturer. Two collections of talks, *The Will to Believe and Other Essays* (1896) and *Talks to Teachers on Psychology and to Students on Some of Life's Ideals* (1899a), furthered his growing national reputation. In 1896, he presented a lecture series on exceptional mental states, which extended the reach of clinical psychology (Taylor, 1982). In 1902, he published a lecture series entitled *Varieties of Religious Experience*. In the last decade of his life, he wrote and lectured on pragmatism, a philosophic movement founded by James, which proposed that meaning should be evaluated by its utility and that truth should be tested by the practical consequences of belief.

After teaching a semester at Stanford University (interrupted by the great earthquake of 1906), he returned to Harvard. Soon thereafter, he retired but continued to write and lecture until his death in 1910.

He was the third president (1894–1895) of the American Psychological Association and was active in establishing psychology as a discipline inde-

Inborn rationalists and inborn pragmatists will never convert each other. We shall always look on them as spectral and they on us as trashy—irredeemably both! . . . [W]hy not simply express ourselves positively, and trust that the truer view quietly will displace the other. (H. James, 1926, Vol. 2, p. 272)

pendent of neurology and philosophy. James's definition of psychology as "the description and explanation of states of consciousness as such" (1892, p. 1) is exciting a new generation of students and researchers.

Intellectual Antecedents

James grew up as a member of a remarkable and gifted family. His father Henry James was one of the most controversial writers on politics and religion in the nineteenth century. Their home was a hotbed of new ideas. James became a passionate and skilled speaker in a family that rewarded and demanded such skills. His brother, Henry James, Jr., more introspective than William, became one of the great masters of fiction. The brothers were in constant communication and remained devoted fans and thorough critics of each other's works (Matthiessen, 1980).

James was familiar with most of the leading philosophers, researchers, writers, and educators of the day and corresponded with a number of them. He frequently acknowledged his debt to this or that thinker but did not seem to be a disciple of any. A single exception may be the French philosopher Charles-Bernard Renouvier, whose work sparked James's early belief in free will. Renouvier's approach to other thorny metaphysical problems influenced James's own brand of pragmatism. In psychology, he was impressed with the work of Wilhelm Wundt, and Hermann Helmholtz, of Germany; the research of Alfred Binet and Jean-Martin Charcot of France; the writings of Alexander Bain of Scotland and Frederic Myers of England; and the contributions of Canadian Maurice Bucke. James read extensively and peppers his work with long quotes from literally hundreds of other writers.

Major Concepts

James was interested in the full range of human psychology, from brainstem functioning to religious ecstasy, from the perception of space to ESP research. He often argued both sides of a controversy with equal brilliance. "There was no limit to James's curiosity and there was no theory, however unpopular, with which he was not willing to play" (MacLeod, 1969, p. v). He pursued most vigorously the task of understanding and explaining the basic units of thought. Fundamental concepts, including the nature of thought, attention, habit, will, and emotion, held James's interest.

For James, personality arises from the continual interplay of instincts, habits, and personal choices. He viewed personal differences, developmental stages, psychopathology, and the rest of personality as arrangements and rearrangements of the basic building blocks supplied by nature and slowly refined by evolution.

In Jamesian theory, there are some contradictions. And James was keenly aware of this state of affairs, knowing full well that what holds for one aspect of his approach may not hold for others. Instead of attempting

It seems to me that psychology is like physics before Galileo's time—not a single elementary law yet caught a glimpse of. (James, 1890)

to create a grand and unified scheme, he indulged in what he called *pluralistic thinking;* that is, holding to more than one theory at a time. James acknowledged that psychology was an immature science, lacking sufficient information in its formulation of consistent laws of sensation, perception, or even the nature of consciousness. Thus, he was at ease with a multitude of theories, even with those that contradicted his own. In an introduction to a book attacking his theories of personality, he wrote: "I am not convinced of all of Dr. Sidis's positions, but I can cordially recommend this volume to all classes of readers as a treatise both interesting and instructive, and original in a high degree" (Sidis, 1898, p. vi).

In the conclusion to the abridged edition of his textbook *Psychology: The Briefer Course* (1892), he admits to the limits of psychology—limits that still exist today.

> When, then, we talk of "psychology as a natural science," we must not assume that that means a sort of psychology that stands at last on solid ground. It means just the reverse; it means a psychology particularly fragile, and into which the waters of metaphysical criticism leak at every joint. A string of raw facts; a little gossip and wrangle about opinions; a little classification and generalization on the mere descriptive level; a strong prejudice that we *have* states of mind, and that our brain conditions them. This is no science, it is only the hope of a science. (pp. 334–335)

James considered many different ideas to be basic to an understanding of psychology. In this section, because there is space only to address a small portion of his treatise, the discussion is confined to major concepts and is highly selective and admittedly incomplete. The concepts are grouped first around the self and then around the elements of consciousness. Finally, a few other concerns, too vital to be left out are addressed. We have touched only briefly upon his contributions to philosophy.

The Self

The self is that personal continuity that we all recognize each time we awaken. James described several layers, seeing the self, like consciousness, to be simultaneously continuous and discrete (Knowles & Sibicky, 1990).

The Material Self

The material layer of the self includes those things with which we personally identify. The material self encompasses not only our bodies but also our homes, possessions, friends, and family. To the extent that a person identifies with an external person or object, it is part of his or her identity.

> *In its widest possible sense, however, a man's Self is the sum total of all that he CAN call his,* not only his body and his psychic powers, but

his clothes and his house, his wife and children, his ancestors and friends, his reputation and works, his lands and horses, and yacht and bank-account. All these things give him the same emotions. If they wax and prosper, he feels triumphant; if they dwindle and die away, he feels cast down,—not necessarily in the same degree for each thing, but in much the same way for all. (James, 1890, Vol. 1, pp. 291–292)

Personal Reflection

Who Am I?

Test James's proposition yourself. Imagine that someone is ridiculing some person, idea, or thing that matters to you. Are you objective in evaluating the merits of the attack, or do you react as if you yourself were under attack? If someone insults your brother, your parents, your hairstyle, your country, your jacket, or your religion, are you aware of the investment that you have in each? Some of the confusion between ownership and identification is clarified by understanding this expanded concept of the self.

The Social Self

"A man's social self is the recognition which he gets from his mates" (James, 1890, Vol. 1, p. 293). We willingly or unwillingly accept any and all roles. A person may have many or few social selves. These may be consistent or inconsistent. But whatever they are, one identifies with each in the proper setting. James suggests that the proper course of action is to pick a self that seems admirable and to try to act like that self in as many situations as possible. "All other selves thereupon become unreal, but the fortunes of this self are real. Its failures are real failures, its triumphs real triumphs" (James, 1890, Vol. 1, p. 310). This is what James called *the selective industry of the mind* (Suls & Marco, 1990). Some researchers have reduced this idea to the distinction between private and public selves (Baumgardner, Kaufman, & Cranford, 1990; Lamphere & Leary, 1990), but that is an oversimplification of James's original observations.

The social self constitutes patterns of personal habit that form the mainstay of our relationships. James viewed it as a shifting, malleable, surface personality, often little more than a set of masks, changed to suit different audiences. He argued that social habits are necessary; they make life orderly. Habit is a cushion; it renders relationships safe and predictable. James believed the constant interplay between cultural conformity and individual expression to be beneficial to both. "The community stagnates without the impulse of the individual. The impulse dies away without the sympathy of the community" (James, 1896, p. 232).

The Spiritual Self

The spiritual self is one's inner and subjective being. It is the active element in all consciousness.

> It is the home of interest—not the pleasant or the painful, not even pleasure or pain, as such, but that within us to which pleasure and pain, the pleasant and the painful, speak. It is the source of effort and attention, and the place from which appear to emanate the fiats of the will. (James, 1890, Vol. 1, p. 298)

One expression of this self is exemplified in religious experiences, which "have no proper *intellectual* deliverance of their own, but belong to a region deeper and more vital and practical, than that which the intellect inhabits" (H. James, 1926, Vol. 2, p. 149).

James remained undecided on the question of the personal soul; however, he did feel that there was something beyond individual identity. "Out of my experience . . . one fixed conclusion dogmatically emerges. . . . There is a continuum of cosmic consciousness, against which our individuality builds but accidental fences, and into which our several minds plunge as into a mother-sea or reservoir" (James in Murphy & Ballou, 1960, p. 324).

Characteristics of Thought

Personal Consciousness

"Every thought tends to be part of a personal consciousness" (James, 1890, Vol. 1, p. 225). Therefore, says James, there is no such thing as individual consciousness independent of an owner. There is only the process of thought as experienced or perceived by an individual. Consciousness always exists in relation to a person.

Changes in Consciousness

We can never have the same exact thought twice. Our consciousness may repeatedly enounter the sight of a certain object, sound of a specific tone, or taste of a particular food, but how we perceive these sensations is different with each encounter. What seems upon cursory inspection to be repetitious thought is actually a changing series of thinking. Each thought within this series is unique and each is partially determined by previous modifications of the original thought.

> Often we are ourselves struck at the strange differences in our successive views of the same thing. We wonder how we ever could have opined as we did last month about a certain matter. We have outgrown the possibility of that state of mind, we know not how. From one year to another we see things in new light. What was unreal has

To give up pretensions is as blessed a relief as to get them gratified. . . . How pleasant is the day when we give up striving to be young—or slender! Thank God! we say, *those* illusions are gone. Everything added to the self is a burden. (James, 1890, Vol. 1, pp. 310–311)

The only thing which psychology has a right to postulate at the outset is the fact of thinking itself. (James, 1890, Vol. 1, p. 224)

Within each personal consciousness thought is always changing. (James, 1890, Vol. 1, p. 225)

grown real, and what was exciting is insipid. The friends we used to care the world for are shrunken to shadows; the women, once so divine, the stars, the woods, and the waters, how now so dull and common; the young girls that brought an aura of infinity, at present hardly distinguishable existences; the pictures so empty; and as for the books, what *was* there to find so mysteriously significant in Goethe, or in John Mill so full of weight? (James, 1890, Vol. 1, p. 233)

The Continuity of Thought

"Within each personal consciousness, thought is sensibly continuous" (James, 1890, Vol. 1, p. 237). Whereas some theorists shy away from the seeming paradox of personality as something continuous and undergoing continual change, James suggested a resolution:

> The passing thought, according to Professor James, is the thinker. Each passing wave of consciousness, each passing thought is aware of all that has preceded in consciousness; each pulse of thought as it dies away transmits its title of ownership of its mental content to the succeeding thought. (Sidis, 1898, p. 190)

What is present at the moment, conscious or not, is the personality. (Carl Rogers, Fritz Perls, B. F. Skinner, and Zen Buddhism provide different conclusions derived from this assumption of the self.)

Each emerging thought takes part of its force, focus, content, and direction from preceding thoughts.

> Consciousness, then, does not appear to itself chopped up in bits. Such words as "chain" or "train" do not describe it fitly. . . . It is nothing jointed: it flows. A "river" or a "stream" are the metaphors by which it is most naturally described. *In talking of it hereafter, let us call it the stream of thought, of consciousness, or of subjective life.* (James, 1890, Vol. 1, p. 239)

Stream of consciousness, a form of writing that attempts to mimic the flow and jumble of thought, arose in part from James's teaching. Gertrude Stein was a major exponent of this genre and was a student of James at Harvard.

In consciousness, the stream is continuous. James (as did Freud) based many of his ideas about mental functions on the assumption of continuous thought. There are gaps in feelings; there are gaps in awareness; but even when there are perceived gaps in consciousness, there is no accompanying feeling of discontinuity. For example, when you awaken in the morning, you never wonder who it is who is waking up. You feel no need to rush to a mirror to verify, to see, if it is *you*. You need no convincing that the consciousness you awoke with is the same as the one you took to sleep.

Personal Reflection
Stream of Consciousness

Try one or all of these stream-of-consciousness excercises. In order to get the greatest benefit from them, share and discuss your findings with other students.

1. Sit quietly and let your thoughts wander for five minutes. Afterward, write down as many of your thoughts as you can recall.

2. Allow your thoughts to wander for one minute. When the minute is over, recall what thoughts you had during that minute. Write down, if possible, the whole series. Here is an example of such a series:

"I will do this one-minute exercise:

. . . pencil to write thoughts down.

. . . my desk has pencils.

. . . bills on my desk.

. . . do I still want to buy fluoridated spring water?

. . . Yosemite last year.

. . . lakes frozen at the edge in the morning.

. . . my sleeping bag zipper stuck that night, freezing cold."

3. Try to control your thoughts for one minute, keeping them on a single track. Write down these thoughts.

Does it seem realistic to consider your consciousness as a stream? When you controlled your thoughts, did they seem actually under your control or did they continue to "flow," moving from one idea or image to another?

Consciousness Chooses

Consciousness is selective: "It is always interested more in one part of its object than in another, and welcomes and rejects, or chooses, all the while it thinks" (James, 1890, Vol. 1, p. 284). What an individual chooses and what determines the choice is the subject matter of most of psychology. James draws attention to the major variables: attention and habit.

Attention

Philosophers before James (John Locke, David Hume, Robert Harley, Herbert Spencer and others) assumed that the mind is passive and experience simply rains upon it. The personality then develops in direct proportion to the amounts of various experiences received. James considered this idea naive and the conclusions patently false. Before experience can be *experienced*, it must be attended to. "*My experience is what I agree to attend to.* Only those items which I *notice* shape my mind—without selective interest, experience is an utter chaos. Interest alone gives accent and emphasis, light and shade, background and foreground—intelligible perspective, in a word" (James, 1890, Vol. 1, p. 402). Although the capacity to make choices is restricted by conditioned habits, it is still possible—and for James essential—to make real and meaningful decisions from moment to moment.

> The mind is at every stage a theatre of simultaneous possibilities. Consciousness consists in the comparison of these with each other, the selection of some, and the suppression of the rest. (James, 1890, Vol. 1, p. 288)

Intellect

There are two levels of knowing: knowing through direct experience and knowing through abstract reasoning. James calls the first level, *knowledge of acquaintance*. It is sensory, intuitive, poetic, and emotional.

> I know the color blue when I see it, and the flavor of a pear when I taste it; I know an inch when I move my finger through it: a second of time when I feel it pass . . . but *about* the inner nature of these facts or what makes them what they are, I can say nothing at all. (James, 1890, Vol. 1, p. 221)

The higher level of knowledge James calls *knowledge-about*. It is intellectual, focused, relational; it can develop abstractions; it is objective and unemotional.

> When we know about it, we can do more than merely have it; we seem, as we think over its relations, to subject it to a form of *treatment* and *operate* upon it with our thought. . . . Through feelings we become acquainted with things but only with our thoughts do we know about them. (James, 1890, Vol. 1, p. 222)

This distinction helps to clarify how differences in knowledge may lead to different social consequences.

Although James's work is rich in metaphors and is still valued as much for its poetry and style as for its content, he is clear in his opinion that the more rational, objective knowledge is the more highly evolved in form. "Though it would be absurd in an absolute way to say that a given analytic mind was superior to any intuitional one, yet it is none the less true that the former *represents* the higher state" (James, 1890, Vol. 2, p. 353).

> Mind engenders truth upon reality. . . . Our minds are not here simply to copy a reality that is already complete. They are here to complete it, to add to its importance by their own remodeling of it, to decant its contents over, so to speak, into a more significant shape. In point of fact, the use of most of our thinking is to help us to change the world. (James in Perry, 1935, Vol. 2, p. 479)

> Who can decide offhand which is better, to live or understand life. (James, 1911)

(In this text, see the sections on Intellect in Freud, Jung, and Sufism for alternative points of view.)

Habit

Habits are actions or thoughts that are seemingly automatic responses to a given experience. They differ from instincts in that habits can be created, modified, or eliminated by conscious direction. They are valuable and necessary. "Habit simplifies the movements required to achieve a given result, makes them more accurate and diminishes fatigue" (James, 1890, Vol. 1, p. 112). In this sense habits are one facet of the acquisition of skills. On the other hand, "habit diminishes the conscious attention with which our acts are performed" (James, 1890, Vol. 1, p. 114). Whether this is advantageous or not depends on the situation. Withdrawing attention from an action makes that action easier to perform but also makes it resistant to change.

> The fact is that our virtues are habits as much as our vices. All our life, so far as it has definite form, is but a mass of habits—practical, emotional, and intellectual—systematically organized for our weal or woe, and bearing us irresistibly toward our destiny, whatever the latter may be. (James, 1899a, p. 33)

James was struck by the complexity of acquired habits as well as by their resistance to extinction. The following is one of his examples:

The only things which we commonly see are those which we preperceive. (James, 1890, Vol. 1, p. 444)

> With a view of cultivating the rapidity of visual and tactile perception, and the precision of respondent movements, which are necessary for success in every kind of prestidigitation, Houdin* early practised the art of juggling with balls in the air; and having, after a month's practice, become thorough master of the art of keeping up four balls at once, he placed a book before him, and, while the balls were in the air, accustomed himself to read without hesitation. "This," he says, "will probably seem to my readers very extraordinary; but I shall surprise them still more when I say that I have just amused myself with repeating this curious experiment. Though thirty years have elapsed since the time I was writing, and though I have scarcely once touched the balls during that period, I can still manage to read with ease while keeping three balls up." (1890, Vol. 1, p. 117)

> *[A stage magician who was the namesake of the famous Houdini.]

Fortunately, we can solve the problem of education without discovering or inventing additional reinforcers. We merely need to make better use of those we have. (Skinner, 1972, p. 173)

As an educator of students and teachers, James was concerned with the formation of proper habits, habits that develop the capacity of attention. He suggested that the systematic training of habits was far more important in education than the rote learning that was still so popular. "Continuity of training is the great means of making the nervous system act infallibly right" (James, 1899a, p. 35). Although much of our lives is determined by habit, we still have the ability to choose which habits to cultivate.

A new habit is formed in three stages. First, there must be need or desire; for example, the desire to exercise regularly or to understand French. Then, one needs information: methods of learning how to maintain the habit. One might read books, attend classes, and consciously explore ways how others have developed the desired habit. The last stage is simple repetition; consciously doing the exercise or actually reading and speaking French until the acts become usual and *habitual*.

Bad Habits

Most obvious and most prevalent among the obstacles to growth in our daily lives are our own bad habits. They are, by definition, those forces that retard our development and limit our happiness. James suggested that we even have the bad habit of overlooking or ignoring our other bad habits. Examples might include overweight people who "don't notice" the size of the portions they serve themselves and poor students who remain steadfastly unaware of when papers are due or when exams are to be given.

Habitual actions are those we do with a minimum of awareness; habit patterns preclude new learning. James stresses that many of our daily routines may actually prevent us from experiencing a sense of well-being by restricting awareness. Resistance to changing a habit becomes critical in that it prevents new possibilities from becoming part of our lives.

Will

James defined will as the combination of attention (focusing consciousness) and effort (overcoming inhibitions, laziness, or distractions). "Acts of will are such acts only as cannot be inattentively performed. A distinct idea of what they are, and a deliberate *fiat* on the mind's part, must precede their execution" (James, 1899a, p. 83). According to James, an idea inevitably produces an action unless another idea conflicts with it. Will is that process that holds one choice among the alternatives long enough to allow that choice to occur. "The essential achievement of the will, in short, when it is most 'voluntary', is to ATTEND to a difficult object and hold it fast before the mind" (James, 1890, Vol. 2, p. 561).

> Suppose, for instance, that you are climbing a mountain, and have worked yourself into a position from which the only escape is by a terrible leap. Have faith that you can successfully make it, and your feet are nerved to its accomplishment. But mistrust yourself, and think of all the sweet things you have heard the scientists say of *maybes,* and you will hesitate so long that, at last, all unstrung and trembling, and launching yourself in a moment of despair, you roll in the abyss. In such a case (and it belongs to an enormous class), the part of wisdom as well as of courage is to *believe what is in the line of your needs,* for

Pessimism is essentially a religious disease. (James, 1896)

only by such belief is the need fulfilled. Refuse to believe, and you shall indeed be right, for you shall irretrievably perish. But believe, and again you shall be right, for you shall save yourself. You make one or the other of two possible universes true by your trust or mistrust. (James, 1896, p. 59)

Strengthening the Will

The development of a strong will was of major concern to James. It continues to be a concern in psychology today. The exact role of intention is still being examined (Cross & Markus, 1990). James understood that being able to do what one wishes to do is not always easy. He suggested that one simple and readily available method to achieve this end was to perform a *useless* task every day.

Be systematically heroic in little unnecessary points, do something every day for no other reason than its difficulty, so that, when the hour of dire need draws nigh, it may find you not unnerved and untrained to stand the test. . . . The man who has daily inured himself to habits of concentrated attention, energetic volition, and self denial in unnecessary things will stand like a tower when everything rocks around him,

Personal Reflection —————————

——————————— A Useless Task

To get a sense of how a useless task might strengthen one's will, try this exercise.

Obtain a small box of matches, paper clips, pushpins, or candies. Place the box on a table in front of you. Open the box. Take out the items inside one by one. Then, close the box. Open it again. Put the items back in the box one by one. Close the box. Repeat this cycle for five minutes.

Write down the feelings this exercise engenders. Pay special attention to any reasons you might have thought of for not completing the task.

If you were to repeat this task over several days, each day you would perhaps discover a host of new reasons for quitting. Although you would find the task difficult at first, over time it would become easier to complete. You also would feel a new sense of personal power and self-control.

The reasons you might invent for not doing this exercise are a partial list of the elements in your own personality that inhibit your will. You have only your will to counter these many (and excellent) reasons. There is no "good reason" to continue the exercise beyond your decision to do so.

and his softer fellow-mortals are winnowed like chaff in the blast. (James, 1899a, p. 38)

The act itself is unimportant; being able to do it, *in spite of its being unimportant,* is the critical element.

Training the Will

Improving voluntary attention includes training the will. A developed will allows consciousness to attend to ideas, perceptions, and sensations that are not necessarily pleasant or inviting and, in fact, may be difficult or even distasteful.

Try, for example, to imagine yourself eating your favorite food. Keep the images and sensations uppermost in your mind for 20 seconds. You will probably find that this is not too difficult. Now, for 20 seconds, imagine that you are cutting the surface of your thumb with a razor blade. Notice how your attention scoots off in every direction as soon as you are aware of the subjective sensation of pain, the color and wetness of your own blood, and the mixture of fear, fascination, and revulsion. Only an act of will can constrain your instinctual desire to move away from the experience.

Unless a person develops the capacity to learn, the content of the teaching is of little importance.

> The great thing in all education is to *make our nervous system our ally instead of our enemy.* It is to fund and capitalize our acquisitions, and live at ease upon the interest of the fund. *For this we must make automatic and habitual, as early as possible, as many useful actions as we can,* and as carefully guard against the growing into ways that are likely to be disadvantageous. (James, 1899a, p. 34)

Surrender of the Will

There are rare times when rather than strengthen his or her will, a person must surrender it, must allow it to be overwhelmed by inner experiences. In his studies of spiritual states, James found that at these moments other aspects of consciousness appeared to assume control. Will is necessary to bring "one close to the complete unification aspired after, [however] it seems that the very last step must be left to other forces and performed without the help of its activity" (James, 1902/1958, p. 170). By complete unification, James means a state in which all facets of the personality seem to be in harmony with one another and the person perceives the inner world and the external world as unified. *Transcendence of limitations, mystical union, cosmic* or *unitive consciousness* are some of the terms used to describe this transformed state. In it, the personality is reorganized to include more than the will and more than personal identity. It is as if one finds oneself to be part of a larger system rather than a single, time-bound consciousness.

The Sentiment of Rationality

A man who thought he was dead was talking to a friend. Unable to convince him otherwise the friend finally asked, "Do dead men bleed?" "Of course not," replied the man. The friend took a needle and jabbed it into the man's thumb. It began to bleed. The man looked at his thumb and then turned to his friend. "Hey, dead men do bleed!"

Why does a person accept one rational idea or theory and reject another? James suggested that it is partly an emotional decision; we accept the one, because it enables us to understand the facts in a more emotionally satisfying way. James describes this emotional satisfaction as "a strong feeling of ease, peace, rest. The feeling of sufficiency of the present moment, of its absoluteness—this absence of all need to explain it, account for it, or justify it—is what I call the sentiment of rationality" (1948, pp. 3–4). Before a person will accept a theory (any of the theories expounded in this book, for example), two separate sets of needs must be satisfied. First, the theory must be intellectually palatable, consistent, logical, and so on. Second, it must be emotionally palatable; it must encourage us to think or act in ways that we find personally satisfying and acceptable.

Consider the way we seek advice. If, for instance, you wanted to get information about the effects of smoking marijuana, who would you go to for such information? Could you predict the kind of information and suggestions that would be offered by your parents, friends who do not smoke marijuana, friends who do, someone who sells marijuana, a police officer, a psychiatrist, a priest or minister, or a person working in a college counseling center? It is likely that you can predict in advance the kind and quality of information that each might offer as well as your willingness to accept the information once you hear it.

Often, we are not consciously aware of this aspect of decision making. We like to believe that we can make decisions based entirely on rational thinking. Yet, there is another critical variable that enters into the process: the desire to find facts that resolve our emotional confusion, that make us more comfortable. The sentiment of rationality involves emotionally changing an idea *before* we can turn to the business of decision making.

Dynamics

Psychological Growth

James rejected absolutes, such as *God, truth,* or *idealism,* in favor of personal experience and discovering how to improve oneself. A recurrent theme in his writings is that personal evolution is possible and that everyone has an inherent capacity to modify or change his or her attitudes and behaviors. He concludes that there is an underlying drive in human beings toward increasing their own well-being.

Emotions

The James-Lange theory of emotion states that an emotion depends on feedback from one's own body. The theory was so called because the Danish psychologist Carl Lange published a similar theory at about the same time (Koch, 1986). It is a biological theory of emotion that includes a psychological component. James says that we perceive a situation in which an instinctual physical reaction occurs, and then we are aware of an emotion (e.g., sadness, joy, surprise). The emotion is based on the recognition of the physical feelings, not of the initial situation.

> Were this bodily commotion suppressed, we should not so much *feel* fear as call the situation fearful; we should not feel surprise, but coldly recognize that the object was indeed astonishing. One enthusiast [James himself] has even gone so far as to say that when we feel sorry it is because we weep, when we feel afraid it is because we run away, and not conversely. (James, 1899a, p. 99)

This seems contrary to the popular conception. Most of us assume that we see a situation, begin to have feelings about it, and then have physical responses—we laugh, cry, grit our teeth, run away, and so on. If James is correct, we should expect different emotions to arise from different physical reactions. Evidence that sensory feedback contributes to the awareness of emotions continues to be verified experimentally (Hohman, 1966; Laird, 1974; Laird & Bresler, 1990) and clinically (Bandler & Grinder, 1979).

Criticism of the theory centers on an assumption that there is no clear-cut connection between emotional states and patterns of physiological arousal (Cannon, 1927). However, James suggests that "the emotions of different individuals may vary indefinitely" and quotes Lange: "We have all seen men dumb instead of talkative, with joy . . . we have seen grief run restlessly about lamenting, instead of sitting bowed down and mute; etc., etc." (1890, Vol. 2, p. 454). Thus, what current researchers are finding is that emotion does not exist without arousal (Schacter, 1971) and that the pattern of arousal is individual, repeatable, and predictable (Shields & Stern, 1979).

Work by Schacter and Singer (1962) has demonstrated that when subjects do not understand the real cause for their emotional arousal, they will label their feelings to fit the external cures. Rather than rely on their internal cues, they are swayed by social and environmental influences, which may actually conflict with their own visceral feelings. So-called misattribution research, in which subjects are given false information about a drug that is administered to or a procedure that is conducted on them, follows James's lead and Schacter's model (Winton, 1990). If subjects are aware of why they are aroused (informed that their feelings are due to side effects of a drug, for example), they are less likely to label their own feelings inappropriately. The event *plus* the individual *plus* the setting will determine the experienced emotion. Our emotions are based on our physical reactions plus our perception of the situation, not on our physical sensations alone. James's general position also seems to be partially borne out by the continuing developments in psychopharmacology. It is more and more possible to evoke specific emotional responses by inhibiting or stimulating physiological processes through the ingestion of certain

In short, there is considerable theoretical agreement with, and empirical support for, the assumption that the experience of emotion is basically an interpretation of behavior. (Averill, 1980, p. 161)

drugs. Groups of drugs are commonly labeled by the changes in moods they produce or suppress. The emotional difficulties that are often experienced by mental hospital patients can be controlled or even eliminated through daily doses of these drugs. There appears to be no doubt that James's insights continue to be at the core of a number of research studies of emotion and arousal (Berkowitz, 1990; Blascovich, 1990; Buck, 1990).

Personal Reflection

Body and Emotion

James says his theory is easiest to observe with the "grosser" emotions—love, anger, and fear. You can experience the interplay between physical sensations and feelings as follows:

Part I 1. Allow yourself to become angry. Visualize a person, situation, or political figure you do not like. Let the emotion build: allow your posture to change, your hands to tighten into fists, your teeth to clench, your jaw to come forward and up slightly. Be aware of these or any other physical changes. If you work in pairs, have your partner take notes as to your posture and how your muscles change.

2. Relax: move around, shake yourself, take a few deep breaths. Let the emotion go.

3. Allow yourself to feel lonely, withdrawn, isolated. (This is probably easier to do lying down.) Curl up your body; draw your knees and head close to your chest. Notice what your hands do.

4. Now, relax as before.

Part II Now, evoke the same feelings; that is, anger and then loneliness while sitting comfortably and relaxed without any physical tension. Compare how it feels to experience emotion with or without the attendant physical changes.

Nonattachment to Feelings

It was James's contention that a balance between detachment and the expression of feelings serves the organism best. He quotes Hannah Smith:

> Let your emotions come or let them go . . . and make no account of them either way. . . . They really have nothing to do with the matter. They are not the indicators of your spiritual state, but are merely the indicators of your temperament or of your present physical condition. (James, 1899a, p. 100)

Emotional Excitement

Although detachment is a desirable state, there are advantages to being overwhelmed by feelings. Emotional upset is one means by which long-standing habits can be disrupted; it frees people to try new behaviors or to explore new areas of awareness. James himself experienced and researched psychological states arising from mystical experiences, hypnosis, faith healing, mediumship, psychedelic drugs, alcohol, and personal crisis. He concluded that the precipitating event was not the critical factor, rather, the response the individual made to the arousal formed the basis for change.

Healthy-mindedness

Healthy-mindedness for James meant that if one acted as though things were well, they would be. Idealism was more than a philosophic concept to James; it was an active force. His own return to mental health began with his decision to hold fast to the ideal of free will. James argued that a positive attitude was more than useful; it was necessary. "I do not believe it to be healthy-minded to nurse the notion that ideals are self-sufficient and require no actualization to make us content. . . . Ideals ought to aim at *the transformation of reality*—no less" (H. James, 1926, Vol. 2, p. 270)!

Pragmatism

Pragmatism, originally developed by James to clarify or eliminate unnecessary considerations about issues in one's life or one's thought, became a school of philosophy in its own right. "Grant an idea or belief to be true, . . . what concrete difference will its being true make in any one's actual life" (James, 1909, p. v)? If no practical differences exist whether an idea is true or false, then, James suggests, further discussion is pointless. From this he proposes a pragmatic or useful definition of truth. "True ideas are those we can assimilate, validate, corroborate, and verify. False ideas are those that we cannot" (1907, p. 199). He understands that there are truths that cannot be assimilated and so on, but he points out that this second class of truths (which he sees as useless) may be cast aside when one is faced with a personal choice or a real decision. Although this point of view may appear obvious to some, it was roundly attacked and criticized at its inception. James writes:

> I fully expect the pragmatist's view of truth to run through the classic stages of a theory's career. First, you know, a new theory is attacked as absurd; then it is admitted to be true, but obvious and insignificant; finally it is seen to be so important that its adversaries claim that they themselves discovered it. (1948, p. 159)

By now, most of us think that pragmatism is part of normal, everyday thinking. We can now add a final stage to James's analysis of a "theory's career": Eventually the theoretical view becomes so ingrained in the culture that no one is given credit for it.

Personal Reflection —————————
————————— Testing the Validity of an Idea

Test the validity of regenerative phenomena in this exercise. Start by taking note of one of James's propositions.

Few of James's propositions are easily testable (Taylor, 1981). One exception is the following:

James says,

The way to success is by surrender to passivity, not activity. Relaxation, not intentness should be now the rule. Give up the feeling of responsibility, let go your hold. . . . It is but giving your private convulsive self a rest and finding that a greater self is there. . . . The regenerative phenomena which ensue on the abandonment of effort remain firm facts of human nature. (1890)

Choose a time when you are engaged in long, difficult activity, either intellectual or physical. If you are a coffee drinker or a candy muncher, pick a time when you really want such a stimulant. Instead of having a stimulant, lie flat on the floor for five minutes, breathe slowly and fully. Do not try to do anything, simply allow your muscles to relax, your thoughts to wander, and your breathing to slow down.

After five minutes, get up and check yourself. Are you refreshed? How does this inactivity compare with getting something to eat? Have you experienced James's *regenerative phenomena*?

Obstacles to Growth

Unexpressed Emotions

Long before the rise of modern psychotherapy as well as *letting-go* therapies, the encounter movement, or twelve-step groups, James saw that it was imperative to release emotional energy. He felt that blocked or bottled-up emotion led to mental and physical illness. He believed that it was unnecessary to express the specific emotion, especially if it might hurt oneself or others. But it was important to find some outlet for the arousal. He felt it was as necessary to express noble feelings as to express hostile ones. If one were feeling brave or charitable or compassionate, those feelings should be translated into action rather than be allowed to subside.

Errors of Excess

It is common practice to label some personal characteristics beneficial and others detrimental. We say that being loving is a virtue, being stingy is a vice. James was convinced that this simple dichotomy was valid only for moderate displays of feeling. An excess of love becomes possessiveness, an excess of loyalty becomes fanaticism, and an excess of concern becomes sentimentality. Each virtue can diminish a person if allowed to assume its extreme form.

Personal Blindness

In an essay that was a favorite of his, James describes a "certain blindness," in which he discusses the inability of people to understand one another. Our failure to be aware of this blindness is a major source of unhappiness. Whenever we presume we can decide for others what is good for them or what they should be taught or what their needs are, we experience a certain kind of blindness.

The blindness we have in relation to one another is only a symptom of a more pervasive blindness, a blindness to an inner vision of reality. For James, this vision was not at all mysterious; it was tangible in the immediacy of experience itself. Our blindness prevents us from being aware of the intensity and the perfection of the present moment. Like Whitman and Tolstoy before him, James advocated grasping nature directly, without the filters of habit, manners, or taste. "Wherever it is found, there is the zest, the tingle, the excitement of reality; and there *is* 'importance' in the only real and positive sense in which importance ever anywhere can be" (James, 1899a, p. 115).

> Life is always worth living, if one has such responsive responsibilities. We are trained to seek the choice, the rare, the exquisite exclusively, and to overlook the common. We are stuffed with abstract conceptions and glib with verbalities and verbosities . . . the peculiar sources of joy connected with our simpler functions often dry up, and we grow stone-blind and insensible to life's more elementary and general goods and joys. (James, 1899a, p. 126)

Symptoms of our blindness may include the inability to express our feelings, the lack of awareness leading to errors of excess, and the willing acceptance of habits that restrict consciousness.

Structure

The Mind Is in the Body

James's own bouts with illness caused him to reexamine continually the relationship between the body and consciousness. He concluded that even the most spiritual person must be concerned with and aware of

Hands off: neither the whole of truth nor the whole of good is revealed to any single observer, although each observer gains a partial superiority of insight from the peculiar position in which he stands! (James in McDermott, 1977, p. 645)

My experience is only what I agree to attend to. (James, 1890, Vol. 1, p. 402)

physical needs, because the body is the initial source of sensation. However, consciousness can transcend any level of physical excitement for a limited period of time. The body, necessary for the origin and maintenance of personality, is subservient to the activities of the mind. For example, intellectual concentration can be so tightly focused "as not only to banish ordinary sensations, but even the severest pain" (James, 1890, Vol. 1, p. 49). There are numerous reports of soldiers in battle who suffer severe wounds but do not notice them until the intensity of the fighting abates. Common also are cases of athletes who break a wrist, a rib, or a collarbone, but who are unaware of the break while engaged in physical activity. Examining this evidence, James concludes that it is the focus of attention that determines whether or not external physical sensations will affect conscious activity. The body is an expressive tool of the in-dwelling consciousness, rather than the source of stimulation itself.

Although James wrote that the body is not more than the place where consciousness dwells, he never lost sight of the importance of the body. Good physical health, rare in James's own life, had its own inner logic "that wells up from every part of the body of a muscularly well-trained human being, and soaks the indwelling soul of him with satisfaction. . . . [It is] an element of spiritual hygiene of supreme significance" (James, 1899a, p. 103).

Personal Reflection ——————————————

—————————————————— Daily Exercise

Decide to exercise for one week, 15 to 20 minutes each day. Choose the kind of exercise you will do: running, swimming, riding a bike, or whatever appeals to you. Do it as well as you can.

Observe: Does anything interfere with your carrying out the activity? What do you feel each time you complete the exercise you have set out for yourself? Does your body have a mind of its own?

To one who proposed that, in the Medical School, lectures be replaced by the "case system," he said: "I think you're entirely right, but your learned professor would rebel. He much prefers sitting and hearing his own beautiful voice to guiding the stumbling minds of the students." (Perry, quoting James, 1935, Vol. 1, p. 444)

The Role of the Teacher

"A professor has two functions: (1) to be learned and distribute bibliographical information; (2) to communicate truth. The 1st function is the essential one, officially considered. The 2nd is the only one I care for" (H. James, 1926, Vol. 2, p. 268). James was first and foremost a teacher. As such, he understood teachers' problems and was acutely concerned with improving the quality of teaching at the primary levels as much as at the college level. His most widely read books were about education and he was in constant demand as a lecturer to teachers. In *Talks to Teachers on*

Psychology and to Students on Some of Life's Ideals (1899a), James applied general psychological principles to the art and practice of instruction. He proposed that children were innately interested in and capable of learning. The task of the teacher, therefore, was to establish a climate that would encourage the natural process of learning. Teaching, therefore, was less a matter of content and more a matter of intent. Teachers should teach behaviors that promote effective learning. "My main desire has been to make them conceive, and if possible, reproduce sympathetically in their imagination, the mental life of the pupil" (James, 1899a, p. v).

James was sympathetic to the fact that certain personality defects seemed endemic to the teaching profession.

> Experience has taught me that teachers have less freedom of intellect than any class of people I know. . . . A teacher wrings his very soul out to understand you, and if he does ever understand anything you say, he lies down on it with his whole weight like a cow on a doorstep so that you can neither get out or in with him. He never forgets it or can reconcile anything else you say with it, and carries it to the grave like a scar. (James in Perry, 1935, Vol. 2, p. 131)

The cardinal responsibility of the teacher is to encourage the student to increase his or her capacity for sustained attention. Sustained attention to a single subject or idea is not a natural state for children or adults. Normal consciousness is a series of patterned interruptions; thoughts shift rapidly from one idea to another. Training is necessary to alter this tendency until longer and longer periods of focused attention can be maintained. The teacher should recognize and inhibit the involuntary lapses of attention for the child's own development. "This reflex and passive character of the attention . . . which makes the child seem to belong less to himself than to every object which happens to catch his notice, is the first thing which the teacher must overcome" (James, 1890, Vol. 1, p. 417).

To aid teachers, James offered some suggestions. First, the content of education must be made relevant to the needs of the students or made to appear so. Students should be aware of connections between what they are learning and their own needs, however remote these connections actually are. This draws the child's initial interest, fitful though it may be at first. Second, the subject matter may need to be enriched in order to encourage the return of students' drifting attention because "from an unchanging subject the attention inevitably wanders away" (James, 1899a, p. 52).

James rejected punishment as a way of teaching, as B. F. Skinner would 50 years later. Instead of punishing students for being bored, James suggested they be given work that would reengage their interest. He suggested that more class time be devoted to active projects than to passive study. The goal, however, is not just to accomplish tasks but to improve the students' underlying capacity to control and direct their

Voluntary attention cannot be continuously sustained, it comes in beats. (James, 1899a, p. 51)

attention. The aim of teaching is to train students in basic learning skills and habits so that they might have the capacity and the motivation to learn whatever they choose to learn.

Evaluation

For James, psychology was bounded by biology on one side and metaphysics on the other; it addressed all areas of *human* existence and experience. James introduced psychology to the United States, teaching the first course and establishing the first laboratory. The span of his interests and his writing is unequaled. He was as concerned about the experiences of the saints as he was about the biological substrata of behavior. After James, psychology was divided up into specialties, like the lands of a great kingdom divided up by the sons of the king into smaller, more manageable portions.

There are lamentably few psychology books one can recommend simply for the pleasure of reading them. James's *The Varieties of Religious Experience* (1902) is one; *Talks to Teachers on Psychology and to Students on Some of Life's Ideals* (1899a) is another. Although many portions of his mammoth textbook are dated, his own remarks, speculations, and colorful examples still are quoted and remembered. His writing is stunning.

James's complete *Principles of Psychology* (1890) included numerous theories in various areas of psychology, each supported by data. New psychology texts include a variety of theories (as does this text); each one supported by much more data. However, even though current theories have more research to substantiate their respective merits, we are still not much closer now to resolving theoretical differences than we were in 1890. (See Wolman & Knapp, 1981, for an example.) Most of the same debates continue unabated today (Staats, 1991).

James advocated an active, involved, psychology-in-the-marketplace role for the science he helped to establish. It mattered to him what people did with their lives, and he felt that psychology could and should be helpful to them. In many ways, we are still in his debt and in his shadow. The broad spectrum of phenomena he laid out for psychology to investigate is wider than most psychologists have dared put forth. James was what we would call today a humanistic psychologist, keenly aware of the moral responsibilities inherent in teaching and counseling others. He was also a behaviorist, convinced that behavior was the primary and fundamental source of information. As well, James was a transpersonal psychologist, sensitive to the reality of higher states of consciousness and intrigued with the effects those states had upon those who experienced them.

His insistence that there was much to be learned from the examination of mental healers, psychics, and visionaries has been validated by contemporary research on altered states of consciousness.

Beyond psychology, James has had a lasting effect on education (through his student John Dewey and Dewey's followers) and on philosophy—not only on pragmatism but on phenomenology as well (Edie,

James' *Principles* is without question the most literate, the most provocative, and at the same time the most intelligible book on psychology that has ever appeared in English or any other language. (MacLeod, 1969, p. iii)

I spent two delightful evenings with William James alone and I was tremendously impressed by the clearness of his mind and the complete absence of intellectual prejudices. (Jung in Adler & Jaffe, 1978)

No one could be more disgusted than I at the sight of the book [*Principles of Psychology*]. *No* subject is worth being treated of in 1000 pages! Had I ten years more, I could rewrite it in 500; but as it stands it is this or nothing— a loathsome, distended, tumefied, bloated, dropsical mass testifying to nothing but two facts: 1st, that there is no such thing as a *science* of psychology, and 2nd, that WJ is an incapable. (James, to his publisher, 1890)

1987). While various of James's ideas have come in and out of fashion in academic psychology, no one (including his most severe critics) ever suggested that the way he portrayed his findings and ideas was anything less than inspiring.

The Theory Firsthand: Excerpts from *Talks to Teachers* and *The Varieties of Religious Experience*

Because of the wide range of James's work, we have included not one but two excerpts. The first is part of a lecture he gave to teachers. It is James at his most moral and most pragmatic. The second is an excerpt from *The Varieties of Religious Experience* (1902), and illustrates some of James's transpersonal concerns.

> It is very important that teachers should realize the importance of habit, and psychology helps us greatly at this point. We speak, it is true, of good habits and of bad habits; but, when people use the word "habit," in the majority of instances it is a bad habit which they have in mind. They talk of the smoking-habit and the swearing-habit and the drinking-habit, but not of the abstention-habit or the moderation-habit or the courage-habit. . . .
>
> I believe that we are subject to the law of habit in consequence of the fact that we have bodies. The plasticity of the living matter of our nervous system, in short, is the reason why we do a thing with difficulty the first time, but soon do it more and more easily, and finally, with sufficient practice, do it semi-mechanically, or with hardly any consciousness at all. Our nervous systems have (in Dr. Carpenter's words) *grown* to the way in which they have been exercised, just as a sheet of paper or a coat, once creased or folded, tends to fall forever afterward into the same identical folds.
>
> Habit is thus a second nature, or rather, as the Duke of Wellington said, it is "ten times nature,"—at any rate as regards its importance in adult life; for the acquired habits of our training have by that time inhibited or strangled most of the natural impulsive tendencies which were originally there. Ninety-nine hundredths or, possibly, nine hundred and ninety-nine thousandths of our activity is purely automatic and habitual, from our rising in the morning to our lying down each night. Our dressing and undressing, our eating and drinking, our greetings and partings, our hat-raisings and giving way for ladies to precede, nay, even most of the forms of our common speech, are things of a type so fixed by repetition as almost to be classed as reflex actions. To each sort of impression we have an automatic, ready-made response. My very words to you now are an example of what I mean; for having already lectured upon habit and printed a chapter about it in a book, and read the latter when in print, I find my tongue inevitably falling into its old phrases and repeating almost literally what I said before.

So far as we are thus mere bundles of habit, we are stereotyped creatures, imitators and copiers of our past selves. And since this, under any circumstances, is what we always tend to become, it follows first of all that the teacher's prime concern should be to ingrain into the pupil that assortment of habits that shall be most useful to him throughout life. Education is for behavior, and habits are the stuff of which behavior consists. . . .

There is no more miserable human being than one in whom nothing is habitual but indecision, and for whom the lighting of every cigar, the drinking of every cup, the time of rising and going to bed every day, and the beginning of every bit of work are subjects of express volitional deliberation. Full half the time of such a man goes to the deciding or regretting of matters which ought to be so ingrained in him as practically not to exist for his consciousness at all. If there be such daily duties not yet ingrained in any one of my hearers, let him begin this very hour to set the matter right. . . .

. . . *Seize the very first possible opportunity to act on every resolution you make, and on every emotional prompting you may experience in the direction of the habits you aspire to gain.* It is not in the moment of their forming, but in the moment of their producing motor effects, that resolves and aspirations communicate the new "set" to the brain.

No matter how full a reservoir of maxims one may possess, and no matter how good one's sentiments may be, if one has not taken advantage of every concrete opportunity to act, one's character may remain entirely unaffected for the better. With good intentions, hell proverbially is paved. . . . When a resolve or a fine glow of feeling is allowed to evaporate without bearing practical fruit, it is worse than a chance lost: it works so as positively to hinder future resolutions and emotions from taking the normal path of discharge. There is no more contemptible type of human character than that of the nerveless sentimentalist and dreamer, who spends his life in a weltering sea of sensibility, but never does a concrete manly deed. (1899a, pp. 33–36)

The following selection includes portions of the final lecture James gave on religious experiences. After having given in his lectures literally hundreds of examples of different kinds of experiences, their effects, and his analysis of them, he attempts, here, to come to some conclusions:

Summing up in the broadest possible way the characteristics of the religious life, as we have found them, it includes the following beliefs:—

1. That the visible world is part of a more spiritual universe from which it draws its chief significance;

2. That union or harmonious relation with that higher universe is our true end;

3. That prayer or inner communion with the spirit thereof—be that spirit "God" or "law"—is a process wherein work is really done, and

spiritual energy flows in and produces effects, psychological or material, within the phenomenal world.

Religion includes also the following psychological characteristics:—

4. A new zest which adds itself like a gift to life, and takes the form either of lyrical enchantment or of appeal to earnestness and heroism.

5. An assurance of safety and a temper of peace, and, in relation to others, a preponderance of loving affections. . . .

We must next pass beyond the point of view of merely subjective utility, and make inquiry into the intellectual content itself.

First, is there, under all the discrepancies of the creeds, a common nucleus to which they bear their testimony unanimously?

And second, ought we to consider the testimony true?

I will take up the first question first, and answer it immediately in the affirmative. The warring gods and formulas of the various religions do indeed cancel each other, but there is a certain uniform deliverance in which religions all appear to meet. It consists of two parts:—

1. An uneasiness; and

2. Its solution.

1. The uneasiness, reduced to its simplest terms, is a sense that there is *something wrong about us* as we naturally stand.

2. The solution is a sense that *we are saved from the wrongness* by making proper connection with the higher powers.

In those more developed minds which alone we are studying, the wrongness takes a moral character, and the salvation takes a mystical tinge. I think we shall keep well within the limits of what is common to all such minds if we formulate the essence of their religious experience in terms like these:

The individual, so far as he suffers from his wrongness and criticizes it, is to that extent consciously beyond it, and in at least possible touch with something higher, if anything higher exists. Along with the wrong part there is thus a better part of him, even though it may be but a most helpless germ. With which part he should identify his real being is by no means obvious at this stage; but when stage 2 (the stage of solution or salvation) arrives, the man identifies his real being with the germinal higher part of himself; and does so in the following way. *He becomes conscious that this higher part is conterminous and continuous with a MORE of the same quality, which is operative in the universe outside of him, and which he can keep in working touch with, and in a fashion get on board and save himself when all his lower being has gone to pieces in the wreck.*

It seems to me that all the phenomena are accurately describable in these very simple general terms. They allow for the divided self and the struggle; they involve the change of personal centre and the surrender of the lower self; they express the appearance of exteriority of the helping power and yet account for our sense of union with it; and they fully justify our feelings of security and joy. There is probably no autobiographic document, among all those which I have quoted, to which the description will not well apply. One need only add such specific details as will adapt it to various theologies and various personal temperaments, and one will then have the various experiences reconstructed in their individual forms.

So far, however, as this analysis goes, the experiences are only psychological phenomena. They possess, it is true, enormous biological worth. Spiritual strength really increases in the subject when he has them, a new life opens for him, and they seem to him a place of conflux where the forces of two universes meet; and yet this may be nothing but his subjective way of feeling things, a mood of his own fancy, in spite of the effects produced. I now turn to my second question: What is the objective "truth" of their content?

The part of the content concerning which the question of truth most pertinently arises is that "MORE of the same quality" with which our own higher self appears in the experience to come into harmonious working relation. Is such a "more" merely our own notion, or does it really exist? If so, in what shape does it exist? Does it act, as well as exist? And in what form should we conceive of that "union" with it of which religious geniuses are so convinced?

It is in answering these questions that the various theologies perform their theoretic work, and that their divergencies most come to light. They all agree that the "more" really exists; though some of them hold it to exist in the shape of a personal god or gods, while others are satisfied to conceive it as a stream of ideal tendency embedded in the eternal structure of the world. They all agree, moreover, that it acts as well as exists, and that something really is effected for the better when you throw your life into its hands. It is when they treat of the experience of "union" with it that their speculative differences appear most clearly. Over this point pantheism and theism, nature and second birth, works and grace and karma, immortality and reincarnation, rationalism and mysticism, carry on inveterate disputes. (1902/1958, pp. 367–369, 383–385)

The Psychology of Consciousness

James studied a wide range of states of consciousness and, in so doing, did not distinguish between abnormal and normal experience. Portions of his work on altered states, religious states, hypnosis, and paranormal states were ignored. As psychology has evolved new methods of investigation, these areas are once again of growing concern. "The study of consciousness as yet has no sure perch anywhere in psychology. Rather it is emerging as a field of study because of the ardent interest of people scattered throughout the many arms of psychology and well beyond" (Goleman & Davidson, 1979, p. xvii). Professional associations such as the Biofeedback Research Society and the Association for Transpersonal Psychology have emerged, publishing journals and supporting new lines of research. There has been a corresponding wave of popular interest, with articles and best-selling books about consciousness appearing regularly.

A few areas have particular implications for personality theory. The research with psychedelic drugs, biofeedback, meditation, and hypnosis has produced findings that question our basic assumptions about consciousness and the nature of reality as we know them. We are utilizing new methods, new instruments, and a renewed willingness to research subjective phenomena in an effort to provide a scientific foundation for James's philosophical speculations.

We cannot yet answer the basic question—the question of what consciousness is—because it may not be answerable; but we are learning more about the contents of consciousness and the forms that it takes. Ornstein (1972) argues that consciousness can never be understood using an objective approach alone. "There is no way to simply write down the answer, as we might give a textbook definition. The answers must come personally, experientially" (p. ix).

> Altered states of consciousness can be triggered by hypnosis, meditation, psychedelic drugs, deep prayer, sensory deprivation, and the onset of acute psychosis. Sleep deprivation or fasting can induce them. Epileptics and migraine sufferers often experience an altered awareness in the aura that precedes attacks. Hypnotic monotony, as in solo high-altitude jet flight, may bring on an altered state. Electronic stimulation of the brain (ESB), alpha or theta brain-wave training, clairvoyant or telepathic insights, muscle-relaxation training, isolation (as in Antarctica), and photic stimulation (light flicker at certain speeds) may bring on a sharp change in consciousness. (Ferguson, 1973, p. 59)

Psychedelic Research

Most cultures, primitive or civilized, have used herbs, seeds, or plants to alter body chemistry, emotional outlook, and levels of awareness (Bravo

The whole drift of my education goes to persuade me that the world of our present consciousness is only one of many worlds of consciousness that exist, and that those other worlds must contain experiences which have a meaning for our life also; and that although in the main their experiences and those of this world keep discrete, yet the two become continuous at certain points and higher energies filter in. (James, 1902/1958, p. 391)

& Glob, 1989; McKenna, 1991). James, himself, experimented with nitrous oxide (laughing gas) and was impressed by his experiences.

> With me, as with every other person of whom I have heard, the keynote of the experience is the tremendously exciting sense of an intense metaphysical illumination. Truth lies open to the view in depth beneath depth of almost blinding evidence. The mind sees all the logical relations of being with an apparent subtlety and instantaneity to which its normal consciousness offers no parallel; only as sobriety returns, the feeling of insights fades, and one is left staring vacantly at a few disjointed words and phrases, as one stares at a cadaverous-looking snow-peak from which the sunset glow has just fled, or at the black cinder left by an extinguished brand. (1969, pp. 359–360)

It appears that some of the distinctions we maintain between ourselves and the outer world are arbitrary and are alterable. Our usual perceptions may be partially a function of the state of consciousness we are in. We see a world of many colors, but colors are only a small part of the spectrum that exists. The finding that a person may lose what he or she calls "personal" identity without feeling a loss of identity (now hard to define) leads us back to James who described the self not as a stable, fixed structure but as a constantly fluctuating field.

When James wrote *The Varieties of Religious Experience* in 1902, he observed that experiencing so-called "mystical consciousness" was a rare and unpredictable event. More recently, the widespread use of psychedelics (especially marijuana) has made experiencing such states—or at least the subjective impression of having experienced such states—more possible. Research into psychedelic states shows that subjects have what they call religious, spiritual, or transpersonal experiences. It has become important to determine the value as well as the validity of these reported experiences now that they appear to be more common (Grof, 1975).

This question is of concern to the religious community as well. Religious conversion, experiences in prayer, visions, and talking in tongues, all occur during altered states of consciousness. The validity of these experiences is the foundation of a number of diverse religious doctrines. The discovery and examination of substances used in religious rituals, which have proved to be active, psychedelic agents, has revived interest among theologians in the origin and meaning of chemically induced religious experience (Doblin, 1991) as well as the ethics involved in having access to such experiences (Clark, 1985; Smith, 1988).

Implications of Psychedelic Research for Personality Theory

Consciousness, time, and space appear to interact. Modern physicists and ancient mystics are sounding more and more alike in their attempts to describe the known universe (LeShan, 1969). Reports of psychedelic experiences suggest that the nature and genesis of consciousness may be more realistically described by mystics and modern physics than by contemporary psychology (Capra, 1975; Zukav, 1979).

The literature and research into various states of consciousness (Lufoff & Lu, 1989; Valle & von Eckartsberg, 1981) suggests that any theory of personality that does not take into account altered states of consciousness is an incomplete description of fundamental human experience. Consciousness may best be described as a spectrum (Wilber, 1977) in which our normal awareness is only a small segment. This normal awareness—unaltered consciousness—seems to be a special case (Bentov, 1977; Tart, 1975) with its own rules and limitations. Although this is an underlying assumption of the Eastern philosophies described in Part II of this book, it is a relatively undeveloped idea in most of Western psychology.

Biofeedback Research

James's theory that emotion depends on feedback from one's body has been expanded in a variety of ways through biofeedback research. Biofeedback is an application of the engineering concept of feedback—the mechanical principle that controls most automatic machinery. A furnace and its thermostat, for instance, form a self-contained feedback system. Biofeedback is the means of monitoring a biological process. For example, when you use your fingers to feel your pulse, you are getting feedback concerning your heart rate.

Through new methods of providing accurate and immediate feedback, researchers found that subjects could control a wide range of physical parameters that included heart rate, blood pressure, skin temperature, and brain-wave frequency (Barber, Dicara, Kamiya, Shapiro, & Stoyva, 1971–1978). It is safe to say that almost any bodily process that can be monitored can be consciously modified and controlled. The fact that people are not aware of how they are controlling a bodily process does not limit their capacity to do so. People and animals can literally *think* their temperatures up and down, slow down or accelerate their heart rates, or shift from one brain-wave frequency to another.

By 1980, the research had spawned a host of clinical applications (Olton & Noonberg) for conditions that included tension and migraine headaches, Raynaud's disease (cold hands and feet), asthma, epilepsy, Parkinson's disease, ulcers, bed-wetting, hypertension, and cardiac abnormalities, including fibrillation. Later extensions, often paired with other relaxation methods, have demonstrated improvements in metastatic cancer (Gruber, Hall, Hersh, & Dubois, 1988), test anxiety (Hurwitz, Kahane, & Mathieson, 1986), rheumatoid arthritis (Lerman, 1987), post-traumatic stress disorder (Hickling, Sison, & Vanderploeg, 1986), as well as a range of phobia, hysteria, and impotence problems (Clonini & Mattei, 1985). It appears that anything that can be brought into sustained awareness can be brought under better control through biofeedback training.

A monkey has learned to fire a single nerve cell to obtain a reward. At Queen's University in Kingston, Ontario, John Basmajian trained human subjects to discharge a single motor nerve cell, selected from the brain's ten billion cells. Miller's rats [Neal Miller of Rockefeller University] learned to form urine at greater or lesser rates, to redden one ear and blanch the other, and increase or decrease the blood in their intestinal lining. (Ferguson, 1973, pp. 32–33)

Implications of Biofeedback Research for Personality Theory

The capacities of the nervous system have been redefined. We used to believe that along with our consciously controllable voluntary nervous system, we had an autonomic or involuntary nervous system that we could not consciously control. However, this distinction has all but vanished. Now it is more accurate to speak of the gross nervous system, which is open to conscious control with little or no training, and the subtle nervous system, which is open to conscious control with specialized training.

All of the "wonders of the mysterious East"—yogis resting on beds of nails, saints being buried alive, devotees able to walk slowly over hot coals—were feats used by adepts to demonstrate the range of human possibilities. As it is now possible to replicate some of these kinds of feats in the laboratory, it behooves us to look again at the implications of these exhibitions (Brown, 1974; Karlins & Andrews, 1972; Rama, Ballentine, & Weinstock, 1976). The evidence for "human transformative capacity" (Murphy, 1992) is so extensive that we need to let go of the definitions of mind-body interaction that were suitable for a far less scientific era.

We may need to redefine what it means to be *in control*. Physical control may be closely linked or may lead to emotional control. If so, there could be advantages to teaching children or disturbed adults basic biofeedback techniques to increase their awareness and their ability to control their own reactions. Initial findings (Kamiya & Kamiya, 1981; Peper & Williams, 1981) indicate positive and lasting results from this training.

James defined will as the combination of attention and volition (wishing). Kimble and Perlmuter (1970) have found that the role of the will is critical to understanding how biofeedback training actually occurs. They note that the role of attention is important in the willing process. They present a trivial example of what can occur if you wish to do something but do not pay close attention.

ARE YOU PAYING ATTENTION?

QUESTION: *What do you call the tree that grows from acorns?*

ANSWER: *An oak.*

QUESTION: *What do we call a funny story?*

ANSWER: *A joke.*

QUESTION: *The sound made by a frog?*

ANSWER: *A croak.*

QUESTION: *The white of an egg?*

ANSWER: . . .

(From Kimble & Perlmuter, 1970, p. 373)

Only if you pay close attention will you escape the pattern established in the series, which tends to elicit the incorrect answer, *yolk*. You may wish to give the correct answer, but it is the combination of your wish (volition) plus your attention that makes it possible to do what you will. (If you wish to further verify this, try reading these qustions to a friend and asking him or her to respond.)

Passive volition is defined as the willingness to let things happen. It refers to the particular state of consciousness that people learn to use in successful biofeedback training. It is attention without effort. An example of a task in biofeedback training might be, for example, to learn to lower the temperature in the right hand. At first people will "try"; the temperature in their right hands will rise. Then, many people will "try not to." This usually results in their temperatures rising as well. Eventually, over the course of training, people learn to stop "trying" and to "allow" their temperatures to fall. Passive volition is not part of our cultural training. We are brought up to be assertive, to succeed, to resist those forces that oppose us. James's distinctions between passive and active willing turn out to be important distinctions.

Most theories of personality that seek to treat mental illness specify the genesis of and contributing factors to mental disorders. Biofeedback research has shown an alternative treatment that focuses on "psychological" symptoms and ignores the psychological origins of the symptoms. As Green and Green (1972) have suggested, because we can become physically ill in responding to psychological stress, perhaps we can eliminate the illness by learning to control the physiological response.

Perhaps some aspects of our personalities can be modified by biofeedback, a form of external, mechanistic, nonpsychological training. Areas usually associated with psychotherapy that are now being researched and targeted for biofeedback include alcoholism, chronic anxiety, drug abuse, learning disabilities, insomnia, obsessive phobic-depressive syndrome, and writer's cramp (O'Regan, 1979). James did the initial research into what was then called *mind cure* (Meyer, 1980); one might conclude that biofeedback training is but one scientific application of James's pioneering investigations.

Meditation

Meditation can be defined as the directing, stilling, quieting, or focusing of one's attention in a systematic manner. It may be practiced either in silence or in the presence of noise, with eyes open or shut, while sitting or standing, and even while walking. There are literally hundreds of techniques, practices, and systems of meditation. Research is beginning to uncover that physiological behaviors are affected by meditation (Shapiro & Walsh, 1981). Most of the early laboratory work was done on one meditation system, Transcendental Meditation (Kanelakos & Lukas, 1974). Apparently, the data obtained are also valid for other systems (Benson,

1975). Later work draws more heavily from research on Buddhist mindfulness practices (Epstein, 1990; Sweet & Johnson, 1990).

With the widespread acceptance and proliferation of groups and teachers who offer training in meditation, large cities and most college campuses house several organizations offering such training. A continuing interest in the practical application of meditation practice in psychotherapy (Carrington, 1978; Delmonte, 1990) and evidence of its utility in the treatment of cancer (Simonton, Mathews-Simonton, & Creighton, 1978) and drug abuse (Benson & Wallace, 1972) ensures its continued use as a therapy technique that is subject to further evaluation (Delmonte & Kenny, 1985; Kenny & Delmonte, 1986).

Implications of Meditation Research for Personality Theory

What are the contents of consciousness? James proposed that we consider consciousness as if it were a stream or a river. Research reports indicate a more complete description might describe consciousness as having many tracks or streams, all flowing simultaneously. Awareness may move from track to track like a searchlight playing over different tracks in a train depot.

What is there in consciousness besides discrete thoughts? Reports from meditators suggest something more than the varied thought forms that float to the surface of the mind. As one explores consciousness, there are changes in the content and in the structure and form of thought itself.

Tart (1972) has encouraged researchers to consider that specialized training may be necessary in order to enter and observe these specific states. Just as a dentist must have special training to be able to detect tiny irregularities in X rays of the teeth, or astronauts need special training to be able to work in antigravity situations, so should scientists, working in *state-specific* science, have appropriate training. James's complaint that the insights generated under nitrous oxide "fade out" may reflect his own lack of training, not just the fleeting effects of the gas.

What effects does meditation have on personal values, life-style, and motivation? Ram Dass (1974) comments that his previous beliefs, developed while teaching Western motivational psychology, were severely threatened by his experiences in meditation. Some of the meditation systems he worked with did not even suggest that the so-called basic drives for affiliation, power, or achievement—or even the biologically rooted drives for food, water, or survival—were necessary for personal well-being. From the writings of Ram Dass (1978), Sayadaw (1954), and others, it is evident that models of personality exist that are based on suppositions beyond those considered here.

Hypnosis

Although hypnosis has been an area of research for over a hundred years, it is still not a well-defined phenomenon. Some of its applications include

---

Of all the hard facts of science, I know of none more solid and fundamental than the fact that if you inhibit thought (and persevere) you come at length to a region of consciousness below or behind thought . . . and a realization of an altogether vaster self than that to which we are accustomed. (Edward Carpenter, 1844–1929)

Within the province of the mind, what I believe to be true is true or becomes true, within the limits to be found experientially and experimentally. These limits are further beliefs to be transcended. (Lilly, 1973)

psychotherapy, aids to athletic training, techniques for modulating pain, and even nightclub entertainment. Well-trained subjects have demonstrated unusual physical, emotional, perceptual, and even psychic capacities while in a hypnotically induced state. Because hypnotic inductions can lead to a variety of altered states, hypnosis is considered a tool for exploring consciousness, rather than a means of inducing any single state.

Subjective reality and the responses of the subject to external stimuli are markedly changed in hypnosis. Tart (1970) describes some of the range of effects.

> One of the standard tests we use, for instance, is to tell someone they can't smell and then you hold a bottle of ammonia under their nose and say, "take a good deep breath." They sit there with a blank face if they're a good subject. (It horrifies me every time I see it done, but it works beautifully.) You can induce total analgesia for pain for surgical operations, for instance. You can have people hallucinate. If you tell them there's a polar bear in the corner, they'll see a polar bear in the corner. You can tamper with their memory in certain ways. . . . You can take them back in time so they feel as if they were a child at a certain age level and so forth. (pp. 27–28)

Implications of Hypnosis Research for Personality Theory

Who is in control of your consciousness? In stage hypnosis, the hypnotist appears to be in full control and can force subjects to do foolish and embarrassing things. Laboratory research indicates that the relationship is a cooperative one. When the subject trusts the hypnotist, he or she will go along with many kinds of suggestions. To some extent, we are all hypnotized by advertising and television (Harman, 1967). How does this kind of conditioning compare to hypnotic induction? If you do what you are told, are you fully responsible for your act?

In dental hypnosis, the patient is taught to move the pain out of the teeth or to "turn off the pain." How is this done? We do not know, but we do know it is successful. If pain is subjective, that is, subject to voluntary control, what does it mean to say, "I am in pain" or even "I am tired" or "I am angry"? The evidence suggests that consciousness *can* be highly selective in what it admits into awareness.

A different approach to pain control, one that you can try for yourself, makes use of the mind's natural tendency to wander. The next time you are in pain—from a burn, insect sting, or a sprained ankle—close your eyes and consciously try to intensify the pain. Concentrate fully on only the pain and the affected part of your body. Experience it as completely as you can. Try to maintain this total absorption for at least 30 seconds. When you relax, the pain will be greatly diminished or gone (Ferguson, 1973).

To what extent is our acceptance of painful stimuli simply a result of not understanding alternative ways of dealing with unpleasant sensations?

In what is labeled *deep hypnosis* (Sherman, 1972; Tart, 1970), personality appears to undergo a series of radical transformations. One by one, aspects of identity seem to be put aside. The sense of time passing, awareness of one's own body, awareness of the room, and awareness of personal identity itself fades away. Although there still is communication between subject and experimenter, even that awareness fades until the experimenter is perceived as no more than a distant voice.

> I asked him about his sense of identity at various points. "Who are you? What's your identity?" That sort of thing. He starts out as himself, ego, and then his sense of identity tends to become less distributed through his body and more just his head; just sort of a thinking part. And that becomes a little more so and then that begins a kind of dropping out until his ordinary identity—let's call him John Smith—steadily decreases and as he goes deeper into hypnosis John Smith no longer exists. But there is a change taking place in who he is. He becomes more and more identified with a new identity, and that identity is *potential*. He's not anybody in particular; he's potential. He could be this, he could be that. He's aware of identifying with this flux of potentiality that could evolve into many sorts of things. (Tart, 1970, p. 35)

What effect does perception have on personality? Most theorists write as if they assume that we all see approximately the same world, see the same colors, have the same sense of time, and so forth. Aaronson (1968, 1979) conducted a number of studies that question this assumption. He has found that hypnotically induced changes in perception (altering the way time, form, or space is perceived) can cause psychoticlike, euphoric, or other short-term changes in personality. Altering perceptual parameters results in emotional and behavioral changes that parallel descriptions of catatonia, paranoia, and other mental disorders. Here is one example of Aaronson's work with a normal, well-adjusted subject.

> Subject 5 reacted [to the hypnotic instruction that there is no dimension of depth] with marked primitivization of behavior. He displayed shallow, inappropriate humor and could not conceive what lay over the brow of a hill or around a corner. He crossed himself repeatedly, although nothing in his background suggested this type of religious symbolism. His affect seemed shallow and blunted, his sense impressions seemed dulled, and his behavior was not unlike that of a chronic schizophrenic. (1979, pp. 227–228)

It may be as fruitful to investigate how others perceive the universe as to investigate their childhood experiences in order to understand their present-day behavior. Do you know anyone who always seems to be hurrying, who cannot slow down? Do you know people who seem unnaturally gloomy or perpetually cheerful? It is possible that individual personalities differ because individual perceptions vary.

The Hidden Observer

In hypnosis, it appears that one part of the personality may be aware of some of what is going on, while another part is absolutely unaware. The early controversial work in this area by James (1899b) languished. He reported on a hypnotic subject whose right hand commented in writing about pinpricks it had been given. When questioned about it, the subject was unaware of the physical sensations and upon reading the writings of his own hand, dismissed them.

Hilgard (1977, 1978) did a series of similar experiments and reported that there seemed to be divided awareness, meaning that there were two parts of the personality and both were equally capable and intelligent, but not aware of each other.

The so-called *hidden observer* was rediscovered by accident:

> We first found the phenomenon in a young man—a blind subject who had achieved hypnotic deafness. He had been unperturbed by noises and by the remarks the students were yelling at him. At one point one of the students said, "How do we know he isn't hearing anything?" So I asked him to raise his finger if he could hear what was being said. The finger went up. Then the subject said, "Would you mind bringing me out so you can tell me what just happened—what caused my finger to lift?"
>
> I then told him that when I placed my hand on his head, I wanted to be in touch with the part of him that had lifted the finger. As soon as I placed my hand on his head, I was able to get from him descriptions of what had been said, how many times I had clapped the wooden blocks together and so on. When I lifted my hand, he reverted to the earlier hypnotic state and said, "The last thing I remember, you told me I would talk to you when you placed your hand on my head. Did I say anything?" (Hilgard, 1977, p. 186)

Do you think there is a part of you that is aware, observing, and yet is unknown to most of you? There is growing evidence that the answer is *yes* (Nadon, D'eon, McConkey, Laurence, & Campbell, 1988; Spanos, Flynn, & Gwynn, 1988). If this is so, then what are the characteristics of that part? What does it know, and how does it affect your behavior?

Multiple Personality

"We are at this time familiar with the notion that a man's consciousness need not be a fully integrated thing . . . but we must now pass on to cases where the division of the personality is more obvious" (James in Taylor, 1982, p. 73).

It must be admitted, therefore, that in certain persons . . . the total possible consciousness may be split into parts which coexist but mutually ignore each other. (James, 1890, Vol. 1, p. 206)

There is ample evidence to suggest that some people seem to have more than one personality; that is to say, they have inside them many personalities, each with a different name, storehouse of memories, and way of thinking and behaving. Even age and gender can differ with each personality. Extreme cases have been fully described by the people "themselves" (Casey, 1991; Chase, 1987); clients with multiple personalities have been described by their therapists (Mayer, 1990; Schoenewolf, 1991) or by objective researchers (Keyes, 1981; Schreiber, 1974). In addition, there exists a large body of clinical reports (Ross, 1989) and psychophysiological research (Coons, 1988; Miller & Triggiano, 1992; Putnam, 1984) detailing the phenomenon.

Apparently, when the human psyche is subjected to severe stress, such as sexual abuse in childhood, or war-related terror, the personality can split. One portion retains the feelings and memories of the traumatic event, while other portions do not. These splits do not seem to fuse back together but continue to maintain a separate existence, developing along separate lines, often having different skills, even knowing different languages (Keyes, 1981). Moreover, laboratory testing has shown that multiple personalities can differ in their reactions to medications, in blood pressure, allergic reactions, even in eyeglass prescriptions (Miller, Blackburn, Scholes, & White, 1991).

Such data stretch the term *personality* beyond its current limits.

Implications of Multiple Personality for Personality Theory

There is an unquestioned assumption that all of the conditions that we class as "abnormal" or pathological are the most extreme variations of normal behavior. For example, paranoia is excessive vigilance, exemplified in extreme distrust of the unfamiliar; hysteria is an excess of emotional excitement; and so forth. If this same assumption is applied to the study of multiple personality, it suggests that a normal capacity for multiplicity exists within each of us.

If we look at some common internal events, this becomes more evident. Have you ever quarreled with yourself? Who is on the other side of the argument? Have you gone to sleep with a problem only to find upon awakening that you have a solution? What does it mean when we say, "I don't know what got into me," or "I cannot imagine how I could have said or done that."

If we consider the reports of people with severe drug or alcohol problems, we often find that one part of them wants desperately to stop the habit, while another part is not at all willing to stop. If this is evidence of multiplicity, then what can be done to ensure, for example, that the part of the person who does the drinking is present during therapy?

Multiplicity may not be a pathology at all, but may be a survival-linked characteristic, a way to function successfully under extreme conditions. This approach to multiple personality could alter some of the goals of psychotherapy as well as other kinds of personal education (Dawson, 1990). There is some evidence that disturbed multiples have exceptional capacities to heal themselves. This might provide an opening into ways to expand human capacities as Murphy (1992) suggests.

The existence of multiple personalities graphically raises the same issue that our examination of other areas of research has also raised. The question, "Who am I?" has answers that may be far more complex and far less obvious than we have hitherto thought possible.

Evaluation

All of the areas discussed in this section espouse concepts that do not fit into the existing paradigms of conventional personality theory. Either the data must be disproved or invalidated or personality theory must enlarge its scope to take in the recent and thought-provoking findings.

Annotated Bibliography

Feinstein, H. (1984). *Becoming William James*. Ithaca, NY: Cornell University Press. An unusual biography that deals primarily with the histories of James's grandfather and great grandfather and their influence on James during his formative years.

James, W. (1958). *The varieties of religious experience*. New York: New American Library (Mentor Books). (Originally published, 1902.) James's lectures on the psychology of religion and religious experience. A full introduction to the more general psychology of altered states of consciousness, although almost all of the many examples come specifically from religious literature.

———. (1961). *Psychology: The briefer course*. New York: Harper & Row. An edited version of the *Principles of Psychology*, his basic textbook. Easy to read and sensible, it contains most of the sections of James that are still of interest to students today.

———. (1962). *Talks to teachers on psychology and to students on some of life's ideals*. New York: Dover. A popular exposition of James's ideas in relation to education. Full of sensible advice about the way to cultivate and train young minds.

McDermott, J. J. (Ed.). (1977). *The writings of William James: A comprehensive edition*. Chicago: University of Chicago Press. The best single-volume collection of James's writings. A good introduction with ample selections from his psychological and philosophical writings.

328 Personality and Personal Growth

Myers, G. (1986). *William James, his life and thought.* New Haven, CT: Yale University Press. James was not systematic in his thinking and changed his positions over the course of his life. Myers has put James into good order, idea by idea. This is not at all about his life, in spite of the title, but is a solid summation of James's ideas.

Perry, R. B. (1935). *The thought and character of William James* (2 Vols.). Boston: Little, Brown. Cambridge, MA: Harvard University Press (abridged), 1948. A masterpiece of exposition that is primarily composed of letters to and from James. This is mainly James but with enough Perry to make it flow easily.

References

Aaronson, B. S. (1968). Hypnotic alterations of space and time. *International Journal of Parapsychology, 10,* 5–36.

———. (1979). Hypnotic alterations of space and time: Their relationship to psychopathology. In J. Fadiman & D. Kewman (Eds.), *Exploring madness: Experience, theory, and research* (pp. 223–236). Monterey, CA: Brooks/Cole.

Adler, G., & Jaffe, A. (1978). *Letters of C. G. Jung* (Vol. 1). Princeton, NJ: Princeton University Press.

Allport, G. (Ed.). (1961). *William James: Psychology, the briefer course.* New York: Harper & Row.

Averill, J. R. (1980). Autonomic response patterns during sadness and mirth. *Psychophysiology,* 99–214.

Bandler, R., & Grinder, J. (1979). *Frogs into princes: Neurolinguistic programming.* Moab, Utah: Real People Press.

Barber, T. X., Dicara, L., Kamiya, J., Shapiro, D., & Stoyva, J. (Eds.). (1971, 1972, 1973, 1974, 1975–1976, 1976–1977, 1977–1978). *Biofeedback and self-control: An Aldine annual.* Chicago: Aldine.

Baumgardner, A., Kaufman, C., & Cranford, J. (1990). To be noticed favorably: Links between private self and public self. *Personality and Social Psychology Bulletin, 16*(4), 705–716.

Benson, H. (1975). *The relaxation response.* New York: Morrow.

Benson, H., & Wallace, R. K. (1972). Decreased drug abuse with transcendental meditation: A study of 1862 subjects. *Proceedings of Drug Abuse, International Symposium for Physicians* (pp. 369–376). Philadelphia: Lea & Ferbinger.

Bentov, I. (1977). *Stalking the wild pendulum.* New York: Dutton.

Berkowitz, L. (1990). On the formation and regulation of anger and aggression: A cognitive-neoassociationistic analysis. American Psychological Association: Distinguished scientific award for the applications of psychology address. *American Psychologist, 45*(4), 494–503.

Blascovich, J. (1990). Individual differences in physiological arousal and perception of arousal: Missing links in Jamesian notions of arousal-based behaviors. *Personality and Social Psychology Bulletin, 16*(4), 665–675.

Bravo, G., & Glob, C. (1989). Shamans, sacraments, and psychiatrists. *Journal of Psychoactive Drugs, 21*(1), 123–128.

Brown, B. (1974). *New mind, new body.* New York: Harper & Row.

Buck, R. (1990). William James, the nature of knowledge, and current issues in emotion, cognition, and communication. *Personality and Social Psychology Bulletin, 16*(4), 612–625.

Cannon, W. B. (1927). The James-Lange theory of emotions: A critical examination and an alternative theory. *American Journal of Psychology, 39,* 106–124.

Capra, F. (1975). *The tao of physics.* New York: Bantam Books.

Carrington, P. (1978). The uses of meditation in psychotherapy. In A. Sugarman & R. Tarter (Eds.), *Expanding dimensions of consciousness.* New York: Springer-Verlag.

Casey, J. with Wilson, L. (1991). *The flock.* New York: Knopf.

Chase, T. (the troops of). (1987). *When rabbit howls.* New York: Dutton.

Clark, W. (1985). Ethics and LSD. *Journal of Psychoactive Drugs, 17*(4), 229–234.

Clonini, L., & Mattei, D. (1985). Biofeedback and cognitive-behavioral therapy. *Medicini-Psicosomatica, 30*(2), 151–161.

Coons, P. (1988). Psychophysiologic aspects of multiple personality disorder: A review. *Dissociation Progress in the Dissociative Disorders, 1*(1), 47–53.

Cross, S., & Markus, H. (1990). The willful self. *Personality and Social Psychology Bulletin, 16*(4), 726–742.

Dawson, P. (1990). Understanding and cooperation among alter and host personalities. *American Journal of Occupational Therapy, 44*(11), 994–997.

Delmonte, M. (1990). The relevance of meditation to clinical practice: An overview. *Applied Psychology: An International Review, 39*(3), 331–354.

Delmonte, M., & Kenny, V. (1985). An overview of the therapeutic effects of meditation. *Psychologia, 28*(4), 189–202.

Doblin, R. (1991). Panke's "Good Friday experiment": A long-term follow-up and methodological critique. *Journal of Transpersonal Psychology, 23*(1), 1–28.

Edie, J. (1987). *William James and phenomenology.* Bloomington, IN: Indiana University Press.

Epstein, M. (1990). Beyond the oceanic feeling: Psychoanalytic study of Buddhist meditation. *International Review of Psychoanalysis, 17*(2), 159–166.

Feinstein, H. (1984). *Becoming William James.* Ithaca, NY: Cornell University Press.

Ferguson, M. (1973). *The brain revolution.* New York: Taplinger.

Fisher, R., & Cleveland, S. (1958). *Body image and personality*. Princeton, NJ: Van Nostrand.

Freud, S. (1922). Dreams and telepathy. In J. Strachey (Ed. and Trans.), *The standard edition of the complete psychological works of Sigmund Freud* (Vol. 18, pp. 196–200). London: Hogarth Press.

———. (1940). Outline of psychoanalysis. In J. Strachey (Ed. and Trans.), *The standard edition of the complete psychological works of Sigmund Freud* (Vol. 23, pp. 141–205). London: Hogarth Press.

Goleman, D., & Davidson, R. (1979). *Consciousness: Brain, states of awareness, and mysticism*. New York: Harper & Row.

Green, E., & Green, A. (1972). How to make use of the field of mind theory. In *The dimensions of healing*. Los Altos, CA: Academy of Parapsychology and Medicine.

Grof, S. (1971). Varieties of transpersonal experience: Observations from LSD psychotherapy. *Journal of Transpersonal Psychology, 4,* 45–80.

———. (1975). *Realms of the human unconscious*. New York: Viking Press.

———. (1986). Psychology and drug research. *ReVISION, 9*(1), 47–63.

Gruber, B., Hall, N., Hersh, S., & Dubois, P. (1988). Immune system and psychological changes in metastatic cancer patients using relaxation and guided imagery: A pilot study. *Scandinavian Journal of Behavior Therapy, 17*(1), 25–46.

Harman, W. W. (1967). Old wine in new wineskins—The reasons for the limited world view. In J. Bugenthal (Ed.), *Challenges of humanistic psychology* (pp. 321–335). New York: McGraw-Hill. (Also in J. Fadiman [Ed.]. [1971]. *The proper study of man* [pp. 132–145]. New York: Macmillan.)

Hickling, E., Sison, G., & Vanderploeg, R. (1986). Treatment of post-traumatic stress disorder with relaxation and biofeedback training. *Biofeedback and Self Regulation, 11*(2), 125–134.

Hilgard, E. (1977). *Divided consciousness*. New York: Wiley.

———. (1978). New approaches to hypnosis. *Brain Mind Bulletin, 3* (7), 3.

Hohman, G. W. (1966). Some effects of spinal cord lesions on experienced emotional feelings. *Psychophysiology, 3,* 143–156.

Hurwitz, L., Kahane, J., & Mathieson, C. (1986). The effects of EMG biofeedback and progressive muscle relaxation on the reduction of test anxiety. *Educational and Psychological Research, 6*(4), 291–298.

James, H. (Ed.). (1926). *The letters of William James* (2 vols.). Boston: Little, Brown.

James, W. Grundzuge der physiologischen psychologie (W. Wundt, Reviewer). In R. W. Rieber, (Ed.). (1980). *Wilhelm Wundt and the making of a scientific psychology* (pp.199–206). New York: Plenum Press. (Originally published in the *North American Review*, 1875, *121,* 195–201.)

———. (1890). *The principles of psychology* (2 vols.). New York: Holt,

Rinehart and Winston. Unaltered republication, New York: Dover, 1950.

———. (1892). *Psychology: The briefer course.* New York: Holt, Rinehart and Winston. New edition, New York: Harper & Row, 1961.

———. (1896). *The will to believe and other essays in popular philosophy.* New York and London: McKay.

———. (1899a). *Talks to teachers on psychology and to students on some of life's ideals.* New York: Holt, Rinehart and Winston. Unaltered republication, New York: Dover, 1962.

———. (1899b). Automatic writing. *Proceedings of the American Society for Psychical Research, 199,* 548–564.

———. (1958). *The varieties of religious experience.* New York: New American Library. (Originally published, 1902.)

———. (1907). *Pragmatism: A new name for some old ways of thinking.* New York and London: McKay.

———. (1909). *The meaning of truth.* New York: McKay.

———. (1911). *Some problems in philosophy.* New York: McKay.

———. (1948). *Essays in pragmatism* (Alburey Castell, Ed.). New York: Hafner Press.

———. (1955). The tigers in India. In R. B. Perry (Ed.), *Pragmatism and four essays from the meaning of truth* (pp. 225–228). New York: Harcourt Brace Jovanovich.

———. (1969). Subjective effects of nitrous oxide. In C. Tart (Ed.), *Altered states of consciousness* (pp. 359–362). New York: Wiley.

Kamiya, J., & Kamiya, J. (1981). Biofeedback. In A. Hastings, J. Fadiman, & J. Gordon (Eds.), *Health for the whole person* (pp. 115–130). New York: Pocket Books.

Kanelakos, D., & Lukas, J. (1974). *The psychobiology of transcendental meditation: A literature review.* Menlo Park, CA: Benjamin.

Karlins, M., & Andrews, L. (1972). *Biofeedback: Turning on the power of your mind.* Philadelphia: Lippincott.

Kenny, V., & Delmonte, M. (1986). Meditation as viewed through personal construct theory. *Journal of Contemporary Psychotherapy, 16*(1), 4–22.

Keyes, D. (1981). *The Minds of Billy Milligan.* New York: Random House.

Kimble, G. A., & Perlmuter, L. C. (1970). The problem of volition. *Psychological Record, 77,* 361–384.

Knowles, E., & Sibicky, M. (1990). Continuity and diversity in the stream of selves: Metaphorical resolutions of William James's one-in-many-selves paradox. *Personality and Social Psychology Bulletin, 16*(4), 676–687.

Koch, C. (1986). Who was the Lange of the James-Lange theory? *Nordisk Psykologi, 38*(1), 41–54.

Laird, J. (1974). Self-attribution of emotion: The effects of expressive behavior on the quality of emotional experience. *Journal of Personality and Social Psychology, 29,* 475–486.

Laird, J., & Bresler, C. (1990). William James and the mechanisms of emotional experience. *Personality and Social Psychology Bulletin, 16*(4), 636–651.

Lamphere, R., & Leary, M. (1990). Private and public self-processes. A return to James's constituents of the self. *Personality and Social Psychology Bulletin, 16*(4), 717–725.

Lerman, C. (1987). Rheumatoid arthritis: Psychological factors in the etiology, course, and treatment. *Clinical Psychology Review, 7*(4), 413–425.

LeShan, L. (1969). Physicists and mystics: Similarities in world view. *Journal of Transpersonal Psychology, 1,* 1–20.

Lilly, J. C. (1973). *The center of the cyclone.* New York: Bantam Books.

Lukoff, D., & Lu, F. (1989). Transpersonal psychology research review: Topic: Computerized databases, specialized collections. *Journal of Transpersonal Psychology, 21*(2), 211–223.

MacLeod, R. B. (Ed.). (1969). *William James: Unfinished business.* Washington, DC: American Psychological Association, pp. iii–iv.

Matthiessen, T. H. (1980). *The James family.* New York: Random House.

Mayer, R. (1990). *Through divided minds.* New York: Avon.

McDermott, J. J. (Ed.). (1977). *The writings of William James: A comprehensive edition.* Chicago: University of Chicago Press.

McKenna, T. (1991). *The archaic revival.* San Francisco, CA: Harper San Francisco.

Meyer, D. (1980). *The positive thinkers.* New York: Pantheon Press.

Miller, S., Blackburn, T., Scholes, G., & White, G. (1991). Optical differences in multiple personality disorder: A second look. *Journal of Nervous and Mental Diseases, 179*(3), 132–135.

Miller, S., & Triggiano, P. (1992). The Psychophysiological investigation of multiple personality disorder: Review and update. *American Journal of Clinical Hypnosis, 35*(1), 47–61.

Monroe, R. A. (1971). *Journeys out of the body.* New York: Doubleday.

Murphy, G., & Ballou, R. (Eds.). (1960). *William James on psychical research.* New York: Viking Press.

Murphy, M. (1992). *The future of the body: Explorations into the further evolution of human nature.* Los Angeles, CA: Tarcher.

Nadon, R., D'eon, J., McConkey, K., Laurence, J., & Campbell, P. (1988). Posthypnotic amnesia, the hidden observer effect, and duality during hypnotic age regression. *International Journal of Clinical and Experimental Hypnosis, 36*(1), 19–37.

Olton, D. S., & Noonberg, A. R. (1980). *Biofeedback: Clinical applications in behavioral medicine.* Englewood Cliffs, NJ: Prentice-Hall.

O'Regan, B. (1979). Biofeedback: The growth of a technique. *Institute of Noetic Sciences Newsletter, 7*(1), 10.

Ornstein, R. (1972). *The psychology of consciousness.* San Francisco: Freeman; New York: Viking Press.

Peper, E., & Williams, E. A. (1981). Autogenic therapy. In A. Hastings, J. Fadiman, & J. Gordon (Eds.), *Health for the whole person* (pp.131–138). New York: Pocket Books.

Perry, R. B. (1935). *The thought and character of William James* (2 vols.). Boston: Little, Brown.

Plutchik, R. (1962). *The emotions: Facts, theories, and a new model.* New York: Random House.

Putnam, F. (1984). The psychophysiologic investigation of multiple personality. *Psychiatric Clinics of North America, 7*(1), 31–39.

Ram Dass. (1974). *The only dance there is.* New York: Doubleday.

———. (1978). *Journey of awakening, a meditator's guidebook.* New York: Doubleday.

Rama, Swami, Ballentine, R., & Weinstock, A. (1976). *Yoga and psychotherapy.* Glenview, IL: Himalayan Institute.

Ross, C. (1989). *Multiple personality disorder: Diagnosis, clinical features, and treatment.* New York: Wiley.

Sayadaw, M. (1954). *Satipatthana Vipassana meditation.* Original edition in Burmese. English edition, nd. San Francisco: Unity Press.

Schacter, S. (1957). Pain, fear, and anger in hypertensives and normotensives: A psychophysiologic study. *Psychosomatic Medicine, 19,* 17–29.

———. (1971). *Emotion, obesity, and crime.* New York: Academic Press.

Schacter, S., & Singer, J. (1962). Cognitive, social and physiological determinants of emotional states. *Psychological Review, 69,* 379–399.

Schilder, P. (1935). *The image and appearance of the human body.* London: Routledge & Kegan Paul.

Schoenewolf, G. (1991). *Jennifer and her selves.* New York: Fine.

Schreiber, F. (1974). *Sybil.* New York: Warner.

Shapiro, D., & Walsh, R. (Eds.). (1981). *The science of meditation: Research, theory, and experience.* New York: Aldine.

Sherman, S. E. (1972). Brief report: Continuing research on "very deep hypnosis." *Journal of Transpersonal Psychology, 4,* 87–92.

Shields, S., & Stern, R. (1979). Emotion: The perception of bodily change. In P. Pliner, K. Blankstein, & I. Spigel (Eds.), *Perception of emotion in self and others* (pp. 85–106). New York: Plenum Press.

Sidis, B. (1898). *The psychology of suggestion.* New York: Appleton-Century-Crofts. (Introduction by William James.)

Simonton, C., Mathews-Simonton, S., & Creighton, J. (1978). *Getting well again.* Los Angeles: Tarcher.

Skinner, B. F. (1972). *Cumulative record: A selection of papers* (3rd ed.). New York: Appleton-Century-Crofts.

Smith, E. (1988). Evolving ethics in psychedelic drug taking. *Journal of Drug Issues, 18*(2), 201–214.

Spanos, N., Flynn, D., & Gwynn, M. (1988). Contextual demands, negative hallucinations, and hidden observer responding: Three hidden observers observed. *British Journal of Experimental and Clinical Hypnosis, 5*(1), 5–10.

Staats, A. (1991). Unified positivism and unification psychology. *American Psychologist, 46*(9), 899–912.

Suls, J., & Marco, C. (1990). William James, the self, and the selective industry of the mind. *Personality and Social Psychology Bulletin, 16*(4), 688–698.

Sweet, M., & Johnson, C. (1990). Enhancing empathy: The interpersonal implications of a Buddhist meditation technique. *Psychotherapy, 27*(1), 19–29.

Tart, C. (1970). Transpersonal potentialities of deep hypnosis. *Journal of Transpersonal Psychology, 2,* 27–40.

———. (1971). Scientific foundations for the study of altered states of consciousness. *Journal of Transpersonal Psychology, 3,* 93–124. (Shorter version in *Science,* 1972, *176,* 1203–1210.)

———. (1975). *States of consciousness.* New York: Dutton.

Taylor, E. (1981). The evolution of William James' definition of consciousness. *ReVISION, 4*(2), 40–47.

———. (1982). *William James on exceptional mental states: The 1896 lectures reconstructed.* New York: Scribner's.

Valle, R., & von Eckartsberg, R. (1981). *The metaphors of consciousness.* New York: Plenum Press.

Wilber, K. (1977). *The spectrum of consciousness.* Wheaton, IL: Theosophical Publishing Co.

———. (1981). *Up from Eden.* New York: Doubleday.

Winton, W. (1990). Jamesian aspects of misattribution research. *Personality and Social Psychology Bulletin, 16*(4), 652–664.

Wolman, B. B., & Knapp, S. (1981). *Contemporary theories and systems in psychology.* New York: Plenum Press.

Zukav, G. (1979). *The dancing Wu Li masters.* New York: Morrow.

Chapter Ten

B. F. Skinner and Radical Behaviorism

B. F. Skinner was for many years the most famous psychologist in the United States. His works had effects that reached far beyond the confines of professional psychology. His distaste for and distrust of mental, subjective, intervening, or fictional explanations led him to base his ideas on the observable behavior of people and animals and to formulate distinct ways of observing, measuring, predicting, and understanding behavior.

No theorist since Freud has been by turns so lauded, quoted, misquoted, attacked, and supported. Yet, Skinner delighted in meeting his critics and debated with major thinkers who opposed his position (Catania & Harnad, 1988; Skinner, 1972d, 1977b; Wann, 1964). The application of Skinner's seminal ideas was widespread. He had great personal charm. And he was willing to speculate on the full implications of his position. These chacteristics, bolstered by his absolute, unshakable faith in his fundamental assumptions, helped to make Skinner a pivotal figure in contemporary psychology.

Freud wrote that his detractors unwittingly proved to be true, by the emotional content of their criticisms, the very propositions of psychoanalytic theory that they so vehemently claimed were false. Similarly, Skinner's critics appeared to him to display the nonscientific and inaccurate ways of thinking that his work attempted to overcome. Both men have been vigorously criticized yet also acclaimed for developing and defending alternative visions of human nature.

Personal History

B. F. Skinner was born in 1904 and raised in Susquehanna, Pennsylvania, a small town in the northeastern part of the state. His father practiced law. Skinner recalls that his home was "warm and stable. I lived in the house I was born in until I went to college" (Skinner, 1967a, p. 387).

His boyhood fascination with mechanical inventions foreshadowed his later concern with modifying observable behavior.

> Some of the things I built had a bearing on human behavior. I was not allowed to smoke, so I made a gadget incorporating an atomizer bulb through which I could "smoke" cigarettes and blow smoke rings hygienically. (There might be a demand for it today.) At one time my mother started a campaign to teach me to hang up my pajamas. Every morning while I was eating breakfast, she would go up to my room, discover that my pajamas were not hung up, and call to me to come up immediately. She continued this for weeks. When the aversive stimulation grew unbearable, I constructed a mechanical device that solved my problem. A special hook in the closet of my room was connected by a string-and-pulley system to a sign hanging above the door to the room. When my pajamas were in place on the hook, the sign was held high above the door out of the way. When the pajamas were off the hook, the sign hung squarely in the middle of the door frame. It read: "Hang up your pajamas"! (Skinner, 1967a, p. 396)

In a survey of department chairmen at American universities . . . Skinner was chosen overwhelmingly as the most influential figure in modern psychology. (*New York Times Magazine,* 1984)

After completing his work at Hamilton College, which sustained and enriched his interest in literature and the arts, he returned home and attempted to become a writer.

> I built a small study in the attic and set to work. The results were disastrous. I fretted away my time. I read aimlessly, built model ships, played the piano, listened to the newly-invented radio, contributed to the humorous column of a local paper but wrote almost nothing else, and thought about seeing a psychiatrist. (Skinner, 1967a, p. 394)

He finally terminated this experiment and went to New York for six months. He spent the summer in Europe and on his return began studying psychology at Harvard Graduate School. His personal failure as a writer led to a generalized distrust of the literary method of observation.

> I had failed as a writer because I had nothing important to say, but I could not accept that explanation. It was literature which must be at fault. . . . A writer might portray human behavior accurately, but he did not therefore understand it. I was to remain interested in human behavior, but the literary method had failed me; I would turn to the scientific. (Skinner, 1967a, p. 395)

During graduate school he worked diligently but not as hard as he liked to recall. In an early autobiographical essay (1967a), he wrote:

> I would rise at six, study until breakfast, go to classes, laboratories, and libraries with no more than fifteen minutes unscheduled during the day, study until exactly nine o'clock at night and go to bed. I saw no movies or plays, seldom went to concerts, had scarcely any dates and read nothing but psychology and physiology.

I'm taking it easy my first semester. . . . After January I expect to settle down and solve the riddle of the universe. Harvard is fine. (Skinner, 1979a)

Much later he amended his description of his graduate years, recalling a normal blend of classes, activities, friends, dull papers, uncompleted work, and dating (Skinner, 1979a).

After receiving his doctorate, he worked for five years at Harvard Medical School, doing research on the nervous system's of animals. In 1936, Skinner accepted a teaching position at the University of Minnesota, where he taught introductory and experimental psychology. He notes with pride that a number of his Minnesota students went on to graduate school and became behaviorists in their own right.

In 1938, he published *The Behavior of Organisms*. This book established Skinner as an important learning theorist and laid the foundation for subsequent publications. Almost all of Skinner's subsequent work can be seen as an expansion, elaboration, and clarification of the seminal ideas in his first major presentation.

After nine years at Minnesota, he accepted the chairmanship of the psychology department at the University of Indiana. Three years later, he moved to a post at Harvard, where he remained throughout semiretirement and until his death. After he stopped teaching, he continued to write. Later publications include a three-volume biography (Skinner, 1976b, 1979a, 1984a), one purposely popular book about the problems of old age (Skinner & Vaughan, 1985), a number of philosophical papers (Skinner, 1986, 1990b), as well as several essays that criticize general psychology, which he felt had lost its way (Skinner, 1987a, 1989, 1990a).

While pursuing his animal research studies, Skinner had time and the creative capacity to apply his ingenuity in other ways. He invented the air crib in 1945. This device eventually catapulted him into national prominence. It was a glassed-in, temperature-controlled crib with a bottom made of absorbent cloth. In it, a child could move freely without cumbersome diapers, pants, and other clothes. The absorbent bottom was easily replaced as the child soiled it. There was a popular rush of interest when the crib first appeared. However, the fact that the child was glassed in, instead of being behind bars (as in the conventional crib), ran counter to many of the public's basic beliefs about child rearing. Although Skinner used it successfully for one of his own children, the crib never became popular. Skinner still regrets that its utility was not better understood (Skinner, 1979a).

Ever the scientist, Skinner reflects on his concerns that led to the invention on the crib:

My experience with American industry has been very sad. Nobody ever took up the air crib properly. (Skinner in Goodell, 1977)

> I must confess also to an ulterior motive. If, as many people have claimed, the first year is extraordinarily important in the determination of character and personality, then by all means let us control the conditions of that year as far as possible in order to discover the important variables. (Skinner, 1979a, p. 290)

He also designed a musical toilet seat for his child, but it was never actually manufactured (Skinner, 1989).

I really wrote *Walden Two* for the sake of feminine liberation but very few women liked it. (Skinner in Goodell, 1977)

In 1948, Skinner published *Walden Two*, which was a novel that he had written several years earlier. It was a description of a utopian community based on behaviorist learning principles. It was Skinner's initial effort to generalize his laboratory findings to human situations. After slow sales in its initial years, the book became increasingly popular and controversial. To date, it has sold over 2.8 million copies. For Skinner, writing the novel was a remarkable experience. "I wrote my utopia in seven weeks. I would dash off a fair version of a short chapter in a single morning. I wrote directly on the typewriter . . . and I revised sparingly . . . I wrote some parts with an emotional intensity that I have never experienced at any other time" (Skinner, 1979a, pp. 297–298). "It was pretty obviously a venture in self-therapy, in which I was struggling to reconcile two aspects of my own behavior represented by Burris and Frazier [the two major characters]" (Skinner, 1967a, p. 403).[1] The creation of Walden Two stood

---

[1]Skinner's first name is Burrhus, his middle name is Frederic.

in stark contrast to Skinner's usual pattern of writing: "In general I write very slowly and in longhand. It took me two minutes to write each word of my thesis and that still is about my rate. From three or four hours each day I eventually salvage about one hundred publishable words" (Skinner, 1967a, p. 403).

Skinner has written a series of books that have defined successively his ideological stance and moved his work further and further from its experimental beginnings. These include *Science and Human Behavior* (1953), *Cumulative Record* (1959, 1961, 1972a), *The Technology of Teaching* (1968), *Beyond Freedom and Dignity* (1971), *About Behaviorism* (1974), and *Reflections on Behaviorism and Society* (1978a). His more personal books include *Particulars of My Life* (1976b), *The Shaping of a Behaviorist* (1979a), *Notebooks* (1980), and *A Matter of Consequences* (1984a).

His willingness to appear in the media (Skinner, 1977a, 1978b, 1979b) has kept his ideas before the general public. He wrote throughout his life, finishing the revisions for his last published paper (1990b) the day before his death at age 86.

Intellectual Antecedents

Skinner feels that he was deeply influenced by his early reading of the English scientist-philosopher Francis Bacon (1561–1626). "Three Baconian principals have characterized my professional life" (Skinner 1984a, pp. 406–412). He described theses principals as follows: (1) "I have studied nature not books"; (2) "Nature to be commanded must be obeyed"; and (3) "A better world was possible, but it would not come about by accident. It must be planned and built, and with the help of science" (pp. 406–412).

Skinner says of himself, "I have . . . asked questions of the organism rather than of those who have studied the organism . . . I classify not for the sake of classification but to reveal properties" (Skinner, 1967a, p. 409). This stance led Skinner to stress careful laboratory experimentation and the accumulation of measurable behavioral data. When we consider the possible richness of human personality, this may seem austere; yet, it is the foundation upon which all of Skinner's propositions firmly rest.

Behaviorism is a formulation which makes possible an effective experimental approach to human behavior. . . . It may need to be clarified, but it does not need to be argued. I have no doubt of the eventual triumph of the position. (Skinner, 1967a, pp. 409–410)

Darwinism

The idea that working with animal studies is relevant to understanding human behavior is an indirect result of Darwin's research and the subsequent development of evolutionary theories. Many psychologists, including Skinner, assumed that humans are essentially no different from other animals. While this extreme position has become less and less acceptable, it is at the heart of Skinner's research and his application of animal reseach to the understanding of human beings.

After the horror of atheism, there is nothing that leads weak minds further astray from the paths of virtue than the idea that the minds of other animals resemble our own, and that, therefore, we have no greater right to future life than have gnats and ants. (René Descartes, "A Treatise on the Passions of the Soul," 1649)

The first researchers of animal behaviors were interested in discovering the reasoning capacities of animals. In effect, they tried to raise the status of animals to that of thinking beings. This idea—that animals have complex personalities—has always been part of our folklore. This anthropomorphizing is most apparent in the visual media and seemed to begin to most popular effect with such animators as Walt Disney. Today, cartoon animals that possess human qualities appear to have flooded both the visual and print media. Gary Larson's "The Farside" comic strip provides a ripe example of how receptive we are to the idea of creatures personified.

We prefer to imagine that animals are like ourselves, rather than the reverse. The behaviorists, however, take the approach that we are more similar to animals than we have been willing to observe or admit. The first examinations of higher thought processes in animals was deterred by the suggestions of Lloyd Morgan and the research of Edward Thorndike. Morgan proposed a *canon of parsimony,* which stated that given two explanations, a scientist should always accept the simpler one. Thorndike conducted research that demonstrated that, although animals seemed to display reasoning, their behaviors could be more parsimoniously explained as the result of noncognitive processes (Skinner, 1964). Consequently, the emphasis shifted. Also, researchers began to speculate freely that human behavior as well could be understood in parsimonious terms, ignoring the little-understood complexities of consciousness.

Watson

The time seems to have come when psychology must discard all references to consciousness. (Watson, 1913, p. 163)

American John B. Watson (1878–1958), the first avowed psychological behaviorist, defined behaviorism as follows:

> Psychology as the behaviorist views it is a purely objective branch of natural science. Its theoretical goal is the prediction and control of behavior. Introspection forms no essential part of its methods. . . .The behaviorist, in his efforts to get a unitary scheme of animal response, recognizes no dividing line between man and brute. (1913, p. 158)

It is a mistake to suppose that there are internal stimuli. (Skinner in Evans, 1968, p. 21)

Watson argued that there was no such thing as consciousness, that all learning was dependent upon the external environment, and that all human activity is conditioned and conditionable in spite of the variation in genetic makeup. Watson, in his time, was a popular and persuasive writer. Skinner was attracted to the broad philosophical outlines of his works (Watson, 1928a) but not to his more extreme suggestions. For example, one of Watson's most widely read books on child rearing contains the following advice: "Never hug and kiss them [children], never let them sit on your lap. If you must, kiss them once on the forehead when they say good-night. Shake hands with them in the morning" (1928b, pp. 81–82).

Skinner criticizes Watson for his denial of genetic characteristics as well as for his tendency to generalize without the support of concrete data.

> His new science was also, so to speak, born prematurely. Very few scientific facts about behavior—particularly human behavior—were available. A shortage of facts is always a problem in a new science, but in Watson's aggressive program in a field as vast as human behavior it was especially damaging. He needed more factual support than he could find, and it is not surprising that much of what he said seemed oversimplified and naive. (Skinner, 1974, p. 6)

Pavlov

Ivan Pavlov (1849–1936), a Russian physiologist, did the first important modern work in the area of behavioral conditioning (1927). His research demonstrated that autonomic functions could be conditioned. He showed that salivation could be evoked by a stimulus other than food, such as a ringing bell. Pavlov was not merely observing and predicting the behaviors he was studying; he could produce them on command. However, as Skinner points out, Pavlov's research had rather narrow implications. It was his good fortune that salivation is naturally one of the most easily conditioned of autonomic functions (in Cohen, 1977).

While other animal experimenters were content with using statistical analysis to predict the likelihood that a behavior would occur, Skinner was fascinated with the step beyond prediction—control. Pavlov's work pointed Skinner toward tightly controlled laboratory experiments using animals. He found that by restricting an animal's environment under limited conditions, he could achieve almost perfectly replicable results. Individual differences could be effectively controlled, and laws of behavior valid for any member of a species might be discovered. Skinner's contention was that, in this way, psychological research could eventually be elevated from a probabilistic science to an exact one.

A prediction of what the average individual will do is often of little or no value in dealing with a particular individual. (Skinner, 1953, p. 19)

Philosophy of Science

Skinner was impressed with the ideas of philosophers of science, including Percy Bridgman, Ernst Mach, and Jules Henri Poincaré. They created new models of explanatory thinking that did not depend on any metaphysical substructures. To Skinner, behaviorism "is not the science of human behavior; it is the philosophy of that science" (Skinner, 1974, p. 3). Behaviorism allows questions to be clearly formulated for which answers can be found. For example, only when biology left metaphysics behind, dismissing its concern with "vital fluids" and other unmeasurable, unprovable, and unpredictable notions, could it become an experimental science.

I often say that when you can measure what you are speaking about, and express it in numbers, you know something about it; but when you cannot express it in numbers, your knowledge is of a meager and unsatisfactory kind . . . but you have scarcely, in your thoughts, advanced to the stage of Science. (Lord Kelvin, 1824–1907)

Skinner contended his position is to be essentially nontheoretical (1950, 1956; Sagal, 1981). He worked from observable data alone. However, his impact on psychology and society arose from extrapolations of his data into theories reaching far beyond the confines of animal research.

Major Concepts

Scientific Analysis of Behavior

A scientific analysis of behavior must, I believe, assume that a person's behavior is controlled by his genetic and environmental histories rather than by the person himself as an initiating, creative agent. (Skinner, 1974, p. 189)

Science is a disposition to deal with the facts rather than what someone has said about them. . . . It is a search for order, for uniformities, for lawful relations among the events in nature. It begins, as we all begin, by observing single episodes, but it quickly passes on the general rule, to scientific law. (Skinner, 1953, pp. 12–13)

Past events are assumed to be sufficient data to begin to predict similar future events.

Behavior, although very complex, can be investigated, like any other observable phenomena.

Since it is a process, rather than a thing, it can not easily be held still for observation. It is changing, fluid, and evanescent, and for this reason it makes great technical demands upon the ingenuity and energy of the scientist. But there is nothing essentially insoluble about the problems which arise from this fact. (Skinner, 1953, p. 15)

"Behavior is that which an organism can be observed doing. It is more to the point to say that behavior is that part of the functioning of an organism which is engaged in acting upon or having commerce with the outside world" (Skinner, 1938, p. 6). The goal is to be able to look at a behavior and its *contingencies* (from a Latin word, meaning "to touch on all sides"). For Skinner, this includes the antecedents of the behavior, the response to it, and the consequences or results of the response. A complete analysis would also take into consideration the genetic endowment of the individual and the previous history of behaviors related to those being studied.

The scientific analysis of behavior begins by isolating single parts of a complex event so that the single part can be better understood. Skinner's experimental research followed this analytic procedure, restricting itself to situations that are amenable to rigorous scientific analysis. The results of his experiments can be verified independently, and his conclusions can be checked against the recorded data.

Freud and the psychodynamic theorists were equally interested in the developmental history of the individual as the basis for action. Skinner, on the other hand, advocated a more extreme position, stating that it is behavior, and behavior alone, that can be studied. Behavior, as distinct from an inner life, can be fully described; that is, it is measurable, observable, and perceivable with measuring instruments.

Personality

Skinner argues that if you base your definition of the self on observable behavior, it is not necessary to discuss the inner working of the self or the personality at all.

Personality, therefore, in the sense of a separate self, has no place in a scientific analysis of behavior. Personality as defined by Skinner is a *collection of behavior patterns*. Different situations evoke different response patterns. Each individual response is based solely on previous experiences and genetic history. To look for "mental or psychic states," says Skinner, is to look in the wrong place. "By emphasizing an inner life as an object of study, [Freud] put science back fifty years" (Skinner, 1953 in Skinner, 1984c, p. 56).

Buddhism, to the surprise of most behaviorists, also concludes that, because there is no observable individual self, the self does not exist. Buddha does not believe that there is an entity called personality; there are only overlapping behaviors and sensations, all of which are impermanent. Skinner and the Buddhists developed their ideas based on the assumption that there is no ego, no self, no personality, except as characterized by a collection of behaviors. Both theories go on to stress that a proper understanding of the causes of behavior eliminates confusion and misunderstanding. The theories, however, diverge widely in their explanation of the causes. (See the section titled, Selflessness in the chapter on Zen Buddhism.)

Explanatory Fictions

Explanatory fictions are those terms that nonbehaviorists use to describe behavior. They are concepts that people make use of when they do not understand the behavior involved or are unaware of the pattern of reinforcements that preceded or followed the behavior. Examples of explanatory fictions for Skinner include *freedom, autonomous man, dignity,* and *creativity*. According to behaviorism, using any of these terms as explanations for behavior, is simply incorrect. "Skinner believes it is a most harmful type of explanation simply because it has the misleading appearance of being satisfactory and therefore tends to retard the investigation of those objective variables that might yield genuine behavioral control" (Hall & Lindzey, 1978, pp. 646–647). The misuse of language is a constantly recurring theme in Skinner's writings.

Unfortunately, references to feelings and states of mind have an emotional appeal that behavioral alternatives usually lack. Here is an example, "If the world is to be saved, people must learn to be noble without being cruel, to be filled with faith, yet open to truth, to be inspired by

When I can do what I want to do, there is my liberty for me, but I can't help wanting what I do want.
(Voltaire, 1694–1778)

great purposes without hating those who thwart them." This is an "inspiring" sentence. . . . But what does it inspire us to do? (Skinner, 1987a)

Freedom

Freedom is a label that we attach to behavior when we are unaware of the causes for the behavior. Although the full argument cannot be presented here, at least one example may clarify Skinner's meaning. A series of studies conducted by Milton Erickson (1939) demonstrated that through hypnosis, subjects could evoke various kinds of psychopathological symptoms. While a subject was in a trance, Erickson would make posthypnotic suggestions. In most cases, the subjects carried out the suggestion and developed the symptom. In no case did the subject recall, when asked, that a suggestion had been given under hypnosis. Whenever subjects were asked what the reasons were for their unusual behavior, they would invent (and apparently believe) a host of explanations. If one simply listened to the subjects' explanations, one would conclude that absolutely all of the subjects were acting of their own free will. The subjects were convinced that their behaviors were due to their own decisions. And the observers, knowing that the subjects had no recall of the preceding events, were equally convinced that *free will* was not the full explanation.

Skinner suggests that the feeling of freedom is not really freedom; furthermore, he believes that the most repressive forms of control are those that reinforce the feeling of freedom. These expecialy repressive tactics restrict and control action in subtle ways, which is not easily discernible by the people being controlled.

> The hypothesis that man is not free is essential to the application of scientific method to the study of human behavior. The free inner man who is held responsible for the behavior of the external biological organism is only a pre-scientific substitute for the kind of causes which are discovered in the course of a scientific analysis. *All* of these *causes* lie outside the individual. . . . Science insists that action is initiated by forces impinging upon the individual, and that freedom is only another name for behavior for which we have not yet found a cause. (Skinner, 1953)

Autonomous Man

Autonomous man is an explanatory fiction that is described by Skinner as an *indwelling agent,* an inner person, who is moved by vague inner forces independent of the behavioral contingencies. To be autonomous is to initiate behavior that is "uncaused": the behavior does not arise from prior behaviors and is not attributable to external events. Skinner found no evidence that such an autonomous being exists, and he was distressed that so many people believed in it.

As soon as one puts aside the indwelling agent, one can freely examine the similarities between the learning patterns of humans and animals. Skinner's research demonstrated that if one plots certain kinds of learning experiences, the shape of the resulting curve (and the rate of the learning) is the same for pigeons, rats, monkeys, cats, dogs, and human children (Skinner, 1956). This parallelism between animal and human learning underlies Skinner's analysis of human behavior. Ever since his first book, *The Behavior of Organisms* (1938), he has performed and has been interested in experiments that postulate no major differentiation between humans and other species. In his book he states, "I may say that the only differences I expect to see revealed between the behavior of rat and man (aside from enormous differences of complexity) lie in the field of verbal behavior" (p. 442). Fifty years later, he was of the same opinion. "There is no place in a scientific analysis of behavior for a mind or self" (Skinner 1990a, p. 1209).

Intelligent people no longer believe that men are possessed by demons, . . . but human behavior is still commonly attributed to indwelling agents. (Skinner, 1971, p. 5)

Dignity

Dignity (or credit or praise) is as much an explanatory fiction as is freedom.

> The amount of credit a person receives is related in a curious way to the visibility of the causes of his behavior. We withhold credit when the causes are conspicuous. . . . [W]e do not give credit for coughing, sneezing, or vomiting even though the result may be valuable. For the same reason, we do not give much credit for behavior which is under conspicuous aversive control even though it may be useful. (Skinner, 1971, p. 42)

In other words, we often praise an individual for the kind of behavior of which the circumstances or the additional contingencies are unknown. By way of contrast, for example, we do not praise acts of charity if we *know* they are done only to lower income taxes. We do not praise a confession of a crime if the confession has come out under extreme pressure. We do not censure a person whose acts inadvertently cause others damage. Skinner suggests that we should admit our ignorance and withhold both praise and censure.

Rights and duties, like a moral or ethical sense, are examples of hypothetical internalized environmental sanctions. (Skinner, 1975, p. 48)

Creativity

With a certain amount of puckish delight, Skinner dismisses the last stronghold of the indwelling agent: the poetic or creative act. It is for Skinner still another example of using a metaphysical label to avoid the fact that we do not know the specific causes of a given behavior.

Skinner derides the opinions of creative artists who maintain their works are spontaneous or that they arise from sources beyond the life experience of the artist. The evidence from hypnosis, the evidence from the vast body of literature on the effectiveness of propaganda and advertising, and the findings of psychotherapy concur that an individual may

I have never been able to understand why he [the poet I. A. Richards] feels that Coleridge made an important contribution to our understanding of human behavior, and he has never been able to understand why I feel the same way about pigeons. (Skinner, 1972c, p. 34)

be unaware of what lies behind his or her own behavior. It is unlikely that poets, or anyone else, are aware of all of their own prehistory. Skinner asks the question, "Does the poet create, originate, initiate the thing called a poem, or is his behavior merely the product of his genetic and environmental histories" (Skinner, 1972c, p. 34)? His conclusion is that creative activity is no different from other behaviors except that the behavioral elements preceding it and determining it are more obscure. He sides with Samuel Butler, who wrote that "a poet writes a poem as a hen lays an egg, and both of them feel better afterwards."

Skinner is convinced that if we would look afresh at this behavior, we would help, not hinder, the production of new artistic expressions. "To accept a wrong explanation because it flatters us is to run the risk of missing a right one—one that in the long run may offer more by way of 'satisfaction'" (Skinner, 1972c, p. 35).

Will

> To say that the "central pathology of our day is a failure of will, which brought psychoanalysis into being," seems more profound than to say that in the world of our day very little behavior is positively reinforced and much is punished and that psychoanalysis came into being to arrange better contingencies. (Skinner, 1974, p. 163)

Skinner considers the notion of *will* a confusing and unrealistic way of viewing behavior. He defines will, free will, and willpower as unobservable, explanatory fictions. These terms imply an inner sense that is important in determining actions; Skinner prefers to assume that no action is free. "When we recognize this, we are likely to drop the notion of responsibility altogether and with it the doctrine of free will as an inner causal agent" (Skinner, 1953, p. 116).

Other researchers, however, have shown that people who believe external forces are responsible for their actions feel less in control of their behavior than people who feel personally responsible for their actions. Davison and Valins (1969) found that "if a person realizes that his behavior change is totally dependent upon an external reward or punishment, there is no reason for the new behavior to persist once the environmental contingencies change" (p. 33).

> What is controversial about Skinner is not so much his view that man is a very superior machine but his views as to what runs the machine. . . . Skinner dismisses all the baggage of consciousness, all feelings, all motives, all intentions as, at best, by-products. (Cohen, 1977)

Lefcourt reviewed studies in which subjects were tested both when they operated under the belief that they could control outcomes and when they could not control these results. These studies suggest that depriving animals or people of the "illusion" of freedom has negative behavioral effects that are measureable. "The sense of control, the illusion that one can exercise personal choice, has a definite and positive role in sustaining life. The illusion of freedom is not to be easily dismissed without anticipating undesirable consequences" (Lefcourt, 1973, pp. 425–426).

Skinner's investigation of will has drawn more criticism than any other aspect of his work. Considerable research literature has emerged investigating what is now called *the locus of control,* or "Who do I think is in charge—me or my environment?" The data continue to strongly favor the position that one's belief in the possibility of directing one's behavior matters (Lefcourt, 1980). Even prominent behaviorists such as Mahoney and Thoresen (1974) talk about self-control and a sense of freedom as the core of successful behavioral manipulation.

Self

Skinner considers the term *self* an explanatory fiction.

> If we cannot show what is responsible for a man's behavior, we say that he himself is responsible for it. The precursors of physical science once followed the same practice, but the wind is no longer blown by Aeolus, nor is the rain cast down by Jupiter Pluvius. . . . The practice resolves our anxiety with respect to unexplained phenomena and is perpetuated because it does so. . . . A concept of self is not essential in an analysis of behavior. (Skinner, 1953, pp. 283, 285)

Conditioning and Reinforcement

Respondent Behavior

Respondent behavior is reflexive behavior. The organism responds automatically to a stimulus. Your knee jerks when the patellar tendon is struck; your body begins to perspire as the outside temperature increases; the pupil in your eye contracts when exposed to a bright light. Pavlov discovered that certain respondent behaviors can be conditioned. His classic experiment conditioned the salivation response in dogs by pairing a bell with the arrival of food. Dogs naturally salivate when food is presented. When Pavlov accompanied bell ringing with the presentation of food, the dogs would salivate to the sound of the bell in the absence of food. He achieved this after only several pairings. The dogs were conditioned so that they responded to a stimulus that previously had evoked no response. Like Pavlov's dogs, we can be conditioned to salivate when we enter a restaurant or hear a dinner bell. Respondent conditioning is readily learned and exhibited. Advertisers use a tactic based loosely on the respondent model. When advertisers link an attractive person with a product, they are trying to form an association and elicit a certain response from consumers. They hope that, through this kind of pairing, consumers will respond positively to the product. Further, advertisers hope that consumers will think that they too will be attractive if they use the product.

> There is no place in the scientific position for a self as a true originator or initiator of action. (Skinner, 1974, p. 225)

Operant Conditioning

Operant behaviors are behaviors that occur spontaneously. "Operant behavior is strengthened or weakened by the events that *follow* the response. Whereas respondent behavior is controlled by its antecedents, operant behavior is controlled by its consequences" (Reese, 1966, p. 3). The conditioning that takes place depends on what occurs after the behavior has been completed. Skinner became fascinated by operant behaviors, because he could see that they can be linked to far more complex behaviors than is true of respondent behaviors. What Skinner concluded is that almost any naturally occurring behavior in an animal or a

> Operant conditioning is not pulling strings to make a person dance; it is arranging a world in which a person does things that affect that world, which in turn affects him. (Skinner, 1972b, p. 69)

human could be trained to occur more often, more strongly, or in any chosen direction.

The following example illustrates some facets of operant conditioning: I am attempting to teach my daughter to swim. She enjoys the water but is unwilling or afraid to get her head or face wet or to blow bubbles under water. This has hindered her progress considerably. I have agreed to give her a piece of candy if she wets her face. Once she can freely wet her face, I will give her a piece of candy but only if she ducks her whole head. After she is able to do that, she will get a piece of candy only for blowing bubbles under water. Stage by stage, she will modify her behaviors, rewarded or *reinforced* by the candies, leading to her learning how to swim.

Operant conditioning is the process of shaping and maintaining a particular behavior by its consequences. Therefore, it takes into account not only what is presented before there is a response but what happens after the response. With my daughter, I am conditioning her behavior by giving her a piece of candy *after* she performs certain acts. The candy is used to reinforce certain of her behaviors in the water. "When a bit of behavior is followed by a certain kind of consequence, it is more likely to occur again, and a consequence having this effect is called a reinforcer" (Skinner, 1971, p. 25).

Extensive research on the variables that affect operant conditioning have led to the following conclusions:

1. *Conditioning can and does take place without awareness.* Numerous demonstrations illustrate that what we perceive depends, in large measure, on our past perceptions, which have been partially conditioned. For example, the way we perceive the optical illusions used by Ames (1951) were thought to be a function of the physiology of vision. (See Figure 10.1.) However, when illusions like the "rectangle" in the figure were shown to people in

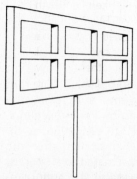

Figure 10.1 "Ames" Illusion This is not a rectangle at an angle. It is a trapezoid looked at straight on. Seeing a rectangle is a conditioned, not an innate response.

cultures where the dwellings and windows were not made with right angles, they did not see the illusion. Perception, in part, is culturally conditioned. A summary of research concludes that conditioning can take place "in human beings . . . in the state of sleep, and in the waking state while the subject is entirely unaware of the fact that he is learning to respond to a conditioned stimulus" (Berelson & Steiner, 1964, p. 138).

2. *Conditioning is maintained in spite of awareness.* It is disconcerting to realize that you can be conditioned in spite of knowing that it is happening and resisting it. One experimenter trained subjects to lift a finger at the sound of a tone paired with a shock. The subjects continued to raise their fingers even after they had been told that the shock had been turned off. They continued to raise their fingers even when asked by the experimenter not to do so. Only after the electrodes had been removed from their fingers could they control their own recently conditioned responses (Lindley & Moyer, 1961).

3. *Conditioning is most effective when the subject is aware and cooperative* (Goldfried & Merbaum, 1973). Efficient conditioning is a collaboration. There is an inherent instability in conditioning when it is not undertaken with full cooperation. The following story illustrates what can happen when cooperation is not obtained:

> A half dozen old and tattered alcoholics in a Midwestern Veterans hospital a few years ago were given an alcohol treatment. [They were administered a drug that induced vomiting anytime they drank alcohol. Eventually, the men were conditioned so that drinking alcohol without taking the drug caused vomiting.] The men were thoroughly conditioned, and just the thought of drinking made them shake.
>
> One afternoon, the old men started talking about their new lives and each discovered that the others hated it. They decided they would rather be in danger of being drunkards again than be terrified of the bottle.
>
> So they plotted an evening to escape. They sneaked out to a bar, crowded together on their barstools, and through their sweating, shaking and vomiting, they bolstered and chided one another to down drink after drink. They downed enough so their fears left them. (Hilts, 1973)

Reinforcement

A reinforcer is any stimulus that follows the occurrence of a response and increases or maintains the probability of that response. In the example of learning to swim, candy was the reinforcer offered after a specific behavior was correctly or successfully exhibited.

When I was a Freudian somebody would say, "I've been thinking about my mother's vagina," and I'd write down "mother's vagina" you know, and pretty soon I've got the patient reinforced so that every time I pick up my pencil [and] he gets a flash . . . [H]e's winning my attention and love . . . [and] pretty soon he's talking about his mother's vagina 15 minutes of the hour. And then I think, "Ah, we're getting some place." (Ram Dass, 1970, p. 114)

Reinforcers may be either positive or negative.

> A *positive reinforcer* strengthens any behavior that *produces* it: a glass of water is positively reinforcing when we are thirsty, and if we then draw and drink a glass of water, we are more likely to do so again on similar occasions. A *negative reinforcer* strengthens any behavior that *reduces or terminates* it: when we take off a shoe that is pinching, the reduction in pressure is negatively reinforcing, and we are more likely to do so again when a shoe pinches. (Skinner, 1974, p. 46)

Negative reinforcers are aversive in the sense that they are stimuli that a person or an animal turns away from or tries to avoid.

Positive and negative consequences regulate or control behaviors. This is the core of Skinner's position; he proposes that all behavior can be understood to be conditioned by a combination of positive and negative reinforcers. Moreover, he asserts, it is possible to explain the occurrence of any behavior if one has sufficient knowledge of the prior reinforcers.

Skinner's original research was done on animals; the reinforcers he used included food, water, and electric shocks. The connection between the reinforcers and the animals' needs was straightforward. A hungry animal learned to do a task, such as open a hatch or push a lever, and was rewarded. The reinforcements are more difficult to perceive when one investigates more complex or abstract situations. What are the reinforcers that lead to overeating? What reinforces a person who volunteers for a life-threatening job? What keeps students studying courses when they have no interest in the content?

Primary reinforcers are events or stimuli that are innately reinforcing. They are unlearned, present at birth, and are related to physical needs and survival. Examples are air, water, food, shelter. *Secondary* reinforcers are neutral stimuli that become associated with primary reinforcers so that they eventually function as reinforcers. Money is one example of a secondary reinforcer; it has no intrinsic value, but we have learned to associate it with many primary reinforcers. Money or the eventual promise of money is one of the most widely used and effective reinforcers in our culture.

The effectiveness of money as a secondary reinforcer is not limited to humans. It has been shown that chimpanzees can learn to work for tokens. They have been trained to spend the tokens in vending machines that dispense bananas and other rewards. When they were denied access to the machines for a time, they would continue to work, hoarding their tokens until the machines were once again available.

Schedules of Reinforcement

How often or how regularly a behavior is reinforced affects how quickly a new behavior is learned and how long or how often it will be repeated (Ferster & Skinner, 1957). *Continuous* reinforcement will increase the speed at which a new behavior is learned. *Intermittent* or *partial* reinforcement will produce more stable behavior; that is, behavior that will continue to be produced even after the reinforcement stops or appears very rarely. Thus, in changing or maintaining behaviors, researchers have found that this scheduling is as important as the reinforcement itself (Kimble, 1961). Playing a slot machine is a model of an intermittent reinforcement schedule. It rewards the player only now and then but often enough so that the act of playing the machine is quickly learned and very hard to extinguish.

Reward (Reinforcement)

Reinforcing a correct response improves learning. It is more effective than punishment (aversive control), because reinforcement selectively directs behavior toward a predetermined goal. The use of reinforcement is a highly focused and effective strategy for shaping and controlling desired behaviors.

Personal Reflection ———————————————————
———————————— Observing and Modifying Behavior

Observing behavior and recording what you observe is the cornerstone of behavior modification. Try this exercise in observing and modifying your own behavior. Use tally sheets or graph paper to record your observations.

Keep a record of the time you spend working on each of your classes. A simple bar graph, marked off in hours, with different bars for each subject would be appropriate. Keep records for a week to establish a baseline. Then decide which class you need to spend the most study time on.

For the next week, each time you study for that class, give yourself positive reinforcement; read a chapter of a novel, eat some candy, take time with a friend, make a phone call, or do whatever appeals to you. *Make sure the reinforcement is something that you really enjoy.* Keep a record of the reinforcers and when you gave them to yourself.

Do you find the amount of time you are spending on this activity increasing? What are the possible causes for this increase?

Behavioral Control

While many psychologists are concerned with predicting behavior, Skinner is interested in the control of behavior. If one can make changes in the environment, one can begin to control behavior. Freedom, for Skinner, means controlling one's behavior.

We are all controlled by the world in which we live, and part of that world has been and will be constructed by men. The question is this: Are we to be controlled by accident, by tyrants, or by ourselves in effective cultural design?

The danger of the misuse of power is possibly greater than ever. It is not allayed by disguising the facts. We cannot make wise decisions if we continue to pretend that human behavior is not controlled, or if we refuse to engage in control when valuable results might be forthcoming. Such measures weaken only ourselves, leaving the strength of science to others. The first step in a defense against tyranny is the fullest possible exposure of controlling techniques. . . .

It is not time for self-deception, emotional indulgence, or the assumption of attitudes which are no longer useful. Man is facing a difficult test. He must keep his head now, or he must start again—a long way back. (Skinner, 1955, pp. 56–57)

What Supports or Impedes Personal Growth?

Growth, in Skinner's terms, means to minimize adverse conditions and to increase the beneficial control of our environment. By clarifying our thinking, we can make better use of the available tools for predicting, maintaining, and controlling our own behavior.

Functional Analysis

Functional analysis is an examination of cause-and-effect relationships. It treats every aspect of behavior as a *function* of a condition that can be described in physical terms. Thus, the behavior and its causes can be defined without explanatory fictions.

When we see a man moving about a room, opening drawers, looking under magazines, and so on, we may describe his behavior in fully objective terms. "Now he is in a certain part of the room; he has grasped a book between the thumb and forefinger of his right hand; he is lifting the book and bending his head so that any object under the book can be seen." We may also interpret his behavior or "read a meaning into it" by saying "he is looking for something" or, more specifically, that "he is looking for his glasses." What we have added is not a further description of his behavior but an inference about some of the variables responsible for it. This is so even if we ask what he is doing and he says, "I am looking for my glasses." This is not a further description of his behavior but of the variables of which his behavior is a function; it is equivalent to "I have lost my glasses," "I shall stop what I am doing when I find my glasses," or "When I have done this in the past, I have found my glasses." (Skinner in Fabun, 1968, p. 18)

Precise descriptions of behavior help make accurate predictions of future behaviors and improve the analysis of the prior reinforcements that led to the behavior. To understand ourselves, we must recognize that our behavior is neither random nor arbitrary but is a purposeful process that can be described by considering the environment in which the behavior is embedded.

Skinner says that explanations that depend on terms, such as *will, imagination, intelligence,* or *freedom,* are not functional. They obscure rather than clarify the causes of behavior since they do not truly describe what is occurring.

Punishment

Punishment does not present information about how to do things correctly. It neither meets the demands of the person doing the punishing nor benefits the person being punished. Thus, it inhibits personal growth.

When people do something wrong, they like to learn how to correct their mistake or how to come to the correct solution next time. Oftentimes, when students have tests returned to them, all they learn is what answers they got wrong. No further explanation is given; the correct solutions are not forthcoming. In such situations, people may feel that they are actually being prevented from learning. Skinner, although often misunderstood, is solidly against punishment in families, in schools, and in social institutions—not on moral grounds but on practical ones—punishment does not work.

Punished behaviors usually do not go away. Unless new learning is available, the punished responses will return, often disguised or coupled with new behaviors. The new behaviors may be ways to avoid further punishment, or they may be retaliation against the person who administered the original punishment. The more a teacher uses punishment the more discipline problems he or she has. The effects of prison illustrate the ineffectiveness of punishment. Prison life punishes people for their prior behaviors but rarely teaches inmates more socially acceptable ways to satisfy their needs. If a prisoner has not learned behaviors to replace those that landed him or her in prison, it is reasonable to expect that once released—exposed to the same environment and still subject to the same temptations—an exconvict will repeat the same behaviors. The high proportion of criminals returning to prison for the same crimes supports these observations.

A related problem is that punishment selectively reinforces and encourages the punisher.

Thus, a slave driver induces a slave to work by whipping him when he stops; by resuming work the slave escapes from the whipping (and incidentally reinforces the slave driver's behavior in using the whip). A parent nags a child until the child performs a task; by performing the task the child escapes nagging (and reinforces the parent's behavior). The blackmailer threatens exposure unless the victim pays; by paying the victim escapes from the threat (and reinforces the practice). A teacher threatens corporal punishment or failure until his students pay attention; by paying attention the students escape from the threat of punishment (and reinforce the teacher for threatening it). In one form or another intentional aversive control is the pattern of most social coordination—in ethics, religion, government, economics, education, psychotherapy, and family life. (Skinner, 1971, p. 26)

Skinner concludes that although punishment may be used briefly to suppress a highly undesirable behavior or one that could cause injury or death, what is far more useful is to establish a situation in which a new competing and more beneficial behavior can be learned and reinforced.

Personal Reflection ———————————————
————————————— Punishment Versus Reinforcement

Part I Punishment   Write down a behavior of your own that you wish to modify. You might choose coming to class late, writing letters during class, eating too much, going to sleep late, or being rude. If you are married, if you live with someone, or if you have a roommate, you can each pick a habit and help each other.

Punish yourself or have your partner punish you each time the behavior occurs. The punishment might be an insult ("Hey, piggy, you're overeating again"), denying yourself some treat, or some other deprivation. An easy punishment is to fine yourself a given amount of money each time the behavior occurs. The accumulated fines can be given to charity. (A variation of this is to give the fines to your partner so that he or she is rewarded every time you are punished. This will make your partner more alert.)

After a week, review your progress.

Part II Positive Reinforcement   Now, choose a behavior that you would like to perform more often, such as exercising.

Begin to reinforce yourself every time you perform the desired behavior. Give yourself, or have your partner give you small gifts: praise, gold stars, or some other reward. Being noticed is among the most effective rewards, so be sure that both you and your partner note the desired behavior when it occurs.

After a week, review your behavior pattern. Have there been any changes? How do you feel about this way of modifying your behavior? Consider the different effects punishment and reward (reinforcement) could have in your life.

Ignorance

Skinner defines ignorance as not knowing what causes a given behavior. The first step in overcoming ignorance is to acknowledge it; the second is to change the behaviors that have maintained the ignorance. Skinner says one way to eliminate some of our ignorance is to stop using words that are nondescriptive, mental terms. Skinner illustrates in the following example how an individual's description of behavior can shape how that person views the causes of the behavior being observed.

> The practice is widespread. In a demonstration experiment, a hungry pigeon was conditioned to turn around in a clockwise direction. A final, smoothly executed pattern of behavior was shaped by reinforcing successive approximations with food. Students who had watched the demonstration were asked to write an account of what they had seen. Their responses included the following: (1) The organism was conditioned to *expect* reinforcement for the right kind of behavior. (2) The pigeon walked around, *hoping* that something would bring the food back again. (3) The pigeon *observed* that a certain behavior seemed to produce a particular result. (4) The pigeon *felt* that food would be given it because of its action; and (5) the bird came to *associate* his action with the click of the food-dispenser. The observed facts could be stated respectively as follows: (1) The organism was reinforced *when* it emitted a given kind of behavior. (2) The pigeon walked around *until* the food container again appeared. (3) A certain behavior *produced* a particular result. (4) Food was given to the pigeon when it acted in a given way; and (5) the click of the food-dispenser *was temporarily related* to the bird's action. These statements describe the contingencies of reinforcement. The expressions "expect," "hope," "observe," "feel," and "associate" go beyond them to identify effects on the pigeon. The effect actually observed was clear enough; the pigeon turned more skillfully and more frequently; but that was not the effect reported by the students. (If pressed, they would doubtless have said that the pigeon turned more skillfully and more frequently *because* it expected, hoped, and felt that if it did so food would appear.) (Skinner in Wann, 1964, pp. 90–91)

Structure

Body

The role of the body in a system based solely on observable data is of primary importance. However, it is not necessary to know the neuroanatomy or the physiological processes that occur concurrent with behavior in order to predict how people behave as they do. In fact, since the personality, as we normally use the term, is for Skinner an explanatory fiction, all there is is the body. Neither mind nor body are separate nor does either have any function other than as the "thing from which behavior originate" (Skinner, 1990).

The body as a body, however, has never interested Skinner. He treats a person as an unopened, but certainly not empty, box. Behaviorists emphasize the inputs and outputs, because these are all that are observable. "Rather than hypothesize the needs that may propel a particular activity, they try to discover the events that strengthen its future likelihood, and that maintain or change it. Thus they search for the conditions that regulate behavior rather than hypothesize need states inside the person" (Mischel, 1976, p. 62).

Relationships and the Psychology of Women

Relationships

Skinner's interest is in the forces that shape and control individuals from outside themselves. For Skinner, there is "no special significance to social behavior as distinct from other behavior. Social behavior is characterized only by the fact that it involves an interaction between two or more people" (Hall & Lindzey, 1978, p. 660).

He devotes considerable attention to verbal behavior (1957) and to the importance of the *verbal community's* role in shaping behavior, especially early language development and other behavior in children. For Skinner, verbal bevhavior includes speaking, reading, writing; anything that uses words. The verbal community is defined as the people who respond to the verbal behavior of others in the same community. For example, a child responds to parents, siblings, other children, teachers, and so forth. He or she responds by changing or maintaining various behaviors. This is common sense, even when expressed in behavioral terms; but Skinner goes on to say that there are *no other relevant variables* beyond a person's past history, genetic endowment, and external events in the immediate environment.

The reinforcements you receive in a social situation depend partly on your behavior and partly on how others react to your behavior. In a conversation, you say something and then you receive feedback. The feedback you receive, however, is based not only on what you said, but also on how the other person behaved after hearing it. For example, you say something as a joke. The other person takes it seriously and becomes upset. You modify your behavior and add, "I was only kidding." Thus, we modify our behaviors in interpersonal relationships as much on the basis of others' reactions as on our own perceptions. This is the verbal community in action.

Although Skinner as a psychologist does not write about social relationships, Skinner as a novelist has his characters in *Walden Two* (1948) discuss them at length. Frazier, the designer of the utopian community, describes the place of the conventional family.

> The significant history of our times is the story of the growing weakness of the family. . . . A community must solve the problem of the family by revising certain established practices. That's absolutely inevitable. The family is an ancient form of community, and the customs and habits which have been set up to perpetuate it are out of

place in a society which isn't based on blood ties. Walden Two replaces the family, not only as an economic unit, but to some extent as a social and psychological unit as well. What survives is an experimental question. (Skinner, 1948, p. 138)

The Psychology of Women

Skinner, in keeping with his atheoretical outlook, did not describe a psychology of women per se. According to Skinner, "a self is a repertoire of behavior appropriate to a given set of contingencies. . . . The identity conferred upon a self arises from the contingencies responsible for the behavior" (Skinner, 1971, pp. 189–190). Thus, a woman's identity is unique and different from a man's identity only insofar as the contingencies responsible for women's and men's behaviors differ. To the extent, then, that a society indeed offers different contingencies to men than it does to women (in terms, say, of roles and behaviors reinforced as culturally appropriate), the "psychologies" of men and women will differ. In the society that Skinner has envisioned in *Walden Two* (1948), for example, the contingencies determining behavior are in fact quite different from those prevalent in contemporary Western society, and conceptions of femininity and masculinity differ accordingly.

Personal Reflection ———————————————
——————————————— Modifying Someone Else's Behavior

Many experiments have established that verbal behavior can be conditioned by selectively rewarding parts of speech or kinds of speech (Berelson & Steiner, 1964). You can experiment with rewarding certain verbal behaviors by simply nodding your head or saying "mmm-hmmm" or "yeah."

Try this exercise. In conversations, indicate agreement by nodding every time a particular behavior is expressed (for example, the use of long, complex words, swear words, or emotional statements). Notice if the number of such expressions increases as you continue to reinforce them.

Emotions

Skinner advocates an essentially descriptive approach to emotions. Instead of treating emotions as vague inner states, he suggests we learn to observe associated behaviors. "We define an emotion—insofar as we wish to do so—as a particular state of strength or weakness in one or more responses induced by any one of a class of operations" (Skinner, 1953, p. 166). He points out also that even a well-defined emotion like

The "emotions" are excellent examples of the fictional causes to which we commonly attribute behavior. (Skinner, 1953, p. 160)

anger will include different behaviors on different occasions, even with the same individual.

> When the man in the street says that someone is afraid or angry or in love, he is generally talking about predispositions to act in certain ways. The "angry" man shows an increased probability of striking, insulting, or otherwise inflicting injury and a lowered probability of aiding, favoring, comforting, or making love. The man "in love" shows an increased tendency to aid, favor, be with, and caress and a lowered tendency to injure in any way. "In fear" a man tends to reduce or avoid contact with specific stimuli—as by running away, hiding, or covering his eyes and ears; at the same time he is less likely to advance toward such stimuli or into unfamiliar territory. These are useful facts, and something like the layman's mode of classification has a place in a scientific analysis. (Skinner, 1953, p. 162)

James and others were on the right track. . . . We both strike *and* feel angry for a common reason, and that reason lies in the environment. (Skinner, 1975, p. 43)

Skinner feels that the current difficulties in understanding, predicting, and controlling emotional behaviors could be reduced by observing behavioral patterns; he doubts that they can be reduced by references to unknown internal states.

Thinking and Knowing

Descriptions of thinking, for Skinner, are as unreliable and vague as descriptions of emotional states.

> "Thinking" often means "behaving weakly," where the weakness may be due, for example, to defective stimulus control. Shown an object with which we are not very familiar, we may say, "I think it is a kind of wrench," where "I think" is clearly opposed to "I know." We report a low probability for a different reason when we say, "I think I shall go," rather than "I shall go" or "I know I shall go."
>
> There are more important uses of the term. Watching a chess game, we may wonder "what a player is thinking of" when he makes a move. We may mean that we wonder what he will do next. In other words, we wonder about his incipient or inchoate behavior. To say, "He was thinking of moving his rook," is perhaps to say, "He was on the point of moving it." Usually, however, the term refers to completed behavior which occurs on a scale so small that it cannot be detected by others. (Skinner, 1974, p. 103)

Skinner defines knowledge as a *repertoire of behavior*. "A man 'knows his table of integrals' in the sense that under suitable circumstances he will recite it, make corresponding substitutions in the course of a calculation, and so on. He 'knows his history' in the sense of possessing another highly complex repertoire" (1953, pp. 408–409).

Knowledge is the behavior displayed when a particular stimulus is applied. Other theorists tend to consider behaviors such as naming the major character in *Hamlet* or explaining the influence of German silvermine production on medieval European history as "signs" or evidence of knowledge; Skinner regards these behaviors as knowledge itself. Another way he defines knowledge is the probability of skilled behavior. To say that a person "knows how to read," to Skinner means that the occasions upon which reading is reinforced tend to produce the behavioral repertoire called reading. Skinner feels that the conventional ways of teaching suffer when the tools of behavioristic analysis are not employed. His concern moved him to devise learning situations and devices that accelerate the pace and enlarge the scope of established learning.

Self-knowledge

Skinner does explore the repertoire of behaviors known as *self-knowledge*. In so doing, he describes a number of cases in which self-knowledge is lacking. "A man may not know that *he has done something* . . . may not know that *he is doing something* . . . may not know that *he tends to,* or *is going to, do something* . . . may not recognize *the variables of which his behavior is a function*" (Skinner, 1958, pp. 288–289). These cases are of intense interest to nonbehaviorists because they are said to be manifestations of various internal states (e.g., complexes, habit patterns, repres-

But if a behavioristic interpretation of thinking is not all we should like to have, it must be remembered that mental or cognitive explanations are not explanations at all. (Skinner, 1974, p. 103)

Personal Reflection ——————

—————————— Modifying a Professor's Behavior

This is a popular stunt designed by behavioral psychology students. Try it. Choose as your subject a professor who ambles about as he lectures. The experimenters in this study will be comprised of as many of the class members as agree to participate. Experimenters can begin by reinforcing the professor's walking toward one side of the room. This can be done as follows: As the professor turns or moves to one side of the classroom, the experimenters should lean forward, write notes diligently, and appear to pay very close attention to what he or she is saying. When the professor moves to the other side of the classroom, experimenters should relax and become much less attentive.

Many classes have found after several lectures that they can keep their professors in a corner for most of the class. You might do well to restrict this exercise to professors of psychology, so that, when it is explained to them, they will not misunderstand your intentions, but will reinforce you with behavioristic goodwill.

sions, or phobias). Skinner labels these incidents simply as behaviors for which there has been no positive reinforcement for noticing or remembering them. "The crucial thing is not whether the behavior which a man fails to report is actually observable by him, but whether he has ever been given any reason to observe it" (Skinner, 1953, p. 289).

Therapy

Skinner considers therapy to be a controlling agency of almost unlimited power. In the relationship, since the therapist is described as a highly likely source of relief, any promise or actual relief becomes positively reinforcing, increasing the therapist's influence.

Since Skinner's theory includes no *self,* the goal of therapy cannot be to make a person feel better, be better adjusted, or achieve insight or self-understanding. From the behaviorist's position, the goal of therapy must be to modify the shape or order of behaviors—that is, to prevent undesirable behaviors from recurring and to have desirable behaviors occur more often. Operating towards these ends, behavior therapy has successfully treated problems including some not readily improved by psychodynamic therapies.

In a far-reaching review of behavior therapies (Rachman & Wilson, 1980), there exists a number of well-designed studies with generally favorable results. These studies explore such areas as sexual dysfunction; sexual deviance; marital conflict; psychotic disorders; and addictive disorders, including alcoholism, smoking, and obesity.

Although there are a number of different approaches to the practice of behavior therapy, it is generally accepted that a behavior therapist is primarily interested in actual behaviors, not in inner states or historical antecedents. According to behaviorists, *the symptom is the disease,* not a manifestation of an underlying illness. The "symptom"—such as a facial tic, premature ejaculation, chronic drinking, fear of crowds, or a peptic ulcer—is dealt with directly. Symptoms are not used as an entree to the investigation of past memories or the patients' existential perspectives.

The therapist is for the patient a nonthreatening audience, which is also true of the psychodynamic therapies. In behavior therapy terms, the client is therefore free to express previously unexpressed behaviors, such as weeping, hostile feelings, or sexual fantasies. However, the behavior therapist is intent upon withholding reinforcement in the face of these expressions. The therapist is interested in teaching, training, and rewarding behaviors that can effectively compete with and eliminate behaviors that are uncomfortable or disabling. For example, progressive relaxation may be taught to lessen specific anxiety reactions, or assertiveness training may help a patient overcome timid behaviors.

The following statements describe the special nature of behavior therapy as well as what it shares with other forms of therapy.

1. Behavior therapy helps people respond to life situations the way they would like to respond. This includes increasing the fre-

quency and/or range of a person's desired behaviors, thoughts, and feelings; and decreasing or eliminating unwanted behaviors, thoughts, and feelings.

2. Behavior therapy does not try to modify an emotional core of attitudes or feelings within the personality.

3. Behavior therapy takes the posture that a positive therapeutic relationship is a necessary, but not sufficient, condition for effective psychotherapy.

4. In behavior therapy, the complaints of the client are accepted as the primary focus of psychotherapy—not as symptoms for some underlying problem.

5. In behavior therapy, the client and the therapist come to an explicit understanding of the problem presented in terms of the actual behavior (e.g., actions, thoughts, feelings) of the client. They decide mutually on specific therapeutic goals, stated in such a way that both client and therapist know when these goals have been attained. (Jacks, 1973)

Personal Reflection —————————————

————————————— Desensitization

This exercise is not intended to show you how a therapist would actually work. It is a way for you to experience some of the dynamics that occur when you focus on a single item of behavior.

One procedure used by behavior therapists is *desensitization*, which is a method that serves to gradually decrease one's sensitivity to a disturbing stimulus.

Part I Identify a Symptom   Think of a fear you have had for some time, perhaps a phobia (phobias are the easiest to work with). Fears of snakes, worms, blood, or heights are good examples. Should you not be able to think of or should you be unwilling to consider a phobia, think of a negative emotional reaction you have to a given situation. For example, you may become anxious every time a police car drives behind you, you may get defensive whenever someone mentions your religion, or you may panic just before you begin an exam. Look for a response that seems repetitive and disturbing.

Part II Relaxation   Sit in a comfortable chair or lie down. Let your whole body relax. Concentrate on one part of your body after another, telling it to relax and noticing the relaxation. Let your toes relax, your feet, your ankles, knees, legs, and so forth. This will take a few minutes. Practice this progressive relaxation a few times. If you cannot tell whether or not a part of your body has relaxed, tense the muscles in that area and then relax them.

Part III Desensitization   After completing the relaxation exercise in Part II, while you are relaxed, think of something that has a very distant relationship to the phobia or habit you are working with. If you have a fear of snakes, think of reading about a small, harmless snake that is found only in a distant country. If you have a fear of police officers, think about a clown dressed like a police officer, giving away balloons at a circus.

Try to maintain an image in your mind related to the anxiety-provoking stimulus, while you stay physically relaxed. If you start getting tense ("Yuck, a snake!"), stop concentrating on the image and focus on relaxing, going back to the relaxation exercise until you are once again relaxed. Repeat this procedure until you can hold the image in your mind while still remaining fully relaxed.

The next step and all of the following steps build on one another. Think of an image or situation that is a little more vivid, and closer to the real object or situation of fear. Visualize or imagine it while you maintain a state of relaxation. Then, visualize and image that is closer still to the actual one, as you continue to be relaxed. For a snake phobia, for example, the remaining successive steps in the desensitization process could include actually reading about snakes, then looking at pictures of snakes, followed by having a snake in a cage across the room from you, then having a snake in the same cage next to you, and finally holding the snake in your hand.

Do not skip steps. Do not go to a later image or situation until you are relaxed in all the earlier ones .

Beyond Behaviorism

The strict or radical behaviorism of B. F. Skinner is at the core of behavior therapies; however, there have been significant liberalizations of his positions that have allowed behavior therapies to become the fastest-growing and most eclectic group of therapies in the English-speaking world.

While it is historically correct to credit B. F. Skinner with the founding of cognitive psychology, it is an honor that appalled him (Skinner, 1978c). In a review of the first century of psychological science, Anastasi (1992) says, "The cognitive revolution has not overthrown behaviorism; it has greatly expanded and enriched the kinds of learning investigated." Skinner, who found cognitive psychology to be a hot bed of murky thinking, revived mentalism, and explanatory fictions argued passionately that almost all of the descriptive words used by cognitive psychologists meant nothing, described nothing, and retarded rather than advanced psychological science (Skinner, 1989). When he offered alternatives, he was disappointed by their grudging acceptance (Skinner, 1987b).

In this textbook, partly in deference to Skinner, we devote an entire chapter to cognitive psychology and the theories of George Kelly. In spite of Skinner's pronouncements, most people, including behaviorists, persist in their belief that thinking, although not easily measured, must be examined nonetheless. The task of the cognitive behavior therapist is to modify behaviors and emotional expressions, but *to do so* while considering the patient's thoughts.

Applied Behavior Analysis

Skinner suggested that it is better to modify contingencies in people's environments than to blame and punish them for deviant behavior. If behavior is due to selective reinforcement, then deviant behavior is a function of the environment. This line of thinking has led to the use of applied behavioral analysis, in which attention is paid to the total environment rather than the psychodynamics of the deviant's behavior.

Skinner did some of the first work in modifying the behavior of persons in institutions. He demonstrated that if one could control the outer environment, one could then control behavior (Lindsley, Skinner, & Solomon, 1953; Skinner, 1984b).

If the reinforcers are changed so that the deviant behavior is no longer reinforced, it should pass out of the behavioral repertoire and stop occurring. Furthermore, the environment can be adjusted to reinforce whatever new behaviors are deemed more desirable (Goodall, 1972a, 1972b). In behavior modification, the focus is on extinguishing behaviors that are in themselves deviant or lead to deviant or criminal activities. These ideas have been and continue to be applied in educational and custodial institutions that include hospitals, prisons, juvenile probation departments, and schools (Gilbert and Gilbert, 1991).

Critics of behavior analysis have argued that the amount of control necessary to eliminate the undesirable behaviors is often excessive. Advocates counter by pointing out that the approach is simply a more comprehensive and formal presentation of what their institutions were originally set up to do. The university is set up to educate students, but it operates inefficiently. The prison is mandated to deter and to reform persons who display criminal behavior, but it often fails. Mental hospitals exist to help return people to adequate functioning, but they frequently do not succeed. The long-standing ineffectiveness of our traditional institutions makes it easier to suggest implementing behavioral models that impose tighter controls over more of the environment. If, for example, a back ward catatonic can be reinforced into speaking, feeding, and dressing himself or herself, it is clearly an improvement for the patient as well as a relief to the staff responsible for his or her care. It is evident that control can change behavior. But critics worry about the ethics of control: How much is too much?

From Programmed Learning to Computer Games

Skinner's most original achievement, derived from his animal experiments, was the development of programmed learning. In its original form, a student sat before a *teaching machine*. A single frame or statement (drawing or problem) was presented to the student. The student *actively* responded (wrote, pressed a button, and so on). After completing a response, the student was then shown the correct response and was invited to check if his or her answer was correct. This feedback occurred *before* the next statement was presented. In every case, the student was shown the correct response. In the early, more simple programs, students moved from statement to statement, having opportunities from time to time to redo or review their errors (Skinner, 1958). Skinner's research showed that people learn more easily and quickly when they are given instant and accurate feedback on their progress. The basic hypotheses in programmed learning are:

1. *Learning is accelerated if discrete units of material are presented.* In programmed learning, simpler units are presented first. Each unit of content is given as a distinct entity, which is embedded in a larger and more complex learning program. Thus, although 4 multiplied by 7 equals 28 is a single equation (unit), it is part of the 4 multiplication table and the 7 multiplication table. These tables are part of a larger group: methods used in performing mathematical calculations. "Lectures, textbooks, and their mechanized equivalents, on the other hand, proceed without making sure that the student understands and can easily leave him behind" (Skinner, 1958, p. 971).

2. *The learner must make a response.* Content is most likely to be retained if the learner actively participates in the learning process. In programmed instruction, the student chooses an answer, writes a response, presses a button, opens a slide, or makes some other response. If the student is not interested enough to respond to the item in the program, then the program waits until the student decides to continue.

3. *Punishment does not lead to learning.* Skinner once remarked that he had observed that drugstores were less likely to be vandalized than schools, because drugstores did not engage in punishment. Programmed learning allows students to reinforce their own learning behavior and to reinforce it at their own pace.

> Programmed instruction is perhaps most successful in attacking punitive methods by allowing the student to move at his own pace. The slow student is released from the punishment which inevitably follows when he is forced to move on to material for which he is not ready, and the fast student escapes the boredom of being forced to go too slow. (Skinner, 1978a, p. 146)

In the preface to their programmed-learning text, Holland and Skinner (1961) sum up the arguments that favor programmed learning:

> Machine programs share with the individual tutor many advantages over other techniques of teaching: (1) Each student advances at his

own rate, the fast learner moving ahead rapidly while the slower learner moves at a speed convenient for him. (2) The student moves on to advanced material only after he has thoroughly mastered earlier stages. (3) Because of this gradual progression and with the help of certain techniques of hinting and prompting, the student is almost always right. (4) The student is continuously active and receives immediate confirmation of his success. (5) Items are so constructed that the student must comprehend the critical point in order to supply the answer. (6) "Concept" is represented in the program by many examples and syntactical arrangements, in an effort to maximize generalization to other situations. (7) A record of students' responses furnishes the programmer with valuable information for future revisions. (The present program has been thoroughly revised twice, and minor changes have been made from time to time. The number of errors made by students was halved (reduced to about 10 percent) as a result of the first revision.) (pp. v–vi)

Augmented Learning

The development of interactive computer learning is a step beyond simple programmed learning. The learner still works with discrete units, still must respond, and still gets immediate feedback; but the computer feedback is much more detailed, individual, and complex than with the teaching machine. The learning experience becomes a dialog between student and computer. The students are not simply informed whether their response is right or wrong. They may receive encouragement, pictures, suggestions, alternative approaches, reminders of previous successes with similar items, or displays of the question in another form. While some programmed texts and teaching machines have failed to maintain student interest, this has not been a problem in computer-augmented situations. (See Figure 10.2.)

The computer's flexibility has other implications as well:

> As a result of more imaginative application, we are beginning to recognize still another aspect of machine teaching that in time will become the most important of all. The child, in intimate dialog with the machine, finds himself in a unique psychological situation. The computer becomes a nonjudgmental reflector of his thoughts. He is encouraged to open up his imagination, to try some of the unlikely possibilities, and to follow his curiosity and see what happens. A wrong answer is as valuable as the right one when the alternatives can be explored and he is shown *why* it is wrong. (Brown & El-Ghannam, 1971, p. 2)

Numerous objections to programmed learning arose. First of all, it was deemed socially isolating; students were encapsulated in their own private world while learning. The benefits of group experience and the uti-

In the light of our present knowledge a school system must be called a failure if it cannot induce students to learn except by threatening them for not learning. (Skinner, 1958, p. 977)

lization of group energy and enthusiasm were missing (as were the negative effects of group pressure and competition). In addition, learning based on a carefully designed hierarchy of linked concepts was progressively less utilized in areas that could not be so clearly defined. Also, students had no opportunity to disagree with the program writer's bias. However, with today's new programs, less defined concepts can be placed into programmed learning tutorials. Students can work in groups or on group projects, sharing their work across a classroom or across the world. Also, interactive programs are now being written that allow users to disagree with the assumptions of the program itself.

Skinner, disappointed with the slow acceptance of teaching machines into education, in a truculent paper, criticized many defects of contemporary education. "[W]ith teaching machines and programed instruction, one could teach what is now taught in American schools in half the time with half the effort" (1984b, p. 948).

This kind of learning is not limited to factual material. The following is part of a program first developed for freshman writing courses at Stanford University. The student, in this case, describes herself as "someone who doesn't ever write poetry."

COMPUTER: Hi! What shall I call you today?
STUDENT: Gail.
COMPUTER: O.K. Gail, this time we're going to talk about what you can and can't see, hear, touch, taste and feel. You just touched the computer terminal. How does it feel?
STUDENT: Like plastic and steel, gray and growling.

COMPUTER: Fine. Now say it in a different way. It feels like . . .
STUDENT: strings of steel licking at my finger bottoms.
COMPUTER: Good. Even more far out? It feels as if . . .
STUDENT: a noise from nowhere beating into an empty room.
COMPUTER: Believe it or not, you've just written a poem. Here it is:
Like plastic and steel, gray and growling.
Like strings of steel licking at my finger bottoms.
Just as if a noise from nowhere beating into
empty rooms.
COMPUTER: Do you want to change the poem to make it better?
STUDENT: You bet I do.
COMPUTER: Good. Use the next three lines to type in your changes.
STUDENT: *Gray and growling, the terminal licks at my fingers.*
Strings of steel, gloved in gray.
Noises from nowhere sing into empty rooms.
COMPUTER: That's the way! Now, Gail, would you like to take an imaginary walk in the woods?
STUDENT: Sure would.
COMPUTER: Good. It's autumn, and as you're walking through the woods, what colors do you see?
STUDENT: Yellow, brown, dashes of rose and red, blue sky.
COMPUTER: What do yellow, brown, dashes of rose and red, blue sky remind you of?
STUDENT: A paintpot drawn by a chariot of the sun.
COMPUTER: Walking in the woods can lead to thoughts of abstract ideas such as death, change, beauty or cycles. Can you think of more? Type them in.
STUDENT: Renewal, quiet, wonder, silence.
COMPUTER: How do you feel when you think about renewal, quiet, wonder, silence?
STUDENT: In awe of the perfect beauty of the unknown.
COMPUTER: Would you like to write a short poem, Gail?
STUDENT: Sure.
COMPUTER: O.K., a suggestion is to type three lines using the colors yellow, brown, dashes of rose and red, blue sky which you mentioned, renewal, quiet, wonder, silence, your abstract ideas, and the feelings you have about renewal, quiet, wonder, silence . . .
STUDENT: *Yellow wheat dies— renewed in bread.*
Brown of the earth—alive in silence.
Stillness broken. The whir of falling red leaves.
COMPUTER: Nice, Gail.

(from Nold, 1974)

Skinner could not have predicted the next step in computer-based learning: the presentation of material in game form. The ingenuity of computer programmers seems the only limit to the kinds of computer-based learning games that can be created. One kind of learning game teaches typing skills. The student types words that become missiles, which repel enemy space attackers. As the student types more quickly and more accurately, the only missiles that will work take the form of longer and longer words typed in the same amount of time. Not only does this next generation of programmed teaching devices minimize punishment, but they also appear to be extremely positively reinforcing. A multi-billion-dollar industry has emerged, partially derived from Skinner's rat and pigeon research, which during World War II was classified and funded by the defense department. Skinner worked with homing pigeons to aid in the effor of making "smarter" bombs. It is ironic, therefore, that Skinner's development of programmed learning has led to the creation of shoot-seek-and-destroy video games.

Evaluation

Skinner's behaviorism has been utilized and applied to create new modes of therapy and instruction. The impact of his ideas has led to modifications of programs in universities, jails, mental hospitals, clinics, and primary schools. Several experimental communities have attempted to make the visions of *Walden Two* a reality (Ishaq, 1991; Kinkade, 1973; Roberts, 1971).

As Skinner extended his interests into the workplace, the classroom, and the home he attracted a horde of admirers as well as critics. His treatment of freedom, creativity, and the self, and his unswerving belief in a world dominated by external forces were chilling and compelling. In 1984, Skinner allowed six of his seminal papers to be sent to a group of professionals who had a stake in behavioral psychology. One hundred and seventy four responded, including "party line eulogists, reconstructed kindred spirits, defectors who had left the behavior analytic fold, unapologetic cognitive scientists, and the never-were behaviorists" (Catania & Harnad, 1988, p. xv). Their detailed comments discussed and dissected every facet of Skinner's ideas: ideological, experimental, and philosophical. Skinner then wrote a response to each and every commentator.

These critiques of Skinner's papers along with his replies filled an entire issue of *Behavioral and Brain Sciences* (1984). Skinner's response to almost all of his critics was that they were either misinformed, misaligned, or just plain wrong. He seemed to delight in this kind of exchange. Having discovered that the more he stood his ground, the more his ideas would continue to attract serious attention, he chose to stand firm on all of his positions, even those that dated back more than 30 years. In his final summation, Skinner writes, "In my experience, the skepticism of psychologists and philosophers about the adequacy of behaviorism is an inverse function of the extent they understand it" (Skinner, 1984c, p. 723).

In his last years, he continued undaunted. In a radio interview conducted a few months before his death, he remarked with amusement, "I will die before my critics can come at me for this last work" (NPR, 1990).

I think the main objection to behaviorism is that people are in love with the mental apparatus. If you say that doesn't really exist, that it's a fiction and let's get back to the facts, then they have to give up their first love. (Skinner, 1967b, p. 69)

Of all contemporary psychologists, B.F. Skinner is perhaps the most honored and the most maligned, the most widely recognized and the most misrepresented, the most cited and the most misunderstood. (Catania, 1984, p. 473)

In his determination to render life more understandable, Skinner proposed a view of human nature that is inherently appealing in its compactness, its directness, and its dismissal of all metaphysical speculation. Firmly rooted in the methodology of modern science, it offers the hope of understanding ourselves without recourse to intuition or divine intervention.

Skinner presented himself as a psychologist whose basic ideas originated from laboratory findings with rats and pigeons. However, with the writing of *Walden Two*, he made a "critical transition, from laboratory scientist . . . to outspoken public advocate for a behavioristic science of human behavior" (Elms, 1981, p. 478). Skinner's own thrust for the past 30 years is best stated in his own words: "I am proceeding on the assumption that nothing less than a vast improvement in our understanding of human behavior will prevent the destruction of our way of life or of mankind" (1975, p. 42).

Just as Freud's suggestion that we are immoral and driven by lust and greed scandalized a generation of Victorians, Skinner's suggestion that we are amoral and are pushed and turned by our external environment has disturbed a generation brought up to admire and value self-generated choices and personal independence.

In a late paper titled, "What Is Wrong with Daily Life in the Western World?" (1986), he cites the alienation of workers from their work. He points to examples of people helping those who would rather help themselves, controlling others by punishment instead of reinforcements, and "reinforcing looking, listening, reading, gambling and so on while strengthening very few other behaviors" (p. 568). He suggested that the solution to all of these quality-of-life issues is to apply what we already know, what has already worked, the extensions and applications of behavioral research. He insisted that differences should be resolved on the basis of actual evidence, not abstract speculations. By forcing the argument back toward science and away from purely emotional discussions, Skinner forged a systematic approach to understanding human behavior that continues to exert considerable influence on current cultural practices and beliefs.

> I am a radical behaviorist simply in the sense that I find no place in the formulation for anything which is mental. (Skinner, 1964, p. 106)

The Theory Firsthand: Excerpt from "Humanism and Behaviorism"

Humanism and Behaviorism
by B. F. Skinner[3]

There seem to be two ways of knowing, or knowing about, another person. One is associated with existentialism, phenomenology, and structuralism. It is a matter of knowing what a person is, or what he is

> He sought a parsimonious, elegant, and useful path to a science of psychology. Most of his efforts were steps in the right direction. (Gilbert & Gilbert, 1991)

[3]From July/August 1972, *The Humanist*. Copyright 1972 by *The Humanist*. Reprinted by permission.

like, or what he is coming to be or becoming. We try to know another person in this sense as we know ourselves. We share his feelings through sympathy or empathy. Through intuition we discover his attitudes, intentions, and other states of mind. We communicate with him in the etymological sense of making ideas and feelings common to both of us. We do so more effectively if we have established good *interpersonal* relations. This is a passive, contemplative kind of knowing: If we want to predict what a person does or is likely to do, we assume that he, like us, will behave according to what he is; his behavior, like ours, will be an expression of his feelings, state of mind, intentions, attitudes, and so on.

The other way of knowing is a matter of what a person *does*. We can usually observe this as directly as any other phenomenon in the world; no special kind of knowing is needed. We explain why a person behaves as he does by turning to the environment rather than to inner states or activities. The environment was effective during the evolution of the species, and we call the result the human genetic endowment. A member of the species is exposed to another part of that environment during his lifetime, and from it he acquires a repertoire of behavior which converts an organism with a genetic endowment into a person. By analyzing these effects of the environment, we move toward the prediction and control of behavior.

But can this formulation of what a person *does* neglect any available information about what he *is*? There are gaps in time and space between behavior and the environmental events to which it is attributed, and it is natural to try to fill them with an account of the intervening state of the organism. We do this when we summarize a long evolutionary history by speaking of genetic endowment. Should we not do the same for a personal history? An omniscient physiologist should be able to tell us, for example, how a person is changed when a bit of his behavior is reinforced, and what he thus becomes should explain why he subsequently behaves in a different way. We argue in such a manner, for example, with respect to immunization. We begin with the fact that vaccination makes it less likely that a person will contract a disease at a later date. We say that he becomes immune, and we speak of a state of immunity, which we then proceed to examine. An omniscient physiologist should be able to do the same for comparable states in the field of behavior. He should also be able to change behavior by changing the organism directly rather than by changing the environment. Is the existentialist, phenomenologist, or structuralist not directing his attention precisely to such a mediating state?

A thoroughgoing dualist would say no, because for him what a person observes through introspection and what a physiologist observes with his special techniques are in different universes. But it is a reasonable view that what we feel when we have feelings are states of our own bodies, and that the states of mind we perceive through introspection are other varieties of the same kinds of things. Can we not, therefore, anticipate the appearance of an omniscient physiologist and explore the gap between environment and behavior by becoming more keenly aware of what we are?

It is at this point that a behavioristic analysis of self-knowledge becomes most important and, unfortunately, is most likely to be misunderstood. Each of us possesses a small part of the universe within his own skin. It is not for that reason different from the rest of the universe, but it is a private possession: We have ways of knowing about it that are denied to others. It is a mistake, however, to conclude that the intimacy we thus enjoy means a special kind of understanding. We are, of course, stimulated directly by our own bodies. The so-called interoceptive nervous system responds to conditions important in deprivation and emotion. The proprioceptive system is involved in posture and movement, and without it we would scarcely behave in a coordinated way. These two systems, together with the exteroceptive nervous system, are essential to effective behavior. But knowing is more than resonding to stimuli. A child responds to the colors of things before he "knows his colors." Knowing requires special contingencies of reinforcement that must be arranged by other people, and the contingencies involving private events are never very precise because other people are not effectively in contact with them. In spite of the intimacy of our own bodies, we know them less accurately than we know the world around us. And there are, of course, other reasons why we know the private world of others even less precisely.

The important issues, however, are not precision but subject matter. Just what can be known when we "know ourselves"? The three nervous systems just mentioned have evolved under practical contingencies of survival, most of them nonsocial. (Social contingencies important for survival must have arisen in such fields as sexual and maternal behavior.) They were presumably the only systems available when people began to "know themselves" as the result of answering questions about their behavior. In answering such questions as "Do you see that?" or "Did you hear that?" or "What is that?" a person learns to observe his own responses to stimuli. In answering such questions as "Are you hungry?" or "Are you afraid?" he learns to observe states of his body related to deprivation and emotional arousal. In answering such questions as "Are you going to go?" or "Do you intend to go?" or "Do you feel like going?" or "Are you inclined to go?" he learns to observe the strength or probability of his behavior. The verbal community asks such questions because the answers are important to it, and in a sense it thus makes the answers important to the person himself. The important fact is that such contingencies, social or nonsocial, involve nothing more than stimuli or responses; *they do not involve mediating processes.* We cannot fill the gap between behavior and the environment of which it is a function through introspection because, to put the matter in crude physiological terms, we do not have nerves going to the right places. We cannot observe the states and events to which an omniscient physiologist would have access. What we feel when we have feelings and what we observe through introspection are nothing more than a rather miscellaneous set of collateral products or by-products of the environmental conditions to which behavior is related. (We do not act because we feel like acting, for example; we act *and* feel like acting for a common reason to be sought in our environmental history.) Do I mean to say that Plato never discovered the mind? Or that Aquinas, Descartes, Locke, and Kant were preoccupied with incidental, often irrelevant by-products of human behavior? Or that the mental laws of physiological psychologists like Wundt, or the stream of consciousness of William James, or the mental apparatus of Sigmund Freud have no useful place in the understanding of human behavior? Yes, I do. And I put the matter strongly because, if we are to solve the problems that face us in the world today, this concern for mental life must no longer divert our attention from the environmental conditions of which human behavior is a function. . . .

Since the only selves we know are human selves, it is often said that man is distinguished from other species precisely because he is aware of himself and participates in the determination of his future. What distinguishes the human species, however, is the development of a culture, a social environment that contains the contingencies generating self-knowledge and self-control. It is this environment that has been so long neglected by those who have been concerned with the inner determination of conduct. The neglect has meant that better practices for building self-knowledge and self-management have been missed.

It is often said that a behavioristic analysis "dehumanizes man." But it merely dispenses with a harmful explanatory fiction. In doing so it moves much more directly toward the goals that fiction was designed, erroneously, to serve. People understand themselves and manage themselves much more effectively when they understand the relevant contingencies.

Important processes in self-management lie in the fields of ethics and morals, where conflicts between immediate and deferred consequences are considered. One of the great achievements of a culture has been to bring remote consequences to bear upon the behavior of the individual. We may design a culture in which the same results will be achieved much more efficiently by shifting our attention from ethical problem-solving or moral struggle to the external contingencies. . . .

Better forms of government are not to be found in better rulers, better educational practices in better teachers, better economic systems in more enlightened management, or better therapy in more compassionate therapists. Neither are they to be found in better citizens, students, workers, or patients. The age-old mistake is to look for salvation in the character of autonomous men and women rather than in the social environments that have appeared in the evolution of cultures and that can now be explicitly designed.

Annotated Bibliography

Catania, C., & Harnad S. (Eds.). (1988). *The selection of behavior: The operant behaviorism of B. F. Skinner: Comments and consequences.* New York: Cambridge University Press. Six of his seminal papers of and comments on each from a number of other authors, as well as Skinner's replies. More than most people would ever want to know about the pros and cons of his basic ideas.

Mahoney, M. (1974). *Cognition and behavior modification.* Cambridge, MA: Ballinger. A thoughtful, solid examination of behaviorism and its development from laboratory to field studies to clinical applications.

Nye, R. (1979). *What is B .F. Skinner really saying?* Englewood Cliffs, NJ: Prentice-Hall. A well-written summary of Skinner's ideas written without much recourse to Skinnerian jargon.

Skinner, B. F. (1948, 1976). *Walden two.* New York: Macmillan. A novel about a full-blown utopian community that is designed and managed by a behaviorist. No plot to speak of, but all facets of the culture are fully described and discussed, from raising children to work schedules to planned leisure.

————. (1953). *Science and human behavior.* New York: Macmillan. The most complete exposition of Skinner's basic ideas.

————. (1971). *Beyond freedom and dignity.* New York: Knopf. An examination of contemporary culture, especially its failure to apply behavioral analysis to personal understanding. A powerful, popular book on the folly of thinking the way most of us still do.

————. (1972). *Cumulative record: A selection of papers* (3rd ed.). New York: Appleton-Century-Crofts. Skinner's choices of what he considers to be his most important papers; covers a number of areas that are not included in this chapter.

————. (1974). *About behaviorism.* New York: Knopf. A direct answer to Skinner's critics. It explores the popular misconceptions that people have about behaviorism. It is a scaled-down version of *Science and Human Behavior,* written for the general public.

References

Ames, A., Jr. (1951).Visual perception and the rotating trapezoidal window. *Psychological Monographs, 65,* 324.

Anastasi, A. (1992). A century of psychological science. *American Psychologist, 47*(7), 842.

Behavioral and Brain Sciences (1984). The canonical papers of B. F. Skinner, 7(4). (Later reprinted: Catania, C., & Harnad, S. [Eds.]. [1988]. *The selection of behavior: The operant behaviorism of B. F. Skinner: Comments and consequences.* New York: Cambridge University Press.)

Berelson, B., & Steiner, G. A. (1964). *Human behaviour: An inventory of scientific findings.* New York: Harcourt Brace Jovanovich.

Brown, D., & El-Ghannam, M. A. (1971). *Computers for teaching.* Transcript of a series of talks presented at the Second Specialized Course on New Technologies in Education at the Regional Center of Planning and Administration of Education for the Arab Countries, Beirut, Lebanon.

Catania, C. (1984). The operant behaviorism of B. F. Skinner. *Behavioral and Brain Sciences, 7,* 473–475.

———. (1988). Preface. In C. Catania & S. Harnad (Eds.), *The selection of behavior: The operant behaviorism of B. F. Skinner: Comments and consequences* (pp. xiii–xvi). Cambridge: Cambridge University Press.

Cohen, D. (1977). *Psychologists on psychology.* New York: Taplinger, pp. 262–290.

Davison, G., & Valins, S. (1969). Maintenance of self-attributed and drug-attributed behavior change. *Journal of Personality and Social Psychology, 11,* 25–33.

Elms, A. (1981). Skinner's dark year and *Walden two. American Psychologist, 36*(5), 470–479.

Erickson, M. H. (1939). Experimental demonstrations of the psychopathology of everyday life. *The Psychoanalytic Quarterly, 8,* 338–353.

Evans, R. (1968). *B. F. Skinner: The man and his ideas.* New York: Dutton. (Edited dialogues with Skinner.)

Fabun, D. (1968). On motivation. *Kaiser Aluminum News, 26*(2).

Ferster, C. B., & Skinner, B. F. (1957). *Schedules of reinforcement.* New York: Appleton-Century-Crofts.

Gilbert, M., & Gilbert, T. (1991). What Skinner gave us. *Training, 28*(9), 42–48.

Goldfried, M. R., & Merbaum, M. (Eds.). (1973). *Behavior change through self-control.* New York: Holt, Rinehart and Winston.

Goodall, K. (1972a). Field report: Shapers at work. *Psychology Today, 6*(6), 53–63, 132–138.

———. (1972b). Margaret, age ten, and Martha, age eight: A simple case of behavioral engineering. *Psychology Today, 6*(6), 132–133.

Goodell, R. (1977). B. F. Skinner: High risk, high gain. In *The visible scientists.* Boston: Little, Brown, pp. 106–119.

Hall, C., & Lindzey, G. (1978). *Theories of personality* (3rd ed.). New York: Wiley.

Hilts, P. J. (1973, May 3). Pros and cons of behaviorism. *San Francisco Chronicle.* (Originally printed in the *Washington Post.*)

Holland, J. G., & Skinner, B. F. (1961). *The analysis of behavior: A program for self-instruction.* New York: McGraw-Hill.

Ishaq, W. (Ed.). (1991). *Human behavior in today's world.* New York: Praeger, pp. 249–256.

Jacks, R. N. (1973). What therapies work with today's college students: Behavior therapy. Paper presented at the annual meeting of the American Psychiatric Association, Honolulu, Hawaii.

Kimble, G. A. (1961). *Hilgard and Marquis' conditioning and learning.* New York: Appleton-Century-Crofts.

Kinkade, K. (1973). *A walden two experiment: The first five years of Twin Oaks Community.* New York: Morrow. (Excerpts published in *Psychology Today,* 1973, 6[8], 35–41, 90–93; 6[9], 71–82.)

Krippner, S., Achterberg, J., Bugenthal, J., Banathy, B., Collen, A., Jaffe, D., Hales, S., Kremer, J., Stigliano, A., Giorgi, A., May, R., Michael, D., & Salner, M. (1988). Whatever happened to scholarly discourse? Reply to B. F. Skinner. *American Psychologist, 43*(10), 819.

Lefcourt, H. M. (1973). The function of the illusions of control and freedom. *American Psychologist, 28,* 417–425.

———. (1980). Locus of control and coping with life's events. In E. Staub (Ed.), *Personality: Basic aspects and current research* (pp. 201–235). Englewood Cliffs, NJ: Prentice-Hall.

Lindley, R., II., & Moyer, K. E. (1961). Effects of instructions on the extinction of conditioned finger-withdrawal response. *Journal of Experimental Psychology, 61,* 82–88.

Lindsley, O. R., Skinner, B. F., & Solomon, H. C. (1953). *Studies in behavior therapy.* (Status Report 1.) Waltham, MA: Metropolitan State Hospital.

Mahoney, M. (Ed.). (1981). *Cognitive Therapy and Research, 5*(1).

Mahoney, M., & Thoresen, C. E. (1974). *Self control: Power to the person.* Monterey, CA: Brooks/Cole.

Mischel, W. (1976). *Introduction to personality.* New York: Holt, Rinehart and Winston.

National Public Radio. *All Things Considered.* Interview with B. F. Skinner, July 27, 1990.

Natsoulsas, T. (1978). Toward a model for consciousness in the light of B. F. Skinner's contribution. *Behaviorism, 6*(2), 139–197.

———. (1983). The experience of a conscious self. *Journal of Mind and Behavior, 4*(4), 451–478.

———. (1986). On the radical behaviorist conception of consciousness. *Journal of Mind and Behavior, 7*(1), 87–116.

Nold, E. (1974). Stanford University Library of Creative Writing Programs. Palo Alto, CA.

Pavlov, I. P. (1927). *Conditioned reflexes*. London: Oxford University Press.

Rachman, S. J., & Wilson, G. T. (1980). *The effects of psychological therapy* (2nd ed.). Elmford, NY: Pergamon Press.

Ram Dass, B. (1970). Baba Ram Dass lecture at the Menninger Clinic. *Journal of Transpersonal Psychology, 2,* 91–140.

Reese, E. P. (1966). The analysis of human operant behavior. In J. Vernon (Ed.), *General psychology: A self-selection textbook*. Dubuque, Iowa: Brown.

Roberts, R. E. (1971). *The new communes: Coming together in America*. Englewood Cliffs, NJ: Prentice-Hall.

Sagal, P. (1981). *Skinner's philosophy*. Waltham, MA: University Press of America.

Skinner, B. F. (1938). *The behavior of organisms: An experimental analysis*. New York: Appleton-Century-Crofts.

———. (1945, October). Baby in a box. *Ladies Home Journal*. (Also in *Cumulative record: A selection of papers* [3rd ed.]. New York: Appleton-Century-Crofts, 1972, pp. 567–573.)

———. (1948). *Walden two*. New York: Macmillan.

———. (1950). Are theories of learning necessary? *Psychological Review, 57,* 193–216.

———. (1953). *Science and human behavior*. New York: Macmillan.

———. (1955). Freedom and the control of men. *The American Scholar, 25,* 47–65.

———. (1956). A case history in scientific method. *The American Psychologist, 11,* 211–233.

———. (1957). *Verbal behavior*. New York: Appleton-Century-Crofts.

———. (1958). Teaching machines. *Science, 128,* 969–977.

———. (1959). *Cumulative record*. New York: Appleton-Century-Crofts.

———. (1961). *Cumulative record* (2nd ed.). New York: Appleton-Century-Crofts.

———. (1964). Behaviorism at fifty. In W. T. Wann (Ed.), *Behaviorism and phenomenology: Contrasting bases for modern psychology* (pp. 79–108). Chicago: University of Chicago Press.

———. (1967a). Autobiography. In E. G. Boring & G. Lindzey (Eds.), *History of psychology in autobiography* (Vol. 5) (pp. 387–413). New York: Appleton-Century-Crofts.

———. (1967b). An interview with Mr. Behaviorist: B. F. Skinner. *Psychology Today, 1*(5), 20–25, 68–71.

———. (1968). *The technology of teaching*. New York: Appleton-Century-Crofts.

———. (1969). *Contingencies of reinforcement: A theoretical analysis*. New York: Appleton-Century-Crofts.

———. (1971). *Beyond freedom and dignity*. New York: Bantam Books.

———. (1972a). *Cumulative record: A selection of papers* (3rd ed.). New York: Appleton-Century-Crofts.

———. (1972b). Interview with E. Hall. *Psychology Today, 6*(6), 65–72, 130.

———. (1972c, July 15). On "having" a poem. *Saturday Review*, pp. 32–35. (Also in *Cumulative record: A selection of papers* [3rd ed.]. New York: Appleton-Century-Crofts, 1972.)

———. (1972d). "I have been misunderstood . . . ," an interview with B. F. Skinner. *The Center Magazine, 5*(2), 63–65.

———. (1972e, July/August). Humanism and behaviorism. *The Humanist, 32*(4), 18–20.

———. (1974). *About behaviorism*. New York: Knopf.

———. (1975). The steep and thorny way to a science of behavior. *American Psychologist, 30*, 42–49.

———. (1976a). Walden two revisited. *Walden two*. New York: Macmillan.

———. (1976b). *Particulars of my life*. New York: Knopf.

———. (1977a). A conversation with B. F. Skinner. *Harvard Magazine, 79*(8), 53–58.

———. (1977b). Hernstein and the evolution of behaviorism. *American Psychologist, 32*, 1006–1016.

———. (1978a). *Reflections on behaviorism and society*. Englewood Cliffs, NJ: Prentice-Hall.

———. (1978b). Why don't we use the behavioral sciences? *Human Nature, 1*(3), 86–92.

———. (1978c). Why I am not a cognitive psychologist. *Reflections on behaviorism and society*. Englewood Cliffs, NJ: Prentice-Hall, pp. 97–112.

———. (1979a). *The shaping of a behaviorist*. New York: Knopf.

———. (1979b). Interview. *Omni, 1*(12), 76–80.

———. (1980). *Notebooks* (Robert Epstein, Ed.). Englewood Cliffs, NJ: Prentice-Hall.

———. (1983). Intellectual self-management in old age. *American Psychologist, 38*(3) 239–244.

———. (1984a). *A matter of consequences*. Washington Square, NY: New York University Press.

———. (1984b). The shame of American education. *American Psychologist, 39*(9), 947–954.

———. (1984c). Reply to Harnad's article, "What are the scope and limits of radical behaviorist theory?" *Behavioral and Brain Sciences, 7*, 721–724.

———. (1986). What is wrong with daily life in the Western world? *American Psychologist, 41*(5), 568–574.

———. (1987a). Whatever happened to psychology as the science of behavior? *American Psychologist, 42*(8), 780–786.

———. (1987b, July/August). A humanist alternative to the A. A.'s twelve steps. *The Humanist*, p. 5.

———. (1989). The origins of cognitive thought. *American Psychologist, 44*(1), 13–18.

———. (1990a). Can psychology be a science of mind? *American Psychologist, 45*(11), 1206–1210.

———. (1990b). To know the future. In C. Fadiman (Ed.), *Living philosophies* (pp. 193–199). New York: Doubleday.

Skinner, B. F., & Vaughan, M. E. (1985). *Enjoy old age: Living fully in your later years.* New York: Warner Books.

Smith, L. D. (1992). On prediction and control: B. F. Skinner and the technological ideal of science. *American Psychologist, 47*(2), 216–223.

Wann, W. T. (Ed.). (1964). *Behaviorism and phenomenology: Contrasting bases for modern psychology.* Chicago: University of Chicago Press.

Watson, J. B. (1913). Psychology as the behaviorist views it. *Psychological Review, 20,* 158–177.

———. (1928a). *The ways of behaviorism.* New York: Harper & Row.

———. (1928b). *Psychological care of infant and child.* New York: Norton.

Chapter Eleven

Cognitive Psychology and the Personal Constructs Theory of George Kelly

by Kaisa Puhakka

Cognitive Psychology

Overview of the Field

Over the past two decades, cognitive psychology has become more and more important. It is vitally concerned with the core elements of consciousness, just as William James was when he created the discipline known as psychology. Cognitive psychology is not, strictly speaking, a theory of personality. It encompasses diverse approaches that share a concern with how the human mind, or consciousness, works. Two areas in cognitive psychology are especially relevant to an understanding of human personality. One involves the mapping of the structure of the intellect, the other involves applying these maps to improve therapy.

After looking at the general issues, we will explore the work of a major theorist, George Kelly, who preceded the research described here but whose work has an essentially cognitive perspective. What unifies all cognitive psychologists is a concern for the principles and mechanisms that govern the phenomena of *human cognition,* which comprises perceiving, thinking, remembering, evaluating, planning, and organizing to name but a few processes (Anderson, 1985; Honeck, Case, & Firment, 1991; Mayer, 1981; Miller, Galanter, & Pribram, 1960; Neisser, 1967).

Rather than attend to the uniqueness and variations of the human personality, cognitive psychologists searched for the principles common to all human cognitive processes. And their search took a decisive turn when a computer scientist and a psychologist joined their efforts in the proposal that the human mind could be viewed as an *information processing system,* much like the computer (Newell, Shaw, & Simon, 1958; Newell & Simon, 1961, 1972). Computer simulation, using a computer to imitate or represent a real-life process, came to be used by many psychologists for testing their hypotheses about how humans perceive, think, remember or use language (Anderson & Bower, 1973; Johnson-Laird, 1977; Lachman, Lachman, & Butterfield, 1979; Quillian, 1969). But the use of computer models has also had its detractors (Dreyfus, 1972; Gunderson, 1971; Neisser, 1976b; Weizenbaum, 1976). They feel that it is impossible for a computer to duplicate all of the subtlety and complexity of human consciousness.

Not all cognitive research has been concerned with general principles. The differences in the way individuals perceive, think about, organize, and evaluate their experience has continued to be a topic of interest among cognitive theorists. These theorists have asked questions like, "Are people pessimistic in their thinking because they feel sad, or do they feel sad because they think pessimistically?" Lively debates over the primacy of cognition versus emotion added momentum to the cognitive movement in the 1960s and 1970s (Lazarus, 1982, 1984, 1991a; Leventhal & Scherer, 1987; Scheff, 1985; Zajonc, 1980, 1984) and generated research on how people cope with stress (e.g., Folkman, 1984; Horowitz, 1979; Lazarus, 1966, 1991b; Lazarus & Folkman, 1984). Debates also focused on how cognitive processes develop in infancy and childhood (e.g., Harris, 1989; Izard, 1978, 1984; Stroufe, 1984; Stein & Levine, 1987; Stenberg & Campos, 1990) as well as on life-span development extending to adulthood and old age (Labouvie-Vief, Hakim-Larson, DeVoe, & Schoeberlein, 1989).

A significant development during the recent decades has been a proliferation of cognitive approaches and techniques in psychotherapy. Beginning with Aaron Beck's (1961, 1967, 1976, 1991) pioneering work in the understanding and treatment of depression from a cognitive perspective, techniques have been developed for the treatment of diverse disorders including marital or couples problems (Beck, 1988), anxiety disorders, phobias (Beck & Emery with Greenberg, 1985), and schizophrenia (Perris, 1988).

These developments in cognitive theory do not constitute a comprehensive theory of personality as did the developments of Kelly. Nevertheless, the computer modeling of human cognition and the advances in cognitive techniques of therapy contain within them powerful explanations of what it means to be human and thus have implications for human personality. We will examine both of these in some detail.

Computer Models and Human Information Processing

Minds and Machines

A. M. Turing (1912–1954) was a British mathematician, logician, and pioneering computer scientist. He invented the prototype for the modern digital computer, the Turing machine. "Can machines think?" he asked. His bold response was that indeed they can. They imitate or *simulate* human thinking so well that the distinction between genuine and imitation becomes meaningless (Turing, 1950/1991).

In 1958, psychologist Allen Newell and computer scientist Herbert A. Simon proposed that human cognition can be viewed as an information processing system and that the behavior of this system can be described "by a well specified program, defined in terms of elementary information processes" (R. Lachman, J. L. Lachman, & Butterfield, 1979, p. 98). The analogy between the human mind and the computer proposed by Newell and Simon spurred a wealth of research and theoretic formulations based on computer models. According to these models, humans, like computers, *encode* symbolic *input, recode* it, make decisions about it and store some of it in memory and, finally, *decode* and give back the symbolic *output* (R. Lachman et al., 1979).

For many information-processing psychologists, the computer came to serve two functions. First, it provided a model that inspired theories about how people talk, think, remember, and recognize. Second, it was a tool by which these theories could be tested. For example, Quillian (1969) expressed his theory of language comprehension in a simulation program called the Teachable Language Comprehender (TLC). This program related "input" assertions to information previously stored in its memory and

I believe that in about fifty years' time it will be possible to programme computers, with a storage capacity of about 10^9, to make them play the imitation game so well that an average interrogator will not have more than [a] 70 percent chance of making the right identification after five minutes of questioning. The original question, "Can machines think?" I believe to be too meaningless to deserve discussion. (Turing, 1950/1991)

came up with a meaningful and relevant "output." The performance of TLC was limited to certain kinds of phrases and sentences. Nevertheless, it was a beginning that held promise of the exciting developments to come in understanding how human language and thinking work.

Since then, sophisticated programs have been developed that can "learn," "recognize" things, reorganize knowledge, even make analogies (Waldrop, 1985). These developments have produced successful programs that "specialize" in particular areas of knowledge, such as medical diagnosis or master chess games, not to mention today's Nintendo games played on the home computers of teenagers and adults.

Criticisms of Computer Modeling

We also happen to believe that, given the present state of psychological theories, almost any program able to perform some task previously limited to humans will represent an advance in the psychological theory of that performance. (Quillian, 1969, p. 459)

But none of this gets at the soul disturbing essence of the question. If a machine can be made to think, then perhaps *we* are machines. (Waldrop, 1985, p. 31)

Numerous areas of technology and the entertainment field have benefited from computer modeling. Few would argue this point. Whether computers have brought us any closer to unraveling the mysteries of the human mind, however, remains a controversial question. Even if computers in some sense "think," do they really think as we do? When it comes to knowing who and what we are, not many researchers agree with Turing (1950/1991) that simulation, no matter how good, is the same as the real thing.

Critics of the computer models point to the contextually determined nature of human responses. For human beings, the horizons of the context are always fuzzy, whereas computers do not deal well with fuzziness. Much of the empirical research with human subjects has occurred under highly artificial laboratory conditions that bypass this problem. But the research also suffers from a lack of "ecological validity" (Neisser, 1976a); that is, it has little relevance to human experience and cognitive performance in real-life situations. Another feature of human cognition that seems difficult—some say impossible—for the computer to replicate is the experience of insight, the "aha!" experience, which comes as a jolt of recognition when we suddenly see how to tackle a problem in a wholly different, far superior way. The insight seems to occur by a "leap" rather than by logically ordered steps. The mind seems truly magical, its processes not mechanically reproducible by a computer!

To these criticisms, the advocates of computer modeling maintain that the mind is not so magical, just hidden from our conscious awareness (Waldrop, 1985). Perhaps, as Freud said, nothing happens by accident in the mind. Perhaps every leap of insight is determined by strictly mechanistic laws operating within the unconscious. And the computer may be able to show what we cannot see—the trudging steps that actually make up the leaps of intuition. That is, the computer may really be able to structurally approximate human cognitive processes.

To this day, the issue of mind versus machine has not been settled. Some psychologists and computer scientists believe that it is only a matter of time before the machinations of the human mind are fully unraveled, whereas others are convinced that no machine can ever have the last word on the human mind. The relationship between mind and machine appears to be such that no final solution seems possible—at least not one that would satisfy everyone. Kelly's (1905–1966) notion of reflexivity suggests why this is so. The computer model proposes to account for how humans construe their worlds. But the computer model itself is a construct. In other words, creating computer models of the mind is a reflexive endeavor in which the mind is seeking to create its own construction processes. Perhaps it could be said that the designing of computer models of the mind is a genuine attempt by human beings to test our machine-making abilities. Thus, we are likening the machine to the mind. On the other hand, when empirical researchers isolate their human subjects from their real-life environments and have them respond in artificial experimental conditions that simulate the circumstance of the computer, then it is a case of molding the mind to fit the machine. In this way, the dialectical dance between mind and machine goes on in an endless reflexive spiral. Out of this dialectic, the machine has emerged as a powerful metaphor for the human mind.

Personal Reflection
Minds and Machines

Here are some questions to ponder about minds and machines.

A machine is designed for a particular purpose. Cars are designed for the purpose of transportation. Computers are designed for various purposes having to do with handling information. Machines serve (more or less effectively) the purposes of their designers.

If the human mind is like a computer, was it, like the computer, created for a purpose?

Who designed it?

If the human mind was not created for a purpose and has no designer, in what sense is it like a machine?

Are there machines that create their own purpose and design?

If the human mind's purpose is the survival of the organism, does the purpose of survival originate inside or outside the mind?

Aaron Beck and Cognitive Therapy

Beck's Discovery

Aaron Beck was trained as a psychoanalyst and, for several years, practiced psychoanalysis in the traditional way by having patients verbalize their *free associations,* communicating whatsoever came to mind. One day, however, something happened that changed his approach. A patient in the course of free associating had been criticizing Beck angrily. After a pause, Beck (1976) asked the patient what he was feeling, and the patient responded, "I feel very guilty." This was not unusual. However, the patient then spontaneously added that while he had been expressing angry criticisms of his analyst, self-critical thoughts had been occurring simultaneously in his mind. Thus, there was a second stream that had been running parallel to the thoughts of anger and hostility he had reported during his free association. This second stream of thought was described by the patient as follows: "I said the wrong thing . . . I shouldn't have said that . . . I'm wrong to criticize him . . . I'm bad . . . he won't like me" . . . etc. (p. 31).

It was this second stream of thought that provided the link between the patient's expression of anger and feelings of guilt. The patient was feeling guilty, because he had been criticizing himself for being angry with his analyst. Perhaps analogous to Freud's *preconscious,* this kind of stream has to do with what people say to themselves rather than what they might say in a conversation with another person. It seems to be a self-monitoring system operating alongside the thoughts and feelings being expressed in a conversation. The thoughts that have to do with the self-monitoring tend to arise quickly and automatically, as if by reflex (Beck, 1991). They are usually followed by unpleasant emotion. Sometimes the patients, either spontaneously or with the prompting of the therapist, express this emotion. But they almost never report the automatic thoughts that precede the emotion. In fact, they are typically only dimly, if at all, aware of them.

Automatic thoughts supply a running commentary on much of what people do or experience. They are present in the experiences of healthy as well as emotionally troubled people. The difference has to do with the kind of messages these thoughts contain and how much they interfere with a person's life. For example, depressed people talk to themselves in highly critical tones, blaming themselves for every mishap, expecting the worst, and feeling that they deserve whatever misfortune befalls them because they are worthless anyway. Severely depressed people tend to talk to themselves more loudly. For them, the negative thoughts are not merely whispers on the periphery of consciousness but are loud, repetitive screams, which can consume much energy and distract the person from other activities.

Automatic thinking and unpleasant physical or emotional symptoms combine to form vicious cycles that maintain and exaggerate the symptoms, resulting sometimes in full-blown emotional disorders. Beck (1976) gives an example of a person who is suffering from symptoms of anxiety, including heart palpitation, sweating, and dizziness. The patient's thoughts of dying lead to increased anxiety, as manifested by the physiological symptoms; these symptoms then are interpreted as signs of imminent death (p. 99).

Cognitive Therapy and Common Sense

The discovery of automatic thoughts marked a shift in Beck's approach to therapy as well as in his view of the human personality. The meanings of these thoughts "did not usually revolve around esoteric themes such as castration anxiety or psychosocial fixations, as might be suggested by classical psychoanalytic theory, but were related to vital social issues such as success or failure, acceptance or rejection, respect or disdain" (Beck, 1991, p. 369).

An important feature of these automatic thoughts is the fact that they are accessible to the patient's own awareness and allow for introspection. Even though they are difficult to notice at first, with some training, these thoughts can be brought into conscious awareness, as Beck discovered. Therefore, the source as well as the solution to emotional problems lies within the sphere of the person's own awareness, within the reach of his or her cognition. This is the principle underlying Beck's cognitive approach to therapy. At the heart of this approach is respect for human beings' capabilities to heal themselves and a celebration of common sense, which embodies the wisdom by which people have, through generations, exercised these capabilities. Beck calls attention to the everyday feats of our cognitive capabilities in the following:

> If it were not for man's ability to filter and attach appropriate labels to the blizzard of external stimuli so efficiently, his world would be chaotic and he would be bounced from one crisis to another. Moreover, if he were not able to monitor his highly developed imagination, he would be floating in and out of a twilight zone unable to distinguish between the reality of a situation and the images and personal meanings that it triggers. In his interpersonal relations, he is generally able to select the subtle cues that allow him to separate his adversaries from his friends. He makes the delicate adjustments in his own behavior that help him to maintain diplomatic relationships with people whom he dislikes or who dislike him. He is generally able to penetrate the social masks of other people, to differentiate sincere from insincere messages, to distinguish friendly mocking from veiled antagonism. He tunes into the significant communications in a vast babble of noises so that he can organize and modulate his own responses. These psychological operations seem to work automatically without evidence of much cognition, deliberation, or reflection. (Beck, 1976, 11–12)

Cognitive Techniques for Therapy and Self-help

A variety of techniques that focus on specific problems and require a relatively short-term therapy period have evolved out of Beck's approach (Beck, Rush, Shaw, & Emery, 1979; Emery, 1981; McMullin, 1986). They aim at modifying the negative or self-defeating, automatic thought processes or perceptions that seem to perpetuate the symptoms of emotional disorders. Either directly or indirectly, these techniques challenge, dispute, or restructure the clients' perception or understanding of themselves and their life situations.

In cognitive therapy, the therapist and the client form a collaborative, almost collegial relationship. The therapist does not presume to know the client's thoughts or feelings but invites the client to explore and critically examine them autonomously. In cognitive therapy, clients are in charge of their own problems; they have direct access to the patterns of perception and thinking that perpetuate any problematic feelings and behaviors, and they are capable of changing these patterns.

Not surprisingly, cognitive therapy has inspired a wealth of self-help literature. In fact, most of the popular literature on how to assert yourself, boost your self-esteem, deal with your anger, get rid of your depression, save your marriage or relationship, or simply feel good is based on the work of cognitive therapists (Burns, 1980; Ellis & Harper, 1975; McMullin & Casey, 1975).

The person who has done perhaps the most to popularize the methods of cognitive therapy is Albert Ellis (1962, 1971, 1974). His forceful tactics of confrontation and persuasion have won him followers among therapists as well as lay people. Ellis's approach is known as rational-emotive therapy (RET). Based on the notion that irrational beliefs cause emotional suffering and behavioral problems, RET uses logic and rational argument to expose and attack the irrationality of the beliefs that maintain the undesirable emotions and behavior. Though more confrontative than other cognitive therapies, Ellis's approach shares the commonsense logic of all cognitive approaches.

This logic can be simply stated in terms of the following four principles (Burns, 1980, pp. 3–4): (1) When people are depressed or anxious, they think in an illogical, negative manner and inadvertently act in a self-defeating way; (2) With a little effort, people learn to rid themselves of harmful thought patterns. (3) As their painful symptoms are eliminated, they become happy and productive again and will respect themselves; and (4) These aims are usually accomplished within a relatively brief period of time, using straightforward methods.

The first step is to become aware of one's automatic thought patterns and identify any patterns of distortion. Burns (1980, pp. 40–41) describes the following ten types of distortions that commonly occur in the thinking of depressed people:

1. *All-or-Nothing Thinking.* Seeing things in black-and-white categories. For example, falling short of perfection means total failure.

2. *Overgeneralization.* One negative event is seen as a confirming instance of a never-ending pattern of defeat.

3. *Mental Filter.* Dwelling on a single negative detail exclusively until negativity colors all of experience.

4. *Disqualifying the Positive.* Insisting that positive experiences do not count for some reason and thereby maintaining a negative belief in the face of evidence to the contrary.

5. *Jumping to Conclusions.* Drawing negative conclusions even though there are no definite facts to support them. This happens, for example, when a person arbitrarily concludes that another person is reacting negatively to him or her without bothering to find out whether it is true. Or, a person so anticipates that things will turn out badly that he or she becomes completely convinced that they will.

6. *Magnification (Catastrophizing) or Minimization.* Exaggerating the importance of things (e.g., one's own slip-ups) or belittling their importance (e.g., one's own desirable qualities).

7. *Emotional Reasoning.* Assuming that one's negative emotions necessarily reflect the way things are: "I feel it, therefore it must be true."

8. *"Should" Statements.* Trying to motivate oneself with "shoulds" and "shouldn'ts," as if one cannot act unless psychological self-force is used. When the "shoulds" are directed toward oneself, feelings of guilt can result; when directed toward others, one can feel anger, frustration, and resentment.

9. *Labeling and Mislabeling.* When referring to an error, instead of describing what happened; for example, "I lost the key," one attaches a negative label to oneself: "I am a loser." If someone else's behavior rubs one the wrong way, a negative label might be attached to this person; for example, "He is a louse." Mislabeling involves describing an event with emotionally loaded language that does not ring true.

10. *Personalization.* Seeing oneself as the cause of an external event that in fact one is not primarily responsible for.

Once the distortions are discovered and correctly identified in a person's habitual, automatic thinking, it then becomes possible to modify the thoughts by substituting rational, realistic thoughts for the distorting ones. For example, a person who was let down by a friend may hold onto the thought, "I am a real sucker and a complete fool." This thought is an example of mislabeling and also of all-or-nothing thinking. A rational, realistic thought that more accurately describes what is going on might be, "I made a mistake in trusting this friend" and "I don't always know when I should or shouldn't trust a person, but with more experience I will learn to make that discrimination better." Cognitive therapists believe that with concentration and some hard work, the automatic thoughts and their distortions can be extinguished, and rational, accurate thoughts can be substituted for them to create and maintain a happier, healthier way of living.

Personal Reflection ————

———————— Patterns of Negative Thinking

Try this experience to get a better understanding of your patterns of negative thinking.

When you are feeling anxious, depressed, upset, or just a little blue, observe the thoughts that spontaneously arise and fade away. Let the thoughts come and go without judging, suppressing, or trying to change them in any way. Simply monitor them for a few minutes.

Take a sheet of paper and divide it into the following three columns: Automatic Thoughts, Cognitive Distortions, and Rational Response.

In the first column (Automatic Thoughts), list the thoughts or recurrent themes as they occur. Then go over your list, and, in the second column, identify the distortions in each thought listed in the first column. In the third column, for each thought, come up with a rational substitute, using accurate, neutral descriptions.

The next time you feel similarly anxious, depressed, or upset about something, try extinguishing any distorted thoughts by first monitoring them and then substituting the rational thoughts for them.

Evaluation

Cognitive psychology offers challenges, but also an optimistic, up-beat vision of the human personality. Human consciousness can be described as a machine, its operations precise and automatic and fully determined by rules and environmental input. If consciousness does operate in mechanistic fashion, then one might rightly ask, "Who controls the machine?" This is the challenging and perhaps unanswerable question. However, many cognitive therapists assert that people can take control of their own cognitive processes much more than has seemed possible. According to these therapists, negative, self-defeating patterns of thinking and acting can be changed to bring about a happier, more fulfilling life. There is no doubt that cognitive psychology has gained mainstream acceptance. Nowhere is this more apparent than in the numerous self-help programs that proliferate outside the confines of academia. It may be that the work described here is having greater impact on the culture than any psychology since Freud, whose works shattered late Victorian rational complacency.

The Personal Constructs Theory of George Kelly

George Kelly's work affirms the basic premise of this book: In the study of human personality, theory tends to reflect the theorist much as a mirror reflects an image. For Kelly, both the person as the theorist and the person as the subject of the theory are in a constant process of change and growth. A theory of the human personality should therefore remain essentially flexible and open-ended.

Central to Kelly's approach is the notion of *personal construct*, or the idea that people *construe* events by anticipating them on the basis of past experience and learning. By *construing*, Kelly means "placing an interpretation" (1955, p. 50). The objective circumstances and conditions of the world matter less than how people interpret them. All experience comes through the tinted glasses of personal constructs; there is no such thing as pure experience apart from its construed meaning.

Kelly viewed human behavior as a quest for understanding. However, *understanding* in this context ranges from a complex, well-formulated theory to a simple feeling of security and satisfaction with the way things are. For Kelly, trying to understand people through a preconceived scientific discipline or methodology is like putting the cart before the horse.

In Kelly's theory, then, the person takes the center stage as an active construer of the world. Psychology's task is to study how people construe their worlds and their sense of self. Kelly's work is infused with a great respect for the person as well as a remarkably undogmatic spirit. He was more interested in making positive contributions than in engaging in controversy or polemics. His was an invitation for "any adventuresome soul who is not one bit afraid of thinking unorthodox thoughts about people who dares peer out at the world through the eyes of strangers, who has not invested beyond his means in either ideas or vocabulary" (Kelly, 1955/1970 p. xi).

Personal construct theory . . . is a notion about how man may launch out from a position of admitted ignorance, and how he may aspire from one day to the next to transcend his own dogmatisms. It is, then a theory of man's personal inquiry—a psychology of the human quest. It does not say what has or will be found, but proposes rather how we might go about looking for it. (Kelly, 1966/1970, p. 1)

Personal History

George Alexander Kelly was born on April 28, 1905, in Kansas. The only child of his devoutly religious parents, Kelly grew up in an atmosphere of hard work and somewhat puritanical attitudes. He was sent away to school when he was 13 years of age. From this point on, he lived away from home most of the time. The self-confidence and down-to-earth practicality that characterize Kelly's later outlook no doubt reflect his early independence as well as rural midwestern roots (Sechrest, 1977, p. 233).

Although he started college as a physics and mathematics major, his interest soon shifted to social problems. He obtained a master's degree in educational sociology from the University of Kansas, and then he held a variety of teaching jobs in Minnesota and Iowa and worked as an aeronautical engineer. In 1929, Kelly went to the University of Edinburgh in Scotland, where he earned another bachelor's degree in education. When he returned to the United States, he enrolled as a graduate student in psychology at the University of Iowa. After only one year of study, he completed a dissertation about the common factors in speech and reading disabilities, and received his doctorate in psychology in 1931 (Maher, 1969).

A remarkable feature in Kelly's background is the apparent absence of significant persons or ideas that would influence his subsequent thinking and theorizing about the human personality. None stand out from his brief course of graduate studies. The behavioristic, or *stimulus-response,* psychology to which he was exposed in his undergraduate days neither inspired nor made sense to him. His first encounter with Freud's theories some three years later only added to his disillusionment with psychology (Kelly, 1963).

The major sources from which Kelly drew ideas and inspiration for his theories were not his formal psychological studies but from a multitude of activities during and between periods of formal study. Among these were the following: soap-box oratory for labor organizers and for governments of prospective American cities, public speaking for the American Banker's Association, and acting in a junior college. He also "dabbled academically in education, sociology, economics, labor relations, biometrics, speech pathology, and cultural anthropology, and had majored in psychology for a grand total of nine months" (Kelly, 1963, p. 48). The breadth and variety of Kelly's educational experience is rarely matched by students today, but neither is the meagerness of his formal studies in the discipline in which he taught and wrote during most of his life.

In 1931, in spite of the depression, he landed a job in his own home state at Fort Hays Kansas State College. This was a small college serving a rural population in the plains of western Kansas, 250 miles from the nearest metropolitan area. Kelly remained at Fort Hays for 12 years, and it is to this period that the origins of his two major contributions, personal construct theory and fixed role therapy, can be traced. Cordial but distant in his relations with academic colleagues, Kelly developed his theory and approach to clinical practice in collaboration with students whom he personally trained (Zelhart & Jackson, 1983).

Immediately upon arrival at Fort Hays College, he took over the clinical program of the psychology department and began to develop innovative programs in research and clinical services. Perhaps the best known of these was the traveling clinics that provided services to the rural counties across Kansas. These clinics were "marvels of organization and must have taken considerable boldness and endurance" (Zelhart & Jackson, 1983). Kelly also established a highly successful satellite system of four or five permanent branch clinics throughout Kansas. Thirty years later, a mental health center model similar in structure and operation to Kelly's clinic system was adopted nationally (Zelhart & Jackson, 1983).

Kelly's students had a great deal of respect and affection for him. They "remark[ed] on his humor, energy, concern for professional conduct, and intelligence. Many describe[d] him as charismatic or inspiring. Clearly George Kelly was a positive and powerful force in the lives of his students and his personality was a key element in the success of his programs" (Zelhart & Jackson, 1983, p. 145).

During World War II, Kelly served in the navy as an aviation psychologist in charge of training local civilian pilots. In 1946, he was appointed professor and director of clinical psychology at Ohio State University. The first task that he undertook upon arrival at Ohio State was to organize the graduate program in clinical psychology. This he accomplished with his characteristic excellence, and, within a few years, this program became one of the leading graduate training programs in the country (Maher, 1969).

At Ohio State, Kelly completed his major contributions to psychology. In 1955, the two-volume work, *The Psychology of Personal Constructs,* was published and gained immediate national and international recognition as a unique and major development in the study of personality (Maher, 1969). In 1965, he took a position at Brandeis University outside of Boston. He died suddenly of a heart attack only months later, in March 1966, leaving incomplete his work on a book in which he planned to collect and edit the papers he had presented and published in the previous decade.

Intellectual Antecedents

Widely read in the various disciplines and well-versed in classical philosophy, Kelly integrated all the influences that came to bear upon him in a highly personal manner. One can truly say that the psychology of personal constructs is an invention of George Kelly (Sechrest, 1977). Nevertheless, there were a number of thinkers whose writings Kelly found inspiring, if not because they opened up entirely new horizons for him then because they resonated with and encouraged the development of his own thinking.

More than most psychologists, perhaps, George Kelly's papers are themselves an autobiography of the man. In them, the reader will find the warmth, humor, and tolerance that characterized him so well to those who knew him best. (Maher, 1969, p. 3)

Moreno and Psychodrama

From his early work with drama students, Kelly had observed the powerful influence that trying on a role can have on a person's experience and behavior. Kelly was also familiar with Jacob Moreno's (1972) work in *Psychodrama,* a method of psychotherapy in which patients enact emotionally significant events in their lives instead of simply talking about them (Blatner, 1988; Kahn, 1964). Moreno viewed spontaneity in action as a major factor that is important to bringing about new learning and integration (Blatner, 1988).

In his own work with students, Kelly observed that taking on a role allows a person to act with a spontaneity that his or her own self-image often does not permit. Once when coaching a cast for the play, *The Enemy,* Kelly chose an extremely shy, inhibited, and socially awkward young man to play the part of a shell-shocked Austrian soldier. To everyone's surprise, the young man did exceedingly well in this role. He seemed to become another person, someone intimately familiar with the trauma of shell shock. Kelly wondered whether the young man had traumatic experiences of his own which "needed to be elaborated within the protective limits of a rehearsal situation" (1955, p. 363).

Kelly's observations, backed by Moreno's work, led him to reject the notion of the human personality as a fixed, substantial entity that predisposes and sets limits to what a person can do. The opposite seemed to be true: What a person does determines what he or she is. Trying on a new role means exploring new ways of acting, which in turn open up new ways of experiencing and being. The concept of role became central to Kelly's theory of how people construe themselves in relation to others.

The Philosophy of Pragmatism

Kelly was familiar with the writings of the great American philosophers, Charles Pierce, William James, and John Dewey. The names of these three are associated with the uniquely American brand of philosophy known as *pragmatism*. Pragmatism emphasizes the practical, experiential nature of truth and eschews abstract, metaphysical speculation. John Dewey's notion—understanding is a matter of anticipating events that might confirm one's belief—especially appealed to Kelly.

The Conduct of Scientific Inquiry

Kelly had a great appreciation for the disciplined manner of scientific inquiry. The systematic, rigorous bent of the scientific approach resonated with the logical, rational style that characterized his own thinking and writing. But his respect for the scientific did not confine him to a narrowly conceived notion about what constitutes scientific method. More generally, it was the scientist's quest for knowledge and understanding that appealed to Kelly. He saw in this quest a profound expression of the human personality. For him, the methods of science were the scientist's constructs. As such, they could never fully explain the personality of the scientist, nor could they fully account for the personality of the research subject, who has his or her own constructs. However, for Kelly, this peculiar state of affairs was no cause for alarm. On the contrary, it presented psychology with an important caveat: It cautioned psychology to remain flexible and open in both theory and approach—a position that Kelly regarded as the hallmark of good science.

Major Concepts

Constructive Alternativism

Kelly rejected the notion that there are absolute, final truths about events in the world. He thought that there are various views or interpretations of events, and none have a monopoly on truth. This is because no person

Both arguments and evidence have been presented in recent years to leave little doubt that almost all methods of psychological enquiry—interviewing, testing, experimentation—are forms of human *relationships*. . . .what is implied is that we come to regard people who take part in our experiments as human beings *just like us*, the experimenters, *even while they are helping us with our research*. This really can be alarming because it means accepting that subjects, like experimenters, can and do continuously think, theorize, anticipate, experiment, react, create, rebel and comply just like everyone else—and what is more, they can and often do all these things in any experiment the psychologist designs. (Mair, 1970, pp. 157, 158–159)

can access truth or reality without viewing or *construing* it in some fashion. Kelly called this position *constructive alternativism*. This does not mean that constructions of truth or reality are arbitrary, or that people are locked up in their own subjective worlds disconnected from other people. Rather, people connect with the world and other people precisely by way of their personal constructs, and some constructs accomplish this more effectively than others.

One implication of constructive alternativism is that all interpretations are subject to revision. This applies to the constructs of individuals coping with their lives as much as to those of scientists trying to make sense of the world. It is a sobering realization that calls for humility and open-mindedness in assessing any views or theories, one's own as well as those of others.

Another implication of constructive alternativism is that an individual has virtually unlimited options for construing his or her life in ways that allow for change and growth. Constructive alternativism conveys a spirit of confident optimism and faith in human capabilities. All persons are capable of changing or replacing their constructions of events and of themselves. In this capacity lies the possibility of freedom: A person's behavior is free to the extent that his or her constructs are flexible or permeable enough to permit new ways of construing events.

Man-the-Scientist and Reflexivity

According to Kelly, ordinary persons and scientists are alike in that both try to make sense of the world by forming hypotheses about how it works, and then they test their hypotheses and revise them if they do not work. He considered human behavior to be essentially a question, an anticipation, or a hypothesis about what any given situation might hold. (Kelly, 1969a).

The psychological study of personality according to Kelly is the study of how persons construe their lives. Like subjects being studied, psychologists construe the human personality in an open-ended way, always ready to revise or replace their constructs as needed. When the psychologist remembers that he or she is first and foremost a person engaged in construction, the flexibility and openness to alternative constructions comes naturally. Perhaps because he saw the openness of constructive alternativism as such a fundamental feature of reality, Kelly was quite undogmatic and not given to polemics in defense of his own particular constructs about personality.

Kelly's notion of what he called *man-the-scientist* highlights a peculiar feature of the scientific method when it is directed to the psychological study of personality. This is called *reflexivity*, which assumes that the psychologist is a person who is engaged in the same kind of activity as is the person who is being studied.

The problem that arises from this notion can be illustrated by the analogy of a hand trying to grab itself, or the eye trying to see itself. The usual

We take the stand that there are always some alternative constructions available to choose among in dealing with the world. No one needs to paint himself into a corner; no one needs to be completely hemmed in by circumstances; no one needs to be the victim of his biography. (Kelly, 1955, p. 15)

Kelly's heresy was to allow the psychologist's subject all the capacities of his investigators. (Sotter, 1970, p. 229)

solution to this problem has been to devise methods or theories that are presumed to be objective in the sense of not being dependent on the personal constructs of the psychologist (i.e., an artificial contraption of some kind is set up to grab the hand). Kelly views this solution as misguided and doomed to failure in that it attempts to comprehend the human personality from the outside without coming to terms with the reflexivity of the endeavor. The reflexivity cannot be avoided due to the inescapable fact that psychologists in the final analysis are engaged in construing just as much as the individuals being studied. Rather than viewing reflexivity as a problem, Kelly embraces it wholeheartedly as a feature of great interest and relevance to psychological inquiry.

The Theory in Twelve Statements

Kelly was meticulous in the articulation of his theory and developed his own terminology with original definitions. The theory of personal constructs is stated in twelve densely packed statements, consisting of a *fundamental postulate* and eleven *corollaries,* which are partly derivatives of and partly elaborations on the postulate. The rest of Kelly's theoretical writings constitute further delineation and expansion of these twelve statements. Kelly's (1955) statements are presented verbatim, accompanied by a brief interpretation, as follows.

1. Fundamental Postulate

A person's processes are psychologically channelized by the ways in which he anticipates events (p. 46).

This is the fundamental postulate for the psychology of personal constructs. It begins with placing the person at the center of things. By *person* Kelly means nothing more nor less than what we ordinarily mean when we say, "[S]omeone we know, or would like to know—such as you or myself" (Kelly, 1966). The person is viewed by Kelly as an event or a process that expresses his or her personality in unique ways of being, by talking and acting in the world. How the personality expresses itself through these myriad ways is psychology's task to understand. According to Kelly, theorizing about biological, social, or unconscious factors outside of the expression of personality sheds little light on how it is conveyed and is therefore irrelevant to the task of psychology.

The term *channelized* in the basic postulate acknowledges that once it is granted that a process is in motion, its direction needs to be specified. Threfore, the process is channelized "in ways of anticipating events" and is thus directed toward the future. People are forever attempting to get a preview of what the world has in store for them. "Anticipation is both the push and pull of the psychology of personal constructs" (Kelly, 1955, p. 49). Usually, the person's subsequent experience either confirms or disconfirms the way in which he or she anticipated the events. The anticipation of events is, in a way, a search for confirmation or disconfirmation. Superficially, this looks like the behavioristic theory of reinforcement in which confirmation of anticipated events works as positive reinforcement and disconfirmation as punishment. But Kelly emphatically rejects the existence of any parallel between personal construct theory and behaviorism. Human beings seek confirmation of even the most feared and seemingly punitive events, and, by the same token, they seek disconfirmation of their most cherished dreams. In such cases, punishment would seem to shape behavior in unexpected ways, providing grounds for reconstruction and creative, new endeavors. Kelly's postulate envisions the nature of life "in its outreach for the future, and not in its perpetuation of its prior conditions or in its incessant reverberation of past events" (Kelly, 1966, p. 11).

2. Construction Corollary

A person anticipates events by construing their replications (p. 50).

Given that life is a process, no two events are exactly the same. What is anticipated are events that are like the ones that have happened in the past. But an event that is like another is also *different* from various others. Here, Kelly is stating the basic principle of construing, which is a process whereby something is perceived as similar to some things and different from others. "Under a system that provides only for the identification of similarities the world dissolves into homogeneity; under one that provides only for differentiation it is shattered into hopelessly unrelated fragments" (Kelly, 1966, p. 11). Identification by similarity and differentiation are both necessary.

3. Individuality Corollary

Persons differ from each other in their construction of events (p. 55).

It is highly unlikely that two persons construct events in exactly the same way. Kelly doubts that any two persons put their construction systems together even in terms of the same logical relationships. But far from finding this to be a cause for worry, Kelly finds it to be an intriguing possibility, "for it seems to open the door to more advanced systems of thinking and inference. . . . Certainly, it suggests that scientific research can rely more heavily on individual imagination than it usually dares" (Kelly, 1966, p. 12).

4. Organization Corollary

Each person characteristically evolves, for his convenience in anticipating events, a construction system embracing ordinal relationships between constructs (p. 56).

Somehow, the numerous constructs a person has must fit into a reasonably coherent whole that enables the person to function and meet life's challenges. The organization corollary states that this involves assigning priorities to the constructs. Some constructs are more fundamental than others. But the doubts, confusions, and deep existential dilemmas that are the common fare of human experience suggest that logic is not all that goes into establishing priorities among the constructs.

Specifically, commitments may take priority over opportunities, political affiliations may turn a person from compassion to power, or moral imperatives may render a person insensitive to the plight of the petty criminal. These, notes Kelly, "are the typical prices men pay to escape inner chaos" (1966, p. 12).

5. Dichotomy Corollary

A person's construction system is composed of a finite number of dichotomous constructs (p. 59).

The dichotomy corollary addresses a key feature of a construct. Namely, it draws a black-and-white distinction that admits no degrees or shadings of gray. This, according to Kelly, is the most frequently misunderstood construct of his theory, because it appears to suggest rigidly categorical thinking. The dichotomy corollary, however, does not describe thinking but instead describes the structure of a construct that may be employed in thinking. A helpful analogy might be a fork in a road on a map, indicating a right and a left turn. Looking at this map for direction, one finds no degrees of left turn or degrees of right turn. One must choose one way or the other. Conceivably, one could decide to move off of the road altogether, which would amount to construing the situation in a new way. Constructs serve as guidelines for discriminating, identifying, understanding, and anticipating events. They are contrasts that one perceives among events, ways of seeing one element as similar to another and different from the rest. (Construing and the nature of constructs will be discussed at greater length in a later section.)

6. Choice Corollary

A person chooses for himself that alternative in a dichotomized construct through which he anticipates the greater possibility for extension and definition of his system (p. 64).

The choice here refers to the alternatives expressed in the construct, or, in the earlier analogy, the right or left fork of the road. The choice therefore has to do with the person's behavior, not with the events or objects that follow once the choice has been made. Only after changing themselves, which means altering their constructs, can people change events around them. Of course, changing one's construct is no guarantee that one's objectives in the world will be automatically accomplished.

7. Range Corollary

A construct is convenient for the anticipation of a finite range of events only (p. 68).

No single construct covers everything that happens in a person's experience. Surprise, puzzlement, bewilderment, and wonder are possible precisely due to the fact that, as Kelly says, the geometry of the mind is an incomplete system. A construct is a distinction that has the effect of distributing objects or events impermanently by way of two associations. It has a *focus* of convenience—a set of objects with which it works especially well. It also has a *range* of convenience that is somewhat large, over which it can work reasonably well.

8. Experience Corollary

A person's construction system varies as he successively construes the replications of events (p. 72).

Constructs are not necessarily fixed but can be modified as they are repeatedly imposed upon events in a person's experience. But the modification of constructs is not something that happens automatically or through mechanisms like conditioning or reinforcement, as the behaviorists would suggest. To change or not to change one's constructs is ultimately a matter of personal choice. This could not be otherwise, for in Kelly's theory, the person, rather than some mechanism outside of the person, is the originator of constructs. How this choice is exercised and whether it is exercised at all has far-reaching consequences for a person's life.

If these constructions are never altered, a person's life may amount to merely a sequence of parallel events that have no psychological impact on his or her life. But if a person engages in what is perceived as the most intimate event of all—unwavering investment in the enterprise, then the outcome, to the extent that it differs from his or her expectation or enlarges upon it, dislodges the person's self-construction. In recognizing the inconsistency between people's anticipation and the outcome, they concede a discrepancy between what they were and what they are. A succession of such investments and dislodgements constitutes the human experience (Kelly, 1966, p. 18).

9. Modulation Corollary

The variation in a person's construction system is limited by the permeability of the constructs within whose range of convenience the variants lie (p. 77).

While people are capable of revising their construction systems, this capacity has limitations. *Permeability* refers to the ease with which a construct can be applied to new events, or its capacity to be used as a referent for novel events. In Kelly's terms, an *impermeable* construct that addresses, for example, the notion of God spells out all things holy in a concrete and literal fashion. Any new ideas that emerge are likely to be excluded from this notion. In a *permeable* construct, this notion of God maintains a focus on all things holy, but the specific targets of that focus—the holy things per se—are open to interpretation. The more permeable the construct, the better it can accommodate new events and allow the person to remain open to experience. On the other hand, an excessively permeable construct is like a sieve that lets through everything and catches hold of nothing. A person who thinks in vague, global terms has excessively permeable constructs, and therefore has difficulty being clear and precise.

10. Fragmentation Corollary

A person may successively employ a variety of construction subsystems which are inferentially incompatible with each other (p. 83).

This corollary simply acknowledges the fact that logic usually plays a rather minor role in the lives of people. A person's responses to events are not necessarily consistent or inferable from other responses he or she has made. Love can unexpectedly turn to jealousy and from jealousy to hate. This kind of irrationality, Kelly notes, is not necessarily a bad thing. People who are wholly integrated are always just themselves, holding surprises for neither themselves nor others who know them. However, it is often the incompatible fragments of people's construction systems that make them great (Kelly, 1966, p. 20).

11. Commonality Corollary

To the extent that one person employs a construction of experience which is similar to that employed by another, his psychological processes are similar to those of the other person (p. 90).

This corollary refers to the construction of *experience,* rather than events. It addresses the possibility that two people who may have confronted quite different events nevertheless end up with similar constructions of their experiences. This accounts for the kind of meeting of the minds that sometimes occurs between people and may become a basis for a lasting friendship or the feeling of being kindred spirits.

12. Sociality Corollary

To the extent that one person construes the construction processes of another, he may play a role in a social process involving the other person (p. 95).

The sociality corollary establishes the basis for Kelly's view of empathy and social relationships. Behavioral psychologists, and often ordinary people as well, construe other people's observable behavior and respond to them on the basis of such constructions. Other people are then regarded as automatons, or puzzles to be pieced together. On the other hand, to recognize the humanity of another person as being no different from one's own is to view the other as a construer of his or her own experience. Relating meaningfully to other people is a matter of understanding how they construe themselves and their world. This has something to do with empathy, the capacity to put oneself in the shoes of another person, or assume the *role* of another. The notion of role has far reaching implications to the construction of self and social relationships and the issue of guilt in Kelly's theory.

Constructs and Construing

The fundamental postulate and the corollaries describe how construction works in people's experience of the world and of themselves. But what exactly are constructs and what is meant by construing? Let us now take a closer look at these key concepts.

Construing involves interpretation, or "erecting a structure within the framework of which the substance takes shape or assumes meaning" (Kelly, 1955, p. 50). Regularity or predictability is an important feature of meaning that has to do with repetition and familiarity. "To construe is to hear the whisper of the recurrent themes in the events that reverberate around us" (p. 76). But the emphasis in Kelly's theory is on the anticipation of events, not on their containment. A meaningful construct embraces the future rather than merely cataloging the past. In this way, constructs connect the past with the future and provide a sense of temporal continuity.

Constructs form the bridge between the private psychological world and the public world of behavior and interaction with others. Kelly (1955) describes constructs as patterns or templates that a person creates and then attempts to superimpose or fit over the world. They are not representations or symbolizations of events but ways of coping with events.

Constructs are ways in which individuals organize experiences according to similarities and differences. *Aggressiveness-gentleness* is Kelly's own illustration that describes the structure of a construct. The construct has two poles, the *likeness end* and the *contrast end*. The things or events that are abstracted by the construct are *elements*. For example, when a person makes a judgment that Mary and Alice are gentle but Jane is aggressive, "three elements, Mary, Alice and Jane are abstracted by the aggressiveness-gentleness construct." A minimum of three elements is necessary for the structure and operation of a construct. This is because "a construct is a way in which at least two elements are similar and contrast with a third" (Kelly, 1955, p. 61).

Usually, only part of the construct is expressed explicitly while the rest of it remains implicit. For example, in the statement, "Mary and Alice are among the gentlest people I know," only the similarity pole of the construct, gentleness, is explicitly stated or *emergent,* whereas the contrast pole, aggressiveness, is submerged or *implicit* in the context. Sometimes the submerged pole is deeply buried, so to speak, and difficult for the person to bring into awareness. For example, a psychotherapy client with a hysterical inclination and a pollyanna complex may insist, "All people I have ever known are very gentle!" This client is likely to be unaware of the aggressiveness pole of the construct he or she is using.

A point that needs to be stressed about constructs is that the way they actually occur in psychological life is not necessarily, or even usually, as articulate and intellectual as Kelly's discussion of them is. Kelly would have been the first to admit that, no doubt, the terse, logically rigorous style with which he presents his theory reflects his own personal manner of construing concepts and is most decidedly not a literal representation of how things are. On the other hand, says Kelly:

> If I had been able to say what I have said in metaphor or hyperbole I might have left the impression that a construct had something to do with feeling or with formless urges too fluid to be pinned down by

labels. But personal construct theory is no more a cognitive theory than it is an affective or a conative one. There are grounds for distinction that operate in one's life that seem to elude verbal expression. We see them in infants, as well as in our own spontaneous aversions and infatuations. These discriminative bases are no less constructs than those the reader may have been imagining during the reading of the preceding paragraphs. (Kelly, 1966, p. 15)

Thus, personal constructs are not all "in the head." They are just as much "in the heart" and "in the gut." Construction occurs even when no verbal labels are available. Infants and presumably also animals engage in such preverbal, or nonverbal, construction. Needs, motivations, emotions, and learning are all aspects of the construction process.

Core Structure and Core Role

Each person has within his or her construction system a core structure through which the person understands the most fundamental features of reality, of the social world, and of the self. This core structure is highly resistant to change and gives expression to the person's basic outlook on life.

Within the core structure are those frames that enable one to predict and control the essential interactions of oneself with other persons and with societal groups. These constitute the person's *core role* (Kelly, 1955, p. 502). How the core role develops is explained by Kelly as follows. A child construes herself as belonging to a family. She construes the behaviors—and as she matures, perhaps the constructs as well—of the other members of the family. She then enacts her presumed part in relation to this construction. She comes to identify herself in the practical terms of this enactment, much before she has the words to say "who she really is" (p. 503). Thus, the more basic features of the core role exist in terms of preverbal constructs.

This notion of core role leads to an interesting interpretation of *guilt* that is notably different from those proposed by psychodynamic theorists. Kelly (1955) defines guilt as follows. "Perception of one's apparent dislodgement from his core role structure constitutes the experience of guilt" (p. 502). The previous example illustrates how the experience of guilt can come about. A child's notion of herself, which reflects her core role, is that she belongs to mother and father and therefore behaves in a prescribed manner. One day, the child (or later, the grown woman) may discover that she is not acting as her parents' child (or what she feels to be decent, proper, or good behavior). According to Kelly, this discovery can go so deep as to affect the person's identity: The person feels as though she is cast out of her core role. Hence, she experiences a level of anxiety far out of proportion to the particular actions that may trigger the guilt.

Further, Kelly's interpretation of guilt explains why certain people, deemed by society as antisocial, might not experience guilt, even after grossly infringing upon other people's rights or well-being. Such people may have as children depended on parents whom they construed as being animal-like. Such parents were only concerned with the bare-bones care of their children, providing food, shelter, clothing, and nothing more. Children construe and enact their roles accordingly, as they grow up in relation to the people they presume their parents to be. Later, when other people point out to them that they are selfish, cruel, and immoral, they may readily agree with these people. However, they do not experience guilt, for these interpretations are not incompatible with the core role structure that such children have developed.

As these examples show, guilt is an affliction of a genuinely social person. It signals a threat to the person's identity as a social being.

Dynamics

Psychological Growth

Personal construct theory envisions the human personality as fluid and open to change and growth through transcendence of the self and what are construed as its current possibilities (Epting & Amerikaner, 1980). Satisfaction or even self-fulfillment cannot adequately define the goal of human life, for these are themselves subject to construction and hence revision and reconstruction. Kelly never loses sight of the fact that for the person as the construer of his or her life and goals, the possibilities for change and growth are always exceeded by the range of the constructs.

Aggressiveness

Personal construct theory celebrates the spirit of inquiry and adventure that turns adversity into opportunity. The theory revises and expands constructs when events fail to confirm them, rather than discard the constructs. Kelly defines aggressiveness as the active elaboration of one's perceptual field (1955, p. 508). As such, it connotes a positive quality in one's approach to life and something that is essential to a person's growth. Unlike psychodynamic theorists, Kelly does not associate aggressiveness with any negative connotations such as destructiveness, hostility, or a drive toward death.

Each person is more aggressive in some ways than in others. And the ways in which people are aggressive depend on the anxieties that are associated with these various forms of aggression. In their aggressive moments, people may actually seek out certain aspects of their anxiety and fuss about them, testing out constructs one after another, rapidly abandoning those that do not fit until perhaps eventually finding one that does. But when the anxiety mounts to an intolerable intensity, the person may completely abandon the construction process and retreat into what seem secure and unchallenged areas. According to Kelly, "the areas of one's aggression are those in which there are anxieties he can face" (1955, p. 509).

People taking on a difficult challenge can serve to illustrate Kelly's point about aggression and anxiety. For example, two friends are trying out for a college sports team. Waiting for the coach, they wrestle and banter with each other. They might say that they are "just warming up," but they eventually respond with excessive aggression, due to the anxiety they are experiencing. In a different situation, a student is sitting quietly, waiting to enter the stage for her senior music recital. She is frozen with stage fright and mechanically repeats in her mind the parts she has learned to play. In this case, her anxiety level is so high that she is forced to fall back on old constructs.

Loosening, Tightening, and the Creativity Cycle

The *Creativity Cycle* precipitates change in a person's construction system. The cycle begins with *loosened* construction and ends with *tightened* and validated construction (Kelly, 1955, p. 528). Loose construction is like a rough sketch that may be preliminary to a carefully drafted design. The sketch permits flexible interpretation because particular features are not yet precisely placed. Dreaming exemplifies loose construction. An example of tight construction would be the carefully drafted design in which each feature is precisely placed, leaving little room for ambiguity or alternative interpretation.

According to Kelly, people who always use tight construction may be productive but they cannot be creative. They cannot produce anything that has not already been blueprinted. "Creativity always arises out of preposterous thinking. If the creative person mumbles the first part of a Creativity Cycle out loud, he is likely to get sharp criticism from everyone who is within earshot" (1955, p. 529). For this reason, many creative individuals keep their loose constructions to themselves, which is not difficult to do as such constructions are often preverbal in nature anyway.

If people who use only tight constructions cannot be creative, neither can people who use only loose constructions. Such people, according to Kelly, would never get past the preliminary stage of mumbling to themselves, let alone progress to the level at which their ideas could really be put to the test. In creativity, as in other kinds of human activity, optimal functioning is a matter of balance. The creative person must have the important capacity to move from loosening to tightening.

Creativity is not the exclusive possession of those who have, or aspire to have, accomplishments in arts, literature, or other creative fields. Creativity abounds in human growth of all kinds, for it is the process whereby individuals can free themselves from rigid, constricted ways of construing and open themselves up to new horizons and ways of being in the world.

Obstacles to Growth

Fear and Threat

The obstacles to growth are usually manifested in the very situations that are opportunities for growth. Such situations call for a change in a person's construction system. According to Kelly, the diagnostic constructs of threat, fear, and anxiety are all essentially constructs having to do with the transitions in one's construction system.

Threat is the awareness of an imminent comprehensive change in one's core structures. Facing one's imminent death, the loss of someone who is construed as essential to one's own survival or well-being, or the loss of wealth or social status that is construed as vital to one's sense of identity, are examples of situations that threaten one's core structures with a comprehensive change.

Fear is like threat, except that fear is a transient, incidental construct rather than a lasting, comprehensive one that seems to take over. An example that illustrates the distinction between threat and fear might be a woman who, while driving in a car, indulges in wild daydreaming and all sorts of crazy, impulsive thoughts. She may feel threatened by the prospect of acting on them. But if suddenly she narrowly misses crashing into another car, she is confronted with a specific situation that arouses fear in her. In both cases, there is a prospect of imminent restructuring of a core structure, but in the second case, this is incidental and passes once the prospect of a crash is no longer imminent. The intensity of the *fear* may, in this incident, feel similar proportionally to that of the threat, but what distinguishes it from a threat is the short-lived narrow variety of events involved.

Anxiety

Kelly defines anxiety as "the recognition that the events with which one is confronted lie outside the range of convenience of one's construct system" (1955, p. 495). This involves a sense of losing a grip on things, or a loss of control.

Loosening is a way in which people can protect themselves against anxiety. As one's constructs become looser, they can be stretched to cover a wider variety of events. Of course, one eventually pays the price if this loosening results in vagueness and incoherence. A person who is aware of the price he or she is paying becomes increasingly anxious; this then means that the protective maneuver is not working. On the positive side, such a person is likely to seek help for the anxiety and benefit from psychotherapy. However, a person who is not aware of the impaired functioning of his or her loosened construction system may not seem to experience anxiety. In extreme cases, this leads to serious communication problems and can ultimately reult in a diagnosis of schizophrenia.

Tightening can also be used as a defense against anxiety. Rather than stretching one's constructs, one may go the route of excluding events that do not fit and developing the precision and detail of one's construction system to such an extent that it "covers all situations." Therefore, one feels in control without having to deal with the nebulous and undefined things of life. A compulsive person whose life follows carefully worked out procedures and is excessively organized, as if into compartments, is most certainly using tight construction to an extreme as a defense against anxiety.

Hostility

Kelly's interpretation of hostility is unique and has significant implications for psychotherapy. Hostility, for Kelly, has nothing to do with aggression or even with the intent to do harm to others. Rather, it is defined as "the continued effort to extort validational evidence in favor of a type of social prediction which has already proven itself a failure" (1955, p. 510). Hostile individuals may insist on being right about something in the face of circumstances that show them to be wrong. But more than insist, they attempt to enforce their constructs upon the world by altering the circumstances to fit their constructs. In trying to alter these circumstances, they may use either overt force or covertly undermining tactics. Usually, the circumstances in question represent another person whose behavior does not fit the hostile person's constructs. "The other person is the victim, not so much of the hostile person's fiendishly destructive impulses, as of his frantic and unrealistic efforts to collect on a wager he has already lost" (1955, p. 511).

Husbands acting as tyrants by abusing their wives and children are obviously hostile individuals. Once this kind of hostility is distinguished from aggressive or destructive impulses, it becomes possible to see the other subtler forms of hostility. Kelly's example of "loving" hostility is a mother who treats her son as if he were her doll, and when the child behaves in an undoll-like manner, she mildly and sweetly reproaches him, shaping, through overprotectiveness, the child's doll-like behavior.

Structure

Body and Mind

Personal construct theory focuses on the viewpoint of the individual; specifically, how this individual construes himself or herself in relation to the world. Therefore, the body as a substantial entity outside of such construction does not enter into the theory. On the other hand, how a person construes his or her own body in terms of such constructs as, say, *healthy-sick* or *strong-weak* can be very important to a person's outlook and well-being.

Just as Kelly refuses to view the body as a physical entity outside of the person's construction of it, he also refrains from theorizing about the mind as a psychological entity or domain that exists independently of personal constructions. Theorizing about how the human mind works or how it relates to the body would amount to nothing more and nothing less than indulging in one's own personal construction. However, personal construct theory is concerned with how people construe their minds and bodies in their lives, and its focus is in the study of this construction process. In this way, personal construct theory is similar to the phenomenological approach in psychology.

Nothing which happens in the brain can be described except in terms supplied by the mind. (Mumford, 1967)

Kelly would say, to find the seat of the mind do not look into the brain, look at those responsible for it. (Sotter, 1970, p. 237)

Social Relationships

Social relationships are a vital part of a person's construction system, as is the testing out of one's constructs within the social system. The communality and sociality constructs reflect Kelly's view of people as essentially social beings who not only respond to one another's misfortune, but are capable of very deep and empathic feelings for one another. Relationships based on the intimate understanding of how other people experience the world should be the basis for society, according to Kelly.

Will

True to his holistic approach, Kelly does not treat will as a distinct entity or attribute that by itself accounts for the construction process. Will is usually understood as some kind of motivating force that sets a process in motion or keeps it going, sometimes even in the face of greater obstacles. For Kelly, the construction process is already in motion and is intrinsically active, because this is what it means to be alive. There is no need to posit a separate factor or process to explain how the anticipation of events begins or what keeps this anticipation going. One might say that life itself keeps it going. Engagement in the world and the commitment to enacting one's anticipation of events, which is so essential for the expansion of constructions and hence for the growth of the person, is manifested in an integral component of the construction process called *will*.

Emotions

Like will, emotions are integrally involved in the anticipation of events and their construction. The construction process is not exclusively, nor perhaps even primarily, cognitive but incorporates emotional components. Some constructions are felt and acted on without ever coming to conscious awareness.

Intellect

Like emotion and will, the intellect is another integral component of the construction process. Accordingly, Kelly is highly critical of attempts to measure intelligence as a distinct trait. The IQ test, in Kelly's view, is a psychologist's diagnostic construct that has little utility for adults and might even hamper learning in children. In the case of children, for Kelly, IQ test results encourage teachers to pigeonhole their students, rather than provide data that could enhance learning.

Self

In the theory of personal constructs, the construer of events is central. But Kelly does not think in terms of a construing entity outside of the construction system. Kelly does envision the self as construer.

The self is a construct. Perhaps more than any other, this construct has a controlling effect on the person, as witnessed by the remarkable variations in people's behavior and experience. This behavior has little to do with circumstance and everything to do with how people view themselves. The controlling effect of the self is a testimony to the power of construction, not an indication that there is some kind of substantial entity or mechanism acting to determine the construct. This view of Kelly's is reminiscent of the Buddhist conception of the self as a process, consisting of a series of perceptions and notions that are devoid of substance.

The self construct has to do with one's core role. Even though the construction of this role goes very deep, it is not static or unchangeable. For Kelly, the role, even the core role that one identifies with, refers to an ongoing activity. Thus, the self is fluid and changeable, not something that binds the person to biology any more than it does to immutable, unconscious dynamics.

Clinical Applications and Therapy

The Rep Test

Kelly developed a test for eliciting and measuring personal constructs in the clinical setting known as *The Role Construct Repertory Test,* or *Rep Test*. An extension of this test that came to be more widely used for research purposes is the Rep Grid Test (Bannister & Mair, 1968).

The procedure involves giving people a list of role titles. The list could be tailored to the situation of the individuals taking the test, so that they could readily identify significant people in their lives to fit each role title. The ways in which the people in the roles are construed are then unraveled and analyzed through a systematic procedure.

The role title list, according to Kelly, represents the cast of characters in the person's life, and the test reveals the person's casting of the parts in the play in which he or she plays the leading role (Kelly, 1955, p. 237). This test can help the client gain insight into his or her important relationships. It is also a tool for exploring the nature of the client's constructs (e.g., finding how permeable or impermeable they are).

Fixed-role Therapy

Personal construct theory views most forms of psychological suffering and maladjustment as involving faulty or no-longer-relevant role constructs of oneself and other people.

Fixed-role therapy is an innovative clinical application of the theory. It is based on the notion that revising or replacing less-than-optimal role constructs can lead to improvement in the person's sense of well-being and in a person's relationship with others. The purpose of fixed-role therapy is to help devise better role constructs and provide a safe environment for trying them out.

Gradually my clients taught me that a symptom was an issue one expresses through the act of being his present self, not a malignancy that fastens itself upon a man. (Kelly, 1969a, p. 19)

Personal Reflection

Your Personal Constructs

Explore your own personal construction of significant people in your life by using the repertory approach as follows:

1. Reproduce on a sheet of paper the Role Construct Grid shown in Figure 11.1. Have 11 index cards or slips of paper available.

2. Write the name of a person you know for each of the 11 role titles shown in the grid on the card or slips of paper. If there is no person in your life who plays one of the 11 roles (i.e., if you have no brother or sister), use someone else who comes close to playing that role in your life. Use each name only once.

3. Shuffle the names and randomly pick three. In what way are two of the people alike, and in what way are they different from the third? Your answer (e.g., kind/cruel, friendly/unfriendly) is a construct through which you relate yourself to these persons and them to one another.

4. On the grid, write your answer (the construct) next to number 1 in the Constructs column.

5. Pick another set of three names and repeat the procedure, writing the construct next to number 2 in the Constructs column. Repeat this procedure for various combinations of three names.

Compare your constructs with a friend or another student.

Did you use several or only a few constructs? How permeable are they? Could you develop new constructs? In what way has your understanding of these roles changed as a result of your exploration?

Self	Mother	Father	Brother	Sister	Boy/Girl Friend	Best Friend	Exfriend	Teacher (of this class)	Boss	Neighbor		Constructs
												1.
												2.
												3.
												4.
												5.
												6.
												7.
												8.
												9.
												10.

Figure 11.1 Role Construct Grid
(Adapted from Chambers & Epting, 1985)

In their daily lives, people are reluctant to try out new ways of being with themselves and with others for a number of reasons. They may have a realistic fear of the punitive consequences that follow when they fail to live up to other people's expectations. This disconfirmation of their self construct undermines their sense of identity and can be very threatening. But enacting a role that both the client and the therapist know to be a fabrication can feel very different. The protective mask of make-believe is crucial for the success of fixed-role therapy. According to Kelly, it provides the safety of a controlled laboratory environment in which the client, like the scientist, can test out his or her hypotheses without fear of the consequences should the experiment fail.

Writing the Fixed-role Sketch

The fixed-role sketch is a crucial element in the therapy. It consist of a written piece, several paragraphs in length, that provides a character description of a person the client is to enact as his or her new role. Before the description is produced by the therapist, the client is asked to provide a character sketch written in the third person. The client's character sketch is then carefully analyzed by the therapist and, based on the analysis, the fixed-role sketch is composed.

The following considerations are important in writing the sketch:

1. *Development of a major theme other than correction of minor faults.* After some experimentation with the fixed-role sketch, Kelly came to the conclusion that the client derived more therapeutic benefit from playing out a role that alters a major theme in the individual's construct of self than from attempts to correct only minor faults.

2. *The use of sharp contrast.* It is easier for a client to play a role that he or she believes to be opposite to his or her character than it is to play at slightly altering the way the person perceives himself or herself.

3. *Setting ongoing processes in motion rather than creating a new state.* The task of fixed-role therapy is to prepare the client to resume the natural developmental processes of which he or she is capable. As much as possible, the role to be played out should encourage movement within the client's existing constructs, making the client an agent of change.

4. *Testable hypotheses for the client.* The new role should not be merely an academic exercise, but it should have a wide range of implications to the anticipation of events in the client's everyday life, in this manner, allowing him or her to test the new role against reality.

5. *Emphasis upon role perceptions.* The role should be constructed so that it enables the client to incorporate other people's con-

struction systems, in this manner, deepening and facilitating the client's interpersonal relationships.

6. *Using the protective mask*. This only indirectly affects the writing of the sketch. The client is to be given the full protection of make-believe. Kelly notes that "this is probably man's oldest protective screen for reaching out into the unknown" (1955, p. 373).

Writing the fixed-role sketch, on Kelly's own admission, "taxes the ingenuity and perceptive capacity of the therapist far more than does the conduct of the interviews" (p. 373). After the clients have indicated their acceptance of the role as sketched, they are asked to play it out continuously over several weeks. Therapy sessions are scheduled for monitoring and encouraging the client's work and for dealing with issues that come up as a result of the role playing.

Personal Reflection —————————
—————————————— Write a Fixed-role Sketch

Explore new ways of experiencing yourself by sketching and acting a role.

Find a partner.

Write a character sketch of yourself, describing yourself as objectively as you can in the third person.

Give this sketch to your partner and, in collaboration with him or her, write a fixed-role sketch following Kelly's guidelines.

Do the same for your partner. Check with each other to make sure you are willing to act the roles.

Then try the roles out over a period of one week. Discuss your experiences.

Therapist

In Kelly's paradigm, the requirements for the therapist are specified in detail. These include acceptance of both the client and the hypothetical role the client will play. The therapist's role is not that of an authority figure, who judges the client's performance; rather, it is that of counselor, who helps the client resume the natural developmental processes he or she is capable of. The therapist must *never* convey to the client that he or she *should be* like the character sketched in the role. According to Kelly, a message of this sort could in one stroke wipe out the therapeutic power of the make believe exercise. Instead, the therapist should encourage the client to *just pretend* to be the character. Additional qualifications for the therapist include "some measure of verbal fluency and acting skill," the ability to convert generalized statements into concrete illustrations, and "a great deal of enthusiastic momentum."

Conclusion

Personal construct theory combines genuinely humanistic themes with a theory that is clearly and rigorously formulated enough to allow empirical testing of many of its implications. This is a rare combination, and it allows Kelly's theory to form a bridge between humanistic psychology and personality theory (Epting & Leitner, 1992). There is a remarkably coherent and fertile relationship between personal construct theory and its applications to research (Carr, 1980). The theory is flexible enough to allow for reconstruction and incorporation of a variety of techniques and approaches to therapy (Karst, 1980). Among these, Kelly's fixed-role therapy is a unique contribution. He enjoys great popularity among writers of personality texts, perhaps because students find the idea of role playing in therapy so engrossing and so different from other approaches.

Yet, Kelly has had a relatively small following, and those who know his work well generally feel that it has received less recognition than it merits (Bannister, 1970; Sechrest, 1977, p. 232). This may be partly due to his terse, logical, and deliberately unpoetic style of writing, which can be difficult to follow. Another reason may be the low profile that both Kelly and his followers have maintained in the literature. His theory has never been surrounded by the kind of heated controversy that, for example, still swirls around the theories of Freud and Skinner. Nevertheless, Kelly's theory has continued to inspire a steady flow of research and clinical applications, which are published in several books and in the *International Journal of Personal Construct Theory*.

Kelly was an original thinker whose ideas set him apart from the main theoretical currents of his field. He was an incisive critic of the mechanistic paradigm that underlies both behaviorism and contemporary information-processing psychology. From the perspective of personal construct psychology, this paradigm is but one of the ways—and a rather constricted way at that—in which the person (or the psychologist) construes the world and the methods for studying it. A comprehensive alternative that subsumes mechanistic psychology under its constructs, personal construct theory stands as a continuing challenge to modern psychological thinking. Kelly's celebration of reflexivity in psychological inquiry places him in the forefront of contemporary, post-modern thinking and of research as well.

The Theory Firsthand: Excerpt from "A Brief Introduction to Personal Construct Theory"

The following excerpt is taken from "A Brief Introduction to Personal Construct Theory," an essay that Kelly completed in 1966, shortly before his death.

The quality of psychological theory which George Kelly most esteemed was fertility. By this he did not mean simply hypothesis generating capacity. . . . He meant rather the capacity of a theory to inspire people, to move them to new ventures, to puzzle them into asking new questions. (Bannister, 1970, p. vii)

The Meaning of Events

Constructive alternativism stresses the importance of events. . . .

When we place a construction of our own upon a situation, and then pursue its implications to the point of expecting something to happen, we issue a little invitation to nature to intervene in our personal experience. If what we expect does happen, or appears to happen, our expectation is confirmed and we are likely to think that we must have had a pretty good slant on the trend of affairs, else we would have lost our bet. But if we think the matter over carefully, we may begin to have doubts. Perhaps a totally different interpretation would have led to an equally successful prediction; and it may, besides, have been more straightforward, or more consistent with our conscience. Or perhaps our vivid expectations overlaid our perception of what actually happened.

So, on second thought, even when events are reconciled with a construction, we cannot be sure that they have proved it true. There are always other constructions, and there is the lurking likelihood that some of them will turn out to be better. The best we can ever do is project our anticipations with frank uncertainty and observe the outcomes in terms in which we have a bit more confidence. But neither anticipation nor outcome is ever a matter of absolute certainty from the dark in which we mortals crouch. And, hence, even the most valuable construction we have yet contrived—even our particular notion of God Himself—is one for which we shall have to continue to take personal responsibility—at least until someone turns up with a better one. And I suspect he will! This is what we mean by constructive alternativism. Our view might even be called a philosophical position of epistemological responsibility.

The Conduct of Inquiry

. . . Constructive alternativism is . . . an invitation to immediate adventure. By not insisting on disproof as a precondition for initiative it saves a lot of wear and tear on nerves and it should release a great deal of scholarly manpower for more productive and less disputatious occupations.

So, under constructive alternativism, even the appearance of some objective certainty may be taken as a flagrant challenge to throw— without waiting for the courage that disillusionment provides—a new light on the very circumstances that make it seem so obvious. Yet constructive alternativism tells us also that the reconstructive enterprise may be forestalled even earlier in the sequence. If one cautiously insists that truth must be compiled and cross-validated in fragments before he ever ventures further in the human quest, he may never reach the point where he can sense the challenge of upending smug certainties. He will be so eager to nail down his bits of truth once and for all that he will never back off and treat himself to a fresh look.

Annotated Bibliography

Beck, A. T. (1972). *Depression: Causes and treatment.* Philadelphia, PA: University of Pennsylvania Press. (Originally published, 1967, as *Depression: Clinical, experimental, and theoretical aspects.*) Presents the cognitive perspective and reviews research on the treatment of depression.

————. (1976). *Cognitive therapy and the emotional disorders.* New York: International Universities Press. A clear and readable interpretation of various psychological disorders from the cognitive perspective, which also describes the principles of cognitive therapy for their treatment.

Kelly G. A. (1955). *The psychology of personal constructs, 2 Vols.* New York: Norton. Kelly's major work, comprising the theory as well as diagnostic and therapeutic applications of personal construct psychology.

————. (1963). *A theory of personality.* New York: Norton. A paperback edition of *The psychology of Personal Constructs,* comprising the first three chapters only.

Maher, B. (Ed.). (1969). *Clinical psychology and personality: The selected papers of George Kelly.* New York: John Wiley & Sons. A selection of articles on theoretical and applied topics written or presented by Kelly from 1957 until his death.

References

Anderson, J. R. (1985). *Cognitive psychology and its implications.* New York: W. H. Freeman.

Anderson, J. R., & Bower, G. H. (1973). *Human associative memory.* Washington, DC: Winston.

Bannister, D. (Ed.). (1970). *Perspectives in personal construct theory.* New York: Academic Press.

Bannister, D., & Mair, J. M. M. (1968). *The evaluation of personal constructs.* New York: N.Y. Academic Press.

Beck, A. T. (1961). A systematic investigation of depression. *Comprehensive Psychiatry, 2,* 163–170.

————. (1967). *Depression: Clinical, experimental and theoretical aspects.* New York: Harper & Row.

————. (1976). *Cognitive therapy and the emotional disorders.* New York: International Universities Press.

————. (1988). *Love is never enough*. New York: Harper & Row.

————. (1991). Cognitive therapy: A 30-year retrospective. *American Psychologist, 46*(4), 368–374.

Beck, A., & Emery, G., with Greenberg, R. (1985). *Anxiety disorders and phobias*. New York: Basic Books.

Beck, A., Rush, A. J., Shaw, B. F., & Emery, G. (1979). *Cognitive therapy of depression*. New York: Guilford Press.

Blatner, A. (1988). *Foundations of psychodrama: History, theory and practice*. New York: Springer.

Burns, D. D. (1980). *Feeling good: The new mood therapy*. New York: New American Library.

Carr, J. E. (1980). Personal construct theory and psychotherapy research. In A. W. Landfield & L. M. Leitner (Eds.), *Personal construct theory: Psychotherapy and personality* (pp. 233–270). New York: John Wiley & Sons.

Chambers, W., & Epting, F. (1985). Personality and personal construct logical consistency. *Psychological Reports, 57,* 1120.

Dreyfus, H. L. (1972). *What computers can't do*. New York: Harper & Row.

Ellis, A. (1962). *Reason and emotion in psychotherapy*. New York: Lyle Stuart.

————. (1971). *Growth through reason: Verbatim cases of rational-emotive therapy*. Hollywood, CA: Wilshire Books.

————. (1974). *Techniques for disputing irrational beliefs (DIB's)*. New York: Institute for Rational Living.

Ellis, A., & Harper, R. A. (1975). *A new guide to rational living*. Hollywood, CA: Wilshire Books.

Emery, G. (1981). *A new beginning*. New York: Simon & Schuster.

Epting, F. R., & Amerikaner, M. (1980). Optimal functioning: A personal construct approach. In A. W. Landfield & L. M. Leitner (Eds.), *Personal construct psychology: Psychotherapy and personality* (pp. 55–73). New York: John Wiley & Sons.

Epting, F. R., & Leitner, L. M. (1992). Humanistic psychology and personal construct theory. *The Humanistic Psychologist, 20*(2, 3), 243–259.

Folkman, S. (1984). Personal control and stress and coping processes: A theoretical analysis. *Journal of Personality and Social Psychology, 46*(4), 839–852.

Gunderson, K. (1971). *Mentality and machines*. Garden City, NY: Doubleday.

Harris, P. L. (1989). *Children and emotion: The development of psychological understanding*. Oxford, England: Blackwell.

Honeck, R. P., Case, T., & Firment, M. J. (1991). *Introductory readings for cognitive psychology*. Guilford, CT: The Dushkin Publishing Co.

Horowitz, M. J. (1979). *Stress response syndromes*. New York: Jason Aronson.

Izard, C. E. (1978). On the ontogenesis of emotion and emotion-cognition relationships in infancy. In M. Lewis & L. Rosenblum (Eds.), *The development of affect* (pp. 389–413). New York: Plenum.

————. (1984). Emotion-cognition relationships in human development. In C. E. Izard, J. Kagan, & R. B. Zajonc (Eds.), *Emotions, cognition and behavior* (pp. 17–37). New York: Cambridge University Press.

Johnson-Laird, P. N. (1977). Procedural semantics. *Cognition, 5,* 189–214.

Kahn, S. (1964). *Psychodrama explained.* New York: Philosophical Library.

Karst, T. O. (1980). The relationship between personal construct theory and psychotherapeutic techniques. In A. W. Landfield & L. M. Leitner (Eds.), *Personal construct psychology: Psychotherapy and personality* (pp. 166–184). New York: John Wiley & Sons.

Kelly, G. A. (1955). *The psychology of personal constructs (Vol. 1).* New York: W. W. Norton & Co.

————. (1969a). An autobiography of a theory. In B. Maher (Ed.), *Clinical psychology and personality: The selected papers of George Kelly* (pp. 46–65). New York: John Wiley & Sons.

————. (1969b). Ontological acceleration. In B. Maher (Ed.), *Clinical psychology and personality: The selected papers of George Kelly* (pp. 7–45). New York: John Wiley & Sons.

————. (1966). A brief introduction to personal construct theory. In D. Bannister (Ed.), *Perspectives in personal construct theory* (pp. 1–29). New York: Academic Press, 1970.

Labouvie-Vief, G., Hakim-Larson, J., DeVoe, M., & Schoeberlein, S. (1989). Emotions and self-regulation: A life-span view. *Human Development, 32,* 279–299.

Lachman, R., Lachman, J. L., & Butterfield, E. C. (1979). *Cognitive psychology and human information processing.* Hillsdale, New Jersey: Erlbaum.

Lazarus, R. S. (1966). *Psychological stress and the coping process.* New York: McGraw-Hill.

————. (1982). Thoughts on the relations between emotion and cognition. *American Psychologist, 37,* 1019–1024.

————. (1984). On the primacy of cognition. *American Psychologist, 39,* 124–129.

————. (1991a). Cognition and motivation in emotion. *American Psychologist, 46*(4), 352–367.

————. (1991b). *Emotion and adaptation.* New York: Oxford University Press.

Lazarus, R., & Folkman, S. (1984). *Stress, appraisal and coping.* New York: Springer.

Leventhal, H., & Scherer, K. (1987). The relationship of emotion to cognition: A functional approach to a semantic controversy. *Cognition and Emotion, 1,* 3–28.

Maher, B. (1969). Introduction. George Kelly: A brief biography. In B. Maher (Ed.), *Clinical psychology and personality: The selected papers of George Kelly* (pp. 1–3). New York: John Wiley & Sons.

Mair, J. M. M. (1970). Psychologists are human too. In D. Bannister (Ed.), *Perspectives in personal construct theory* (pp. 157–183). New York: Academic Press.

Mayer, R. E. (1981). *The promise of cognitive psychology*. San Francisco: W. H. Freeman.

McMullin, R. E. (1986). *Handbook of cognitive therapy techniques*. New York: W. W. Norton.

McMullin, R. E., & Casey, B. (1975). *Talk sense to yourself: A guide to cognitive restructuring therapy*. New York: Institute for Rational Emotive Therapy.

Miller, G. A., Galanter, E., & Pribram, C. (1960). *Plans and the structure of behavior*. New York: Henry Holt.

Moreno, J. (1972). *Psychodrama* (Vol. 1) (4th ed.). Boston: Beacon House.

Mumford, L. (1967). *The myth of the machine*. London: Secker & Warburg.

Neisser, U. (1967). *Cognitive psychology*. New York: Appleton-Century-Crofts.

———. (1976a). *Cognition and reality*. San Francisco, CA: Freeman & Co.

———. (1976b). General, academic, and artificial intelligence. In L. B. Resnick (Ed.), *The nature of intelligence*. New Jersey: Lawrence Erlebaum Associates.

———. (1990). Gibson's revolution. *Contemporary Psychology, 35,* 749–750.

Newell, A., Shaw, J. C., & Simon, H. (1958). Elements of a theory of human problem solving. *Psychological Review, 65,* 151–166.

Newell, A., & Simon, H. (1961). The simulation of human thought. In W. Dennis (Ed.), *Current trends in psychological theory*. Pittsburgh: University of Pittsburgh Press.

———. (1972). *Human problem solving*. Englewood Cliffs, NJ: Prentice-Hall.

Perris, C. (1988). *Cognitive therapy with schizophrenics*. New York: Guilford.

Quillian, M. R. (1969). The teachable language comprehender: A simulation program and theory of language. *Communications of the ACM, 12,* 459–476.

Schank, R. C., & Abelson, R. B. (1977). *Scripts, plans, goals and understanding*. Hillsdale, NJ: Erlebaum.

Scheff, T. J. (1985). The primacy of affect. *American Psychologist, 40,* 849–850.

Sechrest, L. (1977). Personal-constructs theory. In R. J. Corsini (Ed.), *Current personality theories* (pp. 203–241). Itasca, IL: Peacock.

Shepard, R. N. (1984). Ecological constraints on internal representation: Resonant kinematics of perceiving, imagining, thinking, and dreaming. *Psychological Review, 91,* 417–447.

Sotter, J. (1970). Men, the man-makers: George Kelly and the psychology of personal constructs. In D. Bannister (Ed.), *Perspectives in personal construct theory* (pp. 223–253). New York: Academic Press.

Sroufe, L. A. (1984). The organization of emotional development. In K. R. Scherer & P. Ekman (Eds.), *Approaches to emotion* (pp. 109–128), Hillsdale, NJ: Erlbaum.

Stein, N., & Levine, L. (1987). Thinking about feelings: The development and organization of emotional knowledge. In R. E. Snow & M. Farr (Eds.), *Aptitude, learning and instruction: Vol. 3: Cognition, conation, and affect* (pp. 165–197). Hillsdale, NJ: Erlbaum.

Stenberg, C. R., & Campos, J. J. (1990). The development of anger expressions in infancy. In N. Stein, B. Leventhal, & T. Trabasso (Eds.), *Psychological and biological approaches to emotion* (pp. 247–282). Hillsdale, NJ: Erlbaum.

Turing, A. M. (1950). Computing machinery and intelligence. *Mind, 59* (236). In R. P. Honeck, T. J. Case, & M. J. Firment (Eds.), *Introductory readings in cognitive psychology* (pp. 15–24). Guilford, CT: The Dushkin Publishing Co., 1991.

Waldrop, M. M. (1985, March). Machinations of thought. *Science 85,* 38–45.

Webber, R., & Mancuso, J. C. (Eds.). (1983). *Applications of personal construct theory.* New York: Academic Press, pp. 137–154.

Weizenbaum, J. (1976). *Computer power and human reason: From judgment to calculation.* San Francisco: Freeman.

Zajonc, R. B. (1980). Feeling and thinking: Preferences need no inferences. *American Psychologist, 35,* 151–175.

———. (1984). On the primacy of affect. *American Psychologist, 39,* 117–123.

Zelhart, P. F., & Jackson, T. T. (1985). George A. Kelly, 1931–1943: Environmental influences on a developing theorist. *Journal of School Psychology, 23* (4), 297–304.

Chapter Twelve

Carl Rogers and the Person-Centered Perspective

Carl Rogers has had an indelible influence on psychology and psychotherapy, as well as education. He created and fostered *client-centered* therapy, pioneered the encounter-group movement, was one of the founders of humanistic psychology, and was the pivotal member of the first person-centered groups working to resolve international political conflicts.

Throughout his working life, while his interests changed and grew to include not only individual psychotherapy and group therapy but also educational, social, and governmental systems, his philosophical viewpoint remained consistently optimistic and humanitarian.

> I have little sympathy with the rather prevalent concept that man is basically irrational, and thus his impulses, if not controlled, would lead to destruction of others and self. Man's behavior is exquisitely rational, moving with subtle and ordered complexity toward the goals his organism is endeavoring to achieve. The tragedy for most of us is that our defenses keep us from being aware of this rationality, so that consciously we are moving in one direction, while organismically we are moving in another. (Rogers, 1969, p. 29)

It will have been evident that one implication of the view I have been presenting is that the basic nature of the human being, when functioning freely, is constructive and trustworthy. (Rogers, 1969, p. 290)

Unwilling to be limited by the popularity and acceptance of his earlier works, Rogers continued to modify his ideas and to change his approach. He encouraged others to test his assertions, but discouraged the formation of a "Rogerian school" that would only mimic or repeat his own discoveries. Outside of formal psychology his work "has been one of the factors in changing concepts of industrial (even military) leadership, of social work practice, of nursing practice, and of religious work. . . . It has even influenced students of theology and philosophy" (Rogers, 1974a, p. 115).

> What started for me in the 30's as a changing but supposedly well-accepted way of working therapeutically with individuals, was clumsily articulated as my own view in the early 1940's. . . . One might say that a "technique" of counseling became a practice of psychotherapy. This in turn brought into being a theory of therapy and of personality. The theory supplied the hypotheses which opened a whole new field of research. Out of this grew an approach to all interpersonal relationships. Now it reaches into education as a way of facilitating learning at all levels. It is a way of conducting intensive group experiences, and has influenced the theory of group dynamics. (Rogers, 1970)

Through the 1970s and early 1980s, Rogers's interest shifted away from therapy with clients to an international involvement in team building and large-scale community development. His determination to expand his ideas and his belief in the power of individuals to help themselves continue to influence counselors and psychologists worldwide (Caspary, 1991; Macy, 1987).

Personal History

Carl Rogers, the fourth of six children, was born on January 8, 1902, in Oak Park, Illinois, into a prosperous and strictly fundamentalist home. His childhood was restricted by the beliefs and attitudes of his parents and by his own interpretation of their ideas.

> I think the attitudes toward persons outside our large family can be summed up schematically in this way: Other persons behave in dubious ways which we do not approve in our family. Many of them play cards, go to movies, smoke, dance, drink, and engage in other activities— some unmentionable. So the best thing to do is be tolerant of them, since they may not know better, and to keep away from any close communication with them and live your life with the family. (Rogers, 1973a, p. 3)

Rogers was an introspective child and a gifted student who loved books. But he was neither aggressive nor athletic and experienced childhood as lonely. "Anything I would today regard as a close and communicative interpersonal relationship was completely lacking during that period" (1973a, p. 4). To further protect their children from the "corrupting influences of the city and suburbs" (Kirschenbaum, 1980, p. 10), Rogers's parents moved to a farm near Glen Ellyn, Illinois, during his high school years. He maintained an excellent academic record and developed a strong interest in the scientific.

Something of the gently suppressive family atmosphere is perhaps indicated by the fact that three of six children developed ulcers at some period in their lives. (Rogers, 1967, p. 352)

> I realized by now that I was peculiar, a loner, with very little place or opportunity for a place in the world of persons. I was socially incompetent in any but superficial contacts. My fantasies during this period were definitely bizarre, and probably would be classed as schizoid by a diagnostician, but fortunately I never came in contact with a psychologist. (Rogers, 1973a, p. 4)

His college experiences at the University of Wisconsin were meaningful and rewarding. "For the first time in my life outside of my family I found real closeness and intimacy" (Rogers, 1967, p. 349). In his sophomore year, he began to study for the ministry. The following year, 1922, he went to China to attend a World Student Christian Federation conference in Peking. Subsequently, he went on a speaking tour through west China and Asia. The trip served to mellow his fundamentalist religious attitudes and gave him his first opportunity to develop psychological independence. "From the date of this trip, my goals, values, aims, and philosophy have been my own and very divergent from the views which my parents held and which I had held up to this point" (1967, p. 351).

In 1924, he married Helen Elliott whom he had known since grammar school. Both families discouraged Rogers from returning to school after he and Helen were married. They had hoped that he would instead look for work. But Rogers asserted himself and decided to return to school. The couple moved to New York City, where Rogers began graduate studies in theology at Union Theological Seminary. He later chose to finish his work in psychology at Teachers College, Columbia University. This shift was prompted in part by a student-directed seminar that gave him the opportunity to examine his rising doubts about his religious commitment. Later, in a psychology course, he was pleasantly surprised to discover that a person could earn a living *outside* of the church, working closely with individuals who needed help.

His first job was in Rochester, New York, in a child guidance center, working with children who had been referred by various social agencies. "I wasn't connected with a university, no one was looking over my shoulder from any particular treatment orientation . . . [the agencies] didn't give a damn how you proceeded but hoped you could be of some assistance" (Rogers, 1970, p. 514–515). From 1928 to 1939, while in Rochester, Rogers's understanding of the process of psychotherapy changed. He eventually exchanged a formal, directive approach for what he would later call *client-centered* therapy.

> It began to occur to me that unless I had a need to demonstrate my own cleverness and learning, I would be better to rely upon the client for the direction of movement in the process. (Rogers, 1967, p. 359)

While in Rochester, Rogers wrote *The Clinical Treatment of the Problem Child* (1939). The book was well received and led to an offer of a full professorship at Ohio State University. Rogers has said that by starting at the top, he escaped the pressures and tensions that exist on the lower rungs of the academic ladder—pressures that stifle innovation and creativity. His teaching and the stimulation he received from graduate students prompted Rogers to write a more formal examination of the nature of the therapeutic relationship in *Counseling and Psychotherapy* (1942).

In 1945, the University of Chicago offered him the chance to establish a new counseling center based on his ideas. He served as its director until 1957. Rogers's growing emphasis on trust was reflected in the democratic decision-making policies of the center. If patients could be trusted to direct their own therapy, certainly staff could be trusted to administer their own working environment.

In 1951, Rogers published *Client-Centered Therapy*. It contained his first formal theory of therapy, his theory of personality, and some of the research that reinforced his conclusions. In it he suggested that the major directing force in the therapeutic relationship should be the client, not the therapist. This reversal of the usual relationship was revolutionary and attracted considerable criticism. Client-centered therapy questioned one of the most basic, unchallenged assumptions of the therapeutic relationship—that the therapist is all-knowing and the patient is unaware. The general implications of this position, beyond therapy, were spelled out in *On Becoming a Person* (1961).

Rogers's experience in Chicago was exciting and satisfying. He also suffered a personal setback that ironically caused a positive change in his professional outlook. While working closely with an extremely disturbed client, Rogers became enmeshed in her pathology. Close to a breakdown himself, he literally fled the center, took a three-month vacation, and finally returned to enter therapy with one of his colleagues. After the therapy, Rogers's own interactions with clients became increasingly free and spontaneous.

In 1957, Rogers went to the University of Wisconsin at Madison with a joint appointment in psychiatry and psychology. It was a difficult time professionally as Rogers found himself in growing conflict with the psychology department. He felt that his freedom to teach and his students' freedom to learn were being restricted. "I'm pretty good at living and letting live, but when they wouldn't let my students live, that became a dissatisfying experience" (Rogers, 1970, p. 528).

Rogers's rising indignation was captured in the paper, "Current Assumptions in Graduate Education: A Passionate Statement" (1969). Although rejected by *The American Psychologist* for publication, it enjoyed a wide distribution through the graduate student underground before it was eventually printed. "The theme of my statement is that we are doing an unintelligent, ineffectual and wasteful job of preparing psychologists, to the detriment of our discipline and society" (Rogers, 1969, p. 170). Some of the implicit assumptions that Rogers attacked were:

"The student cannot be trusted to pursue his own scientific and professional learning"; "Evaluation is education; education is evaluation"; "Presentation equals learning: What is presented in the lecture is what the student learns"; "The truths of psychology are known"; and "Creative scientists develop from passive learners" (1969, pp. 169–187).

Not surprisingly, Rogers left his tenured professorship in 1963 and moved to the newly founded Western Behavioral Science Institute in La Jolla, California. A few years later, he helped establish the Center for the Studies of the Person, a loosely structured collection of people in the helping professions.

His growing effect on education had become so evident that he wrote a book to clarify the kinds of educational settings he was advocating and was actively engaged in establishing. *Freedom to Learn* (1969) and *Freedom to Learn for the 80's* (1983) contain his clearest statements on the nature of human beings.

His work with encounter groups stems from his years in California, where he was free to experiment, invent, and test his ideas without the interference of social institutions or academia. His encounter research is summed up in *Carl Rogers on Encounter Groups* (1970).

One of his moves away from psychotherapy took the form of exploring the changing trends and values in normal marriages. His naturalistic study, *Becoming Partners: Marriage and Its Alternatives* (1972), is an examination of the advantages and disadvantages of different patterns of relationship.

After splitting his interests for several years, Rogers finally combined his group work and his efforts in educational innovation. Along with some members of the Center for the Studies of the Person, he ran ongoing intensive groups for the faculty and students of a Jesuit training college

> I have often been grateful that by the time I was in dire need of personal help, I had trained therapists who were persons in their own right, not dependent upon me, yet able to offer me the kind of help I needed. (Rogers, 1967, p. 367)

> What do I mean by a person-centered approach? It expresses the primary theme of my whole professional life, as that theme has become clarified through experience, interaction with others, and research. I smile as I think of the various labels I have given to this theme during the course of my career—nondirective counseling, client-centered therapy, student-centered teaching, group-centered leadership. (Rogers, 1980a, p. 114)

and a Catholic school system (elementary levels through to college). He also did extensive consultations for the Louisville, Kentucky, school system (Rogers, 1974b, 1975a, 1975b).

Emboldened by the highly disruptive and yet successful results, Rogers moved away from the *client*-centered relationships that had been the focus of most of his career. He looked instead to *person-centered* situations with their revolutionary implications for every sort of political and social system. His own internal revolution and resulting conclusions are described in *Carl Rogers on Personal Power* (1978).

Until his death in 1987, at the age of 85, he remained at the Center for the Studies of the Person. In the last decade of his life, he applied his ideas specifically to political situations and led successful workshops in conflict resolution and citizen diplomacy in South Africa, Austria, and the former Soviet Union (Macy, 1987; Rogers, 1986, 1987; Swenson, 1987).

Rogers became interested in altered states of consciousness; that is, "inner space—the realm of the psychological powers and the psychic capabilities of the human person" (Rogers, 1980b, p. 12). He also became more open and expressive in his relationships. He says of these shifts, "I am no longer simply talking about psychotherapy, but about a point of view, a philosophy, an approach to life, a way of being in which *growth*—of a person, a group, or a community—is part of the goal" (1980a, p. ix).

He summarizes his own position by quoting Lao-tse:

> *If I keep from meddling with people, they take care of themselves,*
>
> *If I keep from commanding people, they behave themselves,*
>
> *If I keep from preaching at people, they improve themselves,*
>
> *If I keep from imposing on people, they become themselves.*

(Rogers, 1973a, p. 13)

Intellectual Antecedents

Rogers's theory of personality developed primarily from his own clinical experiences. He felt that he retained his objectivity by avoiding close identification with any particular school or tradition.

> I have never really *belonged* to *any* professional group. I have been educated by or had close working relationships with psychologists, psychoanalysts, psychiatrists, psychiatric social workers, social caseworkers, educators, and religious workers, yet I have never felt that I really belonged, in any total or committed sense, to any one of these groups. . . . Lest one think I have been a complete nomad professionally I should add that the only groups to which I have ever *really* belonged have been close-knit, congenial task forces which I have organized or helped organize. (Rogers, 1967, p. 375)

Sidebar quotes:

Our experiences, it is clear, involve the transcendent, the indescribable, the spiritual. I am compelled to believe, that I, like many others, have underestimated the importance of this mystical, spiritual dimension. (Rogers, 1984)

There has never been any one outstanding person in my learning . . . so as I went on there was no one I had to rebel against or leave behind. (Rogers, 1970, p. 502)

He acknowledged that his own thinking had been supported early on by Rank's example as well by later work with a Rankian trained social worker (Rogers & Haigh, 1983). He also noted that Adler's work with children contrasted markedly with the elaborate Freudian procedures that were being employed at the time. This stark contrast affected his own orientation (Rogers in Ansbacher, 1990).

His students at the University of Chicago suggested that his emerging position seemed to echo the ideas of Martin Buber and Sören Kierkegaard. Indeed, these thinkers were a source of support and helped to confirm his brand of existential philosophy. Well into his career, Rogers discovered parallels to his own work in Eastern sources, notably Zen Buddhism and the works of Lao-tse, who was a Chinese philosopher of the sixth century B.C. and believed to be an elder contemporary of Confucius. There is no question that Rogers's work was affected by the work of others; however, his contribution to our understanding of human nature is original and very much his own.

Major Concepts

Fundamental to all of Rogers's work is the assumption that people define themselves through observing and evaluating their own experiences. His basic premise is that peoples' realities are private affairs and can be known only by the individuals themselves. In his major theoretical work, Rogers (1959) defines the concepts that are at the core of his theory of personality, therapy, and personal relationships. These primary constructs establish a framework upon which people build and modify their images of themselves.

The Field of Experience

There is a field of experience unique to each individual; this field contains "all that is going on within the envelope of the organism at any given moment which is potentially available to awareness" (Rogers, 1959, p. 197). It includes events, perceptions, and sensations of which a person is not aware but could be if he or she focused on these inputs. It is a private, personal world that may or may not correspond to observed, objective reality.

This field of experience is selective, subjective, and incomplete (Van Belle, 1980). It is bounded by psychological limitations (what we are willing to be aware of) and biological limitations (what we are able to be aware of). Our attention, while theoretically open to any experience, is focused on immediate concerns to the exclusion of almost everything else. When we are very hungry, our field of experience is completely filled with thoughts of food and how to get food. When we are lonely, our singular focus is how to relieve the loneliness.

Words and symbols bear to the world of reality the same relationship as a map to the territory which it represents. . . . We live by a perceptual "map" which is never reality itself. (Rogers, 1951, p. 485)

The Self

Within the field of experience is the self. The self is an unstable, changing entity. Observed at any moment, however, it appears to be firm and predictable. This is because we freeze a section of experience in order to observe it. Rogers concluded that "we were not dealing with an entity of slow accretion, of step by step learning . . . the product was clearly a gestalt, a configuration in which the alteration of one minor aspect could completely alter the whole pattern" (1959, p. 201). The self is an organized, consistent gestalt, constantly in the process of forming and reforming as situations change.

The self cannot be captured as if by still photography. Because it is a changing, fluid entity, "stills" would reveal nothing of its unstable nature.

Many use the word *self* to point to that part of the personal identity that is stable and unchanging. Rogers's meaning of the word is almost the opposite. Rogers's self is a *process,* a system that by definition is changing. It is this difference, this emphasis on change and flexibility, that is the lynchpin in his theory. From this notion of fluidity, Rogers developed the belief that people are not only capable of growth, change, and personal development, but that such positive change is also a natural and expected progression. The self or self-concept is a person's understanding of himself or herself, based on past experience, present inputs, and future expectancies (Evans, 1975).

The Ideal Self

The ideal self is "the self-concept which the individual would most like to possess, upon which he places the highest value for himself" (Rogers, 1959, p. 200). Like the self, it is a shifting, changing structure, constantly undergoing redefinition. If one's ideal self is very different from the actual self, the person may be uncomfortable, dissatisfied, and experience neurotic difficulties. To be able to see oneself accurately and be comfortable with oneself is one sign of mental health. The ideal self is a model toward which a person can strive. Conversely, to the extent that it is grossly different from one's actual behavior and values, the ideal self may inhibit one's capacity to develop.

An excerpt from a case history may clarify this. A student was planning to drop out of college. He had been the best student in his junior high school, the top student in his high school, and he had been doing extremely well in college. He was leaving, he explained, because he had received a *C* in a course. His image of always being the best was endangered. The only course of action he could envision was to escape, to leave the academic world, to deny the discrepancy between his actual performance and his ideal vision of himself. He said that he would work toward being the "best" in some other way.

In order to protect his ideal self-image, he was willing to give up his academic career. He left school, traveled around the world, and held a host of odd jobs for several years. When he was seen again, he was able to discuss the possibility that it *might* not be necessary to be the best from the beginning, but he still had great difficulty exploring any activity that carried with it the possibility of failure.

The ideal self can become an obstacle to personal health if it differs greatly from the real self. People who suffer from such a discrepancy are often unwilling to see the difference between ideals and acts. For example, some parents say they will "do anything" for their children, but are actually resentful of their obligations; they do not actually do the things they say. The result is a confused child and parents who are unwilling or unable to admit to the discrepancy.

Personal Reflection ———————————

——————————— Self Versus Ideal Self

In order to get an idea of the discrepancy between your ideal self and real self, try this exercise.

Write down a list of your faults or weaknesses. Use full sentences. Here are some examples:

"I'm 10 pounds overweight."

"I'm selfish, especially with my books."

"I will never understand mathematical concepts."

Rewrite the same statements as discrepancies between your real self and your ideal self, for example:

"My ideal self weighs 10 pounds less than I do."

"My ideal self is generous, lending or even giving books to friends who ask for them."

"My ideal self is a good mathematician, not a professional, but able to learn easily and to remember concepts."

Evaluate these statements. Are any of your aspirations unrealistic? Should you modify some of the goals assumed in your ideal-self description? If so, why?

Self-actualizing Tendency

It is human nature to seek greater congruence and realistic functioning. Moreover, this urge is not limited to human beings; it is part of the process of all living things.

> It is the urge which is evident in all organic and human life—to expand, extend, become autonomous, develop, mature—the tendency to express and activate all the capacities of the organism, to the extent that such activation enhances the organism or the self. (Rogers, 1961, p. 35)

Rogers suggests that in each of us there is an inherent drive toward being as competent and capable as we are biologically able to be. As a plant grows to become a healthy plant, as a seed contains within it the push to become a tree, so a person is impelled to become a whole, complete, and self-actualized person. Although Rogers did not include any religious or spiritual dimensions in his formulations, others have expanded his theories to include transcendental experiences (Campbell & McMahon, 1974; Fuller, 1982). Late in his life, Rogers acknowledged that he found, "definitely appealing the view of Arthur Koestler that individual consciousness is but a fragment of a cosmic consciousness" (Rogers, 1980a, p. 88).

The drive toward health is not an overwhelming force that sweeps aside obstacles, for it is easily blunted, distorted, twisted, and repressed. Rogers sees it as the dominant motivating force in a person who is "functioning freely" and not crippled by past events or current beliefs that maintain incongruence. Maslow came to similar conclusions; he called this tendency a small, weak internal voice, one that is easily muffled. The assumption that growth is possible, and central to the purpose of the organism, is crucial to the whole of Rogers's thought.

For Rogers, the tendency toward self-actualization is not simply another motive among many.

> It should be noted that this basic actualizing tendency is *the only motive* which is postulated in this theoretical system. . . . The self, for example, is an important construct in our theory, but the self does not "do" anything. It is only one expression of the general tendency of the organism to behave in those ways which maintain and enhance itself. (Rogers, 1959, p. 196)

Personal Power

As Rogers turned his attention away from strictly therapeutic concerns, his thinking shifted to consider the problems of individuals in political and social contexts. The person-centered approach in society he calls *personal power*. It is concerned with *"the locus of decision-making power:* who makes the decisions which, consciously or unconsciously, regulate or control the thoughts, feelings, or behavior of others or oneself. . . . In sum it is the process of gaining, using, sharing or relinquishing power, control, decision making" (Rogers, 1978, pp. 4–5). Rogers assumed that each of us has an enormous capacity to use our personal power correctly and beneficially if given the opportunity. "The individual has within himself vast resources for self-understanding, for altering his self-concept, his attitudes, and his self-directed behavior . . ." (1978, p. 7). This drive toward self-development is impeded by placing people under others' control. This domination, when overt, as in a dictatorship, is often resisted.

What concerns Rogers are the more subtle and accepted kinds of domination. In particular, he singles out therapists who control and manipulate patients, teachers who control and manipulate students, government bodies that control and manipulate various segments of the population, and businesses that control and manipulate their employees. He predicts that, without these agreed-upon restrictions of personal power, individuals and groups would collaborate and come up with solutions to their problems—solutions that do not demand the domination of the many by the few. This development in his work, from the intimacy of the therapeutic situation to the rough-and-tumble interactions of political, social, and community organizations, is described as radical and revolutionary. He is not suggesting a change in the kinds of control (one government for another) but supports a gradual restructuring of organizations to fully take into account the personal power of the members.

Congruence and Incongruence

Rogers does not label people as adjusted or maladjusted, sick or well, normal or abnormal; instead, he writes about their capacity to perceive the reality of their situation. He defines the term *congruence* as the degree of accuracy between experience, communication, and awareness. A high degree of congruence means that communication (what one is expressing), experience (what is occurring), and awareness (what one is noticing) are all nearly equal. One's observations and those of an external observer would be consistent in a situation that has high congruence.

Small children exhibit high congruence. They express their feelings so readily and completely that experience, communication, and awareness are much the same for them. When a child is hungry, he or she is all hungry, right now! When children are loving or angry, they express these emotions fully and completely. This may account for the rapidity with which children flow from one emotional state to another. Full expression of their feelings prevents the accumulation of the kind of emotional baggage that is carried into each new encounter. Congruence is accurately described by a Zen Buddhist saying: "When I am hungry, I eat; when I am tired, I sit; when I am sleepy, I sleep."

Incongruence occurs when there are differences among awareness, experience, and communication. For example, people exhibit incongruence when they appear to be angry (fists clenched, voices raised, cursing) but insist otherwise, even when pressed. Incongruence is also seen in people who say that they are having a wonderful time yet act bored, lonely, or ill at ease. Incongruence, more generally, is the inability to perceive accurately, the inability or unwillingness to communicate accurately, or both.

When the incongruence is between awareness and experience, it is called *repression* or *denial*. The person is simply not aware of what he or she is doing. Most psychotherapy works on this aspect of incongruence, helping people to become more aware of their actions, thoughts, and attitudes as they affect themselves and others.

The more the therapist is able to listen acceptantly to what is going on within himself, and the more he is able to be the complexity of his feelings, without fear, the higher the degree of his congruence. (Rogers, 1961, p. 61)

When incongruence is a discrepancy between awareness and communication, a person does not express what he or she is actually feeling, thinking, or experiencing. When a person exhibits this kind of incongruence, he or she may be perceived by others as *deceitful, inauthentic,* or *dishonest.* Often these behaviors become the focus of discussions in group therapy or encounter settings. A person who behaves in a deceitful or dishonest fashion may appear to be malicious, but trainers and therapists report that the lack of social congruence—the apparent unwillingness to communicate—actually shows a lack of self-control and a lack of personal awareness, rather than a mean-spirited nature. The person is not able to express real emotions and perceptions due to fears or old habits of concealment that are difficult to overcome. Also, the person may have difficulty understanding what others want, or it may be that the person cannot express his or her perceptions in such a way that others understand (Bandler & Grinder, 1975).

Incongruence may be experienced as tension, anxiety, or, in more extreme circumstances, disorientation and confusion. Mental hospital patients who do not know where they are or what time of day it is, or even who they are, are exhibiting high incongruency. The discrepancy between their external reality and subjective experience has become so great that these patients are no longer able to function without protection.

Most of the symptoms described in the psychopathology literature can be understood in terms of incongruence. The important issue for Rogers is that incongruence demands resolution; the type of incongruence a person exhibits is less relevant. Conflicting feelings, ideas, or concerns are not in themselves symptomatic of incongruence. They are, in fact, normal and healthy. Incongruence occurs when a person is unaware of these conflicts, does not understand them, and therefore cannot begin to resolve or balance them.

Incongruence can be observed in remarks such as, "I'm not able to come to any decisions," "I don't know what I want," and "I never seem to be able to stick to anything." When one is unable to sort out the different inputs one is exposed to, confusion can result. Consider the case of a client who reports, "My mother tells me I have to take care of her; it's the least I can do. My girl friend tells me to stand up for myself, not to be pushed around. I think I'm pretty good to Mother, a lot better than she deserves. Sometimes I hate her, sometimes I love her. Sometimes she's good to be with, at other times she belittles me."

This client is beset with a variety of inputs. Each one is partially valid and leads to congruent action *some of the time.* Sorting out the inputs that the client truly agrees with from those that the client would like to agree with, but does not, is difficult. Recognizing that we have different, even opposing, feelings is healthy and challenging. We behave differently at different times. And this is neither unusual nor unhealthy; but not being able to recognize, cope, or admit to our conflicting feelings can signal incongruence.

Personal Reflection ——————————————
—————————————————————— Congruence

This reflection can help you become aware of the nature of the self as Rogers describes it. It can clarify your ideas about your own congruence.

The list of adjectives in Table 12.1 is a sample of a number of personality characteristics.

Part I 1. Real Self: Check those adjectives that apply to you. These characteristics reflect what you know yourself to be, whether or not anyone else may characterize you as such.

2. How Others See Me: Check only those that you think others who know you would attribute to you.

3. Ideal Self: Check off those attributes that describe you at your best. Remember that this last column is your ideal self, not some plaster saint.

(Note: None of us are any of these adjectives all the time. For example, you do not have to be perpetually *cheerful* in order to select this adjective. If you think you are usually cheerful, then check it.)

Part II Circle the adjectives where there is inconsistency across the columns. These represent possible areas of incongruence in your life. Whether you circle many or only a few is not of great importance. Few people are completely congruent.

From this point on, the exercise is up to you. You can work in small groups to discuss your internal discrepancies. You can write about them for personal use or as a class assignment.

Dynamics

Psychological Growth

The positive forces toward health and growth are natural and inherent in the organism. Based on his own clinical experience, Rogers concluded that individuals have the capacity to experience and to become aware of their own maladjustments. That is, one can experience the incongruences between one's self-concept and one's actual experiences. This capacity is coupled with the ability to modify one's self-concept so that it is, in fact, in line with reality. Thus, Rogers postulates a natural movement away from conflict and toward resolution. He sees adjustment not as a static state but as a process in which new learning and new experiences are accurately assimilated. "The central hypothesis of this approach can be briefly stated. It is that the individual has within him or herself vast resources for self-understanding, for altering his or her self-concept, attitudes, and self-directed behavior" (Rogers, 1984).

ADJECTIVE	1 REAL SELF	2 HOW OTHERS SEE ME	3 IDEAL SELF
cheerful			
persistent			
noisy			
responsible			
absent-minded			
restless			
demanding			
snobbish			
frank			
honest			
excitable			
immature			
courageous			
self-pitying			
ambitious			
calm			
individualistic			
serious			
friendly			
mature			
artistic			
intelligent			
humorous			
idealistic			
understanding			
warm			
relaxed			
sensitive			
sexy			
active			
lovable			
selfish			
shrewd			
affectionate			
opinionated			

Rogers is convinced that these tendencies toward health are facilitated by interpersonal relationships in which at least one member is free enough from incongruence to be in touch with his or her own self-correcting center. The major task in therapy is to establish a genuine relationship. Acceptance of oneself is a prerequisite to an easier and more genuine acceptance of others. In turn, being accepted by another leads to a greater willingness to accept oneself. The last necessary element is "empathic understanding" (Rogers, 1984), being able to accurately sense the feelings of others. This self-correcting and self-enhancing cycle helps people to overcome obstacles and facilitates psychological growth.

Obstacles to Growth

Obstacles arise in childhood and are inherent in the normal stages of development. Lessons that are beneficial at one age can become detrimental at a later stage. Freud described situations in which childhood lessons were carried on into adult life as neurotic fixations. Rogers does not dwell on specific details but sees potential patterns of restrictions occurring as a child grows up.

Conditions of Worth

As the infant begins to have an awareness of self, he or she develops a need for love or positive regard. "This need is universal in human beings, and in the individual is pervasive and persistent. Whether it is an inherent or learned need is irrelevant to the theory" (Rogers, 1959, p. 223). Because children do not separate their actions from who they are, they often react to approval for an *action* as if it were approval for *themselves*. Similarly, they react to being punished for an action as if they were being disapproved of in general.

So important is love to an infant that "he comes to be guided in his behavior not by the degree to which an experience maintains or enhances the organism, but by the likelihood of receiving maternal love" (Rogers, 1959, p. 225). The child begins to act in ways that serve to win him or her love or approval, whether or not the behaviors are healthy. Children may act against their own self-interests, coming to view themselves in terms originally designed to please or placate others. Theoretically, this state of affairs might not develop if the child is always accepted unconditionally, provided that the expression of negative feelings is accepted while the accompanying behaviors are rejected. In such an ideal setting, the child would never be pressured to disown or deny unattractive but genuine parts of his or her personality.

> This, as we see it, is the basic estrangement in man. He has not been true to himself, to his natural organismic valuing of experience, but for the sake of preserving the positive regard of others has now come to falsify some of the values he experiences and to perceiving them in terms based only on their value to others. Yet this has not been a con-

scious choice, but a natural—and tragic—development in infancy. (Rogers, 1959, p. 226)

Behaviors or attitudes that deny some aspect of the self are called *conditions of worth*. Such conditions are thought to be necessary for a sense of worth and to obtain love. Conditions of worth inhibit not only behavior but also maturation and awareness; they lead to incongruence and eventually rigidity of personality.

These conditions are the basic obstacles to accurate perception and realistic thinking. They are selective blinders and filters, used by a needy child to help ensure a supply of love from parents and others. As children, we adopt certain attitudes and actions in order to be worth loving and to retain love. We learn that the adoption of certain conditions, attitudes, or actions is essential to our remaining worthy of love. To the extent that these attitudes and actions are contrived, they are areas of personal incongruence. In the extreme, conditions of worth are characterized by the belief that "I must be loved or respected by everyone I come in contact with." Conditions of worth create a discrepancy between the self and the self-concept.

If you have been told, for example, "You must love your new baby sister or mommy and daddy won't love you," the message is that you must deny or repress any genuinely negative feelings you have for your sister. Only if you manage to hide your ill will, your desire to hurt her, and your normal jealousy, will your mother and father continue to love you. If you admit such feelings, you risk the loss of your parents' love. A solution (which creates a condition of worth) is to deny such feelings whenever they occur, blocking them from your awareness. This means that the feelings, because they must come to the surface in some form, will likely find an inappropriate outlet of expression. You may begin responding in such ways as, "I really do love my little sister; I hug her until she screams," or "My foot slipped under hers, that's why she tripped," or the more universal, "She started it!"

This author can still recall the enormous joy that my older brother exhibited when he was given an opportunity to hit me for something I had done. My mother, my brother, and I were all stunned by his violence. In recalling the incident, my brother remembers that he was not particularly angry with me, but he understood that this was a rare occasion and wanted to unload as much accumulated ill will as possible while he had permission. Admitting such feelings and expressing them as they occur is healthier, says Rogers, than denying or disowning them.

As the child matures, the problem may persist. Growth is impeded to the extent that a person is denying inputs that differ from the artificially "nice" self-concept. In order to support the false self-image, a person continues to distort experiences—the greater the distortion, the greater the chance for mistakes and the creation of additional problems. The behaviors, mistakes, and confusion that result are manifestations of the initial distortions.

The situation feeds back on itself. Each experience of incongruence between the self and reality leads to increased imbalance, which in turn leads to increased defensiveness, shutting off experiences and creating new occasions for incongruence.

Sometimes the defensive maneuvers do not work. The person becomes aware of the obvious discrepancies between behaviors and beliefs. The results may be panic, chronic anxiety, withdrawal, or even psychosis. Rogers has observed that psychotic behavior often seems to be the acting out of a previously denied aspect of an individual's experience. Perry (1974) corroborates this, presenting evidence that the psychotic episode is a desperate attempt by the personality to rebalance itself and allow satisfaction of frustrated internal needs. Client-centered therapy strives to establish an atmosphere in which detrimental conditions of worth can be set aside, thus allowing the healthy forces in a person to regain their original dominance.

Structure

Body

Rogers does not give special attention to the role of the body. Even in his own encounter work, he does not promote or facilitate physical contact or work directly with physical gestures. As he points out, "My background is not such as to make me particularly free in this respect" (1970, p. 58).

Social Relationships

For Rogers, relationships are fundamental. Early relationships can be congruent and supportive, or they can create conditions of worth and personality constriction. Later relationships can restore congruence or diminish it. Interactions with others are crucial to developing awareness and the capacity for high congruence.

Rogers believes that relationships enable an individual to directly discover, uncover, experience, or encounter his or her actual self. *Our personalities become visible to us through relating to others*. In therapy, in encounter situations, and in daily interactions, the feedback from others offers us opportunities to experience ourselves.

For Rogers relationships offer the best opportunity to be fully functioning, to be in harmony with the self, others, and the environment. Through relationships, the basic organismic needs of the individual can be fulfilled. The desire for fulfillment motivates people to invest incredible amounts of energy in relationships, even in those that may not appear to be healthy or fulfilling.

Marriage

Marriage is a special relationship; it is potentially long-term, it is intensive, and it carries with it the possibility of sustained growth and development.

I would like to propose . . . that the major barrier to mutual interpersonal communication is our very natural tendency to judge, to evaluate, to approve or disapprove, the statement of the other person, or the other group. (Rogers, 1952a)

All our troubles, says somebody wise, come upon us because we cannot be alone. And that is all very well. We must all be able to be alone. Otherwise we are just victims. But when we are able to be alone, then we realize that the only thing to do is to start a new relationship with another—or even the same—human being. That people should all be stuck up apart, like so many telegraph poles, is nonsense. (D. H. Lawrence, 1960, pp. 114–115)

Rogers believes that marriage follows the same general laws that hold true for encounter groups, therapy, and other relationships. Better marriages occur between partners who are congruent themselves, have fewer impeding conditions of worth, and are capable of genuine acceptance of others. When marriage is used to sustain incongruence or to reinforce existing defensive tendencies, it is less fulfilling and less likely to endure.

Rogers's conclusions about any long-term intimate relationship, including marriage, are based on four basic elements: ongoing commitment, expression of feelings, avoidance of specific roles, and the capacity to share one's inner life. He summarizes each element as a pledge, an agreed-upon ideal, for a continuing, beneficial, and meaningful relationship.

Dedication of Commitment. Each member of a marriage should view "a partnership as a continuing process, not a contract. The work that is done is for *personal* as well as mutual satisfaction" (1972, p. 201). A relationship is work; it is work for separate as well as common goals. Rogers suggests that this commitment be expressed as follows: "We each commit ourselves to working together on the changing process of our present relationship, because that relationship is currently enriching our love and our life and we wish it to grow" (1972, p. 201).

Communication—The Expression of Feelings. Rogers insists on full and open communication. "I will risk myself by endeavoring to communicate any persistent feeling, positive or negative, to my partner—to the full depth that I understand it in myself—as a living part of *me*. Then I will risk further by trying to understand, with all the empathy I can bring to bear, his or her response, whether it is accusatory and critical or sharing and self-revealing" (1972, p. 204). Communication has two equally important phases; the first is to express the emotion, the second is to remain open and experience the other's response.

Is not marriage an open question when it is alleged, from the beginning of the world, that such as are in the institution wish to get out, and such as are out wish to get in? (Ralph Waldo Emerson, 1803–1882)

Rogers is not simply advocating the acting out of feelings. He is suggesting that one must be concerned about how one's feelings affect one's partner. And one must be equally concerned about the feelings themselves. This is far more difficult than simply "letting off steam" or being "open and honest." Both partners must be willing to accept the real risks involved: rejection, misunderstandings, hurt feelings, and retribution.

Nonacceptance of Roles. Numerous problems develop from trying to fulfill the expectations of others instead of determining our own. "We will live by our own choices, the deepest organismic sensings of which we are capable, but we will not be shaped by the wishes, the rules, the roles which others are all too eager to thrust upon us" (1972, p. 260). Rogers reports that many couples suffer severe strain attempting to live up to the inappropriate images that their parents and society have thrust upon them. A marriage laced with too many unrealistic expectations and images is inherently unstable and potentially unrewarding.

Becoming a Separate Self.   This commitment represents a profound attempt to discover and accept one's total nature. It is the most challenging of the commitments, a dedication to removing masks as soon and as often as they are created.

> Perhaps I can discover and come closer to more of what I really am deep inside—feeling sometimes angry or terrified, sometimes loving and caring, occasionally beautiful and strong or wild and awful—without hiding these feelings from myself. Perhaps I can come to prize myself as the richly varied person I am. Perhaps I can openly be more of this person. If so, I can live by my own experienced values, even though I am aware of all of society's codes. Then I can let myself be all this complexity of feelings and meaning and values with my partner—be free enough to give of love and anger and tenderness as they exist in me. Possibly then I can be a real member of a partnership, because I am on the road to being a real person. And I am hopeful that I can encourage my partner to follow his or her own road to a unique personhood, which I would love to share. (1972, p. 209)

Emotions

The healthy individual is aware of his or her emotional feelings, whether or not they are expressed. Feelings that are denied expression distort perception of and reactions to the experience that triggered them.

An example of this is feeling anxiety without being aware of the cause. The initial cause of the anxiety was *not admitted to awareness*, because it was perceived as threatening to the self-image. The unconscious reaction (McCleary & Lazarus, 1949) alerts the organism to possible danger and causes psychophysiological changes. These defensive reactions are one way the organism maintains incongruent beliefs and behaviors. A person can act on these but be unaware of why he or she is acting. For example, a man might become uncomfortable at seeing overt homosexuals. His own self-report would include the discomfort but not the cause. He cannot admit his own unresolved sexual identity, or (perhaps) the hopes and fears concerning his own sexuality. Distorting his perceptions, he may in turn react with open hostility to homosexuals, treating them as an external threat instead of admitting his internal conflict.

Intellect

Rogers values intellect as a tool that may be used effectively in integrating one's experience. He is skeptical of educational systems that overemphasize intellectual skills and undervalue the emotional and intuitive aspects of full human functioning.

In particular, Rogers finds graduate training in many fields excessively demanding, demeaning, and depressing. The pressure to produce limited and unoriginal work, coupled with the passive and dependent roles forced

Wen you're a married man, Samivel, you'll understand a good many things as you don't understand now; but vether it's worth while goin' through so much to learn so little, as the charity boy said ven he got to the end of the alphabet, is a mater o' taste. (In the *Pickwick Papers,* Charles Dickens, 1836)

Yet, if we are truly aware, we can hear the "silent screams" of denied feelings echoing off of every classroom wall and university corridor. And if we are sensitive enough, we can hear the creative thoughts and ideas that often emerge during and from the open expression of our feelings. (Rogers, 1973b, p. 385)

We all know the effects on children of compulsory spinach and compulsory rhubarb. It's the same with compulsory learning. They say, "It's spinach and the hell with it." (Rogers, 1969)

on graduate students, effectively stifles or retards their creative and productive capabilities. He quotes Albert Einstein as a student: "This coercion had such a deterring effect [upon me] that, after I had passed the final examination, I found the consideration of any problem distasteful for me for an entire year" (1969, p. 177).

If intellect, like other freely operating functions, tends to direct the organism toward more congruent awareness, then forcing the intellect into specified channels may not be beneficial. Rogers's contention is that people are better off deciding what to do for themselves, with support from others, than doing what others decide for them.

Knowing

Rogers describes three ways of knowing, of determining what is real, that are used by psychologically mature people. These are subjective knowing, objective knowing, and interpersonal knowing.

Most important is *subjective knowing*—the knowledge of whether one loves, hates, is disdainful of, or enjoys a person, an experience, or an event. One improves the quality of subjective knowing by getting more in touch with one's inner emotional processes. By paying attention to "gut" feelings, to inner indications, a person perceives that one course of action feels better than another. It is the capacity to know enough that allows a person to act without verifiable evidence. In science, for example, this means following one's hunches in solving specific problems. Research in creative problem solving indicates that a person "knows" that he or she is on the right track long before he or she discovers what the solution will include (Gordon, 1961).

Objective knowing is a way of testing hypotheses, speculations, and conjectures against external frames of reference. In psychology, reference points may include observations of behavior, test results, questionnaires, or the judgments of other psychologists. The idea that the sharing of information with colleagues can be very valuable is based on the notion that people who are trained in a given discipline can be relied upon to apply similar methods of judgment to a given event. Expert opinion may be objective, but it may also be a collective misperception. Any group of experts can exhibit rigidity and defensiveness when asked to consider data that contradict axiomatic aspects of their own training. It is Rogers's experience that theologians, communist dialecticians, and psychoanalysts exemplify this tendency in particular.

Rogers is hardly alone in questioning the validity of so-called objective knowledge, especially in attempting to understand someone else's experience. Polanyi (1958), a philosopher of science, has clarified the different uses and limitations of personal or subjective knowledge and public or objective knowledge. Both types of knowledge are useful for describing and understanding different kinds of experiences. Tart (1971, 1975) describes the necessity of different kinds of training for the sake of simply perceiving, not to mention evaluating, different kinds of subjective experiences.

Who can bring into being this whole person? From my experience I would say the least likely are university faculty members. Their traditionalism and smugness approach the incredible. (Rogers, 1973b, p. 385)

It has been considered slightly obscene to admit that psychologists feel, have hunches, or passionately pursue unformulated directions. (Rogers, 1964)

The third form of knowledge is *interpersonal knowing* or *phenomenological knowing*. This is at the core of Rogerian psychotherapy. It is the practice of empathic understanding: penetrating the private, unique, subjective world of the other to check on one's understanding of the other's views. The goal is not merely to be objectively correct, not just to see if it agrees or disagrees with one's point of view, but to be able to comprehend the other's experience as the other experiences it. This empathic knowing is tested by asking the other person if he or she has been understood. One might say, for example: "You seem depressed this morning, are you?" "It seems to me that you are telling the group that you need their help." "I wonder if you are too tired to finish this right now." This capacity to truly know another's reality is the foundation for forming genuine relationships.

Do not judge another man's road until you have walked a mile in his moccasins. (Pueblo Indian saying)

The Fully Functioning Person

Textbook writers generally class Rogers as a "self" theorist (Hall & Lindzey, 1978; Krasner & Ullman, 1973). In fact, Rogers is more concerned with perception, awareness, and experience than with the hypothetical construct, the "self." As we have already described Rogers's definition of the self, we can now turn to a description of the *fully functioning person:* a person who is completely aware of his or her ongoing self.

> "The fully functioning person" is synonymous with optimal psychological adjustment, optimal psychological maturity, complete congruence, complete openness to experience. . . . Since some of these terms sound somewhat static, as though such a person "had arrived," it should be pointed out that all the characteristics of such a person are *process* characteristics. The fully functioning person would be a person-in-process, a person continually changing. (Rogers, 1959, p. 235)

The fully functioning person has several distinct characteristics, the first of which is an *openness to experience.* There is little or no use of the early warning signals that restrict awareness. The person is continually moving away from defensiveness and toward direct experience. "He is more open to his feelings of fear and discouragement and pain. He is also more open to his feelings of courage, and tenderness, and awe. . . . He is more able fully to live the experience of his organism rather than shutting them out of awareness" (Rogers 1961, p. 188).

A second characteristic is *living in the present*—fully realizing each moment. This ongoing, direct engagement with reality allows "the self and personality [to] emerge *from* experience, rather than experience being translated or twisted to fit a preconceived self-structure" (Rogers, 1961, pp. 188–189). A person is capable of restructuring his or her responses as experience allows or suggests new possibilities.

A final characteristic is *trusting in one's inner urgings and intuitive judgments,* an ever-increasing trust in one's capacity to make decisions. As a person is better able to take in and utilize data, he or she is more likely to value his or her capacity to summarize that data and respond. This is not only an intellectual activity but one that involves the whole person. Rogers suggests that, in the fully functioning person, the mistakes that are made will be due to incorrect information, not incorrect processing.

The good life is a process, not a state of being. It is a direction, not a destination. (Rogers, 1961, p. 186)

This self-trust is similar to the behavior of a cat dropped upside-down to the ground from a significant height. The cat does not consider wind velocity, angular momentum, or the rate of descent, yet on some level these are taken into account given the cat's success in responding. The cat does not reflect on who dropped it from such a height, what the motives might have been, or what is likely to occur in the future. The cat responds to the immediate situation, the most pressing problem. It turns in midair and lands upright, instantly adjusting its posture to cope with the next event.

The fully functioning person is free to respond and free to experience his or her response to situations. This is the essence of what Rogers calls living the good life. Such a person "would be continually in a process of further self-actualization" (Rogers, 1959, p. 235).

Person-Centered Therapy

Rogers was a practicing therapist through most of his professional career. His theory of personality arises from and is integral to his methods and ideas about therapy. Rogers's theory of therapy went through a number of developmental phases and shifts in emphasis, yet there are a few fundamental principles that have remained in place. The following excerpts are taken from a speech Rogers delivered in 1940 in which he described his new ideas about therapy:

> This newer approach relies much more heavily on the individual drive towards growth, health, and adjustment. [Therapy] is a matter of freeing [the client] for normal growth and development. . . .
>
> This therapy places greater stress upon the feeling aspects of the situation than upon the intellectual aspects. . . .
>
> This newer therapy places greater stress upon the immediate situation than upon the individual's past. . . .
>
> This approach lays stress upon the therapeutic relationship itself as a growth experience. (1970, p. 12)

Rogers initially used the word *client* and later the word *person* rather than the traditional term *patient*. A patient is usually defined as someone who is ill, needs help, and goes to be helped by trained professionals, whereas a client is someone who desires a service and does not think that he or she can perform that service alone. The client, although he or she may have problems, is still viewed as a person who is inherently capable of understanding his or her own situation. There is an equality of relating implied in the person-centered model that is not present in the doctor-patient relationship.

The therapy assists a person in unlocking his or her own dilemma with minimum intervention. Rogers defines psychotherapy as "the releasing of an already existing capacity in a potentially competent individual, not the expert manipulation of a more or less passive personality" (1959, p. 221). The therapy is called person-centered because it is the person who does whatever directing is necessary. Rogers feels strongly that "expert interventions" of any sort are ultimately detrimental to a person's growth.

The Client or Person-Centered Therapist

The client holds the keys to recovery, but the therapist should have certain personal qualities in addition to professional tools that aid the client in learning how to use these keys. "These powers will become effective if the therapist can establish with the client a relationship sufficiently warm, accepting and understanding" (Rogers, 1952b, p. 66). Before the therapist can be anything to a client, he or she must be authentic and genuine. The therapist must avoid playing a role—especially that of a therapist—when he or she is with the client.

> [This] involves the willingness to be and to express in my words and my behavior, the various feelings and attitudes which exist in me. This means that I need to be aware of my own feelings, in so far as possible, rather than presenting an outward facade of one attitude, while actually holding another. (Rogers, 1961, p. 33)

Therapists in training often ask, "How do you behave if you don't like the patient or if you are bored or angry? Won't this genuine feeling be just what he gets from everyone else whom he offends?"

The client-centered response to these questions involves several levels of understanding. At one level, the therapist serves as a model of a genuine person. The therapist offers a relationship in which clients can test their own reality. If clients are confident of getting an honest response, they can discover if their anticipation or defensiveness is justified. Clients can learn to expect real—not distorted or diluted—feedback from their inner searching. This reality testing is crucial if the clients are to let go of distortions and to experience themselves directly.

At another level, the client-centered therapist is helpful to the extent that he or she is accepting and able to maintain *unconditional positive regard.* Rogers defines this as "caring which is not possessive, which demands no personal gratification. It is an atmosphere which simply demonstrates, 'I care,' not 'I care for you *if* you behave thus and so'" (1961, p. 283). *It is not a positive evaluation,* because any evaluation is a form of moral judgment. Evaluation tends to restrict behavior by rewarding some things and punishing others; unconditional positive regard allows the person to be what he or she actually is, no matter what it may be.

It is close to what Maslow calls *Taoistic* love, a love that does not prejudge, does not restrict, does not define. It is the promise to accept some-

> The individual has within him the capacity, at least latent, to understand the factors in his life that cause him unhappiness and pain, and to reorganize himself in such a way as to overcome those factors. (Rogers, 1952b)

> When the therapy relationship is equalitarian, when each takes responsibility for himself in the relationship, independent (and mutual) growth is much more rapid. (Rogers, 1978, p. 287)

one simply as he or she turns out to be. (This also resembles *Christian* love described by the Greek word *agape;* see I Cor. 13 and I John 4:7–12, 18–21.)

To do this, a client-centered therapist must always keep in sharp focus the self-actualizing core of the client, while nearly ignoring the destructive, damaging, or offensive behaviors. If the therapist can concentrate on an individual's positive essence, he or she can respond positively, avoiding boredom, irritation, and anger at those times when the client is less likeable. The client-centered therapist is certain that the inner, and perhaps undeveloped, personality of the client is capable of understanding itself. Rogerian therapists admit, however, that they often are unable to maintain this quality of understanding as they work.

Accepting the client means going beyond mere tolerance, which is a nonjudgmental stance that may or may not include real understanding. This is inadequate; unconditional positive regard must also include "empathic understanding . . . to sense the client's private world as if it were your own, but without ever losing the 'as if' quality" (Rogers, 1961, p. 284). This added dimension allows clients more freedom to explore inner feelings. Clients are assured that the therapist will do more than accept them, that he or she will actively try to feel whatever the clients are feeling.

The final criterion for a good therapist is that he or she must have the ability to convey genuine understanding to the client. The client needs to know that the therapist is authentic, does care, does listen, and does understand. It is necessary that the therapist maintain an empathic posture in spite of the selective distortions of the client, the defensive reactions, and the crippling effects of misplaced self-regard. Once this bridge between client and therapist is established, the client can begin to work in earnest.

The foregoing description may sound static and perhaps mechanistic, as if the therapist aims for a certain plateau, reaches it, and then engages in a kind of therapy that is confined by this plateau; it is nevertheless an ongoing dynamic process that continually renews itself. The therapist, like the client, is always striving for higher congruence.

In an early book, *Counseling and Psychotherapy* (1942, pp. 30–44), Rogers outlined characteristic steps in the helping process:

The client comes for help.

The situation is defined.

Free expression is encouraged.

The counselor accepts and clarifies.

Positive feelings are gradually expressed.

Positive impulses are recognized.

Insight is developed.

Choices are clarified.

Positive actions are taken.

Insight increases.

> When I am at my best as a group facilitator or a therapist, I find I am closest to my inner, intuitive self . . . when perhaps I am in a slightly altered state of consciousness in the relationship. Then whatever I do seems to be full of healing. (Rogers, 1984)

Personal Reflection ——————————————————

—————————————— The Client-Centered Therapist

This is a challenging exercise, involving the client-centered approach. It is not intended to give you an idea of what client-centered therapy is like but to give you an inkling of its complex demands, which Rogers viewed as necessary to effective counseling or therapy.

Choose a partner to work with. One of you can choose to be the therapist, the other, the client. You will switch roles so that you both experience both positions. To begin, the client tells the therapist an embarrassing incident from his or her own life that might be hard to relate. For example, you might want to share times when you lied or cheated; or a time when you were accused of being unjust or unkind.

As the therapist, you make every effort to understand what you are being told, listening so that you can repeat what you have been hearing. Repeat back what you are hearing. You want to understand exactly what is said. As a Rogerian therapist, you do not take a stand on the rightness or wrongness of behavior, you do not offer advice, neither do you criticize. Continue to appreciate the client as another human being, no matter what he or she tells you.

This is a difficult exercise. Notice the times when you want to comment, when you have a tendency to judge, feel sorry for, or be disturbed by your client's story. Notice the difficulties in simultaneously being aware of your own experience, remaining empathic, and maintaining positive regard. Be aware of your actual feelings. You may find it is easy to *play* as if you were behaving this way, but it is much more difficult to possess genuine empathy and positive regard in such a relationship.

Reverse roles. The therapist is now the client. Repeat the same procedure. As the client, become aware of what it feels like to be listened to without judgment.

Independence increases.

The need for help decreases.

This suggested series of events displays Rogers's concern that the client determine his or her own path with the therapist's encouraging and supporting efforts.

Some aspects of Rogerian therapy can be learned easily and in fact are used by many therapists. However, the personal characteristics that are necessary to be an effective therapist cannot be easily learned. The capacity to be truly present for another human being—empathic to that person's pain and confident of that person's growth—is a difficult personal demand.

There is a considerable body of research that seems to support these basic assumptions (Mitchell, Bozarth, & Krauft, 1977; Rogers, 1967; Traux & Mitchell, 1971). While Rachman & Wilson (1980), who have a strong behavioristic bias, reviewed major schools of psychotherapy and concluded that the prior research was limited by an inability to define and measure the relevant therapist variables, additional current work (Paterson, 1984; Raskin, 1986) continues to demonstrate a direct relationship between an emphatic therapist-to-client connection and resulting positive personality change for the client.

While the debate may continue among researchers, Rogers's insistence on certain fundamental prerequisites for being a therapist have been absorbed into most counseling training programs, which are organized by laypeople working on hot lines or in local crisis centers; ministers; social workers; marriage, child, and family counselors; and psychologists of many different persuasions. Rogers stresses that therapy is not a science, perhaps not even an art; instead, it is a relationship that depends partially on the mental health of the therapist to plant and nurture the seed of mental health in the client (Rogers, 1977).

Personal Reflection ——————————

—————————— Listening and Understanding

This exercise is adapted from one created by Rogers (1952a). He suggests it is a way to assess how well you understand another person.

The next time you get into an argument with your roommate, your friend, or a small group of friends, stop the discussion for a moment. Then institute this rule:

Each person can state his or her argument only after he or she has accurately restated the ideas and feelings of the previous speaker to that speaker's satisfaction. Before presenting your point of view, you must truly understand the opposition's thoughts and feelings well enough to summarize them.

When you try this exercise, you may discover it to be difficult. Once you are able to see your friends' points of view, you may find that your own opinion has changed drastically. Differences get reduced with understanding. Any differences that remain will be more clear to everyone.

Encounter Groups

Rogers asserted that people, not experts, have inherent therapeutic skills. Because Rogers believed this, it seemed almost inevitable that he would eventually become involved in encounter groups. When he moved to California, he devoted time to participating in, establishing, and evaluating this form of group experience.

Apart from group therapy, the encounter group has a history that predates its popularity during the 1950s and 1960s. Within the American Protestant tradition, and, to a lesser extent, within Hassidic Judaism, there have been group experiences engineered to alter people's attitudes toward themselves and to change how they interact with others. Techniques have included working within small peer groups, insisting on honesty and disclosure, focusing on the here and now, and maintaining a warm, supportive atmosphere (Ogden, 1972).

Modern encounter groups originated in Connecticut in 1946 with a training program for community leaders. This program included evening meetings for the trainers and observers to evaluate the day's events. Participants came to listen and eventually to take part in these extra sessions. The trainers realized that giving feedback to participants enhanced everyone's experience.

Some of the trainers of the Connecticut groups joined with others to establish National Training Laboratories (NTL) in 1947. NTL helped to expand and further develop the T-group (training group) as a tool in government and industry. Participation in these groups gave people experience in observing their own functioning and in learning how to respond to direct feedback about themselves.

What was striking in the T-group experiences was that a few weeks of working with peers in a relatively supportive setting could lead to major personality changes previously associated only with severe trauma or long-term psychotherapy. In a review of 106 studies, Gibb (1971) concluded that "the evidence is strong that intensive group training experiences have therapeutic effects" (in Rogers, 1970, p. 118).

While NTL was forming and developing primarily on the East Coast, Esalen Institute in California was exploring more intensive, less structured group processes. Dedicated to understanding new trends that emphasize the potentialities and values of human existence, Esalen hosted a series of workshops in the 1960s that came to be called *encounter,* or *basic encounter,* groups. Rogers's group work, which developed independently, resembled the basic encounter form developed by Esalen; however, Rogers's groups were more inhibited. His groups reflected some of the structural components (including the unobtrusive role of the leader) of the NTL format.

All encounter groups tend to provide a climate of psychological safety and encourage the immediate expression of feelings, as well as the reactions to these feelings. The leader, whatever his or her orientation, is responsible for setting and maintaining the tone and focus of a group. In this role, the therapist creates an atmosphere that can range from very businesslike to emotional and sexual, fearful and angry, or even violent. The psychological literature offers up groups of all descriptions (Howard, 1970; Maliver, 1973).

The encounter group . . . is one of our most successful modern inventions for dealing with the feeling of unreality, of impersonality and of distance and separation that exists in so many people. (Rogers in Smith, 1990, p. 12)

The basic theoretical concepts that Rogers applied to individual therapy he also applied to group work. In *Carl Rogers on Encounter Groups* (1970) he describes the major phenomena that occur in groups extending over several days. Although there are many periods of dissatisfaction, uncertainty, and anxiety in the group process, each of these gives way to a more open, less defended, more exposed, and more trusting climate. The emotional intensity and the capacity to tolerate this intensity appear to increase the longer the members of a group work together.

The Process of Encounter

A group begins with *milling around;* that is, members wait to be told how to behave, what to expect, how to deal with other members' expectations about the group. There is growing frustration as the group realizes that the members themselves will determine the way the group will function.

Other styles of group leadership lead to other kinds of effects. See Egan (1970); Lieberman, Miles, and Yalom (1973); and Schutz (1971, 1973) for alternative ways of describing, as well as running, group process. The following descriptions apply to groups Rogers either led or observed.

There is *initial resistance* to personal expression or exploration. "It is the public self that members tend to show each other, and only gradually, fearfully, and ambivalently do they take steps to reveal something of the private self" (Rogers, 1970, p. 16). This resistance is visible in most social situations—cocktail parties, dances, or picnics—where there usually is some activity other than self-exploration available to participants. An encounter group discourages seeking any other outlet.

As people continue to interact, they share *past feelings*. These are feelings associated with people in their past. Although the expression of these feelings is important for the individual, they nevertheless represent initial resistance; past experiences and the feelings connected to them are safer, and, because these experiences have a distant quality, they have the advantage of being less emotionally charged.

When people begin to express their feelings in relation to other group members within the context of the group, most often the *first expressions are negative:* "I don't feel comfortable with you." "You have a bitchy way of talking." "I don't believe you really mean what you said about your wife."

"Deeply positive feelings are much more difficult and dangerous to express than negative ones. If I say I love you, I am vulnerable and open to the most awful rejection. If I say I hate you, I am at best liable to attack, against which I can defend" (Rogers, 1970, p. 19). Failing to understand this characteristic of encounter group interaction has led to a number of failed group programs. For example, the Air Force developed race-relations programs, including black-white encounter sessions conducted by trained leaders. The end result of these encounters, however, often seemed to be an intensification of hostile racial feelings on both sides. Because of the complications in organizing encounter groups within the military, these sessions lasted no more than three hours—just enough time for the negative feelings to be expressed and not long enough for the rest of the process to unfold.

As the negative feelings are expressed and the group manages not to crumble, or split apart, *personally meaningful material* emerges. Not all members of the group are necessarily comfortable with these circumstances, but "climate of trust" develops and people start to take real risks.

As meaningful material emerges, people begin to express *immediate feelings* to one another, both positive and negative. "I like that you could share that with the group." "Every time I say something you look as if you'd like to strangle me." "Funny, I thought I'd dislike you. Now I'm sure of it."

As more and more emotions surface and are reacted to by the group, Rogers notes the *development of a healing capacity*. People begin to do things that seem to be helpful, that help others become aware of their own experience in nonthreatening ways. What the well-trained therapist has been taught to do through years of supervision and practice begins to emerge spontaneously from the group itself.

> This kind of ability shows up so commonly in groups that it has led me to feel that the ability to be healing or therapeutic is far more common in human life than we suppose. Often it needs only the permission granted—or freedom made possible—by the climate of a free-flowing group experience to become evident. (Rogers, 1970, p. 22)

One of the effects of the group's feedback and acceptance is that *people can accept themselves.* This self-acceptance can be seen in statements such as these: "I guess I really do try to keep people from getting close to me." "I am strong, even ruthless at times." "I want so much to be liked that I'll pretend half a dozen different things." Paradoxically, this acceptance of oneself, even one's faults, signals one's readiness to change. Rogers notes that the closer one is to congruence, the easier it is for one to become healthy. It is not until a person can admit to being a certain way that he or she can consider alternatives to current behavior patterns. "Acceptance, in the realm of psychological attitudes, often brings about a change in the thing accepted. Ironic, but true" (Nelson, 1973).

As the group continues its work, there is an increasing *impatience with defenses.* The group seems to demand the right to help, to heal, to open up people who appear constricted and defensive. Gently at times, almost savagely at others, the group *demands* that individuals be themselves; that is, that they do not hide their current feelings. "The expression of self by some members of the group has made it very clear that a deeper and more basic encounter is *possible,* and the group appears to strive intuitively and unconsciously toward this goal" (Rogers, 1970, p. 27).

Within every exchange or encounter there is *feedback,* through which the leader is continually being told of his or her effectiveness or lack of it.

It's all right to be me with all my strengths and weaknesses. My wife told me that I seem more authentic, more real, and more genuine. (In Rogers, 1970, p. 27)

Most of us consist of two separated parts, trying desperately to bring themselves together into an integrated soma, where the distinctions between mind and body, feelings and intellect, would be obliterated. (Rogers, 1973b, p. 385)

Each member who reacts to another may, in turn, get feedback about his or her reaction. This feedback may be difficult for a person to accept, but a person in a group cannot avoid for very long being confronted with the group opinion.

Rogers calls the extreme form of feedback *confrontation:* "There are times when the term feedback is far too mild to describe the interactions that take place—when it is better said that one individual *confronts* another, directly 'leveling' with him. Such confrontations can be positive, but frequently they are decidedly negative" (1970, p. 31). Confrontation builds feelings to such a pitch that some kind of resolution is demanded. This is a disturbing and difficult time for a group and, potentially, far more disturbing to the individuals involved.

For each surge of negative feelings, for each eruption of a fear, there also seems to be a following expression of support, of positive feelings, and closeness. Rogers, quoting a group member, says: "The incredible fact experienced over and over by members of the group was that when a negative feeling was fully expressed to another, the relationship grew and the negative feeling was replaced by a deep acceptance for the other" (1970, p. 34). It would appear that each time the group successfully demonstrates that it can accept and tolerate negative feelings without rejecting the person expressing them, the group members grow more trusting and open to one another. Many people describe their group experiences as the most positive, empathic, and accepting experiences of their lives. The popularity of encounter groups lies as much in the emotional warmth they generate as in their capacity to facilitate personal growth.

Are there dangers in the encounter experience? As with any intense form of interaction, there can be and have been unfortunate results. There have been psychotic breaks, suicides, and depressions, perhaps precipitated by participation in an encounter group. In most cases, the encounter experience seems to foster the kind of underlying mechanisms that allow human beings to help one another. That this does not inevitably occur in all cases should come as no surprise. But due to the work of Rogers and others, small group experiences are now understood as one way of developing personal skills and of counseling, motivating, and helping people. Such groups afford people the opportunity to have an unusually intense personal experience.

Conflict Resolution: The International Workshops

In the last decade of his life, Rogers decided to apply his ideas about the healing power of open communication in a group to national and international groups divided by race, ethnic orientation, war, or long simmering hatred. He believed and demonstrated that methods developed to aid individuals in personal growth, with skilled facilitation, could be applied to divided peoples in order to improve communication, develop real trust, and get them working together despite their opposing ideologies.

The groups thus facilitated by Rogers and other staff members of The Center for the Study of the Whole Person included Catholics and Protestants in Northern Ireland, blacks and whites in South Africa, and members of warring nations throughout Central America. He also worked with thousands of Russians in the former Soviet Union. His work was so well received there that a special program featuring Rogers's person-centered techniques was shown on national television.

These international workshops, unlike the formlessly structured traditional encounter groups, were organized around specific agendas that were understood to be political rather than personal.

The results were encouraging. In every group, inevitably the level of rhetoric declined and trust increased. Afterward, participants reported major shifts in their thinking about those whom they had been "against." Many formed new groups, applying the same format to other political and social settings (O'Hara, 1989; Rogers, 1986, 1987; Swenson, 1987).

Rogers took the therapeutic principles proven by clinicians and academic journals to be invaluable in individual practice and used these to make a positive and distinct contribution to world peace and international understanding (Caspary, 1991).

Evaluation

In a conversation in 1966, Rogers described his status:

> I don't have very much standing in psychology itself, and I couldn't care less. But in education and industry and group dynamics and social work and the philosophy of science and pastoral psychology and theology and other fields my ideas have penetrated and influenced in ways I never would have dreamt. (1970, p. 507)

By the time of his death, his work was accepted worldwide (Macy, 1987). In fact, he had established an extensive network for client-centered therapy in Japan (Hayashi, Kuno, Osawa, Shimizu, & Suetake, 1992; Saji & Linaga, 1983).

Critics focus on his view of the human condition, seeing it as less universal than Rogers suggested. To base therapy and learning on the innate capacity of a person for self-actualization is spoken of as hopelessly naive by a number of writers (Ellis, 1959; Thorne, 1957). They argue that Rogers did not take into account the ingrained patterns of psychopathology that can preclude improvement. Also, his theory is criticized for its resistance to rigorous tesing.

> Whether human nature, unspoiled by society, is as satisfactory as this viewpoint leads us to believe is certainly questionable. And it will be difficult either to confirm or to infirm this proposition, on empirical

grounds. . . . The emphasis on self-actualization . . . suffers, in our opinion, from the vagueness of its concepts, the looseness of its language, and the inadequacy of the evidence related to its major contentions. (Coffer & Appley, 1964, pp. 691–692)

Others suggest that self-actualization is neither innate nor a learned desire in human development but derives from a more primary drive, the need for stimulation (Butler & Rice, 1963). At the heart of these criticisms is a distrust of Rogers's steadfast optimism. His unbending belief in the innate goodness of human beings does not echo the experience of those who deride his work or his research. People who do not believe in essential human goodness rarely see it exhibited. They would say that it appears to be present in everyone, but it is latent. Maslow saw human goodness as easily muffled by personal and cultural pressures. And Rollo May says, "The Rogerian agenda hides the power drives of the therapist and not judging is not real." Walt Anderson insisted, "Not judging, not manipulating. This was not taking into account full humanness" (Arons & Harri, 1992). A careful and impartial reading of the results of Rogers's conflict resolution work suggests that treating people as he treated them leads to the results he predicted.

Reading the emotional as well as sensible critics of Rogers, one tends to conclude that either they have seen different kinds of patients or they simply do not accept the Rogerian ideas of trusting others to find their own way (Rogers & Skinner, 1956). Karl Menninger feels that Rogers's insistence on the indwelling thrust toward health is uttering at best a half truth. "Many patients whom we see seem to have committed themselves, consciously or unconsciously, to stagnation or slow spiritual death" (Menninger, 1963, p. 398).

The image of humanity described by Rogers seems to make little sense to his critics. It is therefore doubtful that further research and solid evidence of this humanity would make any difference to his critics. For Rogers, the test of the validity of his position is not dependent on theoretical elegance but on general utility. Rogers's works are constantly gaining in importance and are more widely read each year; and his popularity within clinical psychology continues to increase (Lipsey, 1974).

Although it is clearly an oversimplification, it can be said that just as Freud's ideas met a growing need to understand some aspects of human nature, so too do Rogers's ideas, only his meet a need that can be seen as particularly American. Rogers's philosophy "fits snugly into the American democratic tradition. The client is treated as an equal who has within him the power to 'cure' himself with no need to lean heavily on the wisdom of an authority or expert" (Harper, 1959, p. 83). Rogers's close alignment to the American worldview has helped facilitate the widespread acceptance of his ideas, his ways of doing therapy, and his concern with affirming the capacity and the desire of the individual to be whole.

His intense focus on the person is well expressed in a series of statements Rogers calls *significant learnings*. They are the summation of "the

You [Rollo May] never seemed to care whether the evil impulses in man are genetic and inherent or whether they are acquired at birth. . . . For me their origin makes a great deal of difference. (Rogers, 1982b)

This new world will be more human and humane. It will explore and develop the richness and capacities of the human mind and spirit. It will produce individuals who are more integrated and whole. It will be a world that prizes the individual person—the greatest of our resources. (Rogers, 1980a, p. 356)

thousands of hours I have spent working intimately with people in personal distress" (1961, p. 16). The following are some of his conclusions:

1. In my relationships with persons, I have found that it does not help in the long run to act as though I am something that I am not.

2. I find that I am more effective when I can listen acceptantly to myself, and can be myself.

3. I have found it of enormous value when I can permit myself to understand another person.

4. I have found it enriching to open channels whereby others can communicate their feelings, the private perceptual world to me.

5. I have found it highly rewarding when I can accept another person.

6. The more I am open to the realities in me and in the other person the less do I find myself wishing to rush in to "fix things."

7. I can trust my experience. (pp. 16–22)

His work in conflict resolution led to a set of similiar axioms, some of which Rogers stated as follows:

I am most satisfied politically:

When every person is helped to become aware of his or her own power and strength.

When group members learn that the sharing of power is more satisfying than endeavoring to use power to control others.

When each person enforces the group decisions through self-control of his or her behavior.

When every member of the group is aware of the consequences of a decision, on its members and the external world. (1984)

Rogers concludes his list by saying, "I'm sure many of you regard this list as hopelessly idealistic. But in my experience, especially when a facilitative climate is provided for a group, the members choose to move in somewhat the ways that I have described."

The Theory Firsthand: Excerpts from "Becoming Partners" and "The Linkage to Theory"

The two excerpts included here illustrate different aspects of Rogers's work. The first comes from a chapter on client-centered therapy; the second (not previously published) describes an event that occurred during an extended group experience.

Illustration of the Theory of Therapy[1]

The theoretical concepts that have been defined and the brief, formal statements of the process and outcomes of client-centered psychotherapy are astonishingly well illustrated in a letter written to the author by a young woman named Susan who has been in therapy with an individual who has obviously created the conditions for a therapeutic climate. The letter appears below, followed by an explanation of the way the theoretical statements have operated in her case.

Dear Dr. Rogers: I have just read your book, *On Becoming a Person,* and it left a great impression on me. I just happened to find it one day and started reading. It's kind of a coincidence because right now I need something to help me find *me.* Let me explain . . . [she tells of her present educational situation and some of her tentative plans for preparing herself for a helping vocation] . . . I do not feel that I can do much for others until I find me. . . .

I think that I began to lose me when I was in high school. I always wanted to go into work that would be of help to people but my family resisted, and I thought they must be right. Things went along smoothly for everyone else for four or five years until about two years ago, I met a guy who I thought was ideal. Then nearly a year ago I took a good look at us, and realized I was everything that *he* wanted me to be and nothing that *I* was. I have always been emotional and I have had many feelings. I could never sort them out and identify them. My fiancé would tell me that I was just mad or just happy and I would say okay and leave it at that. Then when I took this good look at us I realized that I was angry because I wasn't following my true emotions.

I backed out of the relationship gracefully and tried to find out where all the pieces were that I had lost. After a few months of searching had gone by I found that there were many more pieces than I knew what to do with and I couldn't seem to separate them. I began seeing a psychologist and am presently seeing him. He has helped me to find parts of me that I was not aware of. Some parts are bad by our society's standards but I have found them to be very good for me. I have felt more threatened and confused since going to him but I have also felt more relief and more sure of myself.

I remember one night in particular. I had been in for my regular appointment with the psychologist that day and I had come home feeling angry. I was angry because I wanted to talk about something but I couldn't identify what it was. By 8 o'clock that night I was so upset I was frightened. I called him and he told me to come to his office as soon as I could. I got there and cried for at least an hour and then the words came. I still don't know all of what I was saying. All I know is that *so much hurt* and *anger* came out of me that I *never really knew*

[1] From *Comprehensive Textbook of Psychiatry* by A. M. Freedman, H. I. Kaplan, and B. J. Sadock, 1975, Baltimore: Williams & Wilkins. Copyright 1975 by Williams and Wilkins. Reprinted by permission.

existed. I went home and it seemed that an *alien* had taken over and I was hallucinating like some of the patients I have seen in a state hospital. I continued to feel this way until one night I was sitting and thinking and I realized that this alien was the *me* that I had been trying to find.

I have noticed since that night that people no longer seem so strange to me. Now it is beginning to seem that life is just starting for me. I am alone right now but I am not frightened and I don't have to be doing something. I like meeting me and making friends with my thoughts and feelings. Because of this I have learned to enjoy other people. One older man in particular—who is very ill—makes me feel very much alive. He accepts everyone. He told me the other day that I have changed very much. According to him, I have begun to open up and love. I think that I have always loved people and I told him so. He said, "Were they aware of it?" I don't suppose I have expressed my love any more than I did my anger and hurt.

Among other things, I am finding out that I never had too much self-respect. And now that I am learning to really like me I am finally finding peace within myself. Thanks for your part in this.

The Linkage to Theory
by Carl Rogers

By summarizing some of the key portions of Susan's letter, the relationship between her statements and the theoretical ones will be evident.

"I was losing me. I needed something to help find *me.*" As she looks back, she realizes that she felt a vague discrepancy between the life she was experiencing and the person she believed herself to be. This kind of vague awareness of discrepancy or incongruence is a real resource for the person who becomes aware of it and attends to it. She also gives clues as to some of the reasons for her loss of contact with her own experiencing.

"My inner reactions meant to me that I wanted to do a certain type of work, but my family showed me that that was not their meaning." This certainly suggests the way in which her false self-concept has been built. Undoubtedly, the process began in childhood or she would not have accepted the family's judgment now. A child experiences something in his organism—a feeling of fear, or anger, or jealousy, or love, or, as in this case, a sense of choice, only to be told by parents that this is not what he is experiencing. Out of this grows the construct "Parents are wiser than I and know me better than I know myself." Also, there grows an increasing distrust in one's own experiencing and a growing incongruence between self and experiencing. In this case, Susan distrusts her inward feeling that she knows the work she wants to do and accepts the judgment of her family as right and sound. . . .

"Things went along smoothly for everyone else." This is a marvelously revealing statement. She has become a very satisfactory person for those whom she is trying to please. This false concept of self that they have unwittingly built up is just what they want. . . .

"I left me behind and tried to be the person my boyfriend wanted." Once more, she has denied to her awareness (not consciously) the experiencing of her own organism, and is simply trying to be the self desired by her lover. It is the same process all over. . . .

"Finally, something in me rebelled and I tried to find me again. But I couldn't, without help." Why did she at last rebel against the manner in which she had given herself away? This rebelling indicates the strength of the tendency toward actualization. Although suppressed and distorted for so long, it has reasserted itself. . . . She was fortunate in finding a counselor who evidently created a real and personal relationship, fulfilling the conditions of therapy.

"Now I am discovering *my* experiences—some of them bad, according to society, parents and boyfriend—but all constructive as far as I am concerned." She is now reclaiming as her own the right to evaluate her own experiences. The "locus of evaluation" now resides in herself, not in others. It is through exploring her own experiencing that she determines the meaning of the evidence being provided within her. When she says, "some parts are bad by society's standards but I have found them good for me," she might be referring to any of several feelings—her rebellion against her parents, against her boyfriend, her sexual feelings, her anger and bitterness, or other aspects of herself. At least as she trusts her own valuing of her experience, she finds that it is of worth and significance to her.

"An important turning point came when I was frightened and upset by unknown feelings within me." When aspects of experiencing have been denied to awareness, they may, in a therapeutic climate, come close to the surface of awareness with resulting strong anxiety or fright. . . .

"I cried for at least an hour." Without yet knowing what she is experiencing, she is somehow preparing herself to come in contact with these feelings and meanings which are so foreign to her concept of self.

"When the denied experiences broke through the dam, they turned out to be deep hurts and anger of which I had been *absolutely* unaware." Individuals are able completely to deny experiencings that are highly threatening to the concept of self. Yet, in a safe and non-threatening relationship, they may be released. Here, for the first time in her life, Susan is *experiencing* all the pent-up feelings of pain and rage that have been boiling under the facade of her false self. To experience something *fully* is not an intellectual process; in fact, Susan cannot even remember clearly what she said, but she did feel, in the immediate moment, emotions that for years had been denied to her awareness.

"I thought I was insane and that some foreign person had taken over in me." To find that "I am a person full of hurt, anger and rebellion," when formerly she had thought, "I am a person who always pleases others, who doesn't even know what her feelings are," is a very drastic shift in the concept of self. Small wonder that she felt this was an alien, a frightening someone she had never known.

"Only gradually did I recognize that this alien was the real *me.*" What she has discovered is that the submissive, malleable self by which she had been living, the self that tried to please others and was guided by their evaluations, attitudes, and expectations is no longer her self. This new self is a hurt, angry self, feeling good about parts of herself which others disapprove, experiencing many things, from wild hallucinatory thoughts to loving feelings. . . . Her self is becoming much more firmly rooted in her own organismic processes. Her concept of herself is beginning to be rooted in the spontaneously felt meanings of her experiencing. She is becoming a more congruent, a more integrated, person.

"I like meeting me and making friends with my thoughts and feelings." Here is the dawning self-respect, self-acceptance, and self-confidence of which she has been deprived for so long. She is even feeling some affection for herself. Now that she is much more acceptant of herself, she will be able to give herself more freely to others and to be more genuinely interested in others.

"I have begun to open up and love." She will find that as she is more expressive of her love she can also be more expressive of her anger and hurt, her likes and dislikes, her "wild" thoughts and feelings, which later may well turn out to be creative impulses. She is in the process of changing from a person with a false facade, a false self-concept, to a more healthy personality with a self that is much more congruent with experiencing, a self that can change as her experience changes.

"I am finally finding peace within myself." She has discovered a peaceful harmony in being a whole and congruent person—but she will be mistaken if she thinks this is a permanent reaction. Instead, if she is really open to her experience, she will find other hidden aspects of herself that she has denied to awareness, and each such discovery will give her uneasy and anxious moments or days until they are assimilated into a revised and changing picture of herself.

This case illustration pictures well the process and some of the outcomes of client-centered therapy. (Rogers in Freedman, Alfred, Kaplan, & Sadock, 1975)

Linda Mourns
by A Participant[2]

I want to write down, while it is fresh in my feelings, an incident which occurred in a large workshop. It was a 17-day workshop consisting of 70 very diverse people, focused on cognitive and experiential learning.

All had been in encounter groups for 6 sessions in the first 6 days. There had been special interest topical groups, and almost daily meetings of all 70 people. These community meetings had become deeper and more trusting. This episode occurred on the 8th day in a morning community meeting.

The group had been discussing, with great sensitivity, listening to all points of view, the issue raised by the fact that some people had brought visitors to the community sessions. Linda had been one of these, bringing her husband to the previous meeting, but she was not present this morning. A consensus was finally reached that in the future (without criticizing any person up to this point), anyone thinking of bringing a visitor should first raise the question with the community. The group passed on to another issue.

At this point Linda arrived, very late. Stephen, trying to be helpful, quickly described to her the conclusion we had reached. None of us gave Linda opportunity to respond though she evidently tried to. The group went on in its discussion. After a few moments someone sitting close to her called attention to the fact that Linda was shaking and crying, and the community immediately gave her space for her feelings. At first it seemed that she felt criticized, but Susan gave her a more complete description of what had gone on, and she seemed to accept that she was not being blamed or criticized. But still she was physically trembling, and very upset because she felt she had been cut off. It was not the first time, she said. She had felt cut off before. Encouraged to say more she turned to Natalie, Carl's daughter, and said, "I've felt you as very cold, and you've cut me off twice. I keep calling you Ellen—I don't know why and when I came to you to tell you how sorry I felt about that, you just said that was my problem, and turned away."

Natalie replied that her perception was very different. "I realized you were quite upset because you called me by the wrong name, but I said that though I could see it troubled *you,* it didn't bother me at all. I realize I haven't reached out to you, and I think you do want contact with me, but I don't feel I have rebuffed you."

It seemed that Linda felt more and more strongly about all this, and that she had not heard, or certainly had not accepted, Natalie's response. She said that she had observed the close relationship Natalie had with Lola, a Chicana, and that perhaps it was only with minority persons that Natalie could relate, rather than to her—tall, blonde, and middle class. This led to an angry outburst from Lola about being stereotyped, and about five minutes was spent in rebuilding the relationship between Linda and Lola. The group brought Linda back to the issue between her and Natalie. It seemed quite obvious that her feelings were so strong that they could not come simply from the incident she mentioned. Robert said he had noticed that he, Linda, and Natalie were all similar—tall, slim, blonde—and that perhaps Linda was feeling that Natalie should at least relate to someone so like her, rather than to Lola, who was short and dark. Linda considered this, wondered if there might be something to it, but clearly was not deeply touched by the idea.

At least two other possible bases for her strong feelings were caringly and tentatively suggested to her. To the first she said, "I'm trying on that hat, but it doesn't seem to fit." To the second she said, "That doesn't seem to fit either."

I sat there feeling completely mystified. I wanted to understand just what it was she was troubled about, but I couldn't get any clue to follow. I believe many others were feeling the same way. Here she was with tears in her eyes, feeling something far beyond some possible imaginary rebuff, but what was it?

Then Annette said, "This may be inappropriate, but I'm going to say it anyway. When you arrived, Linda, I thought you *were* Natalie, you looked so much alike. I feel envious when I watch the beautiful open relationship between Natalie and her father. I had that kind of relationship with my father. I wonder if there is any connection between you and your father and Carl?" "That's it!" Linda sobbed, acting as though she had been struck by a bolt of lightning. She collapsed into herself, weeping her heart out. Between sobs she said, "I didn't really cry at all at my father's death. . . . He really died for me long before his death. . . . What can I do?" People responded that he was still part of her, and she could still mourn for him. Annette, who was near her, embraced and comforted her. After quite a time she quieted down, and then in an almost inaudible voice, asked Carl if she could hold his hand. He reached out and she came across the circle and fell into his arms and her whole body shook with sobs as he held her close. Slowly she felt better and sat between Carl and Natalie, saying to Carl, "And you look like him too, but I never realized *that* was what I was feeling."

As the three sat there with their arms around each other, someone remarked on how much alike Linda and Natalie looked. They could be sisters. Carl said, "Here we are, sitting for a family portrait." Linda said, "But they'll ask, 'Why is that girl in the middle sitting there with such a big smile on her face?,'" and the incident was rounded off as the whole group joined in her sparkling laughter of release and relief.

Carl Rogers's Comments, Later

I was very much involved personally and emotionally in this incident, which has, I believe, been quite accurately described. I have also thought about it much since. It is temptingly easy to diagnose the causes of it: Linda, repressing her pain at losing her father, and seeing a good daughter-father relationship, projects her pain onto Natalie, first by distorting an incident so she could be angry at Natalie, then distortedly expressing her pain through anger at Natalie's close relationship with another woman—etc., etc. To me such "explanations" are irrelevant. But as I try to view it with some perspective it exemplifies many aspects of the existential dynamics of change in personality and behavior.

1. It shows clearly the depth to which feelings can be buried, so that they are totally unknown to the owner. Here it is particularly interesting because it was obvious to Linda and to the group that she was feeling *something* very deeply. Yet she was clearly labelling it in ways which were not truly significant. The organism closes itself to the pain of recognizing a feeling clearly, if that would involve reorganizing the concept of self in some significant way.

2. It is a splendid example of how the flow of experiencing (Gendlin's concept) is used as a referent for discovering the felt meaning. Linda tried on the various descriptions and labels which were given to her and they didn't "fit." Didn't fit what? Clearly it is something organismic against which she is checking. But when Annette pointed— by telling of her own feelings—at another possibility, Linda realized *immediately* and with complete certainty that *this* was what she was experiencing. It *matched* what was going on in her. As is so often true when a person is understood, she was able to follow her experiencing further, and to realize that in addition to the envy, she felt much pain, and that she had never mourned for her father, because he had died for her years before his death.

3. To me this is a very precise example of a moment of irreversible change, the minute unit of change which taken with other such units constitutes the whole basis for alteration of personality and behavior. I have defined these moments of change in this way. When a previously denied feeling is experienced in a full and complete way, in expression and in awareness, and is experienced acceptantly, not as something wrong or bad, a fundamental change occurs which is almost irreversible. What I mean by this last term is that Linda might, under certain circumstances, later deny the validity of this moment, and believe that she was not envious, or not in mourning. But her whole organism has *experienced* those feelings completely and at most she could only temporarily deny them in her awareness.

4. We see here an instance of a change in the way she perceives herself. She has been, in her own eyes, a person with no close relationship to her father, unmoved by his death, a person who did not care. Quite possibly she had also believed she was guilty because of those elements. Now that facet of her concept of self is clearly changed. She can now see herself as a person wanting very much a close relationship, and mourning the lack of that as well as his death. The almost inevitable result of this alteration in her self-concept will be a change in some of her behaviors. What those changes will be can only be speculation at this point—possibly a change in behavior toward older men, possibly more open sorrow over other tragedies. We cannot yet know.

5. It is an example of the kind of therapeutic climate in which change can occur. It is a caring group, a group which respects her worth enough to listen to her intently, even when such listening breaks into the "task" on which the group was working. They are trying very hard to convey as much understanding as they can. Annette's realness in exposing her own feelings is an example of the openness and

"transparency" of the group members. So all the ingredients for growth and change are there, and Linda makes use of them.

6. It is exciting evidence that this growth-promoting climate can evolve, even in such a large group. Sixty-nine people can be therapists, perhaps even more effectively than one, if the group is trustworthy, and if the individual can come to realize that, and to trust their caring, understanding and genuineness.

To me it is a small gem—personally meaningful in my experience, but also rich in theoretical implications.

Annotated Bibliography

Raskin, N. J., & Rogers, C. (1989). Person-centered therapy. In R. Corsini & D. Wedding (Eds.), *Current psychotherapies* (4th ed.) (pp. 155–194). Itasca, IL: Peacock Publishers. Finished after Rogers's death, it is a substantial, well-written summary of his ideas as they relate to psychotherapy.

Rogers, C. R. (1951). *Client-centered therapy: Its current practice, implications and theory.* Boston: Houghton Mifflin. The core volume for what is called Rogerian therapy. Rogers himself sees some of the material here as too rigid. Still a useful and important book.

————. (1959). A theory of therapy, personality, and interpersonal relationships, as developed in the client-centered framework. In S. Koch (Ed.), *Psychology, the study of a science: Vol. 3. Formulations of the person and the social context,* (pp. 184–225). New York: McGraw-Hill. The only time Rogers laid out his work in a formal, detailed, and organized theory. He succeeds, but it remains one of his least read works. The obscurity is undeserved. If you stick with Rogers, eventually you will want to read this.

————. (1961). *On becoming a person: A therapist's view of psychotherapy.* Boston: Houghton Mifflin. A personal, practical, and extensive consideration of the major themes in Rogers's work. A book that is still lucid and useful to people in the people-helping professions.

Rogers, C. R., Stevens, B. (1967). *Person to person.* Walnut Creek, CA: Real Peoples Press (New York: Pocket Books, 1971). A delightful exchange between articles, most by Rogers with fascinating commentaries by Barry Stevens.

————. (1969). *Freedom to learn.* Columbus, OH: Merrill. A set of challenges to educators. Rogers sees that most teaching is set up to discourage learning and encourage anxiety and maladjustment. More strident than his gentler, therapy-oriented volumes.

————. (1970). *Carl Rogers on encounter groups*. New York: Harper & Row. A sensible discussion of the ups and downs of the encounter group. Most of the discussion is drawn from groups that Rogers has run or observed, so it is both representative and explicit. Probably the best introduction to this form of interpersonal gathering in print. Not sensational and not critical.

————. (1972). *Becoming partners: Marriage and its alternatives*. New York: Dell (Delacorte Press). Rogers interviews a number of couples who have taken varying approaches to marriage. He points out the strengths and weaknesses of the relationships. Mainly reporting, he calls attention to those forces that lead to successful or unsuccessful long-term relationships. Useful.

————. (1978). *Carl Rogers on personal power*. New York: Dell. The first book in which Rogers considers the wide social implications in his work. It is subtitled accurately: "Inner strength and its revolutionary impact. The extension of ideas developed in therapy to educational, and political systems."

————. (1980). *A way of being*. Boston: Houghton Mifflin. A collection of essays and speeches that serves as a small autobiography and that illustrates Rogers's growing realization of the social impact of his work beyond psychology. Moving and optimistic, this is his most intimate and gentle book.

————. (1983). *Freedom to learn for the 80's*. Columbus, OH: Merrill. A revision and expansion of the earlier edition. He spends considerable time describing his own work in classrooms, facilitating "responsible freedom."

References

Ansbacher, H. (1990). Alfred Adler's influence on the three leading cofounders of humanistic psychology. *Journal of Humanistic Psychology, 30*(4), 45–53.

Arons, M., & Harri (1992). Conversations with the founders. Manuscript submitted for publication (*Journal of Humanistic Psychology*).

Bandler, R., & Grinder, J. (1975). *The structure of magic* (Vols. 1, 2). Palo Alto, CA: Science and Behavior.

Boy, A. V., & Pine, G. J. (1982). *Client-centered counseling: A renewal*. Boston: Allyn and Bacon.

Butler, J. M., & Rice, L. N. (1963). Adience, self-actualization, and drive theory. In J. M. Wepman & R. W. Heine (Eds.), *Concepts of personality* (pp. 79–110). Chicago: Aldine.

Campbell, P., & McMahon, E. (1974). Religious type experiences in the context of humanistic and transpersonal psychology. *Journal of Transpersonal Psychology, 6,* 11–17.

Caspary, W. (1991). Carl Rogers—Values, persons and politics: The dialectic of individual and community. *Journal of Humanistic Psychology, 31*(4), 8–31.

Coffer, C. N., & Appley, M. (1964). *Motivation: Theory and research.* New York: Wiley.

Egan, G. (1970). *Encounter: Group processes for interpersonal growth.* Monterey, CA: Brooks/Cole.

Ellis, A. (1959). Requisite conditions for basic personality change. *Journal of Consulting Psychology, 23,* 538–540.

Evans, R. I. (1975). *Carl Rogers: The man and his ideas.* New York: Dutton.

Freedman, A. M., Kaplan, H. I., & Sadock, B. J. (1975). *Comprehensive textbook of psychiatry.* Baltimore: Williams & Wilkins.

Fuller, R. (1982). Carl Rogers, religion, and the role of psychology in American culture. *Journal of Humanistic Psychology, 22*(4), 21–32.

Gibb, J. R. (1971). The effects of human relations training. In A. E. Bergin & S. L. Garfield (Eds.), *Handbook of psychotherapy and behavior change* (pp. 2114–2176). New York: Wiley.

Gordon, W. (1961). *Synectics.* New York: Harper & Row.

Hall, C., & Lindzey, G. (1978). *Theories of personality* (3rd ed.). New York: Wiley.

Harper, R. A. (1959). *Psychoanalysis and psychotherapy.* Englewood Cliffs, NJ: Prentice-Hall.

Hayashi, S., Kuno, T., Osawa, M., Shimizu, M., & Suetake, Y. (1992). The client-centered therapy and person-centered approach in Japan: Historical development, current status and perspectives. *Journal of Humanistic Psychology, 32*(2) 115–136.

Holden, C. (1977). Carl Rogers: Giving people permission to be themselves. *Science, 198,* 31–34.

Howard, J. (1970). *Please touch: A guided tour of the human potential movement.* New York: McGraw-Hill.

Kirschenbaum, H. (1980). *On becoming Carl Rogers.* New York: Dell (Delacorte Press).

Krasner, L., & Ullman, L. (1973). *Behavior influence and personality: The social matrix of human action.* New York: Holt, Rinehart and Winston.

Lawrence, D. H. (1960). *The ladybird together with the captain's doll.* London: Harborough.

Lieberman, M. A., Miles, M. B., & Yalom, I. D. (1973). *Encounter groups: First facts.* New York: Basic Books.

Lipsey, M. W. (1974). Research and relevance: A survey of graduate students and faculty in psychology. *The American Psychologist, 29,* 541–554.

McCleary, R. A., & Lazarus, R. S. (1949). Autonomic discrimination without awareness. *Journal of Personality, 19,* 171–179.

Macy, F. (1987). The legacy of Carl Rogers in the U.S.S.R. *Journal of Humanistic Psychology, 27*(3), 305–308.

Maliver, B. L. (1973). *The encounter game.* New York: Stein and Day.

Menninger, K. (1963). *The vital balance: The life process in mental health and illness.* New York: Viking Press.

Mitchell, K., Bozarth, J., & Krauft, C. (1977). A reappraisal of the therapeutic effectiveness of accurate empathy, nonpossessive warmth and genuineness. In A. Gurman & A. Razin (Eds.), *Effective psychotherapy.* Oxford: Pergamon Press.

Nelson, A. (1973). *A conversation with Carl Rogers.* Unpublished manuscript.

Nitya, Swami (1973). Excerpts from a discussion. *Journal of Transpersonal Pycology, 5,* 200–204.

Ogden, T. (1972). The new pietism. *Journal of Humanistic Psychology, 12,* 24–41. (Also appears in *The intensive group experience: The new pietism.* Philadelphia: Westminster Press, 1972.)

O'Hara, M. (1989). Person-centered approach as conscientizaçao: The works of Carl Rogers and Paulo Friere. *Journal of Humanistic Psychology, 29*(1), 11–35.

Paterson, C. H. (1984). Empathy, warmth, and genuineness in psychotherapy: A review of reviews. *Psychotherapy, 21,* 431–438.

Perry, J. W. (1974). *The far side of madness.* Englewood Cliffs, NJ: Prentice-Hall.

Polanyi, M. (1958). *Personal knowledge.* Chicago: University of Chicago Press.

———. (1959). *The study of man.* Chicago: University of Chicago Press.

Rachman, S. J., & Wilson, G. T. (1980). *The effects of psychological therapy* (2nd ed.). Oxford: Pergamon Press.

Raskin, N. (1986). Client-centered group psychotherapy, Part II. Research of client-centered groups. *Person-Centered Review, 1,* 389–408.

Raskin, N. J., & Rogers, C. (1989). Person-centered therapy. In R. Corsini & D. Wedding (Eds.), *Current psychotherapies* (4th ed.) (pp. 155–194). Itasca, IL: Peacock Publishers.

Rogers, C. R. (1939). *The clinical treatment of the problem child.* Boston: Houghton Mifflin.

———. (1942). *Counseling and psychotherapy.* Boston: Houghton Mifflin.

———. *Client-centered therapy: Its current practice, implications and theory.* Boston: Houghton Mifflin.

———. (1952a). Communication: Its blocking and its facilitation. *Northwestern University Information, 20*(25).

———. (1952b). Client-centered psychotherapy. *Scientific American,*

187(5), 66–74.

———. (1959). A theory of therapy, personality, and interpersonal relationships, as developed in the client-centered framework. In S. Koch (Ed.), *Psychology; the study of a science: Vol. 3. Formulations of the person and the social context* (pp. 184–256). New York: McGraw-Hill.

———. (1961). *On becoming a person: A therapist's view of psychotherapy*. Boston: Houghton Mifflin.

———. (1964). Towards a science of the person. In T. W. Wann (Ed.), *Behaviorism and phenomenology: Contrasting bases for modern psychology* (pp. 109–133). Chicago: University of Chicago Press.

———. (1967). Carl Rogers. In E. Boring & G. Lindzey (Eds.), *History of psychology in autobiography* (Vol. 5). New York: Appleton-Century-Crofts.

———. (1969). *Freedom to learn*. Columbus, OH: Merrill.

———. (1970). *Carl Rogers on encounter groups*. New York: Harper & Row.

———. (1972). *Becoming partners: Marriage and its alternatives*. New York: Dell (Delacorte Press).

———. (1973a). My philosophy of interpersonal relationships and how it grew. *Journal of Humanistic Psychology, 13,* 3–16.

———. (1973b). Some new challenges. *The American Psychologist, 28,* 379–387.

———. (1974a). In retrospect: Forty-six years. *The American Psychologist, 29,* 115–123.

———. (1974b). The project at Immaculate Heart: An experiment in self-directed change. *Education, 95*(2), 172–189.

———. (1975a). Empathic: An unappreciated way of being. *The Counseling Psychologist: Carl Rogers on Empathy* (special topic), *5*(2), 2–10.

———. (1975b). The emerging person: A new revolution. In R. I. Evans (Ed.), *Carl Rogers: The man and his ideas*. New York: Dutton.

———. (1977). A therapist's view of personal goals. *Pendle Hill Pamphlet 108*. Wallingford, PA: Pendle Hill.

———. (1978). *Carl Rogers on personal power*. New York: Dell.

———. (1980a). *A way of being*. Boston: Houghton Mifflin.

———. (1980b). Growing old—Or older and growing. *Journal of Humanistic Psychology, 20*(4), 5–16.

———. (1982a). A psychologist looks at nuclear war; Its threat, its possible prevention. *Journal of Humanistic Psychology, 22*(4), 9–20.

———. (1982b). Reply to Rollo May's letter to Carl Rogers. *Journal of Humanistic Psychology, 22*(4) 85–89.

———. (1983). *Freedom to learn for the 80's*. Columbus, OH: Merrill.

———. (1984). A client-centered, person-centered approach to therapy. Unpublished manuscript.

———. (1986). The Rust workshop. *Journal of Humanistic Psychology, 26*(3), 23–45.

———. (1987). Inside the world of the Soviet professional. *Journal of*

Humanistic Psychology, 27(3), 277–304.

Rogers, C. R., Gendlin, E. T., Kiesler, D. J., & Truax, C. G. (1967). *The therapeutic relationship and its impact: A study of psychotherapy with schizophrenics.* Madison, WI: University of Wisconsin Press.

Rogers, C. R., & Haigh, G. I. (1983). Walk softly through life. *Voices: The Art and Science of Psychotherapy, 18,* 6–14.

Rogers, C. R., with Hart, J. (1970a). Looking back and ahead: A conversation with Carl Rogers. In J. T. Hart & T. M. Tomlinson (Eds.), *New directions in client-centered therapy* (pp. 502–534). Boston: Houghton Mifflin.

Rogers, C. R., & Ryback, D. (1984). One alternative to nuclear planetary suicide. *Counseling Psychologist, 12*(2), 3–12.

Rogers, C. R., & Skinner, B. F. (1956). Some issues concerning the control of human behavior. *Science, 124,* 1057–1066.

Saji, M., & Linaga, K. (1983). *Client chushin rycho* [Client-centered therapy], Tokyo: Yuhikaku.

Schutz, W. C. (1971). *Here comes everybody.* New York: Harper & Row.

———. (1973). *Elements of encounter.* Big Sur, CA: Joy Press.

Smith, M. B. (1990). Humanistic Psychology. *Journal of Humanistic Psychology, 30*(4), 6–21.

Swenson, G. (1987). When personal and political processes meet: The Rust workshop. *Journal of Humanistic Psychology, 27*(3), 309–333.

Tart, C. T. (1971). Scientific foundations for the study of altered states of consciousness. *Journal of Transpersonal Psychology, 3,* 93–124.

———. (1975). Some assumptions of orthodox, Western psychology. In C. T. Tart (Ed.), *Transpersonal psychologies* (pp. 59–112). New York: Harper & Row.

Thorne, F. C. (1957). Critique of recent developments in personality counseling therapy. *Journal of Clinical Psychology, 13,* 234–244.

Traux, C., & Mitchell, K. (1971). Research on certain therapist interpersonal skills. In A. Bergin & S. Garfield (Eds.), *Handbook of psychotherapy and behavior change* (p. 299). New York: Wiley.

Van Belle, H. A. (1980). *Basic intent and the therapeutic approach of Carl Rogers.* Toronto, Canada: Wedge Foundation.

Chapter Thirteen

Abraham Maslow and Transpersonal Psychology

Maslow believed that an accurate and viable theory of personality must include not only the depths but also the heights that each individual is capable of attaining. He is one of the founders of humanistic psychology and transpersonal psychology, two major new fields that evolved as alternatives to behaviorism and psychoanalysis.

Before Maslow, Western psychology can be said to have been divided into two great fields: behaviorism and psychoanalysis. Both areas have tended to ignore or to explain away the great cultural, social, and individual achievements of humanity, including creativity, love, altruism, and mysticism. These were among Maslow's greatest interests.

Maslow was a pioneer. He was most interested in exploring new issues and new fields. His work is rather a collection of thoughts, opinions, and hypotheses than a fully developed theoretical system. More an armchair philosopher than a scientist, Maslow rarely came up with final answers. His great genius was in formulating significant questions—questions that are considered critical by many social scientists today.

One reviewer has written,

> Abraham Maslow has done more to change our view of human nature and human possibilities than has any other American psychologist of the past fifty years. His influence, both direct and indirect, continues to grow, especially in the fields of health, education, and management theory, and in the personal and social lives of millions of Americans. (Leonard, 1983, p. 326)

Maslow's approach to psychology can be summed up in the opening sentence of his most influential book, *Toward a Psychology of Being* (1986):

> There is now emerging over the horizon a new conception of human sickness and of human health, a psychology that I find so thrilling and so full of wonderful possibilities that I yield to the temptation to present it publicly even before it is checked and confirmed, and before it can be called reliable scientific knowledge. (p. 3)

Personal History

Abraham Maslow was born in Brooklyn, New York, in 1908, of Russian-Jewish immigrant parents. His father was a barrel maker by trade who moved to the United States from Russia as a young man. He later sent for the woman who would be his wife. In his youth, Abe was extraordinarily shy and very neurotic, ". . . during all my first twenty years—depressed, terribly unhappy, lonely, isolated, self-rejecting" (Maslow in International Study Project, 1972).

Maslow was an extremely bright high school student. He entered New York City College at the age of 18. His father wanted Abe to become a lawyer, but Abe could not stand the thought of law school. When his father asked what he intended to do instead, Abe said he wanted to go on studying "everything."

As a teenager, Maslow fell in love with his first cousin and found excuses to spend time with her family, often gazing love-struck at her but not daring to touch her. He experienced his first kiss at the age of 19, when he finally kissed his cousin. Maslow later described this as one of the peak experiences of his life. Her acceptance of him, instead of the rejection he so feared, was a tremendous boost to his shaky self-esteem. They were married a year later. Marriage and his immersion into psychology began a whole new life for Abe.

In his first year in college, Maslow discovered music and drama. He fell in love with both. It was a love that would remain with him throughout his life. Maslow transferred to the University of Wisconsin, where his interest focused on psychology. He was captured by J. B. Watson's vision of behaviorism as a powerful tool for affecting human life. Maslow trained in the experimental method at Wisconsin and worked in the psychology laboratory there, conducting research using rats and other animals. He received his bachelor's degree in 1930, and his doctorate in 1934, at the age of 26.

After graduation, Maslow returned to New York to work with Edward Thorndike, a brilliant and eminent Columbia University psychologist. Thorndike was particularly impressed with Maslow's performance on the intelligence test that Thorndike developed. By scoring 195 on the test, Maslow had received the second highest IQ score thus far recorded. Eighteen months later, Maslow found a teaching job at Brooklyn College, where he remained for 14 years. New York at that time was a tremendously stimulating intellectual center, housing many of the finest scholars who had fled Nazi persecution. Maslow studied with a number of psychotherapists, including Alfred Adler, Erich Fromm, and Karen Horney. He was most strongly influenced by Max Wertheimer, one of the founders of Gestalt psychology, and by Ruth Benedict, a brilliant cultural anthropologist.

Maslow's interest in the practical applications of psychology dates back to the beginning of his career. Even as a behaviorist graduate student, Maslow was convinced that Freud was right in his emphasis on the importance of sexuality. Maslow chose for his dissertation research the relationship between dominance and sexual behavior among primates. After leaving Wisconsin, he began an extensive investigation of human sexual behavior. Maslow believed that any improvement in our understanding of sexual functioning would tremendously improve human adjustment.

During World War II, when he realized how little psychology had contributed to major world problems, Maslow's interests shifted from experimental psychology to social and personality psychology. He wanted to devote himself to "discovering a psychology for the peace table" (Hall, 1968, p. 54).

Human nature is not nearly as bad as it has been thought to be. (Maslow, 1968, p. 4)

In addition to his professional work, Maslow became involved with family business affairs during a prolonged illness. His interest in business and in practical applications of psychology eventually resulted in *Eupsychian Management* (1965), a compilation of thoughts and articles related to management and industrial psychology. He wrote these during the summer that he spent as Visiting Fellow at a small plant in California.

In 1951, Maslow accepted a position near Boston at Brandeis University, which had just been established, and remained there until 1968. He was chairman of the first psychology department and was instrumental in the development of the university as a whole. Throughout his career, Maslow's pioneering work was generally dismissed as unscientific and considered outside of the mainstream of psychology. He was personally liked by his colleagues and his ideas gradually became better appreciated. Much to his own surprise, Maslow was elected president of the American Psychological Association in 1967 and served for one year.

Maslow left Brandeis to accept a fellowship that allowed him to write full time. In June 1970, at the age of 62, he died from a heart attack.

To Maslow, the labels used for the various schools of psychology were highly limiting. "We shouldn't have to say humanistic psychology. The adjective should be unnecessary. Don't think of me as being antibehavioristic. I'm antidoctrinaire . . . I'm against anything that closes doors and cuts off possibilities" (Maslow in Hall, 1968, p. 57).

I am a Freudian, I am behavioristic, I am humanistic. (Maslow, 1971, p. 144)

Intellectual Antecedents

Psychoanalysis

Psychoanalytic theory significantly influenced Maslow's life and thought. Freud's sophisticated description of the neurotic and maladaptive aspects of human behavior inspired Maslow to develop a scientifically grounded psychology relevant to the full range of human behavior. Maslow's own personal analysis profoundly affected him and demonstrated the tremendous differences that exist between intellectual knowledge and actual gut-level experience.

In 1955, when psychotherapy was still in its infancy, Maslow believed that psychoanalysis provided the best system for analyzing psychopathology and also the best psychotherapy available. However, he found the psychoanalytic system quite unsatisfactory as a general psychology for all of human thought and behavior.

To oversimplify the matter somewhat, it is as if Freud supplied to us the sick half of psychology and we must now fill it out with the healthy half. (Maslow, 1968, p. 5)

The picture of man it presents is a lopsided, distorted puffing up of his weaknesses and shortcomings that purports then to describe him fully. . . . Practically all the activities that man prides himself on, and that give meaning, richness, and value to his life, are either omitted or pathologized by Freud. (Maslow in Krippner, 1972, p. 71)

Social Anthropology

As a student at Wisconsin, Maslow was seriously interested in the work of social anthropologists, such as Bronislaw Malinowski, Margaret Mead, Ruth Benedict, and Ralph Linton. In New York, he studied with leading figures in the field of culture and personality, which is concerned with the application of psychoanalytic theories to the analysis of behavior in other cultures. In addition, Maslow was fascinated by William Sumner's book, *Folkways* (1940) and Sumner's analysis of human behavior: that it is largely determined by cultural patterns and prescriptions. Maslow was so deeply inspired by Sumner that he vowed to devote himself to the same areas of study.

Gestalt Psychology

Maslow was also a serious student of Gestalt psychology, which stresses the importance of studying perception, cognition, and other sophisticated human activities in terms of complex whole systems. He sincerely admired Max Wertheimer, whose work on productive thinking is closely related to Maslow's writings on cognition and to his work on creativity. For Maslow, as for Gestalt psychologists, an essential element in creative thinking and effective problem solving is the ability to perceive and think in terms of wholes or patterns rather than isolated parts.

Another extremely important influence on Maslow's thinking was the work of Kurt Goldstein, a neurophysiologist who emphasized that the organism is a unified whole, that what happens in any part affects the entire organism. Maslow's work on self-actualization was inspired in part by Goldstein, who was the first to use the term.

Maslow dedicated *Toward a Psychology of Being* (1968) to Goldstein. In the preface, he stated:

> If I had to express in a single sentence what Humanistic Psychology has meant for me, I would say that it is an integration of Goldstein (and Gestalt Psychology) with Freud (and the various psychodynamic psychologies), the whole joined with the scientific spirit that I was taught by my teachers at the University of Wisconsin. (1968, p. v)

Kurt Goldstein

A neurophysiologist whose main focus was brain-damaged patients, Goldstein viewed self-actualization as a fundamental process in every organism, a process that may necessarily have negative as well as positive effects on the individual. Goldstein wrote that every organism has one primary drive: "[The] organism is governed by the tendency to actualize, as much as possible, its individual capacities, its 'nature,' in the world" (1939, p. 196).

Goldstein argued that tension release is a strong drive but only in sick organisms. For a healthy organism, the primary goal is "the *formation* of a certain level of tension, namely, that which makes possible further ordered activity" (1939, pp. 195–196). A drive such as hunger is a special case of self-actualization, in which tension reduction is sought to return the organism to optimal condition for further expression of its capacities. However, only in an extreme situation does such a drive become demanding. Goldstein asserts that a normal organism can temporarily put off eating, sex, sleep, and so forth if other motives, such as curiosity or playfulness, are present.

Capacities clamor to be used, and cease their clamor only when they are used sufficiently. (Maslow, 1968, p. 152)

According to Goldstein, successful coping with the environment often involves a certain amount of uncertainty and shock. The healthy self-actualizing organism actually invites such shock by venturing into new situations in order to utilize its capacities. For Goldstein (and for Maslow also), self-actualization does not mean the end of problems and difficulties; on the contrary, growth may often bring a certain amount of pain and suffering. Goldstein wrote that an organism's capacities determine its needs. The possession of a digestive system makes eating a necessity; muscles require movement. A bird *needs* to fly just as an artist *needs* to create, despite the fact that creation can require painful struggle and great effort.

Major Concepts

Hierarchy of Needs

Maslow was deeply concerned that most of what we know about human motivation comes from the analysis of patients in therapy. Although we have learned a tremendous amount from these patients, they clearly do not accurately reflect the motivations of the population at large. In his theory of the hierarchy of needs, Maslow accomplished an intellectual tour de force. He managed to integrate in a single model the approaches of the major schools of psychology—behaviorism, psychoanalysis and its offshoots, humanistic and transpersonal psychology. He tried to demonstrate that no one approach is better or more valid than another. Each has its own place and its own relevance.

Maslow defined neurosis and psychological maladjustment as "deficiency diseases"; that is, they are caused by deprivation of certain basic needs, just as the absence of certain vitamins causes illness. The best examples of basic needs are the physiological ones, such as hunger, thirst, and sleep. Deprivation clearly leads to eventual illness, and the satisfaction of these needs is the only cure for the illness. Basic needs are found in all individuals. The amount and kind of satisfaction will vary in different societies, but basic needs (like hunger) can never be completely ignored.

Physiological needs include the need for food, drink, oxygen, sleep, and sex. In our culture, these needs are satisfied almost automatically for most people. However, if biological needs are not met for a long period of time, the individual becomes almost completely focused on fulfilling them. Maslow argues that a person who is literally dying of thirst has no great interest in fulfilling any other needs. However, once this particular, overwhelming need is satisfied, it becomes less important, allowing other needs to surface.

Maslow's Basic Need Hierarchy

physiological needs	(hunger, sleep, sex, etc.)
safety needs	(stability, order)
belonging and love needs	(family, friendship)
esteem needs	(self-respect, recognition)
self-actualization needs	(development of capacities)

Certain *psychological* needs must also be satisfied in order to maintain health. Maslow includes the following as basic psychological needs: the need for safety, security, and stability; the need for love and a sense of belonging; and the need for self-respect and esteem. In addition, every individual has growth needs: a need to develop one's potentials and capabilities and a need for self-actualization.

By *safety* needs, Maslow means the individual's need to live in a relatively stable, safe, predictable environment. We have a basic need for structure, order, and limits. People need freedom from fear, anxiety, and chaos. As with physiological needs, most people take a smoothly running, stable, protective society for granted. In modern society, the need for safety becomes dominant only in real emergencies, such as natural disasters, epidemics, and riots.

All people have *belonging and love* needs. We are motivated to seek close relationships with other people, and need to feel part of various groups, such as family and groups of peers. These needs, Maslow wrote, are more and more frustrated in our highly mobile, individualistic society. Further, the frustration of these needs is most often found at the core of psychological maladjustment.

Maslow (1987) described two kinds of *esteem* needs. First, there is a desire for competence and individual achievement. Second, we need respect from others—status, fame, appreciation, and recognition. When these needs are not met, the individual tends to feel inferior, weak, or helpless. Maslow pointed out that the esteem needs were stressed by

Living at the higher need level means greater biological efficiency, greater longevity, less disease, better sleep, appetite, etc. (Maslow, 1948)

Adler and relatively neglected by Freud, but that there has been growing appreciation of their importance. Healthy self-esteem comes from personal effort resulting in real achievement and deserved respect from others.

Maslow points out that even if all the above needs are satisfied, people still feel frustrated unless they experience self-actualization: fulfill their own talents and capacities. The form that this need takes varies widely from person to person. Each of us has different potentials. One person may need to be an excellent parent. Another may need to achieve as an athlete, painter, or inventor.

According to Maslow, the more basic needs must be fulfilled before the less critical needs are met. For example, both physiological and love needs are essential to the individual; however, when one is truly starving, the need for love (or any other higher need) is not a major factor in behavior. On the other hand, Maslow argues, even when frustrated in love, we still need to eat (romantic novels to the contrary).

One of Maslow's main points is that we are always desiring something and rarely reach a state of complete satisfaction without any goals or desires. His need hierarchy is an attempt to predict what kinds of new desires will arise once the old ones are sufficiently satisfied so that they no longer dominate behavior. There are many individual exceptions, especially in a culture such as ours where most basic needs are partially satisfied and still serve to motivate without becoming overwhelming. Maslow developed his hierarchy as part of a general theory of motivation, not as a precise predictor of individual behavior.

> It is quite true that man lives by bread alone—when there is no bread. But what happens to man's desires when there is plenty of bread and when his belly is chronically filled? *At once other (and higher) needs emerge,* and these, rather than physiological hungers, dominate their organism. And when these in turn are satisfied, again new (and still higher) needs emerge, and so on. (Maslow, 1987, p. 17)

Metamotivation

Metamotivation refers to behavior inspired by growth needs and values. According to Maslow, this kind of motivation is most common among self-actualizing people, who are by definition already gratified in their lower needs. Metamotivation often takes the form of devotion to ideals or goals, to something "outside oneself." Maslow points out that *metaneeds* share a continuum with basic needs, and that frustration of these needs brings about *metapathologies*. Metapathology refers to a lack of values, meaningfulness, or fulfillment in life. Maslow argues that a sense of identity, success in a career, and a commitment to a value system are as essential to one's psychological well-being as security, love, and self-esteem.

Man's higher nature rests upon man's lower nature, needing it as a foundation and collapsing without this foundation. That is, for the mass of mankind, man's higher nature is inconceivable without a satisfied lower nature as a base. (Maslow, 1968, p. 173)

Growth is theoretically possible only because the "higher" tastes are better than the "lower" and because the "lower" satisfaction becomes boring. (Maslow, 1971, p. 147)

Grumbles and Metagrumbles

Maslow suggests there are different levels of complaints that correspond with the levels of frustrated needs. In a factory situation, for example, low-level *grumbles* might be a response to unsafe working conditions, arbitrary and authoritarian foremen, and a lack of job security from one day to the next. These complaints address deprivations of the most basic needs for physical safety and security. Complaints of a higher level might be lack of adequate recognition for accomplishments, threats to one's prestige, or lack of group solidarity; that is, complaints based on threats to belonging needs or esteem needs.

Metagrumbles speak to the frustration of metaneeds such as perfection, justice, beauty, and truth. This level of grumbling is a good indication that everything else is actually going fairly smoothly. When people complain about the unaesthetic nature of their surroundings, it means that they are relatively satisfied as far as their more basic are concerned.

Maslow assumes that we should never expect an end to complaints; we should only hope to move to higher levels of complaint. When grumblers are frustrated over the imperfection of the world, the lack of perfect justice, and so on, it is a positive sign. It means that, despite a high degree of basic satisfaction, people are striving for still greater improvement and growth. In fact, Maslow suggests that one good measure of the degree of enlightenment of a community is the number of metagrumblers among its members.

To have committees . . . heatedly coming in and complaining that rose gardens in the parks are not sufficiently cared for . . . is in itself a wonderful thing because it indicates the height of life at which the complainers are living. (Maslow, 1965, p. 240)

Self-actualization

Maslow loosely defined self-actualization as "the full use and exploitation of talents, capacities, potentialities, etc." (1970, p. 150). Self-actualization is not a static state. It is an ongoing process in which one's capacities are fully, creatively, and joyfully utilized. "I think of the self-actualizing man not as an ordinary man with something added, but rather as the ordinary man with nothing taken away. The average man is a full human being with dampened and inhibited powers and capacities" (Maslow in Lowry, 1973b, p. 91).

Most commonly, self-actualizing people see life clearly. They are less emotional and more objective, less likely to allow hopes, fears, or ego defenses to distort their observations. Without exception, Maslow found that self-actualizing people are dedicated to a vocation or cause. Two requirements for growth seem to be commitment to something greater than oneself and to doing well at one's chosen tasks. Creativity, spontaneity, courage, and hard work are all major characteristics of self-actualizing people.

Maslow consciously decided to study only those who were relatively free from neurosis and emotional disturbance. He found that his psychologically healthy subjects were independent, self-accepting, had few self-conflicts, and were able to enjoy both play and work. They personally preferred "better" values: They wanted what was considered right, reasonable, and healthy. Only one of Maslow's subjects was an orthodox religious believer, yet virtually all believed in a meaningful universe and in a life that could be called spiritual.

Maslow found that his self-actualizing people enjoyed and appreciated life more. Despite pain, sorrow, and disappointment, they got more out of life. They had more interests and less fear, anxiety, boredom, or purposelessness. They were more aware of beauty and more able to appreciate the sunrise, nature, their marriages—again and again. Whereas most other people enjoyed only occasional moments of joy, triumph, or peak experience, self-actualizing individuals seemed to love life in general and to enjoy practically all its aspects.

Research on Self-actualization

Maslow's investigations of self-actualization were first stimulated by his desire to understand more completely his two most inspiring teachers, Ruth Benedict and Max Wertheimer. Although Benedict and Wertheimer were dissimilar personalities and were concerned with different fields of study, Maslow felt they shared a common level of personal fulfillment in their professional and private lives that he had rarely seen in others. In Benedict and Wertheimer, Maslow saw more than two eminent scientists. He saw deeply fulfilled, creative human beings. He began his own private research project to try to discover what made them so special, and he kept a notebook filled with all the data he could accumulate about their personal lives, attitudes, values, and so forth. Maslow's comparison of Benedict and Wertheimer set the stage for his lifelong study of self-actualization.

Maslow argued that it was more accurate to generalize about human nature from studying the best examples he could find, than from cataloging the problems and faults of average or neurotic individuals.

> Certainly a visitor from Mars descending upon a colony of birth-injured cripples, dwarfs, hunchbacks, etc., could not deduce what they *should* have been. But then let us study not cripples, but the closest approach we can get to whole, healthy men. In them we find qualitative differences, a different system of motivation, emotion, value, thinking, and perceiving. In a certain sense, only the saints *are* mankind. (Maslow in Lowry, 1973a, p. 90)

By studying the best and healthiest men and women, it is possible to explore the limits of human potential. In order to study how fast human beings can run, for example, one should work with the finest athletes and track performers available. It would make no sense to test an average sample from the general population. Similarly, Maslow argued, to study psychological health and maturity, one should investigate the most mature, creative, and well-integrated people.

Self-actualizing people are, without one single exception, involved in a cause outside their own skin, in something outside of themselves. (Maslow, 1971, p. 43)

Maslow investigated students for a study of "Good Human Beings." He found only one clearly usable subject among three thousand undergraduates. Maslow had two criteria for including people in his initial study. First, all subjects had to be relatively free of neurosis or other major personal problems. Second, all those studied had to be making the best possible use of their talents and capabilities.

For his study, Maslow was finally forced to rely on personal acquaintances as well as public figures. This group consisted of 18 individuals: 9 contemporaries and 9 historical figures, including Abraham Lincoln, Thomas Jefferson, Albert Einstein, Eleanor Roosevelt, Jane Adams, William James, Albert Schweitzer, Aldous Huxley, and Baruch Spinoza. It is interesting to note that Maslow's list includes intellectual giants and great social reformers, but no great spiritual teachers or mystics. His interest in transpersonal psychology developed later in his career. Obviously, Maslow's bias toward active, successful, and intellectual personalities as the "best" people has strongly affected his writing on self-actualization. Another psychologist, who valued introverted, emotionally developed, and spiritual qualities in people, would have developed a very different theory.

Maslow lists the following characteristics of self-actualizers (1970, pp. 153–172):

1. more efficient perception of reality and more comfortable relations with it

2. acceptance (self, others, nature)

3. spontaneity; simplicity; naturalness

4. problem centering [as opposed to being ego-centered]

5. the quality of detachment; the need for privacy

6. autonomy; independence of culture and environment

7. continued freshness of appreciation

8. mystic and peak experiences

9. *Gemeinschaftsgefühl* [a feeling of kinship with others]

10. deeper and more profound interpersonal relations

11. the democratic character structure

12. discrimination between means and ends, between good and evil

13. philosophical, unhostile sense of humor

14. self-actualizing creativeness

15. resistance to enculturation; the transcendence of any particular culture

[Self-actualization] is not an absence of problems but a moving from transitional or unreal problems to real problems. (Maslow, 1968, p. 115)

I very soon had to come to the conclusion that great talent was not only more or less independent of goodness or health of character but also that we know little about it. (Maslow, 1968, p. 135)

Maslow pointed out that the self-actualizers he studied were not perfect or even free of major faults. Their strong commitment to their chosen work and values may even lead self-actualizers to be quite ruthless at times in pursuing their own goals; their work may take precedence over others' feelings or needs. In addition, self-actualizers can carry their independence to shocking extremes. Self-actualizers also share many of the problems of average people: guilt, anxiety, sadness, conflict, and so on.

> *There are no perfect human beings!* Persons can be found who are good, very good indeed, in fact, great. There do in fact exist creators, seers, sages, saints, shakers and movers. This can certainly give us hope for the future of the species even if they *are* uncommon and do *not* come by the dozen. And yet these very same people can at times be boring, irritating, petulant, selfish, angry, or depressed. To avoid disillusionment with human nature, we must first give up our illusions about it. (Maslow, 1970, p. 176)

Personal Reflection
Self-actualization

Think of four or five self-actualizing people you have known personally or have heard about. What do these people have in common? What are some of their outstanding qualities? Are they different from your own personal heroes and heroines, or are they the same people? In what ways do these people bear out Maslow's theories? In what ways does each differ from his model of self-actualization?

Self-actualization Theory

In his last book, *The Farther Reaches of Human Nature* (1971), Maslow describes eight ways in which individuals self-actualize; eight behaviors leading to self-actualization. It is not a neat and clean, logically tight discussion, but it represents the culmination of Maslow's thinking on self-actualization.

1. Concentration.   "First, self-actualization means experiencing fully, vividly, selflessly, with full concentration and total absorption" (Maslow, 1971, p. 45). We are usually relatively unaware of what is going on within or around us. (Most witnesses will recount different versions of the same occurrence, for example.) However, we have all had moments of heightened awareness and intense interest, moments that Maslow would call self-actualizing.

2. Growth Choices. If we think of life as a process of choices, then self-actualization means to make each decision a choice for growth. We often have to choose between growth and safety, between progressing and regressing. Each choice has its positive and its negative aspects. To choose safety is to choose to remain with the known and the familiar, but to risk becoming stultified and stale. To choose growth is to open oneself to new and challenging experiences, but to risk the new and the unknown.

3. Self-awareness. Self-actualizing means becoming more aware of one's own inner nature and acting in accordance with it. This means to decide for yourself if *you* like certain films, books, or ideas, regardless of others' opinions.

4. Honesty. Honesty and taking responsibility for one's actions are essential elements in self-actualizing. Rather than posing and giving answers that are calculated to please another or to make ourselves look good, Maslow advocates looking within for the answers. Each time we do this, we get in touch with our inner selves.

5. Judgment. The first four steps help us develop the capacity for "better life choices." We learn to trust our own judgment and our own instincts and to act in terms of them. Maslow believes that this leads to better choices about what is constitutionally right for each individual—choices in art, music, and food, as well as major life choices, such as marriage and a career.

6. Self-development. Self-actualization is also a continual process of developing one's potentialities. It means using one's abilities and intelligence and "working to do well the thing that one wants to do" (Maslow, 1971, p. 48). Great talent or intelligence are not the same as self-actualization; many gifted people fail to use their abilities fully, while others, with perhaps only average talents, accomplish a tremendous amount.

Self-actualization is not a *thing* that someone either has or does not have. It is a never-ending process of making real one's potential. It refers to a way of continually living, working, and relating to the world rather than to a single accomplishment.

7. Peak Experiences. "Peak experiences are transient moments of self-actualization" (Maslow, 1971, p. 48). We are more whole, more integrated, more aware of ourselves and of the world during peak moments. At such times we think, act, and feel most clearly and accurately. We are more loving and accepting of others, have less inner conflict and anxiety, and are more able to put our energies to constructive use.

8. Lack of Ego Defenses. A further step in self-actualization is recognizing one's ego defenses and becoming better able to drop them when

One cannot choose wisely for a life unless he dares to listen to himself, his own self, at each moment in life. (Maslow, 1971, p. 47)

appropriate. A first step is to become more aware of the ways in which we distort our images of ourselves and of the external world—through repression, projection, and other defenses.

Peak Experiences

The term peak experiences is a generalization for the best moments of the human being, for the happiest moments of life, for experiences of ecstasy, rapture, bliss, of the greatest joy. (Maslow, 1971, p. 105)

Peak experiences are especially joyous and exciting moments in the life of every individual. Maslow notes that peak experiences are often inspired by intense feelings of love, exposure to great art or music, or by witnessing the overwhelming beauty of nature. "All peak experiences may be fruitfully understood as completions-of-the-act . . . or as the Gestalt psychologists' closure, or on the paradigm of the Reichian type of complete orgasm, or as total discharge, catharsis, culmination, climax, consummation, emptying or finishing" (Maslow, 1968, p. 111).

Personal Reflection ——————————————
—————————————— Your Own Peak Experiences

Try to recall clearly one peak experience in your life—a joyous, happy, blissful moment that stands out in your memory. Take a moment to relive the experience. Now, consider the following questions.

1. What brought about this experience? Was anything unique about the situation that triggered it?

2. How did you feel at the time? Was this feeling different from your usual experience—emotionally, physically, or intellectually?

3. Did you seem different to yourself? Did the world about you appear different?

4. How long did the experience last? How did you feel afterward?

5. Did the experience have any lasting effects (on your outlook or your relations with others, for example)?

6. How does your own experience compare with Maslow's theories concerning peak experiences and human nature?

To get a clearer sense of peak experiences, compare your experiences with others. Look for differences as well as similarities. Are the differences the result of different situations or perhaps of variations in personality or background? What do the similarities imply about Maslow's ideas or about human potential in general?

Virtually everyone has had a number of peak experiences, although we often take them for granted. One's reactions while watching a beautiful sunset or listening to an especially moving piece of music are examples of peak experiences. According to Maslow, peak experiences tend to be triggered by intense, inspiring occurrences: "It looks as if any experience of real excellence, of real perfection . . . tends to produce a peak experience" (1971, p. 175). These experiences may also be triggered by tragic events. Recovering from depression, a serious illness, or confronting death can initiate extreme moments of love and joy. The lives of most people are filled with long periods of relative inattentiveness, lack of involvement, or even boredom. By contrast, understood in the broadest sense, peak experiences are those moments when we become deeply involved, excited by, and absorbed in the world.

The most powerful peak experiences are relatively rare. They have been portrayed by poets as moments of ecstasy; by the religious, as deep mystical experiences. For Maslow the highest peaks include "feelings of limitless horizons opening up to the vision, the feeling of being simultaneously more powerful and also more helpless than one ever was before, the feeling of great ecstasy and wonder and awe, the loss of placing in time and space . . ." (1970, p. 164).

Plateau Experiences

A peak experience is a "high" that may last a few minutes or several hours, but rarely longer. Maslow also discusses a more stable and long-lasting experience that he refers to as a "plateau experience." The plateau experience represents a new and more profound way of viewing and experiencing the world. It involves a fundamental change in attitude, a change that affects one's entire point of view and creates a new appreciation and intensified awareness of the world. Maslow experienced this himself late in life, after his first heart attack. His intensified consciousness of life and sense of death's imminence caused him to see the world in a wholly new way. (For a more complete description in Maslow's own words, see The Theory Firsthand in this chapter.)

Transcendence and Self-actualization

Maslow found that some self-actualizing individuals tend to have many peak experiences, whereas others have them rarely if ever. He came to distinguish between self-actualizers who were psychologically healthy, productive human beings, with little or no experience of transcendence, and those for whom transcendence was important or even central. The first group was generally pragmatic in orientation. "Such persons live in the world, coming to fulfillment in it. They master it, lead it, use it for good purposes, as (healthy) politicians or practical people do" (Maslow, 1971, p. 281).

Maslow wrote that transcending self-actualizers are more often aware of the sacredness of all things, the transcendent dimension of life, in the

At the highest levels of development of humaneness, knowledge is positively rather than negatively correlated with a sense of mystery, awe, humility, ultimate ignorance, reverence, and a sense of oblation. (Maslow, 1971, p. 290)

midst of daily activities. Their peak or mystical experiences tend to be valued as the most important aspects of their lives. They tend to think more holistically than "merely healthy" self-actualizers; they are better able to transcend the categories of past, present, and future, and good and evil, and to perceive a unity behind the apparent complexity and contradictions of life. They are more likely to be innovators and original thinkers than systematizers of the ideas of others. As their knowledge develops, so does their sense of humility and ignorance, and they are likely to regard the universe with increasing awe.

Transcenders are more likely to regard themselves as the carriers of their talents and abilities, hence they are less ego-involved in their work. A transcender is honestly able to say, "I am the best person for this job, and therefore I should have it"; or, on the other hand, to admit, "You are the best one for this job, and you should take it from me."

Not everyone who has had a mystical experience is a transcending self-actualizer. Many who have had such experiences have not developed the psychological health and the productiveness Maslow considered to be essential aspects of self-actualization. Maslow also pointed out that he found as many transcenders among businessmen, managers, teachers, and politicians as he found among poets, musicians, ministers, and the like, for whom transcendence is almost assumed.

Deficiency and Being Motivation

Maslow pointed out that most psychologies address only *deficiency motivation;* that is, they concentrate on behavior oriented to fulfill a need that has been deprived or frustrated. Hunger, pain, and fear are prime examples of deficiency motivations.

However, a close look at human or animal behavior reveals another kind of motivation. When an organism is not hungry, in pain, or fearful, being *motivations* emerge, such as curiosity and playfulness. Under these conditions, activities can be enjoyed as ends in themselves, not always pursued solely as a means to gratify certain needs. Being motivation refers primarily to enjoyment and satisfaction in the present or to the desire to seek a positively valued goal (growth motivation or metamotivation). On the other hand, deficiency motivation involves a need to change the present state of affairs due to a feeling of dissatisfaction or frustration.

Peak experiences are generally related to the *being* realm, and *being* psychology also tends to be most applicable to self-actualizers. Maslow distinguishes between being and deficiency cognition, being and deficiency values, and being and deficiency love.

Deficiency and Being Cognition

In deficiency cognition, objects are seen solely as need fulfillers, as means to other ends. This is especially true when needs are strong. Maslow (1970) points out that strong needs tend to channel thinking and perception; therefore, the individual is aware only of those aspects of the environment related to need satisfaction. A hungry person tends to see only food, a miser only money.

Being cognition is more accurate and effective because the perceiver is less likely to distort his or her perceptions in response to needs or desires. Being cognition is nonjudgmental, without comparison or evaluation. The fundamental attitude is one of appreciation of what is. Stimuli are exclusively and fully attended to, and perception seems richer, fuller, and more complete.

The perceiver remains somewhat independent of what is perceived. External objects are valued in and of themselves rather than for their relevance to personal concerns. In fact, in a state of being cognition, the individual tends to remain absorbed in contemplation or appreciation, and active intervention is seen as irrelevant or inappropriate. One advantage to deficiency cognition is that the individual may feel compelled to act and try to alter existing conditions.

A section of cancer seen through a microscope, if only we can forget that it is a cancer, can be seen as a beautiful and intricate and awe-inspiring organization. (Maslow, 1968, p. 76)

Deficiency and Being Values

Maslow does not explicitly address deficiency values, though he discusses being values in detail. Being values are intrinsic to every individual. "The highest values [exist] within human nature itself, to be discovered there. This is in sharp contradiction to the older and more customary beliefs that the highest values can come only from a supernatural God, or from some other source outside human nature itself" (Maslow, 1968, p. 170).

Maslow has listed the following as being values: truth, goodness, beauty, wholeness, dichotomy transcendence, aliveness, uniqueness, perfection, necessity, completion, justice, order, simplicity, richness, effortlessness, playfulness, and self-sufficiency.

Deficiency and Being Love

Deficiency love is love of others because they fulfill a need. The more one is gratified, the more this kind of love is reinforced. It is love out of a need for self-esteem or sex, out of fear of loneliness, and so forth.

Being love is love for the essence, the "being" of the other. It is non-possessive and concerned more with the good of the other than with selfish satisfaction. Maslow often wrote of being love as demonstrating the Taoist attitude of noninterference or letting things be, appreciating what is without concern for change or improvement. Being love of nature tends to express appreciation for the beauty of flowers by watching them grow and leaving them, whereas deficiency love is more likely to involve picking the flowers and making an arrangement of them. Being love is also the ideal unconditional love of a parent for a child, which even includes loving and valuing the child's small imperfections.

Maslow argues that being love is richer, more satisfying, and longer lasting than deficiency love. It stays fresh, whereas deficiency love tends to grow stale with time. Being love can be a trigger for peak experiences and is often described in the same exalted terms used for describing deeply religious experiences.

Personal Reflection

An Exercise in Being Love

For Maslow, being love is selfless; it demands nothing in return. The very act of loving, appreciating the essence and beauty of the object of love, is its own reward. In our daily experience, we usually feel a mixture of being and deficiency love. We generally expect and receive something in return for our feelings of love.

This exercise is derived from an old Christian practice designed to develop feelings of pure love. Sit in a darkened room in front of a lit candle. Relax and gradually get in touch with your body and your surroundings. Allow your mind and body to slow down, to become calm and peaceful.

Gaze at the candle flame. Extend feelings of love from your heart to the flame. Your feelings of love for the flame are unrelated to any thought of the worthiness of the flame itself. You love for the sake of loving. (It may seem strange at first to try to love an inanimate object, a mere flame, but that is just the point—to experience the feeling of loving in a situation in which there is no return, no reward aside from the feeling of love itself.) Expand your feelings of love to include the entire room and everything in it.

Eupsychia

Maslow coined the term *eupsychia* (yu-psĭ-kē-a) to refer to ideal, human-oriented societies and communities. He preferred it to *utopia*, which Maslow felt was overused and whose definition suggests impracticality and ungrounded idealism. He believed that the development of an ideal society by psychologically healthy, self-actualizing individuals was quite possible. All members of the community would be engaged in seeking personal development and fulfillment in their work and in their personal lives.

But even an ideal society will not necessarily *produce* self-actualizing individuals.

There is a kind of a feedback between the Good Society and the Good Person. They need each other. (Maslow, 1971 p. 19)

> A teacher or a culture doesn't create a human being. It doesn't implant within him the ability to love, or to be curious, or to philosophize, or to symbolize, or to be creative. Rather it permits, or fosters, or encourages, or helps what exists in embryo to become real and actual. (Maslow, 1968, p. 161)

Maslow preferred eupsychian, or enlightened, management practices to authoritarian business management. Authoritarian managers assume that workers and management have basically different, mutually incompatible goals—that workers want to earn as much as possible with minimal effort and therefore must be closely watched.

Enlightened managers, however, assume that employees *want* to be creative and productive and that they need to be supported and encouraged rather than restricted and controlled by management. Maslow points out that the enlightened approach works best with stable, psychologically healthy employees. Some hostile, suspicious people work more effectively in an authoritarian structure and would take unfair advantage of more freedom. Eupsychian management works only with people who enjoy and can handle responsibility and self-direction, which is why Maslow suggested that eupsychian communities be composed of self-actualizing people.

Synergy

The term *synergy* was originally used by Maslow's teacher Ruth Benedict to refer to the degree of interpersonal cooperation and harmony within a society. Synergy means cooperation. The original Greek word literally means "work together." Synergy also refers to a combined action of elements resulting in a total effect that is greater than all of the elements taken independently.

As an anthropologist, Benedict was aware of the dangers of making value judgments in comparing societies and evaluating another civilization by how closely it conforms to our own cultural standards. However, in her study of other civilizations, Benedict observed that people in some societies were clearly happier, healthier, and more efficient than in others. Some groups had beliefs and customs that were basically harmonious and satisfying to their members, whereas other groups had traditions that promoted suspicion, fear, and anxiety.

Under conditions of low social synergy, the success of one member brings about loss or failure for another. For example, if each hunter shares the daily catch with only his immediate family, hunting is likely to become strongly competitive. Hunters who improve their hunting techniques or discover a new source of game may try to hide their achievements from others. Whenever one hunter is highly successful, there is that much less food available for other hunters and their families.

Under high social synergy, cooperation is maximized. One example would be similar hunting activity to that described previously but with a single important difference—the communal sharing of the catch. Under these conditions, each hunter benefits from the success of the others. Under high social synergy, the cultural belief system reinforces cooperation and positive feelings between individuals and helps minimize conflict and discord.

Maslow also writes of synergy in individuals. Identification with others tends to promote high individual synergy. If the success of another is a source of genuine satisfaction to the individual, then help is freely and generously offered. In a sense, both selfish and altruistic motives are merged. In aiding another, the individual is also seeking his or her own satisfaction.

Synergy can also be found within the individual as unity between thought and action. To force oneself to act indicates some conflict of motives. Ideally, individuals do what they should do because they *want* to do it. The best medicine is taken not only because it is effective, but also because it tastes good.

Dynamics

Psychological Growth

The pursuit of self-actualization cannot begin until the individual is free of the domination of the lower needs, such as needs for security and esteem. According to Maslow, early frustration of a need may fixate the individual at that level of functioning. For instance, someone who was not very popular as a child may continue to be deeply concerned with self-esteem needs throughout life.

The pursuit of higher needs is in itself one index of psychological health. Maslow argues that fulfillment of higher needs is intrinsically more satisfying and that metamotivation is an indication that the individual has progressed beyond a deficiency level of functioning.

Self-actualization represents a long-term commitment to growth and the development of capabilities to their fullest. Self-actualizing work involves the choice of worthwhile, creative goals. Maslow writes that self-actualizing individuals are attracted to the most challenging and intriguing problems, to questions that demand their best and most creative efforts. They are willing to cope with uncertainty and ambiguity and prefer challenge to easy solutions.

Obstacles to Growth

Maslow pointed out that growth motivation is less basic than physiological needs and needs for security, esteem, and so on. The process of self-actualization can be limited by (1) negative influences from past experience and resulting habits that keep us locked into unproductive behaviors; (2) social influence and group pressure that often operate against our own taste and judgment; and (3) inner defenses that keep us out of touch with ourselves.

Poor habits often inhibit growth. For Maslow these include addiction to drugs or drinking, poor diet, and other habits that adversely affect health and efficiency. Maslow points out that a destructive environment or rigid

As the person becomes integrated, so does his world. As he feels good, so does the world look good. (Maslow, 1971, p. 165)

There are two sets of forces pulling at the individual, not just one. In addition to the pressures forward toward health, there are also fearful-regressive pressures backward, toward sickness and weakness. (Maslow, 1968, p. 164)

authoritarian education can easily lead to unproductive habit patterns based on a deficiency orientation. Also, any strong habit generally tends to interfere with psychological growth because it diminishes the flexibility and openness necessary to operate most efficiently and effectively in a variety of situations.

Group pressure and social propaganda also tend to limit the individual. They act to diminish autonomy and stifle independent judgment as the individual is pressured to substitute external, societal standards for his or her own taste or judgment. A society may also inculcate a biased view of human nature as seen, for example, in the Western view that most human instincts are essentially sinful and must continually be controlled or subjugated. Maslow argued that this negative attitude tends to frustrate growth and that the opposite is in fact correct; our instincts are essentially good and impulses toward growth are the major sources of human motivation.

Ego defenses are seen by Maslow as internal obstacles to growth. The first step in dealing with ego defenses is to become aware of them and to see clearly how they operate. Then, each individual should attempt to minimize the distortions created by these defenses. Maslow adds two new defense mechanisms—*desacralizing* and the *Jonah complex*—to the traditional psychoanalytic listing of projection, repression, denial, and the like.

Desacralizing refers to impoverishing one's life by the refusal to treat anything with deep seriousness and concern. Today, few cultural or religious symbols are given the care and respect they once enjoyed; consequently, they have lost their power to thrill, inspire, or even motivate us. Maslow often referred to modern values concerning sex as an example of desacralization. Although a more casual attitude toward sex may lead to less frustration and trauma, it is also true that sexual experience has lost the power it once had to inspire artists, writers, and lovers.

The Jonah complex refers to a refusal to try to realize one's full capabilities. Just as Jonah attempted to avoid the responsibilities of becoming a prophet, many people avoid responsibility because they are actually afraid of using their capacities to the fullest. They prefer the security of undemanding goals over truly ambitious ones that require them to extend themselves fully. This attitude is not uncommon among many students who "get by" by utilizing only a fraction of their talents and abilities. In the past, this was true of many women who were taught that a successful career was somehow incongruent with femininity or that intellectual achievement might make them less attractive to men. (See, for example, Horner, 1972.)

This "fear of greatness" may be the largest barrier to self-actualization. Living fully is more than many of us feel we can bear. At times of deepest joy and ecstasy, people often say, "It's too much," or, "I can't stand it." The root of the Jonah complex is seen in the fear of letting go of a limited but manageable existence, the fear of losing control, being torn apart, or disintegrating.

> Though, in principle, self-actualization is easy, in practice it rarely happens (by my criteria, certainly in less than 1% of the adult population). (Maslow, 1968, p. 204)

Structure

Body

Maslow does not discuss in detail the role of the body in the process of self-actualization. He assumes that once physiological needs are met, the individual is free to deal with needs that are higher in the need hierarchy. However, he writes that it is important that the body be given its due. "Asceticism, self-denial, deliberate rejection of the demands of the organism, at least in the West, tend to produce a diminished, stunted, or crippled organism, and even in the East, bring self-actualization to only a very few, exceptionally strong individuals" (1968, p. 199).

Maslow mentions the importance of intense stimulation of the physical senses in peak experiences, which are often triggered by natural beauty, art, music, or sexual experience. He also indicated that training in dance, art, and other physical media of expression could provide an important supplement to traditional, cognitively oriented education and that physical and sense-oriented systems of instruction require the kind of active participatory learning that should be included in all forms of education.

Social Relationships

According to Maslow, love and esteem are basic needs essential to everyone and take precedence over self-actualization in the need hierarchy. Maslow often deplored the failure of most psychology textbooks to even mention the word *love,* as if psychologists considered love unreal, something that must be reduced to concepts like libido projection or sexual reinforcement.

Will

Will is a vital ingredient in the long-term process of self-actualization. Maslow found that self-actualizing individuals work long and hard to attain their chosen goals. "Self-actualization means working to do well the thing that one wants to do. To become a second-rate physician is not a good path to self-actualization. One wants to be first-rate or as good as he can be" (Maslow, 1971, p. 48). Because of his faith in the essential health and goodness of human nature, Maslow was little concerned with the need for willpower in the process of overcoming unacceptable instincts or impulses. For Maslow, healthy individuals are relatively free from internal conflict, except perhaps the need to overcome poor habits. They need to employ will to develop their abilities still further and to attain ambitious, long-range goals.

Emotions

Maslow emphasized the importance of the positive emotions in self-actualization. He encouraged other psychologists to begin serious research on

The fact is that people are good, if only their fundamental wishes [for affection and security] are satisfied. . . . Give people affection and security, and they will give affection and be secure in their feelings and behavior. (Maslow in Lowry, 1973b, p. 18)

If you deliberately plan to be less than you are capable of being, then I warn you that you'll be deeply unhappy for the rest of your life. (Maslow, 1971, p. 36)

happiness, calmness, joy, and to investigate fun, games, and play. He believed that negative emotions, tension, and conflict drain energy and inhibit effective functioning.

For Maslow, maturity includes "being able to give oneself over completely to an emotion, not only of love but also of anger, fascination . . ." (1966, p. 38). Maslow goes on to point out that it is our fear of deep emotions that leads us to desacralize much of life or to use intellectualization as a defense against feeling. He felt that orthodox science has mistakenly taken "cool" perceiving and mental thinking as the best venues for discovering scientific truth. This limited approach has tended to banish from scientific study experiences of wonder, awe, ecstasy, and other forms of transcendence.

Intellect

Maslow emphasized the need for holistic thinking, dealing with systems of relationships and wholes rather than with individual parts. He found that peak experiences often contain striking examples of thinking that has broken through the usual dichotomies with which we view reality. During peak experiences, individuals have often reported seeing past, present, and future as one, life and death as part of a single process, and good and evil within the same whole.

Holistic thinking is also found in creative thinkers who are able to break with the past and look beyond conventional categories in investigating possible new relationships. This requires freedom, openness, and an ability to deal with inconsistency and uncertainty. Although such ambiguity can be threatening to some, it is part of the essential joy of creative problem solving for self-actualizers.

Maslow (1970) has written that creative people are *problem-centered* rather than *means-centered*. Problem-centered people focus primarily on the demands and requirements of the desired goals. Means-centered individuals, on the other hand, often become so concerned with means, technique, or methodology that they tend to do intensely detailed work in trivial areas. Problem-centering stands in contrast to ego-centering (an example of deficiency cognition), in which individuals tend to see what they wish rather than what it is.

Self

Maslow defines the self as an individual's inner core or inherent nature—one's tastes, values, and goals. Understanding one's inner nature and acting in accordance with it is essential to actualizing the self.

Maslow approaches understanding the self by studying those individuals who are most in tune with their own natures, those who provide the best examples of self-expression or self-actualization. However, he did not explicitly discuss the self as a specific structure within the personality.

Self-actualizing people, those who have come to a high level of maturation, health, and self-fulfillment, have so much to teach us that sometimes they seem almost like a different breed of human beings. (Maslow, 1968, p. 71)

Therapist

For Maslow, as for Rogers, psychotherapy is effective primarily because it involves an intimate and trusting relationship with another human being. Along with Adler, Maslow felt that a good therapist is like an older brother or sister, someone who offers care and love. But more than this, Maslow proposed the model of the Taoist helper, a person who is able to help without interfering. A good coach does this when he or she works with the natural style of an athlete in order to strengthen that individual's style and improve it. A good coach does not try to force all athletes into the same mold. Good parents are much like a Taoist helper when they resist doing everything for their child. The child develops and grows best by means of guidance, not interference.

Although Maslow underwent psychoanalysis for several years and received informal training in psychotherapy, his interests always revolved around research and writing rather than the actual practice of psychotherapy. Maslow (1987) did make an important distinction between what he called *basic needs therapy,* designed to help people meet primary needs such as safety, belonging, love and respect, and *insight therapy,* which is a profound, long-term process of growth in self-understanding.

Maslow viewed therapy as a way of satisfying the basic needs for love and esteem that are frustrated in virtually everyone who seeks psychological help. He argued (1970) that warm human relationships can provide much of the same support found in therapy.

Good therapists should love and care for the being or essence of the people they work with. Maslow (1971) wrote that those who seek to change or manipulate others lack this essential attitude. For example, he believed that a true dog lover would never crop a dog's ears or tail, and one who really loves flowers would not cut or twist them to make fancy flower arrangements.

Evaluation

Maslow's great strength lies in his concern for the areas of human functioning that most other theorists have almost completely ignored. He is one of the few psychologists who has seriously investigated the positive dimensions of human experience.

Maslow's major contributions might be summarized in the following three central ideas:

1. Human beings have an innate tendency to move toward higher levels of health, creativity, insight, and self-fulfillment.

2. Neurosis is basically a blockage of the innate tendency toward self-actualization.

3. Business efficiency and personal growth are not incompatible. In fact, the process of self-actualization brings each individual to greater efficiency, creativity, and productivity.

It has been pointed out that a therapist can repeat the same mistakes for 40 years and then call it "rich clinical experience." (Maslow, 1968, p. 87)

I am a new breed—a theoretical psychologist parallel to . . . theoretical biologists. . . . I think of myself as a scientist rather than an essayist or philosopher. I feel myself very bound to and by the facts that I am trying to *perceive,* not to create. (Maslow in International Study Project, 1972, p. 63)

Maslow's experimental work was mostly inconclusive; *exploratory* might be a better term to describe it, and he was the first to acknowledge this:

> It's just that I haven't got the time to do careful experiments myself. They take too long, in view of the years that I have left and the extent of what I want to do.
>
> So I myself do only "quick-and-dirty" little pilot explorations, mostly with a few subjects only, inadequate to publish but enough to convince myself that they are probably true and will be confirmed one day. Quick little commando raids, guerrilla attacks. (Maslow in Krippner, 1972, pp. 66–67)

There are, of course, some serious disadvantages to the way he approached his experimental work; for example, data from Maslow's small and biased samples are statistically unreliable. His sample of self-actualized people was mainly white middle-class men. Also, not everyone would agree that Eleanor Roosevelt or Abraham Lincoln were good subjects of study after examining their lives in detail. However, Maslow never sought to experimentally "prove" or verify his ideas. His research was more a way of clarifying and adding detail to his theories.

Even so, Maslow sometimes seems very much like an armchair philosopher who remains somewhat aloof from the possible contradictions of new facts or experiences. He was generally clear on what he wanted to demonstrate in his research, but he rarely seemed to find any new data to alter his preconceived ideas. For example, Maslow always stressed the importance of positive triggers for peak experiences: experiences of love, beauty, great music, and so on. Negative triggers tend to be ignored in his writings despite the fact that many people report their most intense peak experiences to be preceded by negative emotions (fear and depression, for example) that are then transcended and become transformed into strongly positive states. (See, for example, William James's *The Varieties of Religious Experience,* 1943.) For some reason, Maslow's investigations seldom seemed to uncover this kind of new information.

Maslow's greatest strength is as a psychological thinker who has continually stressed the positive dimensions of human experience; particularly, the tremendous potential that all men and women possess. Maslow has been an inspiration for virtually all humanistic and transpersonal psychologists. In his book on Maslow and modern psychology, Colin Wilson writes:

> Maslow was the first person to create a truly comprehensive psychology stretching, so to speak, from the basement to the attic. He accepted Freud's clinical method without accepting his philosophy. . . . The "transcendent" urges—aesthetic, creative, religious—are as basic and permanent a part of human nature as dominance or sexuality. If they

are less obviously "universal," this is only because fewer human beings reach the point at which they take over.

Maslow's achievement is enormous. Like all original thinkers, he has opened up a new way of *seeing* the universe. (Wilson, 1972, pp. 181–184)

Maslow has been called "the greatest American psychologist since William James" (*Journal of Transpersonal Psychology,* 1970). Although many might consider this praise somewhat exaggerated, no one can deny Maslow's central importance as an original thinker and a pioneer in human potential psychology.

Recent Developments: The Personal Orientation Inventory

Although Maslow himself did little in the way of formal research, his work has inspired a number of dedicated researchers. Shostrom (1963) developed the Personal Orientation Inventory (POI) as a measure of self-actualization. A significant body of research has been developed using this instrument (Gray, 1986; Kelly & Chovan, 1985; Rychman, 1985).

Transpersonal Psychology

Maslow added transpersonal psychology to the first three forces in Western psychology—behaviorism, psychoanalysis, and humanistic psychology. For Maslow, behaviorism and psychoanalysis were too limited in scope to form the basis for a complete psychology of human nature. Psychoanalysis has been derived largely from studies of psychopathology. Behaviorism has attempted to reduce the complexities of human nature to simpler principles but has failed to address fully such issues as values, consciousness, and love.

In the early 1960s, humanistic psychology emerged out of the work of Maslow, Rogers, and other theorists concerned with psychological health and effective functioning. Many humanistic psychologists have used Maslow's theories, especially his work on self-actualization, as the basic framework for their writing and research.

In 1968, Maslow called attention to the limitations of the humanistic model. He found that, in exploring the farthest reaches of human nature, there were possibilities beyond self-actualization. Maslow became aware that when peak experiences were especially powerful the sense of self dissolved into an awareness of a greater unity. The term self-actualization did not seem to fit these experiences.

Transpersonal psychology adds to the more traditional psychological concerns an acknowledgment of the importance of the spiritual aspect of human experience. This level of experience has been described primarily in religious literature, in unscientific and often theologically biased language. One of the major tasks of transpersonal psychology is to provide a scientific language and a scientific framework for this material.

The human being needs a framework of values, a philosophy of life . . . to live by and understand by, in about the same sense that he needs sunlight, calcium or love. (Maslow, 1968, p. 206)

I should say also that I consider Humanistic, Third Force Psychology to be transitional, a preparation for a still "higher" Fourth Psychology, transpersonal, transhuman, centered in the cosmos rather than in human needs and interest, going beyond humanness, identity, self-actualization and the like. . . . We need something "bigger than we are" to be awed by and to commit ourselves to in a new, naturalistic, empirical, non-churchly sense, perhaps as Thoreau and Whitman, William James and John Dewey did. (Maslow, 1968, pp. iii–iv)

Webster's Ninth New Collegiate Dictionary defines *transpersonal* as "extending or going beyond the personal or individual." It refers to an extension of identity beyond both individuality and personality. One of the basic premises of transpersonal psychology is that we do not yet know the full extent of human potential. This sense of vastness and potential growth within each individual provides a central context for transpersonal psychology. Collections of basic essays and articles on transpersonal psychology include Ornstein (1973), Tart (1969, 1975), Walsh and Shapiro (1983), Walsh and Vaughan (1980). Frager (1989) and Valle (1989) have provided overviews of the field.

Approaches

Major contributors to the field of transpersonal psychology differ in their approaches and interests. The following is a series of excerpts that reflect these varying approaches:

> Transpersonal (or "fourth force") Psychology is the title given to an emerging force in the psychology field by a group of psychologists and professional men and women from other fields who are interested in those *ultimate* human capacities and potentialities that have no systematic place in positivistic or behavioristic theory ("first force"), classical psychoanalytic theory ("second force"), or humanistic psychology ("third force"). (Sutich, 1969, p. 15)

> This field is the study of transpersonal experiences, which involve an expansion of consciousness beyond the usual ego boundaries and limitations of time and space. (Grof, 1975, p. 154)

> Transpersonal psychology is bringing together the insights of the individualistic psychologies of the West with the spiritual psychologies of the East and Middle East. The realization that our own training has been limited and that Western ideas are not the center of the psychological universe is disturbing at first. The feeling passes when one becomes aware of the amazing amount of work that has already been accomplished, but which awaits validation with the scientific and experimental tools of Western psychology, to be fully realized. (Fadiman, 1980, p. 181)

> The term *transpersonal* was adopted after considerable deliberation to reflect the reports of people practicing various consciousness disciplines

Without the transcendent and the transpersonal, we get sick, violent and nihilistic, or else hopeless and apathetic. (Maslow, 1968, p. iv)

who spoke of experiences of an extension of identity beyond both individuality and personality. Thus, transpersonal psychology cannot strictly be called a model of personality, because personalities consider only one aspect of our psychological nature; rather it is an inquiry into the essential nature of being. (Walsh & Vaughan, 1980, p. 16)

In transpersonal psychology, the *search* is the quest for personal growth, or spiritual understanding, or self realization, as it has been described in the world's spiritual traditions, and as it is pursued today, whether assisted by a psychotherapist, guided by a guru, or carried out individually. (Metzner, 1989, p. 329)

The Perennial Model

The underlying concept of human nature in transpersonal psychology is not a new one. It has always existed in human culture. It has been called the "perennial philosophy" (Huxley, 1944), the "perennial religion" (Smith, 1976), and the "perennial psychology" (Wilber, 1977). What is new is the task of bringing together ideas from many different traditions and cultures to form a modern psychological language and scientific framework.

This perennial model includes the following four basic premises (Valle, 1989):

1. There is a transcendent reality or unity that binds together all (apparently separate) phenomena.

2. The ego or individual self is but a reflection of a greater, transpersonal ("beyond the personal") self or oneness. We come from and are grounded in that self. However, we have become estranged from our origins and we need to return to it in order to become fully healthy and whole human beings.

3. Each individual can directly experience this reality or greater self, and this is at the core of the spiritual dimensions of life.

4. This experience involves a qualitative shift in experiencing oneself and the larger world. It is a powerful, self-validating experience.

Not all transpersonal psychologists or scholars of religion agree with the assumption that there is a perennial tradition underlying the diverse forms of religion. At the other extreme is the position that there is *no* fundamental and neutral mystical experience that is then subsequently interpreted by each mystic. The very mystical experience itself is shaped by the mystic's tradition and cannot be taken meaningfully out of its cultural and religious context. (See, for example, Katz, 1978.)

Another transpersonal theorist, Ralph Metzner (1986), has collected descriptions of transpersonal growth, or the transformation of human consciousness. These include such key metaphors as the transforming of a caterpillar into a butterfly; awakening from a dream to reality; moving from captivity to liberation; going from darkness to light; being purified by inner fire; going from fragmentation to wholeness; journeying to a place of vision and power; returning to the source; and dying and being reborn.

A New Paradigm

It should be clear from the foregoing that transpersonal psychology is based on radically different premises from those of other approaches to psychology. It is what Thomas Kuhn (1962) called, *a new paradigm.*

Kuhn defined a paradigm as a set of values and beliefs shared by the members of a scientific community. Both theory and research within any given community will be consistent within this context and within these fundamental beliefs and values. Kuhn has pointed out that critical progress in science often comes from a paradigm shift. Unfortunately, initial resistance to the new paradigm is almost always inevitable. Advocates of the new paradigm are often accused of using unscientific methods or studying unscientific problems.

Tart (1975) has given a detailed analysis of the ways in which the paradigm of transpersonal psychology differs from that of traditional psychology. These include the following:

1. Old: Physics is the ultimate science, the study of the real world. Dreams, emotions, and human experience in general are all derivative.

New: Psychological reality is just as real as physical reality. And modern theoretical physics indicates that the two are not so far apart.

2. Old: Each individual exists in relative isolation from the surrounding environment. We are each essentially independent creatures. (And so we can seek to control the world as if we are not part of it.)

New: There is a deep level of psychological/spiritual connection among all forms of life. Each individual is a *cosmic creature,* deeply embedded in the cosmos.

3. Old: Our ordinary state of conscious is the best, most rational, most adaptive way the mind can be organized. All other states are inferior or pathological. Even "creative states" are suspect, often seen as bordering on the pathological (e.g., "regression").

New: Higher orders of feeling, awareness, and even rationality are possible. What we call waking consciousness is really more like "waking sleep," in which we use but a small fraction of our awareness or capacities.

4. Old: Seeking altered states of consciousness is a sign of pathology or immaturity.

New: Seeking to experience different states of consciousness is a natural aspect of healthy human growth.

5. Old: The basic development of personality is finished and complete in adulthood, except for neurotics, people with traumatic childhoods, and the like.

New: Ordinary adults exhibit only a rudimentary level of maturity. The basic "healthy" adult personality is merely a foundation for spiritual work and the development of a far deeper level of wisdom and maturity.

In various spiritual traditions, authorities point out that our usual state of consciousness is not only limited, it is also dreamlike and illusory. From this perspective, psychotherapies that deal only with personality dynamics are superficial palliatives, much as giving candy to a sick friend is comforting through ineffective in terms of the illness.

Eastern and Western Thought in Transpersonal Psychology

Ken Wilber has been an important transpersonal theorist. In his first major work, *The Spectrum of Consciousness* (1977), Wilber integrates a vast array of Eastern and Western thought into a single model. Wilber sees growth as the healing of a series of dichotomies within the individual. First is the split between conscious and unconscious, or persona and shadow. Next is the division between mind and body. Following this is the separation of organism and environment. The final stage is the attainment of unity with the universe. Wilber argues that each level of consciousness has its own particular issues and problems and its own appropriate forms of therapy or spiritual practice.

Wilber (1980) has also written about human growth and development in terms of two fundamental processes. First, there is the outward arc, the process of personal, ego development. The second process is the inward arc, the process of transpersonal, spiritual development from self-consciousness to *superconsciousness*.

> The story of the Outward Arc is the story of the Hero—the story of the terrible battle to break free of the sleep in the subconscious. . . . The story of the Outward Arc is also the story of the ego, for the ego *is* the Hero. . . . But the Outward Arc, the move from subconsciousness to self-consciousness, is only half of the story of the evolution of consciousness. . . . Beyond the self-conscious ego, according to mystic-sages, lies the path of return and the psychology of eternity—the Inward Arc. (Wilber, 1980, p. 4)

We begin with what Wilber calls the *membership self* as we develop language and become socialized within a particular culture. Next comes the stage of the *mental egoic self,* in which we develop a positive self-concept and a healthy, balanced ego. The final stage of the outward arc is the *integrated self,* the stage of self-actualization, which is generally the highest level of human development described in Western psychology.

The inner arc begins with the stage of the *low subtle-self,* which includes highly developed intuition and various kinds of extrasensory perceptions. Next, the stage of the *high-subtle self* has been described by the world's great mystics in terms of the experience of bliss and visions of divine realms. The final stages are the *low-causal self* and *the high-causal self,* described in mystical literature as the highest levels of illumination and spiritual attainment.

For many transpersonal psychologists, Asian psychologies offer important insights and concepts (see, for example, Frager, 1989; Walsh, 1989; as well as chapters 14 to 16 in this book). Asian psychologies focus more on spiritual levels of experience and little on the pathological. They contain maps of states of consciousness, discussions of developmental levels, and stages that extend beyond traditional psychological formulations. Walsh (1989) summarizes the literature on Eastern meditation and related practices as psychotherapeutic.

Psychedelic Research and the Transpersonal

Another important transpersonal theorist is Stanislav Grof, a European psychiatrist, who has written extensively on psychedelic research and altered states of consciousness. Grof (1985) has described the major characteristics of psychedelic experience. These include transcendence of space and time, transcendence of distinctions between matter, energy, and consciousness; and transcendence of the separation between the individual and the external world.

Grof (1975) has broken down LSD experiences into four categories—abstract, psychodynamic, perinatal, and transpersonal.

1. *Abstract experiences*—which are primarily sensory, including extraordinarily vivid colors or sounds.

2. *Psychodynamic experiences*—which involve reliving emotionally charged memories. They also include symbolic experiences similar to dream images.

3. *Perinatal experiences*—which deal with birth and death. Grof discusses four stages of the birth process. The first begins from the time before labor, the developing child resting comfortably in the womb. It is associated with a sense of the lack of boundaries and with symbols like the ocean. The second stage is the beginning of labor. It is associated with feelings of anxiety and threat, a sense of being trapped. The third stage involves the movement of the fetus through the birth canal. It is symbolized by struggle for survival, crushing pressure, and a sense of suffocation. The fourth stage is the experience of birth, the struggle that finally ends in

relief and relaxation. It may include visions of light and beauty, a sense of liberation or salvation, or the experience of death and rebirth.

4. *Transpersonal experiences*—which include the sense of consciousness expansion beyond ego boundaries and beyond space and time. Other experiences involve extrasensory perception, visions of archetypal images, ancestral memories, memories of prior incarnations, or the sense of merging completely with others.

Grof (1975) has argued that these four levels are closely interrelated. He has found that work with psychodynamic memories tends to lead to perinatal and then transpersonal experiences. Conversely, those who have had profound spiritual or transpersonal experiences find it easier to work with psychological issues.

Psychosynthesis

If humanistic science may be said to have any goals beyond sheer fascination with the human mystery and enjoyment of it, these would be to release the individual from external control and to make him *less* predictable to the observer . . . even though perhaps more predictable to himself. (Maslow, 1966, p. 40)

Another important transpersonal pioneer is Roberto Assagioli (1971). Assagioli was an Italian psychiatrist who studied with both Freud and Jung, and developed the system called, *psychosynthesis*. Assagioli (in Hardy, 1987) distinguishes two levels of work in psychosynthesis: personal and transpersonal. Personal psychosynthesis focuses on the integration of the personality around the personal self. Transpersonal psychosynthesis involves alignment of the personality with the transpersonal self. Assagioli points out that the self at the personality level is basically a reflection of the transpersonal self.

> The fact that we have spoken of the ordinary self and the profounder Self, must not be taken to mean that there are two separate and independent 'I's, two beings in us. The Self in reality is one. What we call the ordinary self is that small part of the deeper Self that the waking consciousness is able to assimilate in a given moment. . . . It is a reflection of what can become ever more clear and vivid; and it can perhaps someday succeed in uniting itself with its source. (Assagioli in Hardy, 1987, p. 31)

Evaluation of Tranpersonal Psychology

It used to be that the transpersonal realm of human experience was the exclusive domain of the priest, guru, or spiritual teacher. Today the transpersonal is very much the concern of psychology. In dealing with human problems involving values, meaning, and purpose, psychological growth inevitably raises issues of a spiritual, transpersonal nature.

Carl Jung has argued that it is only through the transformation of consciousness that we change and grow.

All the greatest and most important problems of life are fundamentally insoluble. . . . They can never be solved, but only outgrown. This "outgrowing" proved on further investigation to require a new level of consciousness. Some higher or wider interest appeared on the patient's horizon. (Jung in Jacoby, 1959, p. 302)

The Theory Firsthand: Excerpt from "The Plateau Experience"

The following quotation is taken from the *Journal of Transpersonal Psychology*. These are excerpts from a discussion between Maslow and several other psychologists.

I found that as I got older, my peak experiences became less intense and also became less frequent. In discussing this matter with other people who are getting older, I received this same sort of reaction. My impression is that this may have to do with the aging process. It makes sense because to some extent, I've learned that I've become somewhat afraid of peak experiences because I wonder if my body can stand them. A peak experience can produce great turmoil in the autonomic nervous system; it may be that a decrease in peak experiences is nature's way of protecting the body. . . .

As these poignant and emotional discharges died down in me, something else happened which has come into my consciousness which is a very precious thing. A sort of precipitation occurred of what might be called the sedimentation or the fallout from illuminations, insights, and other life experiences that were very important—tragic experiences included. The result has been a kind of unitive consciousness which has certain advantages and certain disadvantages over the peak experiences. I can define this unitive consciousness very simply for me as the simultaneous perception of the sacred and the ordinary, or the miraculous and the rather constant or easy-without-effort sort of thing.

I now perceive under the aspect of eternity and become mythic, poetic, and symbolic about ordinary things. This is the Zen experience, you know. There is nothing excepted and nothing special, but one lives in a world of miracles all the time. There is a paradox because it is miraculous and yet it doesn't produce an autonomic burst.

This type of consciousness has certain elements in common with peak experience—awe, mystery, surprise, and esthetic shock. These elements are present, but are constant rather than climactic. It certainly is a temptation to use as kind of a model, a paradigm for the peaking experience, the sexual orgasm, which is a mounting up to a peak and a climax, and then a drop in the completion and its ending. Well, this other type of experience must have another model. The words that I would use to describe this kind of experience would be "a high plateau." It is to live at a constantly high level in the sense of illumination or awakening or in Zen, in the easy or miraculous, in the nothing special. It is to take rather casually the poignancy and the preciousness and the beauty of things, but not to make a big deal out of it because it's happening every hour, you know, all the time.

This type of experience has the advantage, in the first place, that it's more voluntary than peak experience. For example, to enter deeply into this type of consciousness, I can go to an art museum or a meadow rather than into a subway. In the plateau experiences, you're not as surprised because they are more volitional than peak experiences. Further, I think you can teach plateau experiences; you could hold classes in miraculousness.

Another aspect I have noticed is that it's possible to sit and look at something miraculous for an hour and enjoy every second of it. On the other hand, you can't have an hour-long orgasm. In this sense, the plateau type of experience is better. It has a great advantage, so to speak, over the climactic, the orgasm, the peak. The descending into a valley, and living on the high plateau doesn't imply this. It is much more casual.

There are some other aspects of this experience. There tends to be more serenity rather than an emotionality. Our tendency is to regard the emotional person as an explosive type. However, calmness must also be brought into one's psychology. We need the serene as well as the poignantly emotional. . . .

The important point that emerges from these plateau experiences is that they're essentially cognitive. As a matter of fact, almost by definition, they represent a witnessing of the world. The plateau experience is a witnessing of reality. It involves seeing the symbolic, or the mythic, the poetic, the transcendent, the miraculous, the unbelievable, all of which I think are part of the real world instead of existing only in the eyes of the beholder.

There is a sense of certainty about plateau experience. It feels very, very good to be able to see the world as miraculous and not merely in the concrete, not reduced only to the behavioral, not limited only to the here and now. You know, if you get stuck in the here and now, that's a reduction.

Well, it's very easy to get sloppy with your words and you can go on about the beauty of the world, but the fact is that these plateau experiences are described quite well in many literatures. This is not the standard description of the acute mystical experience, but the way in which the world looks if the mystic experience really takes. If your mystical experience changes your life, you go about your business as the great mystics did. For example, the great saints could have mystical revelations, but also could run a monastery. You can run a grocery store and pay the bills, but still carry on this sense of witnessing the world in the way you did in the great moments of mystic perception. (Maslow in Krippner, 1972, pp. 112–115)

Annotated Bibliography

Maslow, A. H. (1968). *Toward a psychology of being.* New York: Van Nostrand. Maslow's most popular and widely available book. It includes material on deficiency versus being, growth psychology, creativity, and values.

————. (1987). *Motivation and personality* (3rd ed.). New York: Harper & Row. A psychology textbook that provides a more technical treatment of Maslow's work, including motivation theory, the need hierarchy, and self-actualization.

————. (1971). *The farther reaches of human nature.* New York: Viking Press. In many ways, Maslow's best book. A collection of articles on psychological health, creativeness, values, education, society, meta-motivation, and transcendence; also, a complete bibliography of Maslow's writings.

References

Assagioli, R. (1971). *Psychosynthesis.* NY: Viking.

Benedict, R. (1970). Synergy: Patterns of the good culture. *American Anthropologist, 72,* 320–333.

Fadiman, J. (1980). The transpersonal stance. In R. Walsh & F. Vaughan (Eds.), *Beyond ego.* Los Angeles: Tarcher.

Frager, R. (1989). Transpersonal psychology: Promise and prospects. In R. Valle & S. Halling (Eds.), *Existential-phenomenological perspectives in psychology.* New York: Plenum.

Goble, F. (1971). *The third force: The psychology of Abraham Maslow.* New York: Pocket Books.

Goldstein, K. (1939). *The organism.* New York: American Book.

————. (1940). *Human nature in the light of psychopathology.* New York: Schocken Books.

Gray, S. W. (1986). The relationship between self-actualization and leisure satisfaction. *Psychology, 23,* 6–12.

Grof, S. (1975). *Realms of the human unconscious.* New York: Viking Press.

Hall, M. (1968). A conversation with Abraham Maslow. *Psychology Today, 2*(2), 34–37, 54–57.

Hardy, J. (1987). *A psychology with a soul: Psychosynthesis in evolutionary context.* New York: Routledge & Kegan Paul.

Horner, M. (1972). The motive to avoid success and changing aspirations of college women. In J. Bardwick (Ed.), *Readings on the psychology of women* (pp. 62–67). New York: Harper & Row.

Huxley, A. (1944). *The perennial philosophy*. New York: Harper & Row.
———. (1963). *Island*. New York: Bantam Books.

International Study Project (1972). *Abraham H. Maslow: A memorial volume*. Monterey, CA: Brooks/Cole.

Jacoby, J. (1959). *Complex, archetype, symbol in the psychology of C. G. Jung*. New York: Pantheon.

James, W. (1943). *The varieties of religious experience*. New York: Random House (Modern Library).

Journal of Transpersonal Psychology Editorial Staff (1970). An appreciation. *Journal of Transpersonal Psychology, 2*(2), iv.

Katz, S. T. (1978). Language, epistemology and mysticism. In S. T. Katz (Ed.), *Mysticism and philosophical analysis*. New York: Oxford University Press.

Kelly, R. B., & Chovan, W. (1985). Yet another empirical test of the relationship between self-actualization and moral judgement. *Psychological Reports, 56,* 201–202.

Krippner, S. (Ed.). (1972). The plateau experience: A. H. Maslow and others. *Journal of Transpersonal Psychology, 4,* 107–120.

Kuhn, T. (1962). *The structure of scientific revolutions*. Chicago: University of Chicago Press.

Leonard, G. (1983, December). Abraham Maslow and the new self. *Esquire,* pp. 326–336.

Lowry, R. (1973a). (Ed.). *Dominance, self-esteem, self-actualization: Germinal papers of A. H. Maslow*. Monterey, CA: Brooks/Cole.
———. (1973b). *A. H. Maslow: An intellectual portrait*. Monterey, CA: Brooks/Cole.

Maslow, A. (1964). *Religions, values and peak experiences*. Columbus, OH: Ohio State University Press.
———. (1965). *Eupsychian management: A journal*. Homewood, IL: Irwin.
———. (1966). *The psychology of science: A reconnaissance*. New York: Harper & Row.
———. (1968). *Toward a psychology of being* (2nd ed.). New York: Van Nostrand.
———. (1970). *Motivation and personality* (rev. ed.). New York: Harper & Row.
———. (1971). *The farther reaches of human nature*. New York: Viking Press.
———. (1987). *Motivation and personality* (3rd ed.). New York: Harper & Row.
———. (1948). Higher and lower needs. *Journal of Psychology,* 433–436.

Maslow, A. H., with Chiang H. (1969). *The healthy personality: Readings*. New York: Van Nostrand.

Metzner, R. (1986). *Opening to inner light*. Los Angeles: Tarcher.
———. (1989). States of consciousness and transpersonal psychology.

In R. Valle & S. Halling (Eds.), *Existential-phenomenological perspectives in psychology*. New York: Plenum.

Ornstein, R. (1972). *The psychology of consciousness*. New York: Viking Press.

————. (1973). *The nature of human consciousness*. New York: Viking Press.

Rychman, R. M. (1985). Physical self-efficacy and actualization. *Journal of Research in Personality, 19,* 288–298.

Shostrom, E. (1963). *Personal orientation inventory*. San Diego, CA.

Smith, H. (1976). *Forgotten truth*. New York: Harper & Row.

Sumner, W. (1940). *Folkways*. New York: New American Library.

Sutich, A. (1969). Some considerations regarding transpersonal psychology. *Journal of Transpersonal Psychology 1,* 11–20.

Tart, C. (Ed.). (1969). *Altered states of consciousness*. New York: Wiley.

————. (Ed.). (1975). *Transpersonal psychologies*. New York: Harper & Row.

Timmons, B., & Kamiya, J. (1970). The psychology and physiology of meditation and related phenomena: bibliography I. *Journal of Transpersonal Psychology, 2,* 41–59.

Timmons, B., & Kanellakos, D. (1974). The psychology and physiology of meditation and related phenomena: Bibliography II. *Journal of Transpersonal Psychology, 6,* 32–38.

Valle, R. (1989). The emergence of transpersonal psychology. In R. Valle & S. Halling (Eds.), *Existential-phenomenological perspectives in psychology*. New York: Plenum.

Walsh, R. (1989). Asian psychotherapies. In R. Corsini & D. Wedding (Eds.), *Current psychotherapies* (4th ed.). Itasca, IL: Peacock Publishers.

Walsh, R., & Shapiro, D. (Eds.). (1983). *Beyond health and normality: Explorations of exceptional psychological well being*. New York: Van Nostrand Reinhold.

Walsh, R., & Vaughan, F. (1980). *Beyond ego: Transpersonal dimensions in psychology*. Los Angeles: Tarcher.

Wilber, K. (1977). *The spectrum of consciousness*. Wheaton, IL: Theosophical Publishing.

————. (1980). *The Atman project*. Wheaton, IL: Quest.

Wilson, C. (1972). *New pathways in psychology: Maslow and the post-Freudian revolution*. New York: Mentor.

Wittine, B. (1989). Basic postulates for a transpersonal psychotherapy. In R. Valle & S. Halling (Eds.), *Existential-phenomenological perspectives in psychology*. New York: Plenum.

Part Two

Introduction to Eastern Theories of Personality

The final three chapters of this book are devoted to the theories of personality developed in three Eastern psychospiritual disciplines: Yoga, Zen Buddhism, and Sufism. Thus, Part Two represents a broadening of the traditional limits of personality theory. This trend can be seen throughout psychology, which is becoming more of an international field of study, less tied to American and Western European intellectual and philosophical assumptions.

Contemporary Concern with Eastern Systems

There is growing interest in Eastern thought throughout the United States. There is a growing proliferation of teachers, books, and organizations based on various Eastern disciplines. More and more Westerners in search of new values and personal and spiritual growth are devoting themselves to the intensive study or practice of an Eastern discipline.

These Eastern theories include powerful concepts and effective techniques of personal and spiritual growth. Both the research into and practical application of these three disciplines have increased in the West.

> There is growing recognition that Western psychologists may have underestimated the psychologies and therapies of other cultures. Certain Asian disciplines contain sophisticated therapies, and experimental studies have demonstrated their ability to induce psychological, physiological, and psychotherapeutic effects. An increasing number of Westerners, including mental health professionals, now use Asian therapies. Benefits include new perspectives on psychological functioning, potential, and pathology, as well as new approaches and techniques. In addition, the study of other cultures and practices often has the healthy effect of revealing unsuspected ethnocentric assumptions and limiting beliefs, thus leading to a broader view of human nature and therapy. . . .
>
> Asian psychologies focus primarily on existential and transpersonal levels and little on the pathological. They contain detailed maps of states of consciousness, developmental levels, and stages of enlightenment that extend beyond traditional Western psychological maps. Moreover, they claim to possess techniques for inducing these states and conditions. (Walsh, 1989, p. 547–548)

These chapters are included to provide you with the opportunity to consider, evaluate, and, to some extent, experience these additional perspectives on personality in the context of a critical and comparative course within psychology. We have ample evidence of the interest and time that students are already devoting to these questions. Yet the degree of fundamental knowledge of the Eastern traditions is often very low in comparison to the amount of interest or even the amount of time many people are spending in these pursuits.

The Study of Eastern Psychologies

Why study religions in a psychology textbook? The term *religion* has strong connotations of rigid dogma, conventional morality, and so on. These do not seem particularly compatible with psychology.

It is important to remember that we are dealing with Eastern *psychologies* rather than Eastern *religions*. Yoga, Zen, and Sufism originated from a common need to understand the relationship between religious practice and everyday life. They do differ from most Western personality theories in their greater concern with values and moral considerations and in their stress on the advisability of living in accordance with certain spiritual standards. However, all three psychologies view morals and values in a practical, even iconoclastic way. They argue that we should live within a moral code because a morally codified life has definite, recognizable, and beneficial effects on our consciousness and overall well-being. Each of these traditions stresses the futility and foolishness of valuing external form over inner function.

These psychologies, like their Western counterparts, are derived from careful observations of human experience. They are built on centuries of empirical observations of the psychological, physiological, and spiritual effects of a variety of ideas, attitudes, behaviors, and exercises.

Each system's ethos is based on the personal experiences and insights of its founders. The vitality and importance of these traditional psychologies rest on the continual testing, reworking, and modifying of their initial insights to fit new settings and interpersonal situations as well as different cultural conditions. The underlying religious traditions for these systems—Hinduism, Buddhism, and Islam—represent the perspectives of millions of people today in over 100 different countries. These three traditions are embraced by the majority of the world's population. They are living realities for their adherents, not academic, scholarly, or impractical abstractions.

Transpersonal Experience

Each of these systems is focused on transpersonal growth, or growth beyond the ego and personality. In contrast, Western psychologists generally discuss growth in terms of strengthening the ego: increased autonomy, self-determination, self-actualization, freedom from neurotic processes, and healthy-mindedness. Nevertheless, the concepts of transpersonal growth and ego strength may be more complementary than conflicting.

Pioneering personality theorist Andras Angyal discusses each of these viewpoints.

> Viewed from one of these vantage points [the full development of the personality] the human being seems to be striving basically to assert and to expand his self-determination. He is an autonomous being, a

self-growing entity that asserts itself actively instead of reacting passively like a physical body to the impacts of the surrounding world. This fundamental tendency expresses itself in a striving of the person to consolidate and increase his self-government, in other words, to exercise his freedom and to organize the relevant items of his world out of the autonomous center of government that is his self. This tendency—which I have termed "the trend toward increased autonomy"—expresses itself in spontaneity, self-assertiveness, striving for freedom and for mastery. (Angyal, 1956, pp. 44–45)

Seen from another vantage point, human life reveals a very different basic pattern from the one described above. From this point of view the person appears to seek a place for himself in a larger unit of which he strives to become a part. In the first tendency we see him struggling for centrality in his world, trying to mold, to organize, the objects and events of his world, to bring them under his own jurisdiction and government [as in ego growth]. In the second tendency he seems rather to surrender himself willingly to seek a home for himself in and to become an organic part of something that he conceives as greater than himself [as in transpersonal growth]. The super-individual unit of which one feels oneself a part, or wishes to become a part, may be variously formulated according to one's cultural background and personal understanding. (Angyal, 1956, pp. 45–46)

This second tendency would seem to be more applicable to those who have already achieved a certain degree of self-possession, maturity, and self-actualization. The development of a strong autonomous personality and sense of self seems to be a prerequisite for this second type of growth.

States of Consciousness

A basic assumption in Eastern psychologies is that there is a broad spectrum of states of consciousness. In addition to the states we experience daily, such as waking, sleeping, or dreaming, there are a variety of meditative and ecstatic states that can have profound, long-term effects on the individual.

William James wrote, "Our normal waking consciousness . . . is but one special type of consciousness, whilst all about it, parted from it by the filmiest of screens, there lie potential forms of consciousness entirely different. . . . No account of the universe in its totality can be final which leaves these other forms of consciousness quite disregarded" (James, 1958, p. 298).

Eastern psychologies claim that our "normal" waking state is filled with daydreaming, fantasies, and habitual, unconscious action patterns. Transpersonal psychologist Charles Tart (1986) has argued that our waking state is more like "waking sleep," "a waking dream," or a "consensus trance." If this dream turns into a nightmare, we call it psychopathology and seek professional help. The universal (and fundamentally distorting) effects of the dream are so pervasive we consider them "normal." People who eliminate this dream state in themselves are said to have become "awakened." The achievement of awakening, also called *liberation*, or *enlightenment*, is the goal of Eastern psychologies.

It is a common prejudice that transpersonal growth and religious experience are not "normal" human phenomena. Many psychologists and other scientists have been strongly influenced by this bias. Furthermore, some feel that transcendant experience is more appropriately explored by theologians than psychologists. This prejudice is strengthened by the fact that virtually the only concepts available to describe transpersonal phenomena come from religious terminology.

> As a matter of fact, this identity is so profoundly built into the English language that it is almost impossible to speak of the "spiritual life" (a distasteful phrase to a scientist, and especially to a psychologist) without using the vocabulary of traditional religion. There just isn't any other satisfactory language yet. A trip to the thesaurus will demonstrate this very quickly. This makes an almost insoluble problem for the writer who is intent on demonstrating that the common base for all religions is human, natural, empirical, and that so-called spiritual values are also naturally derivable. But I have available only a theistic language for this "scientific" job. (Maslow, 1964, p. 4n)

Transpersonal experiences have been important, even central, elements of human life throughout history. Most cultures and societies have been profoundly religious; their value systems have supported such experiences and given them worth. However, modern Western society has been somewhat less open to transpersonal phenomena for the past few decades, which is actually an extremely short span of time in Western history. We should remember that the transpersonal dimension has been of central importance in most societies throughout history.

As a student of personality, it would be as foolish to neglect this sector of consciousness as it would be to ignore psychopathology. It is a reflection on the youth of psychology, not its sophistication, that it has devoted more effort to understanding human illness than human transcendence. The Eastern theories have slowly acquired the tools and concepts necessary to investigate this less concrete and less objective side of human experience.

The following three chapters present comprehensive and practical theories of personality described in psychologically relevant terms. Each system is deeply concerned with questions of ultimate values, with transpersonal experience, and with the relationship of the individual self to a greater whole. Each theory has received considerable attention in the West and many aspects of these systems are already being applied in different facets of psychology.

The test of these Eastern systems is no different than the evaluations you have made of the Western theories presented thus far. You do not have to become a Buddhist to appreciate or to utilize some of the concepts or perspectives found in Zen; you do not have to become a yogi to practice breathing or relaxation exercises. We hope that you will appreciate the Eastern systems of thought as expansions of your own Western psychological background and take from them whatever tools and insights you find of value.

References

Angyal, A. (1956). A theoretical model for personality studies. In C. Moustakas (Ed.), *The self*. New York: Harper & Row.

Campbell, P., & McMahon, E. (1974). Religious type experience in the context of humanistic and transpersonal psychology. *Journal of Transpersonal Psychology, 6,* 11–17.

Goleman, D. (1974). Perspective on psychology, reality, and the study of consciousness. *Journal of Transpersonal Psychology, 6,* 73–85.

James, W. (1958). *The varieties of religious experience*. New York: New American Library. (Originally published, 1902.)

Maslow, A. (1964). *Religions, values and peak experiences*. Columbus, OH: Ohio State University Press.

Tart, C. (1986). *Waking up: Overcoming the obstacles to human potential*. Boston: Shambhala.

Walsh, R. (1989). Asian psychotherapies. In R. Corsini & D. Wedding (Eds.), *Current psychotherapies* (4th ed). Itasca, IL: Peacock Publishers.

Chapter Fourteen

Yoga and the Hindu Tradition

Yoga has two aspects. First, it encompasses virtually all the religious and ascetic practices of India, including meditation, physical discipline, and devotional chanting. Second, Yoga is a specific school of Indian philosophy systematized by Patanjali and first mentioned in India's ancient 3,000-year-old Vedas, the world's oldest recorded literature. The roots of Yoga practice undoubtedly go even farther back to Indian prehistory.

Yoga is a Sanskrit word meaning "to join" or "to unite." The goal of Yoga practice is self-realization, which occurs when consciousness is turned within and united with its source, the Self. One of the classic Yoga authorities has written, "Yoga is *samadhi* (ecstacy)" (Feuerstein, 1989). Yoga also means "method." It embraces the goal of union and the vast variety of yogic techniques meant to accomplish this end. In this sense, Yoga is the technology of self-realization or ecstasy.

In its broadest sense, Yoga embraces all systematic disciplines designed to promote self-realization through calming the mind and focusing consciousness on the Self, the immortal, unchanging essence in all people.

History

The roots of Yoga are very ancient. They go all the way back to the pre-Hindu culture of India. Yoga is an integral part of the rich and complex Hindu tradition. Hinduism encompasses hundreds of different traditions and sacred texts. These are all connected with the Vedas.

The Vedic Period

The Vedas were originally an oral transmission, handed down from teacher to disciple for many centuries. The earliest Vedas date back to 2500 B.C. There are four major sections of the Vedas. The oldest section consists of the Vedic hymns, which include the most sophisticated philosophy. The second section deals with rituals and sacrifices; perfect performance of long and complex rituals was believed essential to ensure good fortune. The third section, on contemplation and inner truth, comprises the forest treatises, written for forest-dwelling ascetics. The last section contains the *Upanishads,* or the *Vedanta,* literally "the end of the Vedas," which discuss the goal of knowing the Self. The Vedas form the basis of all subsequent Indian thought and philosophy.

In the Vedic period, Yoga was closely related to shamanism (Eliade, 1969). Early yogis placed great value on ecstatic trance and the development of supernatural powers through the practice of severe austerities. They believed that individuals could literally compel the Hindu gods to fulfill their requests through superhuman self-discipline and self-mortification. The exercise of austerities and self-control has remained a major part of Yoga practice to this day.

Lead me from the unreal to the real. From darkness lead me to light. From death lead me to immortality.
(*Brihadaranyaka Upanishad,* I:iii, 28)

Personal Reflection ————————————————
————————————————————————— Austerities

General Principles

The simplest, most direct, and most difficult practice of austerity is to give up satisfying one's desires—that is, if you desire food, then you should fast. If you love to sleep, make yourself do with less. Giving up small pleasures and comforts can be an important self-discipline. If you usually get up at 8:00 A.M., try getting up at 4:00 or 5:00 every morning. If you like sleeping on a soft or comfortable bed, start sleeping on a thin mat on the floor.

There are some important cautions in this kind of practice. Austerities can have the side effect of strengthening the ego. Pride in one's accomplishments, pride in suffering, or masochistic enjoyment of austerities for their own sake are all indications of ego involvement. Another thing to watch for is excessive austerity. This is another demonstration of ego and may actually cause mental or physical harm to the individual.

Fasting

Short periods of fasting are an excellent practice of austerity. You can begin simply by deliberately missing one or two meals. A one-day fast is not too difficult for anyone in good health. Drink plenty of water, and drink orange juice if you feel the need for additional nourishment. Fasting for one day a week is an excellent practice. Fasting directly confronts the individual with the need to overcome temptation and to set one's will against the desire for food.

Silence

Silence is another beneficial practice. Try remaining silent for a few hours at home or around friends who understand your intention. Or spend a day by yourself in silence. Carry paper and pencil with you to communicate in writing if necessary. Observe yourself and others, as well as your reactions to conversations. Try to overcome your need to communicate actively. Learn to just *be*, in silence.

The Bhagavad-Gita

The *Bhagavad-Gita* (Mascaro, 1962) is the first and also the most popular work on Yoga. It is a part of the great Indian epic of the second century B.C. called *Mahabharata*. The *Mahabharata* is a magnificent collection of mythology, religion, ethics, and customs. It is about 100,000 stanzas long, almost eight times the length of the Illiad and the Odyssey combined. Yoga and related philosophies are key to the ideas discussed in the epic.

The *Mahabharata* revolves around the story of the five Pandava brothers, their upbringing, education, and many adventures. The *Bhagavad-Gita* can be read as a single great metaphor for the spiritual quest. According to some interpreters, the characters in the Bhagavad-Gita represent various psychological and physical qualities. The five brothers are the five senses and the battlefield is the body and the consciousness of the individual.

The *Bhagavad-Gita* is a dialog between Arjuna (the ego) and Krishna (the Self). Arjuna is a warrior, and Krishna, his charioteer, is an incarnation of God and a great spiritual teacher. Krishna discusses duty and the Yoga of action. He teaches Arjuna the importance of devotion, self-control, meditation, and other yogic practices to serve as an example for others. As charioteer, Krishna symbolizes the *guru,* or spiritual teacher, who can help bring students to terms with the problems and conflicts they encounter in the process of spiritual development. However, the guru, like the charioteer, cannot fight the students' battles for them.

The following are some of the descriptions of Yoga from the *Bhagavad-Gita:*

> For the sage who desires to ascend in Yoga, action is stated to be the means. For him who has ascended in Yoga, serenity is said to be the means. (VI:3)

> When he does not cling to the sense-objects or to deeds and has renounced all desires, then he is called "one who has ascended in Yoga." (VI:4)

> When he has controlled the mind and is established in the Self only, devoid of all desires, then he is said to be a "yoked one." (VI:18)

The *Bhagavad-Gita* includes classic teachings on karma-yoga, the Yoga of action. Krishna advocates action without attachment over inaction and renunciation. The mind is the primary source of all action. The ideal is to develop a pure mind that is without attachment. Then, your whole life becomes a continual Yoga.

> You must [always] do the allotted action, for action is superior to inaction; not even your body's processes can be accomplished by inaction. (III:8)

> Just as the unwise perform [their deeds] attached to action, O Bharata [Krishna], the wise should act unattached, desiring the world's welfare. (III:25)

He who works not for an earthly reward, but does the work to be done . . . he is a Yogi. (*Bhagavad-Gita,* VI:1)[1]

[1]Quotes from the *Bhagavad-Gita* are taken from Mascaro (1962), Prabhavananda and Isherwood (1951), and Feuerstein (1989).

The Classical Period

This era lasted from A.D. 200 until A.D. 800. It was the time of the development of six classical schools of Hindu thought. These are Mimamsa (the philosophy of ritualism), Nyaya (the school of logic), Vaisheshika (naturalistic philosophy), Vedanta (nondualistic metaphysics), Samkya (dualistic philosophy), and Yoga.

Vedanta, Samkya, and Yoga are the most influential schools today. There are strong links between Yoga and the other two. Vedanta teaches nondualism, which describes Reality as a single, indivisible whole. The major Vedanta philosophers also practiced various forms of Yoga for their own spiritual development.

Samkya is mainly concerned with understanding and describing various levels of existence. The goal is not so much to explain the world as to help transcend it by developing discrimination. Samkya and Yoga metaphysics are closely related and in fact both stem from the same earlier, preclassical tradition.

As one of the six schools of philosophy, Yoga refers to the work of Patanjali, scholar of the second-century B.C. and author of at least part of the *Yoga sutras*. The major difference between Samkya and Yoga is their methodologies. Samkya stresses discrimination and renunciation. Yoga emphasizes the necessity of experiencing ecstatic states of consciousness (*samadhi*) that bring deep insight into oneself and the world. Patanjali's approach to Yoga is the main focus of this chapter.

Major Concepts

Spirit

In classical Yoga, there is a strict dualism between Spirit and Matter. Spirit (*Purusha*) is pure consciousness. Spirit knows no limitations or qualifications. Spirit includes consciousness within and beyond the universe; the manifestation of Spirit in the individual is the Self. The Self is changeless, unaffected by physical or mental activity; however, the mind distorts our *awareness* of the Self.

The opposite pole to Spirit is Nature (*Pakriti*). In Sanskrit, *Pakriti* means "that which brings forth." It is related to "procreate." Nature is the ground from which all material forms spring. It is also the source of all nonmaterial forms, including thoughts and emotions. Nature is, like Spirit, eternal and unchanging.

The transcendental Self in each individual is Spirit in essence. The Self is like a wave, a form that the ocean takes on for a time. The Self is pure awareness, pure consciousness.

The classic treatise on Yoga, the *Yoga sutras* of Patanjali, describes Spirit as pure consciousness. Other schools, such as Vedanta, add two

The whole universe is filled by the Purusha (Spirit), to whom there is nothing superior, from whom there is nothing different, than whom there is nothing either smaller or greater; who stands alone, motionless as a tree, established in His own glory.
(Svetasvatara Upanishad, III:9)

Everyone is the Self and, indeed, is infinite. Yet each person mistakes his body for his Self. (Ramana Maharshi in Osbourne, 1962, p. 23)

fundamental characteristics: eternal existence and endless bliss; that is, Spirit is the most enjoyable state of consciousness imaginable—eternal, ever new bliss. The Self shares these characteristics, although we are fated to remain unaware of them until we attain self-realization.

The ideal of Yoga is to seek joy from its source—the Self within. One East Indian parable concerns the musk deer, whose musk glands become active when the mature deer enters the mating season. The deer is so taken with this entrancing scent that it often begins to run through the forest, seeking the source of the odor. The frenzied deer can lose all sense of direction and become entangled in underbrush or even plunge off of a cliff. Frantically seeking the musk without, the deer will never discover the source of the odor, which is within itself.

One authority writes that Spirit is not limited either by form or formlessness. "God, though without form, is with form too; He has the power to take any form according to the wish of the devotee. The yogi who wants to meditate on a form, may choose any form he likes, concentrate on it, and solve his problem" (Purohit, 1938, pp. 37–38). In other words, the individual can concentrate on Spirit represented by a certain form and certain qualities, such as beauty, love, strength, or wisdom.

To the seer, all things have verily become the Self: what delusion, what sorrow, can there be for him who beholds that oneness? (*Isa Upanishad*, 7)

Those who are devotional often choose to worship God with form, a God they can visualize and represent with images and concrete symbols. Others prefer to believe in formless Spirit, to conceive of Spirit in the abstract, as pure light or love or cosmic consciousness. The great Indian yogi Ramakrishna counseled a disciple: "It is enough to have faith in either aspect. You believe in God without form; that is quite all right. But never for a moment think that this alone is true and all else false. Remember that God with form is just as true as God without form. But hold fast to your own conviction" (Nikhilananda, 1948, pp. 61–62).

Three Principles of Creation

Nature (*Prakriti*) has three primary constituents, or principles, the three *gunas: tamas* (inertia), *rajas* (activity), and *sattva* (clarity or light). These three principles function together to generate all activity. All the various manifestations of Nature (matter, thought, and so forth) are composed of different combinations of the three *gunas*.

In the process of creating a statue, for example, tamas can be seen in the untouched, inert stone. Rajas is the act of carving, and sattva is the image in the sculptor's imagination. All three are essential. Pure tamas alone is inert, dead matter. Pure rajas is energy without direction or goal. Pure sattva is a plan that remains unrealized.

Every individual exhibits some balance among these three qualities, although most are dominated by one of them. Sattva is considered the most spiritual. Virtually everything can be classified in terms of the gunas. Rich or heavy foods are tamasic because they are difficult to digest and cause laziness or sleepiness. Spicy, hot foods are rajasic as they lead to activity, strong emotions, or nervousness. Fresh fruit and vegetables are sattvic and promote calmness. Certain places, such as mountains and the ocean shore, are sattvic and thus suitable for spiritual practice.

Consciousness

In Yoga terminology, Mind, or consciousness (*chitta*), embraces all thought processes. Patanjali defines Yoga as "controlling the activities of the mind." This stops the incessant "chatter" of mental activity and brings about a state of deep calm and inner peace. Yoga is the complete focusing of attention on whatever object is contemplated. The final goal is to focus attention on the Self. When mental processes or waves of consciousness are active, the Self is obscured, like a bright light suspended in churning water.

All Yoga practices work toward one end: to quiet the waves and calm the mind. Some schools of Yoga focus on control of the body and others on breathing techniques; still others teach meditation practices. In a sense, all of the Yoga techniques and practices are only preliminary exercises designed to still the mind. Once mind and body are calm and disciplined, awareness of the Self is possible.

> The mind is like a miraculous rubber band that can be expanded to infinity without breaking. (Yogananda, 1968a)

Karma

Karma means action and also its results. Every activity brings with it certain consequences, and every individual's life is influenced by past actions. This influence occurs in part through the creation of subconscious tendencies in the following sequence:

subconscious → waves of → actions → subconscious
tendencies consciousness tendencies

> Before you act, you have freedom, but after you act, the effect of that action will follow you whether you want it to or not. That is the law of *karma*. You are a free agent, but when you perform a certain act, you will reap the results of that act. (Yogananda, 1968b)

In order to avoid the formation of new subconscious tendencies or the strengthening of old ones, the yogi refrains from "acting out." In other words, anger tendencies are strengthened by angry thoughts and feelings and reinforced further by angry speech and actions. The yogic ideal is not suppression of unacceptable tendencies, but transmutation of negative action and thought into positive action and thought. One effective way of dealing with strong emotions is to look calmly and deeply at their roots. Inner awareness can transform subsequent thoughts and feelings. Through self-discipline, right action, and Yoga practice, the individual gradually changes his or her consciousness, transmuting old habits and thought patterns.

Subconscious Tendencies

Control of the waves of consciousness is possible only when the subconscious tendencies are diminished. Such tendencies (*samskaras*) shape mental activity. These subconscious habit patterns are created by past actions and experiences, from this life and from past lives. Tendencies are built up by the continued action of thought waves or waves of con-

> You cannot achieve emancipation unless you have burned the seeds of past actions in the fires of wisdom and meditation. (Yogananda, 1968a, p. 110)

sciousness. For example, anger waves of consciousness gradually create anger tendencies, which predispose the individual to angry reactions.

The discipline of Yoga must include a *complete* reformation of consciousness. Otherwise, the subconscious tendencies eventually will seek to actualize themselves, sprouting suddenly like dormant seeds. Through meditation, self-analysis, and other powerful inner disciplines, it is possible to "roast" such seeds, to destroy their potential for further activity; that is, through fundamental inner change we can grow free of the influence of the past.

In this theory of the subconscious tendencies, Yoga anticipated by many centuries the modern notion of the unconscious. Further, Yoga has gone beyond the insights and goals of most schools of psychotherapy in developing techniques for complete transformation of the unconscious.

The Guru

The word *guru* comes from the Sanskrit root "to uplift." Many teachers in India are called gurus; the name connotes a spiritual teacher, one who can raise the student's consciousness. (In India, teachers of music, dance, and other traditional skills do more than instruct students in technique; they are considered masters of disciplines that affect one's whole life and character.) A guru is considered essential in Yoga for several reasons. The techniques taught are complex and subtle and easily misunderstood if learned from a book. Also, many techniques have to be adapted by the teacher to the specific physical and mental makeup of the students.

The guru is also a disciplinarian, who pushes the student beyond self-imposed limitations. As one who has been through the discipline already, the guru knows through experience the extent of human capacity. Thus, the guru is able to demand that students exert themselves to the limits of their capabilities. In addition, students are inspired by their teacher's living example to realize their highest potential.

There is a beautiful example of the role of the guru found in the *Bhagavad-Gita*. In the great battle, Krishna, the guru, is Arjuna's charioteer. Krishna does not fight but leads Arjuna from battle to battle, testing and strengthening his disciple. At one point, a great enemy warrior throws a magic spear that can pass through all obstacles. Knowing that Arjuna cannot cope with this weapon, Krishna causes the wheels of their chariot to sink deep into the ground so that the dreaded missile passes overhead. In this way, the guru brings the disciple from spiritual trial to spiritual trial, intervening only when the test is too great for the disciple's capabilities.

The guru also fosters the student's emotional and psychological development. The teacher is like a mirror, exposing faults and limitations of the student, but always remaining conscious of the essential purity and perfection of the Self behind such limitations. This kind of discipline can be administered only by someone who is relatively free of ego and strong personal biases or blind spots, which would distort the guru's reactions to the student.

Religion, which is the highest knowledge and the highest wisdom, cannot be bought, nor can it be acquired from books. . . . You will not find it anywhere until your heart is ready for receiving it and your teacher has come. (Vivekananda, 1978a, pp. 35–36)

"Gurus can be had by hundreds and thousands, but Chelas (disciples) there is not one" is an ancient saying. It means that many are the persons who can give good advice, but those who follow it are few. (Ramakrishna, 1965, p. 328)

One of the later Yoga texts, the *Kularnava-Tantra*, classifies six different types of gurus, according to basic function (Feuerstein, 1989). A teacher generally is a composite of several of these. (1) The *Impeller* motivates and inspires the prospective disciple, leading him or her to initiation; (2) The Indicator prescribes the most appropriate form of spiritual practice and discipline; (3) The *Explainer* interprets and clarifies the spiritual process and its goal; (4) The *Revealer* clarifies the details of the process; (5) The *Teacher* supervises the disciple's spiritual discipline; and (6) The *Illuminator* kindles in the disciple mental and spiritual understanding.

> The question is often asked, "Why should we look into the character and personality of a teacher? We have only to judge what he says and take that up." This is not right. If a man wants to teach me something of dynamics, of chemistry, or any other physical science, he may be anything he likes, because what the physical sciences require is merely an intellectual equipment; but in the spiritual sciences it is impossible from first to last that there can be any spiritual light in the soul that is impure. . . . Hence with the teacher of religion we must see first what he *is,* and then what he says. He must be perfectly pure, and then alone comes the value of his words, because he is only then the true "transmitter." What can he transmit, if he has not spiritual power in himself? . . . The function of the teacher is indeed an affair of the transference of something, and not one of mere stimulation of the existing intellectual or other faculties in the taught. Something real and appreciable as an influence comes from the teacher and goes to the taught. Therefore the teacher must be pure. . . .
>
> The teacher must not teach with any ulterior selfish motive—for money, name, or fame; his work must be simply out of love, out of pure love for mankind at large. The only medium through which spiritual force can be transmitted is love. . . . God is love, and only he who has known God as love, can be a teacher of godliness and God to man. (Vivekananda, 1978a, pp. 32–33)

In India the guru's most important attribute is spiritual consciousness. A teacher who has realized the Self transmits a sense of inner peace and bliss. Yogananda describes this kind of inspiration, which he received in his guru's presence: "If I entered the hermitage in a worried or indifferent frame of mind, my attitude imperceptibly changed. A healing calm descended at the mere sight of my guru. Each day with him was a new experience in joy, peace, and wisdom" (Yogananda, 1972, pp. 137–138).

Initiation

Many authorities maintain that initiation is a crucial element in Yoga practice. According to *Kularnava-Tantra,* self-realization is not possible without initiation, and there can be no real initiation without a qualified guru (Feuerstein, 1989).

Initiation is primarily a form of spiritual transmission. The disciple is changed physically, mentally, and spiritually through the guru's transmission of spiritual energy. It also creates a special bond between guru and disciple. The disciple enters the guru's spiritual lineage, a chain which may go back unbroken for centuries.

Schools of Yoga

Several major schools of Yoga developed in India. These suit different personalities. *Karma-yoga*, the Yoga of action, especially suits those with a strong will or those who need to develop their will as their next stage of growth. It is also chosen by those who hold service to others as a central ideal. *Jnana-yoga*, the Yoga of knowledge, suits those with keen minds and provides an essential discipline for those who need to develop discrimination. *Bhakti-yoga*, the Yoga of devotion, is ideal for those with a strong emotional nature. *Hatha-yoga* is for those with strong self-discipline and interest in developing physical mastery. *Kundalini-yoga* generally involves meditative techniques most suited to those with potential for subtle awareness of inner processes. *Raja-yoga* fits those with potential for deep concentration and mental control.

A sophisticated teacher may prescribe a particular form of Yoga practice that builds on a disciple's strengths or assign a specific practice that calls forth underdeveloped attributes. Less sophisticated teachers simply will assign their own practices, without considering individual differences.

> My own temperament is principally devotional. It was disconcerting at first to find that my guru, saturated with *jnana* but seemingly dry of *bhakti*, expressed himself chiefly in terms of cold spiritual mathematics. But, as I attuned myself to his nature, I discovered no diminution but rather an increase in my devotional approach to God. A Self-realized master is fully able to guide his various disciples along the natural lines of their essential bias. (Yogananda, 1972, p. 145)

Everything we do, physical or mental, is karma, and it leaves its marks on us. (Vivekananda, 1978b, pp. 3–4)

Karma-yoga, the Yoga of Action

Karma-yoga teaches us to act selflessly, without attachment to gain or loss, success or failure. The karma-yogi seeks to serve others as well as high ideals. This is a tremendous discipline to learn to overcome our selfishness, laziness, and pride.

Swami Vivekananda writes:

Offer all thy works to God, throw off selfish bonds, and do thy work. No sin can then stain thee, even as waters do not stain the leaf of the lotus. (Bhagavad-Gita, V:10)

> This is the one central idea in the *Gita:* Work incessantly, but be not attached to it. . . . God is unattached because He loves; that real love makes us unattached. . . . To attain this nonattachment is almost a life work. But as soon as we have reached this point we have attained the goal of love and become free. (1978b, pp. 38, 45–46)

Karma-yoga can be an important discipline for all cultures—for those who live in secluded caves in the Himalayas as well as for those who have jobs and families. As long as we are alive we must act. We all can learn to act well.

> Karma in its effect on character is the most tremendous power that man has to deal with. Man is as it were a centre, and is attracting all the powers of the universe towards himself, and in this center is fusing them all and again sending them off in a big current. (Vivekananda, 1978b, p. 5)

The practitioner of karma-yoga need not believe in a particular religious doctrine, or even in God or Spirit. The karma-yogi is transformed by developing selflessness through service rather than through ostensible religious discipline.

Jnana-yoga, the Yoga of Knowledge

The Yoga of knowledge is a discipline of rigorous self-analysis, a path for those endowed with a clear, refined intellect. It is basically a path of discrimination. The jnana-yogi seeks to understand the forces of delusion and bondage and to counter or avoid the influences of passion, sense attachment, and identification with the body.

This yogi is a true philosopher, a deep spiritual thinker who wants to go beyond the visible, beyond the little things of this world.

> Not even the teaching of thousands of books will satisfy him. Not even all the sciences will satisfy him; at the best, they only bring this little world before him. . . . His very soul wants to go beyond all that into the very heart of Being, by seeing Reality as It is; by realizing It, by being It, by becoming one with that Universal Being. (Vivekananda, 1976, p. 395)

The individual seeks the Self by discarding, through intelligent discrimination, all that is not the Self, all that is limiting, perishable, or illusory.

Ramana Maharshi (1879–1950) is regarded by many as India's greatest modern sage and exemplar of jnana-yoga. He taught his followers a technique called *Self-Inquiry,* or *vicara,* for regaining identification with the Self. It is a method of continuously inquiring "Who am I?" and looking beyond the body, the thoughts, and emotions for the source of consciousness. Some of the flavor of this approach can be seen in Maharshi's responses to questions.

"How is one to realize the Self?"

"Whose Self? Find out."

"Mine; but, who am I?"

Self-scrutiny, relentless observance of one's thoughts, is a stark and shattering experience. It pulverizes the stoutest ego. But, true self-analysis mathematically operates to produce seers. (Yogananda, 1972, p. 51)

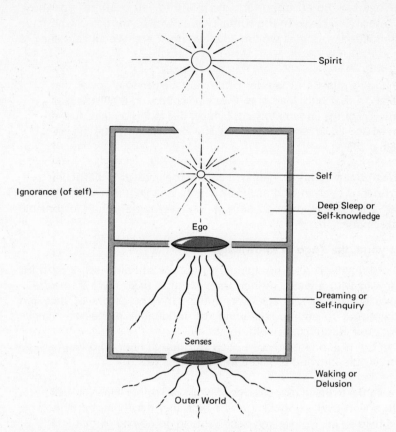

Figure 14.1   A Jnana-yoga Model of the Self and Consciousness (Adapted from Osbourne, 1969, pp. 23–24)

"It is you who must find out."

"I don't know."

"Just think over the question, Who is it that says: 'I don't know'?"

"Who is the 'I' in your statement? What is not known? Why was I born?"

"Who was born? The answer is the same to all your questions. 'However much I may try, I do not seem to catch the *I* [italics added]. It is not even clearly discernible."

"Who is it that says that the 'I' is not discernible? Are there two

'I's' in you, that one is not discernible to the other?"

(Osbourne, 1962, pp. 121–122)

Ramana Maharshi stressed self-realization as a task of removing delusional understanding, not as a matter of acquiring something new. "Once the false notion 'I am the body' or 'I am not realized' has been removed, Supreme Consciousness or the Self alone remains and in people's present state of knowledge they call this 'Realization.' But the truth is that Realization is eternal and already exists, here and now" (Osbourne, 1962, p. 23).

> The first and foremost of all the thoughts that arise in the mind is the primal "I"-thought. It is only after the rise of origin of the "I"-thought that innumerable other thoughts arise. . . . Since every other thought can occur only after the rise of the "I"-thought and since the mind is nothing but a bundle of thoughts, it is only through the enquiry "Who am I?" that the mind subsides. . . . Even when extraneous thoughts sprout up during such enquiry, do not seek to complete the rising thought, but instead, deeply enquire within, "To whom has this thought occurred?" No matter how many thoughts thus occur to you, if you would with acute vigilance enquire immediately as and when each individual thought arises to whom it has occurred, you would find it is to "me." If then you enquire "Who am I?" the mind gets introverted [focused within] and the rising thought also subsides. In this manner as you persevere more and more in the practice of Self-enquiry, the mind acquires increasing strength and power to abide in its Source. (Osbourne, 1969, p. 41)

Bhakti-yoga, the Yoga of Devotion

In contrast to self-discipline, will, or discrimination, bhakti-yoga is a way of reforming one's personality through the development of love and devotion. Its proponents argue that this simple path is most suitable to the modern era, in which few people have time and discipline to pursue fully the other traditional paths of Yoga.

Followers of bhakti-yoga use intense devotion to concentrate the mind and transform the personality. It is easier for most people to love God personified in human form than to love abstract spirit or consciousness. The practice of devotional Yoga is closer to traditional religions than any other form of Yoga. It includes ritual worship, chanting, and the worship of God. The great incarnations of God, such as Rama and Krishna, are a common focus of devotion in some parts of India, and the Goddess Kali, or the Divine Mother, in others.

Long sessions of spiritual chanting typically form an important part of traditional Indian religious practice as well as a basic bhakti-yoga practice. Chants are often simple and repetitive, inspiring concentration on one aspect of the Divine. Chanting practices can also help channel emotions, develop single-pointed concentration, and energize mind and body. A spiritual chant is "a song born out of the depths of true devotion to God and continuously chanted, audibly or mentally, until response is consciously received from Him in the form of boundless joy" (Yogananda, 1963, p. xiii).

By steady and continuous investigation into the nature of the mind, the mind is transformed into that to which "I" refers; and that is in fact the Self. (Ramana Maharshi in Osbourne, 1962, p. 113)

If you must be mad, be it not for the things of the world. Be mad with the love of God. (Ramakrishna, 1965, p. 187)

He is the nearest of the near, the dearest of the dear. Love Him as a miser loves money, as an ardent man loves his sweetheart, as a drowning person loves breath. When you yearn for God with intensity, He will come to you. (Yogananda, 1968a, p. 1)

Hatha-yoga, the Yoga of the Body

The practices of hatha-yoga are designed to purify and strengthen the body for advanced meditation and higher states of consciousness. Enlightenment is a whole-body event. Hatha-yoga is designed to help manifest the infinite Self in the finite body-mind.

The body is seen as a vehicle for vital energies, or *pranas*. Hatha-yoga disciplines strengthen these energies and bring control of them, enhancing physical, mental, and spiritual functioning. According to Yoga physiology, all functions require vital energy. The more energy that is available, the healthier and more effective is the individual.

Practice of yoga *asanas,* or postures, is only part of hatha-yoga. In fact, most hatha-yoga taught in the United States is more a form of gymnastics for physical health than a complete system of Yoga. In addition to postures, classical hatha-yoga includes the practice of strict celibacy, vegetarian diet, breathing and concentration exercises, and techniques for washing and cleansing the nasal passages and the entire alimentary canal from the throat to the intestines. These disciplines form an integrated psycho-spiritual technology designed to move the practitioner toward self-realization.

Each of the classic asanas has many levels of significance. There are various physical benefits, including flexibility, strength, balance, and stimulation of the endocrine and other organ systems. Each posture also has psychological and spiritual benefits. Swami Radha's *Hatha Yoga: The Hidden Language* (1987) explains these various levels of significance for the most common classical postures.

Through hatha-yoga practice, it is possible to develop great mental and physical abilities. However, without mental and spiritual discipline, these abilities can be used to feed the ego. One authority commented that the followers of hatha-yoga he had met "had great powers, strong healthy bodies and immense vanity . . . some more worldly than average worldly men" (Purohit, 1938, p. 30). One of the authors met a yogi of this type in India. The yogi had been a subject of considerable physiological research, demonstrating extraordinary control over his brain waves, heartbeat, and other bodily functions. However, at a major conference on Yoga, the man insisted on challenging all the other yogis present to demonstrate "scientifically" their mastery of Yoga and to determine who was the "greatest yogi."

Mantra-yoga, the Yoga of Sound

A mantra is a sacred phrase or syllable, charged with psychospiritual power. According to Indian metaphysics, the universe is in constant vibration. Correct repetition of a mantra will attune the individual to that cosmic vibration.

The most important mantra in Vedic chanting was *Om,* which is said to be the most basic level of vibration in the universe. Om is still the most widely recognized and most frequently used mantra in India.

Personal Reflection

Meditation Exercises

Heartbeat

Sit with spine erect and body relaxed. Close your eyes and sink your mind into the depths of your heart. Become aware of your heart bubbling with life-giving blood, and keep your attention on your heart until you feel its rhythmic beat. With every heartbeat feel the pulse of infinite life throbbing through you. Picture that same all-pervading life flowing through all other human beings and in billions of other creatures. Open your heart, body, mind, and feelings to receive more fully that universal life.

Expanding Love

Sit erect with eyes closed. Expand your realm of love, long limited by your love for the body and identification with your body. With the love you have given to the body, love all those who love you. With the expanded love of all those who love you, love all those who are close to you. With the love for yourself and for your own, love those who are strangers. Extend your love to those who do not love you as well as those who do love you. Bathe all beings in your selfless love. See your family, friends, all people, all beings in the sea of your love.

Peace

Sit erect with eyes closed. Look inwardly between the eyebrows at a shoreless lake of peace. Observe the waves of peace expanding, spreading from the eyebrows to the forehead, from the forehead to the heart, and on to every cell in your body. As you watch, the lake of peace deepens and overflows your body, inundating the vast territory of your mind. The flood of peace flows over the boundaries of your mind and moves on in infinite directions. (Adapted from Yogananda, 1967)

It is not your passing inspirations or brilliant ideas so much as your everyday mental habits that control your life. (Yogananda, 1968b)

Traditionally, the disciple receives a mantra during an initiation ritual. Some authorities claim that the only real and effective mantras are those sounds that have been received in this way. For others, om and other sacred sounds are not truly mantras; therefore, repeating them will not be effective (Feuerstein, 1989).

Laya-yoga, the Yoga of Meditation

The goal of laya-yoga is to become totally absorbed in a state of meditation. Through intense contemplation, the mind gradually becomes dissolved in transcendent self-realization. According to one scholar, "Laya-Yoga can be understood as the higher, meditative phase of Hatha-Yoga" (Feuerstein, 1989, p. 62).

Kundalini-yoga, the Yoga of Energy

The term *kundalini* means "she who is coiled." According to Yoga physiology, a subtle energy known as kundalini lies coiled at the base of the spine. All energies of mind and body are manifestations of kundalini energy, which can be consciously controlled by an accomplished yogi.

This energy is generally latent. It begins to flow freely as a result of the disciplines of kundalini-yoga. They include meditation, visualization, breathing exercises, and the purification techniques of hatha-yoga. Once fully active, kundalini energy rises through all the levels of consciousness, leading to major physical, psychological, and spiritual changes in the individual. Psychiatrist Lee Sanella (1987) has developed a neurophysiological model that explains the kundalini process as a transformation of the electromagnetic fields of the body.

Kundalini awakening also occurs spontaneously in a surprising number of individuals. Some have engaged in meditation or other Yoga practices, while others have not (Greenwell 1990; Ramaswami, 1989). In a classic account of kundalini awakening, Gopi Krishna (1971) writes:

> Suddenly, with a roar like that of a waterfall, I felt a stream of liquid light entering my brain through the spinal cord.
>
> Entirely unprepared for such a development, I was completely taken by surprise, but regaining self-control instantaneously, I remained sitting in the same posture, keeping my mind on the point of concentration. The illumination grew brighter and brighter, the roaring louder, I experienced a rocking sensation and then felt myself slipping out of my body, entirely enveloped in a halo of light. (pp. 12–13)

The Three Energy Channels.   There are three energy channels that run along the spine through seven consciousness centers called *chakras*. The central channel is the *sushumna*, which is also the path for the ascending kundalini. To the left lies *ida* and to the right lies the *pingala* channel. They are represented by the moon and the sun. These two channels wind around the sushumna in a helical pattern. (See Figure 14.2.)

In most people, their prana, or vital energy, flows primarily in ida and pingala, as their attention is externalized. Through meditation and other inwardly focused disciplines, the yogi brings more and more energy into sushumna. This stimulates the dormant kundalini energy, which then rushes upward through the sushumna channel, leading to a state of samadhi, or illumination. Stimulating the kundalini energy with prana is like bombarding an atomic nucleus with high-energy particles in order to trigger a nuclear reaction (Feuerstein, 1989).

As kundalini reaches the higher chakras, it produces various degrees of illumination. Each chakra is associated with different physical and spiritual attributes; some are related to various senses and elements, and some to other qualities, such as form or color.

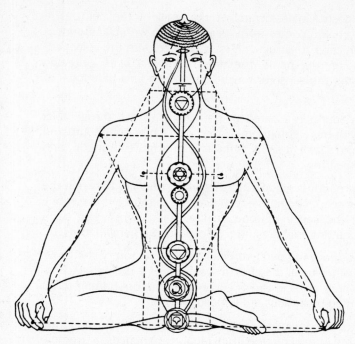

Figure 14.2   The Centers of Consciousness in the Body (From Danilou, 1955, p. ii)

The Seven Chakras[2]

1. *Muladhara* (root-support) is located at the base of the spinal column. It is associated with the element earth, inertia, the birth of sound, the lower limbs, the mantra *lam,* the elephant (symbolizing strength), and the sense of smell. It is portrayed as a deep-red, four-petaled lotus. It is the location of the dormant kundalini.

2. *Svadisthana* (own-base) is situated several inches above the first center. It is associated with the element water, the color white, the hands, the mantra *vam,* a crocodilelike animal (fertility), and the sense of taste. It is pictured as a crimson, six-petaled lotus.

3. *Manipura* (jewel-city) is located at the level of the navel. It is related to the element fire, the sun, the anus, the mantra *ram,* (fiery energy), and the sense of sight. It is depicted as a bright yellow lotus of ten petals.

---

[2]The descriptions of the *chakras* are taken from Eliade (1969) and Feuerstein (1989).

4. *Anahata* (unstruck) is located at the level of the heart. The name of this chakra comes from its association with transcendental sound, which is "unstruck." It is associated with the color red, the element air, the penis, the mantra *yam,* a black antelope (swiftness), and the sense of touch. It is drawn as a blue lotus of twelve petals.

5. *Vishuddha* (pure) is located in the region of the throat. It is associated with the element ether, the color white, the mouth and skin, the mantra *ham,* a snow white elephant (pure strength), and the sense of hearing.

6. *Ajna* (command) is situated in the brain, midway between the eyes. It is the seat of cognitive faculties, the mantra *om,* the subtle senses, and the sense of individuality. It is represented by a downward pointing triangle and a pale-gray, two-petaled lotus.

7. *Sahasrara* (thousand-petaled) is located at the top of the head. It is not actually part of the chakra system. It is a body-transcending center where consciousness is connected to the human form. It is represented by a thousand-petaled lotus.

The seventh center includes the brain. When the brain is stimulated and energized by kundalini, the individual experiences a tremendous change in consciousness, an experience of bright illumination, or *samadhi,* "the blossoming of the thousand-petaled lotus."

Raja-yoga, the Yoga of the Mind and Body

Raja-yoga, or *royal* yoga, emphasizes the development of mental control as the most effective and efficient discipline. It has been called "psychological Yoga." Some consider it a combination of all the schools of Yoga. Others see raja-yoga as but one of the major Yoga schools.

The classic Yoga discipline outlined in the *Yoga sutras* of Patanjali is designed to transform and purify the body and to direct systematically the energy flow within it. This path is systematized by Patanjali in eight limbs of Yoga: (1) abstentions, (2) observances, (3) postures, (4) vital energy control, (5) interiorization, (6) concentration, (7) meditation, and (8) illumination.

They can be thought of as successive levels of achievement, each limb building upon the one that precedes it. The eight limbs are closely interrelated branches of a single discipline; therefore, improvement in one branch tends to benefit the others.

The *abstentions* and *observances* are the moral code that serves as the foundation for Yoga practice. Abstentions include nonviolence, truthfulness, nonstealing, chastity, and nongreed. The observances are purity, austerity, contentment, study, and devotion. They are the yogic equivalent of the Ten Commandments, the principles of right action found in all religions. The abstentions and observances are not an arbitrary system of morality. They are followed for practical reasons to strengthen the effec-

Personal Reflection

Breathing Exercises

Observing the Breath

Sit on a chair or on the floor, with your back straight and your body relaxed. Close your eyes. Exhale and then inhale calmly and deeply for as long as is comfortable without straining. Observe your breath flowing in and out, as if you were on the seashore observing the ocean waves. With each intake of breath, feel that you are breathing in fresh energy and vitality with the oxygen. With each outtake of breath, feel that you are breathing out tiredness, fatigue, and negativity as you expel carbon dioxide. Feel the fresh, vitalizing energy permeating your mind and body as you continue to do the exercise.

Then sit quietly with your mind peaceful and calm.

A master bestows the divine experience of cosmic consciousness when his disciple, by meditation, has strengthened his mind to a degree where the vast vistas would not overwhelm him. Mere intellectual willingness or open-mindedness is not enough. Only adequate enlargement of consciousness by yoga practice and devotional *bhakti* can prepare one to absorb the liberating shock of omnipresence. (Yogananda, 1972, pp. 169–170)

tiveness of the rest of Yoga practice. Without a calm and disciplined daily life, the concentration and peace gained from Yoga practice is soon dissipated, like water carried in a pail riddled with holes.

It is impossible to progress without developing abstentions and observances. However, we cannot expect to master them at first. Nonviolence and truthfulness, for example, are profound disciplines.

The *Yoga sutras* teach that in the presence of one who has mastered nonviolence, no violence can occur. Obviously, the mastery of nonviolence does not occur at a primary level. But the seeds of violence in us—arrogance, anger, rage—can be removed so that there is not a violent cell in our bodies. Violence then cannot arise in our presence because the violence that swells in another person does not find a hook to hang on.

There is great depth to abstentions and observances. They are not simply representations of conventional morality; they are practical principles, which bring a harmony to life that is consistent with the consciousness that Yoga aims for.

Purification of mind and body also prepares the entire system to handle the higher "voltage," the greater power of the full flow of spiritual energy in samadhi.

Posture refers to the ability to sit relaxed and with a straight spine for long periods of time. *The essence of posture is the stilling of both body and mind.* Patanjali writes that "posture implies steadiness and comfort. It requires relaxation and meditation on the Immovable" (*Yoga sutras*, II:46–47).[3] In India, students of Yoga attempt to increase gradually the

---

[3]Quotes from the *Yoga sutras* of Patanjali are taken from Purohit (1938).

Personal Reflection ─────────────────────

───────────────────────────── Concentration

Try this simple exercise in concentration. Look at the second hand of your watch while simultaneously remaining aware of your breathing. See how long it takes before your mind begins to wander.

Very few people can focus their concentration for even a short period of time. Like any other skill, it improves with practice.

(Adapted from Tart, 1986)

time they can sit in a given posture. The student masters a posture upon being able to hold that pose for three hours without stirring.

Control of vital energy is the most unique and most fundamental aspect of Yoga. The original Sanskrit term *pranayama* is often mistranslated as "breath control." Breathing exercises can slow the metabolism and free vital energy; however, this is only an indirect means of controlling vital energy. The breath is just one manifestation of prana, which is the vital force that sustains all life.

The goal is complete mastery over vital energy. It can be attained through various Yoga practices. Accomplished yogis have demonstrated this mastery by stopping their heartbeat or their breathing at will, and in the past some yogis have buried themselves alive for days or weeks. (See, for example, Yogananda, 1972.) Modern physiological studies have confirmed the ability of practicing yogis to control their heart rates and achieve breathlessness. (For a detailed bibliography of research on Yoga and various forms of meditation, see Timmons & Kamiya, 1970; Timmons & Kanellakos, 1974.)

Interiorization refers to the shutting off of the senses. Vital energy is withdrawn from the sense organs and the yogi is no longer distracted by the ceaseless bombardment of outer stimuli. The yogi becomes more and more alive within his or her own mind.

Achievement of interiorization has been verified by Indian scientists who found that brain waves of meditating yogis are unaffected by outside stimuli (Anand, Chhina, & Singh, 1961). Patanjali defines interiorization as "the Restoration of sense to the original purity of mind, by renouncing its objects" (*Yoga sutras*, II:54).

When we sit still, the outward rush of consciousness begins to slow. We learn then to slow down our breathing and to quiet our minds. Interiorization means that consciousness stops flowing out through our senses into the world. We begin to become aware of the source within as the energy flow turns back to the spine and brain.

Concentration is "attention fixed upon an object" (*Yoga sutras*, III:1). There are two aspects of concentration: the *withdrawal* of the attention from objects of distraction and the *focusing* of attention upon one thing at a time. Concentration is a relaxed state, not a struggle or forcing of attention. Some development of interiorization must precede the practice of concentration. When all five senses are active, it is like trying to concentrate with five telephones constantly ringing. External sensations bring thoughts that in turn lead to an endless series of memories and speculations. The sound of a car leads us to think, "Oh, there is a car going by." Then we think about cars we once owned, cars we would like to buy, and so forth.

Meditation is a term that is used loosely in the West. In Yogic terminology, meditation is a highly advanced practice in which only a single thought, the object of meditation alone, remains in the consciousness of the meditator. As concentration develops and becomes deeper and more prolonged, a natural state of meditation is achieved. In meditation, the mind is fully concentrated, completely one pointed. (See Figure 14.3.)

Illumination (*samadhi*) is, in a sense, the essence of Yoga practice. It is the state that defines Yoga, and only those who have attained illumination can be regarded as true yogis. All others are students of Yoga. Samadhi has also been translated as "ecstacy" (Feuerstein, 1989). According to Patanjali, illumination is a state in which "union as union disappears, only the meaning of the object on which the attention is fixed being present" (*Yoga sutras,* III:3).

Realization of the Self occurs once the mind is totally calm and concentrated, reflecting the qualities of the Self within. As the Self is infinite, illumination is not a final or static state. Illumination includes a variety of states of consciousness. Patanjali distinguishes two major kinds of illumination, *conscious* illumination and *supraconscious* illumination. Within conscious illumination, Patanjali describes eight distinct states. The contents in the field of consciousness become more and more subtle as meditation deepens. They progress from consciousness of a thought form,

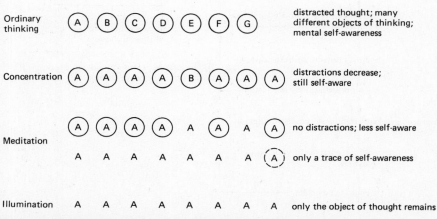

Figure 14.3 Thought Processes in Yoga Practice The circles indicate self-awareness. (Adapted from Taimni, 1961, p. 284)

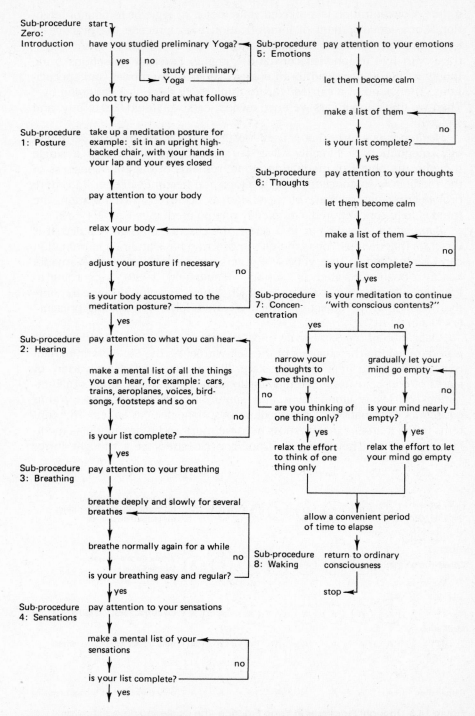

Figure 14.4 The Flow of Meditation Instructions in the "Program for Patanjali," formalized by John H. Clark of Manchester University in a flow chart of the type prepared for computers. (Adapted from Clark, 1970)

such as the image of a deity, to consciousness of abstract ideas, such as love. Eventually, there exists only consciousness of deep joy or peace, and finally, all that remains is consciousness of the Self.

Illumination without content defies description, as there is nothing in the field of consciousness to which words refer. Those who have reached this stage are said to have become totally free of the influences of karma and of their subconscious tendencies.

Dynamics

Psychological Growth

Four Stages of Life

The Yogic way of life best known in the West is that of ascetic renunciation, including celibacy, poverty, and "giving up" the world to devote oneself completely to the disciplines of Yoga. In India, there is another ideal path of spiritual growth, that of a balanced life of worldly service and responsibilities plus the practice of spiritual discipline.

The Vedas describe various types of ascetics who practiced austerities and other Yogic disciplines and were most likely the forerunners of the wandering Yogic ascetics of modern India. The ancient *rishis,* or sages, on the other hand, emphasized the importance of sacrifices and hymns and were more a part of the Indian social order. (For a fuller discussion, see Feuerstein & Miller, 1972.)

There are four stages in this idealized Indian life cycle: *student, householder, forest dweller,* and *renunciant* (Smith, 1958). According to traditional Indian conceptions, each stage should last 25 years, as the normal lifespan was said to be 100 years in the more highly developed past ages.

In many classic Indian works, it is emphasized that an individual must pass through all four stages to achieve self-realization. Each stage has its own duties, and each provides certain essential lessons and experiences.

During the first stage, the *student* traditionally serves as an apprentice, living with a teacher and the teacher's family. In addition to the acquisition of occupational skills, the traditional Indian education is devoted to character building through emotional and spiritual discipline. The goal is to become a mature individual, fully equipped to live a harmonious and productive life, rather than remain a slave to one's moods, habits, and drives.

At the completion of this stage, the apprentice returns home and, after marrying, enters the stage of the *householder*. The duties of the householder include carrying on the family business and raising a family. The householder seeks satisfaction in family pleasures, in achieving vocational success, and in serving the community as an active, responsible citizen. The householder is able to live a self-controlled life due to the character training received during the first stage. He or she has controlled the desire for sex, fame, and wealth and is able to enjoy the pleasures and duties of the householder in a moderate way.

If you run after the world the world will run from you. If you run from the world, it will run after you. (Hari Dass, 1973)

The third stage is literally that of the *forest dweller*. It refers to gradual retirement from family and occupational affairs. When a man and his wife are over 50 years of age, their children have become old enough to assume the family responsibilities. The older couple might retire to a small, secluded cottage in the forest or remain in the family house after withdrawing from all duties and affairs. They remain available to the rest of the family, consulting with and advising their children when needed.

The individual's last quarter century is to be devoted to the fourth stage, *renunciation*. Entrance into this stage is marked by a ritual closely resembling funeral rites. The individual is now officially dead to all social obligations and personal ties, and free to pursue self-realization without external demands or restrictions.

Self-realization

The details of spiritual growth and development vary with different branches of Yoga. For the karma-yogi, growth involves the development of self-discipline, willpower, and selfless service. For the bhakti-yogi, growth is most closely related to an increase in devotion to an aspect of God. For the jnana-yogi, growth is a matter of developing powers of discrimination and self-analysis. In various other schools of Yoga, growth is viewed in terms of developing the ability to meditate, to withdraw one's attention from the world and the senses, and to focus with greater and greater concentration on some aspect of Self or Spirit.

All of the diverse branches of Yoga share certain fundamental principles. The path of Yoga is basically a process of turning the consciousness away from the activities of the external world back to the source of consciousness—the Self. The karma-yogi seeks to act with self-awareness without becoming overinvolved in the action itself or in the possible results of the action. The bhakti-yogi endeavors to keep the mind devotionally focused on a person or representation that symbolizes an aspect of Spirit or Self. The jnana-yogi seeks the Self by bringing the mind back to the roots of thought and rejecting all that is not Self.

Ramakrishna, the great devotional yogi, wrote:

> The secret is that the union with God (Yoga) can never happen unless the mind is rendered absolutely calm, whatever be the "path" you follow for God realization. The mind is always under the control of the Yogi, and not the Yogi under the control of his mind. (1965, p. 186)

The wise man beholds all beings in the Self, and the Self in all beings. (*Isa Upanishad*, 6)

As we mentioned, Yoga literally means "union," union with the Self, or illumination. One classic commentary by Vyasa (in Taimni, 1961) on Patanjali's *Yoga sutras* states that *Yoga is* illumination. All the various paths and disciplines included in Yoga share this fundamental goal of illumination and self-realization.

Obstacles to Growth

Patanjali lists five major afflictions or causes of suffering: *ignorance, egoism, desire, aversion,* and *fear* (*Yoga sutras*, II:3).

The afflictions are gradually weakened by Yoga disciplines, especially austerity and self-control, scriptural study, and devotion. The yogi gradually strengthens subconscious tendencies that oppose the afflictions, weakening their influence. Afflictions have two aspects: gross and subtle. In their gross forms, the afflictions are actual thought waves (of fear, desires, and so forth). In their finer aspects, the afflictions are subconscious tendencies (*toward* fear, desire, and so forth) that remain until the attainment of illumination.

Ignorance

Ignorance is the major obstacle to growth. The basis for all suffering is ignorance, ignorance of our true identity. "Ignorance is the cause, the others are the effects. . . . Ignorance thinks of the perishable as imperishable, of the pure as impure, of the painful as pleasurable, of the non-Self as Self" *(Yoga sutras,* II:4–5).

Consciousness is projected outward from the Self with such great force that it is extremely difficult to direct the mind back to its source. Concern with the external world and with continually active senses has replaced self-awareness. Ignorance is mistaking the effect for the cause; that is, attributing the qualities of the Self to the world by treating the world as the source of experience and remaining unaware of the Self as the ultimate cause.

Egoism

Egoism results from the identification of the Self with the body and the thoughts. "Egoism is the identification of the Seer with the limitations of the eye" *(Yoga sutras,* II:6). Identification with the body leads to fear, desire, and a sense of limitation, and identification with the thoughts leads to restlessness and emotionality.

Desire and Aversion

Desire and aversion are defined by Patanjali simply and elegantly: "Desire is longing for pleasure. Aversion is recoiling from pain" *(Yoga sutras,* II:7–8). These afflictions tie the individual to the constant change and fluctuation of the external world, and they make deep calmness or peace impossible. One major aim of Yoga discipline is to overcome our tremendous sensitivity to pain, pleasure, success, failure, and other changes in the outer world. The yogi seeks freedom from the domination of the world, learning to be in control of physical, mental, and emotional reactions rather than being controlled by them.

Desire and aversion bring about *attachment* to whatever brings pleasure or avoids pain. Attachment arises from the feeling that we must have something for our own pleasure or fulfillment. Overcoming attachment does not mean, however, that Yoga is a negative, joyless self-discipline. The idea of nonattachment means to enjoy whatever one receives, ready to give it up without a sense of loss or sorrow.

Ramakrishna often explained nonattachment through the example of a maidservant who leaves her village to work for a wealthy family in a big

Satisfying the sensory desires cannot satisfy you, because you are not the senses. They are only your servants, not your Self. (Yogananda, 1968a, p. 60)

city. She may grow to love the children of the family and call them "my little boy" or "my little girl" and say "this is our house." But all the while she knows that they are not her own children, that the house is not her own, and that her real home is far away in a distant village. "I tell those who come to me, to lead a life unattached like the maid-servant. I tell them to live unattached to this world—to be in the world, but not of the world" (Ramakrishna, 1965, p. 104).

A young disciple studying nonattachment was shocked to find his guru relishing a meal of exotic fruits and nuts. His teacher seemed to be deeply attached to the food he was eating, rather than properly unconcerned with what he ate. His master explained that nonattachment does not mean dry, joyless experience of good food or other pleasures; rather, it means to enjoy fully what one has and to avoid regret when certain pleasures are no longer available. One who has mastered nonattachment enjoys the present without trying to change it by wishing for more pleasure or less pain.

Fear

The knowing Self is not born; It does not die. It has not sprung from anything; nothing has sprung from it. Birthless, eternal, everlasting, and ancient, It is not killed when the body is killed. (Katha Upanishad, I:ii, 18)

Fear is the fifth affliction. "Fear is that constant natural terror of death, that is rooted even in the minds of the learned" (*Yoga sutras,* II:9). Fear is the result of identification with the perishable body instead of the imperishable Self. In his commentary on the *Yoga sutras,* Purohit writes: "Fear of death is constant in the mind, and as desire and aversion are the result of some experience in the past, so is the fear of death the result of dying in the past" (1938, p. 48).

Structure

Body

Schools of Yoga regard the body in different ways. These attitudes range from outright rejection of the body as the source of desires and attachments to an appreciation of the body as the main vehicle for spiritual growth.

Most Yoga disciplines advocate a moderate approach to the body, neither indulgent nor unduly ascetic. The *Bhagavad-Gita* counsels that "Yoga is a harmony. Not for him who eats too much, or for him who eats too little; not for him who sleeps too little, or for him who sleeps too much" (VI:16).

Social Relationships

Learn to see God in all persons, of whatever race or creed. You will know what divine love is when you begin to feel your oneness with every human being, not before. (Yogananda, 1968b)

Traditionally, Yoga has been associated with isolation from the world, involving meditation in the depths of the forests and in caves on remote mountain peaks. However, the *Bhagavad-Gita* teaches that each individual has his or her own duty in this world; and this duty must be carried out fully whether it involves renunciation or service to others within society.

"And do thy duty, even if it be humble, rather than another's, even if it be great. To die in one's duty is life: to live in another's is death" (*Bhagavad-Gita*, III:35).

Religious devotion can also be learned through social relationships. In the West, we have tended to view God solely as a cosmic father figure, but, in India, the Divine has many faces: parent, child, friend, guru, or beloved. By practicing love and devotion in one's relations with family and friends, the individual learns to expand and spiritualize these feelings, to love others as brothers and sisters.

Those who have attained self-realization understand that their social existence and behavior before realization were largely products of socio-cultural conditioning. After acheiving realization, they are in society but not of society. They truly have free choice. Realized yogis are free to fit conventional patterns of behavior or to behave according to other, inner standards. Their newfound freedom comes from being grounded in Self, grounded in a conscious sense of the peaceful, transcendental center of Being (Chaudhuri, 1975).

Will

The earliest forms of Yoga involved severe asceticism and tremendous will. The concept of *tapas,* ascetic discipline or austerity, still remains central to much of Yoga practice today. Austerity refers to disciplining mind and body, going beyond comfortable limits, and overcoming tendencies of self-indulgence and restlessness. Fasting and holding the body motionless in asana and meditation practice are among the most popular austerities in Yoga today. Exercise of will also provides Yoga students with the direct experience of laziness, resistance to discipline, and similar personality traits. One Yoga master summarized this attitude of disciplined will: "Daily renewed sense yearnings sap your inner peace. . . . Roam in the world as a lion of self-control; don't let the frogs of sense weakness kick you around" (Sri Yukteswar in Yogananda, 1972, p. 149)!

True freedom consists in performing all actions in accordance with right judgments and choice of will, not in being compelled by habits. (Yogananda, 1968b)

Emotions

Patanjali distinguishes between painful and nonpainful waves of consciousness (*Yoga sutras,* I:5). Painful waves are thoughts and emotions that increase ignorance, confusion, or attachment. They do not always seem unpleasant (as in pride, for example). Nonpainful waves lead to greater freedom and knowledge. The greatest obstacles to peace are painful waves of consciousness such as anger, desire, and fear. These can be countered by nonpainful waves such as love, generosity, and courage. Cultivation of nonpainful waves creates positive subconscious tendencies that counteract the negative tendencies. However, the goal of Yoga is to eventually transcend even the positive emotions (Prabhavananda & Isherwood, 1953). It may seem unnatural to transcend feelings of love and joy, but even the most positive experiences tend to bind us to the world of the senses. We must go beyond that to see the Self.

The man who sees Brahman [God] abides in Brahman; his reason is steady, gone is his delusion. When pleasure comes he is not shaken, and when pain comes he trembles not. (*Bhagavad Gita,* V:20)

Another approach to the emotions is to direct their energy to spiritual growth:

> So long as these passions [of anger, lust, and so forth] are directed towards the world and its objects, they behave like enemies. But when they are directed towards God, they become the best friends of man, for then they lead him into God. The lust for the things of the world must be changed into the hankering for God, the anger that man feels in relation to his fellow man should be turned towards God for not revealing Himself to him. One should deal with all the passions in the same manner. These passions cannot be eradicated but can be educated. (Ramakrishna, 1965, p. 138)

Intellect

Do not confuse understanding with a larger vocabulary. . . . Sacred writings are beneficial in stimulating desire for inward realization, if one stanza at a time is slowly assimilated. Otherwise, continual intellectual study may result in vanity, false satisfaction, and undigested knowledge. (Yogananda, 1972)

Intellectual development in Yoga is not a matter of acquiring new information but of attaining understanding through experience. In ancient India, students studied sacred texts by carefully digesting one stanza at a time:

> Dabru Ballav [a renowned teacher] had gathered his disciples around him in the sylvan solitudes. The holy *Bhagavad-Gita* was open before them. Steadfastly they looked at one passage for half an hour, then closed their eyes. Another half hour slipped away. The master gave a brief comment. Motionless, they meditated again for an hour. Finally the guru spoke.
> "Do you now understand the stanza?"
> "Yes, sir." One in the group ventured this assertion.
> "No, not fully. Seek the spiritual vitality that has given these words the power to rejuvenate India century after century." Another hour passed in silence. (Yogananda, 1972, p. 136)

Through Yoga practice, the individual develops self-awareness and increased understanding of the world, gradually overcoming restlessness, lack of concentration, and the mental distortion of desires. Scholars who study scriptures without attempting to put them into practice remain trapped in sterile intellectualism. "They consider philosophy to be a gentle setting-up exercise. Their elevated thoughts are carefully unrelated either to the crudity of outward action or to any scourging inner discipline" (Yogananda, 1972, p. 152).

Teacher

I can cook for you, but I can't eat for you. (Hari Dass, 1973)

A guru is not a magician who transforms students without any effort on their part. Gurus are teachers of subtle truths and practices; as in any learning situation, students' achievements are in proportion to their effort, ability, and receptivity.

The conditions for the taught are purity, a real thirst after knowledge, and perseverance. . . . Purity in thought, speech, and act is absolutely necessary for anyone to be religious. As to the thirst after knowledge, it is an old law that we all get whatever we want. None of us can get anything other than what we fix our hearts on. . . . The success may sometimes come immediately, but we must be ready to wait patiently even for what may look like an infinite length of time. The student who sets out with such a spirit of perseverance will surely find success in realization at last. (Vivekananda, 1978a, pp. 28–29)

Evaluation

The essence of Yoga is reformation of the psyche through a system of concrete, practical exercises designed to transform our consciousness. Yoga treats in depth the relationship of consciousness to vital energy, or prana, which links the physical world and consciousness. Yoga exercises work with subtle energy flow in a uniquely direct way; no other system works as directly and effectively on consciousness.

As the energy and consciousness of the Self flow outward, they become distorted by a series of lenses, our subconscious tendencies, habits, personality, and so on. Subconscious tendencies bias our thoughts, which then affect our actions. Action patterns become habits and habits in turn reinforce the use of distorting lenses. Then the Self, which is pure joy, pure love and bliss, cannot be made manifest within our consciousness or in the world.

The aim of Yoga practice is to reduce the distortion and direct the flow of consciousness to its source, the Self. To reduce distortion, we can cleanse our bodies and our personality tendencies. In hatha-yoga, this cleansing is accomplished primarily through physical disciplines and concentration exercises. In karma-yoga, right action gradually purifies. Bhakti-yoga works through devotion; by embracing the highest ideals psyches are refined. The self-analysis of jnana-yoga can transform personality, much like the process of psychotherapy.

Yoga practice slows the flow of consciousness from the Self to the environment and begins drawing this consciousness back inward. This process is most clearly found in raja- and kundalini-yoga. By turning our consciousness back to its source, the Self, we begin to get in touch with the Self, with joy, bliss, and purity. This in itself cleanses personality.

Most schools of Yoga focus on inner experience at the expense of outward interests, and this may not appeal to everyone. Worldly sensory experiences are seen as distractions from the Self within. This attitude, if improperly exercised, can lead to a retreat from life's problems and a certain kind of passivity. Also, the doctrine of karma, depending on how one approaches it, can mean the passive acceptance of one's lot in life. Although Yoga does include the discipline of action, most branches tend to emphasize inner peace at the expense of outward activity.

Yoga, as practiced in the West, often seems more a system for health and mental concentration than a complete spiritual discipline. Without mental and emotional discipline, or without practice of the moral precepts of Yoga, the practice of postures, breathing, or concentration techniques can result in unbalanced development. These practices alone may not affect the Yoga student's personality and may even reinforce pride and egotism.

In the case of psychotherapy, people generally enter therapy because they are functioning inadequately or are suffering mentally or physically. Yoga traditionally begins with normal, healthy individuals. The aim of Yoga is not the restoration of normality or the improvement of worldly function. The goal is the complete transformation of the individual (Feuerstein, 1972).

The major emphasis in Yoga lies in the practical effectiveness of the techniques. Experience, rather than theoretical knowledge, is at the heart of Yoga. The various disciplines can suit virtually any individual, whether active, intellectual, or emotional in disposition. No other practice contains so many different methods for developing self-discipline, gaining a sense of inner peace, and attaining self-realization.

Success is immediate where effort is intense. (Yoga sutras, I:21)

The Theory Firsthand: Excerpts from *Ramakrishna* and *Ramana Maharshi*

The following passage describes the first experience of illumination of Ramakrishna, the great devotional saint of modern India.

The ideal of man is to see God in everything. But if you cannot see Him in everything, see Him in one thing, in that thing which you like best, and then see Him in another. (Vivekananda, 1976, p. 142)

> Sri Ramakrishna began to spend the whole night in meditation, returning to his room only in the morning with eyes swollen as though from much weeping. While meditating he would lay aside his cloth and his brahminical thread. Explaining this strange conduct, he once said to Hriday: "Don't you know that when one thinks of God one should be freed from all ties? From our very birth we have the eight fetters of hatred, shame, lineage, pride of good conduct, fear, secretiveness, caste, and grief. The sacred thread reminds me that I am a brāhmin and therefore superior to all. When calling on the Mother one has to set aside all such ideas." Hriday thought his uncle was becoming insane.
>
> As his love for God deepened, he began either to forget or to drop the formalities of worship. Sitting before the image, he would spend hours singing the devotional songs of great devotees of the Mother, like Kamalākrānta and Rāmprasād. Those rhapsodical songs, describing the direct vision of God, only intensified Sri Ramakrishna's longing. He felt the pangs of a child separated from its mother. Sometimes, in agony, he would rub his face against the ground and weep so bitterly that people, thinking he had lost his earthly mother, would sympathize with him in his grief. Sometimes, in moments of skepticism, he would cry: "Art Thou true, Mother, or is it all fiction—mere poetry without

any reality? If Thou dost exist, why do I not see Thee? Is religion a mere fantasy and art Thou only a figment of man's imagination?" Sometimes he would sit on the prayer carpet for two hours like an inert object. He began to behave in an abnormal manner, most of the time unconscious of the world. He almost gave up food; and sleep left him altogether.

But he did not have to wait very long. He has thus described his first vision of the Mother: "I felt as if my heart were being squeezed like a wet towel. I was overpowered with a great restlessness and a fear that it might not be my lot to realize Her in this life. I could not bear the separation from Her any longer. Life seemed to be not worth living. Suddenly my glance fell on the sword that was kept in the Mother's temple. I determined to put an end to my life. When I jumped up like a madman and seized it, suddenly the blessed Mother revealed Herself. The buildings with their different parts, the temple, and everything else vanished from my sight, leaving no trace whatsoever, and in their stead I saw a limitless, infinite, effulgent Ocean of Consciousness. As far as the eye could see, the shining billows were madly rushing at me from all sides with a terrific noise, to swallow me up! I was panting for breath. I was caught in the rush and collapsed, unconscious. What was happening in the outside world I did not know; but within me there was a steady flow of undiluted bliss, altogether new, and I felt the presence of the Divine Mother." On his lips when he regained consciousness of the world was the word "Mother." (Nikhilananda, 1948, pp. 9–10)

The next passage is a description of the spiritual illumination of Ramana Maharshi, India's great twentieth-century sage.

It was about six weeks before I left Madura for good that the great change in my life took place. It was quite sudden. I was sitting alone in a room on the first floor of my uncle's house. I seldom had any sickness, and on that day there was nothing wrong with my health, but a sudden violent fear of death overtook me. There was nothing in my state of health to account for it, and I did not try to account for it or to find out whether there was any reason for the fear. I just felt "I am going to die" and began thinking what to do about it. It did not occur to me to consult a doctor or my elders or friends; I felt that I had to solve the problem myself, there and then. The shock of the fear of death drove my mind inwards and I said to myself mentally, without actually framing the words: "Now death has come; what does it mean? What is it that is dying? This body dies." And I at once dramatized the occurrence of death. I lay with my limbs stretched out stiff as though *rigor mortis* had set in and imitated a corpse so as to give greater reality to the enquiry. I held my breath and kept my lips tightly closed so that no sound could escape, so that neither the word "I" nor any other word could be uttered. "Well then," I said to myself, "this body is dead. It will be carried stiff to the burning ground and there

What do you seek here, since this world is not your resting place? Your true home is in Heaven. (Thomas à Kempis in Feuerstein, 1972, p. 9)

burnt and reduced to ashes. But with the death of this body am I dead? Is the body I? It is silent and inert but I feel the full force of my personality and even the voice of the 'I' within me, apart from it. So I am Spirit transcending the body. The body dies but the Spirit that transcends it cannot be touched by death. That means I am the deathless Spirit." All this was not dull thought; it flashed through me vividly as living truth which I perceived directly, almost without thought-process. "I" was something very real, the only real thing about my present state, and all the conscious activity connected with my body was centered on that "I." From that moment onwards the "I" or Self focused attention on itself by a powerful fascination. Fear of death had vanished once and for all. Absorption in the Self continued unbroken from that time on. (Osbourne, 1970, pp. 18–19)

Annotated Bibliography

Eliade, M. (1969). *Yoga: Immortality and freedom*. Princeton, NJ: Princeton University Press. Scholarly treatment of the many diverse Yoga traditions.

Mascaro, J. (1962). *The Bhagavad Gita*. Baltimore: Penguin Books. A good, easily obtainable translation.

Prabhavananda, Swami, & Isherwood, C. (Trans.). (1951). *The Song of God: Bhagavad Gita*. New York: New American Library (Mentor Books). Readable and easily obtainable.

———. (1953). *How to know God: The Yoga aphorisms of Patanjali*. New York: New American Library. Very good, easily obtainable, but a somewhat Westernized translation of the *Yoga sutras*.

Purohit, Swami. (1938). *Aphorisms of Yoga by Bhagwan Shree Patanjali*. London: Faber. Best translation and commentary in English.

Radha, S. (1978). *Kundalini: Yoga for the West*. Spokane, WA: Timeless Books. By far, the most detailed and psychologically sophisticated treatment of kundalini-yoga, the chakras, and the images and symbols of Yoga.

Ram Dass, Baba. (1970). *Be here now*. San Cristobal, NM: Lama Foundation. A modern, "hip" interpretation of Yoga, including sections on meditation techniques and other disciplines, the transformation of Richard Alpert into Baba Ram Dass, a spiritual reading list, and an inspiring interpretation of Indian philosophy and Yoga through integrated text and pictures.

Taimni, I. K. (1961). *The science of Yoga*. Wheaton, IL: Quest. Solid and scholarly translation of the *Yoga sutras*. Extensive commentary.

Vishnudevananda (1960). *The complete illustrated book of Yoga*. New York: Pocket Books. Very good, practical hatha-yoga paperback.

Yogananda, Paramahansa. (1972). *The autobiography of a yogi*. Los Angeles: Self-Realization Fellowship. A classic account of yogis and Yoga training in India. Excellent introduction to the Indian tradition.

References

Anand, B., Chhina, G., & Singh, B. (1961). Some aspects of electroen-cephalographic studies in yogis. *Electroencephalography and Clinical Neurology, 13,* 452–456.

Chaudhuri, H. (1975). Yoga psychology. In C. Tart (Ed.), *Transpersonal psychologies*. New York: Harper & Row.

Clark, J. H. (1970, July 23). Program for Patanjali. *New Society*.

Danielou, A. (1955). *Yoga: The method of re-integration*. New Hyde Park, NY: University Books.

Eliade, M. (1969). *Yoga: Immortality and freedom*. Princeton, NJ: Princeton University Press.

Feuerstein, G. (1989). *Yoga: The technology of ecstacy*. Los Angeles: Tarcher.

Feuerstein, G., & Miller, J. (1972). *Yoga and beyond*. New York: Schocken Books.

Greenwell, B. (1990). *Energies of transformation: A guide to the kundalini process*. Cupertino, CA: Shakti River Press.

Hari Dass (1973). *The yellow book*. San Cristobal, NM: Lama Foundation.

Krishna, G. (1971). *Kundalini: The evolutionary energy in man*. London: Robinson & Watkins.

Majumdar, S. (1964). *Introduction to Yoga principles and practices*. New Hyde Park, NY: University Books.

Mascaro, J. (Trans.). (1962). *The Bhagavad Gita*. Baltimore: Penguin Books.

Nikhilananda, Swami (1948). *Ramakrishna: Prophet of new India*. New York: Harper & Row.

———. (1964). *The Upanishads*. New York: Harper & Row.

Osbourne, A. (1962). *The teachings of Ramana Maharshi*. London: Rider.

———. (1970). *Ramana Maharshi and the path of self-knowledge*. New York: Weiser.

———. (Ed.). (1969). *The collected works of Ramana Maharshi*. London: Rider.

Prabhavananda, Swami, & Isherwood, C. (Trans.). (1951). *The Song of God: Bhagavad Gita.* New York: New American Library (Mentor Books).

———. (1953). *How to know God: The Yoga aphorisms of Patanjali.* New York: New American Library.

Purohit, Swami (Trans.). (1938). *Aphorisms of Yoga* by Bhagwan Shree Patanjali. London: Faber.

Purohit, Swami, & Yeats, W. B. (Trans.). (1970). *The ten principal Upanishads.* London: Faber.

———. (Trans.). (1965). *The Geeta: The gospel of Lord Shri Krishna.* London: Faber.

Radha, Swami (1978). *Kundalini: Yoga for the West.* Spokane, WA: Timeless Books.

———. (1987). *Hatha Yoga: The hidden language.* Porthill, ID: Timeless Books.

Ramakrishna (1965). *Sayings of Sri Ramakrishna.* Madras, India: Sri Ramakrishna Math.

Ramaswami, S. (1989). Yoga and healing. In A. Sheikh & K. Sheikh, *Eastern and Western approaches to healing.* New York: Wiley.

Sanella, L. (1987). *The kundalini experience: Psychosis or transcendence?* Lower Lake, CA: Integral Publishing.

Smith, H. (1987). *The religions of man.* New York: Harper & Row.

Taimni, I. K. (1961). *The science of Yoga.* Wheaton, IL: Quest.

Tart, C. (1986). *Waking up: Overcoming obstacles to human potential.* Boston: New Science Library.

Timmons, B., & Kamiya, J. (1970). The psychology and physiology of meditation and related phenomena: A bibliography. *Journal of Transpersonal Psychology, 2,* 41–59.

Timmons, B., & Kanellakos, D. (1974). The psychology and physiology of meditation and related phenomena: Bibliography II. *Journal of Transpersonal Psychology, 4,* 32–38.

Vishnudevananda, Swami (1960). *The complete illustrated book of Yoga.* New York: Pocket Books.

Vivekananda, Swami (1976). *Jnana-yoga.* Calcutta: Advaita Ashrama.

———. (1978a). *Bhakti-yoga.* Calcutta: Advaita Ashrama.

———. (1978b). *Karma-yoga.* Calcutta: Advaita Ashrama.

Wood, E. (1956). *Yoga dictionary.* New York: Philosophical Library.

Yogananda, Paramahansa (1963). *Cosmic chants.* Los Angeles: Self-Realization Fellowship.

———. (1967). *Metaphysical meditations.* Los Angeles: Self-Realization Fellowship.

———. (1968a). *Sayings of Yogananda.* Los Angeles: Self-Realization Fellowship.

———. (1968b). *Spiritual diary.* Los Angeles: Self-Realization Fellowship.

———. (1972). *The autobiography of a yogi.* Los Angeles: Self-Realization Fellowship.

Chapter Fifteen

Zen and the Buddhist Tradition

Remember thou must go alone; The Buddhas do but point the way. (Shakyamuni Buddha)

Zen Buddhism is primarily concerned with leading others to a direct, personal understanding of Truth. The Buddha's teachings emphasize experience over theology or abstract philosophy. Zen is a school of Buddhism, a particular branch that emphasizes meditation and spiritual practice. In a broader sense, Zen provides an approach to spirituality applicable to all religions and limited to none. As the great Zen philosopher D. T. Suzuki has written, "The basic idea of Zen is to come in touch with the inner workings of our being, and to do this in the most direct way possible, without resorting to anything external or super-added" (1964, p. 44). When asked how one should evaluate religious teachings and spiritual teachers, the Buddha replied:

> You who follow me, consider this carefully. Keep an eye open, seekers of truth. Weigh rumor, custom, and hearsay. Don't let anyone's excellence in the Scriptures mislead you. Logic and argument, supply of elaborate reasons, approval of considered opinion, plausibility of ideas, respect for the leader who guides you—beware of too much trust in them. Only when you *know*, and are sure that you know—this is not good, this is erroneous, this is censured by the intelligent, this will lead to loss and grief—only when you know, should you reject or accept it. (*The Dhammapada*, Lal, 1967, p. 17)

History

Buddhism is based on the teachings of Siddhartha Gautama, the Buddha. The term *Buddha* is a title, not a proper name. It means "one who knows," or one who achieves a certain level of understanding, one who has attained full humanness. There were many other Buddhas before Gautama, and there are still Buddhas to come, according to Buddhist doctrine. The Buddha never claimed to be more than a man whose realization, attainments, and achievements were the result of his purely human capacities. He developed himself into a completely mature human being, which is such a rare achievement that we tend to look on it as somehow superhuman or divinely inspired. The central attitude in Buddhism is that every individual possesses this Buddha nature, the capacity for developing into a complete human being and becoming a Buddha.

The life of Gautama has been recorded as Buddhist religious history; there is little reliable evidence of specific dates and activities. However, his official life story can be read as an illuminating parable of Buddhist ideals and principles.

Gautama was born a prince in a tiny North Indian kingdom in the sixth century B.C. He was married at age 16 to a beautiful princess and lived in his palace surrounded by comfort and luxury. When Gautama had occasion to slip out of his palatial prison, he was suddenly confronted with the reality of life and the suffering of humankind. First, Gautama encountered an old man, worn down by a life of toil and hardship. On his second trip, he saw a man who was suffering from a serious illness. On his third trip,

Gautama watched a corpse being carried in a sorrowful funeral procession. Finally, Gautama met a religious ascetic engaged in the traditional Indian pursuit of spiritual discipline. Gautama realized that sickness, old age, and death are unavoidable endings to the happiest and most prosperous life. The inevitability of human suffering became the fundamental problem at the heart of Gautama's spiritual search. He saw that his present way of life could not possibly provide an answer to the problem of suffering and he decided to leave his family and palace to seek a solution through religious discipline.

At the age of 29, soon after the birth of his only son, Gautama left his kingdom and studied for six years with two different teachers, engaging in severe self-discipline. Eventually, he sat beneath a Bodhi tree and resolved that he would not eat or leave his seat until he reached enlightenment, even if he died in the attempt. Finally, weakened by his long fast, Gautama realized that mortification of the body would never bring about enlightenment, and he accepted some food to give him strength to go on with his spiritual efforts. From Gautama's experience came the Buddhist conception of the Middle Way: seeking a healthy and useful discipline without either extreme of complete indulgence of the senses or self-torture. After deep and prolonged meditation, Gautama experienced a profound inner transformation that altered his entire perspective on life. His approach to the questions of sickness, old age, and death changed because he changed. He became the Buddha.

The Buddha decided to spread his understanding to others, and he taught for 44 years, walking from town to town in India with an ever-growing band of followers. He died in 483 B.C. at the age of 80.

For many centuries, Buddhism flourished in India and spread gradually throughout Asia. Between A.D. 1000 and 1200, Buddhism died out in India, due to a combination of the growing weakness of Indian Buddhism, the revival of Hinduism, and Islamic persecution.

There are two major schools within Buddhism today. The Theravada or Hinayana tradition is found primarily in Southeast Asia, in Sri Lanka, Burma, and Thailand. The Mahayana school has flourished mainly in Tibet, China, Korea, and Japan. The Mahayana school began as a liberal movement within Hinayana Buddhism. This school is less strict in interpreting the traditional monastic disciplinary rules, less exclusive with regard to householders, and more willing to adopt later additions to the Buddhist scriptures. The Mahayanists have also tended to stress the importance of compassion as opposed to a Hinayana emphasis on self-discipline. Originally, these two great traditions were seen as alternative personal interpretations within Buddhism. Adherents of both Mahayana and Hinayana approaches lived together in the same monasteries under the same basic monastic rules.

Zen is one of the major sects of the Mahayana tradition. Zen is said to have been founded in China in the sixth century A.D. by Bodhidharma, an Indian Buddhist monk, who stressed the importance of contemplation and personal discipline over religious ritual. Under the influence of a

Planners make canals, archers shoot arrows, craftsmen fashion woodwork, the wise man molds himself. (*The Dhammapada*, Lal, 1967)

Man's inability to control and discipline his mind is responsible for all his problems. (The Dalai Lama)

series of great Chinese masters, Zen gradually developed as an independent school of Buddhism, with its own monasteries, monastic rules, and organization. By A.D. 1000, Zen had become the second most popular school of Buddhism in China.

In the thirteenth century, two Japanese monks, Eisai and Dogen, traveled to China to study Buddhism. When they returned to Japan, these monks founded temples, taught prominent disciples, and founded the two great sects of Japanese Zen Buddhism, Soto and Rinzai. Master Eisai (1141–1215), who introduced Rinzai Zen in Japan, stressed the achievement of enlightenment through the use of Zen "riddles," or *koan*. Master Dogen (1200–1253), the founder of Japanese Soto Zen, stressed two major points: There is no gap between daily practice and enlightenment, and our right (correct) daily behavior is Buddhism itself.

Just as most of the chapters in this text focus on the work of a particular theorist, this chapter focuses primarily on a particular school of Buddhism, Zen Buddhism, which is only one of a great number of Buddhist traditions and schools. The chapter summarizes fundamental Buddhist concepts and psychology from a Soto Zen perspective.

Basically, there is only one Buddhism. Different teachers and different schools interpret the basic truths of Buddhism to fit their own cultures and societies. Under Recent Developments, we also outline the major contributions of two other schools of Buddhism that are prominent in America, Theravadan and Tibetan Buddhism.

Major Concepts

The Three Characteristics of Existence

There are three major characteristics of existence according to Buddhist thought: *impermanence, selflessness,* and *dissatisfaction.*

Impermanence

Everything is constantly changing; nothing is permanent. Certainly nothing physical lasts forever. Trees, buildings, the sun, moon, stars—all have a finite existence; furthermore, all are in flux at any given moment.

Impermanence also applies to thoughts and ideas. The concept of impermanence implies that there can be no such thing as a final authority or permanent truth. There is only a level of understanding suitable for a certain time and place. Because conditions change, what seems to be true at one time inevitably becomes false or inappropriate at others. Therefore, Buddhism cannot be said to have a fixed doctrine. To truly accept the concept of impermanence is to realize that nothing ever fully becomes Buddha, that even Buddha or truth is subject to change and can still progress.

The Buddhists point out that the primary feature of the universe is change. However, human beings have a strong tendency to conceive of the world as static, to see *things* instead of fluid and constantly changing processes. All the separations we create in our minds are actually connected, interdependent.

Interdependence of All Things.   Perhaps the best illustration of the Buddhist concept of interdependence comes from Thich Nhat Hanh, a Vietnamese Zen master.

> If you are a poet, you will see clearly that there is a cloud floating in this sheet of paper. Without a cloud, there will be no rain; without rain, the trees cannot grow; and without trees, we cannot make paper. The cloud is essential for the paper to exist. . . .
>
> If we look into this sheet of paper even more deeply, we can see the sunshine in it. If the sunshine is not there, the forest cannot grow. In fact, nothing can grow. . . . And if we continue to look, we can see the logger who cut the tree and brought it to the mill to be transformed into paper. And we see the wheat. We know that the logger cannot exist without his daily bread, and therefore the wheat that became his bread is also in this sheet of paper. And the logger's father and mother are in it too. . . .
>
> So we can say that everything is in here with this sheet of paper. . . . Everything co-exists with this sheet of paper. . . . You cannot just *be* by yourself alone. . . . This sheet of paper is, because everything else is. (Hanh, 1988, pp. 3–4)

Selflessness

Other religions have taught that the Self, or soul, is unchanging and imperishable. The Buddhist notion of impermanence, however, is applied to our innermost self as well.

The concept of selflessness holds that there is no immortal soul or eternal Self that exists in each individual. The individual is seen as a collection of attributes, all of which are impermanent and constantly changing. According to the Buddha, the person is made up of five basic factors—body, perception, sensation, consciousness, and mental activities (i.e., ideas, intentions, and so on). The term *I* is merely a useful linguistic device to refer to an ever-changing collection of attributes that comprise the individual.

In other words, our bodies and our personalities are composed of mortal, constantly changing components. The individual is not something other than these component parts. When the parts perish, so does the individual. No part of ourselves goes on forever.

Dissatisfaction

Dissatisfaction, or suffering, is the third characteristic of existence. It embraces birth, death, decay, sorrow, pain, grief, despair, and existence itself. Suffering comes not from the world around us but from ourselves.

Time flies quicker than an arrow and life passes with greater transience than dew. However skillful you may be, how can you ever recall a single day of the past? (Dogen in Kennett, 1976)

It lies in the limited ego—the relative consciousness—of each individual. Buddhist teachings are designed to help us transcend our sense of self. It is only through self-transformation that we can experience a sense of real satisfaction with ourselves and with the world.

To interpret the principle of dissatisfaction to mean only that suffering is an inescapable part of existence is incorrect. The Buddha taught that the source of suffering lies within the individual and optimistically concluded that something can be done about this basic dissatisfaction.

The Four Noble Truths

Gautama searched for a way to overcome the suffering and limitation he saw as an inevitable part of human life. "In what was probably the most important psychological discovery of all time, the Buddha realized the universality of suffering, its cause, its cure, and the way to attain such liberation" (Mosig, 1990, p. 53). He formulated this diagnosis and prescription as the Four Noble Truths.

The first Truth is the existence of dissatisfaction. Given the inner state of the average individual, dissatisfaction, or suffering, is inescapable.

We are what we think, having become what we thought. (The Dhammapada, Lal, 1967)

The second Truth is that dissatisfaction is the result of craving or desire. Most people are caught up in attachment for the positive and pleasurable and aversion for the negative and painful. Craving creates an unstable frame of mind in which the present is never satisfactory. If our desires are unsatisfied, we are driven by a need to change the present. If satisfied, we come to fear change, which brings about a renewal of frustration and dissatisfaction. Because all things pass, the enjoyment of fulfilled desires is always tempered by the realization that our enjoyment is only temporary. The stronger the craving, the more intense is our dissatisfaction because we know that fulfillment will not last.

Like the spider woven in its own web is the man gripped by his craving. (The Dhammapada, Lal, 1967)

The third Truth is that the elimination of craving brings the extinction of suffering. According to Buddhist doctrine, it is possible to learn to accept the world as it is without feeling dissatisfaction due to its limitations. Eliminating craving does not mean extinguishing all desires. When you believe that your happiness depends on fulfilling a desire, or you become controlled by your desires, then they become unhealthy cravings. The normal desire for food and sleep is necessary, however, because we must eat and sleep to stay alive. Desires also help boost our awareness. If all wants are immediately cared for, it is easy to slip into a passive, unthinking state of complacency. Acceptance refers to an even-minded attitude of enjoying fulfilled desires without becoming seriously disturbed over the inevitable periods of nonfulfillment.

The fourth Truth is that there is a way to eliminate craving and dissatisfaction; this is the Noble Eightfold Path, or the Middle Way. Most people seek the highest possible degree of sense gratification. Others, who realize the limitations of this approach, tend toward the other extreme of self-mortification. The Buddhist ideal is moderation.

Avoid these two extremes, monks. Which two? On the one hand, low, vulgar, ignoble, and useless indulgence in passion and luxury; on the other, painful, ignoble, and useless practice of self-torture and mortification. Take the Middle Path advised by the Buddha, for it leads to insight and peace, wisdom and enlightenment. (*The Dhammapada*, Lal, 1967, p. 22)

The Eightfold Path consists of right speech, right action, right livelihood, right effort, right mindfulness, right concentration, right thought, and right understanding. The basic principle is that certain ways of thinking, acting, and so forth, tend to harm others and to injure or limit oneself.

There are three essentials in Buddhist training and discipline: ethical conduct, mental discipline, and wisdom. The divisions of the Eightfold Path fall under these three categories.

Ethical conduct is built on the fundamental Buddhist teachings of universal love and compassion for all living beings. Under ethical conduct are included right speech, right action, and right livelihood.

Right speech means abstention from (1) telling lies, (2) gossip, slander, or any talk that might bring about disunity and disharmony, (3) harsh, rude, or abusive language, and (4) useless and foolish chatter and gossip. We should instead speak the truth and use words that are friendly, pleasant, gentle, and useful. We should not speak carelessly, but consider what is appropriate for the right time and place. If we cannot say something useful, the ideal is to keep "noble silence."

Right action means moral, honorable, and peaceful conduct. This means to abstain from (1) destroying life, (2) stealing, (3) dishonest actions, and (4) illegitimate sexual intercourse. Also we should help others lead a peaceful and honorable life.

Right livelihood means to abstain from making one's living through any means that brings harm to anyone or anything, such as dealing in weapons, intoxicating drinks, poisons, killing animals, or cheating. The ideal is to make a living that is honorable, blameless, and harms no one.

Under the category of mental discipline are included right effort, right mindfulness, and right concentration.

Right effort refers to the active will, used to (1) prevent unwholesome states of mind from arising, (2) get rid of such states if they do arise, (3) facilitate and produce good and wholesome states of mind, and (4) develop and bring to perfection those good, wholesome states already present.

Right mindfulness means to be aware, mindful, and attentive to (1) the activities of the body, (2) sensations or feelings, (3) the activities of the mind, and (4) specific ideas, thoughts, and conceptions. Various schools of meditation—including concentration on breathing, on sensations, and on mental activities—have been developed in different schools of Buddhism in order to develop right mindfulness.

Do not sell the wine of delusion. But there is nothing to be deluded about. If we realize this there is enlightenment itself. (*Diamond Sutra* in Kennett, 1976)

Buddhist psychology distinguishes between generalized activities of the mind and its specific contents. Concerning the activities of the mind, one is to become aware of whether one's mind is given to hatred, delusion, lust, distraction, or any other such negative impulses. In focusing on specific ideas and concepts, one learns how they appear and disappear, how they were developed, how they were suppressed, and so on.

Right concentration leads to four stages of meditation. In the first stage, we discard passionate desires and unwholesome thoughts, such as ill will, worry, restlessness. Feelings of joy and happiness develop. In the second stage, all intellectual activities are dropped. Tranquility and "one-pointedness of mind" are developed, and feelings of joy and happiness developed in the first stage are retained. In the third stage, the feelings of joy, which are active sensations, also disappear. Mindful equanimity and happiness remain. In the fourth stage, all sensations disappear, including happiness. Only pure equanimity and awareness remain.

Wisdom is made up of right thought and right understanding. Right thought includes selfless detachment, love, and nonviolence. Right understanding is the understanding of things as they are, which is acheived by working through the Four Noble Truths. In Buddhist psychology, there are two levels of understanding. The first is knowledge, accumulated memory, and an intellectual grasping of the subject. Deep understanding is seeing a thing in its natural form, undistorted by name and label. This is possible only when the mind is freed from impurities and is fully developed through meditation.

> If we think we hear, we no longer listen.
> If we think we see, we no longer look.
> If we think we know, we no longer search.
>
> (Buddhist saying)

Zen Meditation

Zen comes from the Sanskrit word dyhāna, meaning "meditation" (which evolved to *ch'an* in Chinese and *zen* in Japanese). Meditation is a central discipline in Zen. There are two major practices in Zen meditation, or *zazen* (literally "seated zen"). One can focus on a *koan,* or else simply sit with concentrated awareness and no external focus.

A koan is traditionally contained in a dialogue between a Zen student and Zen master. Some koans are based on questions that were asked by serious Zen students in ancient China. Others are taken from questions posed by a Zen master to stimulate or awaken the student's understanding. The koans vividly and immediately illustrate some aspect of the Zen master's deep understanding of Buddhism. They tend to be paradoxical and beyond logic, forcing the questioner to go beyond the inherent limitations of the categories with which he or she has viewed experience up to that point. Meditation on classical koans is still practiced by present-day Zen students of the Rinzai school of Zen.

One of the most famous koans is known as *Mu:*

A monk in all seriousness asked Joshu: "Has a dog Buddha-nature or not?" Joshu retorted, "Mu!"

The monk was deeply concerned with the Buddhist teaching that all sentient beings have Buddha-nature. (In China at that time, the dog was considered unclean, the lowest of the animals, and the monk was ques-

> For a Zen monk the primary prerequisite for improvement is the practice of concentrated *zazen*. Without arguing about who is clever and who inept, who is wise and who foolish, just do *zazen*. You will then naturally improve. (Dogen in Kennett, 1976)

tioning seriously if such a low creature could be said to have the Buddha-nature.)

Joshu's answer might be translated as "nothing!" or read merely as an exclamation. It is not a simple yes-or-no answer. Joshu does not fall into the trap of accepting his questioner's assumption that there is a particular thing called Buddha-nature that can be possessed. Mu is a vigorous denial of dualistic thinking, a window through which the student can first glimpse Joshu's nondualistic perspective. Another Zen teacher comments, "It is clear, then, that Mu has nothing to do with the existence or non-existence of Buddha-nature but is itself Buddha-nature" (Kapleau, 1965, p. 76).

In meditating on this koan, the individual should not indulge in intellectual speculation on the question and answer or the implications of either. The aim of the koan is to lead Zen students to see their own ignorance, to entice them to go beyond abstract conceptualizing, and to search for truth within themselves. One Zen master gave the following instructions to students working on this koan:

> Let all of you become one mass of doubt and questioning. Concentrate on and penetrate fully into Mu. To penetrate into Mu means to achieve absolute unity with it. How can you achieve this unity? By holding to Mu tenaciously day and night! . . . Focus your mind on it constantly. "Do not construe Mu as nothingness and do not conceive it in terms of existence or nonexistence." You must not, in other words, think of Mu as a problem involving the existence or nonexistence of Buddha-nature. Then what do you do? You stop speculating and concentrate wholly on Mu—just Mu! (Kapleau, 1965, p. 79)

In the Soto school of Zen, students are taught that the most important aspect of Zen training concerns their daily lives, and that they must learn to deal with their own personal koan, the riddle of daily life, as it manifests itself for each individual.

A personal koan has no final solution. The problem can be handled only by changing oneself, by altering one's point of view, which results from changing one's personality. The problem doesn't change, but one's attitude toward it and the way one copes with it does. The individual never fully solves a koan, but learns to deal with the problem at a higher level. For instance, Gautama began his religious quest in the hope of solving the koan of sickness, old age, and death. Even after he became the Buddha, these problems remained unchanged. The Buddha did not become immortal or ageless; however, his new level of understanding transcended his previous personal concern with these problems.

For some people, their personal koan involves a sense of inadequacy, a feeling of not being enough, not knowing enough, not being able to achieve enough. For others, their central koan involves a sense of complacency, a feeling that no further advancement or self-examination, leading to personal change, is needed.

All you have to do is cease from erudition, withdraw within and reflect upon yourself. Should you be able to cast off body and mind naturally, the Buddha Mind will immediately manifest itself. (Evening Service in Kennett, 1976)

As a smith removes flaws in silver, a wise man removes flaws in himself, slowly, one by one, carefully. (The Dhammapada, Lal, 1967)

The Soto approach to meditation can be thought of as "just sitting," without a koan or other exercise to occupy the mind. The meditator strives to maintain a state of concentrated awareness, in which he or she is neither tense nor relaxed but totally alert. The attitude is like that of someone seated by the roadside watching traffic. The meditator observes the thoughts going by, without getting caught up in them and forgetting to remain an aware observer.

Zazen is an expression of faith, of trust in the vastness of the universe and of our own inner nature. "Those who do not have faith will not accept zazen, however much they are taught. If you don't trust this silence and the vastness of existence, if you do not soak yourself in this realm, how can you trust yourself" (Katagiri, 1988, p. 43)?

Visions and similar experiences should not result if Zen meditation is properly performed. Generally, these experiences are the result of tensions that accumulate from sitting improperly in meditation or from daydreamlike states that arise at a certain point in one's meditation. These *makyo*, or illusions, are considered valueless in one's spiritual growth. They are at best distractions and at worst a source of pride, egotism, and delusion. One Zen teacher has pointed out that "to see a beautiful vision of a Bodhisattva does not mean that you are any nearer becoming one yourself, any more than a dream of being a millionaire means that you are any richer when you awake" (Kapleau, 1965, pp. 40–41).

Meditation is an important discipline for developing an inner peace and calm and for learning to concentrate and stay balanced. One first learns to become peaceful and focused in meditation and then to extend that sense of calm awareness to activity. Eventually, nothing can pull an experienced meditator off center. He or she learns to cope with problems and pleasures from that calm base, with a certain amount of detached perspective. "Zazen practice is the direct expression of our true nature. Strictly speaking, for a human being, there is no other practice than this practice, there is no other way of life than this way of life" (Suzuki, 1970, p. 23).

It is important to remember that the practice of meditation is an end in itself, not merely a technique to achieve something.

> In Buddhist meditation we do not struggle for the kind of enlightenment that will happen five or ten years from now. We practice so that each moment of our life becomes real life. And, therefore, when we meditate, we sit for sitting; we don't sit for something else. If we sit for twenty minutes, these twenty minutes should bring us joy, life. (Hanh, 1988, p. 53)

Mindfulness

In one sense, the purpose of meditation is to bring a level of inner calm and heightened awareness into our daily lives. Zen master Thich Nhat Hanh eloquently describes this process:

Personal Reflection ———————————————

————————————————————— Zen Meditation

Try this exercise to learn something about Zen as well as your mind.

First, it is essential that your sitting posture be correct. You should be able to sit comfortably with a straight back, without becoming tense. By straight back, Zen teachers mean that the spine should curve naturally just below the middle back. (Trying to sit with an absolutely straight back will only distort the natural curve of the spine and cause discomfort and tension.)

If you wish, you may sit in a chair. The chief requirement of a correct back can be maintained just as easily using a chair. Find a chair that has a seat that is as flat as possible. A small, flat cushion is optional. Sit forward on the front third of the chair, with your feet flat on the floor. The lower legs should be more or less at right angles to the floor and to the upper legs.

If you are going to sit on the floor, use a small, firm cushion to raise the buttocks. (Meditation cushions are often available at local Zen centers.) It is better to sit on a rug or blanket than on the bare floor. Sit on the edge of the cushion only, with just the tip of the bottom of the spine resting on the cushion. This way, nothing presses on your thighs to restrict the blood circulation. You can place your legs in full lotus (with each foot over the opposite thigh) or in half lotus (with only the left foot over the right thigh). For most long-legged Westerners, it is more comfortable to sit Burmese style, your left foot tucked into the juncture of the right thigh and pelvis and your right leg placed immediately in front of your left leg and parallel to it. Both legs are flat on the ground.

The head should be straight, neither bent forward nor backward. Your head should feel comfortable and almost weightless when it is positioned properly. Place your left hand over your right in your lap, with the thumbs lightly touching, and the palms up.

Sit facing a wall far enough away (about 6 to 9 feet) so that you can focus comfortably your eyes on the wall. Keep your eyes lowered to a comfortable place on the wall. Do not close them completely.

Sway gently from side to side, backward and forward, to find the most comfortable erect posture. Lift up your rib cage slightly to take the pressure off your lower back and to allow your spine to curve naturally. Take two or three slow, deep breaths before you begin to concentrate.

Now comes the part that is easiest to describe and hardest to do. Just sit. Do not try to do anything. But do *not* try not to do anything, either. Just sit with a positive mental attitude. Try this practice for only five to ten minutes each day for a week. It will teach you something about Zen and also about the nature of your mind.

More explicit instructions regarding mental activity during meditation have been given by Kennett:

While you are doing zazen neither despise nor cherish the thoughts that arise; only search your own mind [or heart for] the very source of these thoughts. (Bassui)

Now don't deliberately try to think and don't deliberately try not to think; in other words, thoughts are going to come into your head; you can either play with them or you can just sit there and look at them as they pass straight through your head and out the other side. That is what you need to do—just continue to sit; don't bother with the thoughts, don't be highjacked by them and don't try to push them away—both are wrong. . . .

I have often given the likeness of sitting under a bridge watching the traffic go by. You do have to watch the thoughts that travel back and forth, but not be bothered by them in any way. If you do get caught by a thought—and in the beginning it is quite likely—then OK. Right. So you got caught by a thought. Come back to the beginning again and start your meditation over. It's no good sitting there and saying, "Oh, now there, I got caught by another thought," because you will get caught over the annoyance about the other thought, and so it builds up and you never get back to the quiet within. If you get caught in that way, just come back and start again. (1974, pp. 16–17)

You've got to practice meditation when you walk, stand, lie down, sit, and work, while washing your hand, washing the dishes, sweeping the floor, drinking tea, talking to friends, or whatever you are doing: "While washing the dishes, you might be thinking about the tea afterwards, and so try to get them out of the way as quickly as possible in order to sit and drink tea. But that means that you are incapable of living during the time you are washing the dishes. When you are washing the dishes, washing the dishes must be the most important thing in your life. . . .

"While washing the dishes one should only be washing the dishes, which means that while washing the dishes one should be completely aware of the fact that one is washing the dishes. At first glance, that might seem a little silly: why put so much stress on a simple thing? But that's precisely the point. The fact that I am standing there and washing these bowls is a wondrous reality. I'm being completely myself, following my breath, conscious of my presence, and conscious of my thoughts and actions. There's no way I can be tossed around mindlessly like a bottle slapped here and there on the waves." (1976, pp. 3–4, 23–24)

Enlightenment

The term *enlightenment* tends to be misleading because it seems to refer to some state that one can attain permanently; this would, of course, violate the Buddhist concept of impermanence.

One Japanese word that has been frequently used in Zen is *satori*, which literally means "intuitive understanding." Another term is *kensho*,

Personal Reflection ——————————————

—————————————— Meditation and Activity

You can learn something about applying a meditative attitude to your daily activities by doing this exercise.

Meditation can be seen primarily as a way of developing calmness and a sense of centered awareness by learning not to get caught up in your thoughts and emotions. Once you begin to understand this meditative attitude as you sit quietly, you can begin to extend this feeling to your outward activities as well.

Begin with an hour of daily meditative activity. First, sit quietly for five minutes, then tell yourself that you are going to remain self-aware, an observer of your thoughts, emotions, and activity for the next hour. If something does pull you off center, stop what you are doing and try to regain that sense of calmness and awareness. Initially, try this practice in silence. For most of us, talking almost immediately becomes a distraction.

It is easiest to begin with an hour of quiet physical work—cleaning, cooking, and so forth. Intellectual activity is more difficult and conversation still more so. As you extend this practice to more of your daily life, you can begin to see where you are the most sensitive and easily disturbed. Make a list of these situations and see what the list tells you.

which means "to see into one's own nature." Both terms refer to the individual's firsthand experience of the truth of Buddhist teachings. The experience is not static; it is a progressive, ever-changing, and dynamic state of being, very much like Maslow's concept of self-actualization.

> Enlightenment is perfect peace and harmony. If you think enlightenment is something you can get, then it appears right in front of you and you rush to get it; but the more we rush to get it, the more enlightenment eludes us. We try with greater effort, and finally we become a frantic screaming warrior. Then we become exhausted. . . . But enlightenment is completely beyond enlightenment or not-enlightenment. It is just perfect peace and harmony. (Katagiri, 1988, p. 128)

Manne-Lewis (1986) has outlined five basic principles for the attainment of enlightenment in Buddhism: (1) The state of Enlightenment exists; (2) Enlightenment is attainable by human beings; (3) There are concrete methods for attainment of Enlightenment; (4) There are discrete, ordered stages leading to Enlightenment; and (5) Enlightenment is both a cognitive and affective state.

Enlightenment is not experienced in stages, nor are there types of enlightenment, it is an ongoing flow. (Kennett, 1977b, p. 1)

Enlightenment is not some good feeling, or some particular state of mind. The state of mind that exists when you sit in the right posture is, in itself, enlightenment. (Suzuki, 1970, p. 28)

Arhat and Bodhisattva

The Theravada and Mahayana traditions contain different conceptions of the nature of the ideal human being. The Theravada ideal is the Arhat, one who has completely cut off all the limitations of attachment to family, possessions, and comfort to become perfectly free of this world. The Arhat is basically an unworldly ascetic. Arhat literally means "one who has slain the enemy," or one who has slain all passions in the process of intensive spiritual discipline. The Arhat has liberated himself or herself from pride, selfishness, hate, and greed and has developed wisdom and compassion.

One Buddhist text describes the Arhat:

> He exerted himself, he strove and struggled, and thus he realized that this circle of "Birth-and-Death" . . . is in constant flux. He rejected all the conditions of existence which are brought about by a compound of conditions, since it is their nature to decay and crumble away, to change and to be destroyed. He abandoned all the "defilements" and won Arhatship. . . . Gold and a clod of earth were the same to him. The sky and the palm of his hand to his mind the same. (In Conze, 1959a, p. 94)

Let others gain Enlightenment; I shall not enter Nirvana until the last blade of grass has entered Buddhahood. (Bodhisattva vow in Conze, 1959b)

The Mahayana ideal is the Bodhisattva, literally "enlightenment-being." The Bodhisattva is a deeply compassionate being who has vowed to remain in the world until all others have been delivered from suffering.

In truly understanding the principle of selflessness, the Bodhisattva realizes that he or she is part of all other sentient beings and that until all beings are freed from suffering, he or she can never attain complete satisfaction. The Bodhisattva vows not to enter Nirvana until every sentient being, every blade of grass is enlightened.

> As many beings as there are in the universe of beings . . . egg-born, born from a womb, moisture-born, or miraculously born; with or without form; with perception, without perception, or with neither perception nor no-perception—as far as any conceivable form of beings is conceived; all these I must lead to Nirvana. (Diamond Sutra in Conze, 1959b, p. 164)

Compassion is the great virtue of the Bodhisattva, the result of truly feeling the sufferings of all others as one's own. From the Mahayana point of view, this attitude is enlightenment. In the experience of enlightenment, the world is not transcended, but the selfish ego is.

> When one studies Buddhism one studies oneself; when one studies oneself one forgets oneself; when one forgets oneself one is enlightened by everything, and this very enlightenment breaks the bonds of clinging to both body and mind, not only for oneself but for all beings as well. (Dogen in Kennett, 1976, p. 172)

The Bodhisattva path includes abandoning the world, but not the beings in it. The path of the Arhat emphasizes the quest for spiritual perfection and abandonment of the world, without the emphasis on service. The attitude of the Arhat is that those who desire to help others must first work on themselves. Someone who is lost in delusion is not effective in helping or teaching others, therefore self-development must naturally come first.

These two ideals can be seen as complementary rather than contradictory. The Arhat model focuses on self-discipline and work on oneself, whereas the Bodhisattva ideal stresses dedicated service to others; both are essential ingredients in spiritual development.

Dynamics

Psychological Growth

The path of spiritual growth has been illustrated in the Zen tradition by a series of ten Ox-herding pictures. The Ox is a symbol of the Buddha-nature, and the process of finding the Ox refers to the internal search and spiritual development of the Zen student. Spiegelman and Miyuki (1985), two Jungian analysts, provide an excellent and sensitive analysis of these pictures in terms of the individuation process.

Zen masters have often discussed their students' development in terms of the Ox-herding pictures, which provide clear and graphic illustrations of Zen thinking. One teacher outlined the major points of this series in counseling an advanced Zen student:

> If you continue with zazen, you will reach the point of grasping the Ox, i.e., the fourth stage. Right now you do not, so to speak "own" your realization. Beyond the stage of grasping the Ox is the stage of taming it, followed by riding it, which is a state of awareness in which enlightenment and ego are seen as one and the same. Next, the seventh stage, is that of forgetting the Ox; the eighth, that of forgetting the Ox as well as oneself; the ninth, the grade of grand enlightenment, which penetrates to the very bottom and where one no longer differentiates enlightenment from non-enlightenment. The last, the tenth, is the stage in which . . . one moves, as himself, among ordinary people, helping them wherever possible, free from all attachment to enlightenment. (Kapleau, 1965, p. 231)

Obstacles to Growth

Greed, Hate, and Delusion

Three major sources of suffering, the "Three Fires" of Buddhism, are *greed, hate,* and *delusion.* Some individuals are dominated by greed, others by hate, and others by delusion. Virtually everyone has a mixture of all three qualities, with one predominating, although the balance can

Better than a thousand vacuous speeches is one sane word leading to peace. (*The Dhammapada,* Lal, 1967)

Figure 15.1 Seeking the Ox

This picture represents the beginning of the spiritual quest. The man is now aware of spiritual possibilities and potentials. Having become a spiritual seeker, he has become focused on spiritual attainment. The search itself creates a new obstacle, that of seeking outside oneself for what is within. Those who are searching must eventually come to believe that they can "find" the Buddha-nature within themselves. Kakuan, the Zen master who first drew this series, added commentaries to each picture:

> The Ox has never really gone astray, so why search for it? Having turned his back on his True-nature, the man cannot see it. Because of his defilements he has lost sight of the Ox. Suddenly he finds himself confronted by a maze of crisscrossing roads. Greed for worldly gain and dread of loss spring up like searing flames, ideas of right and wrong dart out like daggers. (Kakuan in Kapleau, 1965, p. 302)

Figure 15.2 Finding the Tracks

The seeker has begun to study Buddhism seriously. Study of various scriptures and accounts of the lives of Buddhist sages brings an intellectual understanding of basic Buddhist truths, although the student has not yet experienced these truths firsthand.

"He is unable to distinguish good from evil, truth from falsity. He has not actually entered the gate, but sees in a tentative way the tracks of the Ox" (Kakuan in Kapleau, 1965, p. 303).

Figure 15.3 First Glimpse of the Ox

The sight of the Ox is the first direct experience of the seeker's own Buddha-nature. The encounter with the Ox is not a result of study or abstract contemplation, but is made possible through direct experience. This first glimpse is for but a moment; it is a realization that comes and goes. Further discipline is required to expand and stabilize this experience.

> If he will but listen intently to everyday sounds, he will come to realization and at that instant see the very Source. The . . . senses are no different from this true Source. In every activity the Source is manifestly present. It is analogous to the salt in water or the binder in paint. (Kakuan in Kapleau, 1965, p. 304)

Figure 15.4 Catching the Ox

Now the Zen Student must make certain that Buddhist self-discipline permeates the whole of daily life. The goal is to extend the awareness of one's Buddha-nature to all activities and to manifest that awareness in all circumstances.

The Ox here illustrates the raw energy and power of Enlightenment. Due to the overwhelming pressures of the outside world, the Ox is hard to keep under control. If disciplined practice is abandoned now, this power and energy may dissipate.

> Today he encountered the Ox, which had long been cavorting in the wild fields, and actually grasped it. For so long a time has it reveled in these surroundings that breaking it of its old habits is not easy. It continues to yearn for sweet-scented grasses, it is still stubborn and unbridled. If he would tame it completely, the man must use his whip. (Kakuan in Kapleau, 1965, p. 305)

The mind is restless. To control it is good. A disciplined mind is the road to Nirvana. (*The Dhammapada* in Lal, 1967)

Figure 15.5 Taming the Ox

An effortless intimacy or friendship with the Ox is now established. The sense of struggle is gone. This is the stage of precise and perfect training. every act, every thought, begins to reflect the True Self. The individual ceaselessly works to manifest Buddhism at all times, without a single interruption. Only because some traces of illusion still remain is there still a distinction between the seeker and the Ox.

"He must hold the nose-rope tight and not allow the Ox to roam, lest off to muddy haunts it should stray. Properly tended, it becomes clean and gentle. Untethered, it willingly follows its master" (Kakuan in Kapleau, 1965, p. 306).

Figure 15.6 Riding the Ox Home

The struggle is over. The student has now become the sage. Although the Ox is still seen as separate, the relation between man and Ox is so intimate that he can ride it effortlessly without needing to pay the slightest attention to where it is going. Life has become simple, natural, and spontaneous. Formal external training is no longer essential once one has become firmly anchored in awareness of the Buddha-nature. The discipline that was once seen as a burden is now embraced as a source of real freedom and satisfaction.

> "Gain" and "loss" no longer affect him. He hums the rustic tune of the woodsman and plays the simple songs of the village children. Astride the Ox's back, he gazes serenely at the clouds above. His head does not turn [toward temptation]. Try though one may to upset him, he remains undisturbed. (Kakuan in Kapleau, 1965, p. 307)

Figure 15.7 Ox Forgotten, Self Alone

The seeker has returned home and the Ox is forgotten. The distinction between religious and worldly categories disappears, as everything is seen to possess the Buddha-nature. Training and discipline have become indistinguishable from daily life. The state of meditation is as normal now as walking or breathing and is no longer associated with any sense of motivation or separation from the goal. Everything is sacred, and there is no distinction between enlightenment and ignorance.

In the Dharma [Teaching] there is no two-ness. The Ox is his Primal-nature: this he has now recognized. A trap is no longer needed when a rabbit has been caught, a net becomes useless when a fish has been snared. Like gold which has been separated from dross, like the moon which has broken through the clouds, one ray of luminous Light shines eternally. (Kakuan in Kapleau, 1965, p. 308)

Figure 15.8 Both Ox and Self Forgotten

This refers to the experience of the void, the essential nothingness of all creation. The individual nature and the Buddha-nature were transcended in the previous stage, and now it is enlightenment itself that is transcended. The perfect circle, made by the single brushstroke of the Zen master, is left open. Because the circle is not closed, further growth is possible. The process of enlightenment is able to go on without becoming frozen or static.

> All delusive feelings have perished and ideas of holiness too have vanished. He lingers not in "Buddha," and he passes quickly on through "not Buddha." Even the thousand eyes [of the Buddhas and Patriarchs] can discern in him no specific quality. If hundreds of birds were now to strew flowers about his room, he could not but feel ashamed of himself.* (Kakuan in Kapleau, 1965, p. 309)

*There is a legend of a Chinese Zen master who was so holy that the birds came to offer him flowers as he sat meditating in his mountain retreat. After he became fully enlightened, the birds ceased their offerings, because he no longer gave off any aura, even of devotion and holiness.

Figure 15.9 Returning to the Source

If the eighth stage is thought of as the static aspect of absolute Truth, the ninth stage may be said to bring a new dynamic appreciation of the world. Nature is not merely void or sacred, it is. If seen clearly, any aspect of the world can serve as a perfect mirror to show us ourselves. There still a subtle duality here between the manifestation of Truth in nature and its manifestation in deluded, suffering humankind. This level must eventually deepen to include our return to human civilization.

> He observes the waxing and waning of life in the world while abiding unassertively in a state of unshakable serenity. This [waxing and waning] is no phantom or illusion [it comes form the Source]. Why then is there need to strive for anything? The waters are blue, the mountains are green. Alone with himself, he observes things endlessly changing. (Kakuan in Kapleau, 1965, p. 310)

Figure 15.10 Entering the City with Bliss-Bestowing Hands

This is the final stage, the stage of the Bodhisattva who is free to associate with and help all other beings without limitation. The city refers to the secular world, in contrast to the secluded Zen temple or contemplation retreat. The Bodhisattva is shown with a big belly and a gourd of wine slung over his shoulder. He is willing to share all the amusements and activities of the world, not because of personal desires or attachments, but in order to teach others.

> The gate of his cottage is closed and even the wisest cannot find him. His mental panorama [concepts, opinions, and so forth] has finally disappeared. He goes his own way, making no attempt to follow the steps of earlier stages. Carrying a [wine] gourd, he strolls into the market; leaning on his staff, he returns home. He leads innkeepers and fishmongers in the Way of the Buddha. (Kakuan in Kapleau, 1965, p. 311)

The Zen master, who realizes that everything is Buddha, can now return to the activities of the early stages with a different perspective.

Cease from evil, do only good, do good for others. (The Three Pure Precepts in Kennett, 1976)

change, depending on the circumstances. Certain situations will awaken an individual's greed, others will stimulate tendencies toward anger or delusion.

Greed is the major problem for most people. Most of us always want more—more money, more food, more pleasure. Children are generally the most obviously greedy, and it is often virtually impossible to satisfy a child's greed. One piece of candy only stimulates the desire for another one. The Buddhist scriptures have described greed types as characterized by vanity, discontent, craftiness, and by love of rich, sweet food and fine clothes (Conze, 1959b).

Those dominated by *hate* have sharp tempers and are quick to anger. For them, life is a continual round of fighting with enemies, getting back at others for real and imagined injuries, and defending themselves against possible attack. Hate types tend to hold grudges, belittle others, and suffer from arrogance, envy, and stinginess (Conze, 1959b).

Delusion refers to a general state of confusion, lack of awareness, and vacillation. Those for whom delusion is strongest find it difficult to make up their minds or to commit to anything. Their reactions and opinions are not their own, but are borrowed from others. Delusion types tend to do everything inattentively and sloppily. Their behavior is characterized by laziness, obstinacy, confusion, worry, and excitability (Conze, 1959b).

At their worst, these tendencies can blossom into what Westerners term *neurosis* or *psychosis*. However, according to Buddhist thinking, even a psychosis is but a temporary intensification of one of these tendencies. It is viewed as a transient state, as are all mental and physical states.

By working on oneself, all three obstacles can be transcended. Greed can be turned into compassion, hate into love, and delusion into wisdom. Self-discipline and the discipline of following the Buddha's precepts offer the opportunity for the individual to confront and control his or her greed. The Buddhist teachings, with their emphasis on compassion and respect for others, provide a way to overcome hate. The realization that all things *are* the Buddha controls the problem of delusion. Everything merits our deepest care and attention, because everything contains the Buddha-nature.

Pride

Pride can be another major obstacle to growth. Pride can lead to a lack of respect for one's teacher and create distortions of the teachings. A Zen teacher will attempt to lead students to see and acknowledge their own pride and egotism. One of the Zen patriarchs points out, "Should the teaching you hear from a Zen master go against your own opinion, he is probably a good Zen master; if there is no clash of opinions in the beginning, it is a bad sign" (Dogen in Kennett, 1976, p. 111).

Pride can enter at virtually any point in training, even after a first-stage kensho. Normally, the direct kensho experience confirms the student's understanding of Buddhism, and the student's convictions about the validity of Buddhist teachings become truly unshakable. However, at this stage, many students tend to believe they have learned everything, that

One man on the battlefield conquers an army of a thousand men. Another conquers himself—and he is greater. (*The Dhammapada*, Lal, 1967)

To see the self is not to be pleased with the self; not to be pleased with the self is to want to do something about the self; and to want to do something about the self is to study Buddhism. (Dogen in Kennett, 1976)

they understand Buddhism fully and no longer need a teacher.

A good teacher will insist that, at this point, the student continues with regular duties and training in order to ensure that pride and ambition do not distort the initial deep understanding of Buddhism. Delusion is extremely difficult to overcome if it develops at this stage, because the student's convictions are now firmly rooted in actual experience. If training continues, one can overcome the inevitable pride and sense of holiness or, what some Zen masters have called, the "smell of enlightenment." The student must be reminded of the doctrine of impermanence and the fact that training in Buddhism is endless.

Structure

Body

The Buddhist concept of the Middle Way is of central importance in one's attitude toward the body. It involves neither full indulgence of all one's desires nor extreme asceticism or self-mortification. The body is a vehicle for service to others and for one's pursuit of truth. It should be cared for with this understanding.

The mealtime ceremonial recited in Zen temples affirms:

> The first bite is to discard all evil;
> The second bite is so that we may train in perfection;
> The third bite is to help all beings;
> We pray that all may be enlightened.
> We must think deeply of the ways and means by which this food has
>   come.
> We must consider our merit when accepting it.
> We must protect ourselves from error by excluding greed from our
>   minds.
> We will eat lest we become lean and die.
> We accept this food so that we may become enlightened.
> (Mealtime Ceremonial in Kennett, 1976, pp. 236–237)

In a commentary on the Zen approach to meals, one Zen master wrote:

> If you can chant the Buddhist teachings while having a meal you are very lucky. . . . If you have breakfast to offer your body and mind to the Buddha, to the universe, how lucky you are. Offering your body and mind to the Buddha is offering your body and mind to emptiness, or in other words, to the pure sense of human action. (Katagiri, 1988, p. 9)

Hyakujo, who was the founder of Zen monastic life, always worked with his monks at manual labor, even when he was in his eighties. Although his students tried to restrain him from working as hard as they

Both your life and your body deserve love and respect, for it is by their agency that Truth is practiced and the Buddha's power exhibited. (Dogen in Kennett, 1976)

did, he insisted, saying, "I have accumulated no merit to deserve service from others; if I do not work, I have no right to take my meals" (Ogata, 1959, p. 43).

Social Relationships

A common misconception found within all meditative disciplines is *quietism,* or withdrawing from the world for fear of disturbing one's meditative peace. Buddhist teaching stresses responsibility, the opposite of withdrawal. Meditation is never an end in itself. One may devote periods of time to meditative practice, with the understanding of the need to work and eventually to help others. Everyone has the Buddha-nature. We should ideally look on all other human beings as the Buddha and say to ourselves, "Here comes the Buddha. How can I help him or her?" The Buddha is not beyond this world of suffering, not beyond the need for help and compassion. Also, being Buddha is not a permanent state (because nothing is seen as permanent in Buddhism).

Someone who is inebriated can be treated as a drunken Buddha. He or she is not permitted to disturb others, but is not treated disrespectfully either. Similarly, one who behaves with wrong or evil intent can be seen as a baby Buddha. The individual needs to be taught, but is never to be punished for the sake of revenge or cast out as evil or worthless. For, if this person is cast out, so too is the Buddha. In these ways, social interactions offer crucial opportunities for practicing Buddhist ideals and principles. They also allow for practicing the calm awareness developed in meditation.

A liar with a shaven head does not make a monk. (*The Dhammapada,* Lal, 1967)

Personal Reflection ————————————
——————————————— Walking Meditation

Try this soothing exercise in walking meditation.

All of our physical experiences can become opportunities for mindfulness practice. Walking is a particularly good practice for maintaining awareness in our daily life.

Walk slowly in a natural setting, in a garden or along a river. Breathe normally and easily. Begin to coordinate your breathing with your footsteps. Then, lengthen your exhalation by one step, without forcing your breath. See if your inhalation also naturally increases.

After ten breaths, again lengthen your exhalation by one step. After twenty breaths, return to normal breathing. Five minutes later you can begin to lengthen your breath again. Always return to normal if you feel the least bit tired. (Adapted from Hanh, 1976)

Will

Dogen writes, "It is by means of the will that we understand the will" (in Kennett, 1976, p. 170). Will develops through the exercise of the will. To grasp the will is to make a real commitment to one's training and to take responsibility for one's own actions, realizing that no one else can do your training for you.

> It is not easy for anyone, however, to cast away the chain of ignorance and discrimination all at once. A very strong will is required, and one has to search single-heartedly for his True Self, within himself. Here hard training is needed in Zen, and it never resorts to an easygoing, instant means. (Shibayama, 1970, p. 31)

One basic Buddhist principle is that daily life and activity should be brought into harmony with ideals and values. Training oneself is not merely a means to an end, but training is an end in itself. Dogen writes:

> It is heretical to believe that training and enlightenment are separable, for in Buddhism the two are one and the same . . . as this is so, the teacher tells his disciples never to search for enlightenment outside of training since the latter mirrors enlightenment. Since training is already enlightenment, enlightenment is unending; since enlightenment is already training, there can be no beginning whatsoever to training. (In Kennett, 1976, p. 121)

There is only one thing, to train hard, for this is true enlightenment. (Evening Service in Kennett, 1976, p. 290)

Personal Reflection

Mindful House Cleaning

There are certain chores that we dislike and have to force ourselves to do. Cleaning house is one of them for many of us. When we do not want to do something, the tendency is to do it badly and half-heartedly. We tend to daydream or to try and rush through the distasteful experience.

Now, take a chore like house cleaning and make it an experience in mindfulness. Divide your work into stages, such as putting things away, dusting, sweeping the floors. Allow yourself plenty of time for each stage. Move slowly, about three times more slowly than usual. Focus your attention completely on each task. For example, when putting a book back on the shelf, look at the book, be aware of what book it is, know that you are in the process of putting it back in a specific place on the bookshelf. Avoid any abrupt or rushed movement. Remain aware of your breath, especially when your thoughts wander. (Adapted from Hanh, 1976)

Training is an ongoing process, because there is no end to the realization of Buddhist principles. Someone who stops and remains satisfied with an initial enlightening experience will soon be left with nothing but a beautiful memory.

A contemporary Zen teacher cautioned one of his disciples: "Your enlightenment is such that you can easily lose sight of it if you become lazy and forego further practice. Furthermore, though you have attained enlightenment you remain the same old you—nothing has been added, you have become no grander" (Kapleau, 1965, p. 231).

O Buddha, going, going, going on beyond, and always going on beyond, always becoming Buddha. (The Scripture of Great Wisdom in Kennett, 1976, p. 224)

Emotions

An important goal of Buddhist training is to learn to be in control of one's emotions rather than be controlled by them. There is nothing wrong with most emotions; however, few people experience their emotions properly or appropriately. They become angry or outraged over trivial matters, suppress their feelings, and carry the emotion into situations that are far removed from the original source of the anger. Through training, the Zen student gradually develops a state of meditative awareness in all daily activities. By becoming more fully aware of emotional reactions to various situations, these emotions tend to lose their hold. One Zen teacher commented that if one does get angry, it should be like a small explosion or a thunderclap; the anger is then fully experienced and can be dropped completely afterward (Suzuki-roshi).

> The precept "do not be angry" means that when anger arises don't *become* anger. Remain still inside and watch the anger arise and depart. See its cause. Anger is always a symptom of something deeper. It is the outward sign that something needs changing. (Sacco)

The ideal Buddhist emotional state is compassion. Compassion can be thought of as transcended emotion, a feeling of unity with all other beings.

Intellect

The study of Buddhist scriptures and intellectual understanding of Buddhist teachings are important first steps in Buddhist training, as mentioned in the commentaries to the Ox-herding pictures. However, reliance on the intellect alone can become a great hindrance to true understanding. Ananda, the most clever and most learned of Buddha's disciples, took almost five times longer than the others to reach enlightenment. After the Buddha's passing, the other disciples went to Ananda, whose memory was so prodigious that he was able to recite word for word all of the talks of the Buddha. But his love of argument and his pride in his learning stood in the way of real understanding.

Although erudition alone is not particularly helpful, intellectual understanding plus the actual practice of that understanding are essential.

Ideally, intellectual understanding deepens and becomes clarified through meditation and training in daily life in accordance with Buddhist principles. One who reads about the concept of compassion without actually serving others understands compassion only as a shallow abstraction. Buddhist teachings are meant to be living truths, actively expressed in people's lives.

Pure intellect and abstract reasoning are seen as useful. But intellect and reasoning alone are not enough to allow us to fully comprehend ourselves and the world around us. The intellect is essentially powerless when it comes to satisfying our deepest spiritual needs. "It is not the object of Zen to look illogical for its own sake, but to make people know that logical consistency is not final, and that there is a certain transcendental statement that cannot be obtained by mere intellectual cleverness" (Suzuki, 1964, p. 67).

Buddhism distinguishes the ordinary conscious mind and the deeper Mind:

> To live a spiritual life is to learn and to practice the Way-mind. The Way is the universal path that is complete serenity and tranquility. It is called Mind. This Mind is not ordinary mind. Mind, as serenity and tranquility, is the original nature of human consciousness. . . .
>
> In the study of psychology, one tries to understand the basis of consciousness, which is called the unconscious. . . . Psychology tries to understand this unconscious level, and to take things from it. When you try to take things from it, this is nothing but the functioning of ego-consciousness. . . . But whatever the ego can pick up and look at is only the surface of Way-mind. Buddhism is to learn serenity and tranquillity directly, and to practice it. (Katagiri, 1988, p. 13)

Self

In Buddhist thought, there is a distinction made between the lesser self and the greater self. The lesser self is the ego, the consciousness of one's mind and body. The lesser self remains focused on the limitations of the individual, the consciousness of separateness between the individual and the rest of the world. This level of consciousness must be transcended in order to develop a real sense of unity with other beings and with nature.

In one sense, the lesser self is created by one's sense of inadequacy. The size of the personal ego directly corresponds with the amount of inadequacy that the individual feels. As we become whole, integrated individuals, our lesser selves naturally diminish in strength. We never lose our egos; however, the mature person is in control of the ego, not run by it.

It is possible to identify oneself with one's greater self, which is as large as the entire universe, embracing all beings and all creation. This level of understanding is an essential element in the experience of enlightenment.

Identification with the greater self does not mean that the lesser self must be done away with. Training brings about a transcending of the less-

Earth penetrates heaven whenever Zazen is truly done. (Dogen in Kennett, 1976, p. 140)

er self so that one is no longer dominated by it. Nirvana is not annihilation of the ego, or smaller self, but transcendence of ego orientation. In Buddhist art, the Bodhisattva Monju is depicted sitting on a ferocious beast. Monju is sitting in serene meditation, although the beast is awake with its fierce eyes open wide. The beast represents the ego, a useful tool that is not to be killed, although it must be watched and firmly sat upon.

Teacher

When you meet a Zen master who teaches the Truth, do not consider his caste, his appearance, shortcomings or behavior. Bow before him out of respect for his great wisdom and do nothing whatsoever to worry him.
(Dogen in Kennett, 1976)

A true Buddhist teacher is one who not only believes in Buddhist principles, but who also is seen by all to live those teachings completely. If he or she fails to live up to this ideal, the teacher must be ready to acknowledge the fault. The pupils approach their teacher as the ideal example to follow, as the living Buddha. However, genuine Zen teachers realize their actual limitations and try never to cut themselves off from their pupils by placing themselves on a pedestal. Disciples must see their teacher's humanness and limitations, yet recognize the Buddha in the teacher in spite of the teacher's faults.

A teacher is primarily involved in his or her own training. Others who recognize certain exceptional qualities in a teacher choose to model themselves after the teacher's example. The teacher does not try to be good for others, or worry about whether or not pupils choose to follow. By example, and by great patience, love, and forebearance, a good teacher can serve as an inspiration so that others will exert their best efforts in their own training. A teacher who tries too hard to teach inevitably creates in pupils a sense of guilt for not living up to various external standards. The teacher can serve best as a standard against which disciples freely choose to measure their own attitudes and training.

To follow a Zen master is not to follow in old ways nor to create new ones; it is simply to receive the teaching.
(Dogen in Kennett, 1976

Dogen stresses the necessity of a teacher:

> If a true teacher is not to be found, it is best not to study Buddhism at all. They who are called good teachers, however, are not necessarily either young or old but simply people who can make clear the true teaching and receive the seal of a genuine master. Neither learning nor knowledge is of much importance, for what characterizes such teachers is their extraordinary influence over others and their own will power. They neither rely on their own selfish opinions nor cling to any obsession, for training and understanding are perfectly harmonised within them. These are the characteristics of a true teacher. (In Kennett, 1976, p. 109)

Students often judge their teacher to decide whether the person is a "Zen master" or not. Some discrimination is, in fact, necessary, because even unprepared and unqualified people may call themselves teachers. But for a pupil to worry about the degree of realization of a qualified Zen teacher is nothing but egotism. The student is really asking "Is this teacher worthy of teaching me?" "Does he or she conform to my standards?" Buddhist teachings hold that anything and everything can teach, if only the student has an open mind.

Originally, there were no statues of the Buddha in Buddhist temples; there were only the footprints of the Buddha. This was a reminder to the student of the principle, "Thou must go alone, the Buddhas only point the way." Also, when there is a concrete image, students begin to believe that a teacher should look like a Buddha and that only those who resemble that image in some way are teachers.

> If you wonder "Can I trust?" you are really wondering, "Can I develop a strong enough opinion to please me?" (Bahaudin, a Sufi master)

Evaluation

One exciting and intriguing aspect of Buddhism is that it fosters a sense of a vital dialectic, the simultaneous appreciation of the real and the ideal and the recognition of the tension between the two. Along with the ideals of Buddhism, the limitations of actuality are acknowledged. The individual must understand and live by this notion: "I am Buddha, and I am not Buddha, and I am Buddha" (Kennett-roshi, personal communication). This dialectic approach manifests itself in virtually all aspects of Buddhist life and thought. It provides a creative tension, at once a way to cope with present limitations, and to move toward the ideal.

To say flatly that "such and such is true" is to ignore the principle of impermanence. This kind of statement is misleading at best. However, the opposite statement is equally misleading. It is better to say, "It is so, and it is not so, *and* it is so." Virtually every statement and every situation can be better understood by applying this dialectic.

> Lo! with the ideal comes the actual, like a box with its lid . . . like two arrows in mid-air that meet. (Sandokal in Kennett, 1976)

There is great depth in the Zen notion that training is enlightenment. The trainee who maintains this attitude avoids getting caught in the trap of working for an unattainable ideal. To work continually for a future goal or reward may mean that one is never fully involved in the present. If the path is not in harmony with the goal, how can one ever reach the goal?

This issue is made clear in a well-known Zen story about Baso, a monk who was making great efforts in meditation. Nangaku, his teacher, asked: "Worthy one, what are you trying to attain by sitting?"

> Baso replied: "I am trying to become a Buddha."
> Then Nangaku picked up a piece of roof tile and began grinding it on a rock in front of him
> "What are you doing, Master?" asked Baso.
> "I am polishing it to make a mirror," said Nangaku
> "How could polishing a tile make a mirror?"
> "How could sitting in zazen [meditation] make a Buddha?"
> Baso asked: "What should I do, then?"
> Nangaku replied: "If you were driving a cart and it didn't move, would you whip the cart or whip the ox?"
> Baso made no reply.
> Nangaku continued: "Are you training yourself in zazen? Are you striving to become a sitting Buddha? If you are training yourself in

> zazen, [let me tell you that] zazen is neither sitting nor lying. If you are training yourself to become a sitting Buddha, Buddha has no one form. The Dharma [Teaching], which has no fixed abode, allows of no distinctions. If you try to become a sitting Buddha, this is no less than killing the Buddha. If you cling to the sitting form you will not attain the essential truth."

(In Kapleau, 1965, p. 21)

Dogen has pointed out that "since Buddhist trainees do almost nothing for themselves, how is it possible that they should do anything for the sake of fame and gain? Only for the sake of Buddhism must one train in Buddhism" (in Kennett, 1976 p. 107).

The Buddhist dialectic also applies to the role of the teacher. As mentioned earlier, the ideal Buddhist teacher recognizes his or her own limitations and acknowledges these limitations to the students. This is a major point of contrast to the Indian Yoga tradition, in which the guru tends to be venerated as the perfect embodiment of all divine virtues and characteristics.

However much any human being might theoretically come to approximate these divine ideals, there is no denying the fact that all religious teachers are merely human. They all have foibles and imperfections. Attempting to maintain a role of holy perfection before one's disciples inevitably leads to a certain amount of posing and hypocrisy. Unless teachers acknowledge their real limitations, they are likely to become egotistical and defensive about their slightest faults or mistakes.

Disciples who view their teacher as perfection itself avoid accepting responsibility for their own development. This is because they can make no real connection between their own imperfections and the ostensible perfection of the master. Therefore, rather than continue the hard work of training and self-discipline, students can convince themselves that their teacher is a "master" who can accomplish all kinds of things that they cannot, so they need not even make the effort.

In Zen, religion and daily life are not separate, they are seen as one and the same. Practical, unspectacular experience is stressed and the esoteric and miraculous aspects of religion are downplayed. A Zen master once said, "My miracle is that when I feel hungry I eat, and when I feel thirsty I drink" (Reps, n.d., p. 68). Life is to be lived with full awareness by accepting and fulfilling the requirements of daily life. The Zen master Jyoshu was once asked for instruction by a new monk.

JYOSHU: "Have you breakfasted yet?"
MONK: "I have had my breakfast."
JYOSHU: "Then wash out your bowl."

The monk suddenly understood the true nature of Zen.

There is no final doctrine or dogma because there can be no absolute truths, nor even an absolute Buddha, in the face of impermanence. Buddhist teachings are oriented to human realities. They are aimed at

To live by Zen is the same as to live by an ordinary daily life. (Evening Service in Kennett, 1976)

eliminating the sense of dissatisfaction and inadequacy caused by a limited, selfish ego. In the passage quoted at the beginning of this chapter, the Buddha is reported to have told his followers not to follow any particular teachings in response to a particular teacher's reputation or skill with words, but to rely on their own judgment and experience. The final criterion for Zen is experience. If teaching and discipline aid people in becoming more mature, more responsible, and more complete human beings, this is considered to be good Buddhism.

Ramaswami and Sheikh (1989) summarize Buddhist psychology:

> The psychology of Buddhism rests on the notions of the absence of a separate self, impermanence of all things, and the fact of sorrow. Human beings suffer because of self-delusion, striving to possess that which inevitably must crumble, and because of desire. The Buddha did not stop with a mere diagnosis. He proclaimed that the cure is to reach a higher state of being, wherein self-knowledge has eradicated delusion, attachment, and desire. (1989, p. 120)

Recent Developments: The Influence of Buddhism

Buddhist thinking has had a significant influence on different areas of psychology. Meditation may provide many of the benefits of psychotherapy. Carrington and Ephron (1975) have explored a number of ways that psychoanalysis and meditation techniques can interact effectively. Fromm (1970) believed that the goals of Zen and psychoanalysis are the same. They include insight into self, liberation from the tyranny of the unconscious, and knowledge of reality. Fromm also pointed out that both Zen and psychoanalysis share the principle that knowledge leads to transformation, and Benoit (1990) has examined in detail the psychology of transformation in Zen.

Gestalt therapy and Buddhism also share basic principles. Both stress the importance of mindful living in the present. For both, awareness is a primary tool for change. Perls (1969) argued that the conscious mind is our enemy, rather than the unconscious. The Buddha also pointed out that it is the conscious mind that clings to cravings and to the false idea of a separate self.

A number of psychologists have begun to synthesize the insights of meditation with cognitive psychology (Brown & Engler, 1986; Goleman, 1988; Shapiro, 1980; Shapiro & Walsh, 1984). Empirical research has demonstrated significant neurological and physiological effects of Zen meditation (Hirai, 1989).

Two other schools of Buddhism have become popular and influential in the United States. These are Tibetan Buddhism and Theravadan Buddhism. A significant number of Tibetan Buddhist teachers have emigrated to the West. They have founded successful Buddhist centers, trained large numbers of students, and written important books. One of the best known is the late Chogyam Trungpa. Trungpa founded the

Naropa Institute in Boulder, Colorado. His books (1975, 1988) have influenced many people interested in Tibetan Buddhism.

The best known Tibetan teacher is, of course, the Dalai Lama, who made world headlines when he received the Nobel Peace Prize in 1989. Other important Tibetan Buddhist writers include Evans-Wentz (1954, 1958, 1960) and Lama Govinda (1960).

There have been a number of works based on Theravadan Buddhism. Daniel Goleman, a well-known transpersonal psychologist, has written about meditation and states of consciousness in the Theravadan tradition (Goleman, 1988; Goleman & Davidson, 1979). Another important figure is Jack Kornfield (1987), who is both a transpersonal psychologist and a Buddhist priest. One of the basic Theravadan Buddhist practices, *vipassana,* or "insight meditation," has become widespread (Dhammadudhi, 1968; Goldstein, 1976; Sayadaw, 1972).

Buddhism has grown substantially in the United States over the past 20 years. It has been accepted more readily than other religions because it has been viewed more as a psychology than as a religion. One Zen master has cautioned that Buddhism as a psychology is limited and that Buddhism must be taught as a religion:

> In a sense, Buddhism as a psychology is still part of human culture, influencing, but not exactly penetrating American life. In order to penetrate American life, Buddhism must be accepted as a religion, and zazen must be practiced as an end in itself. . . . In the nineteenth century, Western people didn't accept Buddhism as a religion because it didn't seem to have prayer; it was not what is called revealed religion. . . . Though Buddhism doesn't seem to have prayer, it does have *dhyana*. *Dhyana* means zazen (meditation), and dhyana is exactly the same as prayer. Shakyamuni Buddha says Dharma is a light you can depend on, the self is a light you can depend on, but this self is really the self based on the Dharma . . . or the Truth itself. So, Buddhism is not a revealed religion, but an awakened religion—it is awakening to the self or to the Truth. (Katagiri, 1988, p. 98)

The Theory Firsthand: Excerpt from "The Wild White Goose"

The following excerpts are taken from the diary—called "The Wild White Goose" (1977a)—of Jiyu Kennett, a British woman who studied for many years at a major Zen training temple in Japan. She is now teaching in the United States at her own Zen temple, Shasta Abbey, in Mt. Shasta, California.

11th January.

Reverend Hajime called me into his room early this evening so that we could get on with the translation for as long a time as possible before the bell [rang] for bed.

"Shakyamuni* Buddha and I are one, as are all Buddhists with both him and me, and not merely all Buddhists but all people and all things both animate and inanimate. And none of us have anything to do with Shakyamuni Buddha." I paused for a moment so that he could thoroughly digest what I had written, then I continued. "Shakyamuni Buddha is of no importance at all at the present time and Shakyamuni Buddha lives for ever in me."

He was silent, simply looking deeply into my eyes; then he spoke softly.

"You should ask Zenji Sama for the Transmission," he said.

[Kennett:] "If Transmission is what I think it is, I do not understand you. As I know of it. Transmission is received when all training is finished and the master wishes to give his seal of approval to a disciple before he goes out to teach. I am anything but ready for that."

[Hajime:] "That is a popular misconception. Admittedly it is the giving of the seals of the master to someone whom he knows has understood his own nature but they are only given when the master is certain that the disciple concerned regards his training as just beginning every minute of his life and not when he thinks of it as being over. In other words, not when he thinks of himself as being enlightened and having nothing more to do. Understand the 'gyate, gyate' of the Hannyashingyo as 'going, going,' not 'gone, gone.'"

[Kennett:] "Doesn't one have to have had some great kenshō [enlightenment] before such a thing takes place? All that happened to me in October was that I realized that there was nothing more I could do but train myself constantly every day of my life and that I was the worst trainee in existence. . . . "

16th January.

. . . There is no part of me that can ever be chopped off. There is no emotion, no feeling, no thought, no word, no deed that does not come out of the Buddha Mind. I said this to [Reverend Hajime], and went on. "Then the sex act is part of the Buddha Nature and expresses the Buddha Nature at every turn, for it is, of itself, clean. What we have done is made it dirty with our own guilts and misuse."

"You are correct."

"Eating and going to the toilet and washing clothes and scrubbing the floor are all part of the 'with' for they are all expressions of the Buddha Nature." I stopped, amazed at myself.

"Go on," he said.

". . . and the sun and the moon and the stars and the earth; and the digging of the earth and the flowing water; these too are all

*In Sanskrit, *Shakyamuni* means "wise man of the Shakyas." It is one of the terms frequently used to refer to the Buddha, Siddhartha Gautama, a prince of the Shakya clan.

expressions of the Buddha Nature, and the tongue I use to speak these words, and the food I eat, and the differences in the tastes; 'by comparing them you can'—Yes! that's what the scripture means. 'By comparing them you can distinguish one from other,'—and yet they're all the same thing; they're all expressions of the Buddha Nature, and there is no way in which they can be separated off from it; and there is no way in which one can separate off any person or being or any living thing . . ."

. . . This is the reason why it is so difficult to keep the Precepts and why the Truth can't be given to us until we have kept them and learned to make them our blood and bones. We don't want to *know* that we can be evil, so where is there any need for Precepts? Thus, no-one can enter into the Truths of Buddhism until he has made the commitment of becoming a priest, otherwise he could use the knowledge of his own indestructibility for all sorts of evil purposes. They would know their own true freedom and they wouldn't care two hoots what they got up to with other people."

"That is completely right. You have understood the 'with' at last. You see, from now on you can carry on from there and there will be no difficulty in understanding, and you will know that you must hold everyone and everything as the 'with' aspect of the Buddha Mind and recognize that, whatever aspect of the Buddha Mind it shows, the Precepts must always hold it within itself."

"Then making the Precepts part of my blood and bones means that the Precepts will eventually fall away."

"Haven't you realized that, in your case, the early moral form of them already has? You have gone on beyond morality."

"I thought they had, but . . . oh dear, there goes the bell. We'd better go to service. Can we continue this later?"

"Tomorrow. I have to go out this evening."

We bowed to each other, the first time he had bowed to me fully, and I left the room.

Annotated Bibliography

Conze, E. (1959a). *Buddhism: Its essence and development*. New York: Harper & Row. An excellent survey of the major Buddhist traditions.

———. (Trans.). (1959b). *Buddhist scriptures*. Baltimore: Penguin Books. Good collection of various Buddhist texts.

Kapleau, P. (Ed.). (1965). *The three pillars of Zen*. Boston: Beacon Press. Includes lectures on training and meditation by a contemporary Zen master and first-person accounts of Zen training experiences.

Kennett, J. (1976). *Zen is eternal life.* Berkeley: Dharma Publishing. Includes an excellent introduction to Zen Buddhist thought, two newly translated classic Zen works, and the major Zen scriptures and ceremonials. For the serious Zen student.

———. (1977). *How to grow a lotus blossom, or how a Zen Buddhist prepares for death.* Mount Shasta, CA: Shasta Abbey Publishing. An account of the mystical experiences of a Zen master, including past life experiences and the deep transformation of mind and body.

Lal, P. (Trans.). (1967). *The dhammapada.* New York: Farrar, Straus & Giroux. Fine translation of a major Buddhist scripture.

Reps, P. (Ed.). (n.d.). *Zen flesh Zen bones.* New York: Doubleday (Anchor Books). A marvelous collection of Zen stories and koans.

References

Benoit, H. (1990). *Zen and the psychology of transformation.* Rochester, VT: Inner Traditions.

Brown, D., & Engler, J. (1986). The stages of mindfulness meditation. In K. Wilber, J. Engler, & D. Brown (Eds.), *Transformations of consciousness.* Boston: Shambhala.

Burlingame, E. (1922). *Buddhist parables.* New Haven, CT: Yale University Press.

Carrington, P., & Ephron, H. (1975). Meditation and psychoanalysis. *Journal of the American Academy of Psychoanalysis. 3,* 43–57.

Conze, E. (1959a). *Buddhism: Its essence and development.* New York: Harper & Row.

———. (Trans.). (1959b). *Buddhist scriptures.* Baltimore: Penguin Books.

Dhammadudhi, S. (1968). *Insight meditation.* London: Committee for the Advancement of Buddhism.

Evans-Wentz, W. (1951). *Tibet's great yogi: Milarepa.* New York: Oxford University Press.

———. (1954). *The Tibetan book of the great liberation.* New York: Oxford University Press.

———. (1958). *Tibetan Yoga.* New York: Oxford University Press.

———. (1960). *The Tibetan book of the dead.* New York: Oxford University Press.

Fromm, E. (1970). Psychoanalysis and Zen Buddhism. In D. T. Suzuki, E. Fromm, & R. de Marino (Eds.), *Zen Buddhism and psychoanalysis.* New York: Harper & Row.

Fromm, G. (1992). Neurophysiological speculations on Zen enlighten-
    ment. *Journal of Mind and Behavior, 13,* 163–170.

Glozer, G. (1974). Sitting on a chair or meditation bench. *Journal of the
    Zen Mission Society, 5*(3), 18–20.

Goldstein, J. (1976). *The experience of insight.* Santa Cruz, CA: Unity
    Press.

Goleman, D. (1988). *The meditative mind.* Los Angeles: Tarcher.

Goleman, D., & Davidson, R. (1979). *Consciousness: Brain states of
    awareness and mysticism.* New York: Harper & Row.

Govinda, A. (1960). *Foundations of Tibetan mysticism.* New York:
    Weiser.

Hanh, Thich Nhat (1976). *The miracle of mindfulness.* Boston: Beacon
    Press.

———. (1987). *Being peace.* Berkeley: Parallax Press.

———. (1988). *The heart of understanding.* Berkeley: Parallax Press.

Hirai, T. (1989). *Zen meditation and psychotherapy.* New York: Japan
    Publications.

Kapleau, P. (Ed.). (1965). *The three pillars of Zen.* Boston: Beacon Press.

Katagiri, D. (1988). *Returning to silence: Zen practice in daily life.*
    Boston: Shambhala.

Kennett, J. (1972a). The five aspects of self. *Journal of the Zen Mission
    Society, 3*(2), 2–5.

———. (1972b). The disease of second mind. *Journal of the Zen Mission
    Society, 3*(10), 13–17.

———. (1974). How to sit. *Journal of the Zen Mission Society, 5*(1),
    12–21.

———. (1976). *Zen is eternal life.* Berkeley: Dharma Publishing.

———. (1977a). *The wild white goose* (Vol. 1). Mount Shasta, CA: Shasta
    Abbey Publishing.

———. (1977b). *How to grow a lotus blossom, or how a Zen Buddhist pre-
    pares for death.* Mount Shasta, CA: Shasta Abbey Publishing.

———. (1978). *The wild white goose* (Vol. 2). Mount Shasta, CA: Shasta
    Abbey Publishing.

Kornfield, J. (1987). *Seeking the heart of wisdom.* New York: Shambhala.

Lal, P. (Trans.). (1967). The dhammapada. New York: Farrar, Straus &
    Giroux.

Leggett, T. (1960). *A first Zen reader.* London: Rider.

———. (1977). *The tiger's cave.* London: Routledge & Kegan Paul.

———. (1978). *Zen and the ways.* Boulder, CO: Shambhala.

Manne-Lewis, J. (1986). Buddhist psychology: A paradigm for the psy-
    chology of enlightenment. In G. Claxton (Ed.), *Beyond therapy.*
    London: Wisdom Publications.

Masunaga, R. (Trans.). (1971). *A primer of Soto Zen.* Honolulu: East-
    West Center Press.

Mosig, Y. (1990, Spring). Wisdom and compassion: What the Buddha
    taught. *Platte Valley Review,* 51–62.

Ogata, S. (1959). *Zen for the West.* London: Rider.

Olcott, H. (1970). *The Buddhist catechism*. Wheaton, IL: Quest.

Perls, F. (1969). *Gestalt therapy verbatim*. Lafayette, CA: Real People Press.

Rahula, W. (1959). *What the Buddha taught*. New York: Grove Press.

Ramaswami, S., & Sheikh, A. (1989). Buddhist psychology: Implications for healing. In A. Sheikh & K. Sheikh (Eds.), *Eastern and Western approaches to healing*. New York: Wiley.

Reps, P. (Ed.). (n.d.). *Zen flesh Zen bones*. New York: Doubleday (Anchor Books).

Sangharakahita (1970). *The three jewels*. New York: Doubleday (Anchor Books).

Sayadaw, M. (1972). *Practical insight meditation*. Santa Cruz, CA: Unity Press.

Shapiro, D. (1980). *Meditation: Self regulation strategy and altered states of consciousness*. New York: Aldine.

Shapiro, D., & Walsh, R. (Eds.). (1984). *Meditation: Classic and contemporary persepctives*. New York: Aldine.

Shibayama, Z. (1970). *A flower does not talk*. Tokyo: Tuttle.

Spiegelman, J., & Miyuki, M. (1985). *Buddhism and Jungian psychology*. Phoenix, AZ: Falcon Press.

Stryl, L., & Ikemoto, T. (Eds. and Trans.). (1963). *Zen: Poems, sermons, anecdotes, interviews*. New York: Doubleday (Anchor Books).

Suzuki, D. T. (1956). *Zen Buddhism*. New York: Doubleday (Anchor Books).

———. (1959). *Zen and Japanese culture*. New York: Pantheon Books.

———. (1960). *Manual of Zen Buddhism*. New York: Grove Press.

———. (1964). *An introduction to Zen Buddhism*. New York: Grove Press.

Suzuki, S. (1970). *Zen mind, beginner's mind*. New York: Weatherhill.

———. (n.d.). *Teachings and disciplines of Zen*. (Lecture). San Rafael, CA: Big Sur Recordings.

Trungpa, C. (1975). *Cutting through spiritual materialism*. Berkeley: Shambhala.

———. (1988). *Shambhala: The sacred path of the warrior*. Boston: Shambhala Publications.

Woodward, F. I. (1973). *Some sayings of the Buddha*. New York: Oxford University Press.

Yampolsky, P. (1971). *The Zen master Hakuin: Selected writings*. New York: Columbia University Press.

Chapter Sixteen

Sufism and the Islamic Tradition

> Know, O beloved, that man was not created in jest or at random, but marvellously made and for some great end. (Al-Ghazzali, 1964a, p. 17)

For thousands of years, Sufism has offered a path on which one can progress toward this "great end" of self-realization. It is a collection of teachings, manifested in many forms, that have a common goal: a transcendence of ordinary personal and perceptual limitations. It is not a set of theories or propositions, but has been variously described as a way of love, a way of devotion, and a way of knowledge. Through its many manifestations, it is an approach that reaches beyond the intellectual and emotional obstacles that inhibit spiritual progress.

It is both fashionable and realistic in psychology to admit how little we know and how much more research is necessary before we can begin to understand human behavior. Sufism, on the other hand, is explicit in what it says it does know. Sufis state that there are teachers who know what is important—that is, they know how to teach their students to reawaken themselves to their natural, alert state. The task of the Sufis is not to understand all of behavior; they need only know how to transmit what al-Ghazzali called useful knowledge. This is the knowledge that can help us unravel our personal and cultural predicaments as well as progress along the path of Truth.

Sufi teachings are not fully systematized; many cannot be communicated in words. The teachings are found in various forms that include rituals, exercises, readings and study, special buildings, shrines, special language forms, stories, dance movements, and prayer.

Sufism is often discussed in terms of a *path*. This metaphor suggests both an origin and a destination. Along the path, one can acquire knowledge of reality. "Real self-knowledge consists in knowing the following things: What are you in yourself and where did you come from? Where are you going and for what purpose are you tarrying here awhile? In what does your real happiness and misery consist" (al-Ghazzali, 1964a, pp. 19–20)? Yet, there are many pitfalls that render us unable, uninterested, or even unwilling to seek this other knowledge. What we have included here is a representative selection of Sufi teachings that have been used to foster inner development.

In our presentation of Sufism, we have focused primarily on a single figure whose psychological orientation is consonant with the general approach of this text. No one teacher, no one approach, no one set of beliefs can be said to "represent" Sufism. There is a growing availability of Sufi writings and Sufi teachings that present a variety of approaches to Sufism, all different from the one presented here. These works include the historical approach of Nicholson (1964a) and Arberry (1970); the philosophical approach of Burckhardt (1968); the personal, contemporary approaches of Meher Baba (1967, 1972), Pir Vilayat Khan (1974), and Siraj-Ed-Din (1970); the more eclectic works by Farzan (1973, 1974) and Perry (1971); and the more devotional presentations of Nurbakhsh (1978, 1979, 1981) and Ozak (1981, 1987, 1991a, 1991b).

A. R. Arasteh and Anees Sheikh are two modern psychiatrists, who are also serious students of Sufism. They outline the following as some of the basic principles in Sufi practice (1989, p. 148):

1. There are as many ways to reach Truth (or God) as there are individuals. All ways involve transformation of the ego and service to creation.

2. We can live in harmony with others only if we develop an inner sense of justice. This only occurs when we have reduced our selfishness and arrogance.

3. Love is one of the underlying principles of morality. Love springs from self-work and expresses itself in service to others.

4. The cardinal truth is self-knowledge. Knowledge of self ripens into knowledge of God.

History

Historians and most Sufi teachers usually describe Sufism as the mystical core of Islam and date its appearance to about the same time that Islam emerged, at about the seventh century A.D., as a major religious force.

Sufism is more prominent in the Middle East and in countries that embrace Islam, but its ideas, practices, and teachers are to be found in India, Europe, and the Americas as well (Shah, 1964). Sufis are scattered among virtually all nations of the world. As with any genuine mystical tradition, Sufism has changed form to fit the cultures and societies in which it has been practiced. Sufism has flourished in more cultures than any other spiritual tradition, and so it has become associated with a greater variety of outward forms. Sufi groups have existed for centuries in the Middle East, North Africa, South America, Europe, Central Asia, India, Pakistan, and Indonesia.

Arasteh and Sheikh provide a psychologically oriented definition of Sufism:

> The various terms for Sufism and its practitioners reflect only external qualities. Sufism is an art of rebirth, a process of regaining one's naturalness, a way out of automation, and a vehicle for creative vision. It is the process of awareness of the world of multireality and the perception of single reality. . . . In essence, Sufism is an inner experience that leads to identification with one's object of desire, the so-called beloved, or if you prefer, the ideal-ego. (1989, p. 151)

Because Sufism has been defined more by its effect than by its form, its teachers often have worked within locally understood traditions to protect its members from harassment during times of religious fanaticism. This was often the case in parts of the Islamic world.

Sufism is not different from the mysticism of all religions. . . . A river passes through many countries and each claims it for its own. But there is only one river. (Ozak, 1987, p. 1)

> Sufis responded to this oppressive environment by cloaking their teachings and their activities in the outward garb of religion. . . . They also cultivated cultural pursuits . . . as a means of maintaining communication with the people at all levels of society. . . . Almost every Persian classic, valued for its beauty and originality, is a Sufic textbook as well as a work of art. (El-Qadiri, 1974, p. 8)

Another working definition of Sufism says that it is "a means of concentrating a certain teaching and passing it on, through a human vehicle, through climates prepared for its reception" (Shah, 1964, p. 285). A further explanation is,

> Sufism is a way of life in which a deeper identity is discovered and lived. This deeper identity, or essential Self, is beyond the already known personality and is in harmony with everything that exists. It has abilities of awareness, action, creativity, and love that are far beyond those of the superficial personality. (Helminski, 1992, p. 171)

Many people define Sufism as Islamic mysticism. For them, Sufism refers to "vibrant and self-aware participation in the depths of Islamic thought and practice. . . . Sufism is the spirituality of the Prophet [Muhammad] himself, handed down by those Muslims who have lived Islam to its fullest" (Chittick in Ozak, 1991b, p. 1).

Look not at my exterior form, but take what is in my hand. (Rumi in Shah, 1970a, p. 31)

Abu Hamid al-Ghazzali

The writings of Abu Hamid Muhammad Ibn Muhammad, known as al-Ghazzali (A.D. 1058–1111), are among the most widely read Sufi teachings. Due to his influence, many Islamic theologians finally accepted Sufism within formal Islam. He is called *The Proof of Islam* and *The Restorer of Islam,* and he is one of the most important figures in Islamic theology. Western authorities agree that al-Ghazzali was among the few Muslim thinkers who exercised profound effects upon later Christian thought. "With the time came the man. He was al-Ghazzali . . . certainly the most sympathetic figure in the history of Islam, and the only teacher of the after generations ever put by a Muslim on a level of the four great Imams [founders of the four major schools of law in Islam]" (MacDonald, 1903, p. 215).

His work altered the public view of Sufism from that of a suspect, even heretical teaching, to a valued and essential part of Islam. "The accepted position of Sufism, whereby it is acknowledged by many Moslem divines as the inner meaning of Islam, is a direct result of Ghazzali's work" (Shah, 1964, p. 148). Although Sufism is accepted by Sufis and others as having existed before Islam and therefore has been practiced in various forms beyond the Arab world, it has flourished and developed mainly within the Islamic world since the time of al-Ghazzali.

Al-Ghazzali was born in the small town of Tus in Iran. His father died when al-Ghazzali was young, and he and his brother were raised by a Sufi who also provided for their early education. Al-Ghazzali was an excellent student; when he was old enough, he went to a larger town to study theology and canon law. He was interested in these areas, he later wrote, because they were the most direct paths to possible fame and wealth. However, his studies offered him other, more personal lessons. For example, once when he was returning to Tus, he was set upon by a band of thieves who took all his belongings, including his lecture notes. Unable to bear the loss of the notes, he ran after the thieves pleading for their return. The leader asked him why pieces of paper should be so important. Al-Ghazzali replied that there was learning in them. "I travelled for the sake of hearing them and writing them down and knowing the science in them" (in MacDonald, 1899, p. 76). The robber laughed at al-Ghazzali and told him that knowledge that can be stolen is not knowledge at all. He returned the notes, but al-Ghazzali took the incident as a message from God; he spent the next few years learning and memorizing his scholarly notes.

After studying under a number of distinguished teachers, he was offered a position at the Nizamiya Academy at Baghdad, the most important seat of Islamic learning. He gained an international reputation as a teacher, and he also gained the respect of politicians and religious leaders. By the age of 34, he had reached the absolute pinnacle of the Islamic intellectual world (Qayyum, 1976). By age 39, he had written seventy books.

In the midst of his growing fame, however, al-Ghazzali became severely depressed; he lost confidence in his teaching, his own training, and his own capacities. Eventually, he grew to doubt even the experiences of his senses. Finally, he suffered a partial paralysis of his vocal cords, which prevented him from teaching. The doctors who examined him could find no physical cause for the symptoms. After two months, he withdrew from the university and let it be known that he was making a pilgrimage to Mecca. Actually, he put all his property in trust, left his family, and became a dervish: a religious wanderer and seeker of truth.

He had studied the systems of formal philosophy and theology, but they seemed no longer fruitful; he had read the Sufi mystics, but knew he could not understand them. "I saw that in order to understand it [Sufism] thoroughly one must combine theory with practice" (al-Ghazzali, 1968a, p. 46). A desire to understand Sufi teachings led to a transformation of his own psychological structure. He was determined to become an initiate: one who has seen and experienced.

Al-Ghazzali found the principles of mysticism easy to learn but difficult to practice:

> I acquired a thorough knowledge of their research, and I learned all that was possible to learn of their methods by study and oral teaching.

"Do you not see," I reflected, "that while asleep you assume your dreams to be indisputably real? Once awake, you recognize them for what they are—baseless chimeras. Who can assure you, then, of the reliability of notions which, when awake, you derive from the senses and from reason?" (Al-Ghazzali, 1968a, p. 18)

> It became clear to me . . . that Sufism consists in experience rather than in definitions and that what I was lacking belonged to this domain, not of instruction, but of . . . initiation. (Al Ghazzali, 1968a, pp. 47–48)

> He proceeded straightway, hiding himself from public view into the wilderness adjoining Damascus and Jerusalem. There in solitude he sought the saints of various creeds, from whom he learnt practices of mysticism on recollection, contemplation and remembrance of the Name of the Lord, and wooed solitude and meekness, practiced the hardest austerities. This led to the development of intuition and unfoldment of hidden faculties within him. (Behari, 1972, p. xxii)

During the next 10 years, al-Ghazzali wrote his most important work, *The Revival of Religious Sciences* (1972), which aligned Sufi experiences with Islamic beliefs and practices. He established a framework in which pathological, normal, and mystical behaviors are linked in a single, unified field of human experience. He reinstated the elements of personal development and transpersonal experiences into an Islam that was rapidly becoming rigid and restrictive. In addition to other scattered writings, he wrote a popular abridged version of *The Revival of Religious Sciences* titled, *The Alchemy of Happiness* (1964a), which describes how one can overcome one's lower nature and find happiness through correct knowledge of the self, God, this world, and the next world.

After 11 years of wandering, he accepted, under pressure from the sultan, a teaching position at Naysabur. Several years later he returned to his birthplace and, in the company of his disciples, lived a religious life until his death at age 55.

Al-Ghazzali attempted to teach others to replace dogma with practice, piety with self-examination, and belief with a relentless examination of the actual situations of daily life. His books are still widely read throughout the Middle East. His ideas extended to the West where they influenced St. Thomas Aquinas and St. Francis of Assisi (Shah, 1964).

Major Concepts

Drawing on al-Ghazzali's model and the work of other teachers, Sufis continue to use orthodox Islamic practices in their own teaching. In order to understand Sufism, it is helpful to know the basic structure of Islam.

Islam

Islam, the Arabic word for "peace" or "surrender," is the religious system associated with its prophet, Muhammad. It is described in the Koran, Islam's holy book, as the original monotheistic religion revealed in constant succession to such teachers as Abraham, Moses, and Jesus.

Muhammad had his initial revelation in the year A.D. 610. The Muslim era dates from A.D. 622, the year Muhammad fled from Mecca to the city of Medina. Islam is a religion that sees humanity as having the necessary intellect to make choices and the will to make correct choices even in the face of conflicting desires.

In one sense, Islam has an exoteric, or outward, set of practices that supports the inner practices of Sufism. Islam provides a way of life that stresses honesty, charity, service, and other virtues that form a solid foundation for spiritual practice. "Sufism without Islam is like a candle burning in the open without a lantern. There are winds which may blow that candle out. But if you have a lantern with glass protecting the flame, the candle will continue to burn safely" (Ozak, 1987, p. 63).

Five Pillars of Islam

There are five pillars in Islam: bearing witness, daily prayer, fasting, charity, and pilgrimage to Mecca. For each of these exoteric practices, al-Ghazzali (1983) provides various levels of esoteric significance and practice.

Bearing Witness, or The Confession of Faith

Entrance into Islam begins with the recitation of these basic tenets of Islamic faith: "I bear witness that there is no god but God" and "I bear witness that Muhammad is a servant and a Messenger of God."

To witness something, we must be awake, conscious. To realize the truth of the assertion, "There is no god but God," is to know first-hand the unity of God. This is, in one sense, not the beginning of Islam but the pinnacle of the Islamic mystical path.

Daily Prayer

Five times a day there is a call to prayer. Prayer times are at dawn, noon, mid-afternoon, dusk, and night. The prayers deliberately interrupt the daily activities to reorient members of the community to their moral and religious concerns. The times of prayer are visible manifestations of the doctrine that all are equal in the eyes of God, irrespective of class, social, and economic distinctions. "Is anything more precious than prayer that any frivolous thought overtakes you at that hour? . . . Prayer is like unto eternity, so when you have entered it how can the uneternal (worldly) thought linger in your mind at the time" (al-Ghazzali, 1972, p. 15)?

Ibn 'Arabi (A.D. 1165–1240) was known as the greatest of Sufi teachers and is ranked with al-Ghazzali as a great philosopher (Chittick, 1989). He has written about prayer:

> Do everything you do in order to come close to your Lord in your worship and prayers. Think that each deed may be your last act, each prayer your last prostration, that you may not have another chance. If you do this, it will be another motivation for becoming heedful and also for becoming sincere and truthful. (Ibn 'Arabi, 1992, p. 8)

Fasting

Each year, all Muslims who are able fast from dawn to sunset during the month of Ramadan. One is also supposed to abstain from sex and from impure thoughts and harmful deeds during this time. It is a difficult practice, intended to help one remain aware of the conflicting forces between the lower and the higher natures. Al-Ghazzali (1986b) describes fasting's intent as follows:

> The fasting of the general public involves refraining from satisfying the appetite of the stomach and the appetite of the sex, as has already been discussed.
>
> The fasting of the select few is to keep the ears, the eyes, the tongue, the hands, and the feet as well as the other senses free from sin.
>
> The fasting of the elite among the select few is the fast of the heart from mean thoughts and worldly worries and its complete unconcern with anything other than God and the last day, as well as by concern over this world. (p. 20)

Charity

Each year, at the end of the month of Ramadan, every household is asked to give a predetermined percentage of its accumulated wealth to the poor. It is said that all things originate from God; having goods and money is seen as a custodianship in that one retains the right to possessions by returning some of them to the larger Muslim community from which they came. "If God had wished he could make all creation rich, but for your trial he has created the poor that you might make gifts to them" (al-Ghazzali, 1972, p. 16).

Ibn 'Arabi (1992) advocates generosity as an act of faith:

> The one who gives from his sustenance attracts more than he has given from the Ultimate sustainer. The miser, in addition to his sin of miserliness, accuses Allah Most High of stinginess and prefers and trusts his miserable goods over the generosity of his Lord. . . .
>
> Therefore, spend from what Allah has given you. Do not fear poverty. Allah will give you what He has promised, whether you or everyone asks for it or does not ask for it. No one who has been generous has ever perished in destitution. (p. 13)

Pilgrimage to Mecca

The city of Mecca in Saudi Arabia is the most holy city in Islam. All Muslims are required to visit it once in their lifetimes, provided they can afford to do so. There are a set of rigorous observances to be followed at the time of pilgrimage, which occurs during a specified week each year. This annual ritual has kept the different Muslim peoples aware of their historical bond. The pilgrimage is a time in adult life when devotion to the spiritual completely overshadows social or commercial interests.

The Koran

It is the Merciful who has taught you the Koran. He created man and taught him articulate speech. The sun and the moon pursue their ordered course. The plants and the trees bow down in adoration. He raised the heaven on high and set the balance of all things, that you might not transgress it. Give just weight and full measure. (Koran, LV: 1)

The Koran, or Qur'an, the holy book of Islam, was revealed to Muhammad so that mankind could know what is true. It contains essentially three levels of instruction. The first is a set of doctrines that describes one view of reality and humanity's special role in it. The second level is a commentary on the opportunities and pitfalls that occur in life. The third level is a tangible manifestation of divinity; the words of the Koran are the direct words of God channeled through the messenger Muhammad.

The Koran discusses religious and secular matters. It includes laws of inheritance, rules for marriage and divorce, and questions of property rights, as well as ethical and religious proscriptions. The central premise of Islam is that there can be no division of church and state; every act, every object, every relationship is part of the divine nature. The possibility of realizing the divine nature at every moment is interwoven into the daily practice of Islam. It is what the Prophet preached and how he lived.

Muhammad

When a person is reading the Koran two angels are kissing his forehead. (Al-Ghazzali, 1972, p. 17)

Muhammad, or Mohammed (A.D. 570–632), transmitted the message of the Koran to humanity. He was not divine, but he was inspired. He is looked upon as the man who comes as close as one can to living the ideal life set forth in the Koran. As a civic leader, he was very much involved with worldly issues; he settled civic disputes, led armies, married and raised children, in addition to instructing his followers in the understanding of the Koran. He instituted and practiced the Five Pillars.

Sufi Teaching and Orthodox Islam

Al-Ghazzali wrote in a time that stressed formal observance of a practice, rather than the capacity of any practice to transform a person's inner being. His stories and illustrative examples serve to remind readers that formal practice, by itself, might be fruitless. One such story tells of an encounter between a Sufi teacher and a conventionally pious man:

> One day a man came to the teacher Bayazid and said: "I have fasted and prayed for thirty years and have found none of the spiritual joy of which you speak."
> "If you had fasted and prayed for three hundred years, you would never find it," answered the sage.
> "How is that?" asked the man.
> "Your selfishness is acting as a veil between you and God."
> "Tell me the cure."
> "It is a cure you cannot carry out," said Bayazid.
> Those around him pressed him to reveal it. After a time he spoke.

"Go to the nearest barbershop and have your head shaved; strip your-self of your clothes except for a loincloth. Take a nosebag full of wal-nuts, hang it around your neck. Go into the market place and cry out—'Anybody who gives me a slap on the neck shall have a walnut.' Then proceed to the law courts and do the same thing."

"I can't do that," said the man, "suggest some other remedy."

"This is the indispensable preliminary to a cure," answered Bayazid, "but as I told you, you are incurable."

(Adapted from al-Ghazzali, 1964a, pp. 128–130)

Women in Sufism and in Islam

It is often difficult to distinguish cultural, religious, and psychological ideas concerning the special status of women; nevertheless, the attempt is nec-essary in examining the role of women in Sufi thought.

From the early rise of Islam as a world religion, there has been a suc-cession of women regarded as saints in Sufi circles and within Orthodox Islam. From Rabia (A.D. 717–801) to the current period, these saints have been venerated and their work regarded with the same esteem as that of their male counterparts (Smith, 1977). An early Sufi teacher made it clear that in the spiritual life there could be neither male nor female (Shabistari in Smith, 1977). In contemporary Sufi teachings and groupings, women are present. The course of training is based on the capacities of the indi-vidual, not on the sex. (Irina Tweedie [1979] has written a vivid and detailed personal account of her own training and development at the hands of a contemporary Sufi teacher.)

Essentially, the rise of Islam changed the status of women, affording them "legal protections in the area of marriage, divorce and inheritance that are considered to mark a vast improvement over the situation of women in pre-Islamic society" (Smith, 1980, p. 517).

Despite their spiritual equality and their improved status through Islam, the position of women in most Islamic cultures is far from equal. As in Europe and the Americas, women have been denied equal access to edu-cation and property rights, as well as the freedom to travel and to develop themselves. There is a growing literature in the West that is beginning to sort out the contradiction between the repressive attitudes still current in many Muslim countries and the fact that religious and spiritual doctrines do not support this repression (Smith & Haddad, 1975).

Knowledge

In *The Book of Knowledge* (1966), al-Ghazzali divides knowledge into two categories: detrimental and useful. Detrimental knowledge is knowledge that distracts from or retards the understanding of our inner selves. Sufism has traditionally viewed scholarly training as antithetical to true understanding, and al-Ghazzali's own legal and scholarly background made him especially sensitive to its limits. He describes three limiting forms. *Logic* is limited, especially in evaluating spiritual questions, because logic does not generally allow the inclusion of novel or seemingly contradictory information. *Philosophy* does not consider realistic situations and is self-limiting because it does not validate its conclusions through actual experience. *Academic knowledge* is vain posturing; it is detrimental when it parades itself as the exclusive path to learning.

Useful knowledge furthers a person's growth. The most important form is *direct knowledge*; it cannot be described but it can be experienced. It cannot be taught but it can be received. Ibn 'Arabi called it knowledge of reality. With it, "man can perceive what is right, what is true, beyond the boundaries of thought and sense" (Shah, 1970a, p. 78). Sufi writings and teaching practices are the records of the ways in which generations of teachers have helped their students to have the experience of direct knowledge coupled with intuitive understanding. Intuition is developed to go beyond the limits of reason; therefore, it can perceive and integrate what reason alone could not accept.

A donkey with a load of books is still a donkey. (Koranic saying)

Personal Reflection ———————

——————————— The Key and the Light

Throughout this chapter we will make use of teaching stories—stories that are told by Sufi teachers for more than just entertainment. Here is one famous story and some ways to work with it (adapted from Ornstein, 1972).

> A man is looking at Nasrudin who is searching for something on the ground.
> "What have you lost, Mulla?" the man asked.
> "My key," said the Mulla.
> So they both went down on their knees and looked for it.
> After a time the man asked, "Where exactly did you drop it?"
> "In my own house."
> "Then why are you looking here?"
> "There is more light here than inside my own house."

The joke is well known in American vaudeville as well as in Sufism. If one begins to work with it, it can be more than a joke, more than a story about a simpleton.

Read the story over a few times. Now imagine that you are searching desperately for something. Consider the following questions:

1. What are you looking for? (Allow an answer, no matter how unusual, to form in your mind.) Where are you looking? Is there a lot of light there? What kinds of associations do these questions evoke? How do you feel now?

2. Now think about a key. What is a key for? What is the key to your life right now? (Again, allow an answer, an image, or an idea to form; take your time.)

3. Now say to yourself, "I have lost my key." What does this evoke in you?

4. Now think, "My key is in my own house." What are your thoughts and feelings?

5. Then put the whole story together: "I am looking for my key—which I really know is in my own house—in places where I know the key is not, but where there is more light." Spend a little more time with the story.

In addition to the personal associations called up by the story, I offer another. . . . Two areas of the mind are opposed, the light, or "day," and the dark, or "night." The key is inside the house, in the dark, unexplored area of our house, of the mind, of science. We are normally attracted and a bit dazzled by the light of the day, since it is generally easier to find objects in daylight. But *what we are looking for may simply not be there,* and often we may have to grope around somewhat inelegantly in the dark areas to find it. Once we find what we are looking for in the dark, we can then bring it into the light, and create a synthesis of both areas of the mind. (Ornstein, 1972, pp. 174–175)

Almost all systems of intuition and direct knowledge describe visionary events, moments of complete clarity. One goal of Sufi training is to hold onto this higher state, to become attuned to this level of reality so that it is not simply relegated to memory. With proper teaching, it becomes a part of ongoing awareness, as readily accessible as normal waking consciousness. The goal is not simply to glimpse or even experience these states but to come to rest in them, to be at home with this other world view. (Note: This closely resembles Maslow's description of *plateau experiences.*)

States of Consciousness

Beyond learning, beyond conventional knowledge, is the clear perception of reality. It can be understood during unusual states of consciousness. The states described here are not separate and distinct from one another but are different ways of understanding a common set of experiences.

Because someone has made up the word "wave," do I have to distinguish it from water? (Kabir, 1977, p. 29)

Certainty

Certainty is having continuous access to direct knowledge. Certainty is immediate; it is knowledge that your whole being possesses (Siraj-Ed-Din, 1970). For example, imagine that you wish to know about peaches. One

What the eye sees
    is knowledge.
What the heart knows
    is certainty.
(Dhun'nun in Shah, 1971a, p. 195)

I laugh when I hear that the fish in the water is thirsty. (Kabir, 1977, p. 9)

way would be to see slides of the varieties of peaches, to study their biology; to learn about the methods of cultivation, where they are grown, how much they cost, what pests they attract, and so on. This would be academic knowledge and useful in its own fashion. However, until you have touched, smelled, tasted, and eaten peaches you do not have direct knowledge of them. Experiencing a peach is comparable to certainty.

Conscious, or Awake, Existence

Being conscious means responding to every situation as it actually is—not as it appears to be, not as one wishes it to be, not as if it were another, similar situation. When one is awake there is little concern with personal identity. Conscious existence has two aspects. The first is a state of union or annihilation (fana) in which individual identity seems merged with the whole of reality. In this state, a person erects no barriers between the self and God, because it is clear that no barriers exist. A person who is truly *awake* is as a drop of water that is aware of being part of the ocean or a column of air that is conscious of the wind.

The second aspect is a state of return or persistence (baqa') in which one is part of the world but not concerned about one's position or rewards in it. The awareness of the divine element in things is so great that personal issues become secondary to caring for others (Arberry, 1966, pp. 131–145; ibn 'Arabi, 1981).

In one sense, Sufism is essentially a path of self-transformation. Arasteh and Sheikh (1989) describe the states of fana and baqa' in psychological terms. Fana is disintegration of one's limited self-concept, social self, and limited intellect. Baqa' is reintegration as the universal self, or activation of one's totality.

The following story indicates the power of a person who has realized both fana and baqa', that simultaneously is nothing and everything:

> At a court banquet, everyone was sitting according to his or her rank, waiting for the king to appear. A poorly dressed man came in and took a seat above everyone else. The prime minister angrily demanded that he identify himself.
>
> "Are you the vizier of a great king?"
>
> "No, I rank above a vizier."
>
> "Are you a prime minister?"
>
> "No, I also outrank a prime minister."
>
> "Are you a king in disguise?"
>
> "No, I am above that rank as well."
>
> "Then you must be the Prophet," the prime minister suggested sarcastically.
>
> "No, I am above even the Prophet."
>
> The prime minister shouted, "Are you then God?"
>
> "I am above that too," the man calmly asserted.
>
> "There is nothing above God!"
>
> The stranger replied, "Now you know me. That *nothing* is me."
>
> (Adapted from traditional sources)

Love

The end point of knowledge in the Sufism of al-Ghazzali is also called love. Similarly, the end point of love leads to the state of certainty. For the Sufi teacher, the two are the same, only the approaches are different. Each path has been taken by different Sufi teachers. The way of knowledge has been most clearly defined by al-Ghazzali; the path of love, by the Persian poet Rumi (A.D. 1207–1273).

For Rumi, love was the only force that could transcend the bounds of reason, the distinctions of knowledge, and the isolation of normal consciousness. The love he experienced was not sensual pleasure. It might be more aptly described as love for all things, for creation itself. Love is a continually expanding capacity that culminates in certainty, in the recognition that there is nothing in the world or in the spirit that is not both loved and loving.

> Thou didst contrive this "I" and "we" in order that
> Thou mightest play the game of worship with Thyself,
> That all "I's" and "thou's" should become one soul and
> at last should be submerged in the Beloved.
>
> (Rumi in Arasteh, 1972, p. 146)

The perception of God as the Beloved, common to both Christian and Sufi writings, comes from direct experience. As you channel your energy into loving God, there appears to be a response, as if you are being loved in return; just as in a personal relationship, the act of loving brings forth or awakens love in another. The reach toward the divine is met with a grasp from that which is called the divine.

A modern Sufi master writes: "The essence of God is love and the Sufi path is a path of love. . . . Love is to see what is good and beautiful in everything. It is to learn from everything, to see the gifts of God and the generosity of God in everything. It is to be thankful for all God's bounties". (Ozak, 1987, p. 7).

When a person comes to a certain distance along the path of love, God reaches out and begins to assist the aspirant by drawing him or her toward his presence. As this occurs, the individual stops striving and begins to allow himself or herself to let go, be helped, be accepted, and be taken in.

> The eyes of the dervish who is a true lover see nought but God; his heart knows nought but Him. God is the eye by which he sees, the hand with which he holds, and the tongue with which he speaks. . . . Were he not in love, he would pass away. If his heart should be devoid of love for as much as a single moment, the dervish could not stay alive. Love is the dervish's life, his health, his comfort. Love ruins the dervish, makes him weep; union makes him flourish, brings him to life.
>
> (Ozak, 1981, pp. 60–61)

Dynamics

Psychological Growth

Stages of Personal Development

Many Sufi teachers have described different stages in the course of personal development. Each stage trains or exposes different facets of the aspirant's character and perception.

We will describe each stage separately in order to facilitate an understanding of al-Ghazzali and others. This does not mean that any single linear pattern is typical or would be the actual experience of a Sufi student. Although other writers describe the stages differently (Arberry, 1970; Rice, 1964; Shah, 1964; Trimingham, 1971), they all acknowledge their debt to al-Ghazzali's earlier descriptions.

Initial Awakening. This stage begins when one concludes that the external world is not fulfilling and decides it is necessary to reevaluate one's life. Such a realization is often preceded by a personal crisis, often coupled with bewilderment about the meaning of existence. It is the beginning of a fundamental reorientation of personal values. What one has strived for may appear to be worthless; what one casts aside as absurd may become filled with meaning. In al-Ghazzali's own case, he gave up his promising and successful career and became a dervish. This was only the beginning of the process of transformation, although it was the most dramatic change in his life. Rumi also abandoned a successful academic career to work with a Sufi teacher.

Patience and Gratitude. One soon comes to the realization that patience is required for progress and that it takes time to overcome personal limitations. Patience is not merely the passive acceptance of one's faults; it is the willingness to accept the fact that inner change takes time and that one's efforts are not immediately rewarded. A person begins to reshape his or her personality gradually, the way a tree is shaped, nourished, and pruned, again and again.

Patience is considered one of the greatest virtues. It is essential for living in the present. Without patience spiritual work is impossible. Impatience means that attention is on the future, which is not yet here. Real prayer or meditation requires present-centered, highly focused attention.

The development of patience is accompanied by a sense of gratitude that one is given the time to make progress at all. Gratitude is related to the belief that *all* things come from God. Gratitude means being grateful for everything one receives, whether the things one receives are pleasant or painful, whether they amount to one's gaining or losing. "If you consider yourself honoured by the diamond and humiliated by the stone, God is not with you" (Attar, 1961, p. 99).

Fear and Hope.   Fear is fear of God. It is not fear of being punished or being sent to hell. Rather, it is the fear lovers feel when they are afraid of losing the other's love. The Sufi master Shibli stated, "Each day that I was overcome with fear, the door of knowledge and insight opened to my heart" (in Shafii, 1985, pp. 183–184).

It is impossible to know the full effects of one's own actions. One hopes that what one does is beneficial, but this hope is linked to the fear that one's action may be detrimental. The hope of success is balanced by the fear of failure; the hope for security is coupled with the fear of stagnation. The task becomes the "avoidance of whatever has the least semblance or suspicion of wrong" (Hafi in Rice, 1964, pp. 40–41).

Focusing on one's faults and shortcomings can be paralyzing. Hope allows one to see oneself clearly and honestly, without becoming paralyzed. "The essence of Sufism is hope" (Shafii, 1985, p. 184).

Self-denial and Poverty.   Self-denial means to serve others rather than always putting oneself first. It is to serve in order to please God, not to please others or to be rewarded or praised. While poverty may be practiced in a literal sense—one may have no or few possessions—what is important is to be free of attachment. "When the heart is cleared (of all except God) poverty is not better than wealth nor is wealth better than poverty" (Hujwîrî, 1959, p. 24). What is important is the loss of desire, not the loss of property. "The vacant heart [is] more important than the vacant hand" (Rice, 1964, p. 42).

Our normal understanding of these matters is satirized in a traditional story about a rich man who asks a poor man the cause of his suffering. The poor man replies, "Half my wages go for food." "I see the cause of your trouble," says the rich man. "You spend your money foolishly. Less than one tenth of my money goes for food."

Trust in God.   (Belief in the Oneness of God.) In this stage, a person seeks neither support nor consolation from the external world. The person seeks everything from God, not from the world. Al-Ghazzali describes three different degrees of trust. The first is the kind of trust you place in a skilled professional, such as a fine doctor or lawyer. The second is the trust of a child in its mother, a total trust and reliance on the mother. The third degree is to completely submit one's will, to be like a corpse in the hands of a washer of the dead. There is no resistance to whatever happens, no expectation.

> This is not like a child who calls upon the mother, but like a child who knows deeply that even if he does not call for the mother, the mother will be totally aware of his condition and look after him. This is the ultimate degree of trust in God. (Al-Ghazzali in Shafii, 1985, p. 227)

This is a period of activity, not a time of indolence, passivity, or dependency. The balance between acting for oneself and trusting in the divine

Higher than the state of asceticism is the state wherein on the approach and departure of wealth the person remains unaffected equally. If it comes he is not glad and if it leaves him he is not sorry. (Al-Ghazzali, 1972, p. 206)

is captured in the saying of Muhammad: "Trust in God but tie your camel first." Trust arises from assuming that your efforts are part of a larger system, the details of which you are unaware.

Love, Yearning, Intimacy, and Satisfaction.   In this stage, the developing personality has only one desire, which is to love God; to love anything other than God is "veiled heresy." It becomes clear that this single desire is the only desire—the only desire that ever truly existed. The earlier stages of giving up attachments, overcoming greed, and awareness of personal sin fade away with the all-encompassing power of this later realization.

Intent, Sincerity, and Truthfulness.   This stage is dominated by a concern for the intent, not the actual form, of action. If one's intentions are correct, then the actual practice is less important. There is less interest in observable behaviors and an ever increasing awareness of the inner meaning of an action.

The following story is about the power of sincerity and the slackening of that personal power when sincerity is diminished:

> A pious woodcutter once heard about a tribe of nearby pagans who worshipped a tree. He decided to cut it down. "I am sure that God will reward me for preventing them from being pagans and worshipping an idol."
>
> As the woodcutter was on his way to cut down the tree, the Devil came up to him and asked, "Where are you going?" The woodcutter said, "I am going to the tribe that worships a tree and cut that tree down." The Devil said, "No, no, don't do it."
>
> "Who are you to tell me what to do. I am going to chop down that tree for God's sake!"
>
> The Devil said, "I am the Devil. I told you not to do that, and I'm not going to let you cut down that tree."
>
> The woodcutter cried, "You! You cannot stop me." He grabbed the Devil and threw him to the ground. The man sat on the Devil's chest and put his axe to the Devil's throat, fully prepared to kill him.
>
> The Devil said, "You are very unreasonable. You are going to try and chop down that tree but the tribe will not let you cut down their god. They may even kill you, and your family will be left destitute. Be reasonable. Leave this project of yours. Also, I'll make a bargain with you. I know that you only make two coppers a day as a woodcutter. You are a devout man and you have a big family, and also you like to help people. Every morning I will put under your bed two gold coins. Instead of going and getting yourself killed, you will get two gold coins. You can spend the money on your family's needs and also help the poor."
>
> The woodcutter replied, "I don't believe you. You are going to cheat me. Everybody knows the Devil is a cheat and a liar. You just want to save yourself."

The Devil said, "No, I am not going to cheat you. Besides, try me. If you don't find the two gold coins each morning, you can always take your axe and try and chop down the tree."

The man agreed. The next morning, he found two brand new gold coins under his mattress. He bought food and clothing for his family and distributed the remainder to the poor. The next morning, when he looked under the mattress, he found nothing. He searched all over the bedroom, but found no gold coins.

Angrily, the woodcutter took up his axe and set off to chop down the tree. On the road, he met the Devil again. This time the Devil was smiling and asked, "Where do you think you are going?"

"You cheat, you liar! I'm going to go and chop down that tree!"

The Devil tapped the man on the chest with his finger and the woodcutter was knocked over. The Devil said, "Look, do you want me to kill you now? Two days ago you were going to kill me. I want you to promise not to harm that tree."

"Oh no, don't kill me. I won't touch the tree. But I just want to ask you one thing. Two days ago I defeated you easily. I just grabbed you and threw you down. Where did you get this tremendous force today?"

"Ah, the day before, you were going to cut that tree for God's sake. Today, you were fighting me for the sake of two gold pieces."

(Adapted from al-Ghazzali, 1972, and other traditional sources)

Contemplation and Self-examination.   Al-Ghazzali describes and considers the distractions that might prevent one from being calm and thus render one unable to perceive inner reality. His concerns are similar to those voiced in Yoga and Buddhism with regard to clearing the mind. He describes various ways of meditation and quotes incidents from the lives of teachers who were well versed in meditation. In one story, al-Ghazzali tells of the saint Shibli who went to Abul Hasan Nuri. Nuri "was seated quiet in the corner of his room, steadfast in concentration and was not moving any limb. He asked him where had he learnt that secret practice? He replied, 'from a cat which was waiting to pounce on a rat'" (al-Ghazzali, 1972, p. 335).

The Recollection of Death.   Contemplating death can be a powerful tool in releasing one from undesirable habits and attitudes. Thinking about one's own death is an exercise in becoming more aware of one's present experiences. It is a way to begin the process of personal growth. In some sense, what al-Ghazzali described is a cycle beginning with conversion and repentance and ending with reflection on death. It can easily begin the other way: reflection on death leading to the psychological state that precedes conversion. Until recently, Western psychology has avoided death. We are a death-fearing culture. Al-Ghazzali suggests the following exercise to engrave the awareness of death into your consciousness:

Remember your contemporaries who have passed away, and were of your age.

Remember the honours and fame they earned, the high posts they held and the beautiful bodies they possessed, and today all of them are turned to dust.

How they have left orphans and widows behind them and how their wealth is being wasted after them and their houses turned into ruins.

No sign of them is left today, and they lie in the dark holes underneath the earth.

Picture their faces before your mind's eye and ponder.

Do not fix hopes on your wealth and do not laugh away life. Remember how they walked and now all their joints lie separated and the tongue with which they talked lightly is eaten away by the worms and their teeth are corroded. They were foolishly providing for twenty years when even a day of their lives was not left. They never expected that death shall come to them thus at an unexpected hour.

(Al-Ghazzali, 1972, pp. 378–379)

Personal Reflection ─────────────
───────────────── Remembering Death

Most of us somehow believe that we will never die. We live as if death were, at best, a remote and far distant possibility. It can help wake us up to contemplate our own death, to make the concept of our last days or hours more real.

Now, imagine that you have died. You have pleaded with the Angel of Death to be allowed to return to life. There are so many things you have yet to do. The Angel of Death grants you one additional day—no more.

Imagine that tomorrow morning is the morning of that extra day. What will you do? How will you spend the day? How will you live with the awareness of your own impending death?

Reflect afterward on what this exercise evokes in you. Does it awaken powerful feelings? Does it provide you with a new perspective on life?

Obstacles to Growth

Heedlessness (Forgetfulness)

Man, like a sleepwalker who suddenly "comes to" on some lonely road, has in general no correct idea as to his origins or his destiny. (Shah, 1972f, p. 133)

The inability to pay attention and to remember what we know are the cardinal problems of humanity. It is the foundation that supports all other human weaknesses and psychopathology. It is inherent in our constitution that we lose sight of our divine origin; even as we remember we begin to forget. The thrust of Sufi teaching is to encourage people to pay attention long enough to *develop* their capacities to remain awake.

Although many systems of morality describe the right way to live, they often fail to show how their principles can be put into practice. A first step in overcoming heedlessness is to learn to recognize it in one's own life. It is as mundane as misplacing one's glasses or as troubling as in the story told about Norbert Weiner, the famous cybernetic researcher: One day he was walking along a path at the Massachusetts Institute of Technology when he met a colleague. They talked for a few minutes and, as they parted, Weiner asked his friend to tell him in which direction he had been walking when they met. Weiner could not recall if he had been on his way to lunch or if he had just finished it.

Some of those who have been influenced by Sufi teachings indicate that the initial task is to wake up enough to be aware of one's predicament. Orage (1965) writes:

> Our present waking state is not really being awake at all. . . . It is, the tradition says, a special form of sleep comparable to a hypnotic trance. . . . From the moment of birth and before, we are under the suggestion that we are not fully awake; and it is universally suggested to our consciousness that we must dream the dream of this world—as our parents and friends dream it. . . . Just as in night-dreams the first symptom of waking is to suspect that one is dreaming, the first symptom of waking from the waking state—the second awakening of religion—is the suspicion that our present waking state is dreaming likewise. To be aware that we are asleep is to be on the point of waking; and to be aware that we are only partially awake is the first conditioning of becoming and making ourselves more fully awake. (p. 89)

As Harman (1967) concludes, "We are all hypnotized from infancy. . . . The apparent corollary is that we do not perceive ourselves and the world about us as they are but as we have been persuaded to perceive them" (p. 323).

Man is asleep, must he die before he wakes? (Muhammad)

Incapacity

Sufi teachers point out that even when a person feels ready to learn Sufism, he or she is not necessarily capable of assimilating Sufi teachings. If the student lacks the capacity to use the teachings, it is like pouring water into sand. There is a saying: "When the student is ready the teacher appears." This does not mean when the student thinks that he or she is ready; it means instead that when the teacher decides the student is ready for learning, the teacher will attract the student. The student's opinion has little to do with his or her actual level of readiness, but the teacher's decision has everything to do with whether the student will begin.

Personal Reflection

Do You Know What You Like, Do You Like What You Do?

Here is an exercise to help you investigate your own heedlessness. Are you constantly aware of the choices and decisions you make?

You wake up in the morning and propose to get up. Ask yourself whether you really wish to get up, and be candid about it.

You take a bath—is it really because you like it or would you dodge it if you could?

You eat your breakfast—is it exactly the breakfast you like in kind and quantity? Is it just your breakfast you eat, or simply breakfast as defined by society? Do you, in fact, wish to eat at all?

You go to your office . . . or you set about the domestic and social duties of the day—are they your native tastes? Would you freely choose to be where you are and do what you are doing? Assume that, for the present, you accept the general situation. Are you in detail doing what you like? Do you speak as you please to other persons? Do you really like or only pretend to like them? (Remember that it is not a question yet of *acting* on your likes and dislikes but only of discovering what they really are.)

You pass the day, every phase offering a new opportunity for self-questioning—do you really like this or not? The evening arrives with leisure—what would you really like to do? What truly amuses you: theater or movies, conversation, reading, music, games, and which ones in particular?

It cannot be repeated too often that the doing of what you like comes later. In fact, it can be left to take care of itself. The important thing is to know what you like. (Orage, 1965, p. 112)

Nafs

The *nafs* is made up of impulses, or drives, to satisfy desires. These drives dominate reason or judgment and are defined as the forces in one's nature that must be brought under control. They prevent one from activating one's totality. The nafs is really a living process, rather than a static structure in the psyche. "The *nafs* is not a thing. The Arabic term is related to words for 'breath,' 'soul,' 'essence,' 'self,' and 'nature.' It refers to a process which comes about from the interaction of body and soul" (Ozak, 1987, p. 31).

The nafs is a product of the self-centered consciousness—the ego, the "I"—and eventually can be controlled. The nafs must be subdued—this is the ideal. *All impulses,* no matter what their effects, can and should be controlled. This is true even if the effects are socially desired and rewarded; they still are an indication of a lack of inner capacity. The goal is to achieve a balance between impulsive excesses and arid detachment.

> The *nafs* is not bad in itself. Never blame your *nafs*. Part of the work of Sufism is to change the state of your *nafs*. The lowest state is that of being completely dominated by your wants and desires. The next state is to struggle with yourself, to seek to act according to reason and higher ideals and to criticize yourself when you fail. A much higher state is to be satisfied with whatever God provides for you, whether it means comfort or discomfort, fulfillment of physical needs or not. (Ozak, 1987, p. 32)

The following nafs categorizations are derived from a number of sources (al-Ghazzali, 1963; Arasteh, 1973; Ozak, 1981, 1987; Shafii, 1974; Trimingham, 1971).

The Commanding Nafs. Descriptions of this level of nafs are similar to descriptions of the id in psychoanalytic theory; they are closely linked to lust and aggression. Al-Ghazzali calls them the swine and the dogs of the soul—the sensual nafs behave like swine, the ferocious ones like fierce dogs or wolves. Wrath, greed, sensual appetites, passion, and envy are examples of these nafs. This is the realm of physical and egoistic desires. We are all dominated by these impulses at times, but it is assumed that we have moments of perspective in which we see this level as the tyranny of the least evolved aspects of ourselves. These basic impulses are not to be denied; however, they are to be properly redirected.

The Accusatory Nafs. At this level, the individual is still dominated by wants and desires, but now the person repents from time to time and *tries* to follow higher impulses. This stage of inner struggle closely corresponds to the stage in the Zen oxherding picture, "Taming the Ox." (See page 560.)

> There is a battle between the *nafs,* the lower self, and the soul. This battle will continue through life. The question is who will educate whom? Who will become the master of whom? If the soul becomes the master, then you will be a believer, one who embraces Truth. If the lower self becomes master of the soul, you will be one who denies Truth. (Ozak, 1987, p. 4)

This level of nafs parallels aspects of the psychoanalytic superego. There is often excessive self-accusation, self-belittlement, or defensiveness, which appears in the form of excessive vanity. Typical manifestations include an insatiable need for praise, hunger for recognition, or a need to control others. "In this stage it is possible for one's motives to become so distorted that it is difficult to distinguish between fantasy and reality" (Beg, 1970). One becomes increasingly dependent on others' evaluations of oneself, and one is unable to accept criticism when dominated by these nafs.

The radical division into good and bad can be the sickness of the Mind. (Erikson, 1964)

The Inspired Nafs.   At this level, the individual is truly motivated by ideals such as compassion, service, and moral values. Though not free of the power of the desires and ego, this new level of motivation significantly reduces their power for the first time. What is essential here is to *live* in terms of these higher values. Unless these new motivations become part of a new way of living, they will wither and die away. Behaviors common to the inspired nafs include gentleness, compassion, creative acts, and moral action. Overall, a person who is impelled by the inspired nafs seems to be emotionally mature, respectable, and respected. (This is similar to the mana personality described by Jung. For many, this is a high state to achieve. The Sufis teach that there is far more potentially available to the aspiring soul.)

The Tranquil Nafs.   The old desires and attachments are no longer binding. This is similar to the stage of trust and gratitude mentioned earlier. The ego-self begins to let go at this stage, allowing the individual to come more closely in contact with the divine. This stage is similar to the stage described in the Zen oxherding picture, "Riding the Ox Home." (See page 561.)

This level of nafs predisposes one to be liberal, grateful, trusting, and adoring. If one accepts difficulties with the same overall sense of security with which one accepts benefits, it may be said that one is dominated by the tranquil nafs. Developmentally, these nafs mark a period of transition. The soul can now begin to "disintegrate" and let go of all previous concern with self-boundaries; it can begin to "reintegrate" as an aspect of the universal self (Arasteh, 1973). In this stage, actions are not performed for conventionally pious reasons but because one is becoming aware of the divine will; one's actions are in accord with the inner natural law.

> The Sufi reaches a stage where one transcends the duality of good and bad and perceives all of the manifest dualities as part of a unitary continuum of existence. Categorizing observations or experiences into good-bad, beautiful-ugly, rich-poor, pleasure-pain disappears. (Shafii, 1974, p. 6)

The Fulfilled and Fulfilling Nafs.   Here the individual has become truly spiritual and whole, within and without. Prayer, service, and spiritual pursuits are pursued because they are now fulfilling in and of themselves. These kinds of activities are now clearly preferred to the desires of the body and the ego.

The path of Sufism is the elimination of any intermediaries between the individual and God. (Ozak, 1987, p. 1)

The Perfected Nafs.   Here all sense of individuality and separateness is dropped. At this stage, the individual has truly realized the truth, "There is no god but God." The Sufi now knows that only the Divine exists, that there is nothing other than God, and that any sense of individuality or separateness is an illusion. This is equivalent to the stage of fana described earlier.

The nafs is parallel to the stages of development described earlier. Each stage of growth has within it nafs, or impulses, that are contrary to the values of that stage. The conflict leads to growth, provided the nafs is subdued, or to regression, if the nafs predominate.

Structure

Body

Al-Ghazzali says that one should consider the body as the carrier and the soul as the rider. "The soul should take care of the body, just as a pilgrim on his way to Mecca takes care of his camel; but if the pilgrim spends his whole time in feeding and adorning his camel, the caravan will leave him behind, and he will perish in the desert" (al-Ghazzali, 1964a, p. 49). Good health is encouraged to the extent that it allows the inner work to proceed without impediment.

Ibn 'Arabi also advocates caring for the body without becoming dominated by concern for it. He taught a middle ground that exists between asceticism and hedonism, an approach which is remarkably like that of Buddhism. "Do not sleep until you are unable to stay awake. Do not eat until you are hungry. Dress only to cover your body and to protect it from cold and from heat" (ibn 'Arabi, 1992, p. 7).

Some Sufi schools employ exercises that entail a "fine tuning" of the body and mind. The so-called "dervish dancing," a combination of music and movement, is the most widely known. "The objective is to produce a state of ritual ecstasy and to accelerate the contact of the Sufi's mind with the world-mind of which he considers himself to be a part" (Burke, 1966, p. 10). An exercise may be movement, movement with music, or music alone.

The body too is a great and necessary principle, and without it the task fails and the purpose is not attained. (Rumi, 1972, p. 31)

The use of dance or movement to bring about this state of ecstasy is described by Burke (1975): "A dance is defined as bodily movements linked to a thought and a sound or a series of sounds. The movements develop the body, the thought focuses the mind, and the sound fuses the two and orientates them towards a consciousness of divine contact" (p. 49). This ecstatic state is a physical condition that allows certain inner experiences to be felt and understood; it is not simply a joyful, hyper-aroused state. The body is not the source of experience; it is the channel through which experience passes.

Social Relationships

Whereas Western psychological theorists as different as William James and B. F. Skinner describe much of personality in terms of social roles, there is far less emphasis on roles in Sufism. Many authors suggest that one simply behaves according to the cultural values of one's own culture. Al-Ghazzali (1976, 1964b) wrote pragmatic letters to government officials and even set out suggestions for rulers that were a mixture of strict adherence to Islamic law and compassionate intuition in specific situations.

Ibn 'Arabi stressed the importance of associating with others who are also on the spiritual path:

> It is best to separate yourself from people who do not believe in what you believe, who do not do what you do, and who are against your faith. Yet at the same time you should not think badly of them or condemn them for what they are. Your intention in ignoring them should be that you prefer the company of believers. (Ibn 'Arabi, 1992, p. 10)

Al-Ghazzali discussed two special situations: the relationship of teachers to students and the relationship between close companions.

> The kernel of the human development called "Sufism" is the basic human unit: the members who meet together and carry on the studies prescribed for them by a contemporary teacher. . . .
>   This is necessary to the realization which comes from being a Sufi. It may be called community, communion, meeting. . . . It is often called the *Jam*—coming together. . . . No higher attainment is possible to man unless the circumstances of the coming-together are correct; unless it is a communion including the right people, at the right time, in the right place. (Foster, 1968, p. 14)

It is the special nature of a Sufi group to be able to work correctly toward a certain goal that produces the right alignment and reduces the likelihood of undesirable developments. What Carl Rogers calls "the innate healing capacity of the group" has been well understood by Sufi teachers.

A teaching story by Sa'di (c. A.D. 1200–1291) catches the matter-of-fact way in which teachers deal with relationships:

> A student said to his teacher: "What am I to do? I am troubled by the people, many of whom pay me visits. By their coming and going they encroach upon my precious time." He replied: "Lend something to every one of them who is poor and ask something from every one who is rich and they will come round thee no more." (1966, p. 131)

The great Sufi saint Shibli also tested the sincerity of his students. Shibli once entered a mystical state and was locked up as a madman. Many of those who had heard him teach went to visit him:

> Shibli asked, "Who are you?"
>   "We are some of those who love and follow you."
>   Shibli began throwing stones at his visitors. They began to run away, crying, "It is true. Shibli really has gone crazy!"
>   Then Shibli called out to them, "Didn't I hear you say that you loved me? You could not even bear a stone or two before running away.

What became of that sincere love you claimed you had for me? Did your love fly away with a couple of stones? If you had really loved me, you would have patiently endured the little bit of discomfort I caused you."

(Adapted from traditional sources)

In addition to the relations between students and teachers, there is the important relationship between companions on the Sufi path. Al-Ghazzali (1975) wrote that real friendship includes the following eight responsibilities:

1. *Material aid*. You have an obligation to help your companions with food, or money, or other things they need for their own survival or development.

2. *Personal support.* "If they are sick, visit them; if they are busy, help them; if they have forgotten, remind them" (p. 33).

3. *Respect.* You should not complain of their faults to them or to others. Also you should not give advice when you know it cannot be acted upon.

4. *Praise and attention.* You should praise the good qualities of your companions and let them know that you care for them.

5. *Forgiveness.* It is helpful to forgive others for their failings.

6. *Prayer.* You should pray for the well-being of your companions with the same fervor as you pray for your own well-being.

7. *Loyalty.* You should be firm in your friendships so that you can be depended on by those who put their trust in you.

8. *Relief from discomfort.* You should not create awkward or difficult situations that involve your companions. You should not be a burden to others.

> You will not enter Paradise until you believe, and you will not believe until you love another. Let me guide you to something in the doing of which you will love one another: salute all and sundry among you. (Muhammad)

This straightforward description of the duties of one person toward another was designed to clarify the value and to emphasize the need for mutual support. Sufism suggests that we need other people for our own sake and to help us put into practice the fruits of our own inner work.

Service to others can become service to God, because there is ultimately nothing other than God. Ibn 'Arabi tells of a conversation between God and Moses:

"O my servant, I was ill and you didn't come to visit me; I was hungry and you didn't feed me.". . . Allah Most High clearly declares that the being of the one who is sick is His being, and the one who is hungry and in need is also He. If the sick and needy are He, then your being also is His being. (Ibn 'Arabi, 1992, p. 35–36)

Another explanation of the power of Sufi groups has been given by a contemporary writer:

> Our tendency is toward personal independence, but in order to know our real Self we need to abandon the ego-protective behaviors that keep us in separation. We need to open ourselves to other beings in this milieu of Love. . . . Only as we begin to open to others in love can the isolated ego be transformed. (Helminski, 1992, p. 15)

Will

Although the term *will* is used in Sufi writings, it is elusive and not subject to a single definition. "'Will,' to the Sufi, will vary in nature, quality and significance in direct relation to the stage which the aspirant has reached" (Khan, 1974). Every act is made up of the conception, the motivation, and the capacity to carry it out.

Free Will

The effort of attention by which we hold fast to an idea . . . is the secret of will. (James, 1899, p. 91)

Free will is assumed to be part of human nature. Humanity is unique in its propensity and capacity to perform actions that are contrary to natural law and incompatible with physical, mental, or spiritual health. Unlike animals, we have the ability to turn away from our own best interests.

Divine Will

Thy will be done
On earth as it is in heaven.
(Lord's Prayer)

In contrast to free will, divine will is described as a fundamental law of nature. A stone falls because it is obeying the divine will manifested as gravity. One definition of a saint might be one whose every action is in conformity with the divine will. Learning to be a saint is learning to be sensitive and to be "attuned" to natural laws of thought and action, laws as regular as the natural laws of electricity and magnetism. Personal will is the driving force behind the eventual surrender to divine will.

One modern sheikh has explained divine will and personal will with the metaphor of an airplane trip. As an individual passenger, you can do virtually nothing that will affect the plane's arrival time. You have neither the skill nor the power to affect the flight itself. But you can decide whether or not to read or write, eat dinner, watch the movie, and so on. In short, you can use your personal will to have a pleasant and profitable time while on the plane, or not. The plane will arrive at exactly the same time in any case.

Emotions

Three things in life are destructive: anger, greed and pride. (Muhammad)

Emotional states are simply states through which a person passes. One's emotional reactions to a situation can serve as an indicator of one's level of attachment or concern. There is some emphasis on the use and the transformation of emotional states. Emotions orient consciousness either toward or away from knowledge of reality. A particular emotion is less important than its overall effect on one's behavior. Al-Ghazzali (1968a) recalls times of bliss and despair, both of which he saw as instrumental in his own realization.

Awareness of one's emotions is important. This awareness is itself transformative, as Perls and other therapists have more recently discovered. "What is essential from you is to be heedful at all times, to be attentive to what comes into your mind and your heart. Think about and analyze these thoughts and feelings. . . . Beware of the wishes of your ego, settle your accounts with it" (ibn 'Arabi, 1992, p. 7).

Intellect

Al-Ghazzali's description of the intellect foreshadows the developmental models of Piaget (Piaget, 1952; Piaget & Inhelder, 1958). He distinguishes four stages of development. First there is a drive for understanding, what Western psychology calls *curiosity* or the need for competence (White, 1959). The second is *axiomatic intellect,* which is the capacity to understand logical relationships. The third element is *empirical knowledge;* it is the aspect that is concerned with external things and events. The last element to appear is the *developed intellect,* which is a higher form of the original drive for understanding. It is this quality of the intellect that guides inner development and allows a person to "conquer and subdue his appetite which hankers for immediate pleasure" (al-Ghazzali, 1966, p. 228).

The developed intellect includes the heart as well as the head. It is an integrated way of understanding oneself, the world, and spiritual knowledge as well. Jelaladin Rumi (1207–1273) is a clear example of the integrated intellect. He was not only one of the world's greatest mystical poets, Rumi was a gifted philosopher and was the founder of the Mevlevi Order, the whirling dervishes (Chittick, 1983).

If your thought is a rose,
you are a rose garden;
if it is a thorn,
you are fuel for the bath stove.
(Rumi in Helminski, 1992, p. 34)

Conventional learning can retard the developed intellect if its function is not understood. Al-Ghazzali again and again upbraids his former scholastic colleagues for their unwillingness to use their learning to reach beyond the empirical and acheive real knowledge (Watt, 1971). He recounts that he needed to pierce his own intellectual training repeatedly with ecstatic and revelatory states until he understood enough to keep his intellect in balance.

Self

There are two ways to describe the self. The first way is to see the self as a collection of socially determined, changeable roles—the self within society. The second is to see the true self, the core of one's being, distinct yet part of a larger entity. Sufi teaching is one way to learn to shift peoples' identification of who they are from the first point of view to the second. As they identify more and more with their inner selves, they do not deny or give up their own personalities. What happens is that as they fully accept themselves for who they truly are, the external attributes of personality (how they speak, how they eat, and so forth) are put into a new

He who knows himself knows his Lord. (Muhammad)

perspective. These attributes assume their natural place in the totality of the personality.

Different Sufi teachers have different personalities, both before and after they are able to identify with the divine. It is only the internal point of identification that has shifted. The personal characteristics of individuals (hair color or skin texture, for example) are part of the new integration of the personality and are relatively unchanged.

Teacher

But how will you ever know him as long as you are unable to know yourself? (Sanai, 1974, p. 10)

A teacher or guide instructs so that students may move closer to realizing their inner nature. A guide, says al-Ghazzali, teaches out of his or her own fullness. Teaching is in itself an expression of the divine will.

Why is a guide necessary? Mohammed Shafii, a psychiatrist knowledgeable in Sufi tradition, suggests:

> The Sufis feel that maturity cannot be achieved alone. They feel there is a need for guidance and discipline. The path is unknown, the night is dark and the road is full of danger. Dangers include preoccupation with selfishness, false visions, misinterpretations of mystical states, arrest in development, fixation in a particular state, appeal to various drugs to create false mystical experiences and not infrequently overwhelming anxiety and insanity. (1968, p. 11)

A Sufi sheikh is like a doctor, and a student is someone who is sick at heart. The student comes to the sheikh for healing. A real sheikh will give a certain diet and certain medications to cure the person's ills. (Ozak, 1987, p. 2)

It is generally accepted that one cannot progress past a certain point without the aid of a teacher. Among many other qualities, a teacher must possess a *sense of occasion*. This is the capacity to know when a lesson, an experience, or an exercise will help the student. Teaching can occur only at the right time, in the right place, and in the right company, or it will be wasted. "The Way requires (1) a teacher who has been that way before; (2) an individual whose consciousness is correctly oriented so that he can make use of the material given to him; and (3) a group of such people" (Abdul-Hamid, 1976, p. 57). Thus, a single exercise or story may prove effective when employed by a teacher; but when used by a student on another occasion, it may have no effect at all.

> One reason for the institution of a Guide is that he knows when to direct the disciple's effort and work, and when not to direct it. He also knows the kind of effort and work which each individual should do. Only the ignorant mistake any work for useful work. (Palawan-i-Zaif in Shah, 1970b, p. 229)

Ibn 'Arabi points out that "those who do not know Him will not see Him, whether by teaching or by learning or by thinking. The one who knows only knows through service to a perfect guide. That one will be enlightened by his light and find the path to truth, find oneness and unity" (1992, p. 46).

Arasteh and Sheikh (1989) comment that although the master-novice relationship may seem to be hierarchical and authoritarian, the inner reality is quite different. In reality, two souls are communicating. One is a channel for a higher level of energy and inspiration. The other receives and progresses. The more the dervish progresses, the less guidance he or she requires. Eventually, one's own heart provides all the guidance necessary.

With a Guide you may become a real man, without one you will remain an animal. (Rumi in Shah, 1970a, p. 37)

Duties of a Teacher

Al-Ghazzali (1966, pp. 145–152) describes eight duties of a teacher. These duties touch upon many of the aspects of Sufi teaching but should not be viewed as any kind of standard list applicable to every Sufi teacher.

1. "The first duty of the teacher is to be sympathetic to students and treat them as his own children." The teacher must care about the students' welfare with the same or greater devotion that a father or mother shows for his or her own children. The teacher must be constantly aware of their failings but, like a parent, must always be able to love the students.

2. "The second duty of the teacher is to follow the example of the Law-giver: he should seek no remuneration for his services . . . and accept neither reward nor thanks." Sufi teachers usually have an occupation and thus do not depend on their students for their livelihood. The teacher should feel gratitude toward the students for their willingness to learn.

3. "[The teacher] should not withhold from the student any advice, or allow him to attempt work at any grade unless he is qualified for it." The teacher, not the student, is the judge of the student's progress.

4. "The teacher, in dissuading the student from his evil ways, should do so by suggestion rather than openly, and with sympathy rather than with odious upbraiding. . . . Open dissuasion destroys the veil of awe, invites defiance, and encourages stubbornness." Before the advent of behaviorism, al-Ghazzali discussed the differential effects of reinforcement and punishment in the learning process. He concluded that punishments inhibit overall learning.

If men had been forbidden to make porridge of camel's dung, they would have done it, saying that they would not have been forbidden to do it unless there had been some good in it. (Muhammad in al-Ghazzali, 1966, p. 149)

5. "The person who is teaching a certain science should not belittle or disparage the value of other sciences before his students." To attack other teachers is demeaning to the teacher and to the students. The task of a teacher is to teach what he or she knows. It is not to pressure the student into doubting other teachers who may benefit the student at another stage in his or her development. It is common in Sufi training for students to be sent to study with others from time to time. The teacher recognizes that

the primary goal is the education of the student. The student must not become sidetracked by becoming dependent on or feeling adoration for the teacher.

6. "He should limit the student to what the latter is able to understand and should not require of him anything which his mind cannot grasp for fear that he would develop a feeling of dislike for the subject, and his mind would become confused." This admonition is similar to the instructions for structuring programmed learning. Each link is designed to prevent the student from progressing until he or she has completed the preceding lesson correctly.

7. "The teacher should give his backward students only such things as are clear and suitable to their limited understanding and should not mention to them anything about the details that are apt to follow but which he deems fitting for the present to withhold. . . . Everyone usually believes himself capable of mastering every science no matter how complex. . . . Even the most foolish and most feebleminded among men is usually the most pleased with the perfection of his mind." If one teaches beyond a person's ability to understand, the effort is wasted. "A donkey stabled in a library does not become literate" (Hadir in Shah, 1970a, p. 273). Material learned prematurely may be misinterpreted and can in itself become an obstacle later on. Ajmal of Badakhshan comments on the necessity of teaching only what can be learned at the time:

> There are three ways of presenting anything.
>
> The first is to present everything.
>
> The second is to present what people want.
>
> The third is to present what will serve them best.
>
> If you present everything, the result may be surfeit.
>
> If you present what people want, it may choke them.
>
> If you present what will serve them best, the worst is that, misunderstanding, they may oppose you. But if you have served them thus, whatever the appearances, you have served them.
>
> (Shah, 1970a, p. 224)

8. "The teacher must do what he teaches and not allow his works to give the lie to his words." The teacher is not just a source of information, he or she is a living example of the effect of teaching. The students and the teacher are all working together. "Teachers talk about teachings. Real teachers study their pupils as

---

The Sufi must act and speak in a manner which takes into consideration the understanding, limitations and dominant concealed prejudices of his audience. (Ibn 'Arabi in Shah, 1970a, p. 33)

well. Most of all, teachers should be studied" (Musa Kazim in Shah, 1970a, p. 221).

Evaluation

Sufism is difficult to evaluate because it has taken so many forms and adapted its teachings to many different cultural settings. Sufism has been presented here as a theory of personality and a way to self-understanding, rather than as a religious doctrine.

Sufism is an ancient tradition; but it has not become so formal, so burdened with old ideas and practices, that it has lost its relevance. It is still responsive to new cultural demands and is still modifying its methods and its message for a new generation of students who can be taught Sufism (Shah, 1981).

It is difficult to accept the emphasis on the need for a living personal teacher. We have become accustomed to the idea that there is nothing that we cannot do for ourselves. Bookstores bulge with shelves of do-it-yourself literature on everything from carpentry to beekeeping, Yoga to childbirth. What Sufism suggests is that we must do the work ourselves, but a teacher can help us to work profitably. It is a common error to think that, because we are working hard and diligently, our work will lead to some personal benefit. No matter how hard we whip our horses, no matter how hard we kick their sides, no matter how fast they go; if we are racing around a circular track, we will not advance beyond the point at which we started.

One begins to appreciate the Sufi point of view by experiencing the distinctions between knowledge and useful knowledge as illustrated by the following story:

> There is little use in teaching wisdom. At all events wisdom cannot be taught in words. It is only possible by personal contact and by immediate experience. (Jung, 1973)

Nasrudin sometimes took people for trips in his boat. One day a fussy pedagogue hired him to ferry him across a very wide river.

As soon as they were afloat the scholar asked whether it was going to be rough.

"Don't ask me nothing about it," said Nasrudin.

"Have you never studied grammar?"

"No," said the Mulla.

"In that case, half your life has been wasted."

The Mulla said nothing.

Soon a terrible storm blew up. The Mulla's crazy cockleshell was filling with water.

He leaned over towards his companion.

"Have you ever learnt to swim?"

"No," said the pedant.

"In that case, schoolmaster, ALL your life is lost, for we are sinking."

(Shah, 1972d, p. 18)

Not only do humorous tales contain valuable structures for understanding. Their use also helps to weed out people who lack a sense of humour. Sufis hold that people who have not developed or who have suppressed their capacity to enjoy humour are, in this deprived state, also without learning capacity. (Shah, 1981, p. 21)

This story raises some questions: What have you learned that is useful knowledge? What have you learned that is extraneous to your life? What have you learned that may, even now, be holding you back?

Sufism proposes that the more we can sift out the true from the unimportant and the false, the closer we are to being able to see the larger picture of humanity, of which our personality is such a small part.

It has been said that in the West we are able to use only very little of the Sufi teaching. It is all too new to us; it contains too many ideas that we immediately dismiss. It is for this reason that some teachers say they are laying the groundwork for later, more direct teaching experiences. One contemporary teacher has said,

> There are different ways of "awakening." Man may be asleep, but he must wake in the right way. One necessity is that when he is awake, he will also have the means to profit by his wakefulness. It is the preparation for this profiting as well as the preparation for waking, which is our current endeavor. (Pendlebury, 1974, p. 74)

In this chapter, we have attempted to present Sufism in as cogent a way as possible, so that as Sufi ideas become more available to the West, you can more easily accept and understand them.

The Theory Firsthand: Excerpts from *Tales of the Dervishes* and *Caravan of Dreams*

Stories, one of the many teaching tools of the Sufi tradition, can be studied, extended into exercises, read aloud, or can be simply enjoyed. They are one way in which students, who know little about Sufism, can be exposed to some of its perspectives and a few of its levels, although not its actual operation.

Stories may be used to evoke specific responses in the minds of listeners, to clarify a point in a lesson, or to keep alive some particular aspects of a teacher's work. If a story is entertaining enough, it will be preserved and passed from generation to generation even if the people who tell it have lost the capacity to understand some of its levels of meaning.

What follows are a few stories from the works of Idries Shah, a contemporary teacher who has revived the use of teaching stories in both Eastern and Western cultures.

The Tale of the Sands

A stream, from its source in far-off mountains, passing through every kind and description of countryside, at last reached the sands of the desert. Just as it had crossed every other barrier, the stream tried to cross this one, but it found that as fast as it ran into the sand, its waters disappeared.

It was convinced, however, that its destiny was to cross this desert, and yet there was no way. Now a hidden voice, coming from the desert itself, whispered: "The wind crosses the desert, and so can the stream."

The stream objected that it was dashing itself against the sand, and only getting absorbed: that the wind could fly, and this was why it could cross a desert.

"By hurtling in your own accustomed way you cannot get across. You will either disappear or become a marsh. You must allow the wind to carry you over, to your destination."

But how could this happen? "By allowing yourself to be absorbed in the wind."

This idea was not acceptable to the stream. After all, it had never been absorbed before. It did not want to lose its individuality. And, once having lost it, how was one to know that it could ever be regained?

"The wind," said the sand, "performs this function. It takes up water, carries it over the desert, and then lets it fall again. Falling as rain, the water again becomes a river."

"How can I know that this is true?"

"It is so, and if you do not believe it, you cannot become more than a quagmire, and even that could take many, many years; and it certainly is not the same as a stream."

"But can I not remain the same stream that I am today?"

"You cannot in either case remain so," the whisper said. "Your essential part is carried away and forms a stream again. You are called what you are even today because you do not know which part of you is the essential one."

When he heard this, certain echoes began to arise in the thoughts of the stream. Dimly, he remembered a state in which he—or some part of him, was it?—had been held in the arms of a wind. He also remembered—or did he?—that this was the real thing, not necessarily the obvious thing, to do.

And the stream raised his vapour into the welcoming arms of the wind, which gently and easily bore it upwards and along, letting it fall softly as soon as they reached the roof of a mountain, many, many miles away. And because he had had his doubts, the stream was able to remember and record more strongly in his mind the details of the experience. He reflected, "Yes, now I have learned my true identity."

The stream was learning. But the sands whispered: "We know, because we see it happen day after day: and because we, the sands, extend from the riverside all the way to the mountain."

And that is why it is said that the way in which the Stream of Life is to continue on its journey is written in the Sands. (Shah, 1970b, pp. 23–24)

The Tale of Melon City

The ruler of a certain city one day decided that he would like a triumphal arch built, so that he could ride under it with all pomp, for the desirable edification of the multitude. But when the great moment came, his crown was knocked off: the arch had been built too low.

The ruler therefore ordained, in his rightful wrath, that the chief of the builders should be hanged. Gallows were prepared, but—as he was being taken to the place of execution—the Master-Builder called out that it was all the fault of the workmen, who had done the actual construction job.

The king, with his customary sense of justice, called the workers to account. But they escaped the charge by explaining that the masons had made the bricks of the wrong size. And the masons said that they had only carried out the orders of the architect. He, in turn, reminded the king that his Majesty had, at the last moment, made some amendments of his own to the plans, changing them.

"Summon the wisest man in the country," said the ruler, "for this is undoubtedly a difficult problem, and we need counsel."

The wisest man was carried in, unable to stand on his own feet, so ancient (and therefore so wise) was he. "It is evident," he quavered, "that in law the actual culprit must be punished, and that is, in this case, quite evidently, none other than the arch itself."

Applauding his decision, the king ordered that the offending arch be carried to the scaffold. But as it was being taken there, one of the Royal Councillors pointed out that this arch was something which had actually touched the august head of the monarch and must surely never be disgraced by the rope of execution.

As in the meantime, exhausted by his exertions, the venerable wise man had breathed his last, the people were unable to apply to him for an interpretation of this new observation. The doctors of Law, however, decreed that the lower part of the arch, which had not touched anything at all, could be hanged for the crime of the whole arch.

But when the executioner tried to put the arch into the noose, he found that the rope was too short. The rope-maker was called, but he soon explained that in his opinion it was the scaffold that was too high. He suggested that the carpenters were at fault.

"The crowd is getting impatient," said the king, "and we must therefore quickly find someone to hang. We can postpone the consideration of finer points like guilt until a later, more convenient, occasion."

In a surprisingly short time, all the people in the city had been carefully measured, but only one was found tall enough to fit the gallows. It was the king himself. Such was the popular enthusiasm at the discovery of a man who would fit, that the king had to conform, and he was hanged.

"Thank goodness we found someone," said the Prime Minister, "for if we had not satisfied the appetite of the mob, they would undoubtedly have turned against the Crown."

But there were important matters to consider, for almost at once it was realised that the king was dead. "In conformity with custom," announced the heralds in the streets, "the first man who passes the city gate shall decide who is to be our next great ruler."

The very next man to wander past the gate was an idiot. He was quite unlike the ordinary sensible citizens with whom we have become familiar, and when he was asked who should be king, immediately said: "A melon." This was because he always said "A melon" to every question. In fact, he thought about nothing else, being very fond of melons.

And thus it came about that a melon was, with due ceremony, crowned.

Now that was years and years ago. Nowadays, when people ask the inhabitants of that land why their king seems to be a melon, they say: "Because of the customary choice. His Majesty evidently desires to be a melon. Certainly we shall allow him to remain one until his further pleasure be known. He has, in our country, every right to be what he wants to be. We are content with that, so long as he does not interfere in our lives." (Shah, 1972b, pp. 83–84)

The Ants and the Pen

An ant one day strayed across a piece of paper and saw a pen writing in fine, black strokes.

"How wonderful this is!" said the ant. "This remarkable thing, with a life of its own, makes squiggles on this beautiful surface, to such an extent and with such energy that it is equal to the efforts of all the ants in the world. And the squiggles which it makes! These resemble ants: not one, but millions, all run together."

He repeated his ideas to another ant, who was equally interested. He praised the powers of observation and reflection of the first ant.

But another ant said: "Profiting, it must be admitted, by your efforts, I have observed this strange object. But I have determined that it is not the master of this work. You failed to notice that this pen is attached to certain other objects, which surround it and drive it on its way. These should be considered as the moving factor, and given the credit." Thus were fingers discovered by the ants.

But another ant, after a long time, climbed over the fingers and realised that they comprised a hand, which he thoroughly explored, after the manner of ants, by scrambling all over it.

He returned to his fellows: "Ants!" he cried, "I have news of importance for you. Those smaller objects are a part of a large one. It is this which gives motion to them."

But then it was discovered that the hand was attached to an arm, and the arm to a body, and that there were two hands, and that there were feet which did no writing.

The investigations continue. Of the mechanics of the writing, the ants have a fair idea. Of the meaning and intention of the writing, and how it is ultimately controlled, they will not find out by their customary method of investigation. Because they are "literate." (Shah, 1972b, pp. 180–181)

Annotated Bibliography

al-Ghazzali. (1964). *The alchemy of happiness* (C. Field, Trans.). Lahore, Pakistan: Muhammad Ashraf. Part of his own abridgment of *The Revival of Religious Sciences*. It is a short vivid book with very few references to purely Islamic ideas.

———. (1971). *Ghazzali's Lhya Ulum-id-din* (Alhaj Maulana Fazlul Karim, Trans.). Dacca, Bangladesh: Mission Trust. Only full translation of al-Ghazzali's *The Revival of Religious Sciences* available.

———. (1972). *The revival of religious sciences* (B. Behari, Trans.). Farnham, Surrey: Sufi Publishing. The best translation of the most important of al-Ghazzali's major works.

Bakhtiar, L. (1987). *Sufi: Expressions of the mystic quest*. New York: Avon. A different approach; symbolic, geometric, and with beautiful illustrations.

Ozak, M. (al-Jerrahi). (1987). *Love is the wine*. (Edited and compiled by Sheikh R. Frager al-Jerrahi.) Putney, VT: Threshold Books. This book is derived from talks given in America by a contemporary Sufi master. It presents the depths of Sufi wisdom in a modern, highly accessible form.

Shah, I. (1971). *The Sufis*. New York: Doubleday. Shah discusses the major traditional Sufi teachers, Sufism's major influences on Western thought, and some of the central ideas of Sufi practice.

———. (1970). *Tales of the dervishes*. New York: Dutton.

———. (1970). *The way of the Sufi*. New York: Dutton.

———. (1971). *The pleasantries of the incredible Mulla Nasrudin*. New York: Dutton. Three collections of traditional Sufi materials brought together by Shah. *Tales of the Dervishes* is a series of traditional teaching stories. *The Way of the Sufi* is a collection of sayings, sermons, meditations, questions and answers, and stories from the major figures and schools of Sufism. *The Pleasantries of the Incredible Mulla Nasrudin* is a collection of short funny stories about the Mulla, a folk hero who is the subject of numerous Sufi stories. Of the three collections, this is the easiest to understand.

References

Abdul-Hamid, Sufi (1976). First statement. In L. Lewin (Ed.), *The elephant in the dark.* New York: Dutton.

al-Ghazzali (1952). *Mishkat al-anwar (the niche for lights)* (W. H. T. Gairdner, Trans.). Lahore, Pakistan: Muhammad Ashraf.

————. (1963). *The foundations of the articles of faith* (N. A. Faris, Trans.). Lahore, Pakistan: Muhammad Ashraf.

————. (1964a). *The alchemy of happiness* (C. Field, Trans.). Lahore, Pakistan: Muhammad Ashraf.

————. (1964b). *Ghazzali's book of counsel for kings* (F. R. C. Bagley, Trans.). London: Oxford University Press.

————. (1966). *The book of knowledge* (N. A. Faris, Trans.). Lahore, Pakistan: Muhammad Ashraf.

————. (1968a). *The confessions of al-Ghazzali* (C. Field, Trans.). Lahore, Pakistan: Muhammad Ashraf. (Also in *The faith and practice of al-Ghazzali* [correctly translated as "Deliverance from error"] [W. M. Watt, Trans.]. London: Allen & Unwin, 1953.)

————. (1968b). *The mysteries of fasting* (N. A. Faris, Trans.). Lahore, Pakistan: Muhammad Ashraf.

————. (1972). *The revival of religious sciences* (B. Behari, Trans.). Farnham, Surrey: Sufi Publishing. Selections drawn primarily from the last half of Ihya'Ulum Ad-din.

————. (1975). *On the duties of brotherhood* (M. Holland, Trans.). London: Latimer.

————. (1976). *Letters of al-Ghazzali* (A. Qayyum, Trans.). Lahore, Pakistan: Islamic Publications.

————. (1983). *Inner dimensions of Islamic worship* (M. Holland, Trans.). London: Islamic Foundation.

Ali, S. N. (1944). *Some moral and religious teachings of al-Ghazzali* (2nd ed.). Lahore, Pakistan: Muhammad Ashraf.

Arasteh, A. R. (1965). *Final integration in the adult personality.* Leiden, Holland: Brill.

————. (1972). *Rumi, the Persian: Rebirth in creativity and love.* Tucson, AZ: Omen Press.

————. (1973). Psychology of the Sufi way to individuation. In L. F. Rushbrook Williams (Ed.), *Sufi studies: East and West* (pp. 89–113). New York: Dutton.

————. (1980). *Growth to selfhood: Sufi contribution.* London: Routledge & Kegan Paul.

Arasteh, A., & Sheikh, A. (1989). Sufism: the way to universal self. In A. Sheikh & K. Sheikh (Eds.), *Eastern and western approaches to healing.* New York: Wiley.

Arberry, A. J. (1966). *The doctrine of the Sufis.* Lahore, Pakistan: Sh. Muhammad Ashraf. (Also, Cambridge, England: University Press, 1977.)

———. (1970). *Sufism: An account of the mystics of Islam*. New York: Harper & Row.

Attar, Farid, Ud-Din (1961). *The conference of the birds* (C. S. Nott, Trans.). London: Routledge & Kegan Paul.

Baba, M. (1967). *Listen, humanity*. New York: Dodd, Mead.

———. (1972). *Life at its best*. New York: Harper & Row.

Beg, M. A. (1970). A note on the concept of self, and the theory and practice of psychological help in the Sufi tradition. *Interpersonal Development, 1,* 58–64.

Behari, B. (1972). Introduction. *The revival of religious sciences* by al-Ghazzali. Farnham, Surray: Sufi Publishing.

Burckhardt, T. (1968). *An introduction to Sufi doctrine*. Lahore, Pakistan: Sh. Muhammad Ashraf.

Burke, O. (1966). Travel and residence with dervishes. In R. Davidson (Ed.), *Documents on contemporary dervish communities*. London: Hoopoe.

———. (1975). *Among the dervishes*. New York: Dutton.

Chittick, W. (1983). *The Sufi path of love: The spiritual teachings of Rumi*. Albany, NY: State University of New York Press.

———. (1989). *The Sufi path of knowledge: Ibn al-'Arabi's metaphysics of imagination*. Albany, NY: State University of New York Press.

Dallas, I. (1973). *The book of strangers*. New York: Warner Books.

Dawood, N. J. (Trans.). (1968). *The Koran* (3rd rev. ed.). Baltimore: Penguin Books.

Deikman, A. (1980). Sufism and psychiatry. In S. Boorstein (Ed.), *Transpersonal psychotherapy* (pp. 200–216). Palo Alto, CA: Science and Behavior.

el-Qadiri, I. H. (1974). *The secret garden*. Introduction by Mahmud Shabistari (J. Pasha, Trans.). New York: Dutton.

Erikson, E. (1964). *Insight and responsibility*. New York: Norton.

Farzan, M. (1973). *Another way of laughter*. New York: Dutton.

———. (1974). *The tale of the reed pipe*. New York: Dutton.

Foster, W. (1968). *Sufi studies today*. London: Octagon.

Gurdjieff, G. I. (1950). *All and everything, the first series: Beelzebub's tales to his grandson*. New York: Dutton.

———. (1968). *Meetings with remarkable men*. New York: Dutton.

Haeri, Shaykh Fadhlalla (1989). *The journey of the self*. Dorset, England: Element Books.

Harman, W. W. (1967). Old wine in new wineskins. In J. Bugental (Ed.), *Challenges of humanistic psychology* (pp. 321–334). New York: McGraw-Hill.

Helminski, K. (1992). *Living presence: A Sufi way to mindfulness and the essential self*. New York: Tarcher.

Hujwîrî (1959). *Kashf al-mahjub* (R. A. Nicholson, Trans.). London: Luzac.

ibn 'Arabi, M. (1981). *Journey to the lord of power* (R. Harris, Trans.). New York: Inner Traditions.

———. (1992). *What the seeker needs* (T. Bayrak al-Jerrahi & R. Harris al-Jerrahi, Trans.). Putney, VT: Threshold Books.

Inhelder, B., & Piaget, J. (1958). *The growth of logical thinking from childhood to adolescence*. New York: Basic Books.

James, W. (1899). *Talks to teachers on psychology and to students on some of life's ideals*. New York: Holt, Rinehart and Winston. (Unaltered republication, New York: Dover, 1962.)

Jung, C. G. (1973). *C. G. Jung's letters* (G. Adler, A. Jaffe, & R. F. C. Hull, Eds.) (Vol. 1). Princeton, NJ: Princeton University Press, pp. 1906–1950.

Kabir (1977). *The Kabir book*. Versions by Robert Bly. Boston: Beacon Press.

Khan, Pir Villayat (1974). *Toward the one*. New York: Harper & Row.

MacDonald, D. B. (1899). The life of al-Ghazzali, with special reference to his religious experience and opinions. The *Journal of the American Oriental Society, 20,* 71–132.

———. (1903). al-Ghazzali. In *Development of Muslim theology jurisprudence and constitutional theory*. Lahore, Pakistan: Premier Book House, pp. 215–242.

———. (1909). *The religious attitude and life in Islam*. Chicago: University of Chicago Press.

Nasr, S. (Ed.). (1987). *Islamic spirituality: Foundations*. New York: Crossroads.

Nicholson, R. A. (1964a). *The idea of personality in Sufism*. Lahore, Pakistan: Muhammad Ashraf.

———. (1964b). *Rumi, poet and mystic*. London: Allen & Unwin.

Nurbakhsh, J. (n.d.). *Sufism and psychoanalysis (Parts 1 and 2)*. Unpublished papers, Department of Psychiatry, University of Tehran, Tehran, Iran.

———. (1978). *In the tavern of ruin*. New York: Khaniqahi-nimatullahi.

———. (1979). *In the paradise of the Sufis*. New York: Khaniqahi-nimatullahi.

———. (1981). *Sufism: Meaning, knowledge and unity*. New York: Khaniqahi-nimatullahi.

Orage, A. R. (1965). *Psychological exercises and essays* (rev. ed.). London: Janus.

Ornstein, R. E. (1972). *The psychology of consciousness*. San Francisco: Freeman, New York: Viking Press.

Ouspensky, P. D. (1949). *In search of the miraculous*. New York: Harcourt, Brace Jovanovich.

Ozak, M. (al-Jerrahi) (1981). *The unveiling of love* (M. Holland, Trans.). New York: Inner Traditions.

———. (1987). *Love is the wine*. (Edited and compiled by Sheikh R. Frager al-Jerrahi) Putney, VT: Threshold Books.

———. (1991a). *The garden of dervishes* (M. Holland, Trans.). Westport, CT: Pir Publications.

———. (1991b). *Adornment of hearts* (M. Holland and S. Friedrich,

Trans.). Westport, CT: Pir Publications.

Pendlebury, D. L. (1974). Afterword. *The walled garden of truth* by H. Sanai (D. L. Pendlebury, Trans.). London: Octagon.

Perry, W. N. (1971). *A treasury of traditional wisdom.* New York: Simon & Schuster.

Piaget, J. (1952). *The origins of intelligence in children.* New York: International University Press.

Qayyum, A. (1976). *Letters of al-Ghazzali.* Lahore, Pakistan: Islamic Publications.

Rice, C. (1964). *The Persian Sufis.* London: Allen & Unwin.

Rumi, Jalal al-Din (1972). *Discourses of Rumi* (A. J. Arberry, Trans.). New York: Weiser.

Sa'di, M. (1966). *The gulistan or rose garden of Sa'di* (E. Rehatsek, Trans.). New York: Capricorn Books.

Salinger, J. D. (1965). *Raise high the roofbeam, carpenters and Seymour, an introduction.* New York: Bantam Books.

Sanai, H. (1974). *The walled garden of truth* (D. L. Pendlebury, Trans.). London: Octagon.

Schimmel, A. (1975). *Mystical dimensions of Islam.* Chapel Hill: University of North Carolina Press.

———. (1985). *And Muhammad is His Messenger.* Chapel Hill: University of North Carolina Press.

Shafii, M. (1963). The pir (Sufi guide) and the Western psychotherapist. *R. M. Bucke Memorial Society Newsletter Review, 3,* 9–19.

———. (1974). *Developmental stages in man in Sufism and psychoanalysis.* Unpublished manuscript.

———. (1985). *Freedom from the self.* New York: Human Sciences Press.

Shah, I. (1964). *The Sufis.* New York: Doubleday.

———. (1970a). *The way of the Sufi.* New York: Dutton.

———. (1970b). *Tales of the dervishes.* New York: Dutton.

———. (1971a). *The dermis probe.* New York: Dutton.

———. (1971b). *The pleasantries of the incredible Mulla Nasrudin.* New York: Dutton.

———. (1971c). *The magic monastery.* New York: Dutton.

———. (1972a). Interview with Pat Williams. In L. Lewin (Ed.), *The diffusion of Sufi ideas in the West.* Boulder, CO: Keysign Press.

———. (1972b). *Caravan of dreams.* Baltimore: Penguin Books.

———. (1972c). *Wisdom of the idiots.* New York: Dutton.

———. (1972d). *The exploits of the incomparable Mulla Nasrudin.* New York: Dutton.

———. (1972e). *Thinkers of the East: Teachings of the dervishes.* Baltimore: Penguin Books.

———. (1972f). First statement. In L. Lewin (Ed.), *The diffusion of Sufi ideas in the West* (pp. 133–145). Boulder, CO: Keysign Press.

———. (1981). *Learning how to learn.* San Francisco: Harper & Row.

Shah, S. (1933). *Islamic Sufism*. London: Rider.

Shea, D. (Trans.). (1943). *The Dabistan*. London: Oriental Translation Fund.

Siraj-Ed-Din, A. (1970). *The book of certainty*. New York: Weiser.

Smith, J. (1980). Women in Islam: Equity, equality, and the search for the natural order. *Journal of the American Academy of Religion, 47*(4), 517–537.

Smith, J., & Haddad, Y. (1975). Women in the afterlife: The Islamic view as seen from Koran and tradition. *Journal of the American Academy of Religion, 43*(1), 39–50.

Smith, M. (1977). *Rabia, the mystic A.D. 717–801 and her fellow saints in Islam*. San Francisco: Rainbow Bridge. (Originally published, 1928, Cambridge University Press, England.)

Trimingham, J. S. (1971). *The Sufi orders in Islam*. New York: Oxford University Press.

Tweedie, I. (1979). *The chasm of fire*. England: Element Books.

Watt, W. M. (1971). *Muslim intellectual: A study of al-Ghazzali*. Edinburgh: University Press.

White, R. W. (1959). Motivation reconsidered: The concept of competence. *Psychological Review, 66*, 297–333.

Credits

Text

al-Ghazzali. *The Alchemy of Happiness.* Copyright 1964, pp. 128–130. Reprinted by permission of Muhammad Ashraf.

al-Ghazzali. *The Revival of Religious Sciences.* Reprinted by permission of Sufi Publishing Co. Ltd.

Alfred Adler. *What Life Should Mean to You.* Copyright 1931, pp. 74–78. Reprinted by permission of Little, Brown & Co.

W. Barlow. *The Alexander Technique.* Reprinted by permission of A. A. Knopf Publishers, © 1973.

Orson Bean. *Me and the Orgone.* Reprinted by permission of St. Martin's Press, Inc.

Erik Erikson. Reprinted from *Childhood and Society,* 2nd Edition, by Erik H. Erikson, by permission of W. W. Norton & Company, Inc. Copyright 1950, © 1963 by W. W. Norton & Company, Inc.

Erik Erikson. *Identity, Youth and Crisis.* pp. 19–22. Copyright 1968, reprinted by permission of W. W. Norton.

Karen Horney. Reprinted from *Neurosis and Human Growth* by Karen Horney, M.D., by permission of W. W. Norton & Company, Inc. Copyright 1950 by W. W. Norton & Company, Inc. Copyright renewed 1978 by Renate Patterson, Brigitte Swarzenski, and Marianne Von Eckardt.

W. James. *Talks to Teachers on Psychology and to Students on Some of Life's Ideals.* Copyright 1899 and 1962, pp. 33–36. Reprinted by permission of Hold, Rhinehart and Winston and Dover Press.

W. James. *The Varieties of Religious Experience.* Copyright 1958, pp. 367–369, 383–385. Reprinted by permission of the New American Library.

C. G. Jung. *Analytic Psychology: Its Theory and Practice.* Reprinted by permission of Random House, Inc. *C. G. Jung Letters: I,* edited by Gerhard Adler, in collaboration with Aniela Jaffe, trans. by R. C. F. Hull, Bollingen Series XCV (copyright © 1973 by Princeton University Press).

Ed Kapleau. *The Three Pillars of Zen.* Copyright 1965. By permission of Beacon Press.

George Kelly. "A Brief Introduction to Personal Construct Theory." In *Perspectives in Personal Construct Theory,* D. Bannister (ed.). Copyright 1970, reprinted by permission of Academic Press.

Jiyu Kennett. *The Wild Goose.* By permission of the author.

Kimble & Perlmutter. "The Problem of Volition," *The Psychological Record,* volume 77, pp. 361–384. Reprinted by permission of Charles E. Rice, Kenyon College.

Stanley Krippner. "The Plateau Experience: A. H. Maslow and Others," copyright 1972, *Journal of Transpersonal Psychology,* Volume 4, Number 2. Reprinted by permission of the Transpersonal Institute, 2637 Marshall Drive, Palo Alto, California 94303.

Swami Nikhilananda. *Ramakrishna: Prophet of New India.* By permission of the Ramakrishna-Vivehananda Center.

A. Osbourne (ed.). *Ramana Maharshi and the Path of Self-Knowledge.* Copyright 1970, by permission of Samuel Weiser, Inc. and Rider Publishers.

Frederick S. Perls. *In and Out of the Garbage Pail.* Reprinted by permission of The Real People Press, © 1969.

F. S. Perls. *Gestalt Therapy Verbatim.* By permission of The Real People Press, pp. 1–4, 68–70, 81–82.

Purohit. *Aphorisms of Yoga.* Copyright 1938, reprinted by permission of Faber.

Carl Rogers. Excerpted from *Becoming Partners.* Copyright 1972 by Carl Rogers, used with permission of Delacorte Press and the Sterling Lord Agency: in Alfred M. Freedman and Harold I. Kaplan, *Comprehensive Textbook of Psychiatry,* 2nd edition, copyright 1975 by the William & Wilkins Co., Baltimore.

Carl Rogers. "Communication: Its Blocking and Its Facilitation." Copyright 1952, pp. 20–25. By permission of Northwestern University Information.

Idries Shah. "The Tale of the Sands" and "The Story of Tea" from *Tales of the Dervishes,* reprinted by permission of the publishers, E. P. Dutton & Co., and by permission of Collins-Knowlton-Wing, Inc., copyright 1967 by Idries Shah; "The Tale of Melon City" and "The Ants and the Pen" from *Caravan of Dreams,* London, Octagon Press, 1968, copyright 1968 by Idries Shah.

B. F. Skinner. "Humanism and Behaviorism." This article first appeared in *The Humanist,* July/August issue, and is reprinted by permission; in T. W. Wann (ed.), *Behaviorism and Phenomenology: Constrasting Bases for Modern Psychology.* Copyright 1964 by The University of Chicago Press.

"The Meaning of Care: Reframing Treatment Models" (pp. 250, 251, 255–257, 266, 267) by I. P. Stiver in *Women's Growth in Connection* by J. V. Jordan, A. G. Kaplan, J. B. Miller, I. P. Stiver, and J. L. Surrey. New York: Guilford Press. Copyright 1991.

Illustration

J. H. Clark. Illustration from "Program for Patanjali." This illustration first appeared in *New Society,* London, the weekly review of the social sciences.

A. Danielou. "The Six Main Centres of the Subtle Body" (illustration) from *Yoga: The Method of Re-Integration.* Reprinted by University Books Inc., a subsidiary of Lyle Stuart.

Ramana Maharshi. In A. Osbourne (ed.), *The Collected Works of Ramana Maharshi.* By permission of Hutchinson Publishing Group Ltd.

Abraham Maslow. Diagram from *Toward a Psychology of Being,* by Abraham Maslow. Copyright © 1968. Reprinted by permission of D. Van Nostrand Company.

Thomas Parker. "The Structure of the Personality" (diagram). Used by permission.

Zenkei Shibayama. *Zen Oxherding Pictures,* commentaries by Zenkei Shibayama, paintings by Gyokusei Jikihara. Used by permission of Sogensha, Inc., Publishers, Osaka, Japan.

I. K. Taimni. *The Science of Yoga.* By permission of the Thesophical Publishing House in Adyar, Madras, India.

Photograph

Association for the Advancement of Psychoanalysis of the Karen Horney Psychoanalytic Institute and Center, p. 130, Brandeis University, p. 463; Dean Brown, p. 366; Culver, p. 1, 289; Jikihara Gyokusei, Zen Priest of Osaka, Japan (paintings, used by permission of Sigensha, Inc., Publishers, Osaka, Japan), pp. 556–565; Deke Simon, Real People Press, p. 264; Wide World, p. 335; John T. Wood, p. 417; UPI, pp. 55, 102, 180, 217; National Museum, New Delhi, Art Resources, p. 507; Carlin, Frederic Lewis, p. 541; The Stone Center, Wellesley College, p. 159; Fort Hays State University, p. 379

Name Index

Subject Index